Un-Blogged:

A Fencer's Ramblings

Written by

HENRY WALKER

Foreword by

KEITH FARRELL

A Sword And Book Enterprises Publication
This edition first published 2019, by Sword And Book Enterprises Pty Ltd, Brisbane Qld Australia.

Copyright © Henry Walker, 2018.
Cover image © Jen Fraser, 2018.
Preface © Keith Farrell, 2018.
Author's portrait © Julia Robertson, 2018.

Neither the author nor the publishers of this text are responsible for any injuries or damage sustained that may occur as a result of using the information found herein. The reader should consult with a qualified physician before attempting any physical activity detailed in this text. Always use safety equipment in any form of weapon sparring.

The author and publisher claim copyright over material which is original and thus written by the author and published by this publisher. All other material previously published not in the public domain is copyright to its original author and publisher. Images which appear in this publication have been taken from original sources, created originally or been given by the owners, and thus are either public domain, owned by the author or have permission to have them. The original free versions of this material may be accessed at https://afencersramblings.blogspot.com and were created for research for the public benefit.

National Library of Australia Cataloguing-in-Publication entry:
Walker, Henry Leigh, 1975— author.
Un-blogged: A Fencer's Ramblings /
written by Henry Walker; preface by Keith Farrell.
Includes bibliographical references and glossary.
Farrell, Keith, 1988— writer of added text.
504 p. 23 cm.

ISBN 978-0-9876447-0-1 (paperback)
ISBN 978-0-9876447-1-8 (e-book)

1. Swordplay; 2. Martial arts - Europe - History; 3. Fencing
Dewey Number: 796.809

Email: hlwalker1975@gmail.com
Website: afencersramblings.blogspot.com

DEDICATION

To my lovely wife Casey who supports
my love of swords and books and
to my readers and donators without
whom this book would not have
been possible.

Contents

Acknowledgements	vi
Foreword	vii
Introduction	1

SECTION 1. Editorial — 5

What is Fencing?	5
Fencing Movies: Problems with Getting it Right	7
Murphy's Laws of Fencing – The "Henry" Version	11
Rapier Combat: A Practitioner's Thoughts	13
Fencing Fest – The Keys to a Great Fencing Event	15
Re-enactment and Its Decline	19
Henry's Rules – The Essentials	21

SECTION 2. Safety — 23

Safety and Fencing	23
The First Defence: Control	25
Brutal Fencing I: A Discussion of Aggression	28
Brutal Fencing II: Aggressive Versus Assertive	31
Brutal Fencing III: A Question of Calibration	32
A "Safe" Sword	34
Proper Fitting Armour	35

SECTION 3. Period Texts — 41

Why Do I Research?	41
Lexicon For Swordplay, Or He Did What?	44
Reading Period Texts – A Question of Language	45
Fencing Manuals: Old and New	47
Watch Your Assumptions	49
What's In a Name?	51
From the Original	53
Fencing Treatise: Part Manual, Part Résumé	55
Musashi for the Rapier Combatant: Fabris From a Chair?	60
Fabris' Single Rapier for the Seated Combatant: A Discussion	63
George Silver: Somewhat of an Explanation	116
Giacomo di Grassi: The Essentials	118
Saviolo: Principles and Practical Elements	121
Musashi for the Rapier Combatant	129
The *Art* of Combat	155
Documentable Combinations: A Discussion of the Rapier & Cane	157

SECTION 4. Technique — 159

What is a Ward?	159
Stand Up Straight and Relax	161
Footwork: Movement in Displacement as an Effective Defence	165
Of the Use of the Off-hand	167
The Sword Parry and Its Execution	183
Calibration and the Correct Execution of the Thrust	186
On the Subject of Cutting	191
Reading the Opponent	195
On Handedness – The Left-handed Fencer	199
No Footwork Fencing, Or Fencing From a Chair	201
True and False Arts: A Discussion of Tempo in the Use of the Feint	204
Rapier & Cloak – A Bluffer's Guide	205
Case of Rapiers: A Bluffer's Guide	210
Sword & Rotella – A Bluffer's Guide	218
Sword Alone Versus Everything	225
On the Manner of Wearing a Sword	230

CONTENTS

SECTION 5. Training — 237
- Fencing Practice — 237
- On Practice — 241
- Fencing and the Learning Process — 242
- Newton's 3rd Law in Fencing — 244
- Taking Hold of Your Training — 246
- Making Plans for Training — 248
- Building an Individual Training Program — 250
- How Many Times This Week? A Question of Practice — 252
- Fencing and Music — 255
- Solo Training: For the Solo Practitioner — 257
- Cross-Training and Other Groups — 259
- Being a Good Training Partner — 260
- Disability Aspects in Fencing — 263
- Females and Fencing — 267
- Building Co-ordination in Fencing — 273
- Relax and Fence — 276
- Move Slow, Learn Fast — 278
- The Myth of Speed — 280
- Are You Using or Teaching a System? — 283
- "Hot" Drills — 285
- What's Next? — 287

SECTION 6. Mind Games — 289
- Why Do Renaissance Fencing? — 289
- What is a Master? — 292
- Fencing Mind Game - The Long Path — 294
- Psychology of Fencing: Things to Consider — 300
- Pressure in Fencing — 303
- On Winning — 306
- Ego: The Good, the Bad & the Ugly — 308
- Renown Versus Notoriety — 311
- Reasons Why I Do Not Do Sport Fencing — 314
- Martial Art Versus Martial Sport — 316
- A Question of Ethics — 318
- What Does Fencing Give the Fencer? — 320
- Virtues Gained from Swordsmanship — 322
- Time and Distance — 325
- Tactics in Fencing — 329
- Motivation and Fencing — 334
- Fencing and Dedication to the Art... Too Much to Ask? — 336
- The Way Forward... — 340

SECTION 7. Teaching — 343
- What is the role of the teacher and the student in fencing? — 343
- Teacher vs Instructor — 345
- Beginning to Teach — 347
- Conduct of Training — 349
- Drill Design and Construction — 353
- Building Self-Confidence — 356
- Biomechanics and the Effects of Body Shape — 359

SECTION 8. Equipment and Curatorial Discussions — 363
- Buying a Sword — 363
- Glove Preparation — 366
- The Perfect Weapon Length: A Discussion of Weapon Proportion — 367
- Saviolo's Weapons — 371
- A Discussion of the Form of the Longsword — 372
- What is a Rapier? — 394
- What is a Feder? — 399
- The Rapier: A Curatorial Discussion — 438
- The Broadsword: A Curatorial Discussion — 455
- The Smallsword: A Curatorial Discussion — 467
- Of Wasters — 481

Glossary — 485
Bibliography and Recommended Reading — 489
About the Author — 494

Acknowledgements

The final production of this book is not the work of a single individual. While the prime writing may have been done by the author, without the audience there would have been no one to write for and there would have been a point to writing in the first place. The simple acknowledgement that a particular post was interesting or was useful was often all that was needed to keep me going and to go and find something to write about for the next posting. Of course, I cannot go without thanking my tireless editors who have combed through my words to find anything which seems odd or out of place.

To Jen Fraser who took some time and explained some important details with regard to the publishing process and then assisted with getting the book set up, there is a special "thank you" to you.

Further I must acknowledge Keith Farrell and the publication of *Encased in Steel: Anthology I*, from which I gained the inspiration for putting a selection of my blog posts into print. This selection of articles is well-worth the read as it contains many different articles of interest to any who wield a sword in this modern age. I recommend it to any who are interested in any facet of European swordplay as it contains many different perspectives upon this subject.

I would also like to thank the most generous authors who gave me permission to use their work in this book, without many of them the articles would be substantially less complete.

In the future there may be further selections of posts made available in this format for readers to access; this is a thought for down the road.

In the meantime the articles on the blog upon which this selection is based will continue appearing so long as I have access to the internet, ideas for material keep presenting, and most importantly readers keep reading what I am writing.

Henry Walker
14 November 2018

Foreword

Henry has been writing and publishing about a variety of issues on his blog *A Fencer's Ramblings* for a number of years now. His articles have spanned many topics, and this book contains over a hundred articles divided into several different thematic sections.

Blogs are an important part of the HEMA community at this moment in time. There are many people who have good and valuable ideas; and to ensure that the HEMA community keeps growing and developing in a safe and productive manner, it is invaluable that people with thoughts and ideas do make the effort to share these with others. Although Facebook is the medium of the day for chats and swift back-and-forths, such discussion is ephemeral and is lost all too quickly, or is otherwise hijacked by people who want to contribute little but memes or pithy one-liners. It is not a good forum for meaningful sharing of ideas. Instead, blogs give people the chance to develop and expound upon ideas without interruption.

By writing an article, one must consider one's thoughts and stances, and turn them into a coherent argument that can persuade others of its validity. Writing can be difficult; there is nowhere to hide when writing, as your text must stand by itself. Without being able to utilise props or speak with hands, or express emotions or humour with a wink or smile as can be done in a video, the text must be concise and effective. This lends an immense weight and value to a well-written piece; while videos often drag on and on with waffle, well-written articles are concise and to the point. They set out the topic for discussion, they discuss the topic, and they either wrap up the topic with a sensible summary or lay out questions for readers to consider and answer for themselves.

The blogs of the HEMA community have supported the development of the community for years. However, as more and more articles are made available, sometimes the older writings are forgotten, even if they contain valuable information and suggestions. Articles may even be lost entirely as websites or blogs close down or go offline. Bringing together a collection of blog articles, editing them for improvement, and publishing them in a paper book like this, ensures that more of the articles from the past several years will be read again and again, and that the ideas will remain accessible to the community.

As an author of both blog articles and printed books myself, I think what Henry has done with his blog is wonderful. I am grateful for the many years of his writing, for so many articles made freely available to the community, and I look forward to the publication of this volume so that these articles gain the permanence of paper in libraries throughout the community.

I hope that those who read this book will experience several "lightbulb moments", as ideas spark in your head; and I also hope that the articles ignite some slow fuses that will burn for a while in the back of your mind until they help new ideas burst into being.

Keith Farrell
4 December 2018
www.keithfarrell.net

Un-Blogged:

A Fencer's Ramblings

Introduction

"A Fencer's Ramblings" is a blog which has been going on row since May 2010. Since that time, and to the date that I write this, there have been about 150 posts of various kinds published, on an average of once a month. Sometimes there were more and sometimes I skipped a few. The only reason that this has kept on going is because of the readership of this blog and no other reason. If no-one read it I would have quit finding things to write about and publish. To date there have been over 100,000 page-views of the various subjects which have been written. I am actually quite amazed at the response that I have had to my writings, and the overly positive responses that I have had to them. If they had not been so, I would not have considered putting this book to print, or even assembling it.

THE SELECTION

For this book I have selected more than 100 of the posts that were published on the blog and added a couple because they were needed to flesh things out a bit for completeness. The regular readers of my blog will note the added ones for sure. All of the article versions of the posts which have been posted here have been edited thus taken from their raw blogged state and made into something even more readable. Some are much the same, some have been extended a little, and some have been improved with more recent research. I like to keep things a little more updated with my own thoughts and also more up to date research, or at least the research which can I put my hands on anyway.

In the case of the articles themselves they were selected on the basis of pertinence to fencing and also level of interest to the reader. I left out posts which were short bits and also book reviews. For the most part I wanted to put in posts which would also spark some level of motivation and possibly a little bit of shock, as most people tend to read passively and I want people to read actively. I want people to go looking for things themselves, thus I have left some the posts open-ended so that you need to go and find the answers yourself.

afencersramblings.blogspot.com

FORMAT

The idea for putting these articles in hard copy format was based on a couple of reasons. For some, reading the articles is easier on paper than on a screen, and also many find it easier to access earlier articles written than in the original format. Another reason for having a hard copy, one which I tend toward myself, is that a hard copy is easier to make notes on for your own thoughts about the subject. For those who are reading an electronic copy of this book, some of these aspects are mute some, not so much.

SUBJECT HEADINGS

Editorials

The collection has been organised under a set of subject headings for ease of finding articles of interest in a particular area. The first is the editorials. These are a collection of articles in which I have expressed my opinions with regard to particular subjects. They discuss things such as fencing in movies, re-enactment, some rules by which I fence and also fencing in general.

Safety

The next subject heading is safety, a subject which I have a particular interest in. This is a subject, which is of great importance regardless of what type of sword you pick up and what type of fencing you may be involved in. It discusses things such as safety in general, protective gear, and the approach the fencer takes to fencing so that they keep their opponent and themselves safe while fencing.

Period Texts

To follow "Safety" is the subject of period texts. For the participant in Historical European Martial Arts (HEMA) these must be the go-to sources for information. These texts explain how weapons were used in pedagogical situations in the periods in which they were set. While we may be able to experiment and find out how weapons may have been employed, the period texts describe how weapons were actually utilized in the periods in which they were used, rather than attempting to find the same answers by trial and error. This selection of articles goes through some of the pitfalls and traps of researching primary materials as well as describing their importance. For the more practically-minded there are also some more informational articles as well.

Technique

For the more practically-minded reader, the section on technique is where you are most likely to head. This has some articles that explain some of the nomenclature used in fencing, and then it describes some of the nitty-gritty about techniques used in fencing. These are essential techniques put under focus so that they can be performed even better. This is followed by some tactical questions and then some information about how to use different forms in combination with the sword. The last two will be a bit of a surprise as one turns this a little on its head and the other gives the correct manner in which to wear a sword.

Training

Training is an essential part of the fencing career of any fencer who wants to improve their skill. It would be pointless to take it up if this was not at least somewhat of an interest. Thus there is a section which addresses training. This asks all different questions about training, how you train, when you train, who you train with, and what you train. Each one of these is a necessary consideration for your training. There are also questions in this section about how you can affect another fencer's training positively or negatively. For anyone who is even slightly serious about their training a glance over these articles would be useful.

Mind Games

There are some who think that fencing is a purely physical pursuit, and they are the ones who miss the subtlety of the art of fencing. They also do not tend to go as far or last as long as those who consider the mind game of fencing. Once the body has been properly trained, or even before this has been completed, the fencer should also be working on their fencer's brain. The fencer needs to think tactically about the opponent, to work out plans of attack and defense. This comes from training the brain. The section called "mind games" has articles on the brain game of fencing, that part which takes over once the physical has gone as far as it can.

Teaching

Teaching is a good way to reaffirm what you know. For some it is a difficult prospect at best, and just as with any other part of fencing it takes training. The teaching section of this collection contains articles pertaining to the teaching of students. These articles will give some ideas about how a class should be structured and also how to take into consideration that all students are not the same. Each one is a skill and each one needs to be learnt.

Curatorial and Equipment

The final selection of articles is about equipment and curatorial discussions of weapons which are being simulated in HEMA. This addresses some weapons directly and asks whether the ideas that we have about certain weapons are as accurate as we might think they are. It also asks some questions about some of the naming conventions which have been given to some weapons and whether they are as accurate as they might be. Needless to say, this is the selection primarily about the weapons rather than the use of them.

ON LANGUAGE...

I feel that I need to add a special note with regard to the language which I use in the following articles. I tend to use the male form, i.e. "he", "man" and so forth. In no way should my female readers feel discouraged that these posts do not speak to them. I use the original Latin root forms of these words with their original intentions. Thus in the case of words such as "chairman", the "man" part of this comes from "manus" to operate rather than any indication of a male form.

I am a firm believer in the quote presented in this marvellous image. As will be noted from my previous posts in three parts about "Females and Fencing" I believe that all have the capacity for excelling in HEMA. I feel that it is necessary that I state this as a special mention at this point in time to clear the air and ensure that when I am speaking to the one I am speaking to all who would join the great fraternity of past, present and future. Swords and fencing are for everyone!

SOMETHING FOR ALL

With eight subject headings covering a wide range of subjects and quite a few articles under each subject, there should be something of interest for every reader who picks up this collection. For some it may be a refresher examination of articles that they have read before. For others it may be to have a look at what has actually been written and gain some ideas about how they can improve. Both of these can be answered within this collection. Needless to say there are at least 37 articles missing from this collection, so after you have finished reading this book, I encourage you to come and have a look at my blog:

"A Fencer's Ramblings"
https://afencersramblings.blogspot.com.au

SECTION 1.
Editorial

What is Fencing?

INTRODUCTION

A question that is not often asked is "What is fencing?" Most often the answer to this question is assumed to be general knowledge by most people. While swordplay, for most people, is not a normal part of their everyday life, there is the assumption that something is known about fencing, as if there is a difference between the two. This blog will address both this particular question and some of the associated elements of fencing which need to be realised.

DEFINITION

There are many assumptions which have been made about fencing over the years. Some of these are reinforced by popular culture in movies and other things. One of the first places that must be investigated is the "dictionary definition" of fencing and what that implies.

> "Fencing is a family of sports and activities that feature armed combat involving cutting, stabbing, or bludgeoning weapons that are directly manipulated by hand rather than shot, thrown or positioned."
> http://en.wikipedia.org/wiki/Fencing

This gives a surprisingly broad definition of what fencing is. What is most relevant at this point in time is that this particular definition of fencing is the one that must be used to appreciate its complete scale. Even for the fencer this is important. Too often we get locked into believing that what we do is the one and only true form of fencing whereas, there are many out there.

NARROW MIND LIMITS VIEW

The much broader view of the idea of fencing allows for a much deeper analysis and discussion of fencing and the potential it has for all fencers and others as well. Where modern usage of "fencing" falls down is as follows:

> "In contemporary common usage, fencing tends to refer specifically to European schools of swordsmanship and to the modern Olympic sport that has evolved out of them."
> http://en.wikipedia.org/wiki/Fencing

This falls down from several different points of view, which I will elaborate on below. First of all it restricts fencing to European schools of swordsmanship. Any Japanese kendoka or Chinese swordsman would also argue the point that theirs is also a form of swordplay, thus fencing. Fencing must refer to all forms of swordplay not only those found in European schools of swordsmanship.

EVOLUTIONIST VIEW

The next point that must be made is the idea that sport fencing "evolved" out of the previous forms. This is inaccurate to say the least. The change from the rapier to the smallsword and thus to later weapons was a result of a change in fashion not evolution of the weapon or increase in skills. Those treatises left by the masters of the Renaissance period will demonstrate that what was taught were complete and complex skill systems. Thus the so-called "evolution" is inaccurate.

The "evolutionary" perspective of fencing primarily comes from nineteenth-century fencing historians, such as Egerton Castle, whose prime aim was to promote and demonstrate classical fencing as the most matured form of the art, thus the art with the foil and the point as the most refined. This particular view can be seen in the history sections of most sport fencing manuals. It also meant that they had to present the arts of the sword of the medieval and Renaissance as backward and primitive leading up to the more refined smallsword and thus on to the foil as the peak of the art. This view is seen in the manner in which the weapons and methods of earlier periods are spoken of as compared to those of later periods. It is a claim of the way the sword necessarily changed to become of greater use to the Art of Fencing.

HOLISTIC VIEW

To approach fencing with a truly holistic point of view it must be appreciated how each of these martial arts relates to one another. The first is through the foundation principles. All the forms of the sword, indeed all forms of hand-to-hand combat, work on the principles of Time and Distance. These two form the foundation of the theory found in all fencing, and indeed all combat. Then there is the universal fencing principle which applies to all and that is the principle of striking the opponent without being struck. With these ideas in mind it is then possible to see where the forms of fencing are all similar. This can also be seen in technique where the techniques of one transfer through to another. Thus it can be seen that all forms are similar in the most elementary parts.

With this in mind it can easily be seen that one form of fencing can assist another, and thus all forms of fencing, due to their similarities. The principles and techniques in many cases make it so that some are simply transferable from one to the other due to the same foundations of Time and Distance. So, too is it the case that their differences enrich the practitioner who appreciates the different forms of fencing available to him.

INDIVIDUAL IMPACT

The individual fencer has more impact than they realise. The individual's action will directly affect those fencers who fence against them. It also follows that it may affect the organisation to which they are associated, and in some instances the actions of the individual may come to affect the entire fencing community. There are many fears and misgivings for fencers in general and the negative actions of the fencer only serve to increase these. Public knowledge of the individual fencer does come through in a positive light on occasion, but also too does it come through in a negative light.

There have been incidents where individuals have attacked others in public with swords and the result of these attacks has been an increase in the restrictions placed on owning and transporting the weapons. In some instances this has been due to the actions of a single individual. Further to this the same can be said of an individual who attends a tournament and injures an opponent. If there are repeated instances of this then the authorities will place restrictions on activities and insurances will increase. Thus the action of the individual matters, and matters greatly. Consider what impact you may have on your club, and the community.

CONCLUSION

All fencers have a responsibility, not only to themselves and the group with which they fence, but to all fencers regardless of their form of fencing. This means that they must watch their actions very closely so that they do not reflect badly on the fencing community. It is also their responsibility to spread knowledge about the art of the sword in all its forms. This means that no fencer should deride another school of thought, Eastern, Western, modern and Renaissance. All forms bring something to the fencing community. It is only through the spread of knowledge about fencing that fencing stays alive and people become more informed about it.

Fencers of all kinds should recognise a kinship amongst those who use swords of all kinds regardless of their form or method of use. There is something to be learnt from all different schools of thought and practice. Every method should be examined with an open mind as only through this study will the fencer truly discover what fencing really is and what they may truly find for themselves.

Fencing Movies: Problems with Getting it Right

INTRODUCTION

Movies with fencing are there for the entertainment of the people who view them. All fencers enjoy a good fencing movie. All remember the fencing scene at the top of the cliff in "The Princess Bride", or some scene in some iteration of "The Three Musketeers". The problem is that quite frequently experienced fencers will look at these movies and see holes in the technique and the actions of the combatants. This article is a brief investigation into the problems with getting such things right, and also continuing to make them saleable for the general public, as unfortunately the educated fencing community seems to be rather small for an entire movie to be budgeted around. Various aspects will be addressed and considered.

CHOREOGRAPHY VS COMBAT

The first problem that is encountered in the making of a fencing movie and making it to suit the fencing audience is the approach. It is a question of choreography versus combat. The purpose of the combat in a movie is to enhance the scene, develop dramatic elements between the combatants involved in the action, and in some part present some of the traits of each of the characters involved. The purpose of an encounter between two fencers is a test of skill, and consideration of their relationship to one another is usually not considered. Thus the big difference here is the purpose of the combat, one set of actions is an attempt to tell a story or develop some part of a storyline, while the other is purely a martial engagement between two individuals where the only concern is striking and not being struck. This situation leads to other elements of great importance to this particular topic.

Intent of Training

Fencers are trained to strike their opponents with their weapons. Admittedly there is a level of control behind this striking, but the intention is to strike the opponent before he strikes you. For the actor involved in a dramatic situation, the last thing they want to do is to actually strike their opponent. Stringent safety precautions are laid into the foundations of the training so that the actors do not strike one another. Anytime that one actor happens to hit the other is usually the result of a lapse in judgement or a break from a set routine. This is a fundamental difference that must be taken into account. Intent is important and the intent of an action more so.

Tactical vs Theatrical

Fencers use tactical considerations for the actions that they will use against their opponent. They will use the most efficient method of striking their opponent while at the same time ensuring that they are not struck. This differs greatly from the actor. The actor has a set of choreographed actions which were developed by the fight director of the movie for the actor to perform to portray the action required by the director. There are no tactical considerations here in the hands of the actor at all. The progression of the actions is controlled not by the person holding the weapon but by someone else, thus the actor is not free to change an action to be more efficient or to avoid an action which will result in defeat. Their fate or more to the point, the fate of their character, has already been determined by the director and writer. One of them will "die" or lose at a time determined by the director. This is obviously not the case for the fencer, who is in control of their own actions and responses to their opponent's actions. The result being entirely determined by the skill performed by the fencers.

BOTH TRAINED BUT DIFFERENTLY

Both actors and fencers are involved in training so that they are prepared for the encounter with their opponent, but the training is different for the two and also the length of training is different. While a fencer will spend months and years perfecting their technique to improve themselves, the actor has a much shorter period of time. While actors are trained in other physical movement, on average the actor has about six weeks to learn all that they need to perform the actions that are set by the fight director and the director of the movie. This truncates the training of the individual quite markedly. It is not to say that there are not actors who are also fencers; Basil Rathbone, and the fight choreographer and stuntman Bob Anderson, clearly prove otherwise. The thing is that the actions learnt by the actor are set moves which are performed for the movie, thus the actions are choreographed rather than intuited.

While there is an introduction to what the actor is supposed to be doing the main focus is on those actions as determined by the director and the fight director. The focus for the actor is this set of moves. If the fencer limited themselves to a predetermined set of actions it would restrict them a great deal and would reduce their effectiveness greatly.

IMAGE FOCUS

The image presented in movies is quite different from the actual nature of fencing. The image depicted by the movie is dependent on many factors and what sort of story the director wants to portray in the movie. This is of great importance. "By the Sword" (1991) depicts some elements of sport fencing in it. Some of the training is addressed, but the main focus in this is to depict the actions of the fencers as having speed and elegance once trained properly. This is reflected by their actions before and after training has been done; still, though the actions are limited by what was required for the movie.

Swashbuckling movie such as "Pirates of the Caribbean" (2003) and "The Three Musketeers" (1993) want to portray something different and thus the actions are different. The most important thing in this respect is that movies tend to focus on the flash and the bash; the sound of steel on steel and the large flowing actions of the characters in the movie. The use of the weapon is characterised by the character being depicted. Certain actions will be used by some characters and not by others; this enables some character development through physical actions. This is all quite different from actual fencing where economy of action is the focus and being the most effective against the opponents being the prime objective.

LACK OF RESEARCH

One problem that seems to come up again and again is a lack of research by the individuals involved in making the movies. This is evident in several places, as will be presented below. Assumptions have been made about weapons and armour and this affects how the action is depicted. A great deal of this is attributable to 19th century fencing historians, but still there are some issues that can be brought to light where there are problems.

Armour

The first assumption which is often made is about armour. It is often assumed to be heavy and thus extremely limiting on the actions of the combatants. Anyone who has used armour which is fitted the right way, and also customised to the wearer, will know that movement, while limited somewhat is not limited to the degree often depicted in movies. Research into the correct construction and wearing of armour is important so that it can be depicted properly. Armour which is constructed properly for the wearer is much less restrictive than several movies would like us to believe. A perfect example of supposed heavy, badly fitted armour can be seen in "A Knight's Tale" (2001) where one of the knights needs to be hoisted on to his horse. While this did happen much later in the Renaissance period where tilting armour was very heavy, it simply was not true for most of it. In fact it is reported that in his prime that Henry VIII could vault into the saddle fully-armoured.

Weapons

The next area which needs to be investigated and researched by those making the movies is about the weapons themselves. Some would have us believe that weapons of the medieval period were heavy and unwieldy. Proper research into their construction and make will reveal that this simply was not the case.

The sword of the medieval period was a precision weapon, and not one used for simple bludgeoning of the opponent. This is also reflected in the many Renaissance period texts on the use of such weapons. Simple bashing at the opponent was not the objective, there was a great amount of technique present as can be seen in the texts presented by such individuals as Liechtenauer, Talhoffer and other masters of the art of the swordsmanship.

Some movies would also have us believe that the thin elegant rapier was as effective at cutting as some of its medieval counter-parts. This is simply not the case. While there were some rapiers which were relatively effective at cutting, its prime function was to stab with the point. The weapon was simply too thin, in most cases, to perform the slashing and cleaving cuts which are so often presented in movies.

Renaissance Martial Arts

Added to all of these misconceptions about weapons and armour, the background of the fight director needs to be taken into account in the examination of the weapons and their use. A fight director whose main area of expertise is sport fencing will depict the use of weapons based on the particular mode of fighting they are familiar with. This is appropriate to some weapons, especially those of the 18th century and later, but those previous cannot have the same said of them. It is important that the fight director actually investigates the weapons being used in the movie so that they can be depicted properly. This is where Renaissance martial artists and other researchers will be of great help to them. Needless to say, only the correct research will enable the weapon and the armour to be depicted properly.

IMPROVEMENTS MADE

While a great deal has been said about the problems associated with weapon-based combat as depicted in movies, it must also be said that there have been some great improvements over the years in the depiction of various period weapons in movies and their associated combats. One example of this is the difference between the 1993 version of "The Three Musketeers" and the later 1998 "Man in the Iron Mask", and again in the later 2011 "The Three Musketeers". The formers' fencing is primarily based on sport fencing as can be seen by much of the action, whereas the latter has a great deal more fighting depicted using the weapons of the period. As research into period weapons improves and becomes evident to fight directors, and directors, the depiction of fencing in movies will improve, so long as this research is taken into account. There have been several movies released relatively recently in which the historical nature of the movie has been more and more evident, along with the use of the weapons in these movies. "Kingdom of Heaven" (2005) is a prime example of this particular trend toward an increase in research in the period being depicted and the use of appropriate weapons and armour in the movie.

CONCLUSION

Movies with fencing in them are very entertaining to watch for the fencing community and also the general public. There are many of them out there, some of them are good, and some of them are not so good. It is important that for the fencer, that these movies are looked at both from the perspective of the educated fencer, but also from how the general public will see it.

Questions about what this movie is attempting to depict as well as what sort of angle the director has taken in depicting the movie are important. If fencing is depicted accurately, much of the general public will not understand what is going on in the movie and thus will lose interest in it. The fight director's art must be respected as the depiction of any form of sword combat on the stage or screen is not a simple thing to achieve, but also considerations should be made on their part so that this depiction will improve and thus represent fencing as it should be. Enjoy movies for what they are, they can teach us much.

Murphy's Laws of Fencing – The "Henry" Version

There are many variants of Murphy's Laws. This is a list which I have assembled based on other lists and also on my experiences in fencing. This will have the laws as well as a little bit of an explanation about where this particular law comes from. In this way, it is hoped that these will be a source of amusement and education simultaneously.

1. If the opponent is within distance, so are you.
2. If you have a tempo, so does the opponent.

Laws one and two are about timing and distance, these are the two key concepts in fencing of all kinds. The important thing here is that they are fluid and what you have the opponent can take, or will also have at the same time. Remember to use these to your advantage.

3. The opponent will attack either when you are ready or when you are not.
4. If you are not attacking, expect your opponent to be.

If you are on guard in front of your opponent, expect that they will attack at their convenience, and not yours. This means you need to be prepared at all times. If you do not have the opponent on the defensive then he will take the opportunity to attack you.

5. Incoming attacks always have the right of way.

Make defence a priority against incoming attacks; the opportunity for riposte or counter should be secondary to not being struck.

6. What can be seen can be hit.

If you leave an opening in your defence, expect it to be struck. Likewise even if it is covered, it can be uncovered and hit.

7. If your attack is going well, your opponent is using second intention.
8. The only plan to rely on is to strike the opponent while not being struck.
9. If you have read your opponent, he has read you.

Plans are awesome in fencing, but remember that the opponent will also have a plan. Expect that your opponent will have some sort of counter to your attack, and you should plan to counter that.

10. Secret Blows, aren't.
11. Ultimate killing moves aren't.
12. The brilliant technique you just learnt has a counter.
13. There is no complex action which cannot be countered by a simple response.

The botta secreta (secret blow) is effective until it is used, therefore it can never be used. Once it is used people will learn it and counter it. There is no technique in fencing which cannot be countered in some fashion. Usually the counter to the action is very simple.

14. You need to know the simple before the complex is useful, but you will only realise this later.
15. The lesson that you need now is the one that will be taught at next week's training session.
16. There is never enough time between tournaments.
17. You will wish you had drilled more.

Training is important, unfortunately for many of us, we only realise that it is the simple stuff which is the most important. It works and it is the basis for the complex stuff. There is always something else to learn, and there is never enough time to learn it all properly.

18. If it's stupid but it works, it isn't stupid.
19. Professionals are predictable; it's the amateurs that are dangerous.

This one is about the unpredictable and unbelievable. Both are dangerous to the fencer. The experienced fencer has a pattern, the beginner for the most part doesn't, and it is that which makes them dangerous.

20. You are always too subtle or too obvious in your feints.
21. What you think is a feint is a real attack.

Feints are a useful technique when performed properly. You have to convince your opponent that it is a valid attack for them to respond.
They are also a problem when used against you. Learn how feints work and what they look like, even if you don't use them, you can figure out how to counter them.

22. Anything you do can get you hit, including doing nothing.
23. Be too focussed on defence and you won't attack.
24. Be too focussed on attack and you won't defend.

Actions in fencing need purpose, but they also need to be tempered with their opposite. You need to act against your opponent, but you need to do this with thought behind it.

25. Your next opponent will always be faster.
26. Progression in a tournament is inversely proportional to the amount of energy you have left.
27. There is always one more round to fence than you expected.

These three apply mostly to tournaments. As you get tired your opponents will seem faster, as such you need to preserve some of your energy for later rounds in tournaments. When you are progressing through rounds of a tournament you are using energy therefore you will always have less, consider this. Of course, you should always be sure when the tournament is finished.

28. Your gear will always wear out just after you have worn it in.
29. The borrowed sword is always less comfortable than your own.

Equipment is of great importance and your own equipment more so. The nature of equipment is that as it gets worn in it will wear out. Always remember to bring all of your own and keep it in good condition as no gear will be as comfortable as yours. This is your responsibility.

30. A cluster of bruises is Nature's way of telling you that you have a hole in your defence.

If you seem to always get hit in the same spot, you should probably have a teacher check what you are doing and what you are not doing in order to get hit there constantly. This is something that you should be aware of.

This is a list of thirty laws which came to my head. They have been clustered to put the like laws together so that they can focus on a single aspect of fencing. There are, no doubt, more laws of this kind that can be applied to fencing. These are, after all the ones which I relate to the most and have thus collected together. Consider this list, examine them, you never know, you may find something useful. There is a much more refined, possibly a little too refined, version of this list in an article in this collection.

Rapier Combat: A Practitioner's Thoughts

INTRODUCTION

The original article that was included with this title was a reprinting an old article that I wrote some time ago. It was primarily designed for an SCA (Society for Creative Anachronisms) audience, but much of what is written in there applies just the same. There are quite a few references to the SCA and the way that this group does things. I hope that this will assist in clearing up some confusion about this particular group also.

PURPOSE

Rapier Combat within the SCA is an attempt to recreate one of the civilian forms of combat that existed in the Renaissance period, in much the same way that much of HEMA does, minus the period forms of address and other period aspects. This form of combat is primarily centred on the rapier and its companions. What should be noted is that more recently other weapons have been included in the Cut and Thrust stream of combat, however the rapier will be the focus, otherwise a lot of confusion will be created.

WEAPONS

In recreating this form of combat, simulated weapons are used in a semi-competitive combat form. The weapons only differ essentially from the real weapons in that the blades have a blunt edge, and a rolled tip, which has a rubber stopper over it. They are very close to the actual weapon in weight and handling characteristics. The older fibreglass blades which were in use are now being phased out, were much lighter than real ones, and were cheaper to purchase. As such the weapons are on par with anything being used by the "more serious" HEMA community.

COMBAT CONVENTIONS

The combat form itself, in tournaments, is an attempt at recreating the lethal nature of the rapier in a combat situation, without the blood and burial costs. A win is scored by "rendering one's opponent disinclined to continue", this could mean a kill or disarm, or sufficient scratches. The whole body is a target, though the groin area is not deliberately targeted. Combatants are assumed to be wearing civilian attire and as such any cut or thrust has to be judged as if the weapon was real and had hit flesh. This means that a combatant has to be really careful.

What we do is kept safe by our safety and armour standards. Most importantly amongst this is the control that we instil into our students while they are in training. The best method to keep safe is to teach and learn control. The armour standard is there just to bolster the safety of the combatants.

RENAISSANCE COMBAT

Where does this form of combat fit into the "medieval" period? Simply, it doesn't. It is a Renaissance form of combat. Earlier forms of combat using thrusting weapons have been theorised as the predecessors of rapier combat. A lot of the techniques which are used in rapier combat were developed as the rapier did. Cut-and-thrust technique is one of the predecessors of the rapier's technique and it is from this that a lot of the style was developed.

The rapier combat which is engaged in within the SCA is based on principles developed by the Renaissance masters combined with the safety standards to ensure that it is as safe as possible. Some of the techniques, which the masters of the Renaissance taught, are not used, as they are much too dangerous to recreate safely.

SOCIAL ASPECTS

There are certain social aspects, which are important to include in recreating this form of combat. These social aspects are important so that the rapier combatant is correct in his manner. Such aspects are honour, courtesy and the gentleman. Another thing that is taken into account is the different schools of rapier combat that existed in the Renaissance period. It is important that people examine these so that their style can more accurately reflect the styles of the period. The most influential schools of the period were the Italian and Spanish. The French school later dominated, but the Spanish school lasted a great deal longer. The German also had its input, but its main contribution was to longsword and other more cut-focussed weapons.

EDITORIAL

Rapier combat fits in the SCA as one of the three combat arts that are offered. The Guilds of Defence for each Kingdom, where they have been created, operate to inspire and encourage rapier combat to develop to a better standard. Membership to the Guild is not compulsory for rapier combatants, but it does give combatants something else to aspire to than just championships and tournament wins.

SAFETY

The Rapier Marshalate is the administration branch of the rapier community. It is this group which administers safety and performs authorisations of combatants. The purpose of the Rapier Marshalate is to ensure that rapier combat is being performed safely and within the standards which have been set.

CONCLUSION

Rapier combat has elements, which you will not find in heavy (fully-armoured) or light combat (missile combatants), but there is no way that it can be persuaded that it is better or worse. Each combat form has elements to contribute. There is so much information about rapier combat in its various forms, and thanks to the Internet there are is large amount of Renaissance period manuals available for research. Combatants often find that the closer they go to a period form the better they do. Aside from all of that, rapier combat can be a lot of fun also.

Fencing Fest – The Keys to a Great Fencing Event

"North of the Border" Rapier Fest
Saturday 7th and Sunday 8th August A.S. XXXVIII
Rapier Training, Tournament and Melee Weekend.
Open to all who have an interest in rapier combat.

A total weekend devoted to the Arte of Rapier Combat. Spread over two days will be training sessions, a tournament or two, melee sessions and a rapier game, a relaxed weekend of fencing and feasting. Lunch is served on both days, with a feast of simple foods on the Saturday night. Billets, booking and information can be arranged by contact with the Steward.

This weekend is open to all ladies and gentlemen who have an interest in rapier combat. Current and future combatants, those who wish to watch and those who wish to learn. There should not be a time during the weekend where an enthusiastic lady or gentleman cannot find something interesting to learn or do. Need to brush-up on a weapon form? Need to authorise in another weapon form? Interested in rapier but did not know where to start? This is your best chance to get all of these things done. More to the point it is the chance to fence, and fence amongst others with the same interest.

INTRODUCTION

Well, for all my non-SCA readers, you will ask "What is Fencing Fest?" for all the ones who know about this event some of this is going to be pretty obvious/dull, but I hope that there will be at least some information useful to all. This article is about an event that I have been running for a while and some of the keys that have made it a success in those years. I hope that my readership will learn from what is placed here and go on to have their own great events.

Before I get on to the nitty-gritty of the event, I need to make something clear. I am not "letting the secrets out" to beat my own drum and show how great I am. The hope is that armed with the information presented here others may learn from it and be able to create great fencing events of their own. This can only be of benefit to the fencing community at large.

WHAT IS FENCING FEST?

Fencing Fest is an event which I have been running or at least been involved in some part now for eight years[1]. The original flyer, with its original name, minus much of the nitty-gritty has been included, above. It is an event which is primarily focused around the arts of defence as they are taught within the SCA and to be more precise within Lochac (which includes Australia and New Zealand). The event itself started as a small local event designed to get fencers together for an event which was focused on fencing rather than any other aspect of the SCA. Over the intervening years the event has grown, dare I say it, to become the primary purely fencing event in Lochac.

WHERE DID THE IDEA COME FROM?

Some years ago I looked about, there were events for every martial endeavour within the SCA, including fencing, it is true, but when it came to events with a focus on one of these arts, this is where it was different. Until Fencing Fest came about there was no event that could be found on the calendar which was totally focused on fencing. There were armoured events and archery events, but nothing for fencers of that kind. This is where the seed was planted.

The origins of Fencing Fest lay in an event which was purely focused on the unarmoured combatants of my local groups, to start with. This would enable the local fencers to get together and fence and learn what they could without any chance of possible interference from anyone else. This is where the "give people what they want comes in". The event was planned around giving people as much fencing as they could handle in the time-frame allowed for the event. In the beginning this was just for local fencers to get together and learn from one another. With the foundation stone laid, it was time to move on to the other things that held the event together. It is these things, these keys, which have enabled Fencing Fest to grow to the event that it has now become.

KEY 1: FENCING

For Fencing Fest, it is the fencing that people come along for more than anything else and as such this must be put first on the priorities above everything else. Fencing Fest has ended up being a success because the event has lots of fencing and that is what people come along for primarily. What kind of fencing? Classes for teaching fencing? A competition-focussed event? Either or both? This depends on your audience.

The early events had a semi-fluid program that was finalised on the first day of the event in order to give people what they wanted. As the event developed and more and more people started to attend a pattern formed where the first day was primarily teaching oriented and the second was more competition oriented. In this way people get a taste of both through the event and thus most are satisfied with the outcome. The balance between the two options should be determined by the people attending the event and what they want, but the organiser should have some at least rough idea of how it all should be planned out.

Importantly keep the program as fluid as you can so that things starting late do not totally throw out the entire program. There will be delays that you cannot predict and

---

[1] *Obviously this was written some time ago, as in 2018 Fencing Fest XV occurred.*

it is important that the program is flexible enough to work with these delays. In a rigid program a delay of a mere half an hour, or even less can cause all sorts of issues. The most important thing with the program is to give the people attending the event what they want above all else, and that is fencing.

KEY 2: COSTS

Contrary to some thoughts about, the price of the event does not guarantee or determine the quality of the event. Some of the best I have been to have been cheap, and some of the most disappointing have been rather expensive. There are some good reasons to keep an event price low, but the best is the simplest. The lower the price of the event for people coming to it, the more people you will get along to the event. In the end this will actually result in the money being made rather than being lost.

Food is something which will be discussed next. Picking a site is important; it should suit the needs of the event and nothing more. There is no reason to pay for facilities or things which the event will not require. Nor is it sensible to pay for any more area than the event will require; doing so with either is a waste of money and will drive your costs and thus the price of the event up. If you keep your costs down, this will keep the price down and thus attract more people to your event. Do research into costs, both of food and sites but also of other events of a similar nature and size.

KEY 3: FOOD

If your event is focused on fencing there is no point in having Master Chef-quality food, especially if this is going to drive your costs up. The attendees at a fencing event will be more focused on the fencing and thus will simply require the food to be filling. There are three simple things to focus on with regard to an event like Fencing Fest.

First, lots. No one who attends the event should go hungry. This means that there should be food enough to fill the people attending the event. Second, filling. This goes with the first one in that the people attending the event will be hungry after fencing and thus will want filling food. The portions of the food should be generous and be of a kind which is filling. Third, simple. Filling rather than pretty; when people are hungry they care a lot less if it is of a period recipe or how much it cost. Thus the three keys to food all link together. Feed the people who attend your event well and they are more likely to come to your next one.

KEY 4: TIMING

The timing of your event on the calendar can have a huge effect upon the success of the event as this can determine who will be available to attend your event. In the case of Fencing Fest, it is placed in early August as this is roughly six months from Rowany Festival, the biggest camping event in Lochac which is in Sydney. It is also placed in August as this is the end of winter and it is more likely to be dry in Queensland, Australia at this time of the year. By placing Fencing Fest here I give the maximum time for saving for the event and also cool but dry weather for fencing.

There is little point planning to have an event, two weeks and even a month close to a major event. People often simply do not have the finances to attend multiple events or even the time to do so. If you plan for your event as far away from big events, especially local ones, as possible you are more likely to get people to come along to your event.

If you want to look further afield you should also consider when major events of other groups are being held. This is a consideration often overlooked to the detriment to an event. The timing is also linked to advertising, which will be discussed below.

KEY 5: CREW

Being the event organiser you will have enough to do organising the event and you will not be able to do it all yourself. This will mean that you will require a crew or team of people to help you with your event to ensure that it runs smoothly. The calendar is littered with events where and organiser tried to do too much.

In your crew you will need people who know their jobs and know them well. Such people will be able to do what is required of them without your supervision and thus the job that they are doing will be one less per member that you have to worry about. In this particular instance it is even good to have smaller teams within the larger team, but all still must know their jobs and know them well. The other thing that you will need for good crew members are people who you can trust to do their jobs and who you can communicate with. This is important when things are going well, but even more important if things are not going well. Just remember that the communication needs to be two-way communication. Having to chase people for information or to do their job is a waste of your time and energy. A good crew is the best asset an event organiser can have.

KEY 6: ADVERTISE

Advertising is something which is often overlooked and also links into the timing aspect. If you plan your event too close, you will not have much time to tell everyone about the event, and the less who know, the less who will attend. The more time that you can give to advertising your event, the more people will know about it, and thus the more people are likely to attend.

There are three things that should be done with regard to advertising for an event. The first is early. As soon as all the details for the event are confirmed the advertising should start. This allows for the maximum amount of time for people to know about the event. It is important that the event needs to be confirmed with all the details for this to work effectively. Half or unconfirmed details do not inspire confidence.

The second is regularly. Regular reminders and updates about your event will constantly bring thoughts about your event to the fore. This is even more important if there is additional information available about the event.

The third is everywhere. Spread the information about your event to as many places as you can. This is even easier now with e-mail and social networks. E-mail lists are a great boon to advertising events and should be used where appropriate. Be careful about electronic advertising however in order that your information does not get marked as spam. Keep it to the point in order not to irritate people as little as possible.

CONCLUSION

What have been presented are the keys which I have used to make Fencing Fest into the great event that it is. I hope that you will find some useful information contained within this and will be able to use it in order to make your own events more successful. With all the information which is available about how to run events and also to plan events, the greatest key is to remember that which will suit your event the best. Once you have found this it should be your focus and every other consideration should have this as a background to the final decision made.

A small side-note that I will add is that Fencing Fest has been used as a model for other events since its sucessful runnings over the past years. Most attributable, it formed the original form of Swordplay, an annual HEMA event which occurs in Queensland, which has now become most definitely a national event, and has attracted international visitors as well. People will notice when an event runs smoothly and they will ask how it works. There is no real reason to keep it a secret, you might as well let it out and let more great events be created, and be satisfied that you had some impact in their creation.

Re-enactment and Its Decline

INTRODUCTION

While this particular subject is not directly relevant to the subject of fencing, it does apply if examined from a certain point of view. For many their swordsmanship actually revolves around one re-enacting group or another, thus the decline of the groups associated has an effect on the availability of participation in the type of fencing that they are interested in. Thus this question forms somewhat of a back-drop of importance to fencing, and indeed different forms of fencing.

In more recent years it would seem that there has been a decline in re-enactment. This would be pointing at a decline in numbers rather than a decline in the quality of the re-enactment. Indeed it is quite the opposite the quality of re-enactment has increased as more and more information and equipment has become available to the re-enactor, and this is part of the problem as to why the numbers are dropping. Interestingly, this has come at the same time that Western Martial Arts (WMA) and HEMA has seen an increase in numbers and interest.

PREVIOUSLY

When I started in re-enactment some 20 years ago, it was reasonably easy for the average person of the street to join a re-enactment group and start participating. In my case the group was the SCA. All that was expected of me at my first event was an attempt at clothing from pre-1600. I managed to rustle up a tunic from a costume set that the family had and a pair of track-suit pants for my legs. All in all, the outfit passed as being "medieval" from a distance, and no one batted an eyelid. It would seem that things have changed quite a bit, even in the SCA.

THINGS HAVE CHANGED

As the ability to construct and availability to gain the equipment has increased, so has the expectations of those within the groups. In my opinion it is partially this set-up cost which is causing people problems in joining the various groups and also maintaining their membership and activity within the groups. Where there's a large initial set-up cost for the group, and an expectation for the purchase of certain equipment to a certain standard, there will be those who simply cannot afford this set-up cost. This instantly restricts who can join and participate within the groups.

Using the SCA as an example, the first thing that is going to be said is that in recent years the membership cost has actually dropped and this should enable people to more easily be able to join the organisation. This is true enough, to become a financial member of the SCA it has become much easier, but why would a person be willing to pay such membership if they cannot afford to feel like they belong? This comes down to the expectations of those within the group more than anything else.

EXPECTATIONS

Previously, it was the case that a newcomer could turn up to an SCA event in clothing which was pseudo-medieval in appearance and there would be nothing said and no one would bat and eyelid. This allowed people from various socio-economic groups to be able to participate within the group and the numbers increased and were maintained at a quite high level. This is would not seem to be the case anymore.

The newcomer arrives and immediately there are expectations laid upon them as to what they need to acquire to fit in. Sure some of the items can be lent on a short-term basis, but still there is the expectation that the individual will fork out in the short-term a quite substantial amount, whether it is fabric, or clothing, or other equipment. For those in a low economic situation this is simply not possible and then they have to rely on the charity of others for an extended period of time and never quite feel like that they "fit". This does not encourage people to stick around particularly much. The indebted state of some is not deliberately placed by others, indeed others will quite happily gift time and materials, but due to not acquiring the materials themselves they still feel like they have a debt to pay off.

ACCEPTANCE AND ENCOURAGEMENT

Aside from the encouragement that people get from the people in the group, there must also be an acceptance of new people. These people, for the most part, will not already have their own gear and their "first attempts" need to be accepted if not praised. Constructive criticism and encouragement is always good as is being helpful. Simple criticism or disparaging remarks, on the other hand, are not. We should not expect our newcomers to turn up in perfect medieval or Renaissance equipment, and we should encourage them to do more and better, but with the expectation that this may take some time.

CONCLUSION

If re-enactment is to survive then we must encourage more and more people to come along and enjoy what we all enjoy. This actually applies to the WMA and HEMA community as well. The more we restrict who will fit within the organisation the more the numbers will decrease. Groups have died due to this particular phenomenon and if we do not want the same to happen to ours, then we must take a hard, long look at ourselves and see what we can do to encourage more people in, rather than scaring them off with high expectations which need to be filled in the short term.

Henry's Rules – The Essentials

INTRODUCTION

In a previous article I mentioned that I would post something of my own rules of fencing and I have had a long think about this particular subject. Much like the Jethro Gibbs (NCIS) list mine is a work in progress and tends to grow and change somewhat as I find new things to add. To reduce this I have decided that I will talk about my essential rules in this short discussion.

THE RULES

1. Don't get hit - defence is most important.
2. Hit the opponent - only real way to victory.

ALL OTHERS ARE SUPPLEMENTARY

All the other rules that I have come up with are supplementary to these two and assist in some way to achieve them. As I have mentioned above I have a much longer list of rules also about 20 in number which I have assembled from various experiences in my fencing career to date. I use them here and there in training my students and obviously during fencing. These rules give some structure both to training and also to teaching and around these I find that if something breaks a rule there has to be good *reason* for it. Rather than listing all the ones that I have to date, there is a more useful purpose that can be gained from this discussion.

DEVELOP YOUR OWN

My personal piece of advice is that each fencer should develop their own list of rules to follow. In this at least one thing is most important, they will not be set in stone, they will change. In the beginning it may be useful to write them down as they develop, or as you come across them. You need to be flexible in your approach and understand that things in your fencing world will change and that will result in a change in some of your rules.

What if they do change? This means going back to where you have written them down and cross the old rules off so you reduce the clutter, but always write down the reason why the old rule was discarded. Don't scribble it out, a single line through it, so you can still read it so you can reflect, and not write the same again. The core rules will stay the same and it is these ones which you should hold most closely to.

Sometimes they will be less like rules and more like short statements about fencing. This is also good. Anything that allows you to put in words what you have in your mind when you are thinking about fencing is good. Not a wordsmith, more of a visual person? So draw it instead. Any way that you can record your thoughts is great. Remember, unless you want to show someone, these are yours.

MOSTLY, BUT NOT JUST TECHNICAL

Most of the rules which are developed for fencing are focused on the technical aspects, but you should also take into account those more social aspects which are of importance.

These will reflect your attitude both on and off the arena of combat. This is to give a broader perspective on what you are doing in your fencing and your interactions with other fencers. The social aspect of fencing is often glossed over in favour of the more technical aspects, but it is of importance for the longevity of your fencing career. Your interactions with others will decide how fulfilling your fencing career is. Nobody wants to fence with a bore and a brute.

CONCLUSION: THE ESSENCE OF FENCING

Two rules. Pretty simple really, they summarise what fencing is all about, striking without being struck. We must consider the other rules which are presented as they assist us in achieving the goal which is presented by the two rules. Consider your own list. Expect it to grow and change. They are a useful way for organising your fencing thoughts. This is something that you need to consider carefully and deeply as it will form a core of your fencing knowledge, even if you don't write them down.

SECTION 2.
Safety

Safety and Fencing

INTRODUCTION

Safety is a concern for all combatants. It does not matter what weapons you use or which School you subscribe to, safety is important. This article will discuss safety and some aspects with regard to it. This is a subject of great significance for all swordsmen as it can affect not only you, but other practitioners. Thus you should always consider your actions before you do something.

Safety is one of the most serious of considerations with regard to all forms of fencing and one that cannot be ignored except at our peril. It is important to all who participate and not just for those safety officers whose job it is to watch over the proceedings. We all need to be aware of the various aspects which affect our safety and also how this affects the entire fencing community as a whole independent of the weapon choice or style being used.

"ARMOUR" AND CALIBRATION

At this particular time I would like to discuss the subject of "armour". In essence this is the protective equipment that we wear to be safe in the practice of our particular art. This takes into account such things as masks, helms, jackets, groin protection and footwear. All of these elements are a part of what we would call protective equipment, what I would like to refer to in the future as "armour". Next there is the subject of calibration, the question of how hard we hit our opponents. Calibration is a measure of how hard we hit our opponents with our chosen weapons. This is a particular aspect which goes hand in hand with the chosen armour for the particular form of fencing which is being done.

There is a scale of calibration as to armour. If we wish to hit our opponents with a certain level of force then the armour must be up to this task. If the striking is heavy, then the armour will have to be heavier than it would have been if the striking was much lighter. This is the first question that we need to ask. Do we increase the armour and increase the calibration or do we reduce the calibration and thus the armour required? This is a question that needs to be answered by the particular organisation doing the fencing and the safety officers within that organisation.

A Sliding Scale

There is a sliding scale which exists which must be paid attention to in the question of establishing an armour standard. If the armour standard increases so too will the calibration and thus the armour will increase and so forth. To limit this it is necessary to remain in control of the calibration of the striking being done. In response to this it is fair to say that the level of calibration used takes an element of control and it is better to have this control than to increase the armour. This must be taught to the students of the school so that they can control their calibration and thus not require an increase in armour.

All this being said, students should not be discouraged from wearing extra armour for their own safety, simply that note should be taken of any trends in the group for any general increases in armour due to an increase in calibration. If this is the case, then it must be time to either discuss bringing back the calibration of the participants, or increasing the armour. Interestingly, while the latter would seem the easier path, the former actually breeds a better kind of fencer who has better control over his actions.

SKILL-FOCUS

In all aspects of our teaching of students control should be the focus, and calibration will emerge from this. It is better that we teach all of our students control in all their actions so that they are able to become better fencers. With regard to engaging an opponent the focus of the training should be on the technique used to gain the hit, rather than the hit itself. This will promote better fencing overall as it is a technique and therefore skill-focused pursuit rather than a result-focused pursuit. Thus the aim should be for the accurate performance of a skill or technique against an opponent rather than just seeking to hit them. This will enable the students to focus on a successful strike on the opponent as the result of the correct conditions being made rather than force being used to ensure the strike.

Accurate Technique

Accurate technique should always be the focus above the use of force used to ensure a successful hit on the opponent. With regard to this accurate technique is more effective that the pure use of force. Technique requires little strength but great knowledge of technique, distance and timing. This should be the focus of our training of students. Due to its basis in the foundation principles of fencing and also skill, technique will always have the advantage over strength and force when it is used. This relates directly back to calibration and by nature safety. If the technique is performed at the correct distance and time, force and thus calibration should be no issue for the user of the technique. Where the lack of technique is compensated for by force then issues will abound.

CONCLUSION

We should all be aware of the various safety issues involved in the performance of our art and not leave these to the safety officers who are delegated to oversee them. If you have concerns about safety you should be encouraged to bring these up with your safety officer. We should strive to teach our students control and thus this will increase our safety in a way that no increase in armour can. The safer we can make our art the more appealing it is for all. If one group is lax about safety in any form this can bring the rest of the practitioners of this art into disrepute or even cause a threat to the existence of our art as it is in the current age. Be aware of safety issues and the important part that you have to play in ensuring that our art is as safe as it can be not only for us but for future teachers and students of our art.

The First Defence: Control

INTRODUCTION

Safety is the concern of all combatants regardless of the nature of their art. This applies to those pursuing both Eastern and Western arts, and regardless of the weapons chosen by the combatants. A lack of consideration for safety aspects will result in injury and the possibility of serious injury or even death. This entry discusses concepts of safety and investigates them to find a foundation from which they are based and one which they should be based.

SAFETY

Standards of safety in fencing, regardless of what form, are based upon what is an acceptable level of injury for the activity which is taken part in. For some this will be to the limit of bones being broken in extreme instances and for others the idea of severe bruising is abhorrent. It is upon this basis that their ideas of safety are built. Obviously there must be some safety standards set for the activity to be encouraged and continued.

This level of injury acceptance goes directly toward the three primary aspects of the safety standard, protective gear, weapons and performance. With regard to these aspects one will always be emphasised over the others. For some it is performance, this will restrict what actions are acceptable and legal within the system. For others the focus will be on weapons and as such weapons are stipulated with particular characteristics, and thus restricted, to be used within that system. Others it is the armour which determines the primary aspect of safety and for these the protective gear will be stipulated depending on the recognised limit of injury.

However in truly intelligent systems it is always an even balance of all of the aspects. Weapons are stipulated but only in comparison to the armour. The performance is then regulated to an acceptable level for the system which will allow the weapons and armour to do their respective jobs. What is important here is that it is the performance, and thus control of the combatants which must be most important. Regardless of the protective gear or weapon standards, a person who is uncontrolled and who does not understand the performance requirements will still be a danger. Thus it must be control which needs to be emphasised in training and also codes of performance which need to be enforced.

ARMOUR AND WEAPONS

With regard to armour and weapons there is always the question of how much of each. Should the focus be upon the weapons or the armour? This has a lot to do with the perceptions of danger on the parts of the combatants.

Should the weapons be light and reasonably forgiving then the armour can be much lighter. Should the weapons be heavier and less forgiving then the armour as a result needs to be upgraded. This is a sliding scale and the direction to which the pointer slides will determine what sort of armour and weapons are chosen as suitable for the activity, as indicated in the previous article. The result will also demonstrate who the focus of safety is: the person doing the striking, or the person being struck.

A Fallible System

Even with armour which is the safest and weapons which are the safest, relying upon the armour and weapons as primary is an issue. This is a fallible system. First, the material in the construction of the armour or the weapon may fail. This is something which we only have a certain amount of control over. Freak accidents will happen. Secondly, the appropriate weapons have to be used in the appropriate manner and the same with the armour should either not suit the purpose for which it is being used, this will cause issues. Finally there is the simple element that a person may forget to don a particular piece of armour, or inspect their own weapon. This can also lead to issues. Once again to comes down to the individual being in control of the situation.

Armour vs Calibration

Finally there is the question of armour versus calibration. If the system is designed that the person being hit needs to feel the impact and they cannot or do not the calibration of the blows will increase. At the point where this becomes an issue, due to injuries, the armour will be increased. This will increase the calibration, and so the process will go around. This can be stopped at the beginning with control on the part of both combatants; hitting and hit.

Weapons and armour are two different sides of the same coin. These are physical items which are used in the performance of the art. Much can be done to determine which armour and weapons are used and thus increase safety, but regardless of the stipulations of the armour and weapons they still only cover so much. It is the combatant who wears the armour and uses the weapons which should be the focus; thus the control of the combatants.

CONTROL

Control is an element which must come from within the student rather than being enforced externally. The way to do this is to have it trained into the students. This means that it must become an element in each lesson. Control must be emphasised in the curriculum that the students are learning. This is the only way that it will become an essential part of them as fencers.

While there does not need to be a specific lesson or lessons on control, it needs to be highlighted in the lessons which are taught. Even such simple elements such as footwork have an element of control to them. Feet need to be placed in the correct positions and the body needs to be moved in a particular manner and with control. This element is obviously required in any element of offensive actions to ensure that they are controlled and delivered properly.

Emphasise Control

The focus on control lays a better foundation for safety for the student and indeed the organisation of which the student is a part. What is even better is that the more that this is emphasised in early lessons, the more that it will grow. Control is something which increases with experience and practice should the trainers put enough emphasis on it.

The question of protective gear vs weapons and calibration is solved by control being an important part of the student's training. Should the students have control they will not have the issues of calibration as their attacks will be controlled in their delivery and thus for the most part should arrive with the correct amount of impact for the system being taught. Should the element of control become a normal and integral part of training a student with control can pick up armour and weapon failures and thus avoid instances of danger; thus control should be the primary safety element.

YOUR RESPONSIBILITY TO THE ART

Whether it is recognised or not, each practitioner/swordsman/fencer has a responsibility to the art that they need to take very seriously and each time a weapon is picked up this responsibility comes into effect. The actions of a single person wielding a weapon can have effects far beyond any single blow delivered, or gesture made. Laws and restrictions have been made because of the rash actions of some stupid individual wielding a sword.

Each individual who involves him or herself in fencing in any form be it sport, historical, Eastern or Western takes upon them the responsibility to see that the art survives. In this they take upon themselves the responsibility to represent the art that they are demonstrating in a good way. Should this not be adhered to they put under threat the entire community. A single act of an individual wielding a sword can have repercussions affecting not only themselves but the wider community.

Every time you pick up a weapon you must ensure that you do your best not to injure your opponent, yourself or anyone who may be standing by. To fail in this places the art under threat of extinction. Already forces have been put in place, which restrict access to the weapons of our art and where we can use them. This is the result of an individual using the weapons with no consider for the repercussions that will result from their actions. Do not be one of these individuals.

CONCLUSION

Keep it safe, keep it controlled. Control is the key to safety in the art that we practice. There is no safety measure, save not using the weapons at all, that has a higher degree of success and safety for yourself and your opponent. Ensure that your practice/bouts/meeting has no way of being interpreted as an offensive gesture to members of the public. Ensure that you are as safe as possible within the practice of your art and you will fulfil your responsibility to the sword community at large.

Brutal Fencing I: A Discussion of Aggression

INTRODUCTION

Aggression is an element which must be taken into account in all forms of fencing. It is also something that can lead to brutal play where there is the high chance that a fencer may injure their opponent. Obviously this is something that we need to avoid for many reasons. This article discusses aggression and how it can be related to this important subject.

SOME REQUIRED

"One problem in fencing is brutal play that leads to injury. This is neither good for the individuals injured, nor good for fencing when fencing's image becomes that of a dangerous activity." (Evangelista, 2000:71)

In the question of aggression there is the question of the use of aggression and also overt aggression. The nature of attacking an opponent implies a level of aggression that is required, if the fencer is totally passive they will not attack their opponent at all and as such from this point of view there is a level of aggression that is required. The problem here is that sometimes a fencer may get taken away by their aggressive state and this can lead to problems. It is this being taken away by the aggression that can lead to overt aggression that needs to be avoided and this is the case for both on and off the fencing arena.

OVERT AGGRESSION

Overt aggression is a situation where the fencer cannot control their aggressive tendencies and this can lead to bad habits forming and also other problems. This form of aggression can lead to brutal play which is something that all fencers should avoid. In this idea of brutal play there are some areas which are undefined. There are some inherently brutal styles of combat, but even these need to be tempered with a level of control in order that the opponent is not injured in the execution of such a style.

"Aggressive: adj. having or showing determination and energetic pursuit of your ends" (wordnetweb.princeton.edu/perl/webwn)

The purpose of facing an opponent in fencing is to match their skills against them. In this the fencer will be striving for victory over their opponent. In the current day and age it is not the purpose to utterly defeat our opponent, or pound them into the ground. This particular aspect ceased as soon as the sword was not used in combat. It is an important consideration that needs to be in the back of the fencer's mind whenever they take to the field. The way that an opponent is defeated will project an image of the fencer to others who are watching, and also the opponent. This image is important as it will be attached to the fencer's reputation as a fencer, regardless of the form of fencing that the fencer is doing. In this the method used to gain victory must be considered, and must be considered to be important to the fencer.

MEANS TO GAIN VICTORY

A clean victory against the opponent where it is reliant on pure technique should be the goal of the fencer regardless of the form of fencing and regardless of the opponent. This form of victory will lead to a greater level of respect and renown for the fencer. If the fencer relies upon pure aggression in their fencing this will be noted by other fencers can result in notoriety rather than respect for the fencer. This form of fencing is less clean, and if the fencer is focussed on the win and nothing more it is what can result out of the encounter. The overt use of aggression in an encounter will be noted by the opponent and the other fencers who are watching the encounter. This also relates to the use of force as related to the use of technique.

The fencer has a choice of using force or technique in an attack and depending on what they choose will decide the result. An attack which uses strength to force its way through the opponent's defence is using the muscles of the fencer to overcome the defence of the opponent. An attack which uses technique to defeat the opponent's attack uses the founding principles upon which fencing is based to strike the opponent.

In the attack using force, the muscles are tensed and are used to a great degree. This form of attack uses a great deal of energy and due to the overt use of muscle and force will tend to be less accurate than the attack which uses technique. It is also the case that often this form of attack will also be delivered against the target with more force and thus a higher likelihood of resulting in injury.

In an attack which is delivered using technique, the muscles and the fencer are much more relaxed. The fencer relies on their control of the weapon and the principles of fencing to deliver the attack. This attack is more likely to be more accurate, and will also be delivered against the opponent with less force and thus less chance of injury to the opponent. The attack with technique relies upon the discipline and control of the fencer.

DISCIPLINE AND CONTROL

Discipline and control are related. To have control takes a great deal of discipline as this control is developed through practice and application of technique. From another point of view control is also necessary for discipline as the fencer needs to control their actions enough to develop discipline in their actions. These two aspects are directly related to the idea of aggression and the results of it.

Where the fencer controls their aggression, they can apply the aggressive tendencies to the performance of a controlled action, which is more likely to succeed. This means that even though they are being aggressive, it is controlled in the application of the technique still however, the fencer needs to be careful that the result of the technique will not injure their opponent. Where control is lost and aggression rules, there will be little consideration of technique and the fencer will use anything at their disposal to strike their opponent. It is important that discipline and control are applied to the aggressive tendencies in order that control is maintained over the weapon.

CONTROLLED AGGRESSION

What is control? What is the control applied to? How can aggression be controlled? Control is the application of self-discipline to a situation. In fencing this means that control is applied to how the body is moved and how the weapon is moved as a result. This control is also over the individual's mental state during fencing. The loss of temper or loss of control over the aggressive nature is a failure of self-discipline on the part of the fencer. Thus it is both physical and mental aspects in the fencer which need to be controlled through the use of self-discipline.

The idea of controlled aggression would seem to some to be an alien concept. The common feeling is that aggression is not controlled at all and the use of such can only be a detriment to the fencer. This is actually not the case. Through the application of self-discipline aggression can be controlled and thus applied with a measure of safety. It is only when the aggressive tendencies take over that the fencer becomes dangerous to them and their opponent. A controlled aggression will mean that the fencer knows how far to go and when to stop before causing a problem. Aggression can be seen to be a bad thing in fencing, but it is really only when the fencer loses control of such aggression that problems will start.

FENCING WITH FRIENDS

One of the most important things about fencing in the modern world is that in general fencing is done with friends. The antagonistic scenario for which fencing was originally designed has fallen by the wayside for the greater part in favour of a sporting or recreational pursuit. What this means is that there is really no reason why a person should be injured deliberately during fencing. More to the point, such behaviour is seen in a negative light.

A certain level of injury is liable to happen due to the contact nature of the recreation, but this should be minimised as much as possible. Part of this can be achieved through protective equipment, but a larger part comes from the control of the actions of the participants. Injuries which result from brutal or overtly aggressive play reflect badly upon the fencer, but they also reflect badly on the activity itself and this is a vital consideration for all fencers, regardless of their type of fencing. Injuries make fencing seem as though it is a dangerous activity and this does not encourage others to join and does nothing for the image of fencing at all. Remember for the most part that fencing takes place with our friends and injuring these people is a bad thing that should be avoided. Injuring friends is a good way to lose them and also have others lose respect for the fencer.

CONCLUSION

It is the duty of the fencer to ensure that they are taking as safe an approach to fencing as possible so that the recreation is able to be maintained and for it to be available for future generations. Aggression is a part of fencing; this is something that cannot be avoided. The act of attempting to strike an opponent with a weapon is aggressive in its nature, but this aggression can be controlled. Due consideration needs to be made by the fencer of their performance of the art, and also especially with regard to the level of control they have over their own aggression. Brutal play should be discouraged strongly in all aspects of fencing, regardless of the type of fencing being performed. Where the aggression takes over the fencer injuries can happen quite easily.

Self-discipline and control are of vital importance to the safe and better performance of fencing.

Brutal Fencing II: Aggressive Versus Assertive

INTRODUCTION
In the previous part of this discussion I wrote about aggression, when I wrote it originally I was not really able to explain what I meant. I was able to explain what I didn't mean, but I was not able to explain what I thought was suitable. This article is an attempt to address this particular issue and hopefully clear up some meaning. This was greatly helped by reading one of the articles in the *Encased in Steel: Anthology I*, which I reviewed.

DEFINITIONS
The Oxford dictionary (www.oxforddictionaries.com) defines the terms as follows:

Assertive: "having or showing a confident and forceful personality"
Aggressive: "Ready or likely to confront; characterized by or resulting from aggression"

One is an expression of confidence and the other is an expression of confrontation. While they could be seen as being quite similar they are actually different. The assertive may attack because he is confident about himself and is thus assured of the result, but he will choose when. The aggressive must attack because he must because that is his way, he has no choice.

ASSERTIVE NOT AGGRESSIVE
So, a person in their fencing when facing and bouting or even competing against another opponent should be assertive rather than aggressive. To be aggressive in this instance is to use power and force where it is not required, to overtly over-power the opponent much as any thug would. To be assertive on the other hand is to assert against the opponent. To present them with valid attacks which they must respond to, to use skill and reason to defeat the opponent, and most importantly while maintaining control of yourself and your weapon. This is the difference that I wanted to achieve.

DIFFERENCE IN ATTACK
The attacks of the assertive fencer may come fast, and they may be unexpected, the actions may force the opponent into a position and so forth, but the assertive fencer will use his skill rather than mere brute force to achieve this. The assertive fencer will still have presence of mind to use complex tactics and change his method depending on the opponent and their reactions. This is what is meant by an assertive swordsman. The other is not a swordsman; it is a brute, a thug with sword.

CONCLUSION
This has taken some time to work out proper meaning, and its application to fencing, but I think what I have expressed here, along with what I have said previously sums my feelings on the matter up quite well. The real swordsman will time his blows

to count, not wasting blows that are not likely to hit, and not attempting to pound his opponent into submission with repeated blows. A single blow which is properly delivered at the correct time with less force is much better than several blows delivered at the wrong time with more force.

Brutal Fencing III: A Question of Calibration

INTRODUCTION

There are two articles on the subject of brutal fencing and its relation to aggression and assertiveness. This discussion is aimed at one particular aspect of fencing and indeed brutal fencing and that is how hard one fencer strikes one another, this is sometimes referred to as *calibration*. Part of this entry goes to the reason why we actually engage in HEMA.

WHAT IS MEANT BY CALIBRATION?

Calibration for the purposes of this post, and indeed in my opinion, is the amount of force sufficient required as struck by one combatant against another combatant for them to acknowledge a blow as "good". This means that the blow would have done them physical harm if the weapon was sharp, in the case of a sword. Of course this means both combatants have to agree on what one another is assumed to be wearing. The level of *calibration* will be different if the combatants are assumed to be wearing some sort of armour as compared to if they are assumed to be not.

For the most part, a lot of HEMA, the assumed armour is nil, the combatants are assumed to be wearing no armour at all. This means that they are wearing normal street clothes, no padding, maybe a pair of gloves. This means there is no armour to cut through, or padded jacket to pound through; just a couple of layers of fabric and then flesh. The armour, or should it be said, protective gear that is worn is worn for protection against injury not for the simulation of any armour.

WHY HIT HARD?

This is an important question which has not really been answered properly at all, and some of the answers which have come back are quite disturbing. Do you want to injure people? If the answer to this question is "Yes", then I hope that I do not meet you and I hope that you do not turn up to my practice because you're not the sort of student I am looking for. There is no reason to injure people at all. It does not show "martial effectiveness" or anything of this kind, in fact you are border-line from having someone call the police for assault and battery.

Armour and Calibration

Combatants wear extra protective gear to protect themselves where they require it; this should not be a surprise. For some out there, they see this as a challenge, "You wear more armour, I'll just hit harder." The first thing to note here is that the attitude is just *wrong*. If you find one of these people, report him to your instructor immediately, if he does nothing, leave the school or group.

The problem we face is that as people increase their *calibration*, so protective gear increases, so *calibration* increases, so protective gear increases, and so on. One has got to give, mostly it is the bodies under the protective gear, resulting in injuries and people out for months at a time, and people leaving in droves because they can't afford the protective gear and don't like being hit that hard. This is a problem which can be stopped at the beginning by controlling *calibration*.

"Martial Effectiveness"
In discussing the question of "martial effectiveness", it does not take as much force to damage flesh as you think. With a thrust it is ridiculously easy. With a cut, it is not much farther off that. We have all seen videos loaded up on YouTube with this sword being applied to that target. The only way to prove this for you is to do it yourself.

Test-cutting has a high degree of relevance for HEMA. How can **you** know what is "martially effective" and how much *calibration* is required to damage a target in the real world unless you have tested it yourself? This means acquiring the appropriate weapons and the appropriate targets to do a proper simulation, something at least close to a scientific investigation.

Technique versus Strength
There is always the question of technique and strength. Where technique is used, strength is not required. The sword is a tool specifically designed to damage an opponent in a particular way and if the techniques are performed properly the sword will work in this way with very little to no strength required. One of the reasons why swordplay appeals to so many is that, for the most part, as long as you can hold the sword up and do the techniques, strength plays a very small factor in what happens.

When a technique is performed and the body is moved correctly with the feet and hands all in the correct time all the strength that is required is applied. I wrote an article about "The Myth of Speed", which can be found in this book. Here, again, is a place where strength is not required it comes through the correct application of technique. So, once again, strength is put on the back-burner.

CONCLUSION
The question really goes; in your performance of HEMA are you using a sword or a long, thin club? A swordsman knows how to apply the correct amount of strength at the correct time to make a particular technique work; he does not simply bash his way through his opponent's defences. A swordsman knows that an excess of strength will actually reduce the amount of speed and precision in his techniques. A swordsman will earn respect from his opponents for striking true but also with an amount of force required to deliver the intent of the blow but with no excess.

The question of *calibration* is one of safety. It questions how hard we really **need** to hit one another. There is no real need to hit one another with any more force than is required for the opponent to feel the intent of the blow. The only reason we should have to wear protective gear is for accidental reasons, i.e. if our opponent or we make a mistake, which we can never protect against. What does this mean? This means that the community as a whole needs to look at just how hard we are hitting and ask, "Does this match with what we are re-creating?" and "Do we need to be hitting this hard?" Personally, I think the answer is "No" to both questions.

A "Safe" Sword

INTRODUCTION
The concept of a "safe" sword is one which is presented again and again to us when considering which weapons we should buy and which weapons should be allowed in tournaments and so forth. This is a concept which badly needs to be addressed and some of the basic notions which are attached to this also addressed. These are weapons which are being discussed, regardless if they have dull edges and blunt points, and they are being used as simulated weapons as well.

THE OBJECT IS SAFE
When a weapon is lying on the ground away from anyone it is safe. This is when a weapon is safe; as soon as a person is involved there is an element where safety is reduced. The safety is reduced both for the person who is picking up the weapon and also for anyone who is around the person wielding the weapon. This is regardless of whether it is a sword, an axe, a mace, an assault rifle, a handgun or even a missile launcher, the same applies.

ALL RELATIVE SAFETY
The weapon may be dropped on the wielder's toe, or even on a by-stander's toe. The relative safety of a weapon has more to do with the person holding the weapon than the weapon itself. A person who is trained in the safe use of a weapon is generally safer than one who is not. A person who has had more experience with a weapon is generally safer than one who is not. It is the person who determines how safe a weapon is or is not. Once again this is with regard to all kinds of weapons, melee or projectile, modern or ancient.

THE SWORD IS A WEAPON
The image, from *The Hogfather* which I posted with the original article is one that I really like a lot, and it is very pertinent with regard to this discussion. It depicts the Hogfather giving a little girl a sword and the parent claiming that it is not safe, and that it's educational due to its lack of safety and so forth. I removed it from here for copyright reasons. A sword is a weapon therefore it is not designed to be safe. Its purpose is to strike another person with the intent to do damage (simulated or not) against them. The aspects of selection which are made for particular weapons due to temper, type of hilt arrangement, edge thickness, and point characteristics cannot change the fact that it is still a weapon, and therefore is still not safe.

The points of construction are merely risk mitigating factors. This simple fact can be seen with children when you give them "toy" or latex swords or even boffer, sooner or later one of them will get hurt. This is because the sword is designed to do damage. The weapon can be selected for temper the point rounded and some sort of blunt placed on it, the edges thickened, and still it is a weapon with the potential to do damage. All that has been done is to reduce the chances of this happening.

RULES AND REGULATIONS – RISK MITIGATION

The same can be said for any rules or regulations imposed by organisations and tournaments with regard to particular weapons which are or are not allowed to be used within the organisation or at the particular tournament. These are, again, risk mitigating factors. These are combined with an expected protective equipment standard and an expected standard of play to attempt to create an environment where catastrophic injury is less likely to occur.

The rules and regulations which are imposed upon tournaments and organisations for the use of swords and the safety equipment required to be worn are no different from those imposed for those for football or any other sport. This is the lowest standard and the lowest method of risk mitigation. The expected standard of play, is again, no different from rules which sports are played; a higher level of risk mitigation, but not much.

EXAMINATION IS REQUIRED

What desperately needs to be noted is, with regard to weapons and especially the weapons chosen by most practitioners of HEMA, it is not the weapons which should be the focus of examination, but the individuals who are wielding the weapons. This is much more effective than looking at protective equipment or changing the point structure of any tournament. Training the users of the weapons to respect the art in which they are training and the weapons they are using is important.

Sure, there may be some weapons which, due to their characteristics, they may be "safer" than other weapons, but it should be noted that this is risk mitigation and not very effective at that. This is at the lowest end of effectiveness on making things safer for participants. The notion of a "safe" sword is false and it is something that as a community we need to get away from and realise the situation for what it is.

HEMA schools should be teaching weapon awareness and respect as one of their first lessons to new students. Everyone should be reminded of this aspect of their training over and over so it becomes habit to treat their weapons with respect and care. A weapon should never be pointed at a target unless you intend to strike it. A weapon should never be left somewhere where someone may trip over it or knock it over. A weapon should always be carried in such a way that it will not be an obstruction to passers-by. Always be sure that the area in which you want to bout or practice is clear of others. These are simple things but students and teachers should always be aware of them.

CONCLUSION: TEACH & LEARN RESPECT FOR THE WEAPON

Much of what has been said above comes down to respect for the sword as a weapon. Regardless if it is sharp or if it has dull edges and a rubber blunt on the end. Both need to be respected as both can cause injury if they are not used with care. Your weapons need to be treated with care and respect. Your fellow practitioners also need to be treated with respect and they will do the same for you. Take care and be aware.

Proper Fitting Armour

PURPOSE

The purpose of this article is to address the question of the proper fit of armour on combatants. Proper fitting protective gear is one of the keys to safety of combatants.

One of the prime issues that will be addressed is that of the proper fitting and constructed gorget. This is a subject, which has emerged both locally and in the wider HEMA community. It is a subject which will be addressed in some detail due to its importance. Armour in general will also be addressed in a general sense to complete the picture.

PROPER FIT

Wearing armour is one thing but wearing protective gear with a proper fit is another. Armour which does not fit properly can impede a combatant's performance as it may rub against the combatant or restrict certain movements. More to the point, protective gear which does not fit properly can offer negligible protection, and in some instances can actually cause safety issues.

Armour is very individual and in most cases needs to be fitted to the individual. Even "off the shelf" armours often need some modification and wearing-in by the combatant before they fit properly and are comfortable. The protective gear must fit the individual and should be fitted to the individual, borrowed protective gear will never be the same and never fit, nor be effective, as your own. This is primarily due to body shape, but there are other factors which can affect this such as age of the armour itself. All new piece of protective gear needs some time to "wear-in". To be really safe, you need your own armour, and you need it fitted to you. As the article below progresses, more will be said of the proper fit of protective gear along with what the armour should be protecting. These two elements work hand in hand as often protective gear which does not fit properly will not cover what it is supposed to protect.

WHAT NEEDS TO BE PROTECTED?

Vital areas are the highest on the list in the answer to this question, but more detail is required. The following will examine what needs to be protected both from a general point of view and also more specifically for weapons of note. It will also address the idea of minimum armour, areas of importance and some recommendations also.

Minimum Armour

Each organisation will, or should, have a document somewhere, or a known standard, which describes the minimum armour which each combatant requires for participation in free-sparring and most forms of bouting in their particular club. The same can be said for HEMA events, once again these describe the minimums required to participate in these events.

These rules, regardless of where they originate, describe the minimums required to participate. What is important is that they are not necessarily the same as a person's personal minimums. Each individual should consider what they require to be safe and if this is above and beyond the minimum, they should feel no issue in wearing such armour, it should actually be encouraged.

The foundation of a minimum armour standard is that the armour is designed to protect those areas most significant with regard to significant amounts of damage to the individual. The protective gear is designed to prevent serious injury as a minimum standard. In this there are areas which are common to all weapons and these are the ones where the most significant amount of damage can occur should they be struck.

The armour needs to be appropriate to the weapon, and thus there will be differences in standards between weapons. This is due to the nature of the weapons being used and the potential damage that the weapon may cause. In this particular case some weapons will require more protective gear, some will require less, and the armour may focus on different areas of the body to be protected. The weapon needs to be taken into account when considering armour.

Areas of Importance

There are some areas of importance which need special attention paid to them when considering armour. These are the focus of the minimum armour requirements. Depending on what weapon is being used will decide how much armour is required.

First of all is the head and neck. Of all the areas of the body this is the most significant. Improper protection of the head can cause serious and lasting injury. The importance of this area will be highlighted in a focused discussion below.

The groin for males is a special consideration for males, as is the breasts for females. Females should also have some consideration with regard to groin protection also. These special areas need to be protected as the damage to these areas can also be long-lasting.

The next area to look at is the limbs and more specifically the elbows and knees. These joints are particularly exposed to damage and need to be protected from percussive hits as they can be damaged relatively easily. The entire joint in the case of both elbows and knees need to be protected.

Protection for the hands and wrists are also important and should be a significant consideration. This is most important for longsword use however the same can be said for any weapon of significant cutting ability. This is less important for the rapier however the hands should still be covered. Suitable hand protection should be a serious consideration for any combatant. Damage can occur to hands and fingers quite easily where proper protection is not being worn. The entire hand and wrist needs to be protected and covered.

Finally, there are feet and ankles. For the most part this can be protected by the correct kind of footwear. Many combatants underestimate the importance of footwear which is suitable to their activity. A lack of decent footwear can lead to damage to both foot and ankle.

RECOMMENDATIONS

While the following are only recommendations, they are some which should be considered seriously, regardless of the weapon being used. While a puncture-proof jacket will protect against a broken blade penetrating the torso, it is also recommended that some supplementary armour be worn on the torso for simple impact protection. This is especially aimed at the protection of the chest, cracked and fractured ribs are no joke. The other recommendation is for lower leg protection. The upper leg is mostly protected by muscle however the shin is quite exposed to damage.

Skin Coverage

The final recommendation that will be made is with regard to skin coverage. This is for protection against burrs and the like from damaged blades. While these lacerations may be small they can be quite significant and have the potential for infection. It is therefore encouraged that all skin is covered at least by a simple layer of material to protect against this. This coverage can also do something to protect against other types of damage to the combatant.

ARMOUR COVERAGE

A piece of armour is designed to cover a specific area of the person wearing the armour. Needless to say, it is important that the protective gear covers the area properly for the area to be protected properly. Needless to say, in the case of those areas mentioned above indicated to be of importance, it is vital that the armour can do its job properly.

The head and neck will be covered by some combination of gorget, mask or helm and coif. This combination of protective gear will be discussed in some detail later on. For now it is important to highlight that the entire neck and head need to be covered in some fashion, and the most vulnerable parts in rigid material. Groin and breast protection need to be fitted properly, and any lack of coverage here or lack of fit will be noticed very quickly.

Knees may be covered by a simple covering, but it is important to ensure that the entire joint is covered this is the same for elbows. Often the protection will protect the tip of the elbow or knee very well, but will leave the sides of the knee or elbow exposed. The same can be said for the upper and lower parts of the knee or elbow. Proper fitting protective gear in both cases will cover all of these areas.

Like the elbows and knees, special attention needs to be paid to hands and wrists. In some cases the hand will be protected well but the wrist will be exposed to damage. With regard to this coverage it is important that the entire hand is protected properly. In this particular case, special attention needs to be paid to the tips of the fingers and thumbs, and also the knuckles. When examining the hands protection do not forget about the sides of the fingers as well.

Overlap

Next in this topic is the discussion of overlap, it is more useful if armour overlaps as this provides better protection and ensures that there is no exposure. This is especially significant when examining skin exposure. Each place where a piece of protective gear joins up with another should be inspected to make sure that when the combatant is stationary and moving there is no exposure and no gapping. In some cases this should also be inspected for individual pieces of armour, especially where they are made from multiple parts.

HEAD AND NECK PROTECTION

With regard to the protection of the head and neck there are three pieces of armour concerned, the gorget, the coif and the mask or helm. In the discussion of these three there needs to be certain things discussed, individually and how they fit together. For the most part the helm or mask is a relatively simple item, so most of the discussion will be on the coif and the gorget, two items which are surprisingly often forgotten. There will, however be some discussion of the mask and helm.

Mask or Helm

When discussing the mask and helm, it is often that the front of the head is the focus of discussion, so much so that the rear of the head is an after-thought. Mostly the head is covered by a fencing mask or similar steel covering, and is often the first piece of protective gear bought. The back of the head needs to be protected by rigid material. This is something that will not flex when it is struck and can take the impact of a weapon. A simple rigid covering would seem to be enough, but padding is also highly recommended for any contact with the rear of the head. This is enhanced by the presence of a coif. Mounting it so force is transferred to the mask and/or gorget rather than the back of the head is even better.

Coif

The coif is a simple cloth covering which is designed most often to go under the mask. This is best made from puncture resistant material for the best effect. Frequently this piece of armour is disregarded as excessive or supplementary, however it is highly recommended that the combatant obtain one. Its purpose is to prevent abrasion of the mask against the combatant's head. It also supplies extra padding for the back of the head, and also coverage for the skin on the head and the neck. As a piece of convenience this item is also good for soaking up sweat. Purpose-made ones can be bought which are made of the same puncture resistant material that is found in fencing jackets[2].

GORGET

The subject of the gorget has been particularly topical and in this particular case will occupy quite a large amount of the discussion. This simple piece of armour can decide the difference between a combatant being seriously injured or even killed or not. To address this properly, this particular piece of armour will be discussed in and of itself.

Minimum

The first thing that needs to be stated is what qualifies as a minimum and what does not. A simple padded collar is not enough. A stiffened jacket collar is not enough. The gorget needs to be rigid and padded on the inside for this piece of protective gear to do the job properly. This is a very simple description for the requirements of a gorget, more detail is obviously required.

Rigid

First is the question of rigidity and what qualifies under this particular heading. With regard to the concept of rigidity, it is a material which will not bend when put under a certain amount of stress, following the safety standards of the fencing mask that would be a 12kg pressure. In this particular instance it would have to withstand the blow of the weapon being used without bending. Materials which would qualify under the concept of "rigid" in this particular case would be: 0.8 mm stainless steel, 1.0 mm mild steel, 1 layer of hardened leather (8oz, 4mm), or their equivalent.

Necessity of Rigid Material

The rigid material is necessary to prevent penetration and crushing damage from a weapon. Penetration is most likely going to come from a broken weapon or one which has had a tip punch through. Crushing damage would be the standard damage which would be caused by the tip or edge striking the target. Such damage applied to the neck can be severely damaging or even lethal.

Coverage

Something has already been said about armour coverage with regard to the other armours discussed and also with regard to the head and neck armours. In the case of the gorget and what it is supposed to cover, this is especially important. The entire neck

---

2 Zen Warrior Armory sells these ones, of which I personally own one: http://www.zenwarriorarmory.com/catalog.php?item=64&catid=39&ret=catalog.php%3Fcategory%3D39

needs to be covered. It is a simple as that. There are areas of special importance which need to be noted.

The front of the neck is especially important and needs to be covered. This includes the hollow of the throat which sits a little lower than the typically considered "neck". It resides at the top of the sternum where the collarbones meet the sternum. This is the first reason why the simple collar gorget is simply not enough. It needs to be extended downward to cover this area at the front, and far enough that a blade cannot slip up underneath it. Usually a simple flap is added to cover this, however it should be considered that something substantial should be added to cover this area.

The back of the neck also needs attention to be paid to it. In this case it is the vertebrae which need to be protected. The protection should extend down to below the shoulders to cover all of the cervical vertebrae, the second reason why the simple collar gorget is not enough. Once again, often a simple flap is added to cover this but it should be covered by something more substantial.

This covers the two really obvious areas which need to be covered. The sides of the neck should not be ignored. While the sides of the neck are protected by substantial muscle, this does not mean that rigid protection should be missed. A substantial hit to the side of the neck can cause quite an issue for the combatant and as such rigid protection should be used for the sides of the neck as well.

COMBINATION

In the combination of gorget, coif and helm or mask the combatant needs to make sure that the armours combine properly and still cover the required areas, both stationary and in movement. This is especially significant when considering the gorget and the helm/mask combination. In some instances there will be a gap left between and this can leave an area of serious vulnerability. The combatant should put all three of the armours on and then have them inspected by a buddy to ensure that they are covered in all areas. Of all the times to ensure that you are covered, the head and neck are the most important.

CONCLUSION

Protective equipment is necessary for the safe participation in HEMA. The problem is that there is the general idea that most of this is a "one size fits all" sort of thing and it is simply not the case. The protective gear needs to be fitted to the combatant to ensure that it covers all of the areas it needs to. This will often have to be done by another person while the combatant wears it as the combatant will not be able to see what is and is not covered.

It is vital that you take the time to ensure that your protective equipment fits properly and covers all of the areas which have been mentioned above if you really want to minimise your chances of having a serious injury. You may have to modify some of your armour to ensure that it fits appropriately and does the job. Some armour will also have some "wear-in" time for you to get used to it. Expect this, new stuff always does.

Take note of the recommendations which have been presented here. Consider whether your armour comes up to scratch. If it does not, it is recommended that you fix it. Above all take care of yourself and your opponents you will both thank each other for it later.

SECTION 3.
Period Texts

Why Do I Research?

INTRODUCTION

Anybody who knows me at all will know that I tend to get into my research projects heavily. I tend to find big projects which are disguised as little ones and then feel that I have to complete them to feel that I have done the job properly. I don't tend to do things small and tend to research things to death[3], of course as would be expected there is a cause behind this. The reasons for this can be found in my own history and interests.

MY HISTORY

I have had a long-term interest in things historical and to understand where this comes from I need to explain a little of my own history. I suppose my first interest in history is a result of the influence of my parents, especially my father who was quite well-read and who had encouraged me to follow my interests in the field, and of course read anything I could lay my hands on. My first real inspiration for history can be found in my first trip abroad.

In 1981, my parents took me and my sister over to the United Kingdom we explored England, Scotland and Ireland. We saw great and popular sites such as the Tower of London, Windsor Castle and the British Museum. What an eye-opener. The trip to Ireland was more of a personal trip and we spent some time in a graveyard scrubbing grave stones looking for ancestors. Now, sounds pretty boring, I can tell you it was quite the opposite, nothing like finding your roots or standing in the house where some of those roots started to inspire a

---

3 The length of many of the articles found in this book will attest to this, along with the extensive bibliography.

deeper love of history. So, this sowed the seeds of my interest, and it was only to be increased as I grew older.

My sixth year of primary school was also a turning point for me as I had a teacher who encouraged my interest in history so I went with it, investing time and energy in my assignments on various topics. Most male kids at this age wanted to be astronauts, policemen or in the army. Me, I decided at that point in time that history would be my thing and I decided that I wanted to become an historian or an archaeologist. It would give me an excuse to research periods of history and have some sort of tangible result as a purpose; needless to say the following years would just increase this desire. The thought of getting my mitts on some actual artefacts of historical significance also sent tingles from my fingers to my spine.

Tailored Education

From that point in time I would attempt to tailor all of my education with an historical bend to it. I took History in grade 10, and would follow this up with both Ancient and Modern History in grade 11 and 12. The other subjects were merely means to an end, to allow me to pursue my love of history even more. This was only to be advanced when I found a social group interested in medieval history.

SCA

I joined the SCA in grade 12. This group is focused on the years 500 to 1600AD or thereabouts so suited me down to the ground. Now not only could I study history but I could go about putting some of my research into practice. Talk about finding a niche. I am still in this group and am really enjoying it, the practical aspects of the research really adds something to it. Nothing like being able to do a bit of experimental archaeology here and there to test theories of your own and having other people willing to participate.

Higher Education

Needless to say my venture into higher education would result in me studying a Bachelor of Arts (BA), with majors in History and Anthropology. More chances to put my zeal into subjects that I enjoyed and further myself to my goal of becoming a historian. It also allowed even more research into areas of interest and allowed me to gain even more tools with which to do so. It would also result in the reason that I tend to research things to death as my training in research would tend to a bend where it was to be done properly. Eventually after graduating with my BA I would eventually get to pursue Honours in History and attain my goal of becoming a historian. No actual paid work at this point in time, due to various medical and other factors, but the research that I do I think fills in this. So with this foundation you can see the reasons for the methodical nature of my research. Now I can really get down to the reasons for my research.

REASONS

The primary reason for my research is expanding knowledge in various areas of history. This interest in historical subjects primarily comes from my unabated interest in history which I think will accompany me for the rest of my life. There are so many things to research and to find out about. I am hoping to fill in gaps in knowledge, primarily my own but also hopefully others as well. Meaning that I tend to look at stuff which has been either overlooked, or things which I think will expand my own understanding of subjects which I have already looked at.

With regard to the particular subjects chosen at a particular time, they come from interest or inspiration depending on the particular subject. I have done some research into terrorism for my own purposes as that has been a big topic over the past decade or so, and I wanted to understand this phenomenon more to understand things happening in world history in the current era. However, for the most part my research tends to be of a medieval or Renaissance flavour as this is my prime area of interest. At the moment I am focusing more on the sixteenth century as it fills in some information which I have become especially interested, mainly due to my association with the SCA and martial endeavours with the civilian weapons of the period. My three blogs, this one, my more personal one which can be found at: http://alifewithfibromyalgia.blogspot.com/, mostly about fibromyalgia (FM), and one about Elizabethan English at: http://oldewordes.blogspot.com/, are a direct result of wanting to get my research into various fields out into the public field for others to read and gain information from them.

Practical Application

In the end I hope that there is some practical application to my research a perfect example of this is my two current projects that I have been working on one which is my "Gentleman's Manual", the discussion version of which is accessible online [4] for people's perusal. This focusses on the idea of turning the fencer into a gentleman, in the Renaissance idea of this.

The other project is what I have called my "Period Manual". It is writing a fencing manual in period form and then presenting a Modern English and Early Modern English version side-by-side in order that people are more able to access Early Modern English and thus more of the period manuals which are available. The fencing manual is based upon what I have learnt over my past two decades or so of fencing and as such is essentially my treatise on the subject. This will be published so that people can buy a fencing manual in both forms and see the similarities between the Modern and Early Modern languages and hopefully be less disconcerted with attempting to tackle one of the treatises. Hopefully by the time that you see this in print, the treatise is already in print.[5]

CONCLUSION

So, why do I research? Primarily to increase my own knowledge but also in the hope that others can gain something from the research in which I have endeavoured. It is my hope that my readers will gain some insight into some of the topics which have been presented and thus be able to wipe away some of the dust and cobwebs of misunderstanding from these topics. It is also my hope that maybe something which I present may inspire someone else to do their own research in order that they can improve their own understanding of a topic which they may be interested in.

---

4   http://dl.dropbox.com/u/32538238/A%20Gentleman%27s%20Handbook%20-%20Discussion.pdf

5   This treatise will be published by Fallen Rook.

Lexicon For Swordplay, Or He Did What?

INTRODUCTION

The following article is about swordplay and the terminologies associated with such. It will also dig a little into the issues of not having a suitable single universal lexicon of swordplay, and indeed having several it in different languages. This creates problems of its own which can cause some to shy away from using them and cause even more problems.

Now we have all been at an event where we have seen two people get into a discussion about what happened during the fencing that day and often it will result in fingers being pointed for the action used to be expressed accurately. This is the result of not having a common language or suitable terms in which to discuss what they are talking about. On the other end one fencer will use an Italian term and the other will look at him strangely because all his study has been in German. In this particular case it comes out as having suitable terms but not a common language both of these can cause issues when expressing an action performed with a weapon.

AN EXAMPLE

To give an example of what is being discussed here. A *beat* is a simple action designed to remove the opponent's blade with force to open a Line. In French it is called *battement*, in German it is called *Klingenschlag*, in Spanish it is called *batimiento*, and in Italian it is called *battuta*. Four (five if you count English) different languages which are four different words for the same thing, they just happen to be in a different language. Things only get more confusing for the new person when a discussion of cuts comes in.

TERMS DEVELOPED

To avoid such confusions, either deliberately or accidentally, some organisations have developed their own language for the various actions with a sword; one example of this is from the armoured combatants of the SCA. Terms have been developed to describe the action of delivering a blow against an opponent, for example the snap, and the wrap. To an uninformed audience these would not make particularly much sense, but the same could be said of many early Italian terms such as the Guardia Porta di Ferro. So in some ways the language is developing the same sort of way; and changes are coming. An example of this can be found in a blog which I read on a regular basis by Cornelius Weber.[6]

THE GOAL IS UNDERSTANDING

The important result of this is understanding. It would take someone quite a while to collect together a complete set of fencing terminologies from the various schools of swordplay in order to have all the terms in all the languages. This would be a great idea and a project well worth looking into however it is not what I am proposing here. For the current period in time it is better that the practitioners do not confuse the language with the swordplay. Hence those involved in Italian swordplay should keep with Italian terms;

---

6   http://corneliusvonbecke.wordpress.com/2011/11/24/to-call-a-spade-a-spade/

those involved in German should keep with German terms and so forth. However, the practitioner should also keep a broad eye open to other terms and pick them up and see how they fit in their own style so that better communication is possible across the styles. Likewise I am not proposing that some other language, a sort of swordsman's Esperanto is developed so that there is a single language for all swordsmen to use.

CONCLUSION

The whole goal of this discussion is understanding. This can be easily related to another article on manuals, "Fencing Manuals: Old and New" and also another one on the language in such manuals. This is important is so that the fencing community is able to converse and understand what is being discussed easily. For this to happen people need to adopt such terms that they can understand themselves, but also such terms that they can pass on to others and relate to the terms being used by them. In this the fencer needs to keep an open mind to what is being said and see the most important relationship of all, the fact that all are doing swordplay and all are related to one another. Once this relationship is recognised and understood then people will be able to see that everyone can learn from anyone who picks up a sword in any style what-so-ever.

Reading Period Texts – A Question of Language

INTRODUCTION

In the pursuit of swordplay from the past, it is necessary at some point in time to consult texts of that period. Sure, we can use secondary sources and other's interpretations but in the end if we really want to get at what the masters and practitioners of the period were getting at then we really need to look at some primary source material, or at least translations of primary source material, where a language barrier exists. It is not *this* language barrier which will be the focus of this discussion. But the difference in expression of language, as it is easy to get caught up in the language of the period, or indeed the translation and/or interpretation of the author of the current form.

LANGUAGE RULES

Language is important and so are the rules associated with that language as it is the rules which hold the language together. Aside from the usual rules of grammar and spelling which need to be interpreted sometimes especially when looking at period texts, there is also the flow and format of the language which is also important to be examined. When examining fencing manuals, there is also an extra set of guidelines which become important to read and gain a useful output from the study of the manual. These are guidelines which apply especially when reading fencing terminology and also fencing actions as performed by the combatants presented by an author.

TEMPOS RATHER THAN ACTIONS

Manuals often have their actions written in tempos rather than individual "turns" or actions. This seems like a small difference, but it can make a large difference in the interpretation of what the combatants are doing. The misreading of this will result in the misreading of actions and results in a misinterpretation of the intent of the author. Reading in tempos changes the time of the action and thus also the tempo of the action. Thus this will affect the resulting sequence of actions.

To read it in a modern manner it may seem that a person makes an action and their opponent replies to that action and the person makes another action in reply to that an so forth. For some sequences this will be appropriate and will apply with no problems however this is not always the case; this especially so for the later period manuals where the use of time becomes increasingly important to the method which is being used; even more so where actions of blade engagement become more complex.

To read in tempos is to realise that the action of one fencer may occur at the same time and thus in the same tempo as their opponent. This will speed up the actions and also allow for more, smaller actions to take place in the same period of time. Thus a fencer may perform an action and as the opponent is responding to the action made by the fencer, the fencer may change his action to defeat the counter made by the opponent. An example of this is that a fencer must begin his counter-disengage at the same time as the opponent starts his disengage for it to be effective. If he waits until it is completed, then it is merely another disengage, and also will be evident to the opponent.

LATER ITALIAN RAPIER

Perfect examples of this sort of writing can be found in the works of Ridolfo Capo Ferro and Salvator Fabris where the initial action of the fencer is designed to make the opponent respond and uncover himself so the following action can be successful. If the same sequence is read as one action by one followed by the action of the other and so forth the sequence will not follow as the fencers will become exposed at some point and this is a breach of good fencing theory.

Thus in reading fencing manuals we need not only to be aware of the actions, but also of the tempos of the actions being performed along with when they are actually being performed. Some sequences will be simple responsive actions, but not all will and this is something that the reader needs to be aware of in their interpretation. Being aware of this particular issue is the first step to being able to read the manual properly.

This is one of the reasons why the author's expressions of theory in the earlier parts of their manuals, often skipped over by many readers and sometimes re-organised and relegated to the rear by some authors and publishers, are so important. It gives the reader the information as to how time relates to the actions and how the time of the fencer relates to that of the opponent and thus the actions of the fencer relates to that of the opponent and vice versa. Such information is vital to understand what the author is expressing in their actions later on in the manual, especially as it relates to tempo.

CONCLUSION

One of the greatest issues that arise in the use of period fencing manuals is language and the issues associated, and this is even the case where the manual is written in English. The language of previous centuries does not always match that of the modern. Indeed the language of the past can be considered almost a foreign language. This can be very disconcerting for many readers and it is often this which scares them away. Problems of changes in language and the differences in language which scare some away need to be broken down to demonstrate that the differences can be identified and settled, thus making period texts more accessible.

The expressions made by the authors need to be demonstrated to fulfil the essential rules of fencing theory, thus a common ground will be laid to begin with. This can be followed by familiar actions noted as familiar. Then the language can be demonstrated to be more familiar, while still being different. It is not for us to be afraid of these differences merely aware of them so we can take them into account when reading, interpreting and then using the information present.

Fencing Manuals: Old and New

INTRODUCTION

The written word has been the most effective method for transmitting information about fencing through time. True, these documents do often come with pictures, but without the words it is much more difficult to understand what the individual is attempting to present.[7]

Fencing manuals have been written by both professionals and gifted amateurs. Regardless, each one teaches something about fencing from a particular point of view.

This article has to do with some of the changes which have happened with regard to the transmission of such information over time, highlighting some interesting points in regards to this. For the purposes of ease of presentation, the discussion will be broadly broken into four sections. The first is about theory content and deals with the presentation of elements of fencing theory. The second will deal with any social elements which may be present in the manual. The third will deal with the method used to convey the information. Some of these will overlap and all will be noted as related to one another. It is not the purpose of this discussion to delve into specifics of any fencing theory or method. This needs to be done on a case-by-case basis rather than in such a general method.

THEORY

Regardless of whether the theory is explicitly presented or whether it is more hidden within the actions presented all fencing manuals have elements of fencing theory present in them. It is these elements of theory which the physical aspects of fencing are hung upon. If the practical element is the meat of the discussion, the theory is most definitely the skeleton upon which this hangs.

In the manuals of the Renaissance period, or at least the later Renaissance period, there were entire sections of the manual which were devoted to the various elements of fencing theory. These would be specifically laid out and detailed before any mention of the practical was made. This was the case even in the later period of the eighteenth century the same sort of idea was made. This highlighted the importance of the reader understanding what the practical elements of fencing were based upon, and thus the importance of theory to the system. It was through such discussions that fencing was demonstrated to be science as well as art.

---

7   *The artist is not always as reliable as the author in getting the message through, especially when the author and artist is not the one and the same person.*

In the modern age, fencing theory seems to be something that only the fencing masters need to know; something that the individual fencer will only pick up through specific studies of fencing theory or through tuition with a fencing master. The theoretical elements seem to be absent from modern fencing manuals, or at least those which are commonly available. If a fencer wants to know about fencing theory then he has to go to specific texts to find the information. Only the practical elements are present in modern fencing books, the theoretical is assumed to be learnt through the repetition of actions and their learning.

SOCIAL

The social element is something which seems to be somewhat odd to find in a fencing manual, but it is present in much the same way as the theoretical elements. Many may ask what purpose there is for social elements to be in a sport manual, and this is one place which demonstrates the difference in attitude to fencing over time. The social element and its presence or absence also describes the change in fencing from martial art with sharp weapons to the commonly known sport of fencing.

In the Renaissance period the weapons were sharp and the potential for injury was high. The social aspects of a person's life dictated what sort of life a person would have and with whom they could associate. The social element found in fencing affected more than just their conduct on the field of combat; needless to say that for the fencer of the Renaissance, social issues were more important. This resulted in these elements being highly prevalent in the manuals of the Renaissance period. This increased even more with the presence of the phenomenon of duelling. The Renaissance author thus devoted a large amount of space to the social elements.

Duelling is not an element which the modern fencer really has to worry about. There are no duels to the death anymore, no conflicts with sharp swords for the purposes of settling matters of honour. The conduct of the fencer, especially the sport fencer does not particularly affect his everyday life, and for the most part only affects a small community. Thus the importance of the social elements of fencing would seem to have lessened. The result of this is that for the most part the only element which could be regarded to as being social in the average modern fencing manual is the discussion of the salute. If anymore is wanted for interest sake or other reasons, the reader has to go searching in more in-depth manuals and books more related to this particular subject.

METHOD

In the discussion of method, it is the method used to convey the information found in the fencing manual which is the subject for this part. This has to do with both the written word and also any pictorial representations present. This may seem less significant than other parts which have been previously discussed, but it is important and also describes a change.

In general, earlier fencing manuals primarily dealt with written words. Later ones increased the presence of pictures to illustrate what was said in the words present. For the later Renaissance manuals the pictures are used as snapshots for examples of what is going on. There are also diagrams for elements of theory present; even with the increase in pictorial representation the words were always more important than the pictures. The word was always used to portray that which the pictures could not.

Modern manuals have a lot of pictures in them; mostly these are photos for the fencer to copy. Diagrams are used to present those elements which the photos cannot present without demonstration. These pictures stand in place of words which were used in earlier manuals for description. The method and presentation of the information has gone from a more written method to a more illustrative method with pictures and diagrams taking the place of the prose that would be found in the earlier manuals. Thus in an opposite fashion the pictures can become more important than the words.

CONCLUSION

There is a large amount of material available and this subject and it only increases as more and more manuals are found and placed in public forums This can only increase the amount of information that the fencer can have to hand at any one time. For those of us interested in the earlier practices various elements need to be understood before the truth of the manual can be found. While it is possible to read the manuals alone it is important to understand that they were not written in a vacuum, and this goes for manuals of all periods and cultures.

This discussion was designed to demonstrate and highlight the differences between the manuals of different periods, in a very general fashion. It is true that some blanket statements have been made and there will always be exceptions to the rule. The change is what is important rather than which has what and what doesn't. It can even be useful for the fencer of the modern period to study those manuals of the older periods to have a greater understanding of what is found in the modern ones. The older manuals do, after all, present a more complete picture of the art of fencing and this should be of importance to all fencers who truly want to understand the art which they practice.

Watch Your Assumptions

INTRODUCTION

We all come to our current fencing through different paths and from different backgrounds. Some come from sport fencing backgrounds; some come from oriental martial arts. The result of this is that well all carry a certain amount of "baggage" with us from previous learning. There is a certain amount where we read something and rather than going off exactly what is read we assume that we know what is being said based on our previous knowledge. Unless it is exactly the same as what we are reading, this can lead us into traps and issues.

PERSPECTIVE

We must remember to read the manuals that we are reading and read them with a similar perspective to the one which the writer wrote them. For example: in the case of an Elizabethan manual, it is important that late Italian knowledge is not read into it, or even later, or German knowledge, or French. This can often happen as a result of our history and our background and thus our assumptions.

The classical fencer, with his foil and epée, has at least four parries which he remembers. The rapier combatant may use actions, which may in part be similar to these, but the actions may not be named or used in the same way. If the classical fencer reads these parries into a rapier manual then he can be horribly confused, or find the actions ineffective. We must ensure that we do not put anachronistic terms, theories and practices into a manual as it will cause problems with the interpretation.

IT'S NOT A PARRY

This particular situation became most evident for me when teaching a class on di Grassi, and more to the point his single sword. This would seem to be relatively simple except my own assumptions got the better of me and began to cause issues. Giacomo di Grassi states for his defence against the attack of the High Ward:

> "For the defence whereof it is needefull that he ſtand at the lowe warde, and as the thruſt cometh, that he encounter it without, with the edge of the ſword, and increaſe a ſlope pace forward, with the hinder foote at the verie ſame time, by which pace he moueth out of the ſtraight line, and paſſeth on the right ſide of the enimie. And he muſt remember to beare alwaies the poynt of the ſword toward the enimie: So that the enimie in comming forwardes, ether runneth himſelfe on the ſword, which may eaſely happen, and ſo much the rather, when he commeth reſolutelie determined to ſtrike, or elſe if he come not ſo farre forwardes that he encountereth the ſword, yet he may be ſafelie ſtroken, with the encreaſe of a ſtreight pace:"
>
> *(di Grassi, 1594)*

So my first reading, all assumptions engaged stated this: Parry the sword in third with a slope pace forward with the hind foot with the point toward the enemy, which he should run upon. If he does not, move forward to strike if he does not. Easy, right? Wrong. Problem here is that with a parry of third, i.e. to the high outside line, with the point nice and high to protect myself, the point tends to be a little high, so there are hilt issues with the opponent's weapon coming in at the downward angle from the High Ward. This did not result in the nice clean execution that di Grassi describes at all. It did not even work with a more minimalised parry of third with the point more toward the opponent. Working through it again, minus the assumptions engaged, if the thrust from the High Ward is encountered with the edge of the blade of the sword in the fashion of a cut, a *mandritta tondo*, not a parry, the action works much more cleanly. The point of the weapon is directed toward the opponent and perfectly set up for the thrust which di Grassi describes in his manual.

ASSUMPTIONS AFFECT INTERPRETATIONS

In this case what happened was I read what di Grassi said, my brain interpreted it through my assumptions based on the training I had and had been previously giving, and turned it into something which was not written in the manual by di Grassi at all. There are no distinct parries described in the Elizabethan manuals. They beat the opponent's blade, they place the weapon in the path of the opponent's weapon for sure, but there is no parry described. If anything all of the so-called parries should be performed in the manner of a cut.

Read what is in the manual, and do what the manual says. Be careful of your own interpretations of the actions which are presented and make sure that they result in the same actions which are presented in the original text. If something does not work it is most likely that you have gotten something wrong rather than the manual has. Check what the original has said and see if something has gone wrong in your interpretation, most likely one of your assumptions has gotten the better of you.

CONCLUSION

Be careful when you are reading and interpreting the manuals and figure out what your assumptions are before they make a mess of things. Or at least be aware of them so that you can understand them and so that you can fix them. Manuals need to be evaluated from the point of view of the time in which they were written and using the terms from when they were written. Mistakes such as these were made by many fencing historians, it would be best for us not to repeat them and gain a greater understanding of these works.

Also remember that in a real fight, they used sharp swords, not blunt ones. This means the threat of an on-coming point was not just the threat of being hit, it was the threat of injury at the least, or death. This is something which is also often forgotten in our relatively safe world of blunted-edged, rubber blunted pointed weapons. In a real fight, their weapons were sharp. This is what they were training for, not to win but to survive. Of all the things forgotten when reading period manuals this is the biggest.

What's In a Name?

INTRODUCTION

We need to be careful about our naming conventions so that we do not misname our sources. Misnaming the sources makes them more difficult to find again. This is irritating for follow-up research. It can become more difficult when we are dealing with foreign names, be they of a different nationality, or from a different time period, and doubly so when it is both. This particular issue can result in a misnaming of a source over a long period of time. There are two examples which will be cited at this point in time, one is French, and the other Spanish.

"LIANCOUR"

The first is an author who is often referred to as "Liancour". His real name is Andre Wernesson, Sieur de Liancour, who wrote *Le Maitre D'armes ou L'exercice de L'Épée Seule dans sa Perfection* in 1692, a treatise on the use of the smallsword. Someone has taken the last part of his name and thought that this was his surname or family name, because it was the last bit of his name. Incorrect. This last part of his name was actually his title. Liancour, or Liancourt, is a geographical location in France. Andre Wernesson is the Lord of Liancour. So the author should be referred to in the text as "Wernesson", sometimes spelt "Vernesson". The first author that I have noted to make this mistake and start the trend was Egerton Castle who called him (de) Liancour in his *Schools and Masters of Defense* in 1881. Then the second was Captain Alfred Hutton continued the pattern in his *Old Sword-Play* in 1891 needless to say the pattern was made.

"NARVAEZ"

The second author is often referred to as "Narvaez". His name is Don Luis Pacheco de Narvaez, who wrote *Libro de las Grandeza de la Espada*, which was printed in 1600, a treatise on the use of the rapier in the tradition of La Verdadera Destreza. Once again, someone not knowing naming conventions has simply taken the last part of the name and used it as the surname. Once again incorrect. Again Narvaez is a geographical location in Spain. Luis Pacheco, is from Narvaez, and has the title of Don. So the author should be referred to as Pacheco. Egerton Castle is also the culprit, in the same book, for the misnaming of Pacheco.

BIBLIOGRAPHICAL INTEGRITY

In our research into various martial arts and the use of the sword we need to examine the sources carefully, but we also need to look at the authors carefully to make sure that we are naming them correctly. This allows anyone who would follow our research later on to find the same sources and gain the same knowledge that we have gained. This is a matter of bibliographical integrity on the part of the researcher to ensure that the correct details are recorded of the source material.

While this discussion has focussed on the names of the authors, it is not just the names of the authors that matter, but also the names of the sources, their dates, their locations and also their publishers that matter. All of these things are important to the location of the source material of research materials. Some think that it is sufficient to place the author and the title of a document in the bibliography at the end of their research. This is simply not the case.

A person who reads this and wants to follow up on the research from that source may find a different edition of the source which has been changed, and thus cannot find the same evidence which was used. A publisher or web address is also required for complete information. If possible it is also useful to have a date of access as things on the internet change quite a bit over time. Making sources easier to find for other researchers encourages further research into fields of endeavour and this can only be of benefit to all areas of research.

CONCLUSION

Misnaming sources by their authors can cause all sorts of issues in finding the sources for other readers and researchers. This could lead them to believe that the source does not exist and even question the research. Take care in your research, and give credit where credit is due, and to the correct author. Such bibliographical integrity is important to all research and ensures that research of any kind can be followed up by interested individuals to see the evidence upon which it was based. Give as much information about your sources as possible as to where to find them it can only benefit research.

From the Original

INTRODUCTION

The following article is designed to address the consideration of the use of primary sources and their importance. This discussion focuses on the importance of knowledge of the primary language of the document and how important it is that unless you are reading the original there *will* be some interpretation. Through this interpretation you already get someone else's idea about what the original author is talking about, without even beginning to discuss interpreting what the text is actually discussing. This is because as soon as a word is translated there is a level of interpretation present.

THANKS ALL AROUND

First of all let me give a lot of respect and thanks to those members of the fencing community who have taken the time to take manuals in foreign languages and translate and make them available for us to use. With regard to this, and in no particular order, I would like to cite the works of individuals such as: Ken Mondschein, Jared Kirby, Tom Leoni, Guy Windsor, Lois Spangler, Chis Slee and Mark Rector. There are others as well. Your contributions to the field are most greatly appreciated and clearly benefit what western martial artists do. Without your efforts there are a lot of fencing manuals which would be unknown, unread and unappreciated; or in some cases known, unread and badly presented due to second-hand and third-hand interpretations.

ALWAYS INTERPRETATION PRESENT

The importance of the use of primary texts in an investigation into any field cannot be overstated. This is one of the reasons why I have gone back to Saviolo of 1595 and di Grassi of 1594. Even the most faithful translation of a text from another language into modern English results in some input from the translator, there is no way to avoid it. It is also the reason why I have made my own study of Elizabethan English to understand the language better, so I can understand my texts better. This can be as complex as the general simplification of word groups to the simple interpretation of single words to mean others. Further to this where there is translation and then interpretation there are further changes made to the original text, there is most definitely input present from the person performing it.

There is a double dose of interpretation where there is a translation from say, Renaissance Italian to modern English, because it often needs to go through a filter of modern Italian in the middle. This means there is first the translation from Renaissance Italian to modern Italian, and then from modern Italian to modern English. Each step away from the original changes the language and thus can change the meaning of what has been said. This can result in some interpretations which may not have been intended by the original author.

INTERPRETATION FAILURES

There are issues that can run rampant in interpretation and translation area. The first is failures in translation where the words have been misinterpreted to mean other things.

Further to this, which often follows, is the failure in the interpretation of the person describing the skills presented in the original text. Often this results in actions which the author did not intend. Added to this there are language issues which must be contended with as some words simply do not translate well into English, many examples of these can be found. You only have to go through the list of Italian, German, Spanish and French fencing terms to see examples which while they do sort of have English equivalents, it is easier to leave them in their original languages.

The change in language from one period to another let alone across different languages can cause issues. Some technical instructions can be interpreted as not being such and thus the author's intention is obscured because of the interpretation of the translator. This is a question of literal translation or interpretive translation. Is the text translated exactly word for word, or does the translator interpret what the author means and translate it as that? These are all issues which the critical reader of the text must contend with when reading from a secondary or tertiary text, some of which can result in a translation being very difficult to use. This is also where the multiple different interpretations of texts come from.

SECONDARY AND TERTIARY TEXTS USELESS?

Does this mean that we should discard all secondary or even tertiary texts? No. They are still useful. They provide interesting different points of view for us to look at. They also provide interesting information which can lead from the interpretation and even further understanding of texts. These secondary and tertiary texts are also a good place for the beginner researcher to begin their research. These are mostly in plain language which makes them easy to understand and thus provide an open door for the beginner so they do not have to attempt to deal with something which is more detailed and thus more confusing for them. These texts still deserve their due and their authors our admiration for the work they have produced.

They are also useful where you may not know the language that the original is written in, clearly. Also useful is where a fencer can access multiple translations of the same text so that they can compare and contrast the translations to find out what is the middle-ground between the translations and thus find a common path amongst them. It is always wise to remember that a secondary text is someone's interpretation of the primary text and not the original text. The only way to actually know what the original text actually said is to read it. Without knowing the language of the original text, comparing and contrasting multiple sources is a good way to find commonalities for a good path through difficult parts which may not make sense.

NOT "OUR" ENGLISH

I have already stated that I have gone back in my research to Vincentio Saviolo's *His Practice in Two Books* of 1595 and Giacomo di Grassi's *His True Art of Defense* of 1594. It is because these manuals are written in English. Now it is true that di Grassi's is a translation of the 1570 Italian version of the manual, but even without reference to the previous manual it stands as a most useful text. What needs to be noted here and this is important is that they are written in Elizabethan English, which is *not* Present Day English. This means that it is not "our" English and this still results in some interesting turns of phrase and other linguistic issues. This has resulted in some interesting situations and many re-reads of the texts, however the language is much closer to my native language and thus I believe these hurdles I can cover (resulting in the study of the language previously indicated).

What this means is, even in this situation the result will be my interpretation of what I have read. Someone may read it differently and come up with a different interpretation. However, I am going from as close to the original source as I can for my information, thus seeking the closest to the original to find out what the author said rather than another's interpretation.

CONCLUSION: CONSIDER THE ORIGINS

In our research we must consider exactly where our information is coming from and, if possible, attempt to access those sources which are the closest to the original texts as possible. This goes for all the research that we do be it with regard to manuals, armour, weapons or techniques. Secondary and tertiary texts should not be discarded out of hand, but their origins should be considered, along with the interpretation of the author of these texts. Care needs to be taken in research, and special attention paid to the sources that we use and their original texts. There are many pitfalls and traps waiting for the unwary investigator and many strange interpretations of what some master may or may not have said. Check your sources. Examine your own findings. Consider again where the information came from.

> *"Truth coherent with the findings of rigorous scholarship is the only effective defence against the academic derelictions of our time."*
> *Claudio Veliz*

Fencing Treatise: Part Manual, Part Résumé

INTRODUCTION

In other articles I have discussed period sources and their uses. These discussions have been focused on the uses of the treatises in a practical sense and also understanding the language within them. There is a slightly different approach that can be taken with regard to the treatises. This approaches the manuals as they are, and how they were presented to the public when they were published originally. It gives something of an explanation to how they are written and what is presented in them. This approaches the treatises as repositories of knowledge and also as documents of purpose, to discuss the reason why they were written.

KNOWLEDGE PRESENTATION

What will be noted in many manuals is the lack of basics presented. Even though there is the demonstration of theoretical knowledge and scientific principles. In this case the treatise is more designed to present the knowledge of the author than to present basic principles. For the most part there is a demonstration of a high level of skill presented in these manuals, rather than the essential skills that a combatant would need to know to learn to survive from the manual. Of course, it could be argued that these basics would be common knowledge, but then why would the same theory associated be presented? This knowledge and skill base presented is designed to present the skills as noble and a noble intention in their teachings. Thus many of these manuals are more résumé than practical manual. Thus is a demonstration of knowledge of the author rather than a manual from which the reader is expected to learn the techniques which are presented.

PROMOTIONAL MATERIAL

The idea of the manual being a curriculum vitae rather than a more practical approach to how the skills should be used is more common in the later manuals of the sixteenth- and seventeenth-centuries, but is also present in earlier ones as well. A perfect example of this is Talhoffer's treatise of 1467 in which skills are presented but also other elements of warfare, such as siege engines. These manuals were designed to present the author as a knowledgeable individual with great skills, designed to draw attention to the author's skill with the hope of future employment. This is perfectly presented if any time is taken to read the dedications in these manuals, in which it is clear that he is selling his skills in book form. In the same way a person presents information in the modern era in a curriculum vitae and cover letter for a job application or introduction to an employer.

Fabris 1606

To give some further examples, Salvator Fabris dedicates his treatise of 1606,

> "To His Most Serene Majesty the All-Powerful Christianus IV King of Denmark, Norway, Gothia and Vandalia, Duke of Slesvik Holstein, Storman and Ditmarschen, Count of Oldemburgh and Delmenhorst, etc."
>
> (Leoni, 2005:1)

Fabris then goes on to discuss the favours bestowed upon him by the king and that his purpose is to demonstrate that his method is the better one having learnt it over a long period of time. He also proposes that the subject is noble in nature and thus the book is an appropriate gesture of his devotion to him (Leoni, 2005:1). Clearly in this instance Fabris is attempting to make sure he has suitably ingratiated himself with Christianus IV so that his employment may continue. That Fabris places in Book Two elements of other arts than the single sword, glossing over basic elements, hints that he knows more and this gives evidence that his treatise is a mere taste of his knowledge.

Capo Ferro 1610

Another fine example of this promotional material masquerading as a treatise is Capo Ferro's treatise of 1610. Again there is the opening dedication present to a lord of influence, "To the Most Serene Lord Don Francesco Maria Feltrio Della Rovere, Sixth Duke of Urbino" (Kirby, 2012:20). So much so is this book about promotion that he discusses this particular element in the opening statements which follow. In Capo Ferro's case he appeals to the Duke to employ him as master to his son, via the book which he has produced. Like Fabris, Capo Ferro demonstrates knowledge of fencing to a high degree in many areas, and points to others that he knows, never actually detailing all of the elements required to fully use the form, such is the case with the rotella, his last form. This leaves the reader wanting more, thus the idea to employ the author of the work.

EPISTLE DEDICATORIE

With these two examples being presented, I am not claiming that these are the only two gentlemen who wrote their manuals to impress or present themselves to great lords or ladies. Indeed publishing a book in the medieval and Renaissance period was a challenge in and of itself as it cost quite a sum of money and to go to such an expense, it would be expected that something would be had out of it so the patronage of a significant individual would be a step in the correct direction. Others were written as thanks for patronage. An example of such is Vincentio Saviolo's manual which is written to Lord Robert the Earl of Essex, in which he thanks him for his patronage (Saviolo, 1595). Such manuals should be studied as documents of their period if not for their discussions of methods of combat.

CONCLUSION

All this being said the manuals and treatises present useful skills that can be learnt and do present a system of defence for certain weapons, thus it is clear that they should be treated partially as practical manual, but also part résumé. In some cases the skills presented cannot be learnt as they are without a teacher, and some where it is claimed that it can be learnt without the assistance of a teacher. The latter type tends to be the more practical and the one where more basics are found. Regardless, both types of treatise are useful not only for their practical skills, but also for the social aspects which are presented. It simply needs to be understood which is which and their multiple uses regardless.

With the discovery of more and more treatises the knowledge of the use of the sword continues to grow and even those manuals which seem obscure and difficult to decipher previously become more readable due to the knowledge gained from other manuals of similar lineages and movement systems. This means that the more that is known from a treatise, the more that is known of other treatises of a similar nature. All of these investigations increase the knowledge of the community at large. The social elements are often over-looked for the immediate practical use of the treatises, but only when we understand the individuals who were using the swords and the reasons why they were using them will we understand why the used them in the fashion that they did.

Musashi for the Rapier Combatant: Adventures in Cross-Training

INTRODUCTION

Musashi for the rapier combatant? What is he on about? These are the first two questions that I would expect to be asked with regard to this particular topic. The idea of this article is to get people thinking about other resources that they might find useful in their study of swordplay. I have actually already written an article entitled "Musashi for the Rapier Combatant" and I was tempted to simply re-print that article here. Instead I have decided to go through the approach that led me to such a conclusion and the article that resulted.[8]

---

8   *The article is actually re-printed later on in this book. So in this way you get both perspectives.*

"LET THE GAZE BE BROAD"

"Let the Gaze Be Broad" is one of the most used sayings found in Musashi's book *Go Rin No Sho*, or *The Book of Five Rings*. From Musashi's point of view it is about being aware of the opponent and also aware of your surroundings when facing an opponent. For the purposes of this particular discussion it is also about being aware of the resources available to you in your research.

People tend to approach the research of fencing and swordplay in general from one of two points of view, a narrow view or a broad view of things. Each one of these approaches has advantages and disadvantages. They are also useful for different things depending on the desired outcome of the particular research.

Narrow View

For the narrow view, people get caught up with the importance of a culturally-centric, weapon-centric, or even "school"-centric approach in their approach. The advantage of this is that they are totally focused on their material and will go into all of the finer details in their particular approach. One problem is that if they are hampered by the source material, being a translation issue or availability; then their research will stop. Every researcher has been here, "I could really do with studying "X" but it is a) written in a language I don't speak or b) simply is not available." Another problem is that they do not experience swordplay from a broad point of view and thus miss the overall picture. For the researcher with a broad point of view, this is less of an issue.

Broad View

The broad point of view looks at all of the source material that is available and thus has much more to look at. The wealth of information can be both an advantage and a disadvantage; the advantage being the quantity of material available and the disadvantage being that there is so much of it that research on a particular topic can last forever and never really finish. The advantage of the broad point of view is that this researcher is able to compare and contrast, and get a view of topics from an overall perspective rather than a focused one. The researcher with the broad point of view is able to use resources from different places in order to build his research and this can lead to using some resources of unexpected usefulness.

GET BELOW THE SURFACE AND BROADEN YOUR HORIZONS

There are resources out there which on the surface look like that they will be of no use to the researcher of swordplay. One of the obvious examples for the researcher of rapier combat is the usefulness of sport fencing materials. The movements expressed in these texts can be quite useful, but the real value is in the drills and concepts which are most useful. From an even broader point of view, you need to look at things from a broad point of view to realise the usefulness of different texts. This is even to the point where seemingly differing weapon systems can be used to assist one another. The trick, of course, is to find these resources to use them.

To find other resources it is first important to ensure that you are looking at things from a broad point of view. To do this you need to look at your topic for study from an over-reaching point of view. Examine it for the key elements which the particular topic is based upon and look for these. If you limit your searches to only one type of material that is all you will get. If, on the other hand you broaden your searches to include different types of materials and different subjects you will find a great deal more.

BROADER TOPICS

The next thing that you need to do is to have a broad outlook in your research and research topics. If you choose "A study of Salvator Fabris" for example, then for the most part, you will only really be looking at a single manual. On the other hand if you choose "A study of the use of 17th century Italian rapier" then you are going to have access to more materials. If your topic is even broader you will be able to use even more materials. Even with the topics suggested, depending on your approach, there are also other additional materials that you might find useful to completely understand the topic.

WIDER RANGE OF MATERIALS

To increase the different places where you can look for materials you must first have a broad point of view. One of the more obvious places to look for material is art and documents of the appropriate period. These are useful as they give background and can also give depictions of the weapons "in action" from a certain point of view. Documentation about the actual weapons used is surprisingly useful to understanding a particular weapon form. Understanding the characteristics of the weapon can be most useful. Another thing to consider is body movement.

The human body, for the most part, can only move in a certain number of ways and to and from a certain amount of positions. When a weapon is added to this, then the number is further reduced. This is one of the reasons why it is possible to do cross-cultural examinations of combat systems; one of the prime examples of this a comparison of the longsword and the katana. This is especially useful in the use of the weapons and the tactics involved in their use.

When further looking at the movements of the human body, a researcher should not ignore an area which has previously been the purview of physiotherapists and fitness instructors, and that is bio-mechanics. This investigates the use of the human body and how it moves most efficiently. This is most useful especially to the modern martial artist, both eastern and western, in order to utilise the body in its movements most effectively and safely. The idea of the importance of body movement is an element that the theorists of the Renaissance period knew, and is one of the reasons that the figures are often depicted naked, to see the muscles in movement.

CONCLUSION

In our research of swordplay, it is important that we do not lock ourselves too much into a single subject, this narrows the vision of what is possible to be found. Of course where a particular topic is specific it is important to stay on the particular topic and thus use appropriate materials. This being said other materials can be used to explain things which are not in the primary source material. This all being said, a broad point of view with regard to the research is useful to the researcher to gain an overall view of swordplay.

Fabris From a Chair?

INTRODUCTION

Many in the HEMA community examine manuals from their own points of view and to understand what the author is saying about fencing. For the most part it is purely so that the individual can understand what the author is on about and possibly put some of what the author has said into practice. The question happens to come to mind about what happens when such information is examined and then attempted only to find out that there is some physical impediment to completing the action, what now?

Performing most of the actions of Fabris is a simple impossibility for me due to my physical condition. My body simply will not allow me to bend in the ways that Fabris would have me do so. For the most part, I will admit, I bought the manual to extract as much information out of it about his blade engagement and counter positions (*contra-postura*) as possible, and this has been most useful. This is somewhat limited as it does not take into account much that could be used from this most informative manual. So to lower the position of my body without having to damage myself, I thought, what about a chair?

WHY THE CHAIR?

One of the prime principles of Fabris is that the lower position of the body is safer than the taller. Sitting in a chair sure lowers the position of the body, and it also allows for the bending of the body as well to make it even smaller. Of course, sitting in a chair and fencing, while possible,[9] does prevent actions from being possible. Any form of major footwork is removed, but it can be compensated for in part by the movement of the body. Approaching the opponent is also not possible due to the seated position. However, even with these limitations, there is a great deal that can be done.

Girata

The most interesting discovery that I made while experimenting with the actions of Fabris is that a form of his *girata* (a turning void) is actually possible from a seated position. This is so long as the movement is based on the movement of the body rather than the feet. The ability to do this particular technique opened much more of the manual as possible from the chair.

DISTANCE

All of the actions of the seated combatant are made at *misura stretta* (narrow distance). This is simply because the seated combatant cannot lunge from the chair, nor can they approach the opponent. What this means is that the seated combatant must wait until the opponent is within the *misura stretta* before launching any offensive action. This means that the seated combatant will be more passive, but does not limit them to only reactive or defensive actions, far from it.

The seated combatant is limited for distance, yes, but this does not stop them from being the first to initiate the action once the opponent comes within their distance. Sure,

---

9   There is an article on the subject later on, and a person only need look at wheelchair fencing in the Paralympics.

the opponent may launch an attack from *misura larga* (wide distance) but the blade of their weapon must enter into the seated combatant's distance before it can strike them, and it is here that the seated combatant can act. Further, body movement can also compensate for some movement of the feet, as in the *girata* described previously.

A BROADER VIEW

The most important thing about this particular discussion is that we should take a more broad view of the period manuals and see how they can work from different points of view. This particular idea can be broadened even more to take into account how different weapons are similar in their uses and how the different techniques may be used. A holistic view of swordplay is most useful to the researcher and a great asset in the understanding of different authors.

INVESTIGATIONS

The first part of the process was to describe to the reader exactly what I was doing, and the perspective I was taking with regard to the manual itself. This was mostly covered in the introduction, but a little more detail is required. An additional part to this particular discussion of intent is discussing the fact that only the single sword will be discussed. This is because it is considered by Fabris that if the single sword is known then the other forms will follow without much difficulty.

Tactical Differences: Seated and Standing

An important part of the introductory part of the discussion was to highlight the tactical differences between the seated and standing combatants. Much of this has been discussed in one of my other articles so I will not go into any detail about it here, for such information I would direct you to the previous article mentioned. Needless to say this is designed to introduce the normally standing combatant to the important changes when being seated.

Theoretical Principles

From this point on there is a discussion of the various theoretical principles which Fabris delves into and must be understood before delving into the more practical aspects of the manual. The discussion of the single sword has already been pointed out. This then needs to be combined with his division of the weapon to understand the various important parts of it. The next part of the discussion follows on with more of the basic elements.

Wards

One of the most basic elements of fencing is those positions that the combatant adopts in the performance of the art, the wards. Now, Fabris calls these guards, but they are wards in effect. While they do protect certain areas they are not the guards found in the modern sport. These are the foundation positions that the fencer will adopt and as such it is important to go into some detail about them, thus there is discussion of the four basic guards, counter-positions, body and sword positions. Armed with this information, the reader can then proceed with more of the theoretical elements.

Time and Distance

Time and distance are the two essential elements from which no art with the sword, true no martial art can escape. To this point there are two separate sections one about distance, or measure, and the other about tempo. It is important also that the reader also understands how these two interact, thus there is also a part within both of these sections about how they both interact. Once these theoretical elements are understood it is then possible to discuss the actions made with the weapon.

Actions of the Weapons

The actions of the weapon go along with the movements of the body and as such it is important that both are understood. The essential offensive action with the rapier is, of course, the thrust and as such there is quite a bit of detail about this particular action. The other offensive action with the weapon is the cut, and while Fabris has some misgivings about its use, he does describe it as a technique that can be used should the opportunity present itself.

With regard to defensive actions, Fabris actually says surprisingly little about them. For the most part with regard to this, Fabris advises the use of the void as a purely defensive action over the parry. He makes some various points about this and also goes into a little detail about the reason for his preference for the void over the parry.

The next set of actions with the weapon once offensive and defensive actions have been discussed are those with regard to blade engagement, such things as finding the blade and the disengage. With very little surprise, Fabris goes into a great deal of detail with regard to all elements of blade engagement as he finds them essential to the proper use of the weapon. These particular elements are most important if Fabris' method is to be understood completely.

Tactical Elements

The tactical elements are those which divide the beginner from the more experienced fencer and it is these considerations which are important to truly understand and be able to plan how to defeat the opponent. To this will be added feints as they are a tactical option more than a specific action. Fabris also goes into a discussion about how the fencer should deal with different sorts of opponents as many Renaissance theorists did.

Use of Wards

The final part of the theoretical part of the discussion covers the guards. There is a great deal of information covered in this particular discussion. Each guard is discussed separately for its advantages and flaws. There is little surprise that Fabris makes his impression of which guard is better than another and so on. He also presents some basic actions which can be performed directly from the guards and their defensive potential. This is designed to lead on to what he calls the "wounds" which are his practical demonstration of the theory previously presented.

CONCLUSION

The brief overview of the project which has been presented here has been designed to strike on the main points of interest in the project which will be presented below. There are some important elements which change from a standing fencer to one who is seated, but these changes are more a change of perspective. There are things which the seated combatant cannot do, but there are still a lot of things which the seated combatant *can*, and this is the point of the exercise. The project is designed to demonstrate what a fencer can do from a chair rather than highlight what they cannot. Perspective is an important element when embarking on any project and the fencer should always be aware primarily of what they *can* do rather than what they cannot.

PERIOD TEXTS

Fabris' Single Rapier for the Seated Combatant: A Discussion

INTRODUCTION

De Lo Schermo Overo Scienza d'Arme of 1606 by Salvator Fabris is an excellent manual about how to use the Late Italian rapier and some companion weapons effectively against an opponent. It is filled with information about how to deal with an opponent in Fabris' particular method, even without any sort of modification, save putting it into English for the English-language audience it is an excellent manual well worth studying. This being said, it is not for every rapier combatant to learn in its original form.

In the approach to studying this particular manual and this particular master, it needs to be considered what sort of student is required, and the simplest answer is fit and able. For an individual who has an infirmity, this particular manual can pose some difficulties. The theory can be applied to areas of their fencing, but not near to its original form. It is true that the theory and several of the methods may be used, but overall it is a small part of what is available.

I happen to be one of those individuals not able to adopt the positions that Fabris requires for his method to work. I can, and have, used his theories on blade engagement, but cannot perform nor stand in the positions that he requires to use much of of the rest of his information. To this particular point, I looked at the low position of Fabris and decided that it may be possible to use more of Fabris' elements from the seated position, lowering the body as he requires without any issue, thus this particular investigation was born. This particular aspect also opens up another option for the seated combatant, whether their seated condition is permanent or temporary.

The purpose of this investigation is so that the method of Fabris, or at least a part of it, may be modified in order that it may be utilised by a seated combatant. This involves modifications of some of the original approaches used by Fabris, and the removal of others. This element of this particular investigation will be discussed early in the investigation so that the reader may understand what I am doing and the differences between the standing and the seated combatant in rapier combat.

The investigation will be focussing only on the single sword of Fabris and more to the point it will be focussing only on Book I. This is an introduction to the techniques of Fabris not a complete investigation. In this investigation, I will only be using the information gained from a single translation of the original material, thus removing the "noise" which occurs when using multiple translations. Thus I am using the 2005 translation by Tommaso Leoni, *The Art of Dueling: Salvator Fabris' rapier fencing treatise of 1606*.

What will be noted is that there will be changes in certain techniques to suit them to the seated combatant. Some of the elements which will be removed from this particular discussion will still be considered due to the theory which is attached to them. Those movements which require excessive movement of the body or those which are reliant on the movement of the legs have been removed due to the seated position. These particular elements will be noted at suitable times throughout the text. The text itself has been reorganised a little for a better flow of discussion, but this is to increase the readability and use of this particular investigation. It is hoped that this investigation will be of use to many people and may open access to this most useful manual to more people.

Before any real discussion of this particular manual from this particular point of view is possible, it is important to note the particular idiosyncrasies that are involved when fighting from a chair. These need to be noted first in order that the perspective of the seated combatant is realised in comparison to that of the standing. Thus the differences between the seated and standing combatants will be noted first. For foundation elements for the seated fencer, there is an article in this book on seated fencing.

TACTICAL CONSIDERATIONS: THE DIFFERENCE BETWEEN STANDING AND SEATED

There are some serious considerations that need to be made before investigating taking a manual made for a person standing on their feet and adapting it for the seated combatant. The differences between the seated and the standing combatants, while obvious in most cases, there are some which are less obvious. All of these need to be taken into account in order to understand the differences so that these can be integrated into the adaptation.

The first and most obvious difference between the seated and the standing combatant is that the seated combatant has no footwork, and for the most part, no movement, at least none which involves the use of the feet. This means techniques such as the classic lunge are not possible due to the required foot movement. This may seem reasonably simple, but this attaches to much larger issues.

Without footwork movement, the seated combatant is reliant on the opponent moving into the *misura stretta*. For this particular reason the seated combatant needs to draw their opponent in so that they are able to attack. What should also be noted is that engagement by the seated combatant will always be at *misura stretta* with the opponent. This means actions need to be changed to take into account this limited use of measure.

Interestingly there is some "footwork" that the seated combatant may perform. This is done by the leaning of the body. If the chair is positioned correctly, there are at least four directions which can be moved in. The forward leaning of the body equates to an advance, the rearward movement the retreat, and movement to either side a traverse. Performed in the same way that a lunge is an extension of the arm followed by the leaning forward of the body, could be equated to a seated form of the lunge, all of the same rules apply. Movements can be even more complex.

In examining Fabris' text I noted that he uses a lot of what he calls giratas. This is a turning of the body with a movement of the feet in similar action to the inquartata. I noted that because the seated combatant is not able to move their feet, this particular technique may not be possible for such a combatant. After some experimentation, it was found that a form of the girata was possible from the seated position, relying on the turning of the body, without the movement of the feet. This opened a great deal more options for the use of Fabris' techniques.

There are some interesting points that must be made in the comparison between the standing and the seated combatants. First of all, as recommended by Fabris, it is actually easier for the seated combatant to adopt and keep a lowered position, simply by their naturally lowered position being seated. This presents some other tactical considerations that must be made.

The lower parts of the body are unlikely targets due to the much lowered position of the seated combatant, also meaning that the dominant part of the opponent's attacks will be directed against the upper parts of the body. The fact that a strike to the leg of a seated combatant does not change a great deal is also a serious consideration. Further, due to the seated combatant not being able to withdraw once engaged, and that movement is limited due to the seated position, it is better to keep the opponent at sword range rather than allowing them to close. Of course these elements can change depending on what combination of weapons is chosen. For the most, part keeping the opponent at sword range is the best option for the seated combatant.

What has been shown above is some of the simple and tactical considerations that need to be made when comparing the seated and standing combatants. These particular elements need to be noted and will form the basis of what is being demonstrated in this investigation. The aspects highlighted in this particular discussion are those which will have a great effect on which parts of Fabris' method will be able to be utilised by the seated combatant. Due to the seated position of the combatant in this investigation certain demonstrations will be left out of this presentation in order to focus on the seated combatant.

SWORD ALONE: THE KEY

The single sword is the basis of all swordplay systems, and as such this investigation of Fabris' techniques will focus on his single sword. As he states himself, "I will start this book with the system for sword alone, from which stems the understanding of all other weapons." (Leoni, 2005:3). There is much that he says about the single sword and in his first chapter as well. This is where the foundation of the system lies, and as such it is of great importance. In fact this particular investigation of the single sword is justified, rather than examining any other combination first in that, "If you are confident with the sword alone, you will find it even easier to use it in combination with another weapon." (Leoni, 2005:3).

From this particular point of view, Fabris then moves on to briefly introduce the four guards, and their importance to his system. It would seem that the combination of the sword along and the four guards are the foundation to the entire system, "All the principles of the sword alone are founded upon four guards." (Leoni, 2005:3). Thus the combination of the two elements form the primary elements of the system, as such it is an examination of the relationship between these two elements which must proceed. This will, of course lead on to other important parts.

First of all, as stated, the system is based upon the single sword and the four guards. The four guards are elementary in this relationship, "no defensive or offensive action can be affected outside of the four guards." (Leoni, 2005:3). It can be seen that all actions are formed from the four guards and that knowledge of these guards will determine what is easiest. Of course the other elements of fencing are important in this particular consideration.

> *"In truth, a knowledgeable swordsman is more free to choose his techniques, because no matter what posture he finds himself, he will be able to maximise the effectiveness through his knowledge of measures, debole, forti, openings and defenses."*
>
> *(Leoni, 2005:3)*

Of course, along with timing, which will be discussed in detail later on, distance, or measure is one of the key elements of fencing, and the use of guard affects the use of measure. Some guards are more suited to different measures and others suited to others. This will affect what techniques are chosen as well.

> "some postures are better than others, and some ways of approaching the measure are safer than others; and that, once within measure, you must conform your strategy to the moves of your opponent, to the opportunities he gives you, and to his distance from you." *(Leoni, 2005:3)*

As previously stated in the tactical considerations, measure for the seated combatant is somewhat limited. The primary actions of the seated combatant will occur at *misura stretta* on the basis that he is not able to move into or use *misura larga* due to the lack of footwork. This does not mean that the seated combatant should ignore elements of *misura larga*, as the opponent may perform actions at this measure. The question of measures will appear in several different sections.

DIVISION OF THE SWORD

Like Di Grassi in *His True Arte of Defence* (1594), Fabris divides the blade into four parts, counting from the hilt toward the tip (Leoni, 2005:4). This numbering means that the first two parts of the blade are the forte, the second two the debole. The middle two would comprise those parts which would be called the mezzo, though Fabris does not mention this. With little surprise, the theory of the sword follows as with many other theorists.

> "There is no blow, whether cut or thrust, no matter how stoutly delivered, that cannot be effectively parried with the first part of the blade – so long as you observe proper form and tempo," *(Leoni, 2005:4)*

Essentially Fabris describes the first two parts of the blade as primarily for defence, and the second two parts of the blade primarily for offence. He goes through each part of the blade describing how they should be used, the second part being useful for defence, the third being less useful for parrying, and the fourth being useless for defence but being the part of the weapon designed for offence. He also states that half the third and fourth should be used for the delivery of cuts (Leoni, 2005:5).

Understanding how the blade is divided assists us with understanding how the author intends the weapon to be used by the combatant. This enables the reader to understand how the weapon will be used and where the primary attacks from the weapon will come. It also tells how the weapon should be positioned for effective defence.

THE FOUR GUARDS

Fabris describes four primary guards which are used. The interesting thing is that while the guards were described by Agrippa as being from the position of the fencer while drawing the sword, Fabris has a different approach as to the origins of the guards. Fabris, rather than being reliant on the position of the combatant, relates them to the sword. "The four guards derive from four perspectives of the hand and the sword, the latter having two edges and two flats, therefore producing four different effects." (Leoni, 2005:3).

With regard to naming conventions, Fabris sticks to a simple numerical system, the first guard being called first and so on. While there are some differences in the origins of the guards, the guards themselves still bear resemblance to those found in the earlier work of Agrippa. First for example places the weapon high, and most importantly, "[point] directed at the opponent – as it should always be directed, in all the guards, especially with the sword alone." (Leoni, 2005:4).

The following guards are much the same as Agrippa except Fabris focuses on the position of the hand more than that of the entire arm or body. These guards reflect the late Italian positioning of the guards and the importance placed on the position of the hand. As with Agrippa, the combatant must pass through the guards to reach the others, first becomes second and then third and then fourth. This relates both to body positions but also to the hand positions of the combatant.

It has been stated previously that for Fabris the guards are one of his core elements and he states as such, "It must be clear that nothing is done that does not proceed from the essence of one of these guards." (Leoni, 2005:4). This means that his system is based on these positions and that all movements, as they must, come from these positions. Of course, there are guards which exist between the standard four.

> *"between the first and second guard there is a mid-point where the hand should stop; similarly, there is one between the second and third and between the third and fourth. So, we could say that there are four "legitimate" guards and three "bastard" ones, the latter sharing some of the qualities of the two guards between which they are formed."* (Leoni, 2005:4)

These "bastard" guards are ones, as stated which exist between the explicitly stated ones. Fabris acknowledges that they exist and that they share some qualities of the original ones, but only discusses what he calls the "legitimate" guards. I would suggest that this is because he does not want to confuse the reader, and also in order to be able to simplify and condense his ideas about the guards, "I will only talk about the four "legitimate" guards, since they possess all the qualities of the "bastard" ones anyway." (Leoni, 2005:4).

The qualities, which Fabris describes gives each one of the guards their particular advantages, and also their disadvantages. Of course discussing them in more general terms, it is important to understand the origin of such qualities. "The quality of a guard not only consists of the position of the hand, but also of the direction of the point, which actually gives a guard the measure of its strength." (Leoni, 2005:4). As can be seen by this statement, Fabris reduces the effect of the guards down to the position of the hand and the weapon as the primary importance.

Of course, to understand the advantage of a particular guard, it is important to also see that this position also relates to how both the fencer and the opponent can attack. This, it will be clearly noted, thus relates the guards also to the lines, "there are only four ways to wound the opponent: inside, outside, below and above. This is done differently depending on the guard." (Leoni, 2005:4). With the guards and their qualities based on the position of the weapon, it could be assumed that the body has less of an importance, but as will be noted, this is not the case, these lines will also be demonstrated to be significant as well.

COUNTER POSTURES

"Forming a good counter-posture means situating the body and the sword in such a way that, without touching the opponent's blade, the straight line between the opponent's point and your body is completely defended. This way, without even moving your body or sword, you are assured that the opponent cannot attack the part of your body directly opposite his point; and if he wants to strike you at all, he has to first move his sword to another spot, thereby lengthening the tempo and giving your ample time to parry." (Leoni, 2005:5)

The good counter-posture, by the nature of its automatic defence also positions the fencer in a position where they can safely attack the opponent without having to concern themselves about their defence as it is already established. Of course this is dependent on the counter-posture being effective once it is established. The defence is the primary concern.

Fabris concerns himself more on the defensive aspects of the counter-posture over its offensive aspects, the first is the position of the weapon, "you must situate the sword so that it is stronger than the opponent's, and is able to resist effectively at the time of the parry." (Leoni, 2005:5). This strong position of defence is to defend the fencer while parrying, but it will be noted that rarely does Fabris mention a defence without a counter, and as such the position also assists with this.

As with all things in fencing, they are dependent on Time and Measure. The time aspect has been discussed a little in the mentioning of having time to parry against the opponent. Measure is also important as this determines where the counter-posture should be formed, "always be mindful to form the counter-posture while far enough from the opponent that he cannot strike you." (Leoni, 2005:6). If the opponent is far enough away that he cannot strike you, then the same will also be true in that you are not able to strike him either, "All of this pertains to a measure that is not quite close enough to enable you to strike the opponent in his mutations" (Leoni, 2005:5). This presents a defensive situation which moves towards an offensive one once the advantage is gained.

The simple thing is that there is no one counter-posture which will defeat the opponent no matter which way he moves. This means that you must modify the counter-posture and remain in control. Where the counter-posture is not effective it needs to be changed, "if your movements are controlled, you can always interrupt the original motion and perform another one as the occasion presents itself." (Leoni, 2005:6). This means that you can change the counter-posture in order to suit the situation which is presented, through this modification of the position you can maintain the advantage over the opponent. "If you can subtly maintain yourself in this counter-posture, you will have a definite advantage over the opponent." (Leoni, 2005:5).

To maintain a constant advantage over the opponent, it is important to know several different options as to how to maintain such an advantage. This comes from an examination of his position and having the knowledge and options in order to change your own position in order to suit the situation.

> *"It is therefore vital to be rich with different resources, to quickly find the advantageous placement against the opponent's and to present him with a new effective counter-posture." (Leoni, 2005:5)*

The counter-posture is more important than most fencers will realise. As a defensive position, performed properly it is extremely effective. The advantage gained in the counter-posture can also be used on the offensive as well, "if you want to safely gain the measure against the opponent, you should first form a counter-posture." (Leoni, 2005:6). The counter-posture forms a defence against the opponent and enables you to approach with more security, and also being able to change in order to take the advantage. The important thing is that, in this counter-posture the body is completely covered by the sword, or it is not effective.

"a counter-posture cannot be deemed "proper" unless the line between the opponent's point and your body is completely covered, although even in this case you are playing with the advantages of the forte against the debole." (Leoni, 2005:15)

BODY POSITION

The position of the sword and the body in the on guard position is significant as it decides what blows can be thrown from the outset, and also how much and what parts of the body are protected in that position. The first part to look at in this particular situation is the body as its position can, in some part, determine where the sword will be placed. For Fabris, he thought that keeping the body as small as possible was the greatest advantage as the large body left more to be covered. "The larger the body, the more difficult it will be for the sword to defend it," (Leoni, 2005:28). What needs to be looked at is exactly what he means by "small".

The small body means showing as little of the body to the opponent as possible and this has the greatest advantage. He stated that the upright body was in a more dangerous position as there was more movement required in order to defend it (Leoni, 2005:28). What this means is that the body is bent over in order to shrink the target area which is presented to the opponent. He presents how this should be achieved for the combatant also. There is an element of comfort present, the important thing is to keep the body low, bent at the waist at a comfortable angle, being that a lowered body presents a smaller target and is less to defend (Leoni, 2005:28).

For the standing combatant this means bending at the waist and ensuring that the feet are spread correctly so that the fencer is comfortable. There is practice required to keep the body low as this is not a natural position at all. The advantages are that with practice it can be a very quick and active position and easy to move from (Leoni, 2005:28). This is where the idea of presenting the same guard from a chair presents its first advantage.

The seated combatant is already in a lowered position by the fact that they are seated in a chair. This means that they have conformed to the first of Fabris' suggestions by staying low. The other advantage in this situation is that the bending at the waist for the seated combatant is less uncomfortable for the back and legs and thus easier to maintain. Fabris states that the weight of the body should be over a single foot so that the other is able to move quickly, thus reducing the tempos in motion (Leoni, 2005:28). For the seated combatant by the virtue of not being able to move very far except in leaning with the body, the weight should be evenly distributed to remain stable. The weight may be moved in moving forward or backward.

With the seated combatant the body position is very low and the target is very small, this conforms to Fabris' tactical ideas about body position. This is closely related to the sword position as it is related to the closeness of the forte of the sword (Leoni, 2005:28).

The forte is used to cover as much of the fencer as possible and this forms a link between sword position and body position. If the body is kept small, then more of it will be defended by the forte. Thus the next discussion is the position of the sword.

SWORD POSITION

With regard to the sword position, Fabris discusses various different options as to how the sword may be placed by the combatant while they are in guard. These sword positions will determine what sort of approach the fencer will take toward their opponent. The question of which has the advantage is something which needs to be discussed.

Holding the sword extended has advantages but is fatiguing, work harder to keep it free (Leoni, 2005:25). Holding the sword extended is tiring on the arm and thus difficult to maintain, especially for the combatant who is not used to it, but there are some advantages gained from this position. With the sword extended it is easy to defend against incoming attacks with only slight motions of the sword and arm, while keeping the point on line (Leoni, 2005:26). This is due to the position of the forte being already extended toward the opponent and therefore able to intercept the opponent's attack before it arrives. Thus the fencer only moves a small amount, enough to defeat the attack (Leoni, 2005:26).

The fencer using the extended guard needs to keep the opponent at distance to maintain the advantage. The sword needs to be position close to the opponent's but maintained free (Leoni, 2005:26). This means that the fencer needs to maintain in control of his own weapon and ensure that the opponent does not gain engagement unless it is presented by the fencer. This particular position is reliant on angles, as Fabris states, "Angles are good for offense but are poor for the defense." (Leoni, 2005:26). Thus the fencer who uses the extended guard must maintain the advantage of the angles over the opponent. This is so that he may stay on the offensive. The advantage that must be maintained is one that unifies all elements of the guard and the fencer, sword, body and foot (Leoni, 2005:27).

While the extended guard has some advantages so are there advantages with keeping the sword more withdrawn and straight. This position is maintained through a direct line from the elbow to the point of the sword. This is used to gain the advantage of the sword (Leoni, 2005:27). Fabris is interesting in his particular decision as to which has the greatest advantage. For his particular position they are all examined and he simply states that there is an advantage to learn all the positions and be able to utilise them (Leoni, 2005:27). Simply due to the explanation and advantages demonstrated the more extended guard has the advantage over the withdrawn. The blade position enables the forte to be utilised in Fabris' system the best, and maintains the fencer in a position able to resist actions by the opponent. Thus for Fabris the arm should be more extended than not with the sword directed against the opponent, this having many benefits over other stances (Leoni, 2005:27).

The guard position with the sword extended, but not completely also has advantages for the seated combatant. With the sword withdrawn, it allows the opponent to close in too far to the seated combatant before the weapon is engaged. The weapon completely extended also is not good for the seated combatant as they are not able to withdraw should the weapon be taken by the opponent, as such having the weapon between the withdrawn and completely extended gives the seated combatant the advantage of keeping the opponent at distance while maintaining control over the weapon.

MEASURES

Distance is one of the key elements in fencing, for the seated combatant, it becomes even more important to know the distance of the opponent. While your position will not change that of your opponent will, and as such it is important to consider where the opponent is. With regard to the position of the fencer, Fabris states,

"After forming a good counter-posture not too far out of measure, you should start cautiously moving your foot forward in order to gain misura larga. However, you should exercise caution if your opponent is static in his guard:" (Leoni, 2005:6)

It is difficult for the seated combatant to move into measure as you are seated, but the same idea can be applied still with regard to ensuring that the measure is made aware of, and utilising the advantage of the static guard. The *misura larga*, or wide distance, is only possible for you where the opponent moves into this position. Even here there is no real offensive action that you can take because to breach this gap footwork is required, "The *misura larga* is that distance from the opponent where you can wound him by stepping forward with the right foot." (Leoni, 2005:6). This is something which is not an option for the seated combatant. Thus the primary actions of the seated combatant will occur at the *misura stretta*, or narrow distance.

It is important for the seated combatant that you know your distance and where you are able to strike against the opponent. The important thing with regard to distance is that while you cannot strike the opponent at *misura larga*, you can still counter the opponent's actions at this measure, "If you are always mindful of that the opponent can do to you, you will be considerably safer because you can more easily counter his moves." (Leoni, 2005:6). The first advantage with regard to distance that you have while seated is the static nature of distance. The other advantage is that every action is in the time of the hand or body; this makes them quite quick, "the movement of the foot is generally longer and slower than that of the blade;" (Leoni, 2005:6). Thus in this way the seated combatant can gain the advantage using tempo.

The actions of the seated combatant will be at the *misura stretta* by the simple fact that you are unable to use footwork in the traditional sense. This distance is measured, according to Fabris as such, "The *misura stretta* is defined as the distance from the opponent where you can wound him by just bending the body forward without moving your feet." (Leoni, 2005:7). This makes this distance perfect for the seated combatant, because bending of the body and extending the arm is the only distance which is possible.

This idea of measure is integrally linked to that of *tempo* or Time, so much so that it is difficult to see where one ends and the other begins. Essentially at the *misura stretta* there is a single *tempo* of action, and this needs to be measured against that of the opponent. The advantage of the lack of foot movement in the seated combatant is that time is in their favour, for the most part.

"If you know for certain that the tempo of his parry and counter is equal to that of your attack, then you can be confident that your sword will arrive on target before he can parry, because you have the advantage of the first move." (Leoni, 2005:7)

The issue with everything for the seated combatant being at the *misura stretta* is that there is very little time to use, and also very little room for error. In this particular case it is small openings that will be made and these need to be taken advantage of, and then changed to another opening if it is closed quickly (Leoni, 2005:7). The movement of the foot, which takes a tempo, where the opponent closes to *misura stretta* leaves options for the seated combatant to consider. The advantage that the seated combatant has is that you can wait for the opponent to gain the correct distance, which will take time, leaving the seated combatant a tempo to consider your options. These options need to be somewhat modified from their original as described by Fabris.

If the opponent closes and attacks simultaneously, then the response for the seated fencer is to parry and counter in contra-tempo, thus availing them of the tempo to defend and respond. If the opponent closes and stops, use the tempo to attack at any opening which is presented, taking the advantage of the time of the hand over the time of the foot. The third option is that if they close then retreat back to *misura larga*, you can take the opportunity to attack on the close, and then re-set as they exit if the attack fails. Most importantly, regardless of the option taken once the attack is completed, "it is necessary while recovering your sword to always withdraw the body as far as you can, and pull back your foot." (Leoni, 2005:8). While the foot movement is useless to the seated combatant, the body can still be withdrawn from the opponent. It can be seen that measure and tempo, or time and distance, interact a great deal, as has been demonstrated, and as such it is most suitable to discuss tempo as the next topic.

TEMPO

Time and distance, tempo and measure, these are the two concepts which fencing is based upon and as such no good fencer will be able to ignore. For this particular part, it will be tempo which will be the subject for discussion. Tempo plays a large role in fencing, only equalled by distance in its importance.

Fabris actually has two explanations for the concept of tempo in with regard to fencing, the first is a more passive explanation, "A tempo is a movement that the opponent makes within the measures." (Leoni, 2005:17), thus basing tempo on what the opponent does, but the second reverses this idea and takes into account the actions of the fencer, "in the discipline, "tempo" also implies an occasion to wound or at least to take some advantage over the opponent." (Leoni, 2005:17). Thus from the explanations it could be reasoned that tempo is both an active and a passive concept, which indeed it is.

The important thing is that the tempo is not a concrete measure of time. It is the measurement of an action. A tempo is the movement of a fencer, whether it is to perform a thrust, parry or any one of the many actions, or combinations of actions, in fencing. The other thing is that, according to Fabris, the time once used in an action cannot be bought back by the fencer, thus the action is committed.

"The reason why the name tempo was given to the movements made while fencing is that the time employed to make one movement cannot be employed to make any other." (Leoni, 2005:17)

What this all means is that fencing can be broken into segments of movement, or tempos, in which the fencer moves, the opponent moves, or both combatants move.

The important thing for the fencer, from the offensive aspect is that the actions need to be timed correctly in order to succeed, "It is therefore important to make sure that the tempo necessary for your attack is no longer than the tempo given by your opponent;" (Leoni, 2005:17). This cannot be isolated from the concept of distance as travelling over a larger distance will increase the amount of time taken to perform the tempo. This is the most important place where time and distance become integrated and hard to separate.

> "Besides estimating the motion of your opponent, you should also evaluate the distance. If you are in the misura larga, and your opponent moves his weapon(s) and his body but not his feet, you cannot be sure to reach him (even if he presents you with an opening)." *(Leoni, 2005:17)*

The fencer needs to estimate the tempos it will take to cross the distance between them and their opponent. This is of great importance as if too much time is used the opponent will be able to easily respond to any action of the fencer. The consideration in this particular instance also needs to take into account the movement of the opponent as well. It is depending on what the opponent moves as much as how much they move is the important part.

> "Whether he moves to settle in his guard, he moves his feet and body, his feet and sword or only his feet – all of these would present you with a good tempo if you see an opening." *(Leoni, 2005:17)*

Tempos are something that a fencer needs to be aware of. You need to be aware of the tempos used by your opponent, but also by yourself. Any movement, shuffling, or other movement is a tempo and this can give an opportunity either to strike or be struck. In many ways the unknown use of tempos is like the "tell" in poker.

> "It is easier to take the advantage of a tempo when the opponent makes it without realizing (provided that he does no retreat while doing so) and when you have the advantage of the counter-posture." *(Leoni, 2005:17)*

It is in this particular situation where the real mental aspect of fencing becomes apparent. Such movements in fencing can be very subtle or they can be quite explicit. There is, however, another side to this and that is where the opponent is deliberately using a tempo in order to lure the fencer in, and this is something that you need to be aware of. These movements are designed to be noticed and designed to be taken advantage of so the opponent may counter the action that follows.

> "It is important to admonish you that there are some who astutely make a tempo to lure you to attack, and as you do so, they will have parried and countered your blow. This is called wounding in contratempo." *(Leoni, 2005:18)*

Contra-tempo literally means against the tempo, and as such describes those actions which move against the tempo of the opponent, "every time you counter an attack ... it is called a contratempo." (Leoni, 2005:18). These particular actions need to be taken especial note of as they can be used both against and by the opponent. This is where knowing the tempos and the amount it takes to perform an action becomes of vital importance.

> "If you want to ward off danger of a contratempo, you have to make sure that the tempo (or movement) of your opponent is long enough to give you time to arrive and that the opponent has not cleverly made the tempo to lure you in." (Leoni, 2005:18)

It is important to discover before you commit to an action whether or not the tempo spent by the opponent is a lure or not. The same can be reversed and used against opponents, but it requires a great deal of subtlety in the actions. It is also important to notice the subtle changes in the opponent in order to ward against the same, "this discipline [contra-tempo and avoidance] relies on great part on the ability to subtly deceive your opponent." (Leoni, 2005:18).

In the *misura larga* there is more time to act as the distance is greater and therefore will take more time for an attack to arrive. Needless to say as the combatants become closer and closer the amount of time will reduce. This is of special importance to the seated combatant, for who most actions will be performed in the *misura stretta*, "In the misura stretta, you can take advantage of any little move or mutation of your opponent, provided that it does not involve his breaking the measure." (Leoni, 2005:18). Essentially at the *misura stretta* there is only really a single tempo to work with, a single movement to be made and countered. It is important in such a situation that the opponent needs to be put on the defensive and therefore be reactive rather than active, "in the misura stretta, it is never good to be the first to move unless this move is an attack." (Leoni, 2005:18).

This idea of being the active combatant rather than the reactive combatant is one which is used by the German schools of fence, especially in their close work with regard to the concept of the Before and After. The *misura stretta*, as has already been noted is an area in which there can be very little if no movement without a purpose. In fact Fabris states that the fencer does not have to wait for a tempo in order to perform an action or attack the opponent, of course there are conditions attached to such actions.

> "Also, in the misura stretta you can perform an attack even without waiting for a tempo, availing yourself instead of the advantage of the counter-posture, the careful planning of your thrust versus his ability to parry and your accurate surveying of the nature and size of the most likely targets. Therefore, in the misura stretta, you can successfully attack your opponent without a tempo, as long as you ensure that your sword can arrive at him before he can parry; it is thus necessary to know that your opponent's sword is far enough from yours that, as you push yours forward, his sword can find yours only at your forte."
> (Leoni, 2005:18)

For the seated combatant, you need to be able to identify weaknesses in the opponent's defences and be able to take advantage of these as soon as possible. The important thing in this particular situation is placement to ensure that the combatant has the advantage in the situation to act safely. Blade engagement and effective use of tempo and action is the most important thing in this particular situation. The attack has to be performed correctly in order to best be able to utilise the situation presented.

OF THE THRUST

The thrust is the primary offensive action when using the rapier; and it is not simply throwing the sword at the target by the use of force. There is technique involved which must be observed so that the thrust is performed correctly and as a result, accurately. This is a particular subject which Fabris had some things to say about.

Fabris divides the use of the point with the rapier into two actions, thrusting and flinging. The first is the thrust performed properly and the second, the same action performed with less accuracy, "There are some who, wanting to execute a thrust, fling their sword-arm forward with force in order to give it more momentum. This is a bad technique." (Leoni, 2005:8). The combatant in flinging is attempting to use strength rather than technique in order for the point to reach its target, and this can result in a list of problems.

Fabris makes a list of the possible problems with regard to the use of flinging rather than thrusting properly. The first problem is that once a sword is flung its direction cannot be changed, this means that the fencer cannot change target if the first one is defended. Another problem is that a flung thrust has little control over it and the thrust is easily deflected. In most instances the forte is stronger than the foible; this is not the case in a flung thrust where the opposite is true. Of course attempting to thrust faster than a person is trained to results in inaccuracy in the thrust and the inability to make successive thrusts without withdrawal (Leoni, 2005:8). Each one of these is a problem for the fencer and a detriment to their overall skill.

Once Fabris has finished discussing the reasons why flinging is not a good technique, he then moves on to discuss various tactical applications of the weapon focussing on tempo and the use of blade engagement. For the most part, Fabris advises against using two tempi, but there are exceptions, "techniques involving two tempi are actually feasible against those who attack with jabs." (Leoni, 2005:8). This, once again, relies upon the bad technique of the opponent, and demonstrates the importance of the proper thrust to the fencer. For the most part, however, he prefers to act in a single tempo. This particular aspect with regard to the use of the rapier is also referred back to the use of flinging as well.

"We can conclude that is much better to parry and counter in the same tempo, although in sword alone this dual action requires great judgement. And as far as thrusting versus flinging your arm, it is comparably better to thrust." (Leoni, 2005:9)

What should be noted here is that Fabris is fully in favour of using technique in all situations. He also uses such technical aspects in all situations. While there will be a discussion about blade engagements further along in the discussion, it is useful to see how the thrust can be changed when it is not flung.

"it is important to retain control of your blade at all times, occupying the opponent's debole, and attacking if the occasion presents itself while always

> keeping your sword free. If, in turn, your opponent doesn't have the skill to keep his own blade free, he will never be able to successfully attack. These rules can only be observed by those who move their sword from one position to another in a measured manner and always retain his control; ... Those are the same fencers who will wound in the same moment that the opponent tries to parry and whose point will continue, without deviating or withdrawing it, to the opponent's body." *(Leoni, 2005:9)*

It is the retaining of control over the blade in the attack which is where the distinction between flinging and thrusting becomes evident. The thrust is a controlled action in which the point is directed toward its target with purpose and control. Flinging involves substantially less control and involves simply throwing the point in the direction of the opponent and this involves substantially less control. The important thing with regard to this is that the action must be completed regardless.

> "once an attack has begun, either by feinting a cavazione or by any other mutation, the point's motion must continue uninterrupted to the opponent's body."
> *(Leoni, 2005:9)*

The advantage of the controlled thrust is that modifications can be made to the attack while in its process. This is not the case for when the weapon is flung. The other thing that should be noted is that when a weapon is thrust, the whole body moves in concert with the action, thus maintaining more control, whereas where the weapon is flung it is only the arm so there is much less control, thus it is much less easier to complete the action with any accuracy.

> "if your sword's motion is underpinned and supported by the movement of the body and feet, it will have more strength and more accuracy. If you master your blade in this manner, it will never fall out of line after an attack." *(Leoni, 2005:9)*

In the case of the seated combatant the foot movement is obviously irrelevant, but the body can still be used to enhance the control of the thrust. This body movement will assist in the controlling of the weapon. In Fabris' case he refers to two different types of attack, the firm-footed and the pass, the firm-footed will be discussed as it is applicable to the seated fencer.

> "A firm-footed attack is performed either by lunging forward with the right foot and withdrawing it immediately afterward, or by just bending the body forward without any movement of the foot." *(Leoni, 2005:22)*

While the foot movement is not possible, the bending of the body is. In this particular manner, the body can stand in for the foot in this particular aspect. Most usefully to the seated combatant who is limited to this particular attack, it is very popular with Fabris. "It is necessary to be proficient with the firm-footed attack because it is the most commonly used attack in duels." (Leoni, 2005:22).

The question that must be asked is why it is necessary to move the body as well as the hand could not just the hand be used in this particular situation? In essence the hand and arm could be the only ones moved, but Fabris advises against this. "The hand is inherently inaccurate, ... This inaccuracy is due to the effects of the wrist, which bends depending on how much it is extended." (Leoni, 2005:22). With the motion of the body included in the thrust the accuracy of it increases due to the motion which is made.

With regard to the position of the body, Fabris also examines the position of the feet in the thrust. This is actually relevant to the seated fencer as either foot may be placed forward depending on how the person sits on the chair. The left foot forward is ill-advised as it shortens the thrust, but it is good for defence (Leoni, 2005:22). With regard to this particular positioning, it needs to be said that due to the fact that this discussion deals with only the single rapier, it is advice for this form that is most prevalent. However, with regard to the rapier and dagger, the left foot forward in the stance is considered more useful, but in general it is better to have the right foot forward (Leoni, 2005:23).

With regard to the void, the seated combatant is somewhat limited in their options for ways in which to void. The foot movement essential in some voids is not possible, but the body movement is, as such the void in its essence can be used. To be used you need to be close enough to wound in the same tempo and redirect the angle of the sword against you (Leoni, 2005:23). More of this will be said in a later part of the discussion, but needless to say it is most useful to know, and to be able to use them effectively.

ON CUTTING

Cutting, with regard to the rapier, has always been a secondary option, with the use of the point being the primary. For the seated combatant this is even more so as cutting often involves movement to position the weapon or defend. This is simply not an option for the seated combatant, movement is quite limited. Regardless, it is important to know how to cut properly should the situation arise.

For Fabris, the cuts are clearly divided by method and target. "The principal cuts are four: the mandritta, roverso, sottomano and montante. Each is used differently and has its own target." (Leoni, 2005:10). Each cut is designed to strike against a different target. Along with the different targets, there are also different methods in which the cuts can be delivered. The combatant needs to consider which method will be used to the greatest benefit.

Cuts can be done from the shoulder, elbow and wrist, and from shoulder with the arm stiff, the point is mostly in-line (Leoni, 2005:10). Of course while the cut from the shoulder keeps the point in-line, it is the slower method. The cut from the elbow is a median point between that of the wrist and shoulder, but it is the cut from the wrist which is preferred due to its flexibility, and thus ability to change target. Fabris also is in favour of the use of the shoulder with the stiff arm due to the position of the weapon during and after the cut (Leoni, 2005:10).

The cut is slower that the thrust and thus will take more time to perform. The most important thing to consider is the timing of the cut to ensure that it arrives before the opponent has a chance to counter it. This means that the tempo has to be of exactly the right length and the opening large enough for the cut.

"If you want to perform an effective cut, you have to wait for the most opportune tempo, since a cut seldom involves a small motion and, once the sword arrives on target, the tempo may already be expired." (Leoni, 2005:11)

This means that the cut requires exact timing for it to be performed correctly. One of the ways to do this is to create the opening for the cut to be delivered to. This can be done through the performance of a feint.

> "A good way to feint a cut, in order to put the opponent into obedience, and while he tries to parry the cut, strike him with a thrust. Alternately, you may feint a thrust and strike with a cut," *(Leoni, 2005:11)*

The problem with the feint is that it requires a tempo to perform, and this gives the opponent time in which they can counter, or perform an action of their own. This means that the timing of the feint needs to be done at the correct time. "Feinting a cut in the first place when the opponent is motionless is not advisable for the two tempi that such a feint requires" (Leoni, 2005:11). The problem with the cut is that while its delivery may only be a single tempo, it is still a slow action. The thrust is a much faster attack which can be delivered to its target more precipitously. Due to this and other reasons, Fabris favours the cut over the thrust.

> "In all respects, thrusting is more advantageous and deadlier than cutting. With a thrust, it is easier to strike quicker and from farther away, and to recover afterwards. Thrusting is a most excellent and elegant attack, since it embodies all the subtleties of fencing." *(Leoni, 2005:12)*

While cutting for the seated combatant should be left as a secondary option, favouring the thrust over it. It is most useful for you to know the cuts so that you know where they will land and thus be able to counter them. It is this particular aspect of the cut that Fabris favours (Leoni, 2005:33).

The defence against the cut is a similarly prepared to the delivery of the cut, the counter which follows should be as precipitous as the offensive action of the opponent. "In order to better parry and counter, you should plan on opposing a stronger cut with a proportionally stronger defense." (Leoni, 2005:33). The element that the seated combatant should gain from this discussion is that the cut is a useful tool, but should not be favoured over the thrust. Knowing the cuts will enable the fencer to be able to counter them.

DEFENSIVE ACTION

The fencer has several defensive options, for the most part they consider of one of two things either voiding or parrying. The void is simply to remove yourself from where the attack will land and as such many of the theorists, including Fabris, do not mention it in a huge amount of detail. The parry, on the other hand, is usually discussed with more detail. With the void being a less likely option for the seated combatant, the parry becomes more important.

> "If you examine the parry, you will find it to be a form of fear, because if you were not afraid of harm, you would not see the need to defend. This type of defense can therefore be dubbed obedience, even servitude, all the more when it is performed out of a sense of necessity,"
> *(Leoni, 2005:12)*

Fabris sees the parry from an interesting point of view being that he relates it to fear, and thus to preventing harm, rather than just in the prevention of harm. The important thing to realise is that he also gives some idea of the most profitable timing for the parry in his explanation, when it is performed out of necessity. Of course he sees this particular aspect of necessity as a negative thing.

> *"if you can put your opponent under the necessity to parry, you will be at a great advantage: as he goes to parry, he creates an opening where he can be wounded, thus rendering his defense ineffectual."* (Leoni, 2005:12)

Essentially what Fabris is saying is that the parry has a disadvantage in tempo and that if you can make your opponent parry out of necessity you will have an advantage. This advantage is found in that the time can be used to change the target of the attack. Of course he states that it is even worse when the fencer has completed the parry and does not counter against the opponent, "some say that parrying is counter-productive, on which I totally agree, especially when it is not accompanied by a counter." (Leoni, 2005:12).

Fabris is talking about fencing tempos as was discussed previously, and he clearly has a distinct favouring for the use of the fewest tempos. From this particular point of view Fabris wants the defence and counter to be performed at the same time, thus using fewer tempos.

> *"With the sword alone, you have to operate very judiciously if you wish to execute these two techniques of defense and offense at one time, which is the only way to operate in order to safely parry."* (Leoni, 2005:12)

With regard to the parry against cuts, Fabris advises the reader that parrying takes much too much time and it is better to void the cut and let it fall away. This is especially so when discussing the single sword (Leoni, 2005:12). This is primarily because the cuts are slower and thus easier to void than the thrust. The other aspect is that the counter against the cut is slower with a parry than it is without one. On the other hand, where the cut cannot be voided, Fabris actually does give some instruction how not to leave the fencer at a loss how to respond.

> *"If you find it necessary to parry a cut, you should place your forte in the spot where your opponent's sword is about to fall and, at the same time, deliver a quick thrust so that your point will make it to the opponent's body before his sword makes it to your forte"* (Leoni, 2005:12)

It has already been stated that the cut should be voided. This clearly states that Fabris is in favour of the use of the void as a defensive action. The action of the void places the fencer in the advantage due to the sword has not been moved; thus is still in-line and prepared for an attack. The cut is slow and allows for plenty of time for the void and a counter, or in some cases a counter and void.

> *"when your opponent attacks you with a cut, he often makes such a wide swing that you can wound him and step back into safety before his sword actually comes down."* (Leoni, 2005:13)

The thrust is a faster action and requires less time than the cut. The point of the weapon can remain in-line for the entire time that the attack is performed. This is not the case with the cut, which must go off-line, at least to a degree, to be executed. This being said, the speed of the thrust does not preclude the use of the void against it, merely that the fencer needs to perform it correctly.

> "voiding the opponent's point with the body becomes preferable for defending against and countering thrusts in the tempo, as long as you know how to do it judiciously." *(Leoni, 2005:13)*

Voiding while seated is difficult but still possible. Standing allows for voiding using the feet in movement. The seated combatant is only able to use the body to move. This being said, the body can be moved quite a distance and in several directions in order to void the opponent's attacks. The important thing is that both of these actions can be performed with equal effectiveness, and can be even more effective when they are performed together, and this is from both a defensive and a counter-offensive point of view.

> "It is necessary to also know how to parry a thrust so you can avail yourself sometimes of this technique (parrying with the sword), sometimes of the other (voiding with the body), as the occasion requires. Safest of all is when both techniques are applied at the same time, because if you parry with the sword while voiding with the body, you defend more effectively and you don't quite upset the position of your sword." *(Leoni, 2005:13)*

The most effective parry and actually the safest parry is the one which is performed at the very last moment before the opponent's blade comes in contact with its target. This is because the later the parry is left, the less chance the opponent has to change his mind about where the attack will land. Further to this if you know that the opponent's attack is not going to land you do not have to parry anyway.

> "If you know that you cannot reach his body with your point, it means that it is not necessary to parry, because it means that the opponent's sword cannot reach you either." *(Leoni, 2005:12)*

If a parry is made against an opponent's attack too far out from the body, the opponent may change the point of attack, as Fabris described previously. This means that the parry should be left as late as possible. However, there are instances in which a fencer may parry early deliberately to set up for a future action, the most important thing in this instance is the commitment to the counter performed, "If you still want to parry even if you know that your point cannot make it to your opponent, you still should move your sword as if you were to wound him;" (Leoni, 2005:13). It is this particular point which divides the early parry which is useful from the early parry which places the fencer in a threatened position.

In Fabris' case not only should the parry be left to the last minute, or not at all if the attack will not reach. He also states that the parry should not be made unless a counter can also be made (Leoni, 2005:13). The parry and counter needs to be performed efficiently and for Fabris that means in a single tempo. Thus the distance for the parry should not only facilitate a safe defence but the surety of a counter against the opponent.

To this point in time, the main focus has been on the use of the sword to parry and the body used to void, but this is not the only way to parry. The offhand can also be used defend against the opponent's weapon. Unfortunately Fabris does not consider this to be a particularly useful method, "I consider this way of parrying with a bare hand to be a truly abysmal way to defend." (Leoni, 2005:14). He then goes into detail about the how against an opponent who defends with the offhand, that they can be defeated.

"Against an opponent who parries with the hand, you should keep your sword slightly at an upward angle, just enough that he cannot pass with the body or counter before you straighten your point against him." (Leoni, 2005:14)

Keeping the sword at a slightly upward angle removes the point and the blade further away from the opponent and thus gives them less opportunity to parry with the offhand. For the opponent to do this they must come within range of the point of the weapon and thus a counter may be made against them. This is designed to remove the effect of the offhand. Not only does Fabris describe defensive operations, but also offensive ones as well.

"when you attack, do so along an oblique line, which will deceive the parrying hand of your opponent, as your sword remains elusive. In other words, once you have found the opponent's sword, gained the distance, found the tempo and a suitable opening, you can perform the attack, taking care that as your sword straightens, its point proceeds forward." (Leoni, 2005:14)

The oblique line is designed that the point will pass the offhand before it can be used, or deceive it for the same purpose, being avoidance. Once the offhand is avoided and the sword is found, the fencer is then in a position from which he can attack with very little difficulty. Once the tempo is gained and opening ensured, there is little that the offhand can do in response.

"All things considered, it is easier and less challenging to wound those who defend with the hand than those who do so with the sword, because the former kind do not avail themselves of their forte." (Leoni, 2005:14)

Fabris clearly dislikes the use of the offhand as a primary defence. He favours the use of the sword for the parry, even though he would prefer that the fencer simply counter the opponent rather than parrying first. In his usual manner, after decrying the use of the offhand, he does go into explain how to use it effectively where it is absolutely required.

"The proper way is to always move your sword in a controlled manner and observe the tempo even if you use the left hand. It is actually important to know how to use the off-hand, but bearing in mind that it has to be employed only in case of emergency and not as habit" (Leoni, 2005:14)

Thus while Fabris states that using the offhand as the primary defence is not a good idea, using it as an emergency use is fine, and thus needs some instruction so it can be performed properly. For Fabris, the use of the offhand is about total control over the opponent's weapon in the close, "The general rule is that it is better not to use the hand at all unless you know that you can reach the opponent's hilt or get into grapples and wrestle him." (Leoni, 2005:14). Of course, using the offhand in the close is not the only place where Fabris finds use for the offhand, he also describes the use of the offhand as being useful in support of the sword in defence. The offhand is used to close a line which the sword cannot while it is being used elsewhere. This is a preparatory defence rather than a responsive one.

"when the opponent performs an attack, it is necessary to parry with the sword and make a counter, but at the same time, place the off-hand so as to protect the most likely opening. This way, the hand defends the body and shuts the opponent's sword out of line without touching it or beating it away, a defense to be used whenever you can if the temp allows it." (Leoni, 2005:15)

FINDING THE SWORD

Blade engagement is a subject in fencing where there has been much debate about what is appropriate and what is the best approach to dealing with a situation. The most important thing about blade engagement, especially for this discussion is that it is about having a superior position of the blade over the opponent. It is from this position that further actions can take place.

For the seated combatant, the superior position is vital. The standing combatant can always make a retreat to disengage from the opponent. The seated combatant does not have this option. The seated combatant must dominate the opponent's blade while the opponent is in the *misura stretta* to succeed. At this distance, the fencer with the best blade position is most likely to come out on top.

"Finding the sword means occupying it. Although this technique is similar to the counter-posture, there are some differences, because it is possible to find your opponent's sword without covering the exact line between the point and your body. However you still have the advantage of the sword because the opponent cannot wound you without passing through your forte." (Leoni, 2005:15)

Finding the sword is the first part of blade engagement and it is important as it will establish the first advantage over the opponent. It is the position of the sword, relative to that of the opponent's that is vital. If the sword is not placed as Fabris describes above, the advantage will not be gained by its position. There is no one position that is stronger than all other positions, there is always a counter to every action, so you must place your sword where it is stronger than that of the opponent's, then their sword is "found".

"You should consider your opponent's sword "found" when your own is situated so as to be stronger than his and cannot be pushed away but, rather, can easily push away that of the opponent." (Leoni, 2005:15)

In the discussion of the finding the sword and its position, the actual position of the weapon is of great importance. It is also of importance as to which side is closest to the opponent's weapon. This difference of which side faces the opponent and their weapon can make a large difference in the result of the encounter between the two blades.

"Be advised that a sword is always stronger on the side to which it points. If you wish to situate your own sword on the stronger side of your opponent's, you have to place your body and your sword so that your sword is as strong as his. This is mostly a matter of how you bend your wrist," (Leoni, 2005:15)

Thus the simple bending of the wrist can determine whether or not the sword is in a strong position and thus the finding of the sword being effective or not. This is very simple. If your sword points at the opponent's left side then the hand should be turned to second so that the true edge faces the opponent's blade and a straight line is formed between the hand point and the target. If the hand was in third, the flat would be against the opponent's blade, and would be in a much weaker position. Having the sword more forward also strengthens its position.

"He who has more of his sword into the opponent's (no matter by how little) will have the advantage of the sword, as long as the opponent's sword is found on its weaker side." (Leoni, 2005:15)

The closer the opponent's foible is to your forte the stronger the position of your sword. Thus the movement of your sword to place the middle of your blade on the foible of the opponent's puts it into a stronger position than that of the opponent. This forward movement of the weapon in order to control the opponent is important as if the opponent achieves the same against you he will have the advantage.

"You can push as much of your sword into his as the initial distance between the swords, as you should do when he comes to find your sword, otherwise he may end up wounding you." (Leoni, 2005:16)

The correct movement at the correct time is of vital importance to gain or maintain the advantage over the opponent's sword. The simple position of the weapon in comparison to that of the opponent's gains the first advantage, but such an advantage can also be lost by the movement of the opponent. Hasty movement is not guaranteed to gain the advantage over the opponent.

"No matter how little space between the two points, if you make the first move to go and find your opponent's sword, he may form an angle with his sword thus fortifying his position and getting his point farther from your sword." (Leoni, 2005:16)

This angle made by the change in position of the opponent's sword changes the engagement and reduces the advantage of the position of the weapon. By making such an angle with the weapon the point is withdrawn and a stronger part of the weapon is moved into position. It is important that you examine your opponent before making any actions in order to gauge their possible reactions, and thus be prepared for them.

> "first assess the distance between your body and the opponent's and between your point and the opponent's body only then begin the movement to find the sword. But when doing so, you should always move your sword cautiously, so as to be able to do a quick mutation in case your opponent decides to use your initial movement as a tempo:" *(Leoni, 2005:16)*

As you move your sword forward to gain the opponent's sword, they may take this action as a tempo in which an attack may be made by them. If you are not aware of this particular possibility the attack will be made and you will not be able to defend against it. To counter this you must be prepared to change the movement into a defense to defend against an attack. The same caution must be made when moving forward to find the opponent's sword.

> "be careful that, as you proceed to find the opponent's sword, your point does not advance so much in the desire to strengthen your sword that the opponent can deceive you by passing your point on either side before you can straighten it against him." *(Leoni, 2005:16)*

The purpose of the action of finding the sword is so that an attack may be made against the opponent, and this should proceed as soon as the opponent's sword is found. The movement to find the sword must be made cautiously so that the opponent cannot change position to counter the action. The opposite to this is of course moving the weapon too slow and thus giving the opponent time to counter the action.

In the discussion of finding the sword, one question that raises debate is to whether or not there should be contact between the two weapons. For some, there must be contact so that the fencer can feel what the opponent is doing, for others, such as Fabris, contact is not required, and in fact, argued against.

> "It is important to remember that, as you find the opponent's sword, you should never touch his blade with yours. The closer he is to you, the safer and surer your advantage if you have your forte subtly situated opposite his debole. Most of the time, if the opponent's sword is not molested, he will not realize that you have found it."
> *(Leoni, 2005:16)*

Fabris states that you should not touch the blade of the opponent. It is merely the position next to the opponent's weapon that is required. This position is all that is required to maintain the advantage over the opponent's weapon. He also states that should they touch this will alert the opponent to the position, and thus he will be prepared for any action made.

Further to his previous arguments he states, "Besides, if you touch the opponent's sword, you somewhat disrupt your own form:" (Leoni, 2005:16). Fabris felt that contact with the opponent's blade will disrupt the actions of the fencer due to the contact made between the blades. This contact may disturb the location of the blade or point of the weapon and thus any action. Further to this, a blade without contact between fencer and the opponent is much freer to move.

"if you keep your sword suspended in the air, you are always more ready in every occasion, your attacks are more in tempo, and you are not forced to control the opponent's blade" (Leoni, 2005:16)

Keeping the blade free is something emphasises greatly, as can be seen by his opinion of finding the sword. By keeping the blade free rather than touching the opponent's weapon the fencer has more options available to him as contact between the blades must not be broken, and thus the advantage is maintained.

"as you are going to find the opponent's point, he moves toward your sword to meet or even bind it with his, you can yield and, going for his body, you can wound him when or even before he touches your sword" (Leoni, 2005:16)

The free blade is abler to move about and thus perform a wider variety of actions. Such a blade is also able to change the engagement between the blades by simple and subtle movement. "He who is subtler in his movements will always be able to keep his sword more free." (Leoni, 2005:17). It is through the subtle movements that the blade is able to be kept free and maintain the advantage of having the blade free.

Finding the blade is of great importance, it is of great use to the fencer and makes other actions much easier than if the blade was not found. "In general, you cannot beat your opponent's sword without moving your own out of line, especially when you do not find the opponent's blade." (Leoni, 2005:9). It is much easier to beat the opponent's sword and keep the blade more in line when the opponent's blade is found because it is a smaller movement to contact the opponent's blade. On the subject of the beat, Fabris also has a further statement to make, especially with regard to blade engagement.

"it can happen that while you are trying to beat the opponent's debole (for if you beat, you should do so to the debole), he pushes forward his forte, thus not only neutralizing your action, but also performing an attack that you won't be able to parry." (Leoni, 2005:9)

This action of pushing forward the forte, the fencer should be aware of especially if the blade is not found and the action is simply performed. Had the opponent's weapon been found, such an action would not have been so much of an issue as the fencer would have been prepared to counter it. The first action of the fencer, according to Fabris should be finding the opponent's blade, "find the opponent's sword, which is the first part of victory." (Leoni, 2005:17). For the seated combatant, finding the sword can present an advantage which is indispensable. Of course to keep the blade free from being found, there is a counter. This is the disengagement, another essential part of blade engagement.

DISENGAGEMENT

The disengagement, disengage or *cavazione* as Fabris calls it is a most useful tool to the fencer. It is also the first in a family of similar actions which are most useful to the fencer, especially when discussing blade engagement. Through these actions a fencer can place his blade in a line, can change a line, and even return to a line when an opponent changes it. It is the performance of these techniques that make them effective, thus important that they are done properly.

> "A successful cavazione has to follow a forward oval motion, so that, at the end of the cavazione, you will have also finished the thrust, otherwise you may not make it there in time." (Leoni, 2005:19)

The *cavazione* is a simple action which takes the blade from one line and places it in another. The point of the weapon usually passes below the blade of the opponent's blade. This action is designed to change the line, usually from a closed line to an open one. Of course this particular action can also be used to keep the blade free. The important thing is that the disengage "family" all link together.

> "If the opponent moves to find or beat your sword and you move your blade to the other side of his before he can accomplish his goal, you will have performed a "cavazione di tempo." A contracavazione is the cavazione you can perform in the tempo of your opponent's cavazione," (Leoni, 2005:19)

While the *cavazione di tempo* or time disengage, is an action which is different as it avoids all blade contact and indeed engagement and as such is different from the other techniques. The *contra-cavazione* or counter disengage, is the counter to the *cavazione* and follows on as a technique, one performs the *cavazione* the other the *contra-cavazione* to counter it. The *contra-cavazione* is designed to return the blade to the line in which it was before the opponent performed the *cavazione*. Of course, as with action in fencing, there is a counter to this particular action.

> "A ricavazione is when the one who first performs the cavazione does so once more during the opponent's contracavazione, thus nullifying the effects of the latter. A half-cavazione is when you do not actually make it to the other side, but stop under your opponent's sword. Committing of the sword is when you start a cavazione, then willingly return to the original side as you see your move either towards your body or your sword." (Leoni, 2005:19)

The *ricavazione* or double disengage, counters the *contra-cavazione*, in essence making another *cavazione* in response to the action. What should be noted here is that one technique counters the previous and is only really useful if the technique before it is performed. The *mezzo-cavazione* is designed to place the blade below the opponent's or above it depending on the original position. It is literally half the action of the disengage. It is designed to attack above or below the opponent's weapon. Committing the sword is an interesting action as it cancels the action of the disengage by returning to its original position. Interestingly enough, there are times when this technique is quite useful.

The *mezzo-cavazione* may be performed when the opponent moves forward and passes the point of your sword before you have completed the action. In this particular situation Fabris advises that you should use the position, thrust and move your body away from the opponent's weapon (Leoni, 2005:19). This is one example of the use of the half-disengage. The *mezzo-cavazione* is an interesting technique as if it is performed at the wrong time it can leave the fencer quite open. This is especially the case where the point is dropped under the opponent's weapon. This results in the *mezzo-cavazione* rarely being the first action being performed (Leoni, 2005:19).

The tactical applications of the disengage and those techniques which are associated with it are as numerous as the techniques themselves and even more so. These techniques also relate very closely to the idea and techniques involved in finding the sword previously discussed. "If the opponent comes to find your sword without moving his feet, you should employ the cavazione to find his sword." (Leoni, 2005:19). This particular motion is only one in a wide variety of options that can be performed while performing these techniques.

Another technique is that if the opponent is stationary you provoke them into making an attempt to find your sword and strike during a *cavazione* during their action. The blade should be returned to the original position and the hilt put against the debole while thrusting (Leoni, 2005:19). This particular technique is designed to commit the opponent to an action and then counter it. The *cavazione* is designed to counter their action while leaving the ability to return to the original line.

What should be noted is there are various techniques and tactics that can be employed in the use of the *cavazione* and its family of techniques. Using the *cavazione* against other actions is also possible and advised in many different situations, the fencer should, however be aware that the opponent may be attempting to get them to perform a technique in order to perform a counter. This is where control over the weapon becomes vital, and also reading the opponent properly.

> *"if you perform a cavazione as your opponent tries to beat your sword, his blade will not find any resistance and will therefore end up out of line, giving you a splendid tempo to wound him. This is also true in case the opponent were only to feint a beat to your sword (to provoke your cavazione) and then beat your sword on the other side. In this case, you should feign the cavazione and actually keep the sword on the same side, it would therefore be his attempt to beat your sword that lands him in trouble." (Leoni, 2005:9)*

The important thing in the situation above is being able to read the opponent and find out what their true intention is. It is covering this intention that leads to the idea of second intention, where the first action sets the opponent up for the second action. This particular idea is also the case when discussing feints, which will be examined in the next section.

FEINTS

Feints are one of the actions in fencing which have been argued for and against ever since people started writing about them. In the Renaissance period there were those who argued for them, those who argued against them, and those who gave the option, but never placed themselves in one camp or another. Fabris is one of those who decided that they are of use, but only if they are executed properly.

The first thing that needs to be done is to define exactly what a feint is to understand what is being discussed. Fabris described the feint as such, "A feint is when you show your opponent that you are attacking one target and you then attack another in the tempo of his attempted parry." (Leoni, 2005:20). The primary element of this is the deception implied, resulting in the defeat of a defensive action. The fact that it is a thrust aimed at one target which changes to another would seem to limit his definition, but he then goes on to describe several different types.

Fabris describes what the problem with certain types of feint is. He does not agree with the use of a stomp as a feint as the fencer may get struck during the tempo of the stomp (Leoni, 2005:20). This is now known as an *appel* in modern fencing. Another feint he disagrees with the use of is a thrust which is withdrawn and followed by another, which he disagrees with due to the tempo taken (Leoni, 2005:20). This is one that many beginning fencers will try. The problem is that it is three different actions and therefore several tempos to its completion. Another common feint is the short attack, where the thrust is made deliberately short in order to bring the opponent out. Fabris states that this is useful against timid or unexperienced opponents but not against experienced ones (Leoni, 2005:20).

What is most useful about Fabris with regard to feints is that he not only describes what can be the problems, but also describes some of the counters. One of the examples of this is the "counterfeint", which is a feint performed to deceive one (Leoni, 2005:20). This is somewhat of a novel approach to the feint, though it describes a valid action that is most interesting. Once Fabris has described these various actions, he then talks more about how to make the feints succeed.

> *"If you wish for your feints to succeed, you should push your sword forward in such a way that, if the opponent allows it to penetrate enough, you have certainty that you are able to resist his parry on your forte. In order for this to happen, you must maintain the sword's forward motion, thus not giving the opponent time to parry and wounding him."* (Leoni, 2005:21)

Fabris description on how to make the feint succeed describes why the feint involving a withdrawal is flawed. The important thing to note is the continual forward motion of the weapon in the action. This motion gives strength to the action, and places the blade in a better position. This forward motion also always presents the opponent with a threat and puts them on the defensive. Of course these defensive actions can also be countered, as opponent moves to parry, change line of attack (Leoni, 2005:2).

Fabris further information about feints is most useful and reminds the fencer that they should always be aware of the actions of the opponent, as well as their own. "As you move to perform the thrust, it is always vital to be ready for a counterattack." (Leoni, 2005:21). This is an aspect of the tempo being used by the feint and the attack, this giving the opponent a chance to respond. The aspect of tempo and the real time taken in the action is important, and thus it is important to reduce this as much as possible. "Another rule for good feints is that the initial target should be a near opening:" (Leoni, 2005:21). This means that the feint should also be near the opening which will be opened should the opponent fall for it. Further to this Fabris advises that in order to take full advantage of tempo, the feint should be done during the tempo of an action of the opponent (Leoni, 2005:21). Of course actions are not the only form of feint. There are also feints when the fencer is still.

> "An invitation is a type of feint where you willingly offer an opening to the opponent within the measures, giving him an opportunity to strike you there. The correct judgement of distance is paramount here." (Leoni, 2005:21)

The invitation is a type of feint which involves the stillness of the fencer. In this stillness an opening is deliberately left for the opponent to attack. The invitation can also be made while the fencer is moving. The important thing here is that the fencer needs to leave an opening which is perceived by the opponent and draws them to attack at that spot. If the invitation is too small it may not be noticed, if it is too big the fencer may not be able to cover it. These can be very useful against over-eager opponents.

> "Invitations are best performed when you see your opponent is impatient to execute an attack, supporting his desire to do so while not giving away your intended feint." (Leoni, 2005:21)

The feint is all about the intent of the opponent and discovering what they intend to do. This needs to be done while covering your own intent in order to be able to strike the opponent where they do not expect to be struck. Discovery of the opponent's intent allows the fencer to be able to discover what the opponent will attack and thus be prepared to cover this target. This is where the great mind games of fencing really occur.

> "it is better to know what to expect rather than wait for something unforeseen and be wounded without knowing how or why. But it is equally important to know how to oppose his design, in order to wound him and save yourself as he tries to carry it out." (Leoni, 2005:22)

TACTICAL CONSIDERATIONS: DIFFERENT OPPONENTS

In the words of Fabris, "it is necessary to mold your tactics to the peculiar characteristics of the person you fight." (Leoni, 2005:29). This means you need to change things depending on who you are fighting based on their stature and attitude. The differences between fighting standing and seated have already been mentioned and these particular elements present themselves again in this particular discussion.

To start with, it is stature that will be examined first. This can have a great effect on how you deal with a particular opponent. A taller person is likely to have a longer reach, therefore Fabris advises that it is best to stay on the offensive and keep your sword free. You should take the tempo as the opponent reaches measure then retreat and keep your distance and wait for the same opportunity (Leoni, 2005: 29). In the reverse of the situation, Fabris advises the shorter person to wait and find the sword, to attack on the pass and control distance (Leoni, 2005:29).

For the seated combatant, both of these have to be modified somewhat so that you can use your advantage. For the most part people will be taller due to the seated position, but you may have a reach advantage which makes you "taller" with respect to reach. Keeping your sword free in both cases is sound advice. You should only stay engaged so long as you have the advantage. The use of distance can be performed from the chair, but it is more about controlling it once the opponent has engaged. See what you can reach of your opponent and use that against them, encourage them to close within your distance and then strike.

The German schools talk a great deal about being hard and soft on the opponent's blade and also the opponent being hard or soft on your blade. Similarly, Fabris discusses dealing with a stronger or weaker opponent. If you are stronger than your opponent, you should find the opponent's sword and control it (Leoni, 2005: 30). This is using your strength against his weakness, of course should the situation be reversed then you need a different approach. Attempting to use strength against a stronger opponent is a waste of time; in fact his strength should be avoided. When you are the weaker, Fabris advises that the sword should be kept free, avoid parrying if possible, void instead. Do not close. Stop hit against attack and wait for the opponent (Leoni, 2005: 30). All of the strategies are designed to avoid his strength.

For the seated combatant, controlling the weaker is more difficult, as is avoiding the stronger. The standing combatant can advance and retreat depending on whether engagement or disengagement from the encounter is required. For the seated combatant this is more difficult, it comes down to more control of the actual fight at the *misura stretta*. Similar tactics can be applied, it is just that the time in which they can be applied, and their application is somewhat more limited.

There are those opponents who will charge in for the kill, and there are those who will sit at a distance and calculate. These are what we call "hot" and "cool" headed opponents respectively. In the case of the hot-tempered opponent provoke him into attacking and wound him as he does so, control the distance and time his mistakes (Leoni, 2005: 30). The hot-tempered opponent is reasonably easy to deal with; you force them to make mistakes. The cool-headed one is more difficult. The cool-headed opponent will not be provoked so easily. Against such an opponent attacks must be made cleanly and with security (Leoni, 2005: 31).

For the seated opponent the same applies in the same manner. The only thing that changes is the use of distance which is shortened quite extensively. The seated opponent needs to know the distance to attack the opponent exactly not to leave them open to a response. In all cases where tactics are being applied, regardless of being seated or standing, the opponent should never be underestimated. You should be cautious and prepare for things that the opponent may do (Leoni, 2005: 31). The cool-headed fencer may give the impression of being hot-headed to force a response which they may be prepared for. Examine what the opponent does and can do carefully.

ON GUARDS: A GENERAL DISCUSSION

The guards and the discussion of them is where Fabris starts to use pictorial representations of the actions which are being described. The previous information was theory upon which the actions which follow are based. It is important that the general discussion is made in order to describe how the guards are presented.

One of the mistakes that were made with regard to Fabris was that it was assumed that the two figures depicted in the guard plates were opponents assuming *contra-postura*, this is actually not the case. The pictures depict the body of the fencer in the same guard from both sides of the body (Leoni, 2005, 31) in order to present them better. This way the reader can see exactly what is happening.

Each one of the plates in Fabris manual[10] is presented with a description of what is happening in the plate. This is not only an explanation of what is happening in the plate, but also the intention of the plates as well (Leoni, 2005: 32). This once again, in order to better present the knowledge to the reader.

From this particular discussion, Fabris then begins to discuss more applicable detail to the application of what is presented. There is a wide variety of positions and techniques presented in the following pictures, the important thing being that all the actions derive from the stances presented (Leoni, 2005: 32). This establishes the basis for the future applications of the guards and the following techniques. Of course, as with most Italian masters, Fabris advises that the "defense and the offense must be performed in one tempo," (Leoni, 2005: 32). This idea of the single tempo is one that will become evident as this investigation proceeds.

The First Guard

In the case of most of the guards, Fabris depicts a first version of the guard, then another with the combatant in the correct position. It is important to look at these images closely to notice the difference between the two. Starting in a logical manner, it is the first guard that will be discussed first.

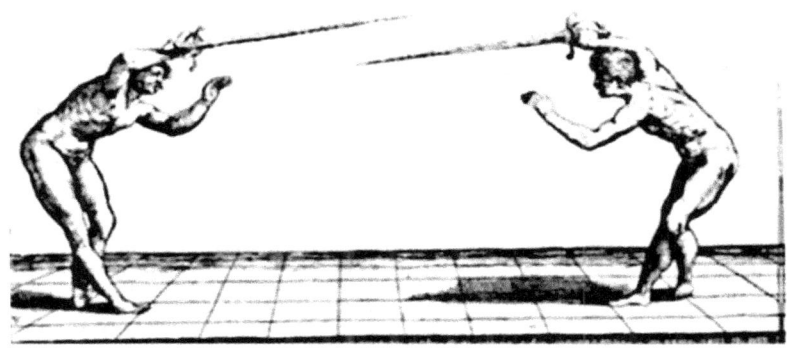

"This guard is not very safe: the sword is too withdrawn, and the body remains uncovered because of the high placement of the sword and the resulting distance between the forte and the body." (Leoni, 2005:34)

This is the position that the body assumes once the sword has cleared the sheath of the fencer and thus is a natural position. This means that the fencer is not in the best position. The sword is out of position due to being too high, this leaves it out of position for parrying, thus Fabris advises the use of the off-hand for this purpose (Leoni, 2005:34). As with most of the guards in this particular position, it is the high line which is covered the best, due to the position of the sword. Due to the position of the arm, this means it is also the outside line meaning that the head is well covered especially on the outside (Leoni, 2005:34).

---

10   All images were sourced from a pdf of the original Italian text.

The position of the first guard, when the sword is simply withdrawn from the sheath is not a purposed position, except for placing the weapon on guard. As far as Fabris is concerned, the purpose of this particular guard is to enable the fencer to break measure with the opponent (Leoni, 2005:34). Due to a seated position of the fencer in this particular investigation, this means that this particular guard is not as useful to the seated combatant as the properly formed guard.

The properly formed first guard has some differences in comparison to the initial version. This is mostly in the form of some simple re-positioning of the body and the weapon. The point of the weapon is extended and the arm kept straight (Leoni, 2005: 35). There are some further modifications made in order to improve the guard as well and each one of these serves a purpose.

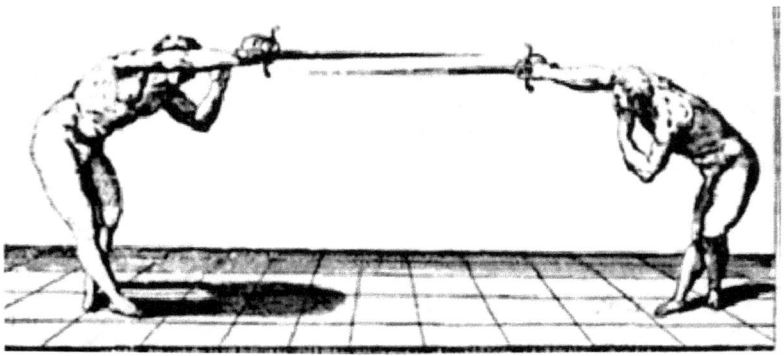

The body is bent further to protect the lower part of the body and the sword in its more extended position defends the head and chest due to the position of the forte (Leoni, 2005:35). This repositioning improves the guard and makes it much more useful to the seated combatant as the head and chest will be the most likely targets for the opponent. Fabris also states that this is an excellent guard for defending against cuts due to its positioning (Leoni, 2005:35). This, however, does not mean that the guard is totally free of issues.

The problem with the first guard is that due to the position of the arm, it is a fatiguing guard to hold (Leoni, 2005:35). For the standing fencer the best method to use the guard is to approach the opponent and extend the step to attack the high outside line. The extended step will also lower the body reducing it as a target (Leoni, 2005:35). Of course this is not an option for the seated combatant. In the seated position, the movement of the opponent must be waited for, the same line can be taken in the attack if the arm is extended, and the body lent forward. The process after the attack is much more useful to the seated combatant.

Fabris advises that on the withdrawal, the fencer should ward against the opponent's attack, finding it and pushing it to the outside and out of line (Leoni, 2005:35). This is actually very useful to the seated fencer as such an approach will clear the opponent's weapon easily, due to the seated position. It is the properly formed first guard which is the most useful to the seated fencer and you should make sure that you are in the correct position in order to use it correctly.

The Second Guard

The second guard derives from the first, as can be expected. It is the second position to which the blade proceeds through the guards. This is the second guard based on the hand placement after the first (Leoni, 2005:36). In a similar fashion it also describes a change in not only the body position and blade position, but also that of the hand.

The second guard is more comfortable being that the arm is less strained due to the arm being in a lower position (Leoni, 2005:36). This places less strain on the muscles, in comparison to that of the first guard. What should also be noted is that the feet are much further apart, thus in a wider step, this makes the guard more comfortable, but also makes the knee more exposed (Leoni, 2005:36). The other thing that should be noted about this particular version of the second guard is that the hand is more withdrawn than in the first guard, but not so much that it is an impediment to an action that may be required (Leoni, 2005:36). It is this more withdrawn position that draws the weight of the sword closer to the core muscles, thus making the position more comfortable for the fencer. As with the properly formed first guard, the properly formed second is also somewhat different.

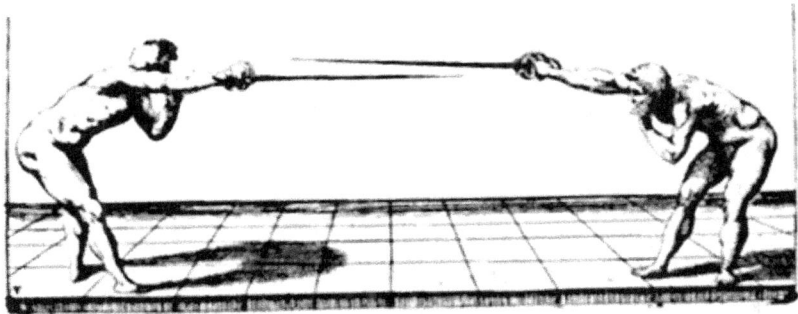

The second guard properly formed is safer but more tiring, for much the same reason as the first, simply the arm is more extended (Leoni, 2005:37). In the second guard, due to its position, the outside line is the weakest and Fabris advises that the sword should be straightened to close it (Leoni, 2005:37). This means that there is an area in which the fencer is vulnerable in this particular ward of course Fabris has an answer to this particular problem.

Fabris states that if the outside line is approached, the fencer should perform a *cavazione* without approaching unless he can strike the opponent in the same tempo (Leoni, 2005:37). The fencer simply changes the line to shore up his defences. For the fencer it is the second and fourth parries which are the most useful to defend the fencer. The guard has few openings and the opponent must move first to reach them (Leoni, 2005:37). This gives the fencer an advantage as it gives you a tempo to act. The defensive options from this particular ward also give the seated an advantage in the use of this ward.

Fabris presents a ward which would seem to be quite odd, due to the position of the weapons. This particular ward is strange to most as the weapons are not pointed at the opponent and seems to offer a large opening. This is actually the purpose of the ward. The ward is designed to lure the opponent to attack (Leoni, 2005:39).

The position places the feet in a wide position which is very stable, but are covered by the position of the body. The lower part of the body is also guarded by this particular position. The upper part of the body seems to be exposed and it is here that the attack is lured to. An attack to head or upper chest defended with left hand, counter by straightening sword into second (Leoni, 2005:39). This presents a very simple response to the action of the opponent. There is another response that can be made against the opponent, but this is more difficult in a seated position. The action is to perform a *girata* in fourth and wound against the opponent (Leoni, 2005:39). There is another response which is much more useful to the seated opponent and that is to parry and counter in second (Leoni, 2005:39), which is a simple but effective response and more useful to the seated combatant.

As with all positions of this particular kind, it is important not to stay in the position for too long. This should be done with the hands and not the feet as you may be struck during the movement. Should you move your feet you should withdraw the feet rather than advancing in order that you are not struck during the change (Leoni, 2005:39). This is all feasible due to the position of the hands in preparation for the response presented by the invitation.

The Third Guard

Each one of the guards as Fabris calls them has a different form. Just because the individual is not placed in exactly the same position does not mean that it is not the same guard. For the most part it is actually the position of the hand, and arm in some instances, which determines what the guard is. With this in mind it should be of little surprise that Fabris describes three different guards of third.

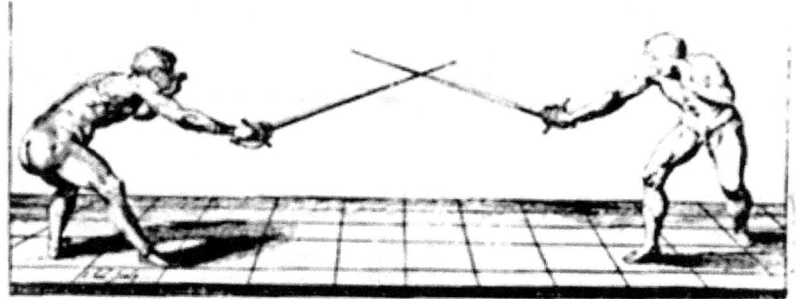

The first version of the third guard that Fabris presents is, as with the previous two guards, one which he determines as not properly formed. The first thing that should be noted is that as with the second guard, and its variants, it is derived from the first guard (Leoni, 2005:42). This means it is once again, the path of the sword travelling through the guards as it moves from one to another.

The third guard, not properly formed, is described as an easy position to adopt (Leoni, 2005:42) and resembles in many ways third guards of many of the Italian masters. The hand is kept low while the tip of the weapon is pointed high, according to Fabris, while this is more comfortable it does leave openings (Leoni, 2005:42). The largest opening is the one above the hilt and it is hard to defend because the movement to do so is slow (Leoni, 2005:42).

This is not the only problem that Fabris highlights with this particular guard. The angle of the sword itself creates this particular opening and it also causes some other problems. One of the first of these is that to parry, the sword must come out of line. The other is that due to the high position of the point it is difficult to perform a *cavazione* (Leoni, 2005:42).

With all of the problems presented, it could be difficult to see how Fabris could actually advocate the use of this particular guard. However, knowledge in fencing is power and with the knowledge of the failures of this particular guard it is possible to counter them. The guard is considered safe because voids and *mezzo-cavazione*, in the correct tempo can be used from this guard, also due to the knowledge of the opening which is created it can be countered (Leoni, 2005:42).

The guard which is presented is quite useful to the seated combatant as the high point position is an advantage as it will always threaten the opponent. Of course, the opening which Fabris describes is present, but due to the much lowered position of the seated fencer this is actually more difficult to gain access to. The seated position also lowers the target further behind the weapon.

The properly formed version of the third guard obviously has quite a few changes to it to remove the issues with the previous guard. The place where this starts is in the formation of the guard itself. When the third guard is taken properly as Fabris describes it, the hilt is higher and the hand is in a true position of third, also the body is more crouched (Leoni, 2005:43). These simple changes creates a much more solid and defendable guard.

The crouched position of the body lowers and removes the targets from the opponent. This properly formed guard leaves very little open, and any attack may be defended against by a small motion of the arm or even the hand (Leoni, 2005:43). Fabris presents many advantages of the third guard and presents it as a primary guard to be used more than the previous two guards. Fabris states that this guard is most useful and is easy to parry from (Leoni, 2005:43). It is also much more comfortable for the fencer than most of those which have been presented.

The properly formed third guard of Fabris is great for the seated fencer as all of the advantages presented by this particular guard are multiplied by the seated position. The crouched position is designed to remove and lower the body. The seated position does that and much more. The body can be crouched comfortably and then even further should the situation require. Just as with the standing fencer the seated fencer closes many lines but even more so due to the lowered position.

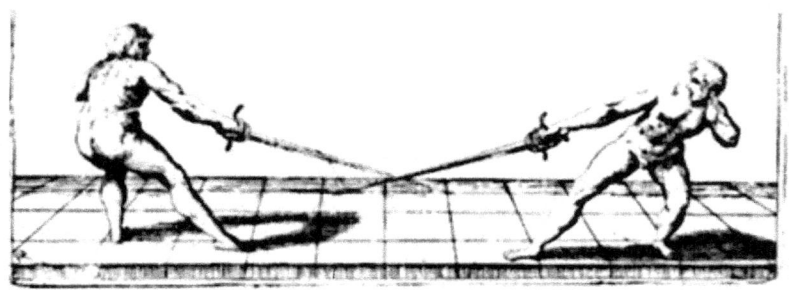

The third version of this particular guard which is presented is a modification of the extended version of the guard. If this particular guard is compared to the original version of the third guard presented many similarities will be noted. The difference between the two guards is that the sword is lowered; this is done in order to prevent it from being found (Leoni, 2005:44).

The first model of the third guard has the body somewhat forward, this version has the body bent back to withdraw it from the opponent's point and the sword lowered to make it harder to find (Leoni, 2005:44). This position places the weight of the body mostly on the back foot, and it means that the easiest movement for the fencer from this position is forward.

As the opponent comes forward, the sword is lifted and then moved forward by the fencer (Leoni, 2005:44). This utilises the pressure placed on the back foot due to the initial guard position. It should not be assumed that this is the only approach as the position lends itself to other options such as voids. The guard has hidden reach which can be increased by leaning the body (Leoni, 2005:44). The leaning is supported by the position of the feet. All of the advantages present make this particular guard effective against many others.

The lowered sword is designed to lure the opponent into range and this suits the seated fencer perfectly. The problem with being seated is mobility; this guard actually gives the seated fencer back some of that mobility by leaning back. The body can then be moved forward as the opponent approaches to attack, thus gaining distance on the opponent. This particular guard is extremely useful to the seated fencer also because the seated position will lower the position of the sword and thus make it almost impossible to find safely.

The Fourth Guard

The fourth guard makes up the fourth of the "legitimate" guards as Fabris would call them. It is the fourth position of the hand that this guard corresponds to and completes the transition from first through second and third to fourth. Interestingly, while there are some modifications of the standard guard, Fabris does not go to mention a not properly formed guard as he does for the previous three guards. He immediately goes into the proper fourth guard.

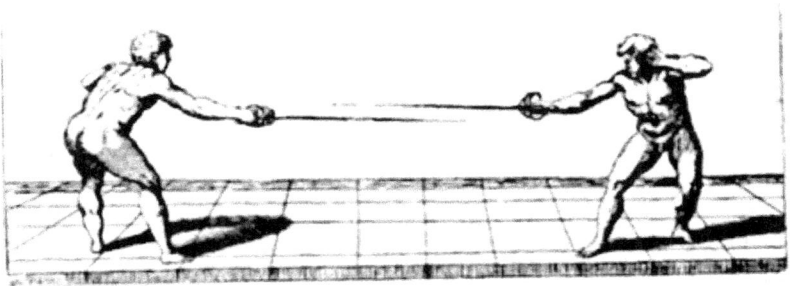

Of the guards presented by Fabris the standard fourth is the most upright of the four guards. This is no doubt due to the position of the weapon. The arm forms an angle which strongly covers the inside line (Leoni, 2005:46). This is both due to the position of the hand and also that of the arm, resulting in the strong position of the weapon, as with many has flaws due to its position. The fencer is more open to the outside and also has a slower *cavazione* (Leoni, 2005:46) due to the position of the weapon.

This also leads to a certain approach that needs to be taken toward the opponent attacking. Fabris advises the fencer to aim at the opponent's right, perform a pass and pass under his sword; the arm is at an angle to protect the body, and straightening angle of the sword to the inside covers the fencer (Leoni, 2005 46). Of course this is not particularly useful to the seated fencer. What can be drawn from this is to remain with the sword aiming at the opponent's right and thus remaining covered along that line. This will also force the opponent's weapon down the inside line and past the body.

The other particularly useful thing about the fourth guard is in the movement of the weapon, especially across the body. This is particularly effective in gaining control of the opponent's weapon and also deflecting it. Fabris states that the fencer's hand turning from fourth to second is stronger, more so if arm straightened along angle of his sword (Leoni, 2005:46). This means that an attack which travels anywhere along the line between these guards will be easily controlled. It is imperative that the fencer ensure that the hand is pointed at the target, as a counter-offensive action this particular turning and moving forward, the fencer should also remember to void the opponent's attack while performing this action (Leoni, 2005:46). For the seated combatant, the control and defensive capability of this particular action is very useful as it deprives the opponent of some of the strength of the attack. While the seated combatant is well covered, some defensive movement of the body should strongly be considered.

Interestingly enough, unlike many of the other Italian theorists, it is not the third guard which is considered to be the safest guard of them all and the one to be preferred. The list of advantages presented, and his own admonition, "Of the four extended guards, this is the safest: there is also no other guard that will allow you to keep your sword quite as ready and free." (Leoni, 2005:47).

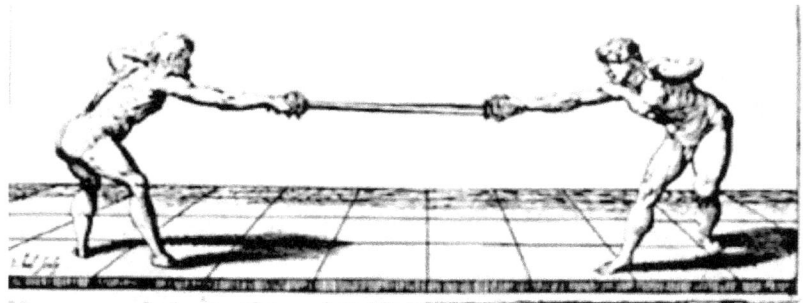

The advantages this guard presents according to Fabris are all founded on sound theoretical advantages. First he presents the argument along the lines of distance claiming that the guard keeps the opponent at distance and that keeping the blade free is easier for being able to see the opponent approach and thus easily being able to *cavazione* (Leoni, 2005:47). Of course this is a simple advantage, further to this simple and elementary advantage, he then presents how the guard is strong in many lines due to its position.

The guard has strength to the outside due to it is closed due to the sword position, and cannot be attacked on the inside line due to the hand position (Leoni, 2005:47). This presents the opponent with a big problem as there are no open lines. The opponent must then do something to provoke the fencer to open a line to make them vulnerable. To do this the opponent must either move the fencer's blade out of line or make them do it (Leoni, 2005:47). This is not a particularly good prospect considering the options of *cavazione* and other such counters to such control.

The extended fourth guard is extremely useful to the seated combatant as it enables the fencer to keep the opponent at distance. For the seated combatant keeping the opponent on the edge of the *misura stretta* is the optimum distance as at the *larga* the seated combatant cannot attack and too close the seated combatant cannot withdraw. This guard presents great advantages by closing the lines and presenting the assets which have been described.

The second modification of the fourth guard relies on the use of movement of the feet to the left or right. This means that it is difficult for the seated combatant to use. This guard is heavily reliant on the use of footwork to be effective as such this particular guard will be left as it is not of much use to the seated combatant. However some of the principles found in this guard are useful.

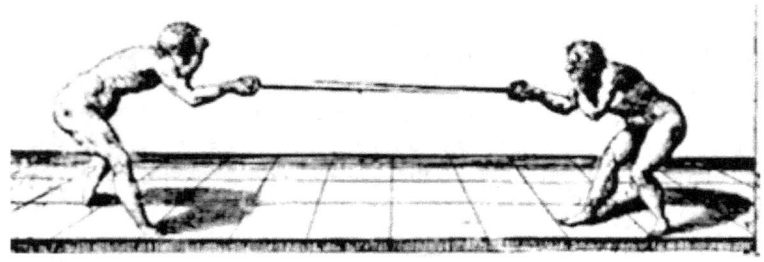

The outside is exposed in this particular guard and thus will draw attacks. This needs to be closed strongly with the arm extended or lifted to wound above the sword (Leoni, 2005:48). This applies to any guard or position which leaves an line open to attack, it needs to be closed strongly and the energy of such a defence directed to a counter-attack. This particular idea is clearly seen in Fabris' response to an opponent who comes to close. The hand is moved from fourth to second moving to the inside of the opponent's weapon and wounding with forward movement (Leoni, 2005:48).

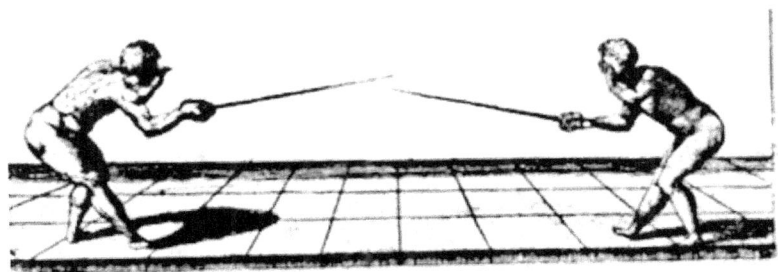

The third modification of the fourth guard resembles the previous guard but is different to the previous one the sword is angled to the inside rather than the outside. This means that the guard is stronger on the inside rather than the outside as in the previous guard (Leoni, 2005:49). Against an opponent using a guard of second the opponent's sword must be found. The opponent actually has the advantage by using second against this guard as the sword will be positioned to easily strike against the fencer (Leoni, 2005:49). The fencer then must use the advantage of the line of the sword to defeat the opponent and void with the body, or wait for the opponent to gain measure and then strike him (Leoni, 2005:49). Fabris also says that for the last one to be used a retreat should be used to step back into safety. In the case of the seated opponent, the attack should be launched as soon as the opponent reaches distance where the body is lent forward, so the retreat may be performed with the body.

This completes the discussion of the individual guards and their various modifications. Fabris' manual moves from here on to what he calls wounds, which are demonstrations of the actions previously described. This gives a practical demonstration of how each one of the movements is performed and against what sort of action by the opponent.

WOUNDS

Fabris' wounds are demonstrations of the theory which has been presented in the previous sections. This demonstrates how, in a more practical sense that the actions which have been described should be used against an active opponent. Not all of the wounds which are presented by Fabris will be used as some are heavily reliant on the use of footwork to be effective. Other ones will be modified to suit the seated combatant.

The descriptions of the actions of the combatants will also demonstrate how the theory which was presented in previous discussions applies in a practical sense. This bridges the gap between the theoretical and the practical in an effective manner. The wounds should be viewed as a demonstration of the theory presented by Fabris and should be seen from an overall perspective, taking into account the actions of demonstrations previous and following.

The First Wound

The first wound presented by Fabris is one in which a firm footed attack of fourth is made against an opponent in the guard of third (Leoni, 2005:54). With regard to the descriptions of the guards in Fabris manual, they are based more on the hand position than the body position. Any sort of idea of which specific guard is being used can only be gained by examining the images supplied. This particular wound uses a feint to open the opponent and then a following attack through the opening. Convincing the opponent to move in response to an action and then capitalising on the tempo of their movement.

Fabris uses his first wound, or demonstration to show how important it is to control the situation and how the theory previous applies to the situation. The important things that this demonstration shows is that the fencer who is stationary and with the sword free has the advantage. This is because once a fencer makes a movement it is difficult to change it, in this particular case the opponent cannot advance and retreat at the same time (Leoni, 2005:54).

The concept of movement verses being stationary also brings to light the importance of tempo. Movement out of tempo is dangerous especially to advance when the opponent has their sword free and is in the *misura larga* (Leoni, 2005:54). Of course, from a seated position this particular aspect is less of a problem as the seated combatant can only move their body to advance or retreat. Of course this means that all the actions happen in the *misura stretta* which increases the importance of correct movements as the slightest movement in *misura stretta* is dangerous, which is something that Fabris also states (Leoni, 2005:55).

Further to this Fabris stresses the importance of paying attention to the actions of the opponent. He states that if the opponent is stationary and has their sword free that the fencer should not feint, this gives the opponent a chance to recover and counter, while the fencer has no recovery from the action (Leoni, 2005:55). Most importantly not only does Fabris state what the fencer should not do but advises how to solve the particular issue. He states that for the feint to work the fencer should wait for the movement of the opponent or to find their sword. Once this is achieved this advantage should never be abandoned. The fencer should advance in the process thus if the opponent does not parry they are struck if they do parry then the line can be changed and the attack made (Leoni, 2005:55).

Fabris' advice with regard to the feint highlights the importance of committing to the attack and ensuring that the feint is perceived as a real attack and can also be used as a real attack should the opponent not respond to it. The feint is concerned with gaining the advantage over the opponent through the use of tempo, making the opponent use tempo in response to an action and thus create an opening for the fencer to attack in the second tempo used in response to the actual attack (Leoni, 2005:55).

Of course for the seated opponent that involves drawing the opponent in to the *misura stretta* and being a little conservative with regard to the use of tempo. This is due to the close confines of the *misura stretta* and the fact that a single tempo is all that is required at this distance. At least the seated opponent does not have to worry about pursuing the opponent if they break distance in response to the attack, which Fabris advises against strongly (Leoni, 2005:55). The fencer should make the attack, recover and then ensure that the opponent's sword is found or the opponent is not in a position to make a further attack.

The Second Wound

Each one of Fabris' demonstrations is designed to teach the reader something specific about what he has previously elucidated in his theory. A perfect example of this is the second wound. This particular demonstration is designed to demonstrate how a *cavazione* is slower than the straight-line thrust (Leoni, 2005:56). This is achieved through the demonstration of a third against third guard encounter between the fencer and his opponent (Leoni, 2005: 56).

The explanation of this is actually in the second method in which the encounter could occur, but serves the purpose of the lesson. In this particular action both fencers start inside, the fencer finds the opponent's sword. In response the opponent performs *cavazione* and moves his right foot forward to strike. In response the fencer uses the tempo of the *cavazione* and foot movement to thrust. This action succeeds in shutting the opponent's weapon out of line and achieving the wound (Leoni, 2005:56).

Of interest is that the first described scenario sees the fencer use a feint followed by a *cavazione* to defeat the opponent's defence (Leoni, 2005:56). This demonstrates that both the feint and *cavazione* are useful actions, but must be performed with respect to the tempos they use and the actions of the opponent.

The wound that has been demonstrated mentions very little in the way of footwork movement for the fencer and therefore is most useful to the seated combatant. For the seated combatant, because the encounter will take place at the *misura stretta* where tempo is extremely important, the lessons learnt in this particular wound are most useful. For the seated fencer the simple action which achieves the desired result is the best choice due to the limited tempos available for the fencers.

The Third Wound

The third wound is one which is set at the *misura larga* and does involve some footwork. This would almost mean that it would not be useful to the seated combatant, but the lessons learnt at this particular distance can be applied at the closer *misura stretta* of the seated combatant. The lesson about distance also applies in this particular situation.

The encounter is a wound of fourth against a third. The encounter starts at the *misura larga*, the fencer motions to find the opponent's sword. The opponent seeing the motion lowers his point to strike against the fencer. The fencer sees the motion and only having moved his point abandons the stringere and uses a straight-line thrust in fourth pushing his hilt against the sword of the opponent (Leoni, 2005:57). The final action of the fencer defends and counters in a single action.

The problem in this particular encounter is that the opponent misjudged the original motion of the fencer who did not move forward in his action. Thus the fencer was able to wait for the motion of the opponent and thus move to strike (Leoni, 2005:57). This can be interpreted as a form of feint, invitation or lure, designed to encourage the opponent to use tempos for an attack which is not actually available. Of course the simple defence is to be aware of the initial action and be aware of the actual measure and tempos used. Thus be able to counter the action simply by moving the weapon and not the body and waiting for the opponent's action.

For the seated opponent, the same lure can be made. Instead of using footwork, the body can be kept upright rather than lent forward, as the opponent engages the body can then be lent forward in the same sort of style as the forward moving attack that is described. Thus the same lesson that applies while standing also applies while seated. Also the same defence against a similar action applies.

The Fourth Wound

The fourth wound operates in much the same manner as the third wound, using the awareness of one of the combatants and the ignorance of the other to achieve the fencer's end. This particular action involves the use of footwork by the combatants, but a similar result can be achieved by the seated opponent through the use of body motion and knowledge of distance. The action takes place with a wound of third against another guard of third (Leoni, 2005:58).

PERIOD TEXTS

Both of the combatants start on the outside, the fencer moves his sword, but not body forward in order to gain the opponent's blade. The opponent moves their foot forward in order to make an action in tempo making a *cavazione*, not realising the distance. The fencer abandons his stringere, drops his point to counter the *cavazione*, lowers their body, pushes forward and wounds the opponent (Leoni, 2005:58).

What should be noted with regard to this action is that it does start in *misura larga*, and there is footwork involved. The seated combatant should be especially aware of their distance in this action waiting for the first action until the opponent is at the very edge of distance. The action then draws the opponent within range at which point the attack can be made against the opponent, thus the same use of distance is achieved without the explicit use of foot movement.

The rule which is described here is that when the opponent has their sword free and does not move their feet, do not close with the opponent. Instead attempt to gain the advantage without closing, rather retreating, the foot being slower than the sword (Leoni, 2005:58). Essentially, Fabris is describing the advantage that the still opponent has over the moving one. The moving fencer has already committed to an action and must complete it or change it, both of these take time. The still fencer has the option of motion and can choose what he wants to do.

Conversely, Fabris highlights another rule which is important, even if it is not immediately relevant to the seated combatant. If stringere is gained and he tries to free it, even if his feet remain motionless you can move forward safely and find his sword on the other side and attack in the next tempo (Leoni, 2005:58). The important thing for the seated fencer is that once the opponent moves within range if stringere is gained then there is an advantage to the fencer, and an attack can be launched at the opponent safely with movement of the body.

All of this highlights a very simple rule of Fabris which is ignored at the fencer's peril, "find your opponent's sword first. If you leave it free, you incur the danger that the picture represents." (Leoni, 2005:58). While Fabris is describing the illustration in his manual, the danger is still the same, the threat of the opponent succeeding due to having free sword, and thus being able to thwart the actions of the fencer, and even wound him. This particular rule applies regardless of whether you are fighting seated or standing, or which theorist or master you subscribe to.

The Fifth Wound

The fifth would is a demonstration of the advantage that a guard of first can have over a guard of third (Leoni, 2005:59). The advantage demonstrated is that a sword in first can easily resist a guard of third due to the mechanical advantage of the position of first. This mechanical advantage can be used in different situations.

Fabris sets the two combatants against one another both in a third guard to the outside, the blades lock together and there is pushing, one of the combatants turns his hand to first moves forward and wounds the opponent (Leoni, 2005:59). This particular action works due to the position of the blade and the strength inherent in its position. The same action in advantage works if the opponent is in second (Leoni, 2005:59).

Fabris goes into a little detail about why this works, and puts it mainly down to the yielding of the sword which works as a result of the resistance applied. He advises that rather than resisting the opponent's blade the fencer should yield or remove the blade altogether and in the action as the opponent's blade falls there is a tempo in which to wound the opponent (Leoni, 2005:59). This is much the same as the German idea of strength against weakness and weakness against strength and how one should be applied to the other and vice versa. In this action the opponent's strength is used to put the fencer in an advantageous position by allowing the opponent to push forward and thus place his foible on the fencer's forte, thus losing any advantage.

The Sixth Wound

The sixth wound is a classic demonstration of how the thrust is faster than the cut. This is a clear demonstration of fencing time. This particular wound takes place finally with a guard of fourth used against a raised sword (Leoni, 2005:60). Of course it is extremely important to look at how the combatants end up in this particular position.

Both of the fencers start with blades to the outside, one combatant raises his sword to cut a *mandritto*, the other uses a stop hit in fourth before the cut is completed (Leoni, 2005:60). Fabris describes performing this action with moving the right foot forward. This is not possible for the seated combatant and thus he must make do with moving his body forward with the thrust.

There is the question about how the fencer who thrusts is not cut by the opponent. It is the hand position of the fencer which protects him against the cut of the opponent (Leoni, 2005:60). The hand in

fourth and high prevents the opponent's cut from travelling through. This is added with the slower speed of the cut to complete the action.

In the action described by Fabris, the opponent uses an elbow cut against the fencer. With regard to this, Fabris makes an important statement about the cuts, especially with regard to timing. The elbow cut is slower than the thrust, but a wrist cut would be simultaneous with the thrust (Leoni, 2005:60). This particular element makes it even more important for the fencer to have his hand and arm positioned properly in order to defend against the cut.

The Seventh Wound

The seventh wound, in a similar way to the sixth wound demonstrates how the cut is slower than the thrust, but also the importance of the position of the sword in defending when making an attack against the opponent. This is demonstrated by an action which results in the combatants ending up with a second against a third which is out of line (Leoni, 2005:61).

Both of the combatants start in third to the inside. The fencer attempts to find the opponent's sword, in this tempo the opponent throws a riverso fendente to the opening at the head and shoulder presented by the finding. The fencer sees this and changes his position from third to second and thrusts against the opponent. The fencer is covered due to the position of his weapon (Leoni, 2005:61).

The cut is slower than the thrust. This is because the sword must be moved out of line before the cut is delivered. This gives the fencer time to counter with the thrust (Leoni, 2005:61). As with the demonstration of time made in the sixth wound, the demonstration of the faster thrust as compared to the slower thrust is clear. It is also important to note that even in the delivery of the thrust, the hand should be placed in such a position as to protect the fencer.

The Ninth Wound

The ninth wound demonstrates the advantage of avoiding the cut rather than parrying it, and having the blade placement in the attack being the defence against the cut. The position resulting from this action is very similar to the previous wound in that it results in one in a guard attacking, in this case fourth, and a fallen third as a result of the completion of the cut (Leoni, 2005:63). This goes to demonstrate that regardless of the line of the cut the fencer is able to defend himself while offending the opponent.

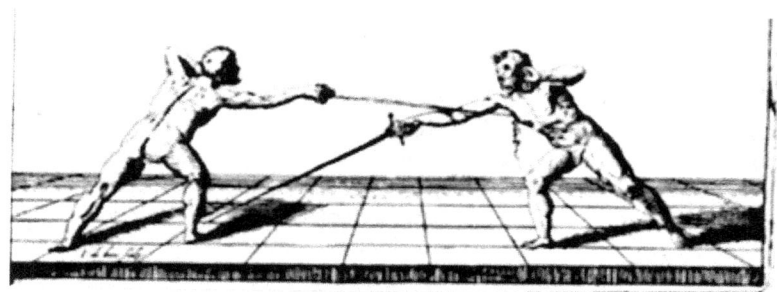

Both of the fencers start in third to the inside, the fencer attempts to find the opponents blade, in *misura larga*. In response the opponent throws a riverso squalembrato at the fencer. The fencer in reply avoids the cut, by maintaining his position, being that the cut will fall short and thrusts in fourth, covering himself by the position of his guard (Leoni, 2005:63). Once again it is an instruction from Fabris to avoid the cut rather than parrying it, thus leaving the fencer with time and position to respond against the opponent. This could give the impression that Fabris discards the cut altogether, but this is not the case.

Fabris actually gives advice about the delivery of the cut and how to make it more effective. Fabris advises that in performing a cut the arm needs to be kept straighter and more in line, thus the cut should be made from the wrist to keep the line more covered in the cut and make it more efficient (Leoni, 2005:63). This wound also demonstrates the importance of being within range, thus the importance of distance, so that the cut will actually strike the opponent.

For the seated combatant the process is much the same as for the standing situation. The opponent's blade is found with an extension, the opponent's cut is avoided by leaning backward, if required. The thrust in fourth is delivered with a forward movement of the torso in order to extend and strike the opponent. The seated combatant needs to be well-aware of his distance in order to achieve his desired result. This applies not only to this situation but all of them.

The Tenth Wound

While some of the previous wounds have demonstrated how a cut is slower than a thrust and as such less effective, Fabris does give at least this demonstration of how the cut can be effective against an opponent. The resulting situation of this particular wound is a mandritta delivered to the head in the third guard (Leoni, 2005:64).

The actions to result in the above proceeds as follows, the opponent moves to find the sword of the fencer, who does not move. The opponent then presses against the fencer's sword to the outside. The fencer yields to the pressure and delivers a cut from the wrist against the opponent, keeping his hilt near the opponent's blade (Leoni, 2005:64). In this particular action, the fencer uses the force applied to his sword to deliver the cut, thus using the opponent's force against him. The position of the hilt prevents the opponent from striking. This is not the only way this action could take place.

Both fencers start third to the inside. The fencer attempts to find the opponent's weapon who performs a disengage while moving his foot forward to wound on the outside. The fencer allows his point to fall, turning his wrist to place his hilt over the opponent's blade, striking with a mandritta fendente (Leoni, 2005:64). Once again, it is the position of the fencer's hilt which keeps him safe from the opponent's action. The action of the cut is once again using momentum which is already in the blade and using it for a purpose.

The seated fencer can proceed in much the same way as described in both actions without any problems. The important thing for the seated combatant is to observe the correct distance in the action and to place the hilt correctly to defend against the offensive action of the opponent while still delivering the cut as described. While the seated combatant can have a stronger position due to the angle, it is important to yield the sword as described in the first description.

The Eleventh Wound

The eleventh wound moves into some more complex ideas presented by Fabris. It deals with some more complex actions such as the invitation. This wound also is one of the first to deal with a complex void called the *girata*. It is a voiding action which is one that needs to be discussed, especially with regard to the seated combatant. The wound results in a guard of fourth defeating one of second (Leoni, 2005:65).

Both fencers start in a guard of third to the outside. The fencer presents an invitation by the angle of his sword. The opponent sees the movement and changes from third to second, closes the line and pushes forward aiming to wound on the outside. The fencer performs a *girata* with the left foot with a *cavazione* with the hand in fourth in response, wounding the opponent (Leoni, 2005:65). The initial action of the fencer is designed to lure the opponent into an attack with feigned weakness. The following actions are performed as a response to the attack delivered against the presented weakness.

Of course, as with several of the demonstrations, this is not the only way that the combatants could end up in the resulting position. Another way the fencers could end up in the same resulting position is as follows. Both fencers start in third to the inside. The fencer attempts to find the opponent's weapon to which he responds with a *cavazione*, turning his hand to second in order to shield against the fencer and wound him. In response to this action, the fencer performs a *contra-cavazione* and *girata* wounding the opponent (Leoni, 2005:65). This particular action has several elements, the blade engagement, using a guard to wound, and the final avoidance and attack of the fencer. It is important that each element is taken into account. What can be noted is that Fabris actions become more complex the further into the manual the reader progresses.

The *girata*, for the seated combatant, is an interesting prospect as it gains some of its effectiveness from the movement of the feet. Obviously for the seated combatant the movement of the feet is not really an option. Of course the action of the *girata* actually has two elements which need to be taken into account. The other part of the action is the movement of the body. This is a part of the action which the seated combatant can quite easily perform and quite effectively.

With the lack of foot movement in the seated combatant, the body movement has to be especially effective in order for the defensive action to work. This means that the seated combatant needs to start with a balanced position and the ability to move the top part of their body in order to be able to avoid the opponent's attack. This action means twisting the body about the waist and hips to withdraw the body from the attack, while presenting the point of the weapon. The shoulders and upper part of the body should also be in motion during the action to be effective against an opponent. Some time should be spent practicing this particular action before attempting it at any sort of speed and against an active opponent.

The Twelfth Wound

The twelfth wound is a demonstration of the effectiveness of the void used against the actions of an opponent. This is performed in combination with the strong position of the sword. The position resulting from this encounter is the fencer in fourth to the outside of the opponent's sword which is in an angled third (Leoni, 2005:66).

Both combatants start in inside third, the opponent in an angled third. The fencer attempts to find the opponent's sword in response the opponent attempts to disengage to the outside. In the same tempo as the disengage, the fencer moves his hand to fourth with his hand to the inside at the same time pushing the right foot forward turning the body away (Leoni, 2005:66). In this method the fencer uses the body movement along with the position of the sword to protect himself in his action.

For the most part, the seated combatant can use this technique and the only part where it becomes difficult is in the movement of the right foot. All the same hand movements can be used. The essential part of this technique is the movement of the body away in combination with the angle of the sword used in opposing the opponent's weapon, the force of which defeats the opponent himself (Leoni, 2005:66).

There is another way that the combatants can end up in the same position, the opponent finds the fencer's sword in third to the outside while the fencer is in second. The fencer yields from second to fourth while performing a *girata*, the thrust is made at the same time that the opponent tries to find the fencer's sword (Leoni, 2005:66). Once again it is a *girata* used to displace the body while using the position of the weapon in order to achieve the goal of defence and striking the opponent. For the seated combatant, there should be no issues as the essentials of the *girata* have been demonstrated as possible in the eleventh wound above.

The Thirteenth Wound

The thirteenth wound is a counter against the use of the *girata* as used by the opponent. This actually poses an interesting situation for the seated fencer as this particular technique relies on the opponent doing the *girata*, something which is not likely to happen due to the position of the seated fencer. This being said there are principles which are applicable. The wound results in a wound to the outside and under the opponent's sword performed in third or fourth against a fourth (Leoni, 2005:67).

The action could proceed in this way the opponent finds the fencer's sword inside, in response to the fencer's *cavazione*. The opponent attacks in fourth underneath, the fencer after the *cavazione*, pulls away to put the sword back in line under the opponent's sword before it arrives on target, lowers both the hand and body finding the opponent's debole with his forte, and wounding in the time of his *girata* (Leoni, 2005:67). This technique is centred on the repositioning of the fencer's sword to have a favourable engagement and lowering the body in order to gain this countering the *girata* of the opponent.

There is another way this action can happen. The fencer finds the opponent sword to the outside while in second. The opponent changes his hand from fourth to second and performs a *girata* to attack the fencer under his sword. At the same time, with his body over his left foot, places his sword back in line to strike under the opponent's sword (Leoni, 2005:67).

This technique is based on the advantage of resetting the sword in-line in response to the opponent's *girata* along with the lowered position of the body and the advantage the combination of these two achieve. For the standing opponent, there is a likely chance that the opponent will void or *girata* to change the engagement. This is less likely for the seated combatant due to the position of the seated combatant to start with. In this particular aspect the seated combatant already has an advantage and lowering only increases this advantage.

The Fifteenth Wound

The fifteenth wound is a wound in a guard of first against one of second (Leoni, 2005:69). It is another demonstration of the advantage of lowering the body to avoid an opponent's attack. However, this particular sequence involves the use of blade position to assist in defence. Both fencers start in inside third guard. The fencer attempts to find the opponent's sword. The opponent uses the tempo to perform a *cavazione* and turn his hand in second to strike over the fencer's hilt. The fencer, seeing the *cavazione* and incoming blow turns his hand to first lowering his body. In this way he uses the sword cover himself and shut the opponent's sword out while the lowering of the body secures him further (Leoni, 2005:69). The fencer uses the lowering of the body and raising of his sword to keep the opponent away. In this way he manages to sure his defence through the use of two defences.

There is a simpler way this particular sequence could have happened as will follow. Starting in the same guards as before, the fencer attempts to find the opponent's sword. In response the opponent attacks with a riverso to the arm. The fencer turns his hand to cover himself with his forte, while wounding the opponent (Leoni, 2005:69). This is a much shorter description, but gives the same result, and uses a similar defence as previous.

For the seated combatant, the same applies as before, but in this case the defence is surer as the blade is used to close the opponent's line. This combination of defences against the opponent's offensive actions means that the fencer is safer in his defence. In the case of the seated combatant the position of the weapon covers the line.

The Sixteenth Wound

The sixteenth wound is a wound of fourth against a second (Leoni, 2005:70). Again it is an answering action to those which have been demonstrated previously. In this particular case it is the response of a *girata* used against an opponent lowering his position utilising the hilt in defence.

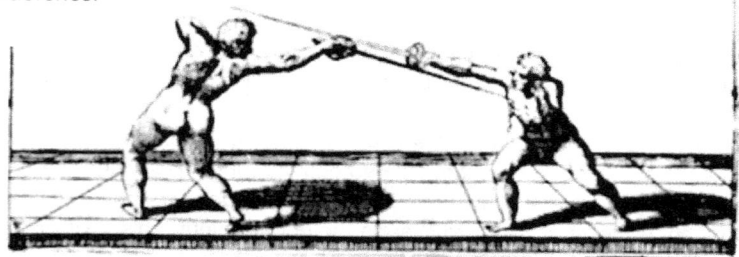

Both of the fencers start in a third guard to the inside. The fencer attempts to find the opponent's sword, in response the opponent, in the same tempo turns his hand from third to second, lowers his body. The fencer sees the motion and does not complete the action but straightens his point putting his hilt to the position of his point performing a *girata* on his right foot placing the hilt on the opponent's debole (Leoni, 2005:70). What can be seen here is that it is both the turning action of the *girata* in combination with the hand position that protects the fencer. The position of the hilt adds to the defence in using the *girata*.

Another way that this could have resulted follows, the opponent starts in second to the inside, the fencer attempts to find the opponent's sword. The opponent disengages in order to wound to the outside. The fencer also disengages and puts his hilt to his point position turning the body and hand at the same time (Leoni, 2005:70). The result is the same as above, the opponent being wounded in the tempo of his own attack. Again it is the hilt position along with the turning of the body that defends the fencer.

Once again the *girata* is used in defence. The seated combatant should pay especial note to the height of the opponent in his attack and ensure that his hand is high enough to defend him. The *girata* can be performed in a form using the body movement as demonstrated in the eleventh wound.

The Seventeenth Wound

The seventeenth wound is a demonstration of the use of the *girata* used without the assistance of blade position. The result of this action is a wound of fourth against a guard of second (Leoni, 2005:71). Fabris gives two demonstrations of this particular action, but the same result and the same core techniques are used.

The sequence that will be used for the demonstration is the first one. Both fencers start third to the inside. The fencer attempts to find the opponent's sword, in response the opponent performs a *cavazione* in second and passes forward with his left in order to wound the fencer. The fencer lowers his point slightly with his arm angled to the inside in fourth and performs a *girata* on the left. The opponent impales himself on the fencer's weapon and the weapon passes by the fencer (Leoni, 2005:71).

What can be seen here is the use of the *girata* performed in the tempo of the offensive action of the opponent. This allows the opponent's blade to pass by the fencer without ever having to be touched. For the seated fencer the *girata's* body movement is possible seated, but care should be taken that the opponent's weapon will be voided properly in the performance of the action.

The Eighteenth to Twenty-Second Wounds

The eighteenth to twenty-second wounds deliver some important ideas and rules for the fencer which should be observed. The actions, however, are not possible for the seated fencer due to the reliance on gross foot movement in all cases. As such it is the rules which are the most useful element gained from these wounds.

The first rule that is described by Fabris in these wounds is that in a defence against a cut, where a parry is necessary, passing closes also results in forte to forte contact (Leoni, 2005:72). The closing action means that the opponent's cut is not allowed to generate enough power from the travel distance. Cuts performed from the shoulder are the easiest to be countered in this particular fashion.

The next rule, taken from the nineteenth wound is also about the forte to forte exchange and states that the *girata* is weaker than passing (Leoni, 2005:73). This is not particularly useful to the seated combatant, but is most useful to know as a standing combatant. For the seated combatant movement of the body forward will result in more strength to the sword.

Fabris advises that the thrust is better avoided by keeping the body low, in fact he clearly states "do not parry if you can at all avoid doing so." (Leoni, 2005:74). Parrying engages the blades and slows the actions down. The simple parry will slow the actions down even more so. It should be noted that Fabris actions when in contact with the blade are typically fluid and in motion.

The twenty-second wound leads on to the ones following in which hand parrying is used as a defence. While Fabris admits that the hand parry is useful in certain circumstances, he says that they should be used not all that much and only in an emergency as they are able to be deceived (Leoni, 2005:76). This means that Fabris would use the hand parry as a supporting action or one as a last action rather than as an initial action.

The Twenty-Third Wound

The twenty-third wound is another demonstration of the usefulness of using the off-hand to deflect the opponent's weapon. In this particular case it results in a wound of third overcoming that of a fourth (Leoni, 2005:77). The first description follows the idea of the off-hand used as supporting the other defences. The second however uses the off-hand as a primary parry.

The action for this particular scenario proceeds as follows, both start in a guard of third to the inside. The fencer feints an attack, fourth to the inside. The opponent counters in fourth through the debole of the fencer's weapon. The fencer lowers his sword in third, places his off-hand against the opponent's sword, lowers his body turning his left shoulder forward to move the sword forward and wound the opponent (Leoni, 2005:77). What should be noted in this particular sequence of events is that the fencer uses his body to push the sword forward, the feet are not moved. This makes this particular approach most useful to the seated combatant.

There is another way that this could have occurred. The fencer who was on the outside, pushes the opponent's sword who performs a *cavazione* and counter to the inside. At the same time the fencer parries with the hand and wounds the opponent underneath his sword (Leoni, 2005:77). This is a much simpler form of events and sees the fencer use the hand as a primary defence while attacking the opponent, which is not typical for the described ideas about parries with the hand.

This particular sequence really requires no modification for the seated combatant to achieve the results as described by Fabris. The only place where a slight modification could be required is in the height difference and using the lowering as the primary defence, a certain amount of care and planning should be used to achieve the desired outcome.

The Twenty-Fifth Wound

The twenty-fifth wound is the last positive demonstration of the use of the off-hand against the opponent's weapon. As with the previous demonstration, the first uses the hand in a supporting fashion and the second uses the hand as an active defence. This wound results in a guard of second against an advanced right-foot extension of a guard of fourth (Leoni, 2005:79).

Both fencers start in a guard of third to the outside. The fencer performs a *cavazione*, in response the opponent attempts to wound in fourth. The fencer turns his hand to second, twisting his body to lead with his left side, turning on the heel of the right foot with his hand on the opponent's blade wounding in second (Leoni, 2005:79). For the seated combatant the hardest part is that the feet will make no difference, but the body can be moved to achieve the end required. This will require some experimentation with a companion in order to work this particular sequence.

Another way this could happen is as follows, both fencers start in third to the inside. The fencer lowers his point and presents an opening. The opponent sees the opponent and attacks, in response the fencer turns his hand to second with the body movement described above, and parries with his off-hand. In this way wounding the opponent and defending (Leoni, 2005:79). This is a simpler and more direct approach to the same result. Once again, for the seated combatant, the body movement is used in the same way as above, this time with the hand being used more actively.

The Twenty-Sixth Wound

The twenty-sixth wound is a demonstration of how the off-hand can be beaten and as such demonstrates the reasons why the off-hand should be used as described by Fabris. This sequence results in a *girata* in fourth against a pass with the left foot in fourth (Leoni, 2005:80). For this particular wound there is only one representation.

The opponent performs a feint outside over the fencer's sword. In response the fencer attempts to parry, to which the opponent places his hand on the inside of the sword to parry at the same time disengages inside in fourth passing over on the left foot. The fencer having gone to defend on the outside and seeing the hand disengages about the hand to point the weapon at the opponent's body and performs a *girata* over the left foot (Leoni, 2005:80). This sequence demonstrates how easily the off-hand can be avoided by the sword, and thus why it should not be the primary defence. Fabris also states that the fencer would not have to aim so low had he not had to find the opponent's debole to enhance his defence (Leoni, 2005:80).

Once again, this particular wound brings up the problem of the *girata* from a seated position. This has already been previously discussed in the eleventh wound, but to reiterate, it is the body which needs to move to avoid the opponent's attack. If the body is moved then the opponent's attack can be avoided without having to move the feet. Of course the *girata* while seated should be practiced to become the most effective that it can be.

The Twenty-Seventh Wound

The twenty-seventh wound is another demonstration of the reason why the off-hand should only be used as an emergency measure or a back-up to the sword. In this particular case it results in a wound of fourth against a third attempting to go under the sword (Leoni, 2005:81). Once again this is demonstrated in a single sequence.

The fencer feints to the right side of the opponent's face. The opponent attempts to parry with his left hand and lowers his body in order to wound underneath the sword and to the inside. The fencer uses the tempo of the off-hand to simply lower his tip between the opponent's arms turns his hand in fourth and performs a *girata* on his left foot in order to wound (Leoni, 2005:81). Once again this is a demonstration of how the opponent's off-hand can be avoided and the reason why it should only be used as a secondary defence to the sword. For the seated combatant, the *girata* has already been demonstrated as possible in the eleventh wound.

The Twenty-Eighth Wound

The twenty-eighth and final wound for the single sword is once again a demonstration of the reason for using the off-hand as a secondary defence to that of the sword. This particular wound ends in a hand in fourth against a deceived left hand with the sword in second (Leoni, 2005:82). Before Fabris goes into the action of the wound itself, he gives some explanatory notes.

Both fencers start in third to the inside, but the one who wants to use his left hand has his sword too withdrawn, thus not able to rely on his sword for defence, his hand is sword hand is too high (Leoni, 2005:82). With this particular description of the opening positions of this sequence, it is of little surprise that it does not end well for the one using his hand as primary defence.

The fencer makes a feint to the right hip of the opponent. The opponent turns his body away and attempts to parry with his left hand, at the same time turning his hand to second to wound the fencer in the chest. The fencer performs a *cavazione* on the side of the fingers of the opponent, and thrusts in fourth in the tempo of the opponent's attack. The fencer also performs a *girata* to remove his body while defending with the hilt. The opponent's sword passes by due to the combination of the *girata* and hilt position (Leoni, 2005:82). Once again the opponent's hand is simply avoided by the fencer. The previous three wounds demonstrate the reason that the hand should not be relied upon for a primary defence but should be used in emergencies or as a support to the actions of the sword.

CONCLUSION

What has been presented is the discussion of how Fabris' theory and method may be utilised by a seated fencer. It should be noted that this is a discussion of the method rather than instructional material, and the instructions which have been given here should be experimented with first to see what sort of mobility is possible. Further fencing from a chair alone is a skill, which the fencer needs practice in, thus if the individual is in experienced in this then it is less likely that the experiment with the techniques which have been described according to Fabris' method are going to work. A solid foundation in the mechanics and theory of fencing from a chair is essential before exploring such advanced techniques for their validity.

George Silver: Somewhat of an Explanation

INTRODUCTION
The manuals written by George Silver are often pushed aside due to their apparent lack of content with regard to the actual use of the sword and other weapons; also often due to their pseudo-political ranting about the "invasion" of the Italians. Were a reader to examine the situation of Silver himself, and the time in which he wrote his inflammatory manuals, more understanding of these treatises is possible. This article is an attempt to bring George Silver under a more understanding light and thus bring some understanding as to the reasons for his treatises, and also to understand some of the uses of these somewhat inflammatory discussions.

FIRST READING AND FURTHER READINGS
Back in the dim, dark days of my fencing history I took up Silver's "Paradoxes of Defence" and began to read. I was pointed toward this as a manual of the period. I read and found no use to me as a user of a rapier besides being told how useless it was and that I should use more native English weapons such as the sword and buckler, and quarterstaff. Needless to say I was not impressed and I was put off the treatise so I put it aside and went on to read something else. Ironically it was to Silver's adversary Saviolo who I turned to.

A little later on I re-read *Paradoxes of Defence* from a clean slate, and a different point of view due to the research I was conducting, and found it an interesting political statement of the times in which he lived, and a kind of last blast of the true native Englishman against the "invasion" of the Italians and their ways. Further, I read his *Brief Instructions Upon My Paradoxes of Defence* and found it to be a much more useful read with regard to the practical application of the sword against an opponent, sure I found some political statements, but the practical nature of the book was much more apparent with the due understanding of the author's position. It is for this reason that I am writing this explanation, to bring Silver back into the light of practicality. First, we need to look at Silver and his manuals in their context, to gain a greater understanding of them.

SILVER IN HIS CONTEXT
Before we can understand George Silver himself, it is important to put him into his context, as his surroundings affected his feelings and his writings. This means a brief look at some Elizabethan history. In the early Elizabethan period there was religious instability with violent arguments between Protestants and Catholics. This was affected by the outside influences of the Spanish, Italians, and to some point the French. In the early part of her reign Elizabeth was not a secure bet for survival as Queen of England. The influences of the Spanish and Italians were felt everywhere from politics to fashion.

The Italian and Spanish fashions were very popular in England during the Elizabethan period. Indeed what we consider to be the classic Elizabethan fashion is a combination of Italian and Spanish put together. To be seen with some Italian influence was to be seen to be cosmopolitan and also very fashionable. These Italian influences seemed to invade all parts of life. Traditionally it was seen that the English weapons, at least focussing on the single hand, were the sword and buckler, but as the influence of the Italians was felt more and more this combination was forsaken for the rapier and dagger. It was here that George Silver was present, his native culture being supplanted by foreign influences.

SILVER'S CHARACTER

The best way to describe George Silver was as a xenophobic/nationalistic military man. To this particular point he had two strikes against the rapier before it was even picked up. Firstly it was foreign, and secondly it was of no use in a battlefield situation. Thus the native combination of the sword and buckler was more useful in war and thus more appreciated. Further the rapier was immediately lethal whereas the sword and buckler seemed to be less so. This was the foundation of his arguments, it could be seen that he felt himself as the defender of English weapons against the invasion of the foreign.

Further to this with the invasion of the foreign cultures also came the invasion of foreign teachers of the new weapons. Such teachers attracted the attention of the upper classes particularly as they had the money to keep up with the fashions. The result of this was they tended to drift away from the English Masters and went over to the Italian ones, giving them money for the privilege of being taught how to use the new, fashionable rapier. So, no doubt there was a little bit of a monetary incentive behind Silver's rantings as well as the Italians were taking money out of the English Master's pockets, and probably his as well.

HIS TWO WORKS

Paradoxes of Defence (1599) was written as a response to the rise of the rapier and the teachers and practitioners of it and the decline of the London Masters of Defence. In this he rails against the teachers of the rapier and their practices which he sees can only lead the practitioners to death. This treatise was more of a political paper rather than a practical manual on the use of weapons. In the treatise he compares "good English weapons" against those of the foreigners and states that the English weapons are of better use. What will be noticed in these comparisons is the presence of weapons which were not civilian but military, thus revealing his military mind and thus the rejection of the rapier as a militarily-useless weapon. This treatise is often seen as a simple rant, but read from his point of view it reveals interesting aspects of the English psyche.

Brief Instructions Upon My Paradoxes of Defence was undated when it was discovered and thus it can only be estimated to have been published a little after *Paradoxes* this placing it c.1600. This treatise is an effort to explain more of what Silver was indicating in his previous manual. What should also be noted is that it is also a response to Vincentio Saviolo's (1595) *His Practice in Two Bookes* as Saviolo is mentioned specifically, and multiple times. Needless to say these two contemporaries did not get on particularly well at all.

There is a relatively well-known challenge in which George and Toby Silver challenged Saviolo to a duel. This duel was to be held in public for all to see so that the Italian methods were inferior. The Silvers went around posting bills advertising the event before even mentioning the challenge to Saviolo. When they actually came to challenging Saviolo, he simply denied the challenge outright; somewhat of an embarrassment for the Silvers. An interesting note, unlike other Italians in the manual, who are reported to have died in duels, mostly to English opponents, the manner of Saviolo's death, is not mentioned, while he is mentioned to have died.

Brief Instructions is more of a fencing manual and gives description and instruction upon the correct use of weapons. In here there are aspects of fencing which are quite useful, and some which are foundation materials for fencing theory. Silver's methods have been researched by some and found to be quite useful and practical and this is enough to give at least this treatise another look. However, it should be noted that this does not mean that there is an absence of his political feelings, quite the opposite actually.

CONCLUSION

While there is a lot of political elements present in both of Silver's manuals, they should not simply be rejected due to this. Indeed the political elements are very useful to the historian especially, but for the fencing student, it explains much of the author's approach to the weapons he describes. If you have read Silver's treatises before and found them of no use, I encourage you to go back and have another look at what he has written as there is a lot of useful information present for both the historian and the historical fencer. If you take into account George Silver's history and his historical surroundings, his treatises make much more sense.

Giacomo di Grassi: The Essentials

INTRODUCTION

Each system proposed by a theorist or practitioner is founded on some basic principles. These principles are what the system is founded upon. Aside from the typical theoretical elements such as time and distance, there are also some foundation practical elements which are the keys to understanding the system which is being presented. These practical elements will appear and reappear throughout the system which is being presented. In the case of Giacomo di Grassi and *His True Art of Defense* (1594), these foundation practical elements are found in his wards and his footwork.

OF WARDS

In di Grassi's opinion the ward is a position in which a person may withstand the attack of the opponent, or may perform a simple action from them to defend. Its second purpose is a place from which to launch an attack against the opponent. This action should be simple enough to cover all parts of the body from the correct ward, and a large action means an inefficient ward. Thus the ward must be formed properly. The ward is a place to settle after an action to consider his next action, or in expectation of the opponent's action against him.

The foundation weapon for di Grassi's system is the single sword, as is found in many manuals. He uses the single sword to depict all of the basic forms which will be presented throughout the following forms. For the single sword there are three wards. Neither in di Grassi's opinion need there be any more, "for that one onlie ſtraight line, which is the ſword, maie not couer, defend and eaſilie offend after anie other maner." (di Grassi, 1594). The three wards of which di Grassi speaks are the High Ward, Broad Ward and Low Ward.

These are the positions from which the fencer will start and therefore are the foundation from which things are learnt.

Even within this foundation there is another foundation element to be found, and that is the basic form of the wards. Each has the right foot forward, the body straight, knees bent and left arm extended toward the opponent. The feet are shoulder-width apart and the left side tends to be more toward the enemy to reduce the profile. What should be noted is that there is also an option available for the right foot to the rear rather than forward.

The High Ward

The High ward (depicted at right) is formed from the drawing of the sword from the scabbard, just like Agrippa's first ward and also the first ward just as in Agrippa. In di Grassi's opinion this only just qualifies as a ward due to its open position, however used correctly it can defend the whole person. To achieve this, the point of the weapon must be turned downward toward the opponent. Thus the ward is formed with the arm high from the shoulder with the knuckles of the sword hand high in first position however the point of the weapon is not parallel to the ground or horizontal. It is positioned obliquely, pointed downward toward the opponent

From this position he states that the fencer should gather his hind foot to his forefoot, and make a thrust "above hand" or as an imbroccata, with the hand in first position at the enemy. In this as in all the other wards a line should be drawn from the point of the weapon toward the enemy, this may be bent to strike another part, but the point should follow this line directly against the opponent. The point must be pointed downward at the enemy, lest he pass beneath it and strike the fencer before it descends, however it should also not be too low, or it may be beaten off by the opponent's sword. From this position the fencer may also beat off the opponent's weapon downward using the force and create an opportunity to strike.

The Broad Ward

The Broad Ward is the second ward. It is called "broad" because the arm is stretched wide from the right side. It is important that the arm is stretched directly perpendicular to the shoulder. This position would seem to give the opponent an opportunity to strike, but while the arm is wide from the body a straight line to the opponent is still present. The point of the weapon must be pointed at the opponent, and pointed toward his left side to be more easily able to strike and defend. If the point is left straight from the hand, the fencer is much too open and may easily be hurt by the enemy, with the point inward, it may defend the body.

The Low Ward

The lowe ward.

The Low Ward or "lock" ward is the strongest and surest of any of the wards. It is the easiest to stand in and may most easily defend and offend. It is formed in many ways by many different teachers; many readers will know this ward as third or *terza*. In di Grassi's case, the arm should be places directly down from the shoulder toward the knee, but on the outside of it. The point should be somewhat raised and bearing toward the left side of the opponent. From this position it is easy to defend and easy to thrust.

FOOTWORK

"Moſt great is the care and conſiderations which the paces or footſtepps requier in this exerciſe, becauſe from them in a manner more thſ from anie other thing ſpringeth all offence and defence." (di Grassi, 1594)

Footwork is the key to di Grassi's system and from it comes all offence and defence, as will be noted in the writings of the author. Very rarely does di Grassi describe or indicate any movement without some consideration of the movement of the feet. In this however, it is always controlled and purposeful, using as little time in the motions of the footwork as possible.

The body should be stable with the right shoulder toward enemy to make a smaller target. It should be bent backward rather than forward, being away from danger and it should be kept firm and stable regardless of the movement made. The body should be kept stable in its ward rather than bending and changing as this takes time this motion of the body is directed by the head as with all motions.

The idea of stability presented in the movement and positioning of the body is further enhanced by di Grassi's advice with regard to the actual step itself. He states that the fencer should step comfortably to ensure no chance of falling, and this should be a self-managed length of step. The length of the step should be natural to the combatant, not lengthened or shortened to match the opponent. The movements will seldom be straight.

The Whole Pace
The Whole pace is to take the hind foot from behind and place it before the fore foot, keeping the fore foot still in the motion.

The Half Pace
The Half pace is to take the hind foot close to the fore foot, or the fore foot backward to the hind foot. This motion may be extended by moving the same foot forward or backward. This may be straight or crooked in the motion.

The Retreat
The Retreat step is made straight backward, "back pace is framed more often straight than crooked". (di Grassi, 1594)

The Slope or Crooked Pace
The Slope or Crooked is made with the hind foot going forwards but crossing as it goes forward, out of straight line. Diagonal step made by the rear foot.

The Compass Pace
The Circular or Compass is made by making a circular movement with either fore or hind foot to the left or the right. This will move the body to the left or right dependent on the side moved to. The combatant may compass forward or backward.

CONCLUSION
The information which has been presented is the essential practical parts of the system which is presented by di Grassi. The actions of the cuts and thrusts are also important however their actions, for the most part, are common knowledge. The actions and positions which have been presented here form the foundation of the system, as it will be noted that if weapon forms using the sword accompanied by another device are read, it is the same footwork which is used and also the same wards. These have been presented here for a greater understanding and increased familiarity with these elements.

Saviolo: Principles and Practical Elements

INTRODUCTION
Saviolo is a master of particular interest to me as his method appealed to me[11]. In this article I will be presenting some of the research that I have made about Saviolo, giving some information about his method and how it is applied. Various points will be made about this system which will be of interest to various people, and I hope that the information present will be of interest. All of the references and the image in this article come straight from Saviolo's treatise of 1595.

PART I: PRINCIPLES

Introduction
Vincentio Saviolo is a master of the Renaissance period. More specifically he is one from the Elizabethan period. He taught in London and held a school at Blackfriars, which is on the south bank of the River Thames. Of especial note is that the same region held

---

11   In fact, if you are interested in Saviolo, keep your eye out for a future publication of my interpretation of Saviolo's First Book.

a theatre which was sold to William Shakespeare. Saviolo published his own treatise *His Practice in Two Bookes* in 1595, and his name is present in the works of George Silver who was a contemporary of Saviolo, and who was discussed in an article previously.

Saviolo's treatise is a composite treatise encompassing principles from at least two, possibly three, different schools of thought brought together to form a single system. This in and of itself makes Saviolo's technique interesting and of note to the Renaissance fencer. The treatise and the information contained within are presented as a discussion between a master and his student. In this particular case it is Saviolo talking with his student Luke. Unlike many manuals the principles are not presented singularly but are presented within the text as a practical representation of what a person should do against their opponent. There are some which are elucidated simply, but for the most part they are within the discussion between the master and the student.

The three schools of thought from where Saviolo draws his information are the Italian, Spanish and German. Each one of these is used for a particular application and then are combined together to form the overall system. The Italian school is present in Saviolo's use of the thrust, and more to the point, the dominance of the thrust over the cut in the use of the rapier. The footwork is primarily circular to gain an advantage over the opponent due to the angle of one opponent to another, thus presenting principles present in the Spanish school. Finally, the method of cutting presented by Saviolo is designed to defeat the opponent while defending at the same time and also before the opponent has time to respond, thus presenting elements from the German school. This makes for what should be a very complex system. Externally the system is quite simple, but internally once deeper reading is made of it, the hidden complexity within the system is exposed.

Entropy: The Conservation of Energy

To understand both the simplicity and complexity of the system presented by Saviolo, it is first important to examine the general principles upon which the system is based. The first of these principles is about entropy and emotional control. Entropy is using only the amount of energy that is required in order to achieve an objective; in this particular case it is to defeat the opponent.

> *"this I would advise you, when you would make these passages, or put your weapon under your enemies, that you doe them not in vaine nor without some advauntage." (Saviolo, 1595)*

This passage states that the combatant should not perform actions without gaining some advantage over the opponent. The energy of the combatant is thus maintained and not used for actions which would not gain him some advantage. In achieving this principle, the combatant will retain a larger store of energy and thus will last longer against the opponent than if he used energy to perform actions which did not achieve something. One place where this can be present is in the use of fury to defeat the opponent, thus Saviolo warns against this.

Control of Emotion

"Wherefore as well in this ward as in the other, take heede that you suffer not your selfe to bee blinded and carried awaie with rage and furie." (Saviolo, 1595)

When a combatant is enraged, they lose the ability to reason and thus make decisions to their advantage. This particular aspect will mean that control is lost over the use of the weapon and thus over the situation and this can easily lead to the combatant being struck by the opponent. It is important that the combatant go into the combat "cold" and not be taken away by anger or similar emotions so that they can maintain control over themselves. This is an aspect where some Spanish influence could be claimed.

To Strike and Not be Struck

> "In this sorte the saide scholler shall learne to strike and not be stricken, as I alwaies advise the noble-men and gentlemen whit whome I have to deale, that if they cannot hit or hurt their enemy, that they learn to defend them selves that they be not hurt." (Saviolo, 1595)

To strike and not be struck is the principle on which all fencing is based, and in the case of a real combat using sharp weapons it is of great importance. Saviolo is instructing the combatant to ensure that if they are not able to strike their opponent without being struck themselves then they should not attack. This is a principle of great importance to all fencing, and is what we should all base our fencing. It is not optimum for the fencer to strike the opponent while being struck. Thus the guard against the opponent should always be maintained, even in offence. It is no surprise that this particular principle is present in Saviolo's treatise.

Just Distance

> "Moreover, you must observe just distance, which is, when either of you stand in such place, that stepping forward a little, you maye reache one another," (Saviolo, 1595)

All forms of fencing are based on two basic principles, timing and distance; and neither can be denied. In all cases the correct distance between a combatant and their opponent must be observed. In the case of Saviolo, this correct or "just" distance is a distance at which the opponent may be struck with only a simple movement of the feet and an extension of the arm. This particular distance is common amongst fencing treatises. Saviolo cautions against the combatant coming too close to the opponent as well, and then makes note of another important principle which will be discussed next.

Timing

> "Moreover, hee must beware of coming too much within his just distance, because if he hit his adversary, hee may bee hitte againe by his adversarye: wherfore I will teache you how to offend and defend in the same time." (Saviolo, 1595)

Timing is the other half of the equation so to speak. Distance and timing work both separately and together and the ignorance of either by the combatant is done at their peril. Saviolo discusses time throughout his treatise, but is never particularly specific about what each time is and how it functions. He presents the elements of time as part of the description of the execution of the action he is describing. This is an important note to make as it demonstrates how important principles may be hidden within the text when not explicitly presented.

> *"At the same time that the scholler removeth his foote, the teacher shall play a little with stirring of his body, and with his lefte hand shall beat away his schollers rapier from his right side, and shall remove his right foot behinde his left striking a crosse blow at the head."* (Saviolo, 1595)

With the essential more academic principles of Saviolo's system presented, it is now possible to move on to more practical matters with regards to the information which is presented in his treatise. Not all of the practical elements will be presented as some of them are taken for granted and do not really aid in this particular discussion. The more practical elements of Saviolo's treatise will be left for later in this discussion, along with a final wrap-up of the information which has been presented over both.

PART II: PRACTICAL ELEMENTS
Introduction

With the background set, and the principles in place, it is now possible to delve more deeply into the system which was developed by Saviolo. The principles are laid out first and understood to understand the practical side of the system. There will be elements that will be left out of this discussion as they serve no purpose in going into them in detail in the discovery of Saviolo's method of fence. Thus it will be those elements which are essential to his system that the detail will be centred upon.

Externally Saviolo's system is simple, but when you examine it in more detail, the hidden complexities emerge. As with the previous part it is important to start with the principles, or in this case the basic elements before moving on to the more complex aspects of the system. First is starting with Saviolo's wards.

The First Ward

The first ward the Saviolo presents is a teaching ward, simple as that. It is designed to place the student in the correct position so that they have all the elements in place. This is important as it places the student in the correct position for applying the techniques that follow.

> *"I come therefore to the point and say, that when the teacher will enter his scholler, he shal cause him to stand upon this ward, which is very good to bee taught for framing the foote, the hand, and the body:"* (Saviolo, 1595)

Without teaching this ward the student will be unprepared to perform the following wards and to understand how they are used. Once the student can place himself in the correct position, it is then possible to move on to the combat ward which Saviolo advises for use in combat. Once again, it is important to stress that the first ward is purely a teaching ward and designed to teach the student the correct position for their body.

The Second Ward

The second ward is Saviolo's primary combat ward. This is the one that he advises for use in combat against an opponent. It should be noted that this ward carries through many of the same elements as found in the teaching ward, thus it can be seen that one is based upon the other. If we examine Saviolo's description of his second ward, these elements can easily be seen.

> "Therefore if the maister desire to make a good scholler, let him begin in this sorte, causing his scholar to place his right legge formoste, a little bending the knee, so that the heele of his right foote stand just against the midst of his left foote, holding his sword hand close on the outside of his right knee, with his swoorde helde in shorte, least his adversarye should gaine the same, ever keeping the poynte directlye on the face or bellye of his enemye, and the maister shall dispose of him selfe in the same manner, as well with his foote as with his poynt." (Saviolo, 1595)

As in the first ward the right or sword side leg is placed forward, with the knee bent slightly. This is the same as the teaching ward. This is the same with the position of the feet and demonstrates how the first ward teaches the student where to place themselves. The hand position with the weapon held in close and the off-hand slightly more extended means that it is the off-hand that will be used for the primary defence against the opponent rather than the use of the sword. The withdrawal of the weapon also denies the opponent blade engagement from the out-set. As with many of the masters, the point is directed against the opponent in order to threaten them and also to place in in a position to attack.

The Third Ward

The third ward has two purposes, and it is important to realise them to use the ward properly. The primary reason for the third ward is so that the combatant can easily perform a lunge or "stoccata at length" as Saviolo calls it. From this position, the combatant is also prepared to perform a *punta riversa*. This is a ward in the truest sense as it is a position from which an attack is made rather than a static defence. In many ways this position should not be adopted but moved through.

> "I will not faile in anie part to make you understand the excellencie of this third warde, which notwithstanding is quite contrarie to the other two. Because that in this you must stand with your feet even together, as if you were readie to sit down, and your rapier hand must bee within your knee, and your point against the face of your enemie: and if your enemie put himselfe upon the same ward, you may give a stoccata at length betweene his rapier and his arme, which shall bee best performed and; reach farthest, if you shift with your foot on the right side." (Saviolo, 1595)

This ward differs in its foot position from the other two as they are quite close together. The hand position is very similar to the previous two wards as it is withdrawn to deny blade engagement from the enemy. The position of the feet clearly demonstrates that it is a preparation for the use of the back foot to push the combatant forward in the performance of an attack. Saviolo's "stoccata at length" will be discussed in more depth in a later section of this part.

Saviolo's System

Saviolo's system is entirely based on the use of the sword in conjunction with the off-hand. All of his techniques are based on the premise that the hand is the primary defence against thrusts, and the sword is more of an offensive object rather than defensive. This particular idea transfers and follows through to his rapier and dagger which follow the same principles, using the dagger in the off-hand as defensive and the sword as offensive in most situations.

The entire system revolves around the use of the off-hand parry, void with movement off-line and the stoccata in offence against the opponent. Clearly the only difference in the use of rapier and dagger is that there is a dagger in the off-hand. This results in a system which, from the outside, is extremely simple. This simplicity of purpose is demonstrated in the forms of attack also.

In offence while the stoccata is the primary attack, there are others. In Saviolo's system the attacks are simplified to four thrusts and three cuts. This makes for a very simple system. To start with the cuts, there are three, the mandritta, the riversa and the stramazone. The mandritta is an attack which, for the right-hander, is delivered against the opponent's left side, a forehand blow. The riversa is the reverse of this and is delivered against the right of the opponent, a backhand blow. Saviolo does not discriminate amongst the angles at which the blow is delivered, merely the direction. The stramazone is a cut delivered with the tip of the weapon, and there are no directions supplied. In this the reader is left to make their own decision as to where the blow should be delivered against the opponent.

Saviolo uses four thrusts, two which are simple thrusts, and two which require the use of footwork. The two which are simple thrusts are the stoccata and the imbroccata. The stoccata, Saviolo's preferred attack, is delivered against the opponent from a low position to a high position. This means that this is a rising thrust. It is usually delivered below the opponent's hilt, but its targeting is not restricted at all. The imbroccata is a descending thrust as such it is delivered from a high position to a low position. This is usually delivered above the opponent's hilt, and the most likely targets are the head and upper body, though the targets are, once again not restricted. The *punta riversa*, like the riversa as a cut attacks the right side of the opponent. This is performed with a sloping step forward and to the right of the opponent. The other thrust with movement is the long stoccata.

The Long Stoccata

> *"stoccata at length betweene his rapier and his arme, which shall bee best performed & reach farthest, if you shift with your foot on the right side."*
>
> (Saviolo, 1595)

The long stoccata, or "stoccata at length", or lunge is an explosive extension of the arm and body designed to quickly deliver the point of the weapon against the opponent when at increased distance. This particular technique allows the combatant to strike the opponent at longer range than with just using the simple stoccata. This is a technique which needs to be delivered suddenly and without warning.

> "if you would deliver a long stoccata, and have perceived that your enemie would shrinke awaie, you may, if you list, at that verie instant give it him,"
> (Saviolo, 1595)

This is a technique which until very recently was thought to be restricted to the treatises of later period masters such as Giganti and Capo Ferro. Clearly the technique is clearly demonstrated in Saviolo's treatise. This leads on to the advanced techniques which are present in Saviolo's treatise but not explicitly described.

The Beat

The beat parry and beat attack are forms of swordplay which are considered either very simple or very advanced, depending on who is discussing them. Saviolo uses the beat parry in many instances in order to both defend and also create an opening in the opponent. The best example of this is as such;

> "when you finde his point long, you maie breake it aside with your swoorde,"
> (Saviolo, 1595)

This is essentially Saviolo stating that if they give you their sword by extending it toward you, you should beat the sword to the side. This simple technique opens the opponent up to an attack. While the technique seems simple as just smacking the opponent's blade away, there is some care that should be taken in its performance.

> "let him beware that he doo not beate aside his teachers weapon toward the point, because he shoulde be in danger to receive a thrust or stoccata either in the face or belly." (Saviolo, 1595)

What Saviolo is saying is that you should not beat the opponent's sword too close to the point because this will not have as great an effect as beating it lower on the sword. He actually states that the beat should be done against the opponent's weapon toward the tip, but not too far up. This demonstrates a clear understanding of this particular technique. The other advanced techniques take a little more interpretation on the part of the reader.

Hidden Complexity

It has been claimed by some that Saviolo's system is extremely simple and that he does not use any advanced blade techniques, merely relying on beating the opponent's sword out of the way or waiting for the opportune moment to strike. This is actually quite false and if the treatise is read properly it will be noted that there are more advanced techniques of the blade present.

> "but rather passe on him with your point above his sword, turning wel your hand as in an imbroccata," (Saviolo, 1595)

This is a clear description of the use of a bind. The sword is passed over the opponent's blade and then the hand is turned downward against the opponent's blade. The simple blade contact along with the turning motion would result in the control of the opponent's blade and thus a bind against the opponent's sword.

Another example of an advanced technique present in Saviolo's manual is the pressure glide. This technique, as with the bind, is not explicitly demonstrated or presented merely the technique is within the text leaving the reader to interpret what Saviolo is saying.

> *"thrusting with the point of his Rapier at the belly of his teacher, turning readily his hand that the fingers be inward toward the body, and the joint of the wrist shall be outward."* (Saviolo, 1595)

Both elements of the pressure glide are present in this description. First, there is the thrust pushing toward the opponent, and then there is the contact of the blade with the turning of the hand to increase the pressure on the opponent's blade. This turning action of the hand and wrist results in a displacement of the opponent's blade and thus an opening in the opponent's defence, the exact reason for the performance of a pressure glide and the exact method also. This demonstrates the complexity of Saviolo's techniques which are hidden within the simple system which is immediately present.

Three Schools in One
There are three schools of thought present in Saviolo's treatise, the Italian, German and Spanish. It is only through the combination of the principles of each one of these schools that we are able to understand the manual in its entirety. Each one of the elements present enhances the system and allows it to deal with different approaches. It is also important to realise that the system is based on those principles highlighted in the first part of the discussion and without these founding principles it is impossible to understand what Saviolo's aim was and how he meant to achieve it through his system. Each one of these principles adds something to the system and allows it to be complete under the theory which surrounds fencing. It is important to understand these principles in order to completely understand the system.

CONCLUSION

The practical elements which have been highlighted in this part describe a system which is based on some very simple techniques for the base elements of the system, but these hide the complexity which is somewhat hidden within the system. In this way Saviolo's system is complexity within simplicity. The basic elements need to be understood first to realise what the system is based upon, only then is it possible to apply the more complex aspects of the system in a combative situation.

This discussion of Saviolo's treatise, the practical elements anyhow, has been designed to highlight the system which was developed by Saviolo and presented in his treatise. Further to this it is important that the main understanding of the system can only really be gained by a study of the period manual itself. Secondary sources, such as the information supplied here, can assist with this understanding, but only through reading the manual itself is it possible to really understand the system. This blog has been designed to introduce this particular manual to the readership that a better understanding of Saviolo may be gained.

Musashi for the Rapier Combatant

INTRODUCTION

The following discussion is designed to introduce Musashi's techniques to the rapier combatant and demonstrate how they are useful. When people research, they tend to be much too focussed on what they are studying and as such they miss some important elements. This is especially the case in this situation. It is only through the acknowledgment of the multiple places that principles cross over that it is possible to truly understand sword combat. This is especially the case when examining the relevance of Musashi to the rapier combatant.

There are many principles that do cross over from one form to the next. In this particular element it must be realised that sword combat is sword combat and a great deal of the principles are universal no matter what the weapon is. What makes this investigation even more interesting is that on the level of philoscphy and the elemental principles there are many commonalities.

To begin with Musashi's philosophy of sword combat will be discussed. The thought processes that an author goes through are almost as important as what is written. From this discussion of the philosophy of Musashi various important and relevant elements will appear. The next part of the process is to examine Musashi's combat principles and to realise that they do have a great deal of relevance to the rapier combatant. Here is another place where the relevance of Musashi will be demonstrated. The final element that will be discussed is Musashi's techniques and they will be shown to be relevant to the rapier combatant. While it is not possible to directly convert these techniques it is important that we understand that the principles of the techniques do apply.

PHILOSOPHY

Musashi's philosophy of fighting and the use of the sword can be seen as very deep and difficult to understand. If it is approached from this point of view, there is no real hope of every being able to truly understand what he is talking about and what he is teaching. We must examine what Musashi says and understand it both from his point of view and our own.

"I take up my brush to explain the true spirit of this Ichi School as it is mirrored in the Way of heaven and Kwannon." (Musashi, 1974:35). The important part of this statement is the idea of the "true spirit" and what that means. Through understanding this we can understand what the art of the sword is all about. This "true spirit" is what the art of the sword is about.

The importance of a normal approach to training and fighting is emphasised by Musashi throughout his work. This normal approach means to be calm but determined and not recklessly enter into a situation.

"In strategy your spiritual bearing must not be any different from normal. Both in fighting and in everyday life you should be determined though calm. Meet the situation without tenseness yet not recklessly, your spirit settled yet unbiased."

(Musashi, 1974:53)

It would seem that this is the part where the philosophy is truly entered into, but as can be seen it is saying that fighting should be approached the same way as everything else. It is important to have confidence in what you are doing and not be flustered or apprehensive. It must be understood that fighting is all a process just like everything else in life.

"What is big is easy to perceive: what is small is difficult to perceive." (Musashi, 1974:44). This is an extremely obvious seeming statement, but even so it is important. Related to fencing, it must be realised that large movements are much easier to see and predict than small ones. This is also the case for learning small amounts of learning are more difficult to perceive than leaps in achievement, but often it is the smaller ones, which are more important.

We must understand where we are going and this requires some sort of plan. "The carpenter uses a master plan of the building, and the Way of strategy is similar in that there is a plan of campaign." (Musashi, 1974:41). This is especially important in training and fighting. Even a general plan is useful. If the process is not planned problems can arise, and things are missed.

Musashi has nine statements, which he feels are essential to learning the art of the sword. It can be seen that each has an important element that we should follow if we are to achieve mastery. These statements are clearly linked to Musashi's philosophy of mastering strategy and the art of the sword.

"1. Do not think dishonestly." (Musashi, 1974:49). You only know what you really know and this is only tested in combat. This is a statement about self-deception; thinking that you are better than you are does not make it so.

"2. The Way is in training." (Musashi, 1974:49). Training is vital to maintenance and advancement of our skills. There are no exceptions to this particular statement, no matter how much natural talent a person has.

"3. Become acquainted with every art." (Musashi, 1974:49). Broaden your horizons; there is much that can be learnt from others. Learn other weapons and realise that these will all improve each other. Learn other skills especially those that teach you patience.

"4. Know the Ways of all professions." (Musashi, 1974:49). Examine how others can help. See how other things are related. Examine what other people do and how what they do helps or can help you with what you are doing.

"5. Distinguish between gain and loss in worldly matters." (Musashi, 1974:49). Examine the true meaning of these words. How do they benefit you? Can a loss be examined in a different light? A loss at practice is not a loss but a chance to learn. Appreciate it if there is someone who can challenge you and make you work hard.

"6. Develop intuitive judgement and understanding for everything." (Musashi, 1974:49). Intuition is "learned instinct" and it is a great asset. Let it feed your mind. Understand the why and the how and investigate them. Delve into things so that good decisions are easier to make this will help you in fighting.

"7. Perceive those things which cannot be seen." (Musashi, 1974:49). Examine things beyond the physical, and use all of your senses. One of the most important senses that we have in fencing is feeling. Feel through the blade; listen to the sound of the blade.

"8. Pay attention even to trifles." (Musashi, 1974:49). Small elements are as important as large ones, especially in mistakes or technical errors. The change of angle by a few degrees can make a difference. Small mistakes can develop into bigger mistakes and cause you some real problems later on.

"9. Do nothing which is of no use." (Musashi, 1974:49). There must be a reason for everything that you do, especially when fencing. Do nothing that gains you nothing. Every movement of the body or sword should gain you something. Only use those actions, which achieve something for you, no matter how small.

Within the framework of the overall philosophy of Musashi, one cannot ignore the concept of strategy and how Musashi relates to this particular subject. In many ways, Musashi's philosophy is his philosophy of strategy, but it is much more than just this. He states that; "Strategy is the craft of the warrior." (Musashi, 1974:37). In this he underwrites the importance of strategy to swordplay and its importance to be studied by the student of the blade. The two cannot be separated neither strategy from the warrior, or the warrior from strategy, they are so integral to one another. Further to this initial concept, Musashi illustrates the importance of strategy and what it is based upon;

"studying the Way of strategy is based on overcoming men. By victory gained in crossing swords with individuals, or enjoining battle with large numbers, we can attain power and fame for ourselves and our lord. This is the virtue of strategy" (Musashi, 1974:38)

It is important that we understand that strategy is not some ephemeral concept that is not concretely based. We must understand it from its most basic element, overcoming men. This is what strategy is used for. The attainment of power and fame are results of the successful application of strategy and hence the virtues of it. We must see that this applies both to single combat and engagements of multiples. On this particular basis and concept, we must address his next point with regard to strategy. "If there is a Way involving the spirit not being defeated, to help oneself and gain honour, it is the Way of strategy." (Musashi, 1974:49). Strategy teaches us how to beat the opponent and develops the confidence to do so. This is what truly helps you and gains honour.

Accompanying the concept of strategy is how people view it. In the initial instance the singular individual does not seem all that powerful, even with strategy to back up his pursuits, but the concept must be broadened to understand its true effects. "To master the virtue of the long sword is to govern the world and oneself, thus the long sword is the basis of strategy." (Musashi, 1974:47). While this was very much so in Musashi' time, it can be seen as pertinent in own time. This can also be viewed from another perspective. Just as for Musashi the long sword is the basic weapon, so too this opinion can be used for the rapier as all the combinations are based on the rapier. If we master the rapier, we can master its other forms. Again we must look at strategy from a much broader view to see what Musashi is really talking about.

"Polish your wisdom: learn public justice, distinguish between good and evil, study the Ways of different arts one by one. When you cannot be deceived by men you will have realised the wisdom of strategy." (Musashi, 1974:54)

Deception is a part of combat and everyday life. When you cannot be deceived you will not be tricked and will see how the principles apply. This is important for the rapier combatant so that he will not be tricked on or off the field. This will assist you to see what is true and what is deception. For you to do this you must broaden your view.

To see how to apply the principles of strategy we must have a broad view of things. It is important that we are able to see the importance of strategy in all situations, "if you know the Way broadly you will see everything." (Musashi, 1974:47). Do not become too focussed, we need to see the principles of sword combat in different things. This is how we can truly become to understand strategy and its benefits.

> "In the first place, people think narrowly about the benefit of strategy. By using only their fingertips they only know the benefit of the five inches of the wrist." (Musashi, 1974:69)

It is easy to see how strategy is applied to combative situations of all kinds, be it swordplay or competitive sports. Think beyond this to be able to truly apply strategy. What Musashi is referring to is more than just the physical mechanics of swordplay, but also how the benefits of strategy are applied to much broader things than swordplay. "The true value of sword-fencing cannot be seen within the confines of sword-fencing technique." (Musashi, 1974:40). We must look beyond fencing to see how the skills may be applied. See what is learnt from practice and on the field and how it applies to other things. Fencing also gives us increased fitness and health benefits, and makes the body more limber. These are just a few of the "outside" applications.

The ability to have both a broad view of things and the ability to focus are essential. It is necessary to change focus from the small details to the larger picture and back again. This is especially the case when we become too focused. Break focus to gain the larger picture and then refocus on where it matters. We are often beset by theories presented by many people, some of these theories seem sound, and yet others do not. Knowing the difference is what Musashi refers to as the Void. "By knowing things that exist, you can know that which does not exist. This is the void." (Musashi, 1974:95). The void is about knowing the difference between that which does exist and that, which does not. Through this knowledge advantage can be gained. We need to apply what is known to see what will work and what will not work.

All forms of sword combat are both a physical and mental process, and both must be used if we are to succeed. This particular element is an integral part to Musashi's philosophy of combat. It is important to investigate this part to understand what Musashi is talking about.

> "It is said the warrior's is the twofold Way of pen and sword, and he should have a taste for both Ways. Even if a man has no natural ability he can become a warrior by sticking assiduously to both divisions of the Way."
> (Musashi, 1974:37)

The first part of this quotation says that we should both fight and write and should know both. We should all seriously consider putting our thoughts on paper, not only for ourselves but to benefit others from our point of view. Another way to interpret this is in the light of the physical and the mental. Both are important. The second part means that even without natural ability, it is possible to succeed, as long as we stick to what we are doing, especially with regard to both the physical and mental attributes.

> *"It is difficult to realise the true Way just through sword-fencing. Know the smallest things and the biggest things, the shallowest and the deepest things."* (Musashi, 1974:43)

If we only focus on the physical elements of fencing it is difficult to see the mental attributes and hence a deeper meaning will be missed. Analyse the physical and the mental and to investigate these things thoroughly. Sparring is essential but practice, research and analysis are also extremely important. The idea of research into sword practices is something, which is reiterated throughout Musashi's book. "You must do sufficient research." (Musashi, 1974:43). This applies to understanding all forms. Research is not necessarily in the book sense but also in the physical sense. We need to not only know how an action is performed but why and when.

The learning process is something that we can never depart from. "Study strategy over the years and achieve the spirit of the warrior." (Musashi, 1974:66)

Learning to fence is a long process and the only way to learn is to do one thing at a time. "Step by step walk the thousand-mile road." (Musashi, 1974:66). Learning to fence properly will take time but you must begin and continue to achieve what you set out to do. You must take time to learn and understand to achieve victory. This process of learning must be both a physical and mental process.

> *"The Way of the warrior is to master the virtue of his weapons. If a gentleman dislikes strategy he will not appreciate the benefit of weaponry, so must he not have a little taste for this?"* (Musashi, 1974:41)

We must learn to master the weapons as they are. It is also important to master strategy to appreciate the benefit of the weapons and see how they are best used. Therefore we must have a little of the mental to appreciate the physical in the learning process.

You must learn the basic elements before anything else. These elements are the essential ones. Move in a natural fashion, feel and observe the timing and distance. You will learn as you fight opponents and see how the principles are applied. There are those who will think that once they have learnt the basics that they know everything, and just because an approach works that it will continue to work. "Someone once said "Immature strategy is the cause of grief." That was a true saying." (Musashi, 1974:40). Things must be learnt completely before they can be really applied. Another way of saying this is that "a little knowledge is a dangerous thing". Only through learning all of the elements will a person really be successful.

It is only through the attainment of all of the skills of fencing that we will be successful. "The carpenter's attainment is, having tools which will cut well, ... Things are similar for the trooper. You ought to think deeply about this." (Musashi, 1974:42). The student's attainment is having skills that work for him. These skills can be said to be the student's "tools". The important thing here is that it is only when the skills are learnt that the student can attain victory. More important is that the skills are not only learnt but learnt well.

> *"The attainment of the carpenter is that his work is not warped, that the joints are not misaligned, and that the work is truly planed so that it meets well and is not merely finished in sections. This is essential."* (Musashi, 1974:43)

For the student and fencer this means to have learnt all of the skills involved in the art and being able to perform them when fighting. It is important that the learning is done well. If the skills are only learnt in the most rudimentary fashion, then the student will not be able to perform them well. It is important that we do not deviate from this process even a little.

> *"If you study a Way daily, and your spirit diverges, you may think you are obeying a good Way but objectively it is not the true Way. If you are following the true Way and diverge a little, this will become a large divergence."*
> (Musashi, 1974:44)

The "true Way" for fencing is the art of the sword. You must study how the sword works and not be taken in by fads. These are divergence. If you diverge a little, problems will be created and these will become larger problems. Learn the correct things and stick to them. It is easier to fix a problem in the earlier stages than to have to fix them later. This is also the case for understanding the principles of combat. "If you interpret the meaning loosely you will mistake the Way." (Musashi, 1974:53). It is important to fully understand concepts in order to be able to apply them. If you do not achieve this you will misinterpret and not be able to apply the skills at the right time or in the right fashion. Confusion with advanced concepts is usually the result of not understanding the basic ones fully. "Strategy is different from other things in that if you mistake the Way even a little you will become bewildered and fall into bad ways." (Musashi, 1974:53). You must adhere to what is taught in the principles of combat especially in the initial lessons. To mistake these will result in confusion and bad habits.

While for many fencing is a hobby that they take seriously enough when they are engaged in it, in some cases they will become bored with the lessons. If the lessons are skipped then there will be problems later on. It is important to focus on what we are doing to truly learn the art of the sword.

> *"More than anything to start with you must set your heart on strategy and earnestly stick to the Way. You will come to be able to actually beat men in fights, and to be able to win with your eyes. Also by training you will be able to freely control your body, conquer men with your body, and with sufficient training you will be able to beat ten men with your spirit."* (Musashi, 1974:49)

You must stick with what you are learning and not deviate. You will begin to see holes in the opponent's defence. Training prepares the body for what it is required to do. Defeating men with your spirit is about mental dominance; with this your confidence will be able to defeat your opponent before they start. While it is advantageous to be able to learn with someone else, it is also possible to study and learn by yourself and still achieve victories.

> *"you can become a master of strategy by training alone with a sword, so that you can understand the enemy's stratagems, his strength and resources, and come to appreciate how to apply strategy."* (Musashi, 1974:70)

You can learn about others by learning about yourself. You use the sword techniques to find his strategy, strengths and weaknesses, and how to apply strategy in any situation. If you learn all of the essential basics well on your own and then apply them in a combat situation you will be able to see how the enemy fights. Thorough this you will be able to apply what you have learnt. "What remains is sword-fighting ability, which you can attain in battles and duels." (Musashi, 1974:67). True fighting ability is realised in combat and only through combat. Combat is an essential part of the learning process, whether you win or lose. Things are difficult at first, but training will gradually reduce the difficulty. When you are used to using the weapons they will become less difficult to use and you will be able to utilise them effectively.

> *"It will seem difficult at first, but everything is difficult at first. Bows are difficult to draw, halberds are difficult to wield; as you become accustomed to the bow so your pull will become stronger. When you become used to wielding the long sword, you will gain the power of the Way and wield the sword well."* (Musashi, 1974:46)

Once you have learnt all of the skills and principles well you are in the position to be able to train others. "When the carpenter becomes skilled and understands measures he can become a foreman." (Musashi, 1974:42). What is most important in this particular situation is that it is only after all of the skills and principles are learnt that you can teach. The teacher must know and understand the skills and principles to teach.

Practice is essential to learning and the maintenance of the skills that have been learnt. Without practice it is not possible to see whether the lessons have been learnt completely. It is also important that the practice becomes a normal part of life, "you must train day and night in order to make quick decisions. In strategy to treat training as a part of normal life with your spirit unchanging." (Musashi, 1974:44). Quick and accurate decisions are a key to success. Training must be treated as a part of normal life so that it becomes normal. It is possible to train during normal life, or make normal life training. Consider how to apply this thought.

> *"Any man who wants to master the essence of my strategy must research diligently, train morning and evening. Thus he can polish his skill, become free from self, and realise extraordinary ability. He will come to possess miraculous power."* (Musashi, 1974:70)

Practice must also be regular. The process of learning strategy is the same for all. You must research, and train. You must polish the skill through training and learn to see the elements at work. This is how to realise extraordinary ability, only through hard work, study and training. There is no other way to achieve. Learning and practice go hand in hand and this is important. As such, it is also important that practice is as important as learning. It is a slow accumulative process. "With your spirit settled, accumulate practice day by day, and hour by hour." (Musashi, 1974:95). This is the way that true skill and mastery is achieved.

For a student to learn properly it is necessary to have a real teacher. Musashi also went into some detail with regard to how a student should be instructed. "The teacher is as a needle, the disciple is as thread. You must practice constantly." (Musashi, 1974:41). This means that the student will follow the teacher's instruction and that it is necessary that the student should practice constantly. It is important that skills are learnt from teacher to student, there is no other way. "The method of teaching my strategy is with a trustworthy spirit." (Musashi, 1974:92). The student must trust what the teacher has to teach for them to excel. It is important that this bond of trust is established early on in the training.

Pupils must be taught as they progress. Teaching easy things so that they understand and then more complex things, just as in the assembly of houses so too is the fighter assembled from his lessons. It is necessary that the teacher considers this and establishes the lessons as such. The advantages and limitations of the student must be taken into account, especially in the learning of the lessons. Many think that there is an inner meaning to what is being taught by the teacher and there are great secrets in the teaching. "There is no inner meaning in sword attitudes. You must simply keep your spirit true to realise the virtue of strategy." (Musashi, 1974:93) There are no "secrets" it is simply necessary to learn the principles and to follow these principles. The combat principles are vitally important to understanding any form of sword combat and they must be taken into account, and Musashi has much to say about them.

COMBAT PRINCIPLES

"If you master the principles of sword-fencing, when you freely beat one man, you beat any man in the world. The spirit of defeating a man is the same for ten million men." (Musashi, 1974:43)

The combat principles are what the art is based upon. If these are truly mastered then it is possible to beat any opponent. It is important that the principles used to defeat one opponent are the same as defeating any opponent. This is regardless of their skill level or experience the principles still apply from one to another combat situation. The combat principles advocated by Musashi are designed for combat in all senses of the word.

"The true Way of sword fencing is the craft of defeating the enemy in a fight, and nothing other than this. If you attain and adhere to the wisdom of my strategy, you need never doubt that you will win." (Musashi, 1974:83)

It is often seen that fencing is about defence, but it is also important that offence is important, as can be seen above. The first part is very simple and reminds us that it is in defeating the enemy that the skill is shown. This part is also showing that fencing is about defeating opponents and nothing simpler. The second is also important as it shows the importance of adhering to what is taught by strategy to win. These principles are vital to combat, in all its forms. "Without the correct principles the fight cannot be won." (Musashi, 1974:87). This is the same for all combat.

Some may claim that the use of such decisive skills and the use of weapons are evil, but this is not true. Musashi addresses this concept linking it to what he calls the void. "In the void is virtue, and no evil. Wisdom has existence, principle has existence, the Way has existence, spirit is nothingness." (Musashi, 1974:95). This is the way of fencing. There is no evil, only principles of how things are.

In the application of the skills of fencing and strategy it is important that things will not always go our own way and as such, it is important that you can use the principles of strategy even when you are hard-pressed. You must learn to detach yourself and apply the principles to the situation and act on learned instinct. This is the only way that you will be able to change the situation and be able to counter-attack.

Timing is elemental to all forms of combat and it must be mastered to master the use of weapons. "There is timing in everything. Timing in strategy cannot be mastered without a great deal of practice." (Musashi, 1974:48). This is an extremely important element as it is present in all forms of combat. "In all skills and abilities there is timing." (Musashi, 1974:48). This is one element that cannot be escaped and Musashi says quite a lot about timing throughout his treatise.

"All things entail rising and falling timing. You must be able to discern this. In strategy there are various timing considerations. From the outset you must know the applicable timing and the inapplicable timing, and from among the large and small things and the fast and slow timings find the relevant timing,"
(Musashi, 1974:48)

Being able to tell the difference between fast and slow timing is important. It is less the timing itself and more how timing is applied that is important. The relevant timing is most important to the situation it being fast or slow. If we can master timing it will make it much easier to defeat the opponent, this also includes the ability to be able to change the timing as required.

"You win battles with the timing in the Void of the timing of cunning by knowing the enemies' timing, and thus using a timing which the enemy does not expect."
(Musashi, 1974:49)

In this Musashi talks about changing and breaking time and rhythm. If the fight progresses it will develop a rhythm, if you can break this rhythm unexpectedly you can attack. This is a sure way to be able to beat an enemy. A simple break in timing can disrupt the enemy enough for him to leave a hole in his defence, which can be exploited.

"Knowing the times means, if your ability is high, seeing right into things. If you are thoroughly conversant with strategy, you will recognise the enemy's intentions and thus have many opportunities to win." *(Musashi, 1974:74)*

Everything in strategy is based on time, and if you can see this clearly you will see what the enemy will do before he does it. This will open many opportunities for attacks. By the use of timing we can anticipate what the enemy will do and counter it before it has taken full effect, this can be extremely effective when executed properly. "Many things are said to be passed on. Sleepiness can be passed on, and yawning can be passed on. Time can be passed on also." (Musashi, 1974:77). This can be achieved in timing. You can influence the timing of a bout by movement and action or inaction. It is possible to slow the bout down and then as the opponent relaxes you attack quickly, catching them off-guard. Musashi goes into quite a bit of detail about this particular aspect and it is something that cannot be ignored.

> *"In single combat, start by making a show of being slow, then suddenly attack strongly. Without allowing him space for breath to recover from the fluctuation of spirit, you must grasp the opportunity to win."* (Musashi, 1974:77)

Change the timing in the bout to unsettle the opponent. When the opponent is unsettled you have an opportunity to attack. This disruption will unbalance the opponent and lead to opportunities to attack. It is important to realise that a sudden change in timing can upset the enemy's defence and allow for openings to be created, but it is also important that the motions are deliberate and not rushed. This is one place where true skill is demonstrated. "Really skilful people never get out of time, and are always deliberate, and never appear busy." (Musashi, 1974:91). Where the skills are used purposefully and deliberately a person can be seen as fast. This is the result of precise techniques rather than speed. Surprisingly, Musashi does not talk much about distance unless it is associated with timing, this is important to realise as one will affect the other and vice versa.

> *"The spirit of "Glue and Lacquer Emulsion Body" is to stick to the enemy and not separate from him. When you approach the enemy, stick firmly with your head, body and legs. People tend to advance their head and legs quickly, but their body lags behind."* (Musashi, 1974:62)

This is all about timing and distance and ensuring that the combatant moves as one so he's not stretched out and unstable. You need to move as one to ensure that you maintain accurate distance to the opponent. This ensures a solid attack and defence. It can be seen here that distance is mentioned, but not without a reference to timing, this is important, as it is difficult to understand one concept without referring in part to the other. To truly master combat and strategy it is important that the concepts of timing and distance are properly understood and that they can be both seen in action.

When weapons are considered some people prefer some weapons to others. In the case of rapier combatants some will prefer a longer weapon to an average length weapon because they believe that this will give them some advantage. Musashi addresses this idea and clearly sets down a principle of weapon preference.

> *"you can win with a long weapon, and yet you can also win with a short weapon. In short, the Way of the Ichi school is the spirit of winning, whatever the weapon and whatever its size."* (Musashi, 1974:46)

What Musashi is saying is that the use of the weapon is more important than its size. The important this is that you must know how to use the weapons accurately rather than relying on length or shortness. This is important, as there will be times when your weapon is longer or shorter than the opponent's. This does not mean that either opponent will necessarily win; what matters is how the weapon is used. Further to this particular principle, Musashi clearly states that you should make no real preference for weapons but study them all equally, and use those weapons, which you use best.

"You should not have a favourite weapon. To become over-familiar with one is as much a fault as not knowing it sufficiently well. You should not copy others, but use weapons which you can handle properly." (Musashi, 1974:48)

To focus on one weapon is to be blinded to others. Remember that knowing other weapons is part of the secret to defeating them. People will have their own preference for length and weight. Use the weapon, which is best suited to you. It is important that you should not be taken in by fads for excessively long weapons nor excessively short weapons this is vital. You must use the length and weight of weapon, which is best for you. There has always been debate about having a longer weapon and this providing some advantage. This, according to Musashi is a weak way of thinking.

"Some other schools have a liking for extra-long swords. From the point of view of my strategy these must be seen as weak schools. This is because they do not appreciate the principle of cutting the enemy by any means."
(Musashi, 1974:85)

The use of extra-long swords is about keeping the enemy at range. To truly fight we must also fight the enemy at close ranges. Thus being able to fight at all ranges and not being reliant on a maximum length weapon. It is of no use only to fight at range, as if the opponent closes in you will not be able to defend yourself nor attack when the moment presents itself. This applies equally to both long weapons and short ones.

"Some men think that if they go against many enemies with a shorter long sword they can unrestrictedly frisk around cutting in sweeps, but they have to parry cuts continuously and eventually become entangled."
(Musashi, 1974:87)

The shorter the weapon's thought is more defensive as the correct time has to be waited for, rather than taking the offensive. Defence must be maintained for a longer time with the shorter weapon to be able to close range. This is where the combatant with the shorter weapon will become entangled with the opponent and not able to attack. An even length weapon is the best one, which is suited to the particular combatant so that they are able to fight both at range and also close whenever either is necessary. In addressing weapons specifically, once the debate about length has been decided, it is necessary to examine how the weapons are used.

"The Way of strategy is the Way of nature. When you appreciate the power of nature, knowing the rhythm of any situation, you will be able to hit the enemy naturally and strike naturally." (Musashi, 1974:44)

Fencing is reliant on timing and distance. Once you appreciate this you will be able to see it in any situation and you will be able to use this to hit the enemy. It is important to be able to use time and distance to strike. The appropriate timing is that which is suited to the particular encounter, and to strike when the timing and distance is suited to it.

When we carry two weapons it is best to make use of both of them, otherwise it is useless to carry a second weapon, as it will only slow you down. This is an important consideration in the use of any combination of weapons or defensive items. "This is a truth: when you sacrifice your life, you must make fullest use of your weaponry. It is false not to do so," (Musashi, 1974:45). Use the weapons to their best advantage. You have two hands, utilise them both in attack and defence. This is especially important. If you carry two weapons, use them both. What also needs to be realised in this situation is that there is a time and a place for the weapons being used. "There is a time and a place for the use of weapons." (Musashi, 1974:47). This is specific. Certain weapons are best used at certain times. This applies to defensive as much as offensive items. The dagger can only be used at close range so trying to use it at range is useless. This is about knowing the weapons and how they are used most effectively.

> "Knowing the Way of the long sword means we can wield with two fingers the sword we usually carry. If we know the path of the sword well, we can wield it easily." (Musashi, 1974:56)

This is the same for the rapier. If the sword's balance is well known then it is easy to move. It also refers to not fighting the weapon when using it. Each weapon is balanced in its own particular way and it will want to move according to this balance. It is important that we allow the weapon to move, as it will and not to fight it. Fighting the balance of the weapon is useless and will not only tire you but also make the weapon more difficult to use. "If you try to wield the long sword quickly you will mistake the Way. To wield the long sword you must wield it calmly." (Musashi, 1974:57). It is important to use the weapon within its own characteristics. This applies to all weapons. You must wield the weapon calmly so that you remain in control of the weapon and use correct techniques. Let the sword follow the path that it dictates. This will make the movements of the weapon smooth. The balance of the weapon will dictate how it is best moved.

> "However you hold the sword it must be in such a way that it is easy to cut the enemy well, in accordance with the situation, the place and your relation to the enemy." (Musashi, 1974:58)

Essentially whatever ward you use should utilise the weapon effectively no matter what the opponent does. To do this you must hold the weapon correctly. The ward can be changed to suit the circumstances and how the combatant feels. Think through the techniques to the next step and do not use single actions, you must consider what the initial technique does for you.

When using the weapon it is also important to consider the techniques and executing them with conviction. Musashi refers to this in reference to the difference between the cut and the slash. The cut is decisive, the slash less so. This is considering the attack in its execution. A committed attack is much more effective than a responsive attack. The responsive attack must be followed by a committed attack, the first against a secondary target, and the second against a primary target. If you do not commit to the attack then it will never be effective. The ultimate idea with regard to this is Musashi's principle of the 'one cut'. "You can win with certainty with the spirit of "one cut"." (Musashi, 1974:66). One blow will seal the bout but you need to know how and where he blow must be delivered.

Clearly following on from the use of weapons and the idea of delivering a single blow to end an encounter is the concept of offence. This is something that Musashi discusses in much detail, as would be expected. One of the most important parts is that "cutting down the enemy is the Way of strategy, and there is no need of any refinements of it." (Musashi, 1974:88). What Musashi is saying here is that while there are many techniques that can be used against an opponent, it is the most effective method of defeating the opponent that is the best. This idea is further demonstrated, by his stressing the importance of taking to the attack and not waiting and staying on the defensive.

> *"we cannot get a decisive victory by cutting, with a "tee-dum tee dum" feeling, in the wake of the enemy's attacking long sword. We must defeat him at the start of his attack, in the spirit of treading him down with feet, so that he cannot rise again to the attack." (Musashi, 1974:74)*

It is difficult to gain victory while being on the defensive. You must attack the enemy at the beginning of his attack and take the initiative so he must stay on the defensive, and not let go. This particular idea of taking the lead in a conflict and not allowing the enemy time to react is something that Musashi emphasises repeatedly. This will be discussed more later on. In the same vein as this particular thought is the idea of not allowing the enemy a second attack, and keeping him on the defensive.

> *"You must achieve the spirit of not allowing the enemy to attack a second time. This is the spirit of forestalling in every sense. Once at the enemy, you should not aspire just to strike him, but to cling after the attack." (Musashi, 1974:74)*

Once you have defeated the enemy's attack, counter-attack and stay on the offensive. It is important that you attack and continue to attack until the enemy has been defeated. Give them no room to breathe, give them no room to attack a second time. This is clearly associated with the idea of recovery and not allowing the enemy to recover. This particular aspect is one, which Musashi emphasises repeatedly.

> *"In single combat, the enemy sometimes loses timing and collapses. If you let this opportunity pass, he may recover and not be so negligent thereafter. Fix your eye on the enemy's collapse, and chase him, attacking so that you do not let him recover." (Musashi, 1974:75)*

When you see a break in the enemy's timing, you must attack and not allow the enemy to recover the timing. Stay on the offensive and do not allow the enemy to recover. You must stay on top of him and crush him utterly. If this is not done he may recover and change the advantage. It is important that once the advantage of offence is gained that it is utilised and used to its maximum capacity. The enemy should be allowed no time to recover from the attack. "This means to crush the enemy regarding him as weak." (Musashi, 1974:80). This particular idea sounds particularly brutal, but it must be understood that underestimating the enemy, allowing him to recover gives him a chance to learn from the attack and possibly break through. It is important that the enemy is not allowed to recover otherwise he may beat you.

> "if the enemy is less skilful than yourself, if his rhythm is disorganised, or if he has fallen into evasive or retreating attitudes, we must crush him straight away, with no concern for his presence and without allowing him space for breath. It is essential to crush him all at once. The primary thing is not to let him recover his position even a little." (Musashi, 1974:80)

Musashi is talking about staying on top of the enemy and not allowing him to recover. Once the advantage is gained it should be used to utterly defeat the enemy. Do not draw back even a little, stay on the offensive. This must be done as soon as it is perceived that the enemy is on the retreat. Allowing the enemy to recover allows him to re-evaluate and possibly gain the offensive. It is important that this is not allowed.

One way to achieve this is through attacking secondary targets before the primary is attacked. Musashi states, "it is easy to win once the enemy collapses. This happens when you injure the "corners" of his body, and thus weaken him." (Musashi, 1974:78). "Injuring the corners", means weakening the enemy by attacking secondary targets. Once the enemy is reduced it is much easier to win than if you attack directly. It is important to follow the attack up in order to defeat him. While an attack to the body will defeat the opponent quickly, it is not easy to get to. If the enemy's hands are attacked first, it is then much easier to attack the body.

What is most interesting is that Musashi spends very little time on defence. His primary focus is on the attack. It could easily be said that from Musashi's point of view a good offence is the best defence. The principles of defence need to be extracted from the others, but what he does say about defence, is in what he calls the "Body of a Rock". This idea refers to having a defence so solid it is like a rock and being so dedicated to doing what you are doing that you cannot be moved. Clearly defence is important to Musashi, but only to wait for the opportune moment to attack the opponent.

While it is of vital importance to know what we can do, it is also important to know what the opponent is able to do. This concept of knowing the opponent is something that Musashi spends some time on. "It is difficult to know yourself if you do not know others." (Musashi, 1974:44). As a combatant, you need to broaden your research, learn the way others train and fight. This will assist you to know what works for you. You will also know how they fight and be able to defeat them. "In strategy you must know the Ways of other schools," (Musashi, 1974:85). This way you will know their techniques and be able to use this as an advantage.

> "Small people must be completely familiar with the spirit of large people, and large people must be familiar with the spirit of small people. Whatever your size, do not be misled by the reactions of your own body." (Musashi, 1974:54)

As can be seen from above, it is not only important to know the combatant in a specific sense, but also in a general sense. By spirit, Musashi is referring to attributes, advantages and limitations. You must be able to see what another will move like and not be misled by the reactions of your body. You must learn to control your body so that you will react in accordance with your training, rather than your automatic reflexes.

Once you know the enemy's techniques and how they will move, it will be much easier to take advantage of the situation. "Discern the enemy's capability and, knowing your own strong points, "cross the ford" at the advantageous place," (Musashi, 1974:73). Use the situation to your advantage when the timing and distance is right for it. To know this timing it is essential that you know the opponent. This means that you will be able to attack him at the right moment. "To cross at a ford means to attack the enemy's weak point, and to put yourself in an advantageous position." (Musashi, 1974:73). In the essence of knowing the opponent it is important how you view the opponent. This self-knowledge is essential. How you consider the enemy is important. You must consider his position. If you consider your enemy to be superior, he will defeat you. Have confidence in your own abilities.

Once you truly know the opponent you will anticipate what he will do and counter it. This is about knowing the enemy's intention. Sometimes it is important to discover the enemy's intention. If you cannot see what the enemy's intention is, make a feint so that he will react. From what you are shown you should see his intention and from this you can counter it and win. Where you can see the enemy's intention you can attack it and defeat it before he has time to use it. More to the point, as Musashi refers to it as 'The Commander Knows the Troops', once you know the enemy's intention you will control him and force him to create openings in his own defence.

As important as knowing the opponent is knowing the terrain upon which you will fight. "Examine your environment." (Musashi, 1974:70). It is important to examine the field, especially in the case of broken ground. Through this you will take advantage of the environment. Use the environment to your advantage. In the case of a tournament, examine the field for where it may be unstable so that you can stay away from these areas. Musashi talks about using the environment to the combatant's advantage.

> *"When the fight comes, always endeavour to chase the enemy around to your left side. Chase him towards awkward places, and try to keep him with his back to awkward places."* (Musashi, 1974:70)

This is the best way to use the environment to your advantage, corner the opponent and chase him into inconvenient positions. Establish a dominant position from which to attack. It is important that you control the environment. If possible force the opponent into places where he cannot move easily. To do this it is important to have taken the lead in the combat. It is much more difficult to control the opponent if you are reactive and he is active.

> *"In contests of strategy it is bad to be led about by the enemy. You must always be able to lead the enemy about. Obviously the enemy will also be thinking of doing this, but he cannot forestall you if you do not allow him to come out."* (Musashi, 1974:72)

Take and keep the initiative. Lead the enemy about and keep him reactive while you stay active. Stop the enemy's attack before it is complete, pre-empt the attack. Further to this, once you have taken the initiative it is important to keep it. Keep the enemy on the defensive. ""To Hold Down a Pillow" means not allowing the enemy's head to rise." (Musashi, 1974:72). This is referring to initiative and not allowing the opponent to take the initiative but to keep it.

Once you have gained the initiative and the lead you must do everything to ensure that the enemy cannot take it from you. "The important thing in strategy is to suppress the enemy's useful actions but allow his useless actions. However doing this alone is defensive." (Musashi, 1974:73). In essence you must take control of the situation and block only those attacks, which are potentially effective. Once you have gained control you can manipulate the situation to your advantage. Only once you have done this is it possible to win.

It is only once that some advantage has been gained that it is possible to win a bout. It is important that this advantage is sought through all means possible. "By "to strive for height" is meant, when you close with the enemy, to strive with him for superior height without cringing." (Musashi, 1974:62). This is less striving for physical height and more for advantage. You should close with confidence and place yourself in a good position to attack. This will force openings and allow for an attack. Close combat is one situation where it is vital to have confidence and some sort of advantage over the opponent. Without this element, the encounter will go badly.

> *"When you have come to grips and are striving together with the enemy, and you realise that you cannot advance, you "soak in" and become one with the enemy. You can win by applying a suitable technique while you are mutually entangled."*
> *(Musashi, 1974:78)*

This is focusing on close-quarter combat where it is difficult to use the point. When you become engaged at close range you must move as the enemy does to achieve the advantage. Only by achieving "priority" can you be able to attack successfully. It is important that the point is abandoned in this situation, as there is no advantage gained by its use. Without the correct use of weapon and tactics it is difficult to win at close range, there is no room for error. "What is mean by "mingling" is the spirit of advancing and becoming engaged with the enemy, and not withdrawing even one step." (Musashi, 1974:80). Attack the enemy at his strong point and then attack another at his periphery. Engage with the enemy and fight through him. Stay engaged with the enemy without withdrawing. This sort of attitude is the most elemental for close combat. Change the point of attack to keep the opponent on the defensive. Also, you must stay engaged once the advantage is gained and use it to the best of your ability.

> *""To release four hands" is used when you and the enemy are contending with the same spirit, and the issue cannot be decided. Abandon this spirit and win through an alternative resource."*
> *(Musashi, 1974:76)*

There are times in combat where you will arrive at an impasse with your opponent. When you and your opponent use the same techniques it is difficult to win. In this situation you need to change tact to win. You must apply this when your techniques do not seem to be working against the opponent. The ability to change tactics when required is vital as it is useless to continue with a tactic that does not work.

"we can confuse the enemy by attacking with varied techniques when the change arises. Feint a thrust or cut, or make the enemy think you are going to close with him, and when he is confused you can easily win."
(Musashi, 1974:79)

Varied techniques are the key. If you change your approach constantly the opponent will not know how to respond, this will make him unsettled and much easier to beat. Where possible, change the technique as you are fighting. Changing tact will also keep the opponent on the defensive, as he will not know how to respond, this means that he will not be able to attack. This will make it much easier to lead the opponent. "The "mountain-sea" spirit means that it is bad to repeat the same thing several times when fighting the enemy." (Musashi, 1974:80). If your attack fails, it is useless to repeat the same attack. If you do your enemy will gain your measure and counter you easily. Change your method of attack. Changing tactics is most important where you are faced with an opponent of equal skill, if you become deadlocked and stay that way, the outcome will be more of luck than anything. It is vital in this situation to be able to change tactics.

"To renew, when we are deadlocked with the enemy, means that without changing our circumstance we change our spirit and with through a different technique."
(Musashi, 1974:81)

Where there is no possible resolution we must change our approach to win. This is especially the case in close work, you must change to break a deadlock but keep the advantage. This also applies at range. To change tactics you must know more than one set of techniques. Vary what you learn so that you can change your approach. This is where it is important not to become too specialised, "if you learn "indoor" techniques, you will think narrowly and forget the true Way. Thus you will have difficulty in actual encounters." (Musashi, 1974:47). The way it is trained is how it will be used. f too much specialisation is had you will not adapt to different situations. Remember to take into account other aspects and forms of the art, especially in training.

There are various combat principles, which have been presented here. It is important that each one of these principles influences Musashi's techniques. To really understand a particular technique, we need to know what it is based upon, and this is found in the combat principles. Each individual must refine the general work down to this set of principles so that the essence of the techniques is understood and the reason that the types of techniques are presented.

TECHNIQUES
Basic Techniques

Now that Musashi's combat principles have been established to some degree, it is now possible to examine the techniques that he advises the swordsman use. Through this investigation it will also be possible to see how these techniques are useful for the rapier combatant. In some instances the ideas presented will have to be somewhat modified to suit the rapier rather than the Japanese sword. What will also be noted is that in certain circumstances these changes to the techniques will not be required. This will demonstrate some of the similarities between the Japanese sword and the rapier. It is best to examine these techniques in the same order that they would be taught. Hence the stance will be examined first.

"Adopt a stance with the head erect, neither hanging down, nor looking up, nor twisted. Your forehead and the space between your eyes should not be wrinkled. Do not roll your eyes nor allow them to blink, but slightly narrow them. ... features composed, ... Hold the line of the rear of your neck straight: ... Lower both shoulders and, without the buttocks jutting out, put strength into your legs from the knees to the tips of your toes. Brace your abdomen so that you do not bend at the hips." (Musashi, 1974:54)

The stance suggested by Musashi can be adopted and used effectively by the rapier combatant. The same principles apply for both stances used in rapier combat and that suggested above. It is a very settled stance. What should be noticed is that he makes the position solid, but still allows movement in the legs. This position is very relaxed. An interesting point with regard to the stance is that Musashi believes it should be normal for the combatant.

"In all forms of strategy, it is necessary to maintain the combat stance in everyday life and make your everyday stance your combat stance. You must research this well." (Musashi, 1974:54)

The stance must be normal to be effective. See where you are comfortable and apply this. The principles for both the everyday stance and the combat stance should be the same. This requires research to find the correct stance. You must be relaxed in your stance, as you will adopt it many times, it is important that it feels normal for you.

"Placing a great deal of importance on the attitudes of the long sword is a mistaken way of thinking." (Musashi, 1974:88). While it cannot be denied that the stance is important, but they are only as useful as what follows them, as such the stances should not be learnt in isolation. Once the stances are known, it will be much easier for you to break through the opponent's guard; "you must move the opponent's attitude. Attack where his spirit is lax, throw him into confusion, irritate and terrify him." (Musashi, 1974:89). Once you know what a stance protects and where it is open you can counter it. It is impossible to achieve this without knowing how the stances are used and what techniques they lend themselves to. "Whatever attitude you are in, do not be conscious of making the attitude; think only of cutting." (Musashi, 1974:56). Do not focus on the ward or guard, more on how you will use the weapon from the guard. As with the commonality of terza in rapier combat, so too does the katana have a common guard or attitude as Musashi calls them, "The Middle attitude is the heart of attitudes." (Musashi, 1974:56).

One of the elements of the stance Musashi mentioned was how to hold the face. He actually has quite a bit to say about this, he places great importance on the gaze of the combatant and how it is utilised. "The gaze should be large and broad. This is the twofold gaze "Perception and Sight". Perception is strong and sight weak." (Musashi, 1974:54). You can see and you can perceive, the first is weaker than the second. You need to be able to take in the entire picture. While you can see something it may not be perceived and if not it will not be taken not of.

Looking is as important as what to look at, while some advise to look at the weapon, Musashi says to keep track of it but not to focus on it. "It is important in strategy to know the enemy's sword and not to be distracted by insignificant movements of his sword. You must study this." (Musashi, 1974:54). You need to be aware of the opponent's weapon but not be distracted by insignificant movements. This takes practice. It is necessary to know where the opponent's weapon is but not be transfixed by it. In this it is necessary to take in the whole picture at once and this is not easy to learn. "It is necessary in strategy to be able to look to both sides without moving the eyeballs. You cannot master this ability quickly." (Musashi, 1974:55). You need to observe the opponent completely by simply looking forward. This is not an easy thing to master. This is especially important where two weapons are involved.

> *"In single combat you must not fix your eyes on details. As I said before, if you fix your eyes on details and neglect important things, your spirit will become bewildered, and victory will escape you." (Musashi, 1974:90)*

If you fix your eyes you will respond to even small movements of the enemy and will not know what his true intention is. If this happens, you will become confused and will not be able to defeat the opponent. This is very important, that the eyes should not stay focussed on one element while fighting. "If you fix the eyes ... your spirit can become confused and your strategy thwarted." (Musashi, 1974:89). If you keep your eyes fixed you will miss important details in the periphery.

Once the correct stance is known, next is the important element of knowing how to hold the weapon properly. It is important to realise that if the weapon is not held properly then it will not be able to be used properly. Musashi has some points to mention with regard to the grip.

> *"Grip the long sword with a rather floating feeling in your thumb and forefinger, with the middle finger neither tight not slack, and with the last two fingers tight. It is bad to have play in your hands." (Musashi, 1974:55)*

The grip of Musashi is useful especially with regard to the first three fingers. The difference with the rapier is that the last two fingers should be loose. Some play is also useful. The best grip is firm but not tight. It can be seen here in the difference between the grips that how the weapon is gripped is particular to the weapon itself. What is interesting, however, is that many of the principles that apply to one apply to another. "Generally, I dislike fixedness in both long swords and hands. Fixedness means a dead hand. Pliability is a living hand. You must bear this in mind." (Musashi, 1974:55). This refers to having the hands too tight. Some movement in the hands is necessary to wield the sword. This is interesting as it somewhat contradicts what Musashi stated previously. What is most important is that the principles of the grip can be used. This is the same with footwork.

> "With the tips of your toes somewhat floating, tread firmly with your heels. Whether you move fast or slow, with large or small steps, your feet must always move as in normal walking." (Musashi, 1974:55)

Musashi's approach to footwork is useful. He is referring to keeping the feet fluid in motion and to move them naturally. With regard to large or small steps, this more refers to the individual and how they move normally. What Musashi is saying is that the footwork should be like normal movement. This is clearly demonstrated throughout what he says about footwork.

> "Yin-yang foot means not moving one foot. It means moving your feet left-right and right-left when cutting, withdrawing, or warding off a cut. You should not move one foot preferentially." (Musashi, 1974:56)

This encourages the use of both feet in movement; that in each movement both feet should be used. It also makes an important link between the feet and sword motion and how they are connected. It is important to be able to move off both feet. This element of natural foot movement is extremely important to Musashi, "the footwork does not change. I always walk as I usually do in the street. You must never lose control of your feet." (Musashi, 1974:90). Essentially what Musashi is saying is to move normally and move your feet according to what is required at the particular moment in the fight.

With regard to specific techniques, Musashi discusses many and describes how they should be used to the swordsman's advantage. One of these sets of techniques is known as his five approaches in which he describes five different ways to attack the enemy. What is also interesting is that he starts each one from a different position.

> "1. The first approach is the Middle attitude. Confront the enemy with the point of your sword against his face. When he attacks, dash his sword to the right and "ride" it. Or, when the enemy attacks, deflect the point of this sword by hitting downwards, keep your long sword where it is, and as the enemy renews the attack cut his arms from below." (Musashi, 1974:57)

Keep the sword point toward the opponent's face, as the enemy attacks beat his sword to the right and pressure it. The second attack is to deflect the point of the enemy's sword by hitting downward and keep your sword down, as he attacks again attack upward into the arms. This would be best executed from terza. These attacks would most likely result in a great deal of close work and would rely on the combatant knowing exactly what they are doing.

> "2. In the second approach with the long sword, from the Upper attitude cut the enemy just as he attacks. If the enemy evades the cut, keep your sword where it is and, scooping up from below, cut him as he renews the attack. It is possible to repeat the cut from here." (Musashi, 1974:57)

From a high ward attack in stesso tempo using an imbrocatta. If you miss, keep the sword low and attack upward as he attacks again. The attack can be repeated from here. It is important to know timing for this to work. The opponent's sword will have to be met at the correct time for this one to work well.

> "3. In the third approach, adopt the Lower attitude, anticipating scooping up. When the enemy attacks, hit his hands from below. As you do so, he may try to hit your sword down. If this is the case, cut his upper arm(s) horizontally with a feeling of "crossing". This means that from the Lower attitudes you hit the enemy at the instant he attacks." (Musashi, 1974:58)

From terza, with the point low, attack the opponent's hands as he attacks. If he tries to deflect you, half-disengage and thrust or cut at his arm. These attacks are executed in stesso tempo. It is important that the counter-attack at the hand is performed at the same time as the opponent's attack, and the second attack should be prepared for just in case.

> "4. In this fourth approach, adopt the Left Side attitude. As the enemy attacks, hit his hands from below. If as you hit his hands he attempts to dash down your sword, with the feeling of hitting his hands, parry the path of his long sword and cut across from your shoulder." (Musashi, 1974:58)

Adopt a quarta guard, as the enemy attacks; hit his hands from below in stesso tempo. If he attempts to parry your attack, use the momentum of the parry to half-disengage, parry his sword and attack his upper body or cut at his neck. It is important to notice that with this as most of these descriptions, Musashi has a back-up plan just in case the opponent counters the first movement.

> "5. In the fifth approach, the sword is in the Right Side attitude. In accordance with the enemy's attack, cross your long sword from below at the side to the Upper attitude. Then cut straight from above." (Musashi, 1974:58)

Adopt a seconda or broad ward, as the enemy attacks bring the sword across low, parrying the opponent and then rolling up to prima. Then attack from above. These techniques need to be done in consideration with the opponent's timing. Footwork will change the motion and change some thrusts to cuts and vice versa. Musashi does not detail the footwork used in these encounters. What is most interesting is that Musashi does fill in some of the responses from the opponent possible. This is an important consideration in any preparation for an attack.

Forestalling

To forestall means to anticipate, or to guard against while attacking. Musashi gives three methods of forestalling the enemy. This requires that the combatant is able to anticipate the enemy's attack and then be able to counter it.

"In strategy, you have effectively won when you forestall the enemy, so you must train well to attain this." (Musashi, 1974:72). Forestalling essentially means stopping the enemy in his tracks, this requires timing and practice to find the right timing. If you can forestall the enemy you can easily win while he is reactive and you are active. The three methods for forestalling the enemy are made at different times during the encounter. "The first is to forestall him by attacking." (Musashi, 1974:71). This means to attack the opponent and set him up, manipulate the position. Musashi calls this Ken No Sen. He states that,

"you can win quickly by taking the lead, it is one of the most important things in strategy. ... You must make the best of the situation, see through the enemy's spirit so that you grasp his strategy and defeat him." *(Musashi, 1974:71)*

Stay calm and attack the enemy before he can move. You can also move in quickly but keep some in reserve for when he attacks. Lastly, attack in smooth motion and when you gain the correct distance speed up and beat the opponent with speed. The last is to attack and pressure the enemy without letting up. In this particular technique, the combatant must move first, but it is not always necessary to attack first. It is also possible to forestall the enemy as he attacks. "Another method is to forestall him as he attacks." (Musashi, 1974:71). Essentially to wait for the attack and block it before it takes effect, this particular technique is referred to by Musashi as Tai No Sen. As the enemy attacks, move away then quickly attack. Or as the enemy attacks, attack strongly to disrupt his timing and take this advantage in order to win.

The third method follows the third timing, when the two combatants attack at the same time. "The other method is when you and the enemy attack together." (Musashi, 1974:71). Use initiative and the force of both attacks to stop the opponent, this technique is known as Tai Tai No Sen. When the enemy attacks quickly, attack strongly aiming for his weak point and strongly defeat him. If the enemy attacks calmly observe his time and motion, join the time and motion then move quickly and strongly into the attack. It is essential that the combatant know his own timing and the timing of the opponent to achieve these methods of forestalling.

Timing

This particular element of timing is something, which is reiterated over and over through Musashi's techniques. It is clear that timing is one of the vital elements that the combatant must know in order to win. ""In One Timing" means, when you have closed with the enemy, to hit him as quickly and directly as possible," (Musashi, 1974:59). Once you have closed within range, strike quickly before the opponent has time to react. This must be done in an instant. It is important in all close encounters that the initiative is taken to win.

The idea of timing can be used in different ways to defeat the opponent. One particular skill is to break time. "When you attack and the enemy retreats, as you see him tense you must feint a cut. Then, as he relaxes, follow up and hit him." (Musashi, 1974:59). This technique is "breaking time". The opponent reacts to the initial movement and this is followed by the real attack. Most feints work in this manner. It is also important to remember the timing of the body and hands.

> "Also "the long sword in place of the body". Usually we move the body and the sword at the same time to cut the enemy. However, according to the enemy's cutting method, you can dash against him with your body first, and afterwards cut with the sword." (Musashi, 1974:61)

This is all about timing and force. Usually the timing is with body and sword. But you can force the blade aside with forward motion and then be able to attack. Consider ways to achieve this. One method, which can be used, is to use a pressure glide or similar action, in which forward motion and pressure from the blade is used to force the opponent's blade aside.

It is useless to apply force when the combatant is not fully committed to the attack. To achieve the required pressure for the attack, the combatant must commit totally to the attack. This must also be done with an element of calm.

> "when the enemy attacks and you also decide to attack, hit him with your body, and hit him with your spirit, and hit from the Void with your hands, accelerating strongly." (Musashi, 1974:60)

This is less an actual attack and more about the response to the situation. It is important to act calmly and not get flustered. It is also about putting everything behind the attack to increase its speed. The only way to achieve this is through committing to the attack. How the combatant also responds to the opponent's attack is important, to achieve a good counter a firm commitment must be made to the attack.

Close Combat
When actions are performed with the blade, the combatant must not stretch himself out. This leads to inaccuracy in the technique and can also leave the combatant's blade in a vulnerable position where the blade may be manipulated by the opponent as such it is important that the blade is kept close to the centre of mass. "The Chinese Monkey's Body is the spirit of not stretching out your arms. The spirit is to get in quickly, without in the least extending your arms," (Musashi, 1974: 62). This technique is about not engaging only with the blade but keeping it close to the body. This is essential in defence. In offence it is about gaining control solidly before attacking. With the weight of the body behind it, this makes a solid control of the opponent's weapon.

> "When the enemy attacks and you also attack with the long sword, you should go in with a sticky feeling and fix your long sword against the enemy's as you receive his cut. The spirit of stickiness is not hitting very strongly, but hitting so that the long swords do not separate easily." (Musashi, 1974:62)

This technique is about control and feeling through the blade. Once the blades come in contact the "stickiness" forces the blades to stay in contact in which control and feeling is gained. While the blades are engaged it is possible to gain control so that you can attack. It is also the case that while the blades are engaged as such, it will be much more difficult for the opponent to attack.

Defence

What is most interesting is that Musashi focuses mainly on offence rather than defence, and this is an interesting point. With regard to defence he mentions various methods about how to parry. The first is a beat parry by forcing the blade forward forcing the opponent's blade to the right, much in the same way as a beat-pressure glide. The second is to beat the opponent's sword back towards him on a straight line. The third is to make a counter-attack at the opponent's face, voiding the attacking blade. It can be seen that even in defence, Musashi is thinking about offence and how to turn the defence into an offensive move. Musashi also refers to what he calls a "smacking parry" this is also much like a beat.

> *"By "smacking parry" is meant that when you clash swords with the enemy, you must meet his attacking cut on your long sword with a tee-dum, tee-dum rhythm, smacking his sword and cutting him." (Musashi, 1974:64)*

He says to meet the opponent's sword in a rhythm. If you beat and beat again you will easily be able to attack. This will work in much the same way as a beat attack, keeping your point on-line with the second beat. The second beat should position your blade for an attack. What must be noted in this example is that it is not simply a parry, but also to set the opponent up for an attack.

Attack

Musashi describes several different cutting techniques. What is most important about all of them is that they have a time and a place to be used. It is also important to realise that each has its individual purpose. If the wrong cut is used for the wrong purpose then there is no hope of success in the encounter. The first cut is the Flowing Water Cut.

The Flowing Water Cut is used when you are close and there is blade-to-blade contact. Musashi is talking about the enemy withdrawing and then stepping in to cut on the pass. This is especially so if the opponent forces the blades apart. It can be seen here that this cut would be useless when the opponent's blades are not in contact. The Fire and Stones Cut is an attack of force. It is designed to force the blade through the enemy's defence to attack him. Clearly this needs to be done with speed and force combined.

"The Red Leaves Cut means knocking down the enemy's long sword. The spirit should be getting control of his sword." (Musashi, 1974:61). Unlike the Fire and Stones it is designed to push the opponent's blade downward, rather than force it away, the object in this case is firstly to remain in control. Once the control has been established over the opponent's sword more pressure can be applied to force the opponent to drop their sword.

> *"If you then beat down the point of his sword with a sticky feeling, he will necessarily drop the sword. If you practise this cut it becomes easy to make the enemy drop his sword." (Musashi, 1974:61)*

The Continuous Cut is less of an actual cutting technique and more about the use of the weapon. It is designed to remind the combatant that there is always a chance to attack multiple targets. It is important to remember that a thrust can be changed into a cut and that every time an edge or point passes by the opponent there is potential for an attack. It is important to interpret what Musashi has to say and then apply it as it suits the form of combat. The Body Strike is a perfect example of this.

"The Body Strike means to approach the enemy through a gap in his guard. The spirit is to strike him with your body." (Musashi, 1974:63). While bodily contact is not allowed in this manner, the technique can still be used blade on blade. Approach and engage the blades in a strong position, from here force forwards into and through the opponent. This will have a similar effect to the technique described by Musashi. It is important to be able to apply the techniques with the resources available.

> "To stab at the face means, when you are in confrontation with the enemy, that your spirit is intent on stabbing at his face, following the line of the blade with the point of your long sword." *(Musashi, 1974:63)*

The description above is very similar to a stesso tempo attack to the face. The following part indicates that the attack will intimidate the opponent and allow you to gain control of the situation and that this will lead to openings to attack.

The idea of intimidating the opponent into breaking him is something that Musashi places a great deal of emphasis on. He states that, "you must use the advantage of taking the enemy unawares by frightening him with your body, long sword, or voice, to defeat him." (Musashi, 1974:78). For the rapier combatant, one method of achieving this is through the use of the *appel*, a stomping movement with the foot. This fright can also be achieved through other quick movements, which will startle the enemy.

> "You must stab the enemy's breast without letting the point of your long sword waver, showing the ridge of the blade square-on, and with the spirit of deflecting his long sword. The spirit of this principle is often useful when we become tired" *(Musashi, 1974:64)*

This is not only about thrusting in an easy fashion against the largest target using the blade to deflect the opponent, but also the use of the correct attack for the situation. It is easier to hit a large target, hence the use of this when tired. The idea of deflecting his long sword is about making sure that the thrust goes through to the enemy cleanly and is not intercepted. What is also important is to think about how the enemy will respond to an attack.

> ""Scold" means that, when the enemy tries to counter-cut as you attack, you counter-cut again from below as if thrusting at him, trying to hold him down. With very quick timing you cut, scolding the enemy." *(Musashi, 1974:64)*

This technique can be used when a beat is used against you. When he beats you, revive your attack by first blocking his weapon and then beating against it hard. Then you will be able to attack. If you consider how your enemy will respond to a particular attack, then you will be in a position to defend against it and also counter it. This is where swordplay truly reveals itself in a combatant, the ability to think about techniques like chess moves.

Melee

Melees always change the dynamics of an encounter. In a single encounter there is only one opponent to worry about in a melee there are more. This requires particular techniques in order to be able to deal with them. Musashi describes the basic techniques for dealing with more than one opponent.

> "The spirit is to chase the enemies around from side to side, ... Observe their attacking order, and go to meet those who attack first. Sweep your eyes around broadly, carefully examining the attacking order, and cut left and right alternately with your swords. Waiting is bad. ... Whatever you do, you must drive the enemy together," *(Musashi, 1974:65)*

In melee do not wait to be attacked but attack those who come first. Attack with both hands attacking both sides alternately. Push the enemies together and attack on their edges so that they are restricted. Break from the encirclement by attacking through them.

CONCLUSION

The object of this investigation was to introduce Musashi's techniques to the rapier combatant and demonstrate how they are useful. The first part of the document deals with Musashi's philosophy of combat. This was followed closely by the combat principles and specific techniques, which Musashi advises. It is important that each one of these steps was taken to gain a more full idea of the basis for Musashi's techniques. It would have been less useful to focus purely on the techniques, as this would have left no basis to understand what the techniques were based upon.

The view of this document was quite broad to enable the best use of Musashi's techniques and to gain the best understanding of what he was alluding to in his treatise. It is important to realise that even though Musashi's techniques focus on the use of the Japanese sword, the rapier combatant can use these techniques, as there is a common element amongst all forms of sword combat.

With regard to Musashi's philosophy of sword combat, it is important to see that many of the ideas presented in this section can be applied to the use of the rapier in rapier combat. It is also important that these philosophical ideas were presented in the initial stage so that his combat principles may be better understood, and therefore a better appreciation of his techniques can be gained.

It can be easily seen in Musashi's combat principles, as they have been presented, do cross over to rapier combat, and many of the same principles apply to both. The prime example of this is in the discussion of timing and distance, which are elemental to all sword combat. The other principles, which he raises such as the size and use of the weapon, are also equally applicable to rapier combat as they are to the use of the katana. It is important that these principles are completely understood before the techniques are addressed otherwise it would be much more difficult to see how they apply, and to apply them also.

In addressing Musashi's techniques, it was important to look at particular selections of techniques together due to their commonalities and their basis. For example, it was important to look at the basic techniques before moving on to more complex ones so that a firm basis may be established in the understanding of the techniques that are being suggested. Clearly it was important to look at these techniques together to get an overall picture of the techniques being presented. It is then up to the rapier combatant to understand how these techniques can be applied in the use of the rapier. Some suggestions were made as to how these techniques could be used, but it is also important for the individual to figure how they could be used also.

The aim of this particular document was to broaden the perspective of the reader and make them more aware of the universal nature of sword techniques, specifically between the rapier and the katana, and as a whole. It is important that sword combat cannot be investigated in a vacuum, but must take into account the universal principles. This will also enable the combatant to investigate useful techniques from seemingly vastly differing weapons and to apply them to the use of the rapier. Useful techniques for the use of the rapier can be more easily seen in weapons of similar form, such as the foil or epee, but it is also important to realise that other weapons such as the katana and longsword can also be used equally effectively.

The *Art* of Combat

INTRODUCTION

Art and what it is has been a question which has plagued theorists, and philosophers, for many years and no doubt will continue to plague them as art changes and changes again. This article addresses the idea about the art being found in different places and namely in the combat manuals of the medieval and Renaissance periods. These manuals depict not only the combat styles of the period but also the dress and also the artistic styles of the periods in which they were first written.

A BROADER SEARCH FOR ART

In the search for the art of the medieval and Renaissance period most people go to the typical sources, examining known artists of the period. Names such as Da Vinci, Michelangelo, Giotto and Dürer others are very well known for their art, some of which have become famous and stayed as such even into our own period to become recognised, at least throughout western countries. Art can also be found in other sources. Manuscripts of the period are one good example; another is the combat manuals of the period, a source which is often overlooked in the search for art.

Examples of the art of which I speak can be found as early as the fifteenth century and indeed earlier an example of this can be found in Figure 1 [12].

Figure 1: Fiore dei Liberi

---

12 http://www.getty.edu/art/collection/objects/132276/fiore-furlan-dei-liberi-da-premariacco-decorated-text-page-italian-about-1410/

Figure 2: by Albrecht Dürer

This is a page out of a manual from 1410 written by Fiore dei Liberi. Now many Western Martial Artists will know of this manual and will know of the art which can be found within it. However for them it is the application of the techniques which are present rather than the artwork which is more significant for them. The artwork which is present and the skill it took to present such art cannot be denied. The gold-leaf in the letters alone on this page along with the flowing script allow this page to be deserving of the title of "art" let alone the detail of the art which it contains.

THE *MARTIAL* ARTIST

What is even more interesting is that well-known artists of the period even dabbled in the martial arts as well. It is well known that Benvenuto Cellini an Italian artist of some note was involved in at one significant duel in his history in which he killed a man. What is less known is that the renowned artist Albrecht Dürer actually wrote and did the art for a fencing manual of his own "Oplodidaskalia sive Armorvm Tractandorvm Meditatio Alberti Dvreri" or the MS 26-232. This is a single page out of the manual[13], is presented in Figure 2.

The links have been included with the images, in the footnotes, both for referential purposes and also so that you are easily able to follow the links to their sources. This image not only shows the techniques from the manual, but also presents dress from the period. These images of combat, while directed at the martial artist should be examined more deeply for detail as to what other information that they can give.

SIGNIFICANCE OF AUTHORSHIP

The significance of the authorship of this manual is not only that respected artists were involved in the arts of combat themselves, but were also interested and invested enough that they would use their art to represent it in print, not a small prospect in the period. Indeed artists were put on retainer by men of note so that martial deeds could be recorded, and also that commissions made of the theorists of the period could be reproduced with significant quality. One need only examine the images which have been presented. While Dürer may have been an artist most of the masters were not and would have commissioned artists to reproduce their works for them, a significant investment.

---

13   https://wiktenauer.com/wiki/File:MS_26-232_85r.png

CONCLUSION

The martial arts of the medieval and Renaissance periods have and are being revived by people devoted to their arts, mostly in the search for instructions as to the use of arms. More and more of these manuals are discovered and investigations made into them as time goes by. As the arts of combat are revived by the martial artists, mainly through the discovery and exploration of manuals and manuscripts of the period, so too should the art which is present in such manuals and manuscripts be recognised for the artwork which is present in them even if the subject is a little distasteful to some. From the martial artists' point of view also, the art which is present in the manuals which they are using, must also be recognised and the manual recognised as a significant document and artwork, not merely an instructional manual. The same can be said for those who research art of the same periods, investigations into martial manuals of the periods should be made to recognise the art which is contained within the documents which have been produced.

Documentable Combinations: A Discussion of the Rapier and Cane

DISCLAIMER:

This discussion is a discussion about the standard forms used in rapier combat within the SCA; as such the discussion will be more focussed on the conventions and rules of the SCA rather than any other organised form of combat. The discussion is not encouraging the removal of any combination of weapons or form from combat due to their documentable or non-documentable nature. Something can be learnt from all forms regardless. This is designed to be a discussion of an intellectual nature exploring what is and is not available with regard to the documentation available and what we as fencers can imply or infer from what is available to make such undocumented forms legitimate.

SEVEN STANDARD COMBINATIONS

In SCA Heavy Rapier which is the standard form of rapier combat used in Australia, with the adjunct of Cut-and-Thrust Combat being an additional form of combat. Within the standard form of Heavy Rapier there are seven recognised "standard" combinations being: single rapier, rapier and gauntlet, rapier and dagger, case of rapier, rapier and buckler, rapier and cloak, and rapier and cane or baton. This is not to imply that other forms do not exist or indeed are used. These are the seven recognised as "standard" for SCA Heavy Rapier purposes. As time goes on and other weapons are discovered and used more forms are introduced, but the seven remain as the standard ones.

DOCUMENTATION

Documentation is available for all but the rapier and baton combination within the SCA period. The single rapier is the standard one which most theorists begin with or at least appears somewhere in their work; almost as popular as the single rapier is rapier and dagger, which is mentioned by most including Capo Ferro and Fabris to mention only two. Rapier and gauntlet is mentioned by Saviolo, and Silver, if only in passing. Though Saviolo's single rapier does focus on the use of the off-hand in defence as primary the adjunct of a gauntlet is expected. Case of Rapier is mentioned in di Grassi and also Agrippa, as is rapier and cloak. Finally rapier and buckler is mentioned in di Grassi and even earlier in Marozzo. This presents a true glossing over of the theorists for these forms as they are represented in these and more.

RAPIER AND CANE: PLAUSIBLE

Arguments for the use of the rapier and cane can be found in the simple idea of an item found at hand placed in the off-hand. It may not be a specific cane but a stick or other object. Indeed even a rolling pin would suffice in this particular form to be useful. Turning further to the plausibility of the combination is the idea of the baton and its use by constabulary. The final argument for its use is with the walking cane which may or may not be a post sixteenth-century affectation of gentlemen of the period. With these merely presented while not clearly documented, or at least in my own research, the rapier and cane combination is at least a plausible combination.

"A DOCUMENTABLE FORM"

The question we must ask ourselves with regard to the documentation of how a weapon or weapon combination is used is what we define as suitable documentation. There are primary and secondary documents which present evidence for particular forms, and in these instances the primary is always better, however good secondary sources can also be useful. Further to this we can, as presented above, apply rules of plausibility with regard to a form also, however the rules of plausibility cannot be used as clear documentation alone such needs to be supported by some historical documentation of some description.

Primary documentation consists of documents, paintings, and other objects from the period which is being discussed. These materials have been recognised as such by some professional, and are usually found in a museum or other historical collection. These form the most reliable form of documentation as they were written or constructed in the period concerned.

Secondary documentation consists of articles which report about a particular period but are not from that actual period. Such materials need to have been recognised as authentic in nature; and also reliable in nature also. Some such secondary materials also come from the period but are reports from second-hand accounts. Such also need to be verified as a personal perspective can lead to errors. This is the reason why in research a person needs to be careful with secondary materials when conducting research.

CONCLUSION

We need to keep a reasonably open mind to the possibility of a combination of weapons in what we do so that we are more fully able to explore the combat which we are involved in. Each form has its own particular idiosyncrasies and these need to be accepted and learnt from. To out-right deny a form simply because it does not have detailed documentation presented limits us to what we can use does not allow for invention or experimentation, both of which are most useful. This experimentation should always, of course, be tempered with sense and intellectual discovery to prevent outright flights of fantasy. Explore different combinations and seek new meanings within them. There are many possibilities out there.

SECTION 4.
Technique

What is a Ward?

INTRODUCTION

The question would seem to have a relatively simple answer, however there is some contention with regard to the use of terms here, and that is what will be discussed in the following. There is often much confusion with regard to the terms "ward" and "guard". For some they mean exactly the same thing, for others they mean different things. To understand both terms it is necessary to look at both terms rather than just assume knowledge of one term or the other. As a result there will be a discussion of both of the terms presented below. What is important is that there are some important differences between the two terms and that they are actually separated by type of weapon, by time, and by what they actually do.

WARD

A ward is a position from which an attack or defense is launched. This is the best definition of what a ward is. A more in-depth definition of this would also include that this is a position which the combatant moves through from one action to another. What this means is that a set of actions might look like this: Ward - attack - ward - defense - ward - attack, and so forth. What is important is this is not a "guard".

The ward is a position which is associated with weapons prior to the smallsword, after which the positions became much more formalised and became guards, as will be explained below. These wards were designed so that combatant could strike against an opponent or their weapon in a clean action to make an attack or defence resulting in ending up in another ward, thus prepared for another. The position presented in this image, to the left, from Joachim Meyer's treatise of 1600, and clearly this position protects no lines, but is a position from which a cut from below may be launched which could be used as a parry or an offensive cut. Similar positions can be found with the longsword, where the combatant can deliver an action to defend themselves or offend the opponent but one is necessary rather than simply being defended by their current position. Needless to say, the ward is a

position which is more associated with a cutting-style weapon than a thrusting one, but is still accurately used with regard to the rapier.

GUARD

A guard is a position in which one line is closed, thus the fencer is defended along that line due to being in that position, not requiring movement. The guard "Invitation to Sixte" protects the high outside line due to its position. If an attack is launched at the fencer along the high outside line the fencer does not have to move to defend himself. This is a guard. A ward does not do this, in most instances. It should be noted that only when a person is in the correct position of the guard is the line covered.

The guard is a position which came into play at the time of the smallsword. This will be noted as the positions of the guards are the same as the parries. Thus the line which is covered by the parry is also covered by the guard as they are one and the same position, in most instances. The example to the left is Angelo's guard of Quarte of 1787, closing off the high inside line. The profiled position of the body combined with the position of the sword makes the guard position different to the ward and closes the line indicated previously. There are some exceptions to this, as usual. These positions originated from similar positions to the wards of the previous weapons, but are not the same. The ward of quarta with the rapier is different to this position, even with the late period masters.

EXAMPLE: LOW WARD

The Low Ward, or Terza, is the favourite ward of many of the fencing masters and theorists, due to its simple application in offense and defense. The example to the right is Giacomo di Grassi's Low Ward from his (1594) *His True Art of Defense*. From this position it is convenient to parry to defend any line and also make attacks along any line that the combatant may want to. However an attack must be defended and it must be defended by some action *made* by the combatant. This is not a guard, it is a ward. The defense must be made it is not already set by the position adopted.

CONCLUSION

While many may use the terms "ward" and "guard" together to describe the same thing, or even the same position, they are not actually the same. There is a clear difference as to what a real ward is and what a real guard is, and they are not the same. The swordsman should realise which he has adopted when he is facing his opponent, this can make a large difference. In a real guard he is defended along a single line due to his position. In a ward it is a position from which an attack or defense is launched.

The lowe ward.

When discussing the position a combatant has adopted it becomes important to be accurate with the description of what they are doing and the position they have adopted. Using the correct term is important, especially at this very basic level for essential comprehension. This may seem like a high level of semantics but in the comprehension of the words when discussing and using them, if a student hears one and assumes it is the other it can lead the student into trouble and confusion as to the status of the technique. It is necessary to ensure the correct word is being used for the correct technique.

Stand Up Straight and Relax

INTRODUCTION

Most of the time when we are told to stand up straight, relaxing is not going through our minds. This is usually someone telling us to improve our posture or stand at attention. In these particular situations the body goes rigid and upright. For fencing the two, upright and relaxed, need to be accommodated to achieve the most effective guard, or ward position. The relaxed position is also necessary so that we can move from that position easily to another for our next action. Relaxed muscles are more efficient and faster.

NOT RIGID

Being rigid in the on guard position is detrimental to your fencing. When you are rigid, your muscles are already tensed and are already burning energy. This means that they are not ready for movement which leads to slower movement, which can decide whether you are struck or not. It also means that you are burning much needed energy of which you have a limited supply. This energy needs to only be used when you are moving.

To counter-act this you need to relax your body, so only those muscles that need to be working are actually working.

STAND TALL

Standing up straight means that you are standing tall, your chest is expanded and you have an air of confidence about your stance. Both of these elements are important in the on guard stance. With the chest expanded it is much easier to breathe, this means you have more energy due to the increase in breath and thus increase in oxygen going to your muscles. Your muscles are also not tensed as much if you were slouching, this goes especially for those which are over the shoulders and the lower back.

Standing tall means that the weight of your body sits upon your spine rather than being held up by your muscles. This means larger muscle groups can be activated to hold your posture, but more easily. Using your spine and skeleton to hold you up is much easier than using your muscles, which happens when you slouch. This is the reason why people get a sore back from standing up; it is because of the pressure on the lower back from slouching. Standing up straight also takes the pressure off your neck which means the muscles in your neck can relax a little as your spine takes some of the weight of your skull.

COMBINE RELAXED AND TALL

So, the trick is to combine the relaxed but upright position into the on guard position. This may sound like a contradiction, but it is not. First of all, spread your feet to shoulder width, remember to keep the front foot pointed at the opponent. Bend your knees somewhat, but not so much that they become tensed. You should still move your feet easily. Your body should be in an upright position, with your spine vertical, head supported also. Push your chest out, and roll your shoulders down and in. This should expand your chest and make it easy to breathe. Keep your head upright. Now, breathe deeply in and hold it, then let it out slowly. Do this a couple of times and mentally relax all of your muscles. What you should find as a result is that the body is relaxed and ready for action and is also upright.

DON'T CROUCH

The common mistake that is made in the on guard position is that the shoulders are slouched forward. This pushes the shoulders forward, and also the head forward. The position that results also constricts the breathing of the fencer and makes it more difficult for them to breathe. Standing in this manner also tenses muscles, tightening them and making it harder to move. This is usually found in beginners, or fencers who face up against a more experienced opponent. What they are trying to do is shrink themselves into a smaller package and hide. Needless to say, this does not result in good fencing.

To get out of this habit you have to mentally focus on standing up straight and getting others to tell you when you are crouching, it will take time to break this habit, but it will be worth it in the end. At your practice, spend some time standing in your on guard position with your rear shoulder against a wall. You should be able to feel the pressure of the wall against that shoulder and your back when you are standing straight. Practice some fencing actions to feel the difference. Do this once every lesson or so to get into the habit of standing straight. It will help improve your fencing.

CONCLUSION

Standing up straight in your on guard stance, you will breathe better and move more efficiently. The other thing is that standing up straight gives you an air of confidence and makes you feel more confident, neither of which is a bad thing in fencing. A relaxed but upright position is advantageous for all the reasons above, but the same principles can be applied to any on guard position that is found in fencing. Expand the chest, keep the head up and relax.

Footwork: Movement in Fencing

INTRODUCTION

Footwork is vital in fencing and it is often overlooked in importance in comparison to the use of the sword. It does not matter what form of fencing is being performed, footwork is of great importance. This article will be focussing on footwork and its importance. It will also address the differences and advantages and disadvantages of practicing footwork both indoors and outdoors. For some may not realise the difference, but there is one, especially if you have your tournaments outdoors and practice indoors.

PRACTICE, PRACTICE AND MORE PRACTICE

Footwork is undoubtedly important. The practicing of footwork at a training session tends to be rather boring. It usually involves moving up and down the training area over and over again. This is designed to implant the footwork into the muscle memory of the fencer. Once the basic motions have been practiced and perfected, more interesting things can be done with it such as distance games of various kinds. The thing about this practice is that the fencer needs to be able to move without thinking. This means that the footwork movements need to be so familiar to the fencer that they do not have to think about them, while footwork motions remain correct, this takes a lot of practice. The footwork should eventually become like walking, a part of your normal movement.

"With the tips of your toes somewhat floating, tread firmly with your heels. Whether you move fast or slow, with large or small steps, your feet must always move as in normal walking." (Musashi, 1974:55)

STABILITY AND SAFETY

Practicing and using footwork is the ability to move freely over the field. Now, anyone can walk or run across a field, this is undoubted as it is something which we learnt when we were small children. Footwork in fencing is about taking this ability and making it more efficient and also about making it effective. Footwork is also teaching the body to be stable while moving across the field. This means that footwork enhances the ability of the fencer, and it also protects the lower limbs through this movement. Accurate footwork is about safe and efficient movement across the field. Simple things such as turning the foot in the direction of the opponent creates a biomechanical situation where the body is better protected from injury and damage.

CONTROL OF DISTANCE

> *"DISTANCE. The space for attacking or defending that separates two fencers. Learning to establish proper distance is vital to successful fencing. ... it is up to each individual to find the most advantageous spot for him to wage his offensive or defensive campaign." (Evangelista, 1995:177)*

Distance is controlled by footwork. The arm of the fencer is only so long and so is their weapon. If the fencer stays stationary, the opponent only has to stay out of range of the arm and weapon. If the fencer moves with their feet they can change the distance.

Footwork does the major part of moving the body of the fencer. Without the correct footwork, it is difficult for the fencer to move properly. It is also through the use of footwork that the fencer controls distance in the bout. Through this the fencer can close or withdraw at the time and place of their choice. Through this use of distance the fencer is then able to control the bout.

INDOORS AND OUTDOORS

For the most part, the question of training and fighting indoors or outdoors is pretty much mute for the sport fencer. So this particular aspect is more directed at the medieval, Renaissance and Classical fencer whose tournament field may be indoors or outdoors. The question of where training will actually take place is usually up to the person or organisation which organises the training. This may mean that you may end up training either in a hall or outside. There are some important differences that must be realised between these two.

Indoors

Training indoors has some advantages. The floor is flat and this can affect many things. It is much easier to practice perfect footwork on a flat floor, and to some point it is also easier on the joints of the fencer. The other great advantage of training indoors is that the training is not affected by weather. This means pretty much regardless of what the weather is like outside training can go on. Of course if the tournaments are to be fought outdoors, this can also lead to some issues.

Outdoors

Training outdoors involves usually uneven ground. This can place extra stress on the joints of the fencer, and it can also be more difficult to present technically perfect techniques. The fencer who trains outside is also affected by weather and inclement weather means that sometimes training is not possible on that particular site. However, the big advantage that outdoor training has over indoor training is that it reflects the effect of outside conditions on the movement in fencing. This means that the fencer's footwork is prepared for uneven terrain and knows how to move efficiently across this.

Preparation for Unexpected

For the most part, for the Renaissance fencer, the field on which tournaments are fought is outside. This means that the fencers who train outside are already prepared for the conditions presented by the field. For the indoor practicing fencers this can present somewhat of a challenge to them as they are not used to fighting on uneven ground.

TECHNIQUE

> *"if you learn "indoor" techniques, you will think narrowly and forget the true Way. Thus you will have difficulty in actual encounters."*
> (Musashi, 1974:47)

It is true that the event organisers will attempt to find the most even ground possible, but this is not always guaranteed. The result of this is that the advantage will go toward the fencers who train outdoors. A way that this advantage can be gained by all fencers is for all fencers to do a proportion of their fencing outside. For those fencers who have the access to do both indoor and outdoor training this presents an advantage over both the people who train only indoors and also those who only train outdoors.

CONCLUSION

Footwork is of vital importance to the fencer and it is something which should not be glossed over. For the fencer to move properly over the field they must have practiced their footwork. This must be done with correction so that the fencer learns the correct actions and can move efficiently and safely over the field. The practice for footwork should be done under as many conditions as possible, indoors and outdoors. This will enhance the fencer's ability to move over a variety of terrain, and thus move efficiently over it.

Displacement as an Effective Defence

INTRODUCTION

One of the simplest defences in fencing is not to be where the attack is delivered. This article is about the use of voids and other forms of displacement as a form of defence. Performed effectively, displacement, or the void, can be an extremely effective form of defence and can also set up for a counter-attack while the void is being executed. There are various considerations that need to be made when using this form of defence.

SIMPLE AND COMPLEX

Voids or displacements can be used effectively both as a form of defence and also to set up for a counter-attack. Voids can be extremely simple or quite complex in their execution, and various forms of displacement are discussed. The simplest form of void is the retreat. In this distance is increased between the combatant and their opponent so that the attack is avoided by a simple increase in range. This is one of the basic forms of footwork that is taught in the early stages of learning how to fence, but surprisingly enough, it is often forgotten as a simple form of defence against the opponent's attack. All of the tools available to the fencer should be used to be effective.

Displacements can be very simple, as in the retreat, or quite complex as in the form of the *inquartata*, or *volte* as it is called in French. A simple movement of the body can be used to avoid an attack, or this can be combined with the use of the feet in combination with the body movement. Both forms of avoidance need to be considered for their effectiveness and how they can be most effective in their execution. Each element must be considered for them to be effective.

TIME AND DISTANCE

As in all parts of fencing, timing and distance are of great importance, and this also applies to the use of the void. If one of these elements has been perceived badly then problems can occur. With regard to distance it is important that in the use of the retreat, for example, that the distance is increased enough that the opponent's attack still does not strike its intended target.

Timing is also of equal importance in this situation. The combatant must use the correct timing for the void to be effective when it is used. The fencer must wait for the attack to come and only move at the last minute to ensure that the defence is effective. This is the same with all forms of defence. Particular to the void, an early movement can allow the opponent to change their direction and still strike the fencer with the same attack. Without the awareness of these particular principles and how they apply to the use of the void, the void will be substantially less effective.

SIMPLE

In order of simplicity, after the retreat comes the body or part void. This is a simple movement of the body part out of the way of the opponent's attack. This is most commonly performed with attacks to the limbs, but can also be effectively used to move the torso away from the opponent's attack. In the defence of the limbs it involves simply moving the limb out of the way. For the body in involves bending the body out of the way of the opponent's attack. This can be performed without the feet moving.

Simple movement of the body or part is useful especially where the sword or the off-hand cannot reach or be moved quickly enough to defend the intended target. These movements can also leave the fencer's sword in position to deliver a counter-attack against the opponent while the void is being performed. A slightly more complex version of this movement involving slight movement of the feet is the stop hit. In this the body is displaced while a counter-attack is delivered against the opponent.

COMPLEX

The *Inquartata* is the Italian term, and *volte* is the French term, as stated previously, these actions are actually the same thing, but have terms associated with the language being used. This action is a combination of the use of the feet and the body to displace the combatant to avoid the opponent's attack. In the use of these techniques it is useful to keep the point on-line as this gives the fencer access to a counter-offensive option while the action is being performed.

The full version of the *inqartata* is a radical movement of the feet and body to displace it from the opponent's attack, but there is a smaller movement that can also be used effectively. This defence is the *half-inquartata* or *demi-volte*. This involves a simple movement of the rear foot behind the front foot to turn the body away from the opponent's attack. Once again, as in all cases of voids the weapon should be kept on-line to counter-attack. The more complex motion of the feet and body is the full version of both. This is a larger movement of the rear foot behind and across, ending up almost perpendicular to the front foot. This results in a greater movement of the body due to the greater movement of the feet.

The footwork in all forms of the *inquartata* and *volte* are the vital element which ensures a greater success of this particular action. The movement of the feet should be simple, as in all forms of footwork. One of the greatest mistakes in performing this technique is that the body is used to move the feet into position, the opposite is actually what should happen. The movement of the feet moves the body. The body may be moved some to increase the effectiveness of the technique, but it must be primarily the movement of the feet that creates the effect. Balance must be maintained in this technique, as in all others, and this is achieved by effective use of the feet and the correct maintenance of the centre of gravity over the middle of the feet. Being unbalanced during or at the end of this technique can leave you vulnerable to your opponent's following attack.

CONCLUSION

The length of this article belies the use and effectiveness of this particular technique. It is not one that should be glossed over in any way whatsoever. A fencer with effective voids who has practiced them well and has a good application of timing and distance can actually successfully defend himself without any consideration of the use of the sword or the off-hand. This leaves the weapon free for counter-offensive actions against the opponent. Serious consideration should be made by the fencer about the use of the void. Even if it does not become the primary defence of the fencer, it can seriously enhance the fencer's ability to avoid an opponent's attacks. Of course, most effectively, the void can actually be combined with other forms of defence to be even more effective. Practice and research your displacements and you will become a much more secure fencer.

Of the Use of the Off-hand

INTRODUCTION

"V. I will tell you, this weapon must bee used with a glove, and if a man should be without a glove, it were better to hazard a little hurt of the hand, thereby to become maister of his enemies Swoorde. than to breake with the sword, and so give his enemy the advantage of him."

(Saviolo, 1595)

The following lesson could be seen as an introductory to Saviolo however the parry with the off-hand is not restricted to Saviolo, other masters also described its use. Fabris argues against the use of the off-hand to parry, but includes techniques on how it should be used in four different instances. Capo Ferro demonstrates and describes techniques using the off-hand to parry or grasp with on four different plates. Thus the use of the off-hand is actually more widespread than most would give credit

In the standard modes of rapier training the off-hand is often neglected or brushed over in favour of the sword parry. Indeed the techniques involved with the use of the hand parry are often simplified almost to the point of ignorance of their use. However it is a useful technique and gives the user an additional defence when used. The use of the off-hand for parrying can also be beneficial to use of off-hand equipment later on as the hand is already active.

The use of the off-hand is even presented in most of the guards presented in rapier combat as they present the off-hand in front of the body ready for use, rather than behind the body. Even if it is static the off-hand can provide a defence if it is accidentally hit rather than the body, however it is a much more active use which will be the focus here.

Saviolo is the most active user and advertiser of the use of the off-hand. Indeed he even often prefers the use of the use of the off-hand parry to the use of the sword for the same action in many instances. His principle use is based upon the idea that it is better to use the hand and keep the sword free and point on-line and thus threatening the opponent easy for use. This lesson is designed to introduce specifics and present the off-hand as a useful, if often forgotten, option for the fencer to use.

OFF-HAND DEFINITION AND GENERAL USE

Before the details of the use of the off-hand can be discussed some important definitions and principles need to be addressed. The first part of this is to define exactly what is meant by the off-hand. The off-hand is that part of the body which extends from the points of the fingers to the wrist bone, in most instances. However, should a parry be missed with the hand and caught with the forearm and still successfully made, then it can also include this.

In the use of the off-hand against the opponent's blade, the palm of the hand is the optimum contact surface. This is due to the padding which is present on the palm of the hand and also the increased control in using the palm of the hand. Firstly, if the back of the hand is used, the knuckles can come into contact with the opponent's weapon and this will sting. Secondly, the back of the hand gives no option to grasp the opponent's weapon and gives less control.

While the parry with the hand is a technique which can be used and is an effective defence in and of itself; it is even more effective when combined with another technique. In defence the off-hand parry can be enhanced by the use of a void, for example. This is a technique which needs to be added and used with other techniques; use the hand, sword and other techniques together and it will be substantially more effective.

When the hand parry is considered one subject which always eventuates is the subject of the parrying gauntlet. This is a subject, which is best discussed and defined early in the lesson. The parrying gauntlet is not required for the off-hand to be effective, but can be used as an adjunct to enhance its use.

Parrying Gauntlet

There are several different types of gauntlet that can be used on the off-hand in order to enhance the techniques which will be discussed here. The most common type of gauntlet recognised is made of mail however there is also the gauntlet of plates of steel, of leather, and even combinations of the above. Each has its own advantage and disadvantage.

The gauntlet of plate is rigid and is protected from thrusts and cuts on the outside where it is plated, however where it is not protected is on the inside, here the user may be cut. The gauntlet of mail covers the entire hand and protects it well from cuts however it is vulnerable to thrusts. Hutton mentions in *The Sword and the Centuries* of a glove of "stout leather" used to protect the hand when it is in use. However this could be mistaken for a normal leather glove so is often overlooked. The combination of a plate gauntlet with a mail palm would seem to be the ultimate choice in this situation, however there is a weight consideration to take into account. What also needs to be considered are the conventions which may be used with the item.

In normal SCA rapier combat the parrying gauntlet is considered to be a glove of mail worn to protect the hand up to and including the wrist bones. This gauntlet protects the wearer's hand from cuts and can allow the combatant to grasp the opponent's weapon. The grasping of the opponent's blade is a convention that must be agreed to before the bout starts, as are any other conventions, such as plate being protective against thrusts which may be agreed to by both combatants. If there is no agreement then the convention is not used.

The use of the gauntlet will be mentioned in those instances where it is specific to it however all of the techniques can be used with the parrying gauntlet. The parrying gauntlet should not be considered to be required for the use of the off-hand more as a supplementary item to enhance the ability of the off-hand. Always practice the hand parry with and without a parrying gauntlet. Further, do not rely on the grasping ability of the gauntlet, as will be described, be able to use the parries as normal as well, this can only be an advantage.

THEORY

The use of the off-hand in fencing is based upon elements of fencing theory as are all sound techniques. It is the application of these theoretical elements which is important. Time and distance are as applicable to the use of the off-hand as they are to the use of any other element of fencing technique. Further to this the use of the off-hand can be related in to the use of the sword.

The first relationship between the off-hand and the sword is that there is the availability of an option for a beat parry or parry with opposition with both. This means that both can be used to beat or control the opponent's weapon. There is also that the hand can be seen as a pure forte, in much the same way that a dagger is. However, just as control is tenuous at the debole of the dagger so too is it tenuous at the tips of the fingers. What this also means is that there is a great deal of leverage possible on the opponent's weapon with the off-hand, just as with the dagger.

Just as with the parry with the sword, the fencer needs to wait for the opponent's weapon to arrive before making his parry. In this it is just as much a mistake to reach with the hand in a parry as it is with the sword. Thus all the principles of timing and distance apply just as much to the use of the off-hand as they do to the sword.

In the use of the hand, a person may consider that the hand might be hurt in the process however, it is better than the opponent's weapon striking something more vital. This is one of the primary principles in the use of the off-hand. This principle is supplemented with the idea that two hands can be used, one for attack and one for defence. The off-hand parries leaving the weapon free for attack; this is the principle which Saviolo points to the opening quote, and performed in the same tempo this can be extremely effective.

There are some simple principles which need to be followed to use the off-hand effectively in combat:

1. Contact the flat not the edge – this is regardless whether a parrying gauntlet is worn or not. It is safer and reduces potential damage to the hand.
2. Move from the elbow as the primary method of use – the shoulder is slower and less efficient.
3. Move the opponent's attack away from the body not across – use the shortest route possible.
4. In defence wait for the opponent's attack to arrive – don't reach for the opponent's weapon.
5. Always remember that there are two options, beat and control – choose depending on the situation and know how to use both.

There are other elements which are important which will be noted in the following but these are the essential principles. For example, it is best that you do not parry your own sword with your hand, however you may find a situation where parrying the opponent's weapon into yours gains you more control. Always consider the particular situation that you are in.

Entanglement

Entanglement is something which some fencers fear, however entanglement is a position which can be an advantage or a disadvantage depending on the control and the situation. In close combat situations, which are sometimes the result of using the off-hand, are situations in which control over the opponent's weapon, your own, and the situation is vital. If one element is missing then trouble is usually the result. Accidental entanglements are those which cause the most problems, deliberate entanglement on the part of one fencer is different. Consider what the entanglement will gain you before engaging.

In the use of the off-hand you must consider how you will get around the opponent's weapon and of course your own. This often results in questions of whether it is better to move the hand first or the weapon and which one should be in front. This is dependent on the particular situation that you find yourself in. In general if the offhand is used first then the sword must go below the arm, if the sword is first then the sword will usually go above. This is dependent on the situation, of course. The most important thing is not to put yourself in a situation where your resulting attack will contact you. The weapon must be given a clear line to the target, or one that can be cleared without compromising the defence.

In the close, the prime location you should attempt to place the opponent's weapon against their body. Obviously they will be attempting to do the same with their own to complete their own attack. If you can control the opponent's weapon enough to place it against the opponent's body, not only will you have gained control over their weapon, but you will also have the potential for damaging them with their own weapon.

Some will state that it is best to move the opponent's weapon away from your own. This is dependent on the situation. There are times when the extra leverage provided by your sword against the opponent's sword can result in a great advantage. This situation can also result in the chance for an opportunity to change control items to or from the off-hand in order to change the situation. In all instances you should consider what advantage, or disadvantage occurs from your movements, and also those of the opponent.

TECHNIQUE

With the elements of theory enumerated it is possible to start to examine the practical elements in the use of the off-hand. Essentially, the off-hand is used in two techniques which are related to one another. The first is the parry and the second is the action of control. The parry, and choice of parry, will often determine whether an action of control is possible. To begin with the parry will be dealt with.

Parry

In parrying using the off-hand is much like using the sword. It has the same options available to it, and same principles apply. It is possible to perform a beat or a parry with opposition, and it is also possible to perform a purely defensive parry or one of a more active nature. Before the specifics of these different parries are examined the overall elements need to be examined.

There have been some principles described above and these apply to the use of the off-hand in all instances, however more detail is required. Firstly the hand should be held with an open palm, the fingers may curl a little, but the open palm is the primary method that will be used. The open palm reduces the instinct to always grasp the opponent's weapon. In the use of the off-hand it is the palm that should be placed against the opponent's weapon; this should be done in a smooth, sweeping motion to allow the best contact.

Drill 1: Hand on the Blade

1. Two fencers stand across from one another one with the weapon extended but not fully, the other in his normal ward. They should be close enough that they can reach each other with the point of their weapons.
2. The fencer from his normal ward should extend his hand and place the palm against the opponent's weapon, first the inside then the outside of the blade.
3. The action should be performed gently, only contact is needed. This focussed on the action of placing the palm on the opponent's blade.

This first drill is designed to familiarise the combatants with placing their hand against the opponent's weapon with the palm and on different sides of the weapon. This only covers a single position but highlights the basic concept of the use of the hand against an opponent's weapon. The next part of the process is the parry itself.

Beat or Control?

There are two options which have been described the beat and the control, or parry with opposition. Each has its advantages and disadvantages. The beat removes the opponent's weapon with impact and force and diverts the opponent's blade off-line; this is the faster parry however control is lost over the opponent's weapon. The parry with opposition or control parry retains the opponent's weapon and thus control however there is the potential that the hand can be cut and it is slower. In actual fact it is better to know both types of parry and when they are advantageous than to purely focus on one.

Parry Execution

The parry with the off-hand is designed as an action to remove an incoming threat against the fencer. This needs to cover all four lines to some degree however the fencer should be careful about over-reaching. This is especially important for the low line parries. As described defensively the fencer should wait for the incoming attack and then defend against it. The active beat and control will be discussed further along.

In the previous drill the hand was placed against the flat of the blade so that the combatant can see how the hand is placed against the opponent's weapon. The execution of the parry is much like this. The execution of the parry, regardless of whether it is a beat or opposition parry is the same, the change being made toward the end of the parry.

From a normal terza (or third) ward, to protect the high inside line the hand should be turned so that the palm comes into contact with the opponent's weapon and then is pushed over the shoulder of the off-hand. This is the easiest of the parries as it takes minimal movement of the hand and arm.

To protect the high outside line the hand should be pushed across the body to come in contact with the opponent's weapon and then pushed past the sword side of the body. Care should be made that the combatant does not inadvertently parry their own weapon. To avoid this, the sword should be dropped a little or lifted a little depending on where the attack is aimed at.

With regard to the low line parries, no hand parry should be made lower than where the wrist sits on the fencer when his arm is placed down at his side. To attempt to parry lower will lower the head toward the opponent's weapon. For the low inside line the arm is dropped toward the opponent's weapon the palm is turned toward the weapon and pushes it to the off-hand side. This is often performed as a sweeping action. For the parry to the low outside line, the arm and hand with the palm is dropped and pushed across the body so that the palm pushes the opponent's weapon past the sword side of the body.

Drill 2: Simple Parry Action
1. Stand with a partner at a range where each can strike the other with a fully extended blow.
2. One of the partners should make slow thrusts toward the partner and the partner should parry each one using his off-hand. The attacks should be slow but deliberate toward each line.
3. The focus of the drill should be parrying the opponent's weapon away from the fencer using the palm of the hand in each line. Placing the palm against the opponent's weapon and pushing it, or guiding it, away is sufficient at this stage. Speed can be increased once the partners are comfortable with the parries.

Opposition Parry

The opposition parry is the parry which has been described in both the description of the parry and also the drill above. The only real difference is that the off-hand will stay in contact with the opponent's blade for an extended period of time rather than simply leaving it once the threat has passed.

The purpose of the parry with opposition is to gain and maintain control over the opponent's weapon. This relies on the off-hand maintaining contact with the opponent's weapon in the process. It is this parry which is used to push and control the opponent's weapon. The important thing, at this stage, is that this is performed with an open hand, using the palm of the hand to control the opponent's weapon. Grasping is a skill which will be discussed further along as it is a more complex action.

For the most part the parry with opposition is used passively and thus defensively against the opponent's weapon. The control elements and moving the opponent's weapon come as a result of the passive nature of this parry. It can be used more offensively, but you need to place yourself in the correct position to do this. For the most part this consists of taking control of an extended weapon and pushing and controlling it to where you want. This will be discussed more under actions of control.

Beat Parry

The beat parry is one of the options available. This parry is designed to remove the opponent's threat with velocity and impact of the parry against the weapon. This technique is often the first that will be used by fencers as it is relatively simple but still requires technique.

The effect of the beat should be made at the very end of the parry rather than performing a full-blooded swipe at the opponent's weapon. Just as with the beat with the sword the impact should come from the wrist, in this case sending the palm against the opponent's weapon with velocity. Saviolo states, "then must the scholler with his left hand beat aside his masters rapier, not at the point, but in the strength and middest of the weapon," (Saviolo, 1595). The beat is better performed against the opponent's weapon on the debole or mezzo for greatest effect.

In the performance of this parry you need to come into contact with the opponent's blade on the flat. To come into contact with the edge will sting the palm and even worse if the fingers come into contact. You should always aim to parry with the palm rather than the fingers.

Drill 3: Beat Parry: Defensive
1. Stand with a partner at a range where each can strike the other with a fully extended blow.
2. One of the partners should make slow thrusts toward the partner and the partner should beat parry each one using his off-hand. The attacks should be slow but deliberate toward each line.
3. The focus of the drill should be parrying the opponent's weapon away from the fencer using the palm of the hand in each line. Speed can be increased once the partners are comfortable with the parries.
4. Once comfortable with the basic defensive parries, the partners should experiment with the directions that the opponent's weapon can be beaten.

Placing the hand into correct position for the defensive parry has already been described. However, just as with the sword there is also a pre-emptive or active beat. The active beat can most effectively be used against an opponent whose weapon is left out of good control, or in an overly extended ward. In this beat parry you should aim to remove the opponent's weapon by striking it with the palm, preferably against the debole for the greatest effect, as described by Di Grassi, "men do much use at this weapon, to beate off the poynt of the sworde with their handes:" (Di Grassi, 1594). The direction that the beat is made is dependent on what you have planned for after the beat is made.

Drill 4: Beat Parry: Offensive
1. Stand with a partner at a range where each can strike the other with a fully extended blow.
2. One should be in an extended ward. One of the partners should beat the one whose blade is in the extended ward. The goal should be to beat the opponent's

weapon off-line.
3. Once comfortable with simply beating the blade away, the partners should practice deliberately beating the opponent's blade in different directions to see the effect.

Actions of Control

The beat parry does not maintain control over the opponent's weapon and this is its greatest failing. The parry with opposition maintains control over the opponent's weapon and thus leaves you with more options as to what actions can be performed. However, the beat parry should not be disregarded as it also has its own advantages.

The actions of control primarily begin with the use of the parry with opposition with the hand however this is not the only way that they can begin. This part of the lesson will focus on the use of the off-hand as the primary and continuing contact. The hand is placed upon the opponent's weapon as is described in the parry with opposition above. The contact must be on the flat of the blade and with the palm of the hand for greatest control; this contact needs to be maintained so that you can push the opponent's weapon to the location desired. This contact enables you to retain control and knowledge of where the opponent's weapon is.

Drill 5: Weapon Movement
1. Partners stand across from one another in their normal wards.
2. One makes a slow thrust against the other who uses a parry with opposition against the attack.
3. The partner who parried now moves the opponent's weapon around using the control of the palm. The sword should not be grasped. Movements should be made in all directions.

The drill above introduces the idea of the movement and control of the opponent's weapon to places where you wish it to go. The hand should be placed about the debole or mezzo at this stage for the simple movements of the opponent's weapon, however this is not the place where the greatest control over the opponent's blade is gained but it is the most likely first contact with the opponent's weapon.

Control over the opponent's weapon increases the further down the blade you go. With your hand at the point the opponent has a lot of movement, as your hand moves closer and closer to their hilt they lose more and more control over the weapon. This is due to an increase in leverage on your part and a decrease in leverage on theirs. The location of the maximum control over the opponent's weapon is to place your hand on their hilt or pommel. As a result the hilt is where you should be aiming for control of the opponent's weapon.

Drill 6: Leverage
1. Partners stand across from one another, only one weapon is required. One holds the weapon the other places his hand on the point.
2. One who is holding the weapon should move the weapon about. One with the hand on the weapon should notice the movement, and then move his hand down to the debole and repeat the process.
3. The change in leverage should be noted by both of the combatants involved. The

process should be repeated until the hand reaches the hilt of the weapon. The increase in control of the combatant with his hand on the blade should be noted.

What has been described and demonstrated is the increase in control over the opponent's weapon the closer to the hilt that the off-hand comes. Logically this would mean that the greatest control would be to place your hand on the opponent, however this is not actually the case. For simple practical reasons if you place your hand on the opponent's arm he may swap the weapon to the other hand thus renewing the threat. While fleeting contact is allowed within the rules of the SCA, it is best to aim for the forte of the weapon with the hope of gaining the hilt, thus contacting the weapon and not the individual. This will gain the greatest advantage. The clever fencer will actually practice swapping the weapon to the other hand in case his person is contacted by the opponent.

With contact made upon the opponent's weapon the question of location becomes apparent. The goal of moving the opponent's weapon is to place you in the position of greatest advantage. Where this may be will be dependent on the particular situation that you find yourself in.

In general it is best not to tangle yourself in your opponent's weapon. This would seem to say to move the weapon as far away from your weapon as possible, but this may not be always the case. The simplest movement in defence is to move the opponent's weapon toward their sword side and attack down inside of the opponent. This is the simplest approach when both combatants are right-handed. This approach works for both inside and outside lines.

Drill 7: Parry and Riposte
1. Partners stand across from one another in their ward at a combat distance.
2. One person makes an attack against the other to the inside line. The defender parries to the off-hand side with his hand controlling the weapon and then makes a riposte to the inside line.
3. The partners then re-set and the attacker makes an attack to the outside line.
4. The defender parries with the off-hand, controlling the weapon and attacks to the inside below the arm of the opponent.

The drill above results in simple parry and riposte techniques, but can lead to more advanced movements thanks to the result of the opponent's weapon being in the off-hand. Another approach is to gain the opponent's weapon and then use the weapon against them by crossing it over and using to block the opponent's off-hand side. This is most useful when the opponent is carrying a supplementary item.

Drill 8: Parry and Control to Block Off-hand
1. Partners stand across from one another in their ward at a combat distance.
2. One person makes an attack against their opponent. The defender parries with the off-hand and then carefully, maintaining control over the opponent's weapon crosses it to the opponent's off-hand side.
3. The defender should step toward the opponent's off-hand side to increase the leverage with a diagonal step. From this position an attack can be made either over or under the arm with either cut or thrust.

The drill above gives the primary control over the opponent's weapon and demonstrates one approach to controlling the opponent's weapon and then using the situation to your benefit. There is an element of entanglement in this approach, ensure that the situation is to your benefit in the end.

Just as with the beat parry, there is an offensive version of the parry with opposition. This action is designed to actively gain control over the opponent's weapon, and just with the beat parry it is best performed when the opponent's weapon is extended from them. This is not simply reaching out and grabbing the opponent's weapon, instead it is placing the hand on the opponent's weapon, gaining control and moving it to a position advantageous to you.

Drill 9: Parry with Opposition to Gain Control
1. The partners should stand across from one another in their wards. They should be at a combat distance.
2. One should have their sword more extended. The other should move forward and gain control with the off-hand. The sword should then be moved out of line and to a position more advantageous so that an attack can be made.

The direction and location which the opponent's weapon is moved to is dependent on the attack or action that is to follow the action. In the simplest form this action will simply open the opponent up to an attack. More pressure can be gained upon the opponent's weapon by forward movement. Care needs to be taken to ensure that the opponent's weapon is controlled before any forward movement is made.

Defence

What have been described thus far have been offensive ideas about how to use the hand, based on a simple defence against an attack by an opponent. What have been missed up to this point are the defences against the techniques which have been described. These techniques are just as important as, if not more so than the offensive actions. Defence in the close against techniques such as those which have been described work off some general defensive principles.

1. Place your hand on the opponent's weapon, as with offence try to aim as low on the weapon as possible. This helps prevent the opponent from continuing their action.
2. Regain control of your own weapon. You need to get your own weapon back to gain more control of the situation.
3. Move either toward or away from the opponent. Moving away is not always the best option as it may give the opponent the chance to attack. Moving toward the opponent can cramp them and will also increase your own leverage.
4. Move circularly to increase the control of your own weapon and to decrease that of the opponent. Moving toward your sword side will increase the pressure of your own weapon upon your opponent, however releasing this pressure may regain the weapon.
5. Gain control of as many elements present as possible. This refers back to the previous principles but encourages the use of multiple at once.

These are the general defensive principles in the use of the off-hand especially at the close. The same principles also apply at distance and should be used here also. Anytime that your opponent places their hand on your weapon, you should be considering what your hand is doing and where it is. You should be considering where the opponent's attack will arrive to and defend that line.

The defence against the parry and riposte using the off-hand is relatively simple. Consider where you are open in your attack and be prepared to defend that area with your own off-hand, you may have to shift your position to achieve this. This is actually simpler against a beat parry than against the opposition parry as the opponent's hand is cleared away.

Drill 10: Parry and Riposte Counter
1. Partners stand across from one another in their ward at a combat distance.
2. One person makes an attack against the other to the inside line. The defender parries to the off-hand side with his hand controlling the weapon and then makes a riposte to the inside line.
3. The other partner defends against the riposte using his off-hand.
4. The partners then re-set and the attacker makes an attack to the outside line.
5. The defender parries with the off-hand, controlling the weapon and attacks to the inside below the arm of the opponent. As previous, the defence against the riposte is made with the off-hand.

The drill above should be practiced using both beat and opposition parries on the part of both partners and against different lines. This will enable both fencers to see the actions involved and to consider what could come from this position. In the discussion of position, blocking the off-hand was the next technique which followed. The counter against this technique is to simply follow the first principle and to place your off-hand on the opponent's weapon and thus counter the pressure that he is applying. If this is not possible then placing the hand against an open line is the next best option.

Drill 11: Parry and Control to Block Off-hand Counter
1. Partners stand across from one another in their ward at a combat distance.
2. One person makes an attack against their opponent. The defender parries with the off-hand and then carefully, maintaining control over the opponent's weapon crosses it to the opponent's off-hand side.
3. The defender should step toward the opponent's off-hand side to increase the leverage with a diagonal step.
4. To counter the increasing pressure the off-hand should be placed on the defender's sword to counter an attack while stepping circularly away.

The defence against the offensive beat parry and offensive opposition parry all work on similar principles. For the most part they work on the action involved by the opponent and what he gains through his action. The offensive beat parry is used to displace the weapon by force. If the same force applied is not resisted by the fencer through the loosening of the wrist the point of the weapon will come back on-line again. In the meantime the off-hand should be used to defend against the following attack.

Drill 12: Offensive Beat Parry Counter
1. Stand with a partner at a range where each can strike the other with a fully extended blow.
2. One should be in an extended ward. One of the partners should beat the one whose blade is in the extended ward. The goal should be to beat the opponent's weapon off-line.
3. Against the force of the beat the wrist should be loosened so that the point can be controlled back on-line using the force of the beat. The off-hand should be prepared to intercept the opponent's attack.

The counter to the offensive beat parry is relatively simple on the basis that the offensive action works on relatively simple principles which can be countered easily. Against the offensive opposition parry a little more consideration needs to be made as to the counter to the action, however once again this counter is derived from the principle of the action. The parry with opposition is designed to gain and maintain control. This can be countered by removing the weapon and thus the object of control or forcing the weapon to a place of better leverage against the action. In both instances the off-hand should be prepared to counter any attack.

Drill 13: Counter to Parry with Opposition to Gain Control
1. The partners should stand across from one another in their wards. They should be at a combat distance.
2. One should have their sword more extended. The other should move forward and gain control with the off-hand. The sword should then be moved out of line and to a position more advantageous so that an attack can be made.
3. In response to this the weapon can be withdrawn from the opponent's hand thus removing control, or it can be forced forward with hand and arm to a place of better leverage. Both techniques should be considered and attempted. The off-hand should be in position to counter any following attack of the opponent.

These actions are designed to counter those which have been taught previously. In the case of both sets of actions, they are based on simple and similar principles. These actions are designed to introduce the idea of the use of the off-hand as further, more complex actions are possible but they are based upon the simple ones and as such these must be established first.

ADVANCED ACTIONS

There are many further actions which can be utilised in the use of the off-hand; two specific areas will be addressed along with some general ideas and discussions of these more advanced techniques. These are more the combination of simple techniques utilised together for a greater effect. These techniques will obviously be based upon the same principles as the simple techniques, merely expanded to include more techniques and possibilities.

Counters to Counters

The first area of discussion is the concept of the counter to beat a counter. Actions have been discussed. Counters to these actions have been discussed. By applying the same principles and examining the situation counters can be made to these counters. This cycle can continue until one combatant has run out of ideas and breaks off, until a stalemate has been reached and both combatants break off, or until one of the combatants succeeds in his action.

The most important thing in this is as with all combats is to ensure your safety first. The first thought should be to counter the action of the opponent's sword and then consider attacking. If both can be achieved simultaneously then you will have a great advantage. In the situation of breaking off remember to ensure your safety in the process of breaking off and also once completed.

Beat and Opposition Follow-Up

The basic techniques have been described for both the beat and opposition parries in both their defensive and offensive forms. One example has been given of where to direct the force in the pushing to the off-hand side of the opponent. This is only one option of many that may be used. The direction of the parry and the control should be dependent on what the fencer has planned to follow the action.

The parry may be followed by a simple control, contact with the weapon, or even a second parry with the hand depending on the chosen situation. This is where it is important to know how to control the direction in which the opponent's weapon will travel and to have some idea of what to follow this action with. Some ideas about this particular concept will be discussed below in the combination and application of the sword and the hand.

Blade grasping

> *"Moreover, having the use of your lefte hand, and wearing a gantlet or glove of maile, your enemy shall no sooner make a thrust, but you shal be readye to catch his swoorde fast, and to command him at your pleasure:"*
>
> (Saviolo, 1595)

Saviolo explains the operation of the parrying gauntlet succinctly. The purpose of the gauntlet is to gain the opponent's sword by grasping it and controlling it. However, there is a little more detail that should go into the consideration in the use of the gauntlet. Some of this has to do with the simple use of it, but a little also has to do with the safe use of it.

First of all the gauntlet and blade grasping is designed to give the user solid control over the opponent's weapon whether or not they are wearing the gauntlet. The same actions can be performed with a standard glove but the user needs to be aware of the threat to the hand. There is one great advantage and one major disadvantage to this controlling action. The greatest advantage is the solid control over the opponent's weapon and thus able to move it about, however this solid control also tells the opponent exactly what is going on and gives them a chance to react to the action of the grasp. Of course there is also the obvious potential for the hand being cut if the gauntlet is not being worn.

In practicing blade grasping it is best to consider the advantages that you possess before you begin. The first question is whether a gauntlet is being worn and how this will change the operation of it. To begin, with it is best to practice without grasping the opponent's blade. This prevents the embedding of the idea of the necessity of grasping and thus inability in other actions. Use the previous drills to get used to the idea of using the hand first. Once this has been achieved you can consider grasping and controlling.

Drill 14: Control of the Weapon
1. Partners stand across from one another in their ward at combat distance.
2. One makes an attack at the other which is parried with the off-hand.
3. Once parried the opponent's blade should be grasped, and then moved about to get an idea of how the opponent's weapon is controlled in the grasp.
4. Follow the same action with grasping about different parts of the blade. This is designed to enable the different levels of control and different positions that the opponent's weapon can be moved to.

The choice of grasping or not grasping is always present with the open hand regardless of whether a gauntlet is worn or not, but you need to make considerations with regard to this. First of all the question of permitted use within the rules structure must be answered. The other real question is as to what advantage there is in the grasping of the current opponent's weapon. In some situations it is actually better to retain lighter control rather than grasping. Grasping is a solid control action and sometimes it is an advantage to have a more mobile ability to the control action. Choosing when is important.

Drill 15: Grasping and Release
1. Partners stand across from one another in their ward at combat distance.
2. One makes a thrusting attack at the other which is parried with the off-hand.
3. Once parried the opponent's blade should be grasped, and then moved about to get an idea of how the opponent's weapon is controlled in the grasp.
4. The same attack and defence should be made, except this time the blade is not grasped on the initial contact merely controlled with the hand. Slide the hand down the weapon and grasp lower on the blade.
5. The same action can be performed up and down the blade. The important thing is to get the idea of the grasp and release of the opponent's weapon and the advantages that both give.

Blade grasping clearly gives some great advantages over the opponent and solid control over the opponent's weapon, however just as with any other skill it should be combined with others and used when it is best suited to the situation. Just as with any other skill it is also one that needs practice to become effective. The use of blade grasping will often result in the actions of closes and gripes and you should consider the consequences of the use of blade grasping and apply this to the current situation.

Sword and Hand
The following part of the lesson will discuss the use of the sword and the hand together. Most of the actions previously have used the sword and the hand together but in a passive sense. The following considerations are for actively using the sword and hand together.

The first point of call for this discussion is what will be called a "1-2". In this action the sword or the hand is placed on the opponent's weapon in defence and then the contact is swapped to the other. This can be performed with initial hand contact or initial sword contact. This response is designed to enhance your response to the opponent's attack. These actions can be extended to include three or more points of contact either using the hand or the sword twice depending on the desired result and time available.

For these actions to work you must consider the placement of your sword and also your hand to ensure that they do not get entangled in the process of the action. If your hand or your sword is placed incorrectly you will end up entangling yourself or even possibly damaging yourself. You need to consider the final result for the action to be placed correctly. Some of this was discussed in the discussion of entanglement early in the lesson. Because the sword is the offending object it is usually best placed in front of the hand to give access to the opponent, so the hand is placed behind the point of contact for the sword, or the sword is placed in front of the point of contact of the hand.

Drill 16: Hand and Sword: The "1-2"
1. Partners stand across from one another at combat distance.
2. One person makes a thrusting attack against the other to a high line.
3. The defender parries with the sword and then places their off-hand on the opponent's weapon to control it and then makes a riposte. The hand must be placed behind the position of the sword.
4. The partners reset and the attacker makes another thrusting attack to the high line.
5. The defender parries with the hand and then places their sword on the opponent's weapon to control it and then makes a riposte. The hand must be placed behind the position of the sword.

This drill demonstrates two simple "1-2" combinations using an initial contact with the sword and an initial contact with the weapon. Further techniques can be added to these to make the action more complex and you should investigate these using the same drill. The sword and the hand are best used in combination and the options open up the more this option is used.

The actions so far described in the drills deal primarily with the use of the off-hand as the primary point of contact. This is so that the off-hand is actively used, however it should be noted that complex sword actions can be used in combination with the off-hand to increase the effect of the off-hand. There are many different actions which can be used to achieve this however the bind is often the most useful. In this action the sword is used to parry to set up for a bind in which the sword is delivered to the off-hand for control.

Drill 17: Parry and Bind with Off-hand Contact
1. Partners stand across from one another at combat distance.
2. One person makes a thrusting attack against the other to a low outside line.
3. The defender makes a simple parry to defend. From the parry position a bind is made against the opponent's weapon designed to move the blade up and across to the defender's waiting off-hand. This technique will also work against an attack made to the high outside line.

It is the action of the bind which places the sword into the fencer's off-hand. Performed and positioned correctly, there is actually very little movement that the off-hand needs to make as the bind will deliver the opponent's blade to the hand. This action frees the sword up for further actions while maintaining control over the opponent's weapon. You should consider what other actions can be used to extend the control over the opponent's weapon.

There is a technique which uses both the hand and the sword together to get an increased effect which is primarily considered to be a longsword technique, but can also be used with a rapier. This technique is half-swording. In this technique, the hand is placed about the blade of the fencer's sword up around the mezzo or debole to gain more leverage to this part of the weapon. The part of the blade between the hands can also be used for leverage against the opponent's weapon. This technique is most effective where two combatants have come together at the close.

One time where the use of the half-sword is particularly effective is where the combatants have come close the fencer has his hand on the opponent's hilt and is applying pressure with his weapon against the other's to gain position. If the off-hand is removed from the opponent's hilt and placed about the mezzo then extra leverage can be applied and a greater chance for an attack may be made. The important thing here is the increase in pressure while maintaining control. The above description can be used as a drill for demonstration and practice of the technique and to figure out other ways that it can be used.

CONCLUSION

The off-hand is useful but is often overlooked in favour of using the sword for an action. What has been presented is a lesson about how the off-hand can be used effectively, especially when used in combination with other techniques. The documentation from period masters is clear that the use of the off-hand is a technique which needs attention paid to it for a fencer to reach their potential.

Just as with any technique in fencing the use of the off-hand needs practice and this lesson has described several drills which can be used to familiarise you with the use of the off-hand and then used to continue the practice and thus increase the proficiency with the off-hand. In this practice it is important that the people involved understand what is happening and the goals for it to ensure that the goals are reached. Once proficient with the use of the off-hand the techniques will be performed as naturally as any other technique.

While each person will find that they will have favourite techniques which will seem to work particularly well for them, you should attempt to use as many as possible to increase your ability. Only through the practice of each technique will a level of ability and familiarity be built. Practice varying techniques and discovering new ways to use the techniques; this is best done with a partner with a similar goal.

The advantage of using the off-hand in fencing from the simplest point of view is that it gives other options and responses to actions which the opponent may perform. Further to this there are also times where the off-hand will actually have an advantage over the use of the sword; this is especially the case where the sword is freed for use due to the use of the off-hand.

This lesson was designed to reveal different possibilities in the use of the off-hand in fencing and to re-establish its position as a valid technique. Too often the use of the off-hand is overlooked, ignored or pushed aside in favour of other techniques, or taught ad hoc to fill in a technique. The use of the off-hand is worth the attention paid to any other technique. Indeed those who develop the skills associated with the use of the off-hand will have a great advantage over those who give it a mere cursory glance.

TECHNIQUE

The Sword Parry and Its Execution

INTRODUCTION

The sword parry is one of the primary defences of the fencer in all forms of fencing, be it rapier, foil, or even the katana. This is a technique which is taught in the earlier part of a person's fencing career and it is important that the parry is performed properly for it to be effective. This article will be discussing the execution of the parry and some points about such. This discussion will include some diagrams to assist the discussion.

THE SWORD PARRY

A sword parry is a (mostly) defensive use of the weapon to stop or deflect an opponent's incoming attack. This technique can be used effectively against both thrusts and cuts. The technique in principle is relatively easy. It involves placing your weapon in a position where you will intercept your opponent's weapon before it strikes you to stop or deflect their attack. The principle is relatively easy the execution of the parry can be somewhat more complex.

Purpose Affects Position

Much of the purpose of the parry has been discussed above, but we must look at it a little deeper. The primary purpose of the parry is to defend against an opponent's attack. In its execution, that our safety against the opponent's attack is the primary purpose of the parry. The setting up for a riposte or following action needs to be a secondary consideration in comparison to the defence that the parry supplies. This needs to be realised and will affect the execution of the parry depending on what your considered primary purpose is. This will be revealed in a later part of the discussion on this particular subject.

Simple Parries

With regard to sword parries there are many different kinds. This discussion will be focussing on the simple or standard parries. There are other parries available to us, such as hanging parries. These work on very much the same principles as the standard ones, but due to their different execution, they will not be addressed in any sort of detail. The standard parries will also be the focus due to their commonality with the various forms of fencing which are available to the fencer.

FOUR LINES, TWO EDGES

There are four lines which need to be covered, and at least two parries per line, one with the true edge and one with the false edge. In all cases the parry must cover the line, to be effective as a parry, and this relies upon proper execution of the parry. In all cases it is important to examine the position of the hand in relation to that of the parry.

In the case of true edge parries the knuckles of the fingers should be facing the opponent's blade. In a false edge parry it should be the knuckle of the

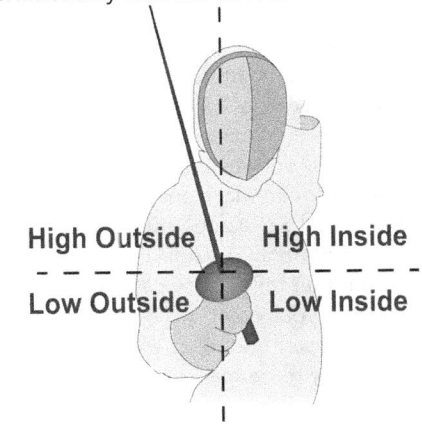

thumb which is facing the opponent's blade. This will ensure that you have an edge to the opponent's blade. The hand position in the parry is vital and must be considered.

There is the question about whether a parry needs to be done with the edge or whether it can be done with the flat of the blade. The edge of the sword is much stronger than that of the flat, and thus makes a more secure parry. This being said, there are parries which when done with the flat are quite effective, but as a rule it is better that the parry is performed with the edge.

BEAT OR OPPOSITION

The next question that comes up is whether the parry should be executed as a beat or with opposition. Both of the methods have their advantages and disadvantages, and these will be discussed. The principle of the beat parry is that the edge of the blade is struck against the opponent's moving it away by the impact of one blade against the other. This is an effective technique because it forces the opponent's blade off-line by the shock allowing the fencer to make a counter-attack against the opponent. The disadvantage of this technique is because the blades do not remain in contact, knowledge of the location of the opponent's blade through the use of *senso di ferro* or *sentiment du fer* is lost. It is also relatively easy for the opponent to use the impact to roll the blade back on line. This parry can be used as an offensive action.

The parry with opposition contacts and prevents the opponent's blade from contacting its target by placing a wall against the attack, also forcing the opponent's blade off-line. The advantage of this technique is that due to remaining in contact with the opponent's blade it is easy to know exactly where the opponent's blade is. This also allows for the use of techniques which rely upon blade engagement. The greatest disadvantage of this particular technique is that it can allow for a slower riposte, and also gives the opponent some *senso di ferro* by the contact between the weapons. In general, while the beat parry is easier to execute and learn, the parry with opposition tends to lead to more advantages and more options for the fencer. This being said, both techniques can be used effectively.

KEEP IT SMALL

In the execution of the parry, it is important to keep the parry small. The opponent's blade only needs to be deflected enough, and just enough to avoid striking the fencer. The blade does not have to be forced particularly far to be forced away from its intended target. This means that in execution the parry needs to be minimalist in its execution.

There are a couple of reasons for this. The first reason is one of entropy. A smaller parry takes less energy to perform; this allows the fencer to conserve energy for future actions which require more energy. Another reason for keeping the parry small is that it will take less time to execute, thus giving the fencer more time to perform other actions against the opponent. The final reason that will be discussed has a great deal to do with the action that follows the parry once it is performed. If a parry is kept small, it is much easier to keep your point on line against the opponent, and thus make any counter-offensive action faster and more effective. With these reasons in place it is clearly advantageous for the parry to be made as small as possible.

TECHNIQUE

WAIT

The beginner fencer will come out and chase the opponent's blade to make a parry. This means that they will parry very early. The more experienced fencer will wait for the opponent's attack to come and then parry only at what they conceive as the last moment in which they can parry. This is about what is called parrying "late" it is late in the action of the opponent.

This relates to what I tend to refer to as the "panic space". This is the zone in which the fencer sits in which if any attack is made the fencer will respond to. In the beginner fencer, this will extend to up to a foot out from the fencer. As the fencer becomes more and more confident in their skill, the "panic space" will reduce allowing them to parry later and later. The most experienced fencers will have a "panic space" which extends as little as 5cm from them.

The advantage of parrying late is that you are less vulnerable to complex actions. A person who parries late is less vulnerable to a feint than a person who parries early. The late parrying fencer is also less vulnerable to changes in tempo. Because the attack is allowed to come close to the fencer it is easier to determine whether the attack is a feint or not. The fencer should only parry a valid attack, i.e. one that will actually strike them. This is achieved through parrying late. The late parrying fencer also achieves a better mechanical advantage over the opponent due to the later parry resulting in the opponent's blade being caught further down the forte of the defender and further up the foible of the opponent.

PARRY ANGLE

Now that both time and distance have been discussed with regard to the parry, now it is time to discuss the angle of the blade in the parry. This is an important consideration and will come back to the discussion on the primary purpose of the parry. The larger the angle of the parry the more defense which is afforded to the fencer; the smaller the angle of the parry, the faster the riposte will be. Thus defense decreases as the speed of the riposte increases. This has been placed on a chart for your interest.

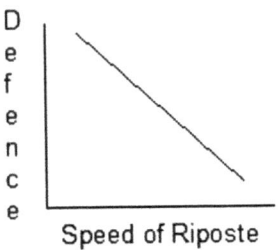

As can be seen by the chart, a parry which has a high degree of defence has a low speed of riposte, but a parry which has a high speed of riposte also has a low degree of defence. This comes back to whether the primary purpose of the parry being performed is for defence or for setting up for a following action. In the beginner fencer it is more important to focus on the defensive characteristics of the parry than the action which follows it. The more advanced fencer needs to balance the relationship and figure out what is most appropriate for them at the time. Into this discussion is also the fact that the larger the angle of the parry, the more of the fencer the blade will protect.

As can be seen in the diagram to the right, the more that the angle of the blade in the parry increases, the more of the fencer the blade protects. With a point high and thus large angle of the blade, the parry protects a large amount of the fencer; whereas, if the angle is reduced, less of the fencer is protected. Of course

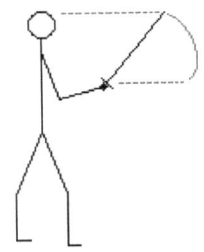

referring back to the other diagram, this will also mean a slower riposte in response to the increased defense. It is better that we teach our students that it is better to have a sure defence than a speedy riposte. With a focus of striking without being struck, this is the only sure way to achieve this end.

CONCLUSION

The purpose of this article was to discuss the general characteristics of the sword parry and how it should be performed properly against an attack delivered by an opponent. Various elements have been discussed in some detail and so that the parry is performed correctly and effectively. What is really important is that the purpose of the parry must be established and expressed to our students so that they understand that defence is the primary purpose of the parry.

A lot of practice is required to perfect the parries and time needs to be spent on this on a regular basis. The sword parry is an effective technique when performed properly and this discussion has highlighted various points of importance in consideration of this technique. Each point is important in its own right, but also in relation to the whole. Focus on effective parries and your fencing will improve and your defence will be effective against your opponents.

Calibration and the Correct Execution of the Thrust

INTRODUCTION

Everyone has been struck a too hard by their opponent before, and indeed the same could be said of us in the same situation. This article, as noted by the title will focus on calibration in the execution of the thrust. The thrust is the primary attack in many forms of fencing and knowing the correct calibration so that we do not injure our opponents is important and is something that needs to be discussed. This discussion will address various details with regard to the execution of the thrust and examine how we can minimise the chances of over calibrating our thrust, or in more simple terms stop or at least reduce hitting too hard.

The two root causes of over-calibration in the thrust come from a problem with knowledge of Distance or from the technical execution of the thrust. Each one of these will be addressed with some pointers about how these can be improved and why there may be problems. The last part of the article will address some problem solving suggestions as to how we ourselves can prevent over calibration and how we can fix the same problem in our students. Time and Distance are the two root principles of fencing and any flaw in them will be expressed when we come up against an opponent. In this particular case it is Distance which needs to be addressed.

DISTANCE

Knowing your Distance is about situational awareness; knowing your own Distance with a thrust, and also the Distance to the opponent. This particular element will be affected by other things going on during the bout such as movement and each one of these elements needs to be addressed in some form. The lunge is equally important in this equation but at the moment it is the thrust that is the focus as the lunge is simply a thrust with a forward step added to it. The same elements which will be raised apply equally to the lunge as they do to the thrust.

Own Distance

The first element is your own Distance. You need to know how far your point will be away from your body at the full extension of your thrust. If your opponent is within the distance of your thrust it is important that you realise this and do not extend to your full length, otherwise you will strike your opponent too hard. This is the first element, and is forms some of the basis of the others. Once you know your own Distance you can move on to the examination of the opponent.

Distance to Opponent

You need to be aware of the Distance to your opponent in comparison to your own thrusting distance, as stated if they are too close you will over calibrate if you fully extend your thrust. Thus both elements need to be taken into account at the time that the thrust is made.

Movement

The final element of Distance that needs to be taken into account is movement. Both combatants will be moving, during the bout and this will change the Distance between you and your opponent. This is most easily seen in the use of the retreat in response to a thrust. You need to be aware of your own movement during the execution of the thrust, but also the movement of the opponent, especially if they close distance as you are thrusting.

SITUATIONAL AWARENESS

The elements described above; your distance, the distance to the opponent and movement, all form a part of situational awareness and it is a lot of information that you need to assimilate in a short amount of time. Situational awareness is also important to be aware of the environment. For the classical and sport fencers, this means being aware of your position on the piste. For the Renaissance fencers it is being aware of any boundaries or obstructions that may be present on the field which you are using.

These elements also need to be taken into account, but for different reasons. Situational awareness is something which is important as you need to know the distance elements in a very short amount of time, in fact when the thrust is delivered, and even a little before it is delivered. With the awareness of distance discovered, the next element that needs to be addressed is technique.

TECHNIQUE PERFORMANCE

The correct performance of the thrust and indeed all skills in fencing is vital. For the current discussion, the correct technical execution of the thrust is vital to correct calibration. Technique is vital to the correct execution of the thrust and it is something that needs to be examined in some detail. It seems like a simple action, but there is a level of skill in it. The thrust must be examined in some detail to see how it works and how this may affect our end result.

Accuracy

Accuracy is an element which extends from proper technical performance of the thrust, and while it is not the focus of this discussion it does have elements which are important. An accurate, but slow thrust is substantially more important that a fast but inaccurate one. The accuracy allows us to hit the target that we are aiming for and this can be important in calibration so that we strike the target at the correct distance rather than some closer one by accident. Thus it can be seen that accuracy in the thrust can be of great importance in its execution and calibration of the thrust. To investigate this, the technical detail must be addressed.

Execution

The thrust is not merely shoving the point of the weapon at the opponent. There are various elements which come into play in the execution of the thrust and only if all of these elements are combined together properly will the thrust be executed properly. Each one of these elements can affect the calibration of the thrust, some will more than others. Each part of the thrust needs to be examined to understand the action properly and to do it properly.

Point to Target

In the execution of the thrust the point should move in a straight line from its starting position to its target with very little deviation. This will ensure that the point has travelled the shortest distance to its target. This is important for accuracy and also speed. A change in direction of the thrust can also affect calibration as the point may gain more velocity, or it may change the distance. Thus it is important that the point travels in the shortest line to its target.

Extend the Arm

The thrust must be performed as a simple extension of the arm toward the target. This keeps things simple and efficient and leaves the least amount of room for errors in its performance. It is better not to think about hitting a target merely extending the arm and thus the point into a position into space which happens to be occupied by the opponent. In this way your mind does not think about hitting a target and focuses more upon the correct execution of the action, and this will help you a great deal.

The primary muscles that should be used in the performance of the thrust are the shoulder muscles. The arm should be lifted by these muscles to push the point toward its target. The wrist and elbow should be merely used to direct the point toward the target. Thus it can be seen that the correct execution of the thrust involves the movement of the shoulder more than any other part of the arm. This keeps the action simple in its performance. Problems in the execution of the thrust will be discussed further on.

Speed

Speed is an element which gets too much focus made of it. A fast thrust is useful, but only if it is accurate, and thus we should aim for accuracy more than speed in the performance of the thrust. A slow thrust is easier to control, whereas a fast thrust is harder to control because the mind starts to focus more upon the speed of the thrust rather than its execution. This can be one of the causes of over calibration. At slower speeds you can focus more on the performance of the thrust and making sure that the target is struck and with the correct calibration. Going too fast is one place which will have some discussion in the problem areas which arise and can cause you to hit too hard.

PROBLEM AREAS

There are many problem areas in the execution of the thrust. As teachers and students we should be aware of them in ourselves as well as our students. Some of the problem areas will be highlighted here, with some solutions to these problems discussed in a later part of the discussion.

Chambering
The first problem that will become present is what is called chambering the thrust. This involves one of two actions. The first form involves the bending of the elbow before the thrust is performed. The thrust is then pushed toward the opponent using both the shoulder and the elbow. This form of thrust will tend to be very hard in its performance due to the extra muscles put into play. The other form of chambering involves swinging the arm backward a little before the thrust is made, once again this can lead to over calibration due to the extra velocity added to the thrust.

Swinging
Swinging is another problem which will surface both on its own and also with chambering the thrust. Simply swinging the arm is no good, this often comes from practicing the thrust without executing each on singularly. Simply swinging the arm releases a great deal of control and as with chambering it can lead to hitting too hard.

Elbow Thrust
Attempting to deliver the thrust from the elbow by its simple extension, or driving the wrist forward are both problems that can lead to inaccuracy and over-calibration. The first results in a snapping action which creates a great deal of velocity and very little control. This performance method can also lead to the fencer developing "tennis elbow" and similar problems with the joint.

Wrist Driving
Driving the wrist forward is related to throwing the thrust. This is very much simply attempting to throw the point at the opponent. Due to all of the force being at the front, the over-balancing and over-extension in the action will lead to a high velocity and also hitting too hard. This problem and the "elbow thrust" often result from the fencer attempting to thrust faster than their technical skill at their current level will allow them safely. This is a problem where, because the speed is the aim of the thrust, technique gets left behind and the fencer will attempt to muscle the thrust through to its target. The overt use of muscle is what leads to the over calibration in the thrust.

Scooping
Use of the wrist in this method can also lead to "scooping" the point, where the point of the weapon dips downward or is pushed upward before the thrust is made. This leads to an inaccurate thrust and the creation of velocity which can lead to over calibration in the thrust. It also gives a very predictable path which an observant opponent can easily counter.

SOLUTION

Start with Awareness
Various problems have been highlighted in the delivery of the thrust. Each one of these problems has a solution to it to correct the problem which is present in the fencer, but the

first thing that needs to be done is to be aware of the problem. The opponents of the individual will realise the problem as they are being struck too hard, but the fencer themselves may not realise what this is or think it is their problem. Where the fencer does not realise, they should be approached in a friendly manner and be made aware of the problem.

Observe

Once the awareness of the problem has been made the next step is to see what the problem is exactly. This involves close observation of the fencer. It is possible to see the problems in a bout, but it is much easier to do in a drilling situation. The fencer should make some thrusts against a stationary target to examine the thrust and see if it is a technical problem, and then against moving targets to see if it is a Distance issue. Once the root cause has been found it is then possible to look at problem solving. As with any other technical skill in fencing the best way to improve the skill is to use drills.

Distance Drills

Distance drills are very easy to set up. The fencer should stand at a distance away from a stationary target and then approach it. Once they think that they are at the correct distance a thrust should be made. This should be done slowly at first, and then speed up. A further drill involves the use of two combatants who move toward one another and the fencer who is the focus will say "Stop." when they think they are at the correct distance. A situational awareness drill involves the fencer closing their eyes and several people moving about them once they stop the fencer should open their eyes and say who is at the correct distance, too close or too far away.

Technique Drills

Technique drills involve focusing on the thrust itself and how it is performed. In these drills a stationary target should be used so that the Distance does not change. Depending on what the problem is will depend on what should be the focus of the drill.

Where it is one of the other joints leading the thrust, in extreme instances these joints can be immobilised so that the fencer does not use them. The teacher should be watching the fencer perform the thrust and giving corrections as they are being performed. This should be done until the fencer can perform the thrust without the problem surfacing in the thrust.

The thrust should be performed at very slow speed at first so that the fencer can focus on what they are doing. As they get more comfortable and are able to perform it properly, the speed of the action should be increased. The increase in speed should stop once the fencer is focusing too much on the speed rather than the technique as this is the limit of their technical skill, at this point in time the speed should be then reduced until the fencer is able to perform the action properly again. In all cases, the focus should be on technique rather than speed.

CONCLUSION

In most forms of fencing, the thrust is the primary attack and thus it is important that it is able to be performed without the opponent being struck too hard. This involves the thrust being performed at the correct Distance and using the correct technique. Distance and technique are the two root causes of over calibration in the thrust and need to be examined in some detail if we are all to improve as fencers. As we progress, consideration of the thrust is often left behind, but it is of great importance that we come back to this most basic skill on a regular basis in order that we can refine our skill and ensure that we are performing the action properly.

If problems arise in the performance of the thrust, go back and see how it is being performed and fix the problems. These problems need to be fixed as early as possible so that they are not allowed to become habits. It is never good to strike the opponent in a bout too hard; this is a consideration that should be made by all fencers no matter what weapon that they are using.

On the Subject of Cutting

INTRODUCTION

The subject of this discussion is cutting. It is a subject which has been debated long and hard, both in the Renaissance period and the modern period. For the purposes of this article I will be mainly focusing on cutting from a Renaissance perspective and also specifically focusing on the use of the rapier.

One of the most important things about this discussion is that it is necessary that it is done from an open-minded perspective to get the greatest benefit from it. As such there will be some points which will be raised which may cause some arguments. Please bear in mind as you read that I am attempting to give the most event-handed discussion of the subject possible and that possibly some of the points raised should be considered as such.

TEST CUTTING VALIDITY

Method

Various organisations and individuals have performed test cutting experiments with regards to the use of the cut with the rapier and this will be the first subject for discussion. It is the methods of these test cuts that will be the focus of the discussion. One of the most important things that need to be taken into account for proper test cutting is the proper method of performing the cuts. If the cuts are not performed properly the test can in no way be valid. This has to be balanced with various other factors in order that the test cutting itself is representational.

Weapon

Not only does the method have to be valid but this also needs to take into account the weapon being used and the various variations on the weapon possible. In essence a sample of weapons should be taken rather than one single form being taken as representational of all of the forms of that weapon. A perfect example is the rapier in this case. The classification of the weapon is difficult as it came in many forms. Some had longer blades. Some had thicker blades. Some had edges which would be suitable for cutting and others did not. Unless this is taken into account the test cannot be truly valid for all weapons of that particular type.

Situational

Next it is important to balance this to the combat situation in which the weapon was used. To be valid the test must be performed in a manner which at least resembles the action and situation in which the cut would be performed. This also must take into account any preventive equipment or lack thereof, such as clothing that would have or not been worn at the time.

If a cut would most likely have been aimed for example at the body then the target should be placed in a particular way that it would reflect such and placed in such a manner that it would represent a human body. This means that there needs to be some way to prevent it from moving and also allow the action to be performed against it. Without these factors being taken into account it is impossible to say that the test is representational.

TECHNIQUE AND BIAS

The method of performing the cut does need to be taken into account so that the test can be valid. The test will be invalidated if the cut is not performed as it would be in the situation where it would be used. This means that the correct technique needs to be used applying the correct amount of pressure against the target. If either of these is missing then the test cannot be seen to be valid. This requires research into how the cut would have been performed using a real weapon against a real human being.

Personal Bias

In this, it is here where personal bias has the most effect. If the tester does not think that a method is valid there is no way to guarantee that the cut will be performed correctly as sub-consciously if they do not think that the method is valid they will want it to fail the test. This means that the tester needs to be open-minded throughout the test in order that it can be valid through proper performance of the actions required.

Group Bias

There are various reasons why a particular form of cut may or may not be used by a particular group or organisation. This may be based on various different factors that need to be taken into account when examining what is being done. One factor is the weapons being used in the bouting. If the weapons are not suited to the performance of a particular cut it can be easily expected that that form of cut will not be used by that group. This can be based on the make or design of the weapon being used.

Historical Bias

Another factor that should be taken into account is the school of thought behind the organisation using the weapon. The late Italian schools of fence did not use the cut particularly much and this will influence the type of cut that is being used, how much it is practiced, and the situations in which it is or is not used. This will be different to a more German approach where the cut is more important to the style being performed and thus its use will be more prevalent.

Administrative and Safety Bias

Finally there are administrative and safety issues that may be present in the organisation which prevent certain types of cut being used. These are typical to the organisation or group and will determine which cuts are considered valid and which ones are not. This simply results in the group being unused to the cut being performed.

CORRECT METHOD ESSENTIAL

With regards to cuts the most important thing of all types of cuts is the correct method so that they are effective. Without this it is impossible to perform them properly or effectively. There are various factors that need to be taken into account. Technical detail needs to be considered in the performance of all kinds of cut, and these technical details are best expressed in the various factors highlighted below.

Hacking Versus Cutting

First there is the question of hacking in comparison to cutting. This relies upon the purpose and method used for the particular type of cut. Simply bashing away at the opponent with the edge of the weapon is a waste of time, at least with a rapier, and thus the cut must be performed properly and with purpose, the purpose being to cut the target. This purpose must be realised and paramount for the individual even where the damage is only simulated as it will be for most modern martial practice.

Weapon Appropriate

The next thing that needs to be taken into account is that the method is appropriate for the weapon itself. This is important as the wrong type of cut performed with the weapon can lead to all sorts of problems not to mention potential damage to a weapon which money has been invested. This means that the method of cutting is very much dependent on the weapon being used. It is useless to attempt to perform cleaving cuts with a weapon for which it is not the purpose.

Situationally Appropriate

Finally, situational importance, the cut must be appropriate to the situation in which the combatant finds themselves in. This must factor in various aspects such as distance, leverage and pressure. There are cuts which are best performed close to the opponent and there are those which are best performed further away, these aspects need to be taken into account in the consideration of which cut will be performed. If the distance is wrong or the leverage is not adequate or the pressure of the blade against the target is not correct then there is no way that the cut will be able to be performed correctly or properly in that situation. Thus situational importance is vital in the correct performance of the cut, or any attack for that matter.

WEAPON DESIGN

The weapon has been discussed briefly, now it is important to go into more detail. There is a great impact on cutting from the design of the weapon. It must be remembered that there are many different weapons which were called rapiers, and several different forms in which they came, some of which were elucidated above.

Blade Design

Obviously the thing that has the greatest effect is the blade design. The width is important in determining the types of cut that will be valid for it. This needs to be balanced with the edge itself, and whether it has a real one or not, whether it is sharp or would have been sharp. This also needs to be balanced with the angle of the edge to see how well it would cut using different methods. This needs to be considered along with whether the weapon is suited to the particular form of cut chosen. Some weapons will be able to perform several different types of cut well and others will be more restricted in their proper use. This may, and often does even come down to the individual weapon.

HISTORICAL EVIDENCE

Various historical sources describe cutting in their texts and describe the manner in which the cut should be performed. It is important to examine these important documents to find how the cuts should be performed. Of course, the interpretation of these texts will also have a great impact on how the cuts will be performed.

Some give clear examples of how the cut should be performed and others merely hint that cuts were performed but give no description at all. The important thing here is that due to cuts being mentioned in various texts with regard to the use of the rapier, di Grassi and Saviolo being only two examples, the idea that the cut is not a valid attack or technique in the use of the rapier is ludicrous.

PUSH AND DRAW CUTS

The most debated forms of cut for the rapier which are argued about by modern theorists and practitioners are the push cut and the draw cut. Some believe that they are a by-product of some forms of fencing performed; others believe that they are legitimate methods which have been changed to suit the current age. The question that would be posed is that if they are such a non-technique for the use of the rapier, why have they travelled down and been described in so many manuals? This goes back to some of what was said before.

A Slicing Cut

These are slicing cuts performed with pressure against the target. The blade is not merely placed against the target and then drawn or pushed. This comes back again to the correct method for their use and also the weapon. A draw or push cut will only work particularly well with a weapon which is sharp on its edge, and sharp in the form of a razor as the cut is designed to slice.

Appropriate Target

In test cutting for this particular form of cut the target, method and weapon are important. The target would be presumed to be an individual wearing a light shirt as may be worn for a duel, thus the preventative measures are important. The position of the target is also important that it will represent such an individual standing up.

Appropriate Weapon and Technique

The weapon needs to be sharp on the edge so that the weapon will actually cut using this method, thus it needs to be suitable for this form of cut. Finally the cuts must be performed correctly with the correct amount of pressure and leverage against the target. Only once all of these elements are brought together will it be seen whether or not this is a valid method for cutting, and there may be some who will be surprised by the results.

TEST CUTTING NECESSARY

There are various methods of cutting, the impact cut, tip cut, push cut and draw cut. The only way that we will ever know what is or isn't a valid method is for test cutting to be performed where discovery of new information rather than the debunking of a particular method is the aim of the experimentation being performed. Test cutting is also the only real way to understand what these weapons would do against their designed target, the human body, without causing all sorts of legal issues.

CONCLUSION: HEALTHY DEBATE IS GOOD

The debates about various methods of cutting with various weapons will be debated in the future along with many other elements of fencing that present themselves. This is due to the many different points of view that are available in the modern world. The most important thing with regard to this is that we keep our minds open to these different points of view as they can only enrich our understanding of fencing.

Debate is healthy as it allows us to examine various subjects and hopefully come up with some answers in some situations, but always with different points of view. This is healthy for all practitioners and to close our minds to these possibilities is to close our minds to a wider world of different options.

Reading the Opponent

INTRODUCTION

Everybody has been in this situation before... You are called up for your bout, you get yourself ready, you wander out on to the field, the various litanies are read, the marshal then calls you to on guard, and then "Fence!" You stand there looking at your opponent thinking "What do I do now?" This is the first place where reading the opponent becomes a practical thing, of course, if we are smart we observe our opponents off the field as well. This discussion will be focussed on those aspects of reading the opponent which occur on the field. It is not designed to tell you how to deal with every opponent, just how to get the information so you have some ideas about how to deal with your opponents.

IMPORTANCE

The first question that is asked is why is reading the opponent important? There are various reasons that answer this particular question. The first and most practical one is that so we do not launch into an attack and skewer ourselves on the opponent's point in the process. This can be avoided through reading of the opponent and knowing how he will react. This leads on to another aspect that of predicting what the opponent is likely or not likely to do.

The ability to predict what the opponent can or cannot do is dependent on reading the opponent. If we can see what the opponent can or cannot do, we can plan for those things that they might do. The element of prediction comes from reading the opponent both stationary and in action, each one of these elements will tell us something about the opponent.

SENSES

There are two main senses which are of greatest use to the fencer in reading the opponent and one which is less useful. The two which are the most useful are sight and touch, the one which is least useful is hearing. Hearing is limited due to the head protection which is worn when fencing, this muffles the ability to hear and reduces the effectiveness of this particular sense.

Sight is the most obvious one as we are looking at our opponent and seeing what they do or do not do. The sense of touch is also important as we can also feel where the opponent may move and how they move through contact through the weapons. Each one of these two most useful senses will be addressed in turn, giving some ideas about how they can be used to read the opponent.

SIGHT

The first sense that will be discussed is sight. This is more than just looking at your opponent, it is observing them. In this it is important to look at details but also at the whole picture as well. The details assist with building a complete picture of the opponent.

Feet and Legs

We will start from the ground and work upwards. You can tell things from the position of the feet of your opponent. Is their front foot pointed at you? Is their back foot in line with their front foot? Are they standing flat-footed, or are they more on the balls of their feet? Each one of these elements will tell you something about the opponent.

If their front foot is not pointed at you then their facing may be different. This can also affect the accuracy of their thrust. If their feet are in line with one another the opponent may have a tendency to use more linear footwork. If they are standing flat-footed they will move slower than if they are on the balls of their feet. Needless to say the primary information you will get from looking at the feet will be about movement. Similar information is gained from looking at the legs. Are the opponent's knees bent? Are they bent deeply? This will give you some indication about how well the opponent will move and also some indication of how quickly.

Body

The next element to look at is the body. This is the primary body mass that the opponent carries during fencing. This should also partially consider the head of the opponent, but staying with the body, questions can be asked. Is the body upright or bent? Is the opponent slouching or hunched? Where is their body mass located?

The location of the body mass will determine which foot, if either the weight is placed, this will give some idea as to whether the opponent is more likely to move forward or backward. The bending of the body can indicate some of this direction; this can also give you some idea about what they are trying to protect the most. A slouching or hunched opponent may be tired or scared; this will affect their fencing ability. Moving on to the head, the position of the head will tell you much of what has also been discovered by the position of the body due to its weight. If you can see your opponent's face you can see what sort of expression they have and this will tell you about the opponent and their feelings about the bout.

Arms and Hands

Hands and arms are important. They are a direct connection between the body and the weapon of the opponent. These limbs will determine where the weapon is and is not able to be placed. How is the opponent holding the weapon? This can give some indication about what they are likely to do. Where are the arms placed in the on guard position? How does the opponent move them? Each one of these will tell you where the next movement may be. Is the hand and arm extended from the body, or withdrawn? Are they in an advanced position or more refused? This may give you some indication about what sort of blade engagement, if any, you will get out of your opponent.

Assemblage

The next part of the observation is assembling all of the information that you have gained by observation to get some idea of your opponent. Each piece of information will fill something in about the opponent and how they may move. Their position will tell you which direction is easiest for them to move to and where they are likely to go to. This relates to their ward and *contra postura*, which will be discussed in more detail further on.

The overall picture is important, but it must take into account the different elements and details in order to complete the picture. Nothing at this point in time has been said about movement, but the observation process should continue when the opponent is moving. The idea of activity versus inactivity will be something that will be discussed later on.

Equipment

While it can sometimes be misleading, information about the opponent can also be gained from examining the equipment that they are using. How well does the mask or helm fit? What about the fit of the jacket? Does it look like the equipment belongs to them or is just borrowed? What sort of state of repair is the equipment in? Each one of these elements can tell you something about the opponent; if the equipment is borrowed and does not fit as well as it could, this could result in some restriction on the opponent. It could also indicate that the opponent is only new to fencing. If the equipment is not in a particularly good state of repair this can tell you things about the opponent and their attitude to what they are doing. All of these elements can tell you something about your opponent.

TOUCH

Touch is the other sense that does us most good in fencing. This is primarily achieved through the use of *senso di ferro*, or *sentiment du fer*, or *tacto*. The idea of feeling through the blade is an important one and a skill that every fencer should seek to develop as it can tell us a great deal about our opponent. Both prolonged and incidental contact between the blades can tell us something about the opponent.

This skill, if well developed, can act like an extra sense and can help us predict what our opponent may do, or is likely to do. Simple things such as the blade quivering can tell us that the opponent may be afraid, nervous, tired or be overly excited. Is the contact between the blades weak or strong? This can tell us whether the opponent may attempt to use force against the blade to open a line. How the blades contact is important as well as where they contact. The movement of the blades against one another is also important. All of this information is gained through the use of *senso di ferro*.

CONTRA POSTURA

Contra postura is an idea which was expounded by Salvator Fabris and is a most useful concept. To use it properly we have to understand its underlying principles. The main idea of *contra postura* is to place you in a position which both actively and passively resists the position of the opponent.

The principles behind *contra postura* are that your blade should be on-line while the opponent's blade is forced off-line by the simple position of the weapon and the body of the fencer. In essence in a correct *contra postura* you should be able to make a simple unhindered attack against the opponent. If they were to attack at the same time their attack should pass you by because you have closed the line. This is all about examining the ward of the opponent and placing yourself in a position to resist this. The whole idea is reliant on the accurate observation of the opponent.

The greatest effect of *contra postura* is that you place yourself in a position where you can attack the opponent safely while guarding yourself against the attack of the opponent. This is the primary purpose of the use of *contra postura*. The only way for the opponent to attack you is to change their position, this results in an action which involves the opponent using a fencing tempo to achieve this. Depending on the particular position will determine where the opponent will have to move to perform this action, resulting in an element of prediction, which you can then use to counter them. This leads on to the concept of second intention also as you are making the opponent perform an action which you can then counter with a following action, thus the first action sets up for the following one. *Contra postura* is a most useful tool, if it is used properly, and can lead to a great advantage over the opponent.

ACTIVITY AND INACTIVITY

The idea of movement has been briefly discussed in various parts above. It is now time to examine what activity and inactivity can tell us about the opponent. If you perform an action and the opponent does not respond this can tell us something about them, as well as if they actually respond to the action can tell us something about them.

What the opponent does and how they do it are simultaneously important as this can allude to the skill level of the opponent and how they move. This will assist us in telling us what they are and are not likely to do, and how they may or may not respond to an action. If you perform an action to elicit a response from the opponent to perform a following action, and the opponent does not respond, this tells us something about the opponent and how we should respond in future. Thus it is important that both action and inaction can tell us something about the opponent.

LEADS?

The question that needs to be asked once all of this information has been assimilated is where does all of this lead? There needs to be a point behind spending so much time in reading the opponent. The first thing that reading the opponent does is it allows us to feel out the opponent. To find out where they are strong and where they are weak.

The smart tactician will then attack where the opponent is weak and avoid where they are strong. It is sometimes necessary to feel out the opponent by performing actions, these actions should be designed to see how the opponent will respond and thus gain information about them. This can lead on to further actions which can result in a plan being formed as to how to defeat the opponent. The information gained through reading the opponent can allow us to form attacks and defences against the opponent. Further to this, with the full facility of reading the opponent in action and the correct responses elicited, it is then possible to move on to second intention and other advanced ideas.

CONCLUSION

Reading the opponent is an essential skill that every fencer will eventually have to develop if they want to become more successful. Each time we face an opponent we should be observing the opponent, finding out their strengths and weaknesses. The reading of the opponent on the other side can also tell us things about ourselves and where we need to improve. This can be a great asset to us as it allows us to improve every time that we face an opponent. It should always be a learning experience for us every time we face an opponent.

Each one of the elements is important in telling us how to deal with our opponents. Each one must be taken into account so that we have the most complete picture of the opponent. Only with this information to hand are we able to make intelligent decisions as to how to deal with our various opponents.

On Handedness – The Left-handed Fencer

INTRODUCTION

The left-handed fencer is always tricky. This is the case for both fighting against them, and also teaching them. Due to the dominant presence of right-handed fencers, the left-handed fencer is one that the right-hander will run into on relatively rare occasion. For those groups who have left-handed fencers present, you have an advantage over those who don't as you will become used to facing them. From the teacher's point of view teaching the left-handed this presents some issues in their teaching. This article will be a discussion of the issues associated in both teaching and combat against the left-hander.

TEACHING

Teaching a left-handed fencer while you are right-handed is always a tricky situation. It requires a switching over in your mind about how to teach the fencer. For some of the demonstration you may have to switch hands to demonstrate the technique so that they can understand what is happening. This will also assist you in learning about fighting with the left hand yourself, which is to your advantage.

Most importantly, you should never force a left-handed student to fence right-handed because it will make the teaching more difficult. Take this on as a challenge for your teaching so that you can learn something for yourself in the process. There may be some swapping of sides during drills and this is fine, learning the opposite hand is useful for all fencers. The best conceptual way to think about the left-hander is to look at the change in lines as this is the real difference and go from there. It is a mirror image.

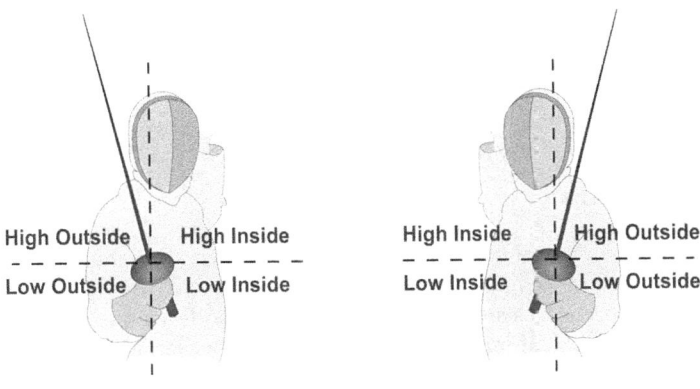

Lines for the Right-hander   *Lines for the Left-hander*

Lines

The lines are opposite, but also the same. The outside line is still to the outside of the weapon, in the case of the right-hander this is to the right, in the case of the left-hander this is to the left of the sword. Obviously the inside line is the opposite side also, but the same principles apply. When teaching a right-hander it is sometimes more effective to stand next to the student to show them the technique, in the case of the left-hander it may actually be more effective to stand opposite them and thus use the mirror effect of the position.

In the case of companion weapons in rapier combat the companion weapon will be on the "wrong side" this will require some adjustment for their effective use. It may require the crossing of the hands and devices to use them effectively. Another method for achieving this is to change the on guard position and movement to promote the off-hand; this will take practice and experimentation to achieve effectiveness.

COMBAT

The combat against the left-hander is an interesting prospect, just as with teaching the left-hander the combat against the left-hander takes a change in perspective. For some it makes no perceivable difference to them. In most cases there is a difference but the change for them is subtle enough that they do not consciously notice it. There are differences that should be made especial note of in how to deal with a left-handed opponent. These changes will assist you to deal with the change in perspective.

Guard

To start with you need to change your on guard position slightly. You need to stand more profiled in stance; this involves moving the feet slightly. This position should remove the inside line away from the opponent. The guard should be pushed more toward the outside line to close it due to the position of the left-handed opponent; further to the importance of the outside line with regard to the left-handed opponent.

Lines

In the case of the left-handed fencer, he will seek the outside line as it is the easier target due to the on guard position. The most important thing is that the easier target for the right-hander against the left-hander is also the outside line. This makes things most interesting for the combatants. You should seek movement toward the outside line to be more effective in the attack. The inside line of the left-hander is far away and puts you in a position where you could be easily struck by the opponent.

The only way that the inside line should be approached or attacked is when you have blade engagement with the opponent. This engagement needs to entirely close the line against the opponent to be effective. The essence here is that the line needs to be closed entirely so that you are protected.

LEFT VS LEFT

An interesting point that should be made in this discussion is that the left-handed fencer will usually be facing right-handed opponents rather than left-handed ones. This is an important consideration as it often results in the left-handed fencer having problems with facing other left-handed opponents. This is due to the change in position that results from facing a left-handed opponent.

Ironically, the left-handed fighting another left-handed comes down to the same situation as a right-handed facing a right-handed opponent. In this the left-handed opponent should consider examining how right-handed opponents deal with other right-handed opponents and apply the same principles, but in a mirror image.

CONCLUSION

The left-handed fencer is an interesting prospect from the point of view of the combatant and also the teacher. In all cases, much can be learnt from both situations.

So that we become better at both facing and teaching left-handed fencers, we should endeavour to seek them out and learn as much as we can from them. This goes for both right-handed and left-handed fencers. Hopefully this discussion will have given some ideas about how to deal with the left-handed student and opponent. The important thing to note is that both teaching and fighting against the left-hander requires a slight change in perspective to achieve the goal that is sought.

No Footwork Fencing, Or Fencing From a Chair

INTRODUCTION

The first thing that is going to be said by the reader is "Didn't you not so long ago write an article about the importance of footwork?" The answer to this is "Yes." Am I going to deny the importance of footwork to normal modes of fencing? Not at all; this article reinforces another article about disability and fencing, which can also be found in this book, and also the discussion about Fabris from a chair, it lays the foundation work for the Fabris lesson.

The qustion arises, just because you cannot walk for some reason, either permanent or temporary, does that mean that you should stop fencing, or fencing training for you is not possible? Not at all; there are ways around this. From the point of this particular article so long as you can sit up and hold a sword you can still fence in a form. This article is designed to show you how to do this. The more able fencer will also find that fencing from a chair is a useful training tool.

LEG REPLACEMENT

The first part of the process is replacing the bits of the body that don't work. In this particular case it is replacing the legs that are not working. To this point the chair is used. This has some advantages over legs actually. The chair is more stable as it has four legs and is thus less likely to fall over. Your legs do not have to be used and thus any injured joints do not have stress placed on them.

Of course there are some disadvantages as well. With the increased stability also come the lack of footwork and thus the inability to move as far as you otherwise might, footwork in its normal form is not possible. This means that you are a stationary target for the most part, though as will be explained there are some options available for the sitting fencer. The final disadvantage is the possible increased luggage when you travel, but this is more of a side note.

CHOOSING A CHAIR

Choosing the chair needs to be done carefully, just any chair will not do. While your favourite laid-back chair may be awesomely comfortable, it may not be the most appropriate for fencing from. The first thing is that the chair must be stable on the ground. A wobbly chair may collapse from beneath you and take you with it causing injury and you do not need this sort of threat in the back of your mind when you are fencing.

Secondly, is that the chair must allow you to sit up straight in the chair's normal mode of operation. This means that it should have a straight back or none at all. This will enable you to breathe better and present yourself better to your opponent. The lack of a back will actually have an advantage in some instances allowing you to lean back further than if one was present.

Thirdly, is to examine the arms which may be found on some chairs for resting the arms on. It is preferable that the chair does not have arms as these will get in the way of your own arms. While it may provide a minimum of protection the presence of the arms on the chair will be more of a hindrance than a help. Having your arms hindered will prevent you from using your arms effectively and most of your defence will rely upon the effective use of your hands and arms.

THE SITTING WARDS

Now that your chair has been selected it is time to start the process of learning to fence from it. As with all forms of fencing, the ward, or guard, is important to the fencer. For the sitting fencer, the position of the lower limbs is just as important as if they were standing. Your legs should be lined up with the front legs of the chair. Make sure you have the chair turned so your dominant shoulder is closer toward your opponent. This will profile your body to them slightly. The top half of the body should assume the normal position for your ward of choice.

In selecting a ward when sitting in a chair you should consider your position and what you have to protect. Selecting a high ward may place the blade across the line of the opponent, but it will also allow them easy access to it. This is beside the fact that it will be tiring. A low ward is much preferable as the arm can relax more and the blade is withdrawn more. This means that the engagement can be chosen by you at the correct time. The other thing is that a low ward may lure your opponent into easy striking distance.

SITTING "FOOTWORK"

What? How can you do footwork when sitting down? When sitting, remember it is possible for you to lean your body forward, backward and sideways. The forward and backward will serve for your advance and retreat. The sideways movement will serve for voids. In this way you can actually change your distance, however so slightly that you do. Sit in your chair and see how far you can lean in each direction.

With this in mind, it is actually possible to do a lunge from a chair. It works the same way as it would if you were standing. Extend your point toward your target and lean with your body. Just as with the standing version the hand should always lead the body. Especially when performing this action from a chair, you should lift your hilt in to protect yourself.

OTHER FENCING ACTIONS

For the most part, the other actions in fencing work much the same as they do when you are standing up. Parries are the same for the upper part of the body. Parries for the lower parts, if used, will just have to be a little shallower than when you are standing. As stated you can lean your body to the left, right and rear to void, though this will clearly demonstrate the advantage of going perpendicular to the opponent's attack.

Actions using the blade of the weapon will work the same as they have previously. This is because the hand actions are not changed. You just have to remember that you don't have to go so low with many of them and if you do you may run into problems.

TACTICS FOR THE SEATED FENCER

Where the two fencers are seated in chairs, they should be placed an extension and a lean away from one another. This allows for some movement and use of distance. Where there is the normal situation of a seated fencer against a standing one. The standing one has the advantage of movement and a much greater use of distance and height. The seated fencer has the advantage of having a set distance so has one thing less to worry about.

The only way that the seated fencer can get the advantage in distance is to lure their opponent in so an attack may be made. This is the primary method that the seated fencer has to use. This can be achieved by body position, arm positon, sword position or all of them. Blade engagement is one way in which this can be achieved.

CONCLUSION

Fencing without footwork is possible, not generally advised for the individual who has the option of movement, but for the fencer without that option, it is. Fencing from a chair is an option for those individuals with mobility impairment. In this way they can participate, and quite effectively, in fencing. This idea is not actually new, as can be seen by the wheelchair fencing at the Paralympics, as has been mentioned in another article. For the Renaissance fencer a suitable period-looking chair is even an option.

Fencing is something which many can participate in, with the right attitude and approach. This has been a rather short guide to fencing from a chair, but it should give some ideas about where to approach this particular problem from. What should also be noted is that fencing from a chair can be used effectively as a drill and exercise for all fencers to improve their hand actions. With the use of the feet completely removed the fencer will then have to rely on their hand actions, thus improving them in the process. Perspective with regard to fencing is important and ability should be the focus rather than what the fencer cannot do.

Below: Author, fencing from a chair against Duncan Bailey, with Steve Pye watching. Rowany Festival, 2005 (AS XL)

True and False Arts: A Discussion of Tempo in the Use of the Feint

INTRODUCTION

Feints are a subject which come up in discussions with regard to the tactics of fencing quite often, and one which I have not really discussed in detail. To fill this particular hole in my explanations of fencing I present the following on the subject of the True and False Arts. This is examining one element of the feint, but it is one that needs to be considered as it is vital to how feints work, or don't.

THE TRUE AND FALSE ARTS

> "I am constrayned to divide this Art into two Arts of Sciences, callinge the one the True, the other, the False art: But withall giving everie man to understand, that falsehood hath no advauntage against true Art, but rather is most hurtfull and deadlie to him that useth it."
>
> (Di Grassi, 1594)

The first question is what is this all about, True and False arts? Discussion of Tempo? Put simply, tempo is a concept, which is integral and one of the founding elements of fencing, essentially to understand this discussion the reader must understand that *all actions in fencing take time*. This is something which di Grassi states as his fifth advertisement.

As for the True and False Arts, this is a discussion which has raged since the Renaissance, and will continue to rage amongst those who use the rapier, indeed any sword. What is most interesting about this argument is that it abates a little in the time of the smallsword, though there are still active proponents against it. In the modern era, there is even less argument against the use of the False Art.

To discuss the True and False Arts, first the two must be divided, so that they may be compared and seen in contrast. In essence, the True Art is the use of the blade using direct attacks against the opponent, and the False Art is the use of the blade using feints and misdirection. If the two concepts, tempo and the False Arts, are combined then it will be understood as to what this discussion is about.

FEINTS AND THOUGHTS

The feint can be used to quite good effect to deceive the opponent into opening themselves up for an attack. This is using the False Art. There were Renaissance masters who thought that the False Art was something, which a person should stay away from, for various reasons including that it was dishonourable. On the other hand there were other masters that said that a combatant who masters both the True Art and the False Art was a much better swordsman than one who stuck to one or the other. The other argument against the False Art, that being the one regarding tempo, and the focus of this discussion, was that using the False Art lost time in the attack and therefore reduced its effect.

TECHNIQUE

"Tempo is lost due to lack of practice, owing to which one's body is not yet made limber, or if students adopt some bad habits, futilely pursuing feints, disengages, counterdisengages, and similar things." (Capo Ferro, 1610)

FEINTS CAN LOSE AND GAIN TIME

Each movement of the blade takes time, so a thrust takes time; the parry takes time, and so on. If a feint is used time is lost in the attack if the feint could not hit the opponent, but if the feint is convincing enough, then the opponent will attempt to parry. When the opponent uses the parry and the blade then moves to another line of attack, the feint has actually increased time for the defence and reduced it for the attack. If the feint is not effective in presenting itself as an attack, then the opponent will wait for the real attack, and the defender keeps the time advantage.

In the first scenario, the combatant gains time through the use of the feint; and in the second he loses time due to the use of the feint. The combatant should be aware of this if they are going to use the False Art. It has its advantage, but it also has its disadvantage. The combatant needs to make the feint convincing enough that the opponent has to parry it for the feint to work, otherwise it is simply extra blade work and lost time.

CONCLUSION

The use of the feint is dependent on the use of time in fencing. It is the use of time in the efficient movement of the sword of the attacker to make his motions and it is also in the efficient movement of the sword of the defender to make his motions in defence. In a simple mathematical sense, the feint is bound to fail as the attacker has to make two actions, first the feint, then the real attack, to the defender's single action, his defence, unless he can blend his feint into his attack in a single motion.

If, however, the defender can be convinced to defend to somewhere they are not needed to defend, then the attacker can make an advantage with the first action, and even the playing field a little bit, reducing the actions to two and two a-piece. It is in the convincing of the feint and the efficiency of the action is where the attacker can make up his advantage. This is where the real secret of the feint lies.

Thus in the end it still lies in the simple statement made by di Grassi, "every motion is accomplished in time." (di Grassi, 1594). It is how the fencer uses this time which is important. This goes for all fencing, not just feints. The simplest defence against the feint is even easier than making one, it is simple, don't parry the feint, wait for the real attack. This, again, relies on time.

Rapier and Cloak – A Bluffer's Guide

INTRODUCTION

While there will be reference to three manuals of the Renaissance period, this investigation is an introduction to the use of the cloak, based on the general principles found in these manuals. This is designed to give you and understanding of how the cloak operates so that you can use it in a competent fashion. More specific lessons on particular masters are of benefit to study, however having a foundation in the use of the cloak will make these more in-depth lessons more useful.

The rapier and cloak combination is one of the more difficult to use, but it can also be one of the most satisfying if performed correctly. There is an inherent amount of flair in the use of the cloak due to the nature of the combination, and much care needs to be applied in its use. There are those who do not like this particular combination and those who like it very much. This is up to personal preference. As with other combinations, there is much, which can be said about it, from the holding of the cloak, to its use.

SOURCE MATERIAL

The source material which is presented in this discussion uses as close to primary materials as possible. Issues with regard to this particular element of the discussion will be noted below in the bibliographic discussion. Further to this these primary materials will be in a distilled form, extracting the most important parts from each and using this as the framework upon which the investigation is based.

This examination focusses on three masters works with regard to their use of the sword and cloak. Chronologically they are Agrippa's *Trattato di Scientia d'Arme* of 1553, di Grassi's *His True Art of Defence* of 1594, and finally Capo Ferro's *Gran Simulacro dell'arte e dell'uso della Scherma* of 1610. Most of the information found in these manuals is from the point of view of matched weapons i.e. sword and cloak versus sword and cloak, but the information found within can also be applied to other situations with a little modification. The best and most in-depth discussion comes from di Grassi. The other two give basic instruction and ideas about how to use the cloak.

BIBLIOGRAPHICAL ISSUES

In the study of the sword and cloak there are some bibliographical issues that need to be taken into account before any real study can be achieved. One of the first things is with regard to the weapon, the second with the device in the other hand, and lastly there is a language issue that needs to be taken into account. These need to be addressed in some fashion before a real study can take place.

First of all is the language. Of the four manuals which have been used for this investigation only one of these is written in English, that of di Grassi's 1594 manual. Even that is actually a translation of the 1570 Italian manual of the same name. All of the others have been translated from Italian to English in the modern period, by some very knowledgeable people admittedly, but there is still the interference of the translation of the language to take into account.

Further to this language issue, and directly related is the names of the devices being used, the sword and the rotella. Often "spada" in Renaissance manuals is translated as "rapier" where in actual fact it simply means "sword". This investigation is more focused on the use of the rapier and cloak and as such the words "sword" or "rapier" will be used in reference to the weapon used.

As for the cloak itself, there is some discussion and confusion as to whether it is more appropriately called a cape or cloak. The Italian manuals use the word "cappa" while di Grassi uses "cloak", in various spellings. In some ways this is a question of the object itself rather than a bibliographic issue, as is presented below. For the purposes of this investigation the generic "cloak" will be used.

TECHNIQUE

CLOAK OR CAPE?

There are many different types of cloak and cape, depending on size, weight and construction, and the choices between these will be of a personal nature. The main difference between a cloak and a cape is the size, the cloak being larger. A larger cloak will protect more, but it will be heavier and easier to entangle. A smaller cloak will protect less, but will be lighter and move faster. In general the item will be called a cloak for convenience.

The cloak should be constructed of a material which will resist tearing but should also be light enough that it can still be used. The use of the cloak should be considered in its construction. It is advised that cloaks of various constructions and sizes be used before one is constructed to figure out which will suit you the best. The masters do not actually describe the size or construction of the cloak and thus it must be inferred from images or what they write. There is an equal chance that they could be talking about a cape or a cloak. Simple advice dictates that the best cloak to use for the techniques of the master is one which is appropriate to them and also appropriate to you.

HOLDING THE CLOAK

The cloak may typically be held in one of three different ways, wrapped around the arm, draped over the arm, or held in the hand. Each one of these has advantages and disadvantages, which need to be considered. Wrapping the cloak around the arm will allow for the greatest control, but will limit the range and agility of the cloak. Draping the cloak over the arm will allow for a similar amount of control as wrapping, but will give the cloak more range and agility. Holding the cloak in the hand, gives the cloak the best range and agility, but the least amount of control, it is also the easiest to move the cloak from one position to another by this method, and also to throw the cloak.

The choice of how the cloak is held will determine what is possible. Rather than focusing on a single method of use a more broad approach will be used. The cloak, as instructed by di Grassi may be wrapped about the arm, held in the hand or even simply placed folded over the arm. This allows more utility in the use of the cloak rather than restricting it. The best thing to do is to hold the cloak however is most suitable for what you want to do with it at the time.

WARDS

Just as the method of holding the cloak will determine what is possible with it, so too will the ward play a part. The position of both the cloak and rapier will determine what you are able to do with both of them and what sort of access you have to both offensive and defensive actions. In order to gain an appreciation for the options available it is useful to examine what the Renaissance masters had to say about the ward.

Agrippa
Agrippa has his cloak wrapped

around the hand, and also used in combination with the dagger. The cloak is kept low and the rapier adopts a high or low position. He also depicts taking the cloak off the shoulder and shows it to be about thigh length.

This depiction of the cloak is useful for sizing as to usage. Both the sword and cloak are placed in a terza position and centralised.

di Grassi

Giacomo di Grassi depicts two wards but describes three wards in his text. Each one of the wards moves the position of the weapon rather than the position of the cloak, depending on the ward. The cloak however is positioned extended from the body, but also with the arm bent to cover the body with the position of the cloak for all of the wards. This extended position is similar to that shown by Agrippa. Capo Ferro's ward is in a similar position.

Capo Ferro

Capo Ferro places the cloak at the same level, with the cloak draped over the arm, with it extended or retracted. Either the cloak or the rapier may be retracted depending on which item would be used to catch the opponent's blade. The change in position will

allow the combatant to change easily between the two items. Having both extended could lead to entrapment of both rapier and cloak, but gives the opportunity to use both easily. Draping the cloak makes the cloak freer to move than being wrapped, but still will limit its movement. This will also still retain some of the control of the wrapped method.

Common Elements

The common element in all the wards is the position of the cloak. For the most part it is extended. However there are also wards where the cloak is more withdrawn. This is determined by what the ward is most suitable for and how the cloak is likely to be utilised. The position of the weapon is commonly placed in terza, a good central position with access to variations in attack and defense. It is an advantage to change the ward to suit the situation, and thus it is advised that the wards demonstrated as well as others are examined and utilised.

DEFENSE

With regard to defense there are all of the usual options, plus a couple which are unique to this combination. Obviously there is the void, footwork and the sword parry, as with any other use of the rapier. For the cloak and rapier you add the parry with the cloak and also the parry with the combination of cloak and rapier.

For the most part the masters advise that the parry with the cloak is most suitable for any attack which is below the shoulder as lifting the cloak to defend the head will obscure vision. There are a couple of instances where the cloak is used higher than the shoulder but these are usually exception rather than the rule. In these instances the sword is used to parry, and as is described by Capo Ferro the use of the guardia di testa, or head guard, may also be used to defend the head.

Clearly where the cloak is used as a defense, the position of the sword should be considered in order not to entrap it along with the opponent's weapon. Those times where the cloak and rapier are used together it is the cloak which is the primary parry while the rapier supports the defense. In this way the sword can then be withdrawn and used for the counter-attack.

In using the cloak defensively, wait for the opponent to attack and then use the cloak to block or deflect the opponent's attack. The weight of the cloak should be focused on the debole of their weapon. The motion should be a sweeping one, away from the body. The cloak can also be used to deflect the opponent's blade. This should be performed with either the loose part of the cloak or the part, which is over the hand. The cloak will take time to move and it needs to be made correctly so that the blade of the opponent is collected with the maximum amount of weight behind it. Once again the aim should be contact with the debole as primary. The cloak will require practice to use.

Practice with the cloak alone in parrying first to understand and feel how the cloak will move and how much time it will take to move. Practice with the cloak in all of the different methods, wrapped, draped and held in the hand. Once it is easy to move the cloak, then the rapier should be added, ensure that the rapier is not entangled when parrying otherwise this will cause a lot of problems.

OFFENSE

Clearly the best offensive actions with this combination are made with the rapier. These attacks are all the same as found with any other combination. However it should also be noted that there are offensive actions which can be made with the cloak. The actions of the cloak are most often used to enhance the attack with the rapier which follows immediately behind it.

In the use of the sword when used in combination with the cloak, you should make sure that the cloak is clear of the line of attack in order that it does not become entangled. For the most part the best attacks made in combination with the cloak are also made with a forward motion of the feet in order to clear the cloak. An attack can easily be fouled by the bad positioning of the cloak when the attack is made.

The most dramatic use of the cloak is when it is thrown. This is mostly made against the opponent, either directly against them or against their weapon. This action is designed to entangle either the opponent or their weapon to allow an attack with the weapon to be more effective. The throwing of the cloak is something which requires practice to gain the target and not to foul your own weapon. The other offensive actions of the cloak are designed directly against the weapon and thus will be discussed in the next section.

ENGAGEMENT

With little surprise all the actions of the sword alone may also be used when the cloak is also being used. Being that these are discussed with regard to the single weapon these will not be detailed here. However what will be discussed are those actions of the cloak which may be used which involve the use of engagement of the opponent's blade.

While the throwing of the cloak, as indicated above is the most dramatic action of the cloak, there are others which can also be performed. The cloak can be used to beat the opponent's weapon off-line to allow for an attack. The ideal for this is the same as the beat performed with the sword. The weight of the cloak makes this particularly effective however the action can be quite slow and can leave you vulnerable, thus must be performed at the correct time.

Simple forms of blade engagement may also be performed with the cloak. Stringere is possible with the cloak allowing for an attack with the rapier to follow it. Likewise it is important that the cloak be directed against the debole of the opponent's weapon to be most effective. In this way the cloak can be used like a gauntlet as it has the advantage that the hand is safe from being cut through it.

CONCLUSION

The rapier and cloak form is a complex combination, and is one, which will require time and practice to perfect. This combination can be used to great effect, and against any other weapon form. The combatant should learn to use each method of using the cloak, and then learn how to counter them so that both sides of the rapier and cloak are understood. The cloak is a great entangling combination, but must be used properly otherwise this effect can quite easily backfire on the combatant, and leave them with no defense. Practice and learn with the cloak and it can become one of the most thrilling and satisfying weapon forms.

The lesson which has been presented will give the basic attributes of how the rapier and cloak are used in combination. This has merely scratched the surface of the many possibilities in the use of the rapier and cloak. While the description above has described direct actions against an opponent while using the cloak, the cloak may also be used as a form of deception and thus its contact with the opponent's weapon will be incidental, this is another way in which the cloak may be used. More research and experimentation than has been described here is required in order to truly understand the operation of the rapier and cloak.

Case of Rapiers: A Bluffer's Guide

INTRODUCTION

The case of rapiers is a challenging weapon form to learn and one which is quite difficult to master. Indeed the authors of the reference material to be used in this lesson advise the reader that this weapon form should only be used by a practitioner who is sufficiently trained and experienced in their use, to quote di Grassi "he which is not much practised and exercised therein, ought not to make profession of this Arte: for he shall find himself to be utterly deceived." (di Grassi, 1594).

The case of rapiers is essentially the use of two rapiers at the same time however it is not always as simple as this. These weapons are often matched in length, but not necessarily. In a way it is similar to the rapier and dagger combination in that there are two offensive items to use, but it is also different in that both weapons are long.

TECHNIQUE

This is a weapon form which has been discussed by several theorists and masters of the Renaissance period. For the purposes of the following investigation the focus of the research will be on one of these, Giacomo di Grassi. The single source was chosen as it supplies a relatively simple approach to the use of the case of rapiers, and provides a solid foundation for the theoretical elements found in its use. This lesson will also take into account my own experiences in the use of the case of rapiers, which has been noted to be somewhat different to most.

The focus of this lesson is the investigation of the use of the weapon form in a practical manner. To find a foundation, it will be based upon having opponents with matched weapons in the active descriptions of the form on the basis that the manuals describe this. This is most useful as it describes not only how to attack but also to defend against the same combination. Before this is possible it is important that a more general approach is taken to the form, thus the operation of the weapons alone, before coming to a place where contact with another opponent is possible.

BIBLIOGRAPHIC ISSUES

In the study of the case of rapiers there are some bibliographical issues that need to be taken into account before any real study can be achieved. One of the first things is with regard to the weapon, and then there is a language issue that needs to be taken into account. These need to be addressed in some fashion before a real study can take place.

First of all is the language. *The True Art of Defence* by di Grassi was originally written in Italian and published in 1570. The 1595 version of the manual which is being used for this investigation is an English translation of this manual. This is important as it means that however skilled the translator of the language there will be some interference between the different versions of the manual. Indeed there are even issues as the 1595 version was written in Elizabethan English which is different to the modern language. This issue does form a barrier to the research, but not one which is insurmountable.

Further to this language issue, and directly related is the names of the device being used, the sword. Often "spada" in Renaissance manuals is translated as "rapier" where in actual fact it simply means "sword". This is the case for the translation from the 1570 Italian to the 1595 English. While it would be more accurate to refer to this description as a case of swords lesson, the rapier is the focus and while cutting actions are primarily the purview of the sword, the cutting actions can be performed with a rapier. Aside from this, the fact that it is referred to as a rapier in the 1595 version makes the discussion of the weapon valid.

PRINCIPLES

The case of rapiers would seem to be one of the most complex systems devised, and in some ways it is, however what should be noted about this is that as with any system it is based on principles and for the most part these principles are relatively simple. While the principles do not explain the entire system they are advantageous in gaining an understanding of the foundations of the system.

The simple thing is that the case of rapiers places a sword in each hand this is clear and evident to all. Regardless of the length of the weapons and whether they be matched or not it is two swords. These weapons have the ability to both strike and defend the wielder.

It is important that both hands can be used to attack and defend for maximum effect, "a man ought to accuſtome his bodie, armes and handes aſwell to ſtrike as defend." (di Grassi, 1594).

The case of rapiers is two weapons, as stated, two weapons which can both attack and defend. What needs to be realised here on a conscious level is that the weapons are one in each hand and each can be used independently and in combination.

> "For ſeeing they are two weapons, & yet of one ſelfſame kind, they ought equally and indifferently to be handled, the one performing that which the other doth, & euery of thſ being apt aſwel to strik as defend." *(di Grassi, 1594)*

This means that the weapons can be used alone against the opponent doing what needs to be done or they can also be used in combination. The used in combination is the more effective choice but the independent option should not be forgotten. In combination, the actions of one weapon should be supported by the actions of the other weapon. Thus where one is used to defend so the other should strike, and where a weapon is used to strike, so should the other defend. This allows for the maximum benefit possible from using two weapons.

As with any weapon form in the arts of the Renaissance period, circular and sloping footwork is the best approach to the opponent. In the case of two weapons of length this is vital. To approach directly upon the opponent is substantially less effective than to use circular or sloping footwork to change the facing and thus gain an advantage over the opponent.

The case of rapiers is a complex weapon form, but the basics should never be forgotten, they still apply. The simple actions which work at single rapier work just as well with the case of rapiers. In all instances the single weapon can dominate and beat the double weapons so long as the one using the single does not forget the foundation elements. This is the same with ward choice, using one which confirms to the basic principles and works for you is best, remember to move through them rather than remaining static.

These are the base principles which will form the foundation of the information which follows. The principles will be found in the various elements and elucidated upon so that their real meaning can be completely understood. Without the principles which have been presented this system works substantially less well.

WARDS

In the case of the wards for the case of rapiers, they are wards in the truest sense; they are positions from which a defence or offence is launched not positions of safety. Giacomo di Grassi uses his wards as positions from which the action is started. These are foundation positions which enable the weapons to be used against the opponent. Regardless of the ward chosen there are some important factors which need to be taken into account.

The first factor has already been iterated in that they are positions from which an action is made, not guards and thus positions of safety. The combatant should always remain alert and aware of the actions of the opponent regardless of the position he is in. Further to this the combatant needs to be aware of the position of his weapons.

The weapons need to be held in such a way that they are not easy to tangle. This issue of tangling must be taken into account whether it is an active action of the opponent in order to immobilise the weapons or an inadvertent action of the combatant making an action of his own. In this they need to be kept separate in some fashion, in order that one weapon does not foul the action of the other or by its action become entangled in the other.

In the discussion of the sword there is always the consideration of lines. These are important for defensive and offensive purposes. In the typical situation the lines are based on the position of the primary weapon. In the case of using two swords, both are essentially the primary weapon thus resulting in a complication. In essence due to the doubling of weapons the lines are doubled; one for each weapon.

The place where this is of most importance is the inside and outside lines. This is not to say that there is less significance for the high and low lines. Each weapon has an inside and outside line. What needs to be noticed here is that the inside lines will occupy the same space as they cover the same area. It is possible to make all four parries with each weapon, thus two parries could be used to cover a single line. More of this will be discussed later on.

di Grassi

In his manual, di Grassi discusses three wards, as he does through the entire manual. These wards are the High, Broad and Low wards. In all cases it is the rear weapon which is the focus of this description. The forward weapon, regardless of the hand, will adopt a Low ward, which is slightly more extended in the double Low ward. The rear weapon accompanies the rear foot. The only ward which is actually depicted in his manual is the High ward. The following is the depiction from the 1570 manual.

The High ward as presented has the left foot forward with the left sword in a Low ward, while the right sword is in the High ward position. The rear arm is high above the head in the position of first while the other is in the usual position of the Low ward. This footwork position remains the same for all of the wards as does the rear foot accompanying the "descriptor" weapon at the rear.

The Broad ward as described has the same footwork position as above and the same position for the left-hand sword in the Low ward. The rear arm is extended from the body to the right in a position of second with the point aimed at the opponent. The arm needs to be extended in this position for the ward to be formed properly.

The Low ward, and di Grassi's preference for ward, is slightly different from the others but the same principles apply. Once again the footwork position is the same with the left to the front and the right to the rear. In this case the weapons are both in the Low ward position and the forward weapon should be pressed forward a little from the front leg for clearance. This ward is clearly demonstrated as the preferred ward as it is used to oppose the other two wards using contra-postura, and also di Grassi spends more time discussing the Low ward than any other ward.

Others

There are other wards which can be used indeed Marozzo describes a ward for each hand alluding to the use of two weapons independently in the process. Other wards which may be adopted are ones such as the open ward in which one weapon is placed to the front aligning with the foot on that side and one is placed to the rear in a "long tail" position. As a combatant you should experiment with many different wards to see which ones work the best for you. Remember to move through the wards to a position which is most advantageous to you.

FOOTWORK

The footwork position for the wards described actually forms the foundation for the footwork which di Grassi describes in his manual. The weapon in the offensive position is the one to the rear, and the most advantageous way to bring this weapon into play is through the use of a passing step with the rear foot. This simple fact results in most of the footwork found in di Grassi being passing steps. He does also use more direct steps but usually to set up for the use of the passing step.

The description in his manual discusses the use of one foot moving, this is for timing purposes and when the position of the feet is found, it means that the passing step is the clear choice in most instances. He does use slope paces and circular movements both with the forward and rear feet, however in order to place the primary weapon, the rear one, into the attack a passing step is made in some form or another.

For the combatant using case of rapier, the most important thing to see is that circular and sloping footwork is secret to gaining the advantage over the opponent. Going straight at the opponent is like two warships standing within gun range and using broadsides at one another, while one side may win this is not going to be without casualties on both sides. To be effective you need to shift yourself into a position of advantage, simply put this is where you can gain dominance with one of your weapons over the pair of the opponent's or where both of your weapons are in a position to attack where only one of the opponent's is. For the most part this involves gaining the inside with at least one of the weapons. The best way to achieve this is through the use of circular and sloping footwork. Defensively footwork is also an important part of the defensive apparatus available.

DEFENSE

Considering defensive options, the first point that must be reiterated is that the lines are doubled due to the use of two swords. The result of this is that the parries are doubled meaning that there are two parries for each line one using each sword; this results in an increase in the defensive options available, however you need to be careful as this can also result in entanglement of the weapons. The same can be said of any combination. It is best to practice the parries with the weapons first alone and then with the other present.

In the case of di Grassi, he uses several different defensive techniques. First of all is the beat against an incoming attack. This is much like the beat attack and beat parry; in fact it is a combination of these concepts. The utility of this particular technique is that it clears not only the opponent's weapon but yours as well allowing for a hole in which an action with the other weapon may be performed. In effect this action is both offensive and defensive in nature.

While the parry with opposition is not named specifically this technique is used in an active way rather than a passive way. This technique is much like that of stringere in that it forces the opponent's weapon off-line however this is more of a defensive action in this case. Clearly this action requires timing to perform properly.

The final defensive action which is useful to you is the combination of voids and footwork. This is designed to displace the body while placing it in a position of advantage. Either footwork or a void alone can be used to defend against an opponent's attack but the combination of the two is more effective.

Each defensive option should be practiced both alone and with a partner to test it out against an attack being made. This practice should start slowly and then increase. In these actions the defensive partner should also be considering their own final position and where they can move from there in order to make a counter.

OFFENSE

Just as defense is doubled so too is offense, being that there are two weapons both with edges and points this results in there being offensive actions present for both weapons. While the edge can be used, it is the point which is the primary used. The thrust is easier to perform with case of rapier as it uses less room and thus is less likely to entangle.

In his manual di Grassi indicates that there are cuts which can be used at the case of rapiers but he does not present a single example of a cut being actually used in his description of the weapon form. This clearly demonstrates the dominance of the thrust over the cut in the use of the case of rapier. Likewise he indicates that a person with the practice and skill can execute two attacks simultaneously, however he also does state that this requires practice.

As with any other weapon form the position of the weapons needs to be taken into account, both the opponents and the combatant's. Obviously it is useless to make an attack against a line which is closed, but you must also consider what you are exposing in the process of making the attack. Clearly the attack should only be made after some sort of defensive action is made to make you safe, as di Grassi states, "for first a man must endeavour to defend himself, and then to strike others." (di Grassi, 1594). To make the best choice for attacking the opponent, practice with a partner in both defending and attacking should be made.

TIME AND ENGAGEMENT

So, this section is called "time and engagement", however it will be covering quite a bit more than that. This will also deal with how the weapons are used as a system and some of the general points of note about the combination which either do not exactly fall into one of the previous categories or needs further explanation with a wider focus. This will also be about putting the previous information together in a more usable format.

The often case, especially with newer combatants is that the weapons are used for a single purpose only. One is used for attack and the other is used for defence. The only change to this will be a changing of hands and thus roles. This is a very basic use of the combination and while the weapons are both being used much improvement can be made.

The sword is simultaneously offensive and defensive. It means that both hands can operate offensively and defensively. For the most part, until this is acknowledged in a conscious manner, the actions available will be limited.

To be effective with case of rapiers you need to work with both hands offensively and defensively for maximum effect. This means that both hands need to be used offensively and both need to be used defensively. In this the weapons need to be used combined and separately, this opens a lot more options for you. For the most part to use the combination, the actions of one weapon need to be supported by the actions of the other weapon. It is through this that it is possible that the opponent can be put into a position by one weapon and then struck with the other.

However, singly each weapon can be used to great effect. Thus the weapons can be used on their own for great effect both offensively and defensively. Even a person who is armed with a single sword can defeat one who is armed with two; this through the application of the weapon to the situation. Keeping these points in mind will allow you access to a lot more option that applying any sort of artificial limitations on their use.

Time

As with any combination time is an important factor. With regard to this there are some points which are useful in application to the use of the case of rapiers. With regard to the hand and foot, di Grassi uses them accompanied, right hand with right foot and vice versa. This allows for the full extension of the weapon in its movement. This also allows for better timing in both attack and defence. There are instances where this is not the case and these should also be noted in practice.

For di Grassi the actions of the weapons are usually double time, one weapon defends and the other follows through with the attack once the defence has been made. There are instances of counter-time and single time present however it is double-time which dominates. Of course, with practice the other times can be effective and come to be used.

Engagement

With regard to engagement, this is considering any time that the weapons come into contact with one another. There is very little evidence of absence of blade in di Grassi; he prefers solid contact between the weapons to know where they are. The first element of note with regard to this is the use of the beat action, be this a parry or an attack, it is one which appears regularly often as the primary defensive action with the weapon. He does use other actions such as presses and elements of stringere but these are not named as such. The important element for di Grassi is, as stated, solid contact with the opponent's weapons.

The idea of the doubled lines has been noted previously in both the defensive discussion and also under the wards. This particular element leads to how to gain advantage over an opponent who is using the same combination. This requires the use of sloping or circular footwork to change the facing and thus gain the best line on the opponent; this line is the inside line and the forward weapon should always be moved to a position where it can gain this position.

The final element which defeats experienced and inexperienced combatants alike is that the weapons need to be kept separate in some fashion so that they are not entangled. This entanglement can be due to the action of the opponent or the action of the combatant. This primarily happens due to a lack of consciousness of the position of the other weapon when an action is made, or when an action is completed. It is for this reason that the Low ward starts with one weapons slightly extended and the other more withdrawn.

CONCLUSION

The case of rapiers is an interesting and exciting weapon form. It is also one of the more complex ones available. The information presented here is designed to introduce you to the use of the case of rapiers rather than claiming to be everything possible. The best way to learn about how the case of rapiers works for you is to use them against an opponent, however it is important to remember the essential points.

The basic elements are the key to the useful and effective functioning of the case of rapiers. There are two weapons and two hands therefore there are always two options, one for each weapon. The weapons can be used both separately and also together, in this there are offensive and defensive options for each weapon. It is this multitude of options which makes the form so complex and so challenging. The problem being that an incorrect choice can lead to real problems.

The base ward that you choose needs to be comfortable and the weapons need to be in a good position to prevent entanglement. More to the point the wards need to be moved through and each stop needs to be a firm position from which an effective offensive or defensive move can be made. The ward must allow you to move effectively in offensive and defensive actions.

As in all cases it is footwork which is the key to being effective. It is through this movement that you can position yourself effectively. In the case of this weapon form the use of circular and sloping footwork which is the most effective and will gain the most positive results. Moving directly against the opponent, especially armed with the same weapon combination will gain you little.

In defense it is most effective, as with any other form to use all forms of defense. Thus parries and voids are effective, but so can the use of footwork and body position. These need to be taken into account for you to be effective, as with any other form the rounded defense is the most effective. In case consideration of defense, not blocking avenues of offense also needs to be considered along with ensuring that there is no entanglement in the process.

In offense the blade is used either with the point or the edge. In the case of rapiers the point is more effective due to the nature of the form and the positions of the weapons. Cuts are less useful due to time and position. As was indicated in defense above, the action of offense needs to be considered so that it does not hinder you in the process or after-effect.

In the case of time, all forms are used and can be used effectively. With regard to the case of rapiers is that the hand and foot move together, right with right and left with left. This gains you length and dominance in the process. The extension using same foot and hand is also more effective due to the momentum of the blade. Further this leads to engagement, in which the position is important for both offensive and defensive actions. The weapons can be used in many ways and thus many forms of beat and control should be used for the weapons to be effectively used. Once again, as with all elements of this form, the position of the other weapon is of great importance.

Practice is required for the case of rapiers to be used effectively indeed di Grassi expresses this particular fact as indicated in the introduction. Both weapons need to be used effectively along with the body in order to be effective. The tactical side of the case of rapiers needs consideration and practice is required to find how the form is most effectively used.

Sword and Rotella – A Bluffer's Guide

INTRODUCTION

The sword and rotella, or round target, is a combination which is not common to Renaissance manuals. This is a "bluffer's guide" to the use of the sword and rotella meaning that it is light on the detail in most places and gives you a general idea about how to use this particular combination. The work is, however, based on research from suitable materials as will be demonstrated.

> "It very often happens that one's own weapons make war to the selfsame ones who do not know their use well. Therefore, I have judged it not to be outside of the purpose to mention some particulars of the rotella, as it is a most perilous weapon to those selfsame ones who have not done any kind of practice."
> – Capo Ferro, 1610 (Kirby, 2012:142)

The sword and rotella is a system which has a relatively long heritage, most of the information been found in Renaissance manuals. What this means is that there is quite a bit of information to cover for the understanding of the system if each master was to be examined in detail. This is not what this investigation will be aimed at.

The discussion here is designed to reveal the essentials of the system. These essentials are what make the system what it is and are found in various manuals but it is the common elements which reveal the system for what it is. This investigation has taken four manuals from the Renaissance period and through an examination of each manual distilled and found the essential elements. Thus the system which is presented here has been developed from the examination and common and foundation elements from each of the four manuals.

This is more of a generalised discussion of the system overall rather than an in-depth discussion of individual techniques. The discussion presented is designed to give the reader an overall understanding of the system. This understanding can form a foundation from which other systems can be examined.

The order of presentation is: examine the background issues in the investigation and then examine the sword and rotella as a system. Individual elements of the system will be examined in some detail for completeness to give understanding as to how the sword and rotella work as a system. This means that while there will be practical elements presented and these can be used it is the understanding of the system which is the goal of this discussion.

SOURCE MATERIAL

The source material which is presented in this discussion uses as close to primary materials as possible. Issues with regard to this particular element of the discussion will be noted below in the bibliographic discussion. Further to this these primary materials will be in a distilled form, extracting the most important parts from each and using this as the framework upon which the investigation is based.

This examination focusses on four masters works with regard to their use of the sword and rotella. Chronologically they are Marozzo's *Art dell Armi* of 1536, Agrippa's *Trattato* di *Scientia d'Arme* of 1553, di Grassi's *His True Art of Defence* of 1594, and finally Capo Ferro's *Gran Simulacro dell'arte e dell'uso della Scherma* of 1610. Most of the information found in these manuals is from the point of view of matched weapons i.e. sword and rotella versus sword and rotella, but the information found within can also be applied to other situations, with a little modification. What should also be noted in these manuals is that the earlier manuals contain more with regard to the use of the rotella whereas the later manuals contain less. However the information which is contained within these manuals is most useful to this investigation and development.

BIBLIOGRAPHIC ISSUES

In the study of the sword and rotella there are some bibliographical issues that need to be taken into account before any real study can be achieved. One of the first things is with regard to the weapon, the second with the device in the other hand, and lastly there is a language issue that needs to be taken into account. These need to be addressed in some fashion before a real study can take place.

First of all is the language. Of the four manuals which have been used for this investigation only one of these is written in English, that of di Grassi's 1594 manual. Even that is actually a translation of the 1570 Italian manual of the same name. All of the others have been translated from Italian to English in the modern period, by some very knowledgeable people admittedly, but there is still the interference of the translation of the language to take into account.

Further to this language issue, and directly related is the names of the devices being used, the sword and the rotella. Often "spada" in Renaissance manuals is translated as "rapier" where in actual fact it simply means "sword". This is the reason that this investigation is being referred to as a sword and rotella manual, thus covering both of the weapons concerned.

As for the rotella itself, it is called this in Italian. It is called a "Shield" generically, a "target" in Old English and a "rodela" in Spanish. All of the terms refer, more or less, to the same item. Due to the more Italian focus the shield will be referred to as a rotella, as it has previously and will in future be.

WHAT IS ROTELLA?

The rotella is a round shield. Its size varies from approximately 20" to 30" or roughly 50-cm to 76-cm. The grip is most often a loop of leather but may be a solid handle. There is a second loop of leather which sits about the elbow; this is sometimes replaced with an adjustable strap. The outside of the rotella is constructed of steel or wood.

The rotella and its use is the only, to date, documentation of the use of a shield in combat aside from the buckler. However, as will be demonstrated, the rotella differs from the buckler in use. While this style of combat is more readily associated with military-style encounters, there is evidence, as presented in these civilian manuals of its use for civilian combats as well.

VERSUS BUCKLER

One of the great mistakes made with regard to the rotella is that it is often assumed that it is used the same way as the buckler. This is incorrect. There are some significant differences that must be noted between the rotella and buckler to completely understand how the rotella is used.

Simply based on physical size the buckler is small and the rotella is large. This alone will result in differences. The simple thing is that a small defensive object will be more mobile than a larger one. The result of this is that the buckler will be more active that the rotella which will be more stationary.

The size will affect the nature of the use of the item, but the use will still be based on the same foundation theory of such a defensive device. Thus similarities can be drawn between the use of one and the use of another. Ken Mondschein has noted that the use of the rotella as used by Agrippa is similar to the Bolognese judging from Marozzo's assaulti; however the rotella is more to the fencer's side whereas the buckler is placed out in front of the fencer.

What will also be noted through this investigation is that the similarities will be present amongst the masters indeed if there were no similarities it would be difficult to draw a common use of the item, and thus a universal approach to its use. It is the similarities which will be the focus but differences will also be noted.

WARDS

There are several wards available for the use of the rotella. Each of the four masters described at least one if not several wards which can be used at sword and rotella. For the purposes of this examination the ward which will be used is one which is based upon the essential principles which each of these wards is based. This is in essence designed to simplify the system in order that one ward is used.

Marozzo

Marozzo focuses on three wards, coda lunga stretta, coda lunga alta and porta di ferro stretta, however this being said in his description of the actions he also passes through and uses six others. The three named here, though are the three which for the most part he starts from or ends up in. It is the form of the dominant wards which is important.

Agrippa

Agrippa uses four guardia in his manual as his primary. These are described previously in his manual and are given simple alphabetic indications. As the wards are presented as single sword or sword and dagger, it is up to the reader to interpret where the rotella is placed. However after the examination, it will be noted that the same foundations upon which Marozzo bases his wards will

TECHNIQUE

also be found in the wards of Agrippa.

di Grassi

Further along in the chronology is di Grassi and later is Capo Ferro, by this time the amount of wards for the combination have been reduced. Di Grassi mentions the use of three wards, but is essentially focussed on a single ward being his Low Ward. Capo Ferro uses a couple of wards in his use of the rotella but his sesta is his favourite ward. As can be seen the system has been refined to present the essential parts of the system, and in a similar fashion one ward will be indicated here. Of the holding of the rotella Capo Ferro states;

"the rotella must be held embraced with the left arm somewhat curved, in a way that looks somewhat towards your left side, but not so curved that it impedes the eye so that you cannot discern whatever part of the enemy you want to proceed to strike." – Capo Ferro, 1610 (Kirby, 2012:142)

Common Ward

The essential ward for the use of the sword and rotella is formed as such, the sword foot is placed forward of the off-hand foot with the toe pointed at the opponent. The feet should be comfortably spaced, neither too close or too broad. As with any good ward, the knees should be bent slightly.

The rotella is held extended from the body rather than close to it, with the arm slightly bent in order to bring the rotella slightly across the body to cover it, at least the off-hand side. The position of the rotella should not restrict the view of the opponent, if this is the case the rotella should be moved out slightly. Having the rotella against the body is dangerous, as is resting on the thigh.

For the most part the rotella remains stationary for other wards, should they be taken the sword moves around it. The most common position would be in guard of terza or equivalent. This means that the hilt of the sword should be about the hip or slightly extended with the point upwards. The Broad Ward or broad seconda is discouraged as it takes the weapon too far out of line. From this position you should have full utility of both sword and rotella.

FOOTWORK

The footwork used with the rotella is the same as the footwork used for any other form. In the case of the use of the rotella passing and circular footwork tend to dominate due to the nature of the combination, but more direct approaches are also possible. The footwork is used, as per usual, to suit the situation. For the most part the approaches will consist of passing steps using biomechanical advantage to enhance the position of the sword and rotella against the opponent.

This being said the paces should not be ignored as they also have their purpose especially in those cases where the position needs to be maintained while approaching the opponent. Gathers and slips are used in both offence and defence with the rotella positioning the body through small movements to take advantage of the opponent. Footwork, as usual, will also affect the effectiveness of the defences made and can also be used as defence.

DEFENCE

As with the footwork the defences in the use of the rotella are much the same as they are with any other form. Footwork is used both alone and with voids to enhance both. This is the simplest form of defence and all four of the masters mentioned here advocate the use of the void in some form.

There is little use describing voids except to say that the position of the rotella in relation to yourself and the opponent needs to be taken into account. If the rotella is left exposed the arm holding the rotella can actually come under threat from the opponent's attack. Likewise it is important, for obvious reasons, not to lose vision of both the opponent and the incoming attack.

The sword can be used to parry the opponent's attack as per usual. These can be made as parries in the usual fashion or as part of a cut. These actions should consider the position of the rotella to be effective. Unintended contact between sword and rotella can be detrimental to the effectiveness of the parry. Likewise, and on the same note a parry can be deflected off the sword and toward the rotella should the choice be made to enhance the parry or plan for a further action.

The parry made with the rotella is something which needs to be seriously considered. The rotella is large and slow and thus an action with the rotella requires thought. So much so that in some instances it is actually advised against.

In most cases the rotella will occupy a more or less stationary position only changing for the changing of a ward or position of the body. This stationary position passively denies the line to the opponent. Most of the movement should be made around the rotella rather than moving it.

Should the rotella be used to parry the action should be small in nature and accompanied by footwork to enhance the action. The rotella can also be used in a beat parry through the full extension of the arm. Once again the action should be used to deny the line to the opponent.

Counter actions against the opponent especially in mezzo tempo are useful. These should be primarily directed against the opponent's sword arm to stop the incoming attack. True an attack against the body or head of the opponent will debilitate him, but the incoming attack may still be completed.

Marozzo in his defensive actions mentions a discouragement cut. This cut a riverso spinto, a riverso delivered with a forward slicing action, is used to discourage the opponent from closing or attacking. This action is most often used, and most useful when coming back into guard in order to gain the time to do such. Delivered with the correct timing such a cut can also result in a counter-cut against the opponent.

OFFENCE

The offensive actions of the sword and rotella are much as expected, the same as any other combination. The most interesting thing is that most of the attacks are either made high against the head and face, and low against the legs. This is really to be expected as these are the two areas left relatively open in the rotella. There are some actions directed against the body but these require manipulation of the opponent's rotella.

The earlier manuals, as can be expected have more of a cutting element while the later manuals focus more on the thrust. This is not to say that the reverse does not happen just that it is much rarer. With regard to the attacks themselves the most interesting point comes from Agrippa where he positions his fencer for a throw against the opponent.

For the most part the dominant thrust is the stoccata, a rising thrust usually from below under the rotella and against the opponent's face. In some ways this is more of a generic thrusting attack and could be directed against the body should the opportunity present itself. While there are few cuts mentioned in di Grassi, as he considers them too easy to defend, they are mentioned in Capo Ferro targeting the legs. Cuts are made with both true and false edges, and made usually against the head or legs. However a note should be made as indicated above as to cuts made against the attacking arm and hand of the opponent. Feints are used to enhance the attack, usually a thrust to the head followed by a cut low.

TIME AND ENGAGEMENT

With regard to these two subjects, and indeed the subject heading, there is a lot which can be discussed both specific and general. For the purposes of this part time will consider fencing time and parts associated with it while engagement will consider actions of the blade and rotella against the opponent's devices. This allows for a little breadth in both discussions so the important elements can be highlighted.

Time

In the combat with sword and rotella there are examples of the use of all forms of time. It would seem, however that counter-time, half-time and single time are the dominant forms of time. Each one of these uses the motion of the opponent in some fashion to generate an action so that a response may be made against it. These forms of time are very active moving from an action in one form of time to another in quick succession, sometimes as part of a plan and sometimes in response to the actions of the opponent.

What should also be noted is that there are active and passive modes of time present in the action. There are times when the fencer will wait for the opponent to attack and then react to the motion given, but there also actions which are active where the fencer makes the first action against the opponent. These initial actions are usually designed to elicit a response from the opponent so further actions may proceed. If the response is not forthcoming then an action can be completed as an attack. This is especially the case in the use of feints. If there is no response to the feint it is completed as an attack against the opponent, thus these actions can be feints or complete attacks depending on what is required.

Engagement

Engagement for this discussion, as indicated, rather than being focussed on a single set of actions, it will related to all actions related in the engagement of the devices either sword, rotella or both. This enables a better overview of these actions rather than attempting to detail each individually. Allowing for a broader perspective of the subject also allows an overview of the actions.

Engagements with the opponent's devices are typically of a solid nature or in absence. The use of absence is often enhanced through the use of falsing. This is not to claim that the action is either one or the other and thus the action is limited. There are elements of glancing and leading actions also. However where there is contact between the devices it is most often solid and uses an element of force to achieve the desired end.

As for detailing specific actions with the sword and rotella there are a few which dominate the actions. This is actually the result of the presence of the rotella as it limits the action of the blade due to its presence. This being said, there is evidence of the use of stringere and also the disengage in some form for control of the engagement. The beat is also used by the sword. What should be noted here is that most the actions used by the sword are actually also performed with the rotella as well. Clearly a disengage in the classic sense is not possible with the rotella, but the other actions mentioned here are, and are present in the primary material.

CONCLUSION

The previous information is a very brief discussion of the sword and rotella. In some ways it could be called a "bluffer's guide" to the system. Its purpose is for the reader to examine the system from a general point of view and to understand how the system works. The aim here has been to present a system based on the works of several masters to distil to a singular system and thus give basic instruction as to the use of the sword and rotella.

The earlier parts of the discussion examined the various issues with regard to studying the system and the reasons for how the investigation proceeded. This also allowed for some foundations to be laid as to exactly what was being examined and from what point of view. Without this introductory material the following would be less useful.

Each one of the masters which has been mentioned is useful in their own right. For the simplest approach di Grassi is best. His approach goes for the immediate fundamentals of how to deal with attacks and defences from specific guards, while demonstrating a clear preference for a single one. In a similar way Capo Ferro really gives an overview of the system, but his investigation seems to be rather rudimentary. The same simplified nature could be accused of Agrippa in his approach however it is clear that his examination can only really be understood alongside the rest of his work. Marozzo presents the most complex and in-depth system using multiple guards and presenting problems and solutions using each one. Just as with Agrippa this is a system that needs to be understood from the point of view of his entire system rather than just the sword and rotella.

The examination here only forms the basis of the system. While the system which is presented here is useful and covers the essential elements, it is presented more as a discussion. A more practical approach is required for a real understanding of the system and how it operates. To this point a more practical and lesson-orientated approach can be taken. Further study should also be made into the primary materials to really understand the system; this discussion is only the beginning in order to be able to successfully apply the system against an opponent.

Sword Alone Versus Everything

INTRODUCTION

The following is about fighting against different forms. While the initial focus will be on fighting single sword against others, there will be a further discussion later on based on more general combat conditions. Some people will be intimidated by an opponent who is holding an item in the off-hand while they are not. They should not be; there are still elements which allow a fencer with a single sword not only to survive but to prevail and dominate. The single sword is known as the "queen of weapons" and there is a good reason for it.

FOUNDATION POINTS

The first thing that I would point out is that we have spent more time using a single sword, be it with a parrying gauntlet or without than any other form in rapier combat. In our training mode, we start with the single sword as it teaches principles which will apply to all of the other following forms. This means that it is the form which we have had the most practice, not to mention that while our opponent may have had a lot of practice with whatever form they are using their main form for practice will also have been the single rapier. So no matter what your opponent brings out against you; remember that proportionally, if not in actual fact, you have had more practice with your single than they have had with their other form.

Some of the newer fencers will be intimidated by an opponent taking an offhand device when they only have a single sword. Part of the point of this discussion is to reassure these individuals that there is nothing to be worried about, only to be aware of the other item that they have in their hand. The most important thing to remember in all situations is that in both cases the opponent has only got two hands. This means that when the opponent has two weapons the offhand becomes more significant, as does the use of the weapon that you have.

ADVANTAGES AND DISADVANTAGES

When examining what the opponent has chosen to take it is important to take in what advantages the form has and what disadvantages the form has. For example, in a defensive combination such as sword and buckler, the buckler cannot be used to strike, and if it can, only when very close. Therefore should have less regard paid to it. This doesn't mean that it should be ignored, just that the weapon is really the main threat in that situation.

Once you have ascertained these advantages and disadvantages you should play toward the opponent's disadvantages and attempt to minimise the advantages. This particular situation is the same in all accounts with all opponents in all weapon forms. We need to maximise our own advantages while minimising those of the opponent.

To discover the advantages and disadvantages of each form it is necessary to examine them in a little detail. This is best done as a general look and then given some more detail to find the specific characteristics of each one. In this way we are able to see the characteristics from both a generalised point of view and also a more specific point of view. The best way to do this really well is to have a go at the forms yourself and figure out what these characteristics are.

Defensive Combinations

First we will look at defensive combinations as they are often the first that a fencer will come across. What is most significant about the defensive combinations is that there is one weapon and one defensive item being used. The most important fact here is that the defensive item is defensive and not an immediate threat in the same way that a weapon is. This places you on the same field as the offhand is a defensive tool in the same way that a buckler or a cloak.

So in this way aside from the extended reach, or slightly improved physical protection the defensive options against an open hand are pretty much neutral. The real threat from these combinations is when they come into contact with the weapon and are used to control it. Obviously the way to avoid this is to avoid the item being used to control your weapon. More detail will be given to these forms later on.

Offensive Combinations

Offensive combinations are where people have the most problems, it is usually the thought of two weapons that is the issue, but even this can be dealt with intelligently if you know what to look for. The main thing with offensive combinations is that there are two weapons to your one. This means that there is double the amount of threat from your opponent. As has been stated you can counter one with your weapon and one with your offhand when it is required, or the other way around if you prefer.

In most instances combatants will attack with one and then the other but not at the same time, this means that you actually have the time to counter both weapons with one item if you are practiced enough. This of course comes down to your level of practice. The trick in this situation is making your defence effective and succinct so that you are not over-extending yourself. If you move too far you will leave yourself exposed. This combined with the avoidance of control as explained under the defensive items will allow you to deal with these forms as well.

EXAMINE EACH FORM

It is important to look at each form in some detail to understand the specific advantages of each of the forms. These will be summarised a little, so to keep this discussion succinct. The characteristics of the weapon in the offhand itself give a great deal away as to where its advantages and disadvantages lie. Case of rapier has reach. Dagger and buckler are better at closer ranges, and cloak has the advantage of volume and a little reach. Of course, now that we can see the advantages it is easier to see the disadvantages. With regard to the following combinations, it is the ones which you would most likely find used which will be presented below.

Case of Rapier

The case of rapiers is the most intimidating form for the fencer with a single rapier to face due to the double long weapons against the single however it can be defeated by a single weapon. It is also the most wholly offensive combination that a fencer can arm himself with in the fight with the rapier. You should not simply throw yourself into the fray as this will result in yourself being struck. Some time should be taken to correctly study the form for its advantages and disadvantages.

You should also move to a position where one weapon is closer than the other. Once this is achieved then the fencer can use single sword techniques against single weapons; this can be either line. The engagements will work the same as they would with a single weapon but you should always be aware of the other weapon. You can also, with a great deal of care, work between the weapons as the inside lines are often forgotten.

Remembering you have two hands, you should put your weapon on one weapon and your hand on the other weapon. In this you do not need to attack, merely to spoil the opponent's chance to attack. Simple contact against the opponent's weapons will often achieve this. Through this spoiling the opponent can be frustrated into a mistake or even entanglement, this is obviously an advantage which you can use to your advantage.

It will be noted that in the use of two weapons and two long ones at that, the form is entirely more offensive than defensive. This presents one of the keys to the way to defeat the opponent with case of rapiers. If the opponent is kept on the back foot, thus in the defensive, it will make it difficult for him to make an offensive action against you. In this method you take the initiative and keep it from the opponent. You must make the opponent use both weapons to defend himself with to not allow them to offend with the weapon.

The first thing that will be noted is that in the use of two long weapons the opponent will have the advantage at longer distance while the closer distance to the opponent he will lose this advantage due to the length of the weapons. Thus, if you can get inside the range of the opponent's weapons his advantage will increase markedly. Even though the case of rapiers has a lot of advantages and offensive potential, it also does have disadvantages. The studious and careful fencer can find situations where he can have the advantage even in this situation.

Sword and Dagger

With regard to the offensive devices of the off-hand the most common that will be encountered is the rapier and dagger. This is much more common than the case of rapiers. This gives the opponent the ability to strike at both a short range and also at long range. Clearly the dagger can also be used to defend. Even with this increased advantage the fencer with the single sword can still prevail.

The dagger cannot strike at longer distances so it should simply be avoided. You should do your best to avoid contact with the dagger at all and while staying at distance this will do a lot to neutralise its advantage. The disengage can be used effectively against the dagger. Against the single long weapon single sword techniques can be used against the opponent while staying out of contact with the dagger. You should move to a position where the sword is on the dominant side to neutralise the use of the off-hand. The shorter reach of the dagger will make it difficult for it to be brought into play.

To further gain advantage the primary attack of you should be to the outside line where the dagger has difficulty reaching, or to the inside line close to the opponent's sword where the dagger will have difficulty being used without entangling the sword. If you can force the opponent to self-entangle, this will give you a great advantage and, no doubt, an opportunity to strike in safety against the opponent.

Sword and Buckler

The buckler is a defensive item which is often used with the rapier, while in a period form it was used to strike against the opponent when close, as a direct threat it is absent simply due to distance. From this point of view it can be ignored. Avoidance is the best option in the fight against the buckler where the fencer only has a single weapon.

You should move to the sword side of the opponent to neutralise the effect of the buckler as much as possible. Once this is achieved, you can then use single sword techniques. To bring it back into use, the opponent will have to shift their position, and may foul their own weapon in this shift of position. However, another approach can be used against the buckler which works due to the nature of the item. The disengage can also be used against the buckler in order to avoid contact with it.

The point of your weapon can actually be hidden behind the buckler and thus out of view of the opponent, thus using the buckler against them. From here you can make actions and initialise movements which the opponent cannot see due to the buckler. Thus, the covering aspect of the buckler is used against the opponent. The same effect can be used if you make attacks which move close to the position of the buckler, thus using the buckler against the opponent.

Anytime that the opponent blocks his vision with the buckler you will have a chance to make an action and has an advantage, you should use these opportunities as much as possible. Some of these positions can be forced. The same can be said for anytime that the buckler is moved into a position where it will foul the movement of the sword. Movement to the sword-side and attacks close to the sword can work effectively.

Anytime that the buckler comes into contact with your weapon, you should disengage and re-position your weapon to neutralise the effect of the buckler; it is also often a good idea to withdraw, if possible to at least wide distance, to increase the distance and the immediacy of the possible following attack of the opponent. This applies to the use of any off-hand item, disengage and withdraw from the encounter to counter the effect of the item. This will also remove you from any possibility of a buckler strike.

Sword and Cloak

The cloak is a unique device in that it is flexible and has the greatest volume of all of the devices. It can also have the advantage of reach. The cloak can be used to entangle a weapon, cover the opponent's weapon and thus intention, can be used to weigh down a weapon, and even block the vision of its opponent. For all these advantages the cloak can be slow in motion and also difficult for the opponent to control. If you notice either of these things you have an advantage.

Rapier and cloak is another defensive combination that the fencer may be faced with an opponent carrying. The purpose of the cloak is to block sight, and to bind and entangle the weapon. In some instances it may be thrown to achieve its goal, but still it is a defensive item so from the point of being struck to be killed, it can be ignored.

The prime mode of dealing with an opponent's cloak is to avoid it as much as possible if the opponent cannot come into contact with your weapon then it is difficult for them to perform most of the effect of the item. As with the other combinations, you should move to the side where the opponent's sword is to neutralise the effect of the cloak in the off-hand, to use the cloak effectively the sword will have to be moved and this can result in the opponent becoming entangled in his own cloak.

In the case of the cloak, it is effective at defending against cuts, but not so much against thrusts, so the off-hand can be attacked with a thrust to harm the hand. Care should be taken in this attack not to become entangled in the cloak in the process, a quick withdrawal after the attack will help. With the change in position and the opponent's weapon being primary, and the cloak being neutralised, simple single sword techniques can then be used against the opponent.

In general contact with the cloak should be avoided to avoid any chance of deflection or entanglement. However the position of the cloak as placed by the opponent can be used by the fencer to obscure the position of his weapon and indeed in cases even his entire body. This is using the cloak's ability to block sight lines against the person who is using the cloak. This can be achieved in a similar manner to that described in the use against an opponent using a buckler above. Once again, it should be emphasised that should the opponent's cloak come into contact with the fencer's weapon and start to become entangled he should withdraw into a secure guard.

GENERAL APPROACH

The important thing here is that you need to realise the advantages and disadvantages be aware of them and utilise the situation to your own advantage. This is the same with all forms of fencing. In all cases you need to be aware of the situation and manipulate it to your own advantage to maximise your ability to succeed in the encounter. This is how you win in all forms of fencing regardless of the weapons in the encounter.

In the simplest terms the best weapon or combination is the one you can win with or the one you are most comfortable with. This is one of the true keys to success in fencing. Of course you should also practice with other forms to get more comfortable with them and also fencing against them so that you can face different weapon forms and be comfortable facing them as well. The best method of knowing how to deal with a weapon form is to learn it, from this perspective it is much easier to take it apart and then find its weakness, and thus find ways to defeat it.

CONCLUSION

Fencing with the sword alone is often seen as the purest expression of the art. Fencing against different combinations will not only open your eyes as to the ability of the single sword, but will also improve your fencing as it will stretch your ability to meet the challenge of the opponent's chosen combination. There is no combination of weapons in fencing which cannot be beaten with the single sword, it is merely an application of the principles of one against the other to find the advantages and disadvantages of both to find out how to take the advantage and win. This is the attitude that you should take when an opponent faces you with a combination of weapons when you hold a single sword.

Find his weaknesses and exploit them. Enhance your own advantages in the process. Through this you will achieve victory.

On the Manner of Wearing a Sword

The following is the lesson version of the discussion which I had previously made on the manner of wearing a sword. This takes a much more practical approach to the subject and includes references for anyone who might be interested in a little more research, or where I got my findings from. This lesson is more focussed at a recreationalist approach to the subject, but still applies overall. Overall the same material is discussed with additions to fill it out with more practical advice.

INTRODUCTION

"The man dancing the Balletti gravi will wear the cloak, and the sword in the manner which is demonstrated in the design of the Balletto of the Bellezze d' Olimpia: and dancing Cascarde, or Gagliarda, they will carry that as is demonstrated in the design of the Cascarda Alta Regina: keeping it as most it will please him either under the right arm or under the left; which one does not matter much: neither dance without this ever, because it makes a most brutish sight. Dancing gagliarda, and finding the sword, he shall hold that with the left hand, such that he would not let it go wandering: and finding it again in the Ballo to have little field, keeping it with the hand, it will return some with the point towards the forward part, such that it not offend the bystanders." (Caroso, 1581)

The wearing of a sword is a subject which is often overlooked with regard to weapons, but is one which needs some attention paid to it. Some would think that this is a subject where the knowledge is automatic, but there is a great deal more attention that needs to be paid to it. The wearing of a sword, especially in public is a skill not unlike those designed to teach how to use the sword, thus it is a skill which needs instruction, especially for the modern wearer who is not used to the issues associated.

Caroso, in the above statement, gives some very specific instructions for wearing the sword and cloak when dancing. Some of the information presented above will be re-presented below as it is applicable to the situation. Caroso's instruction is primarily discussing the wearing of the sword and cloak while dancing whereas this investigation will cover a much broader consideration of wearing the sword, while covering some specifics as well.

APPROPRIATENESS

The first question that must be dealt with in regards to wearing a sword is whether or not it is appropriate to wear a sword in the first place. There are times when it is appropriate to wear a sword and there are also times when it is most definitely not appropriate. In this, there are times in medieval and Renaissance instances, as they are being recreated, and times in the modern world when it is and is not appropriate to wear a sword and the level of censure can be severe for some of these.

Most of the appropriateness of wearing a sword comes from the perceived social norms and conventions of the situation, as well as some legal ones. It is not normal for a person to be seen walking down the street in the modern world with a sword, this would obviously be a breach of a social norm. More to the point in this particular situation a person could also be pulled up by the local constabulary and could be charged with "going armed in public with intent to cause fear", which while it is a misdemeanour is still a serious situation to put yourself in. However, should the same person be found wearing medieval or Renaissance dress and the appropriate weapon at a medieval or Renaissance event or fair, then the situation would be different and the person would blend in. Consider whether the situation is appropriate before girding yourself with your weapon.

Weapons and Alcohol

Weapons and alcohol simply do not mix. There are many stories of people being injured and/or killed when weapons and alcohol are mixed. Some of these stories are from the medieval and Renaissance period and some are from the modern period. The two should be kept from one another regardless of the social situation, thus it is advised that the weapon be put in a safe place before going anywhere near a bar or tavern. Wearing a sword into such a situation has too high a potential for causing issues. The owner of the weapon should even consider putting the weapon away in a safe place should they be in a private situation where alcohol will be served.

Costume

> "While some military swords were worn as costume decoration from the end of the fifteenth century, the rapier and dagger combination were specialist weapons designed for use away from the battlefield."
> (Patterson, 2009:58)

Surprisingly enough, even when associating with a medieval or Renaissance recreation group the consideration of appropriateness still applies and needs to be considered. The first question that needs to be asked is whether the wearing of a sword is appropriate for the attire which is being worn in the first place. The common wearing of swords in a civilian situation did not really come about until the Renaissance period, as indicated, and even in that it was not really until the later period that it became common. Thus the period of the costume with regard to wearing a weapon is something that needs to be considered. You should investigate whether or not it would be appropriate for your own costume.

Rank

> "as economic development generated wealth for the middle classes, many aspiring gentlemen incorporated the rapier and dagger into their everyday dress ... As clothing accessories they were decorated as a set and worn in a fashionable sling called a hanger. Their decoration might also match the spurs in their boots, the pendants around their necks, and the embroidery in their clothes" (Patterson, 2009:58)

With regard to the suitability of the attire for wearing a sword with it there is also the question of rank, or to be more general, social status. Wearing a sword with a peasant outfit would look almost as out of place as being heavily jewelled. Thus we must consider whether the attire which is being worn is appropriate to be accompanied by such a weapon.

With regard to the question of rank, there are some obvious ranks which would carry swords as part of their outfits. These would be knights and the nobility. However there are also lower ranks that would wear weapons, such as the gentry. In fact a gentleman of the later Renaissance period would not be seen in public without a weapon at his side. However, to add to this we must consider the image which is being presented in this instance and whether such a weapon is suitable for it. Clearly a person should consider whether they will wear a sword in the presence of royalty as this can cause some issues as well. Obviously only people of the appropriate rank should even consider doing so. It is better to assume that you do not have the appropriate rank than to wear the weapon and possibly cause issues.

MOUNTING

Now that the appropriate situations have been considered it is possible to look at the mounting of the weapon, or how it is worn. This would seem to be an automatic sort of thing, but actually there are things which need to be considered. The appropriate mounting for the weapon must be considered to control the weapon. Having a weapon in an in appropriate mounting not only looks bad but also can lead to a lack of control of the weapon which can be disastrous. Thus the appropriate weapon must be placed with the correct mounting.

Suitable to Weapon

"Most medieval swords were strapped to the wearer with belts attached directly to the scabbards. They sat on the left hip, slightly angled forward so they could be controlled and drawn easily. Later swords were usually suspended from the belt at a more horizontal angle, either by various arrangements of straps or by a baldric, a broad strap hung from the right shoulder and running round the body across the left hip." (Ducklin and Waller, 2001:34)

In the case of all swords, this must start with a scabbard. This protects the blade of the weapon and prevents a piece of steel being exposed to damaging or being damaged by passers-by. The next part is what sort of hanger is appropriate, or even if one should be used. For most medieval swords, the scabbard was mounted directly on to the belt as they had a belt designed for the purpose. In the case of the rapier and later weapons a hanger was attached to the scabbard and this was mounted on to the belt. The owner of the weapon should research for the appropriate mounting rig for the weapon.

Position

Once the correct mounting rig has been chosen then it is necessary to consider the position of the weapon. In the case of the rapier the hanger and belt made it possible to shift the position of the weapon to suit the user and also the situation. The first thing that must be considered is to ensure that the wearer has easy control and access to the weapon. The weapon in its mounting should not be able to waggle about freely; this is the reason for the second strap often found on hangers. The handle of the weapon should be placed so it is easily accessible to the drawing hand. This position should also position it where the pommel can be accessed for control by the off-hand. This will enable the wearer to control and move the weapon out of the way should it be placed in a position where it may strike another.

AREA OF EFFECT

The area of effect of the weapon or increased personal space is something that needs to be taken into account. The position of the weapon in its mounting will often result in the weapon trailing behind the wearer, or this may be caused by the placing of the hand upon the pommel. Either way, the presence of the weapon increases the personal space of the wearer. It is actually due to this area of effect that swords were shortened in the later seventeenth century to allow for less problems with people being struck by the scabbards of the weapons, and it is the different personal space between the current period and the period in which swords were worn that needs to be considered.

While wearing the weapon, the wearer needs to be aware of their increased area of effect, this is especially so when moving through crowds. It is at these times that control must be maintained over the weapon to ensure that it does not strike anyone. The wearer of the weapon should always be aware of the position of the weapon and its increased area of effect. Look about yourself and consider your personal space when wearing the weapon and how much it has increased. This becomes especially apparent in movement.

Movement

"One of the most common faults among actors and actresses wearing slung swords is to the tendency to hold the weapon firmly by the grip in an attempt to stop it flapping around. The proper method is to allow the forearm or the hand to stay in light contact with the hilt between the weapon and the body. In this way the sword can be controlled by applying pressure to keep it lying close across the back of the hip or buttocks, especially if the performer wishes to make a bow without a sword coming into contact with those behind him." (Ducklin and Waller, 2001:34)

In moving, the wearer of the sword needs to be aware of his surroundings. Special consideration should be made with regard to any movement which may cause the weapon to swing out and strike someone or something. In all considerations of movement care should be taken. Indeed it is a skill like any other and needs to be practiced. Consider those movements which could cause the weapon to become uncontrolled or cause issues for others about you.

Weapon Control

In walking the off-hand should be placed gently on the pommel of the weapon so that it can be controlled. Ducklin and Waller (2001) instruct the use of the forearm, but the effect is the same, control over the weapon. This prevents the weapon contacting and possibly tripping the wearer but also allows the wearer to move the weapon out of the way should an obstruction be present. In most cases it is best to move the pommel forward and upward slightly thus reducing the area of effect of the weapon when moving through a crowd of people, or to force it behind slightly. The scabbard of the weapon should also be directed closer to the wearer, but not so much that it will obstruct him.

Stand normally with your weapon in its mounting. Place your hand on the pommel and push downward and glance behind to see the increased personal space. Release the hand from the pommel and then lift the pommel forward to see the decrease in personal space. Next walk with your weapon to see how it moves in its mounting without any control over the weapon and follow this up with control by the hand or forearm. Take note of the difference in personal space. Consider how the different movements would take effect in a crowded room or other place.

ACTIONS
Standing
In standing the wearer of the weapon is not moving so things should be simple however there are still considerations to be made. In standing the weapon should be placed so that its area is reduced so that someone passing to the rear of the wearer will not trip over the scabbard. A useful technique in this regard is to move the weapon forward and tuck it around the leg closest to the weapon, even if it is just the point hooked over the foot or ankle. Should this be too uncomfortable, the movements described using pressure on the pommel or handle can also be utilised. If the wearer is standing out in the open then there needs to be less stringent control of the weapon, but awareness of those around you should still be taken in.

Sitting
Sitting is where there can be some consternation about what to do with the weapon. If the weapon is worn in the mounting, the weapon should be pushed forward so as not to trip anyone passing behind the wearer. It is even an advantage to take the weapon out of the mounting rig then sit and place the weapon either immediately to the side or between the wearer's legs. Care should be taken that no one can knock the weapon if it is placed to the side of the wearer, and also how much room there is under the table. Placing the weapon on the top of the table is only an option when food is not being served and there are not too many others about, especially if they are wishing to do the same. Consideration should be made for placing the weapon away from the table if there is a secure place where it can be placed. A deal of practice should be taken by the wearer in sitting and then standing again as it is here that problems can really occur. Try with the weapon in the mounting and with it in your hand. Once again it is control over the weapon which is of greatest importance.

Bowing
Bowing is an action which takes practice to perform with or without a weapon being worn. In the case of wearing a weapon, special consideration needs to be made about the movement of the weapon so that it does not detract from the action of the bow nor becomes a problem for others who may be near. In bowing with a weapon the handle should not be gripped so that the weapon sticks out when the bow is performed. The weapon pointing up in the air detracts very much from the bow.

The easiest way to perform the bow with a weapon is to bend the top half of the body forward while bending the left leg at the knee. The right leg is kept straight as the body is lowered. The arms part to the sides of the body. The hand or forearm is used to gently move the weapon in a small arc behind the wearer, thus keeping control of the weapon and reducing any chance of it striking another. This is especially important in crowded situations. You should practice the bow both with and without the weapon at your side so that you can see the difference. Any hand gestures should be made with the right hand, while the left controls the weapon.

CONCLUSION: TAKE CARE...

The instruction and discussion which has been presented with regard to wearing a sword presents concepts which must be taken into account anytime that a weapon is worn. Indeed the opening parts of the discussion consider whether it is appropriate to wear a sword at all. Each of the points which have been illuminated in the discussion needs to be taken into account.

For the first time sword-wearer, or even the more experienced one, it is better that you get some practice in wearing and moving with a weapon before you go into a crowded situation. This is a skill like any other with regard to a weapon and it needs practice. The most important thing that needs to be considered with regard to this is the increased personal space due to the weapon.

Before you even put the weapon on, consider whether it is appropriate for the weapon to be worn, if it is not leave the weapon behind. In examining the weapon, is it in a scabbard? Is it in the correct mounting for the weapon? If you do not have a scabbard or the correct mounting the weapon should not be worn. In wearing the weapon, how much more space does the weapon take up? How will you control the weapon? Consider these important points before moving toward a group. Are you comfortable wearing the weapon and moving with the weapon? If not, it is better that you do not wear it.

The wearing of a sword is designed for the most part in the modern world to increase the effect and authenticity of the costume being worn. We have no other real reason for wearing a weapon. If the wearing of the weapon does not enhance the costume consider leaving it behind. Ceremonial purposes would be the only other reason for carrying the weapon.

What have been presented are some instructions about how the weapon should be worn and the considerations that need to be made with regard to this. In all instances the wearer of the weapon should be aware of his surroundings and other people near him so as not to strike them inadvertently with the weapon. With regard to this utmost care should be taken. Practice is required to be able to wear the sword properly and be able to control it effectively. It is advised that the wearer make time to practice these things before actually entering the situation where the weapon is worn.

SECTION 5.
Training

Fencing Practice

INTRODUCTION
Practice, it is something that we all need to become better fencers and also to maintain the level of skill that we have attained. What follows will address the idea of practice and what people do at practice to discuss how our attitude toward practice and what we do affects our fencing. The attitude which we take to our practice sessions is of vital importance and will determine how much we will learn.

The first thing that we must ask is what our practice/training sessions is designed for. This is where we must start to see the mindset which is behind the thoughts of going to practice in the first place. If we are to truly utilise a training session properly it is necessary to understand that we are not merely there for honing our current skills but also learning new skills and experimentation with these new skills. These two should always be achievement goals for a fencing practice.

LEARNING NEVER STOPS
The learning process for the true student of the sword will never stop as there is always something out there to learn. If you stop learning, this will lead to stagnation in your knowledge-base, and also stagnation in the process of becoming a better swordsman. When a fencer starts the volume of information seems to be inexhaustible and seems like that the fencer knows nothing and there is a lot to learn. As the student progresses this volume of information seems to shrink gradually until it seems like there is less and less to learn, but is this really true? While at this stage the essential skills have been learnt and a collection of advanced techniques have also been learnt, where does the fencer go from here? The answer to this is experimentation, the other part of practice.

afencersramblings.blogspot.com

While it is vital that we hone the skills that we already possess so that we can become technically proficient in them and can to call upon them, the process of learning does not stop here. It is at this point in time that we need to go out and seek new skills to learn to enhance our repertoire. Of course once these new skills have been learnt, we need time to see how they work, the perfect time for this is at practice. Experimentation is the key to expanding your knowledge and repertoire. It is important that we are willing to experiment with new skills to progress in the learning process. The best place for this, of course, is at practice.

Where a new skill is put up against an opponent and works, something is learnt, that the skill was performed correctly and effectively in that situation against that opponent. Where the attempt fails something is also learnt, that maybe it was not the correct time, or distance, or the opponent had a counter for it. In both cases something is learnt. The only way this sort of information is gained is if the fencer is willing to experiment with the new skills, without this experimentation, the fencer will stagnate, so we must experiment and be willing to fail in the experiment.

TWO PATHS FOR LEARNING

Next it is important to examine the question of how we learn fencing. In essence there are two paths that a person may take to learn more fencing, once the basics have been learnt. The first is through experimentation through bouting, and the second is through learning a sets of skills one after the other. The first one has the great appeal of being out on the field with an opponent having a great time matching skills against them. The second does not have this as it involves a level of instruction, drills and set pieces that must be followed, which seems to be substantially less satisfying, especially to the newer fencer. The question here is which one really has the advantage in the long run.

Learning through bouting with different opponent has the advantage of putting the skills in the situation where they will end up in the long run anyway. This tends to mean that the skills will be in a situation of working to solve a particular problem. This method allows for a great deal of experimentation as long as the fencer can keep to the goal of experimentation and learning. Sadly, in most situations this is not the case and the result of the bout actually becomes more important than the learning process. It also means that the skills that are learnt in this sort of environment are not based on principles but on what worked at the time. This can lead to sloppy technique, or "what works", and often does.

Learning through bouting is actually a slower and harder process while it seems faster as the body has to learn things on the fly. This is because the skill is learnt at speed where the fencer really does not know exactly why they have done what they have done, and in a lot of instances does not know exactly what they have done. This leaves out avenues for discovering why the technique actually worked and how it worked against the opponent. This coupled with the fact that the only reason that it worked may have been due to the sloppy technique of the opponent, does not lead to a solid base for learning.

Learning through learning a specific technique can seem tedious and boring to some as it seems that there is no practical application immediately to the skill being learnt. The skill is discussed, described and then demonstrated. Only then are the students involved at which point in time they have to follow the instruction and perform the action slowly at first and then speed up to do it properly, all the time being corrected by the teacher. This process sounds slow and painful, but in actual fact the student will actually learn faster due to the amount of detail presented. The reasons why the skill works will be explained along with how to use it properly and when it should be used. All this information will be present before the student even takes the field.

This learning process allows for refinement of the technique based on the information given. This method followed by practicing and experimentation based on the technique is a more effective learning process as all the knowledge is present before the action is performed at speed. Learning set skills and then bouting focusing on those skills is more likely to lead to experimentation as the focus is on the skills rather than the result of the bout.

BOUTING

Bouting, bouting is fast, bouting is fun, bouting allows us to match our skills against an opponent, but there is a great deal of difference between the types of bout. There is a lot of difference between a bout at training and a bout in a competition due to the difference on the focus of the bout. While bouting in training is focused on the learning process, competitive bouts are more focused on the result rather than how the fencer gets to that result.

Both fencers must decide what the focus of the bout is before they start. If one is there for the win and the other wants to practice a particular technique this can lead to problems, as the opponent may not present opportunities where the particular technique can be used. It is important where bouting is done for practice purposes that the focus of both combatants is upon the skills being learnt and how the fencer gets to the end result. Bouting with a new skill should always come after a period of drilling that skill.

DRILLS

Drills are important in the learning process as they focus on a particular skill which is being learnt. The focus of the drill must be on the skill being drilled rather than the result. This will focus the participants on the skill rather than the result of the drill. It is necessary that both participants in all drills understand what their part in the drill is and do not exceed this part so that both may learn. If one of the participants does not allow the skill to be performed how it is supposed to neither of the participants will learn what is supposed to be being learnt. Even where the result is one being struck things can be learnt, such as possible ways to defeat it even if they are not used in the drill.

Both participants need to be aware of what is being learnt in the skill and keep their minds open to what further things can be learnt from what is being taught. This can only be achieved where both participants in the drills participate to 100% of their ability following the requirements of the drill so that it is done properly and the correct responses are elicited. The attacks in drills must be credible along with the defence against them, if the defence fails then the attack should succeed, this is a part of the learning process. If the attack is not credible then the person who is defending will not learn the correct response to the attack. As such an attack must be delivered to a relevant target and at the correct distance so that the defender must defend to defeat the attack. A failure to defend actually enhances the learning experience as the defender learns what they did wrong in defence. Drills are about repetition, but it is important that the repetition is done properly for the skills to be learnt properly.

Specific skill sets need to be learnt and then drilled so that they are repeated so that the fencer can call upon that skill when it is needed. It is vital that the correct response is elicited for each attack or defence that it is used so that the skill is learnt properly. Repetition on it is own is useless, it is important that the repetition is the repetition of the correct action on the part of both participants in a partner drill, or the action of a single participant in a solo drill, to correctly develop the correct muscle memory for that particular skill, and it is important that it is done right the first time and every time. It takes something like 500 repetitions to place something in muscle memory, and takes about 100 times that to remove something or replace it. In other words it is better that a person does the correct action properly the first time and every time after that so as not to have to go back and take more time to remove a bad habit.

REASONS

As fencers we need to focus on the reason for going to practice, and also the reason for practice itself. It is important that the correct focus is made with regard to practice so that we can gain the maximum benefit from the practice we do engage in. While learning through bouting is a fun way to do things, learning through specific skill sets and lessons is actually a better way to learn. Remember the reason why you are doing drills and ensure that you are participating to 100% of your capacity in the drill so that both participants are able to learn the correct thing. Remember practice does not make perfect, perfect practice makes perfect.

CONCLUSION

There has been a lot discussed here with regard to practice, and there is a lot to consider. Each element should be taken into account each time you go to practice. Keep your mind open to elements which you may not have examined before. Take a lesson a second time and examine it from a different point of view and you may find that you have missed something. It is much easier to learn when there is some structure to your practice.

While learning "on the fly" is a lot of fun and presents a great challenge, it is not the greatest way to do things. It may seem quicker because you can get out there and fence, and you may have some quick victories in the beginning, but many of the nuances of fencing will be lost. A more structured method will yield greater results as the reasons will be better founded in theory, especially when they are presented by a teacher who knows what they are talking about.

Take your time and do your drills properly. Give your partner in the drill your full attention. You will benefit as they will more likely give you the same benefit. Drills are designed to focus on one aspect of fencing and are not a combat situation, adding things in will alter the drill and deviate from their purpose. Stick with the plan, the teacher has a reason for the drill and the way in which the drill is done.

When it comes to bouting, talk to your partner. If there is something you want to work on, tell them. You are both here to practice maybe there is something that they want to work on as well. Be generous with your partners in bouting and you will find your bouting experience to be much more rewarding to your learning and fencing experience. Never stop practicing. Never stop learning.

On Practice

INTRODUCTION

Practice is important. It is something which we hear and something which we are told again and again. This post is going to examine some of the details with regard to practice, how it is performed and why it is performed. Many will just skip over this one, but I suggest that you do not, as practice *really is that important*.

1. IMPORTANCE

Everyone needs to practice. It does not matter if you are the newest of the new or the most aged or experienced practitioner. Skills decay if you do not use them and thus practice is important. This also means that you should also practice everything that you have learnt. When you do not use a skill, it will decay and will not be as sharp the next time you try to use it.

2. REGULARITY

Regular practice of short amounts is better than long bursts infrequently. You should practice every day, an hour is best, 30 minutes if it is all you can squeeze in. It does not have to be anything complex merely using some footwork and making some defences and attacks will do on the physical side. This is on top of any practice that you may attend during the week at a school.

With regard to school training, if you can get it, it is preferable that you get at least two training sessions, but the optimum number is three. This allows for learning and then practicing your new techniques and then integrating them with your old techniques. If your school does not give you this option, you need to find time to do the extra training yourself, find drills that you can do at home.

3. MUSCLE MEMORY

There is a thing called "muscle memory". When you practice something enough, you will get to a stage where you can do the action without thinking about it, naturally this is a great advantage in any form of swordplay. It takes about 500 repetitions of an action to put it into your muscle memory, but you must practice it accurately. Any mistake you make in the action will also be practiced into muscle memory as well and it will take 50,000 repetitions to remove a mistake from muscle memory, so it is best to do it right the first time. Any action which is placed in your muscle memory can be performed without thought, this means you will react quickly to the stimulus given by your opponent; another reason why you must practice accurately and why your partner must give you the correct stimulus when you practice.

4. WHAT TO PRACTICE

In a word, *everything*. This being said some elements need more focus than others. Foundation elements should always be practiced more than peripheral elements because they form the basis of the peripheral elements. There is little point in practicing a counter-disengage if you cannot do a disengage, or practicing a *punta riversa* if you cannot do footwork properly. Things which are new will always require a little more attention when they are fresh because they are new, but this does not mean you should ever neglect your foundation elements.

5. HOW TO PRACTICE

Most importantly, with a sharp focus on practicing and what you are practicing. We are often distracted by what is fun or what is more engaging. If we are engaging in bouting with the purpose of working on a particular technique then both swordsmen need to work on that technique and not get distracted by other things. Likewise during drills we need to focus on what the drill is about and what each person's job is, if both do not do their jobs the drill will not be effective. Even when practicing alone the same focus is required. Pick a technique and work on that until you have completed practicing it and not before.

6. WHEN TO PRACTICE

Practice should be like sleep for military-types in field, whenever you can and however you can. You may not have access to an opponent, but there are still skills you can practice. You may not have access to a sword, but there are still skills you can practice. You may be stuck on a plane or a bus, but there are still things you can practice. If you are serious about your practice, there is always something that you can be practicing at almost anytime, anywhere that you are. Naturally, you will get some odd looks, but at least you are getting practice in. If you are serious about your art there are a lot of simple things in every-day life that can be turned into practice.

CONCLUSION

There have been six headings which have been presented with regard to practice and statements made with regard to each of them. Each is as important as the one before it and the one after. They are in no particular order really. If you hit a spot where you are having problems, go to your instructor or teacher and ask them how best to practice a particular skill or even set of skills. Better yet, I would advise you to sit down with them and work out a training program. This way you will always have a goal to work toward. For some the motivation is internal for others it needs to be external, most of all find your own and practice, it is the way to be a better swordsman.

Fencing and the Learning Process

INTRODUCTION

What follows will address the idea of fencing and the learning process. More to the point, it will have a look at the attitude of the fencer toward fighting different opponents and how this can affect the learning process. This is something that you should consider if you want to expand your learning experience past drills and exercises and become a real tactician, and a real swordsman.

CHOOSE AN OPPONENT

In fencing, when you are bouting, there will always be a choice between the easy win and the hard fight. Who you go out to seek to fight? Do you seek simply to win, or do you seek a challenge and the opportunity to learn from the encounter? If you are simply looking for the win, then it is more likely that you will seek opponents that you can easily beat whereas if you are seeking a challenge and an opportunity to learn this will inevitably lead you to finding the harder opponent.

While the instant win gives you some sort of ego gratification it is a much shorter path. If you go out and seek the harder opponents not only is a win against them more gratifying, a loss can also lead you to learn something from the encounter, this will enable you to learn more and improve, a much longer term goal. Seek the harder opponent and be grateful for their presence as it gives a much wider opportunity for you to learn than fighting those that you can easily beat, which leads on to something else.

CHOOSE TECHNIQUES

Everyone knows that they have a set of techniques which are reliable for them, which in some cases will guarantee victory over the opponent. So, should you use these same techniques and be satisfied with the victory, or should you look to learn new things and put them to the test against an opponent? As with fighting opponents who are easier, the win is instant gratification whereas the other will extend your fencing experience.

Even where the technique does not work something is learnt. Was it the way the action was performed? Was it the timing or the distance at which the action was performed that needs to be corrected? These are things we can learn from extending yourself and trying new things, this is vital to the learning process. Even where the loss is to an easier opponent something can be learnt when using a new technique, so the expansion of ones repertoire is a good thing and will help you down the path. Remember, in bouting, the purpose is to learn and to practice. This is the perfect time to make mistakes and try out new techniques or work on things which maybe you are not so good at.

In bouting tell your opponent that you want to work on something in particular, and they may also want to work on something. You can then give each other opportunities to work on the skill-sets which you have both chosen to improve your skills in these areas. This is not an opportunity that you would get in a tournament. Maximise your chances to learn from these experiences. Sure it is fun to have a bit of a hit, but it is also a chance for you to focus on something and improve it also, and your bouting partner can help.

EXTENDING YOURSELF

In essence what is being discussed here is how you progress in your fencing and nothing more. Fighting the same opponents with the same techniques will refine the techniques, it is true, but it does not extend you from where you are at the moment. To extend yourself, means to put you in a situation where the outcome is not certain so that you can learn something from the encounter. This is what extends your experience and invites you to excel in what you are doing. You must seek the harder opponent and newer techniques to progress in your training and learning process it is the only real way to learn. If you seek the same opponents and use the same techniques you will stagnate and not learn and not progress, this is not what you should be about as a fencer.

FURTHER HORIZONS

As you improve and gain experience and skill it will be difficult to find opponents who challenge you, this is where things become more difficult and the advancement process becomes more difficult. It is at this point that it is of vital importance that you seek new horizons, new skills and new opponents to face and test your skills against. Be happy that if there is someone out there who can give you a real challenge in your fencing and who makes you bring out your best in your fencing, this is the only way to improve. It is even better if this person is in your on school or club because then you can see them on a regular basis.

The advantage of having a local "rival" is that as one of you improves the other has to get better. Then to match up again, the other has to improve again. This process repeats over and over again, the two bouncing off one another's improvement. In this way one helps the other to improve. When they train together this can be both a gift and a curse, because they will learn each other's moves. The problem is that they will also become too in-tuned with one another that they may become blinded by one another, thus missing what others are doing.

Starting again is hard and it is a difficult process. It is an even harder process the further along you go with a particular weapon. Your body will be trained with certain responses and so will want to respond with these. You will have to re-train it to do other things due to the different style or weapon, but the extension in your knowledge will improve your skills overall and knowledge of the sword always feeds back upon itself regardless of what weapon it is.

CONCLUSION

Remember that a loss is only a loss if you do not learn something from the encounter with your opponent. Even if you have to go and discuss with your opponent how you were defeated or what you did wrong. This is not too much to ask if you really want to improve your fencing. Fencing is a learning experience more than anything else and we all have a great deal to learn, realise this and you are in for a long and fruitful journey. Think that you are the font of all knowledge and that your skills are complete and you are going to find yourself upset and your fencing career shortened considerably.

Think about your learning process, and ask yourself whether you are maximising your chances to learn.

Newton's 3rd Law in Fencing

INTRODUCTION

The following article will focus on a single point in fencing which is of importance. One of the fundamental things about fencing is that there is no ultimate killing move. There is always a counter to every single attack performed. This sounds strange considering that there were masters who used to have schools in which they taught their *botta secreta*. There is a defence to every attack it is just a matter of finding it. This is one of the things which are so exciting about fencing; it is about putting the techniques together so that they can work and achieve the fencer's aim. So this blog will be focussing on action and counter.

A MUCH USED STATEMENT

"To every action there is an equal and opposite reaction."

This statement has been used many times with regard to many things, primarily it has to do with physics, but it has been used to describe other things as well. This particular statement is as applicable to fencing as it is to human interactions as it is to physics. There is an action which can be used in response to any other action in fencing, no matter how simple, or complex, it may be. This is one of the most essential points that as teachers, we must instil in our students, and as fencers, we must understand. It is one of the keys to the development of the fencing mind.

We must develop our enquiring minds to go and seek answers to questions in swordplay. Most of them will be physical, as in "How do I answer this attack?", but some of them will also be more of a mental kind as well. While this article does focus on seeking answers to the physical questions these mental questions should not be pushed too far aside. A fencer needs an active mind to answer the physical questions and so exercises of the mind are useful if nothing else.

ATTACK AND DEFENCE

So first, there is attack and defence. A scenario, a thrust is made this is a very simple attack to which there are at least three defences regardless of the form of fencing you are doing. The attack can be parried, voided or retreated from. Each one of these either displaces the body or displaces the attack. For this particular purpose the parry will be used.

So, the attack is parried, this allows the defender to mount a counter-attack, the riposte. With regard to this discussion, tempo is not going to be mentioned so bear with me. Even in a *stesso tempo* response there is still the element of a parry and a riposte, they are simply blended together. Of course the individual receiving the riposte can perform anyone of the three actions described in defence, the ceding parry being the most useful if blade engagement is to be maintained. From the ceding parry another counter-attack may be made.

With the simple description above, it can be seen that each attack has a counter, this counter then builds to a counter-attack, and against this there is also a counter. There is no action in fencing which is performed which cannot be countered in some manner. It is up to the fencer to find this counter and use it against the attack. In many ways it is like the arms race. One builds a weapon, the other builds a weapon to counter it and so forth. Luckily in this competition the world is not under threat.

BLADE ENGAGEMENT

Even in the actions used in blade engagement the same sorts of things can be seen. There is an action followed by as response followed by a response to the response and so forth. *Stringere* is performed to open a line on an opponent. A *cavatione* is performed to counter the *stringere* to change the engagement and close the line again. A *contra-cavatione* is performed to counter the *cavatione*. A *ricavatione* is performed to counter the *contra-cavatione*, and then just when you think it is all finished, a simple *cavatione* will start the entire process again.

So, it has been demonstrated that in blade engagement there is always a counter to the action performed by a fencer. The fencer merely has to have the skill and the ability to think of and use the counter at the appropriate time to counter the action of the opponent. The same was demonstrated with regard to attack, defence, counter-attack, and counter-defence. In all cases it must be remembered that every action in fencing can be countered. This may take some time for the fencer to wrap their head around this particular concept.

CONCLUSION

The fact that eventually every action will be able to be countered some way is one of the most fundamental points in fencing and for some it is the reason why the actions keep going. In the beginning when the skills are low such things will seem like they have no answer, but it should be remembered that there is always an answer to every action. In many cases it is just a matter of building up the skills of the body and also those of the mind for the fencer to perceive these answers.

In many ways the action posed by the opponent is a question and the action performed by the fencer is an answer to that question. This is a debate performed with steel in the same way that any debate is performed. There is always an answer all you have to do is go out and find that answer. This is a search for a solution in which both the body and mind are involved. What is interesting, and sometimes infuriating, is that sometimes the answer that we are looking for is not the complex answer that we are seeking, but a simple one that we cannot see because we are looking for the complex answer, "missing the forest for the trees".

Taking Hold of Your Training

INTRODUCTION

There is a time in your fencing career when *you* need to take hold of *your* training. What this means is that you need to take hold of the direction in which the training goes. This discussion is designed to address this particular concept and present some ideas about how you can take a hold of your training and thus push it in a direction which interests you.

TRAINING IS PERSONAL

The first thing is that training is actually a very personal thing and that you are person who gets benefit out of training. Sure, the teacher or coach may get some satisfaction out of your progress, but in the end it is really up to you. This is the most important thing and the reason why eventually you need to take ownership of your own training and give it some personal direction.

To begin with the teacher supplies the direction because you do not understand those skills that you will require. In this particular element the teacher will supply the basic elements of training and through such the basic skills which are required. Once these basics have been learnt then you need to have some idea about where you want to go after the basics. The new direction will always be based on the basic skills which you have learnt, but will tend to go in a direction different and more personal than previously.

DIFFERENT DIRECTIONS

There are many different directions that the training can go once the basics have been learnt. For the more Renaissance oriented fencer there is the question of whether a particular school or nationality will be the focus. Or you may focus toward a particular skill-set or weapon combination. Or you may even decide that a particular manual may be your focus. Each one of these gives different options for you and gives a slightly different direction. In this particular situation is that you have to choose the direction. The teacher may suggest or encourage, but in the end it is *your* decision.

For the fencer who is primarily training alone the taking a hold of training has to happen a lot sooner. This is because it is only you who can really motivate you to do the training in the first place. In this particular situation there really is no teacher or coach that can give the direction for you. Other teachers or fencers may supply suggestions, but in the end it is all up to you. You need to decide where you are going and what to work on next as there is no one else to supply the plan of where to go.

YOU NEED A DIRECTION

To continue to progress you require some sort of direction. Even if that direction is merely to improve the skills that you have already, this is still a direction. The best direction for you to go in is one which you are self-motivated to go in. The teacher can supply ideas and encouragement, but in the end you must make the decision and then stick to it. This requires you to have the motivation to start and continue along your chosen path.

In the end you must choose the direction in which you want to go. You should get some ideas about what options are open to you from various sources. These ideas can be based on a particular direction based on a specific text, general improvement or at a specific goal that you want to achieve. You should take the time to put the suggestions on paper to compare them. This way there will be a clear idea about the choices open to you. Once you have an idea about where you want to go it is time to plan.

PLAN

It is necessary to plan the direction that you want to take. If there is no plan made of the direction it is difficult to see any sort of improvement. It is also difficult to see what end result is planned and whether you have deviated from the direction chosen. The plan is what will keep you striving toward their goal and also having some idea about where that is.

In choosing this direction for training it is a good idea to get some help and advice. This should preferably be from your teacher. There are others who can supply some ideas about the direction and the plan to make to get there. People who are on the same path are also useful as they are currently doing it and will have ideas about good things and bad things. The same can be said for people who have travelled in the same direction, experience is very useful in this endeavour.

Some people like to make plans and keep the ideas in their heads or some other loose form. The best idea is to put it on paper. In this way the plan is obvious and presented to you so you can see exactly what they need to do next and what is coming up. Putting the plan on paper also gives it a solid quality. This being said, it is also important that the plan has some ability to be modified if required, some level of flexibility to meet different challenges along the way. Things happen which are not controllable, illnesses and injury will mean that the plan may have to be changed or put on hold for a period, and it is important to take these things into account.

Once the plan has been put on paper it is important to work towards the goal described. It is also important that it is not packed away and then never seen again. The plan should be placed somewhere it is easy to get a hold of it and to examine what is happening and whether the plan needs to be modified. Integrate the plan into normal training this way the plan will be followed by habit rather than being something separate from normal training. It is also important to discuss the plan that has been worked out with your teacher or coach. This way they will know what is going on, what is being worked upon and will be able to help with it. They may also be able to help with it and assist in improving the plan.

CONCLUSION

You will come to a situation where you have completed all of the basic training which enables you to fence at a reasonable level. It is at this time that you really need to take control of your own training. What happens after this will determine the length of your fencing career. If you are clever you will look at many different options and discuss these with various people. In the end the decision is yours and this is of great importance. Remember to plan the direction, put it in some solid form, and then work towards it. Don't be afraid to ask for help.

Making Plans for Training

INTRODUCTION

Making plans for training is a good concept as it provides advantages, but it needs to be done right. The advantage of making a plan for your training, rather than just filling in holes where they are perceived is that it gives a plan for the future. This provides a direction for the training and a simple process to follow. This plan can provide a reason for going to training, and going on a regular basis, which is a good thing in itself. Where it is filling holes then there is required motivation to pick something, where there is a plan, it is just the next lesson in the plan. This provides things to do at training, especially where the motivation may not be there to figure something out to do. This also means that the training is directed at a target.

TARGETS

Targets are important as they give us something to aim at. For some, they can be non-specific, but for most they need to be specific about where it is all going. As far as overall targets are concerned "I want to get better at my fencing." is a target which we all have as who does not want to get better at their fencing? This target does not provide particularly much direction. To provide direction, it is useful to be somewhat more specific, this is achieved by dividing goals up into long term and short term targets or goals.

Long Term

Long term targets are those which will not happen soon and will require a lot of work and are something to strive toward. These are often hopeful goals of where a person may want to end up sometime down the track. In many ways this is somewhat "cloud shooting" dreaming about the day that you will hit the top of the ranks in your particular form of fencing. Of course for some, this will be out of reach so this needs to be tempered a little with sensibility. These long term goals should not have a time limit on them anything under a year or even more.

Short Term
Short term goals are those which will happen sooner than the long term goals, but they may not happen in a couple of months or possibly even a couple of years. These goals need to be realistic so that you can work toward them in an active fashion. It is these goals that the plan for training is written to actively pursue. Each short term goal should be achieved with a plan. Each one of these short term goals should build to fulfil a long term goal. In this way there is an overall plan and more specific ones as well. The short term goals may or may not have a time limit, or date of completion on them. For some the introduction of a time is useful, for some it is not. Just remember to be at least a little flexible.

FLEXIBILITY

Being flexible in your plan is always useful. Things will happen in life which will interrupt the progress of your fencing plan. This can be major life-changing things or even simple things such as the flu. Due to these particular factors it is important to be flexible in your plan in order to take into account the unexpected. This means that if you propose a date; make sure that there is room in there to make changes as they are required. If one week off due to being ill makes a mess of the plan, then you need to be more flexible about it. Of course, simply putting things off because you don't feel like it is a way that will cripple the plan, so you also need to temper this flexibility with motivation and control over yourself.

LESSONS

Once all of the goals have been decided and dates set for the completion of the goals, next it is important to look at the lessons themselves; most of the time these lessons will be able to be taken from the standard training program. In most instances it will be a simple tightening of the expectations of these lessons. Often it will be an increase in the performance aspect with regard to form. There will also be those lessons which will have to be modified to suit the training program and the goals set. In these particular instances tailor the lesson to suit what you want to achieve out of it. Use what works. Sounds silly? Use those techniques which have worked for you in the past to learn. For some it is simple repetition in drills, for some it will be to put the skill into a more active situation such as bouting.

Remember this plan is being tailored to suit you. Make sure that the lessons build on one another. The lessons should be connected in some way. One lesson should attach to the next to get to the one after that. Parry + Thrust = Riposte is a simple example of two lessons combining to result in a third. The lessons should build on one another in order to get you to your goal. Think of this like building a wall. Each brick lends its strength and the wall would be faulty if it was missing. This needs to be one of the most important considerations in your plan.

CONCLUSION

Plans help us to achieve goals. Some will muddle through and find their way through other means, but a plan is always a useful thing. The plan will set simple goals for the fencer for each lesson. Each lesson will be built to assist in achieving that overall goal. It is direction which a plan most supplies and often gives a person the motivation to do what they need to do in order to achieve their goal.

1. Establish goals.
2. Make a plan.
3. Find lessons to suit the plan, or make lessons to suit the plan.
4. Stick to the plan.
5. Expect to have to change things as you go.

Building an Individual Training Program

INTRODUCTION

The individual training program is different from the group training program as it is designed to fit an individual. This means that the specific requirements of the individual must be taken into account. For the student to get the greatest benefit from the program it is important that it suits them. This can be somewhat trying if sufficient information is not gained from the student to start with. The teacher should not be attempting to build the training program without communication with the student. In this way the program will fit the student better and go further to achieving their aims and also keeping them interested in it.

The individual training program must suit the individual and thus must be individual in nature. This will mean that the program will change dependent on the particular student. There are several different aspects that must be taken into account for the program to suit the student the best and these will be discussed in a little detail. For the program to be the best for the individual student all of the elements present in the training program must suit the student. This means that information is required from the student for this to happen.

BACKGROUND INFORMATION

The first element that must be taken into account is the student's background. Do they have previous experience in any relevant areas that may assist them? Are there any elements in their background that may hamper their development due to thought processes or physical elements present?

Students with experience in martial arts of any kind will already have some background in movement and bio-mechanics. Also they will also have certain movement patterns and thought processes that will have an impact on what they are to learn. This is the same for students who have previous experience in fencing. How this will affect their program and ability will be dependent on the type of fencing they have done, and to some degree the school of thought. Other sports can also have an impact on the program depending on the sport. All of these background elements will have developed a level of conditioning which can be an asset or a detriment depending on their training.

PRESENT AND POTENTIAL ABILITY

The student's present ability and potential ability is important and must be taken into account. Their present level of ability is important and must be taken into account so that the skills that will be taught are appropriate to the student. This is to ensure that the program does not deal with skills which are too far out of their current ability. This is also dependent on their potential ability.

A student who is currently at a lower level may be able to deal with skills at a higher level if the program allows them to build up to the higher level, but this must be present in the program to allow them to do this. If the program is to be built around a particular manual, such as a period manual especially, this must also suit their ability so that they can perform the skills present. Finally in this particular element, personal issues must be taken into account. This includes such things as disabilities, fencing knowledge and also time constraints. All of these elements will affect how the program is built and what sort of program is used.

INTEREST

The final personal element that must be taken into account before developing the program is interest. What sort of level of interest in fencing does the student have? This will affect how rigidly they will stick to the program and also how much they will be willing to spend time doing it.

In general, the student with a passing or social interest in fencing will not request a personal training program, and will also have more difficulty sticking to the program. The dedicated fencer will go out of their way to make time to train and do what is present in the training program. Their level of interest will also affect how far they want to go with the program.

Interest areas are also important. It is less useful to attempt to teach the French school of fencing to a person who is more interested in the Italian or German. Specific areas of interest are useful as they allow the student to focus on one particular area and this also allows a more focussed training program to be constructed.

PURPOSE

Once all of the more personal details have been taken into account with regard to the student, it is then possible to examine the program itself. The purpose of the training needs to be considered next. This is the foundation principle upon which the training program is based. The basic requirement for this to be possible is communication with the student to find out exactly what they want out of the training program. It is through this process that goals for the training program are set. This will affect what type of program is developed and the focus of the training program.

If the student has a specific goal, this is useful as it means that the training program can be tailor-made to strive toward that particular goal. If the student has a more general goal, then the program will be more fluid and will involve skills of general development. It is important that the purpose of the training program is established for both the student and the teacher, in this way they both know the goal of the training program. Once this is established, it will then be possible to examine the type of training program that will be required in order for the goal to be achieved.

Initial Training

There are essentially three types of training program that will be developed for the individual student. The first is the initial training. This is designed to introduce the student to the skills of fencing for the first time. This type of program will introduce the basics of fencing and how the skills all work. In some cases this type of training may be included into the other training program types.

Re-Training

The second type is the re-training type. This is designed for the student who has been away from fencing for an extended period of time and is designed to re-introduce them to the skills that they may or may not know. The re-training program may also be used for those who have been rushed through their initial program to go over basic skills to establish a foundation from which to progress further.

Development

The final type of training is the developmental type. This is designed for the advancement of the skills of the student. In this case the student has already learnt the basics and is looking at advancing their skills to a higher level. This form of training tends to be the most intense version of the program types as the skills are at such a high level and more is required of the student.

CONCLUSION

The individual training program must be developed between both the student and the teacher. If either attempts to do this alone the ultimate goal may be missed. The most important thing is that the training program must suit the student more than it is required to suit the teacher. This means that the goals of the student must come first.

Pushing a student into a premade training program is generally futile as it may not have those things that the student is interested in learning or may not go toward the goals that they have set for themselves. While in general every form of training should be suited to the students which are present, the individual training program takes this idea to its upper limit as it is purely focussed on the individual.

It must be collaboration between the student and the teacher at all times. Both the student and the teacher have important roles to play in the development of the individual training program and this is very important. Of course, the first thing that needs to happen is that the student actually requests the training program in the first place. Teachers are not mind-readers.

How Many Times This Week? A Question of Practice

INTRODUCTION

Practice is something which has been mentioned time and again to us all in many different activities. If you were to go back through the articles in this book, you will note I have mentioned it many times. For the most part these articles have been focused more upon how a person should practice and what they should practice. This post will focus on a different point of view on the same subject, frequency.

REGULARITY

The first thing that must be said about the frequency of practice is that regular practice is great. It gets your body and mind into a pattern that it can work with and work to. This enables the body and the mind to prepare for the practice and thus be prepared to learn and enhance skills which have already been attained. However regularity is not the only key, there is the question of frequency.

FREQUENCY

Regularity of practice is only the first step, frequency is also important. Some will decide that only one session a week is all that they can do. This will result in a truly slow rate of progression unless they are doing some substantial work at home. In reality three sessions are required to really improve, more sessions after that are only improving on that. For the most part, many schools run two sessions a week which students are expected to attend. One of these will focus on the learning aspects while the other will focus on the more practical aspects. The third session, the students are expected to make up in solo drills on their own at home.

What you will find is that if you attend one session a week and do no work at home, you will often have to do repeats of skills to truly learn them. If you do one session a week and then go home and do some sort of solo practice on the new skill, this will establish this new skill in a rudimentary form in your skill-set. To really establish a skill you will need three sessions and one of these being drills with a responsive partner to find action and reaction. If your school does not have the sessions in the week to do this then it is up to you do make the time.

HOMEWORK

We all get homework from school and other learning institutions; this is to encourage us to practice what we have learnt so that it will make connections in our brains. Fencing is no different. You need to do work at home between practices to establish skills for yourself. There are some very simple things that you can do to practice fencing at home.

1. **Sitting in Stance** - Sit on a chair in your usual on guard stance and do whatever that you were normally going to do with the upper part of your body. I have found this usually works best on an office chair in front of a computer or television.
2. **Footwork in the House** - Use your fencing footwork to move around the house. This will make the movements natural to you so that you do not have to think about them.
3. **Hand and Foot** - Move your hand before your foot. This adds on to the previous one. Always remember to move your hand before your foot in your actions. Approach the fridge, extend your hand, step closer to it. Approach a bookshelf, extend your hand, step closer to it. Do this consciously.
4. **Hanging on a String** - Hang a piece of string, attach a tennis ball to it, have a stick the same length as your sword next to it. Every time you pass the stick, pick it up and strike the ball 5 times from proper distance on guard. Once you are striking it more times than not, change it to a lunge. Then shrink the target and repeat.
5. **Stationary Target** - Cardboard box flattened approximately the same size as your

torso. Hang it on a wall. Divide it into quadrants. To start, simply thrust at the box from on guard. Once you can hit the box without missing aim for each individual quadrant. Add footwork once you can strike each quadrant and strike each quadrant on the move, including on a lunge.

These are five simple physical practice elements that you can do so that you can practice solo at home. If you do not have a sword, the weapon can be swapped for a stick of the same length of sword that you would normally use. These drills are simple and apply to all fencers regardless of their level.

EXERCISE THE MIND

"Accidents happen" an unfortunate but true fact of life. Regardless of how we protect ourselves injury and illness are only a step around the corner. The result of these is often time off where we cannot do the physical practice which the art of the sword requires however there is not an end to it. There is always the mind to exercise.

Studies have shown that individuals who exercise their minds as well as their bodies do much better than those who just exercise their bodies. Reading about the actions of fencing and practicing them in our minds actually goes some distance to assisting us in our training. It familiarises us with the ideas of fencing and the theoretical aspects and these explain the physical. If you cannot go out and actual do fencing you should be at least reading or thinking about it.

CONCLUSION

So, practice needs to be regular and frequent to be effective. This is the same with any sport or hobby that you may pursue. Three times a week is the most effective amount if you want real progression in your fencing. You need at least one for learning a skill and two for practicing it before it will become cemented. If your club or group does not offer sessions three times a week then you need to make up the time somewhere.

The first place where you can, and should, be doing this is with doing practice at home. There are five simple exercises which have been presented which are easily able done at home. These will help with the foundation skills up which all of the other skills are based. Remember to focus on the skill which is being learnt in the exercise and not the result so that you are learning the correct thing. These exercises can be expanded into other areas. Just don't be surprised if you get some funny looks.

No one is going to be 100% all of the time, thus we are not going to be able to practice using our bodies to our fullest capacity. This is where exercising the mind comes in. Reading about fencing, even if you are not studying it intently to learn exactly what's being said, still gets the mind thinking about fencing. This will assist you in your training. Researching elements in your fencing is always a good idea as you can find different perspectives, and it also exercises your mind which is good for your fencing.

To reach the best that you can be, it will take a lot of work. This work needs to be regular and it needs to be frequent. It is just the way it has to be. If it is less regular or less frequent, it will take longer, it is as simple as that. Most importantly of all, there is only one person who can do the practice and make the time to do the practice and that is *you*.

Fencing and Music

INTRODUCTION

There is no doubt that music has an effect on us all. Indeed that one odd body fact that I read somewhere, and have been meaning to fact-check, is that the human heart will beat alongside with the bass of the music which is being played, or something similar. Music can inspire us toward different feelings and also emotional states, this particular effect is deliberately used in movies all of the time. So, I did some reading and had some thoughts and decided that it was time to look at it in relation to fencing.

RESEARCH

Farrell

Conveniently, not long after this little gem popped into my head I came across an article entitled, "Western Composers and Western Martial Arts"[14] in *Encased in Steel Anthology I*. Interestingly enough there were aspects of what was said in here which lined up quite well with what I was going toward. While Keith Farrell's article deals more with the comparison of the dates of music with the dates of treatises to understand their social context and also for a better understanding of their footwork and movement (Farrell, 2015:87), mine was more toward asking questions of how peoples bouts compare to music and what influences it can have on training.

Flavel

Toward the avenue of my own thoughts I stumbled across an article in *Australasian Scientist* called "Turn Down the Volume?" which studied the effect of music on study and the performance of students. Needless to say, this article was more along my own lines of thinking as I was also wondering if the playing of music would enhance my students' training or detract from it. Some of it was most helpful with regard to this, as it stated with regard to gene expression and "changes also inferred potential benefits relating to memory, learning and general brain health." music possibly aids in protecting and improving the brain (Flavel, 2015:15).

WHICH MUSIC?

Clearly there is evidence that music being played is a good thing and can be an aid toward the student's learning. The question next was what music should be played during the practice? Going back to the two useful sources of information there is an examination of the relationship between the manuals and the music in Farrell (2015) as indicated above, Medieval Music is reflected in style of fighting, rhyming method presented in manuals and in music as well (Farrell, 2015:89). This would make medieval music perfect for this kind of fighting. Similarly, Renaissance Music was more complicated also found in music, repetition found in manuals also found in music (Farrell, 2015:90). This meant that the first choice for music should be from the Medieval and Renaissance periods as this should help with ingraining

---

14 I recommend having a look at this article if you get the chance the relation between fencing notation and dancing notation has been noted in several works. The rhythm of music of different ages seems to line up with the actions of fencing in thos ages as well.

a thought about the sort of feel of the fencing in the students as they listen to the music.

Of course, this was all a place to start, and to start only. For myself it is also an examination of how music relates to the bouts we fight. What sort of music is your bout like? What sort of music should it be like? We often imagine that our bouts should be musical with one person playing off the other, like a dancing madrigal from the Renaissance period. How often does it turn into something that belongs at a death-metal concert? This is the reason why I wanted to play music at practice, to see the effect of it not only upon their learning but also their bouts.

THE MUSIC ADVANTAGE

Personally, I have found music to be a boon when I study. I use it when I write. I use it when I read. I have found that the right sort of music is most useful in keeping my brain active in the right sort of way and focused on what I am doing. The hope was to find the key to this and give it to my students at training and thus give them the advantage of the right music to train with.

Flavel (2015) states that music beforehand to make you feel good improves performance, the choice of music is up to the individual (Flavel, 2015:15). This can also work for practice and also tournaments also. The trick is selecting the correct music for what you are about to embark upon. For myself, I have a selection of music which I used to like playing before tournaments. Much of it was metal and mostly very up-beat. This was designed to get my heart pumping and also my mind focused on what I was doing. This is one that you can do for yourself, find what works for you.

CONCLUSION: FUTURE EXPERIMENTATION

I hope to be running an experiment as to the effect of different types of music on training. This experiment will be given details as to what I hope to achieve and will stretch over an extended period of time. My students have already been subjected to the unofficial start to this experiment as I have been taking my laptop to the hall and playing different music with training. My *very* rough and *very* initial findings are that Classical and Renaissance music seems to have no effect, whereas Metal and other "heavier" styles seem to be highly motivating.

For the most part I have been playing Classical music as background music for our training sessions. I have found this most suitable as the students do not get distracted. I have found at times when I play more modern music students tend to get distracted by familiar lyrics and find it difficult to keep them to the task at hand. The music tends to get changed when they are bouting to something a little more up-beat to encourage more movement. This I have found to be quite effective.

Music does have a positive effect on the training atmosphere. I have had students actually come up to me and tell me that they miss the music in the background when it is not present. This makes me think that the music is also useful in creating a more welcoming rather than intimidating atmosphere for the newer students as well. Music has a great effect, try it at your next training session and see what your results are.

Solo Training: For the Solo Practitioner

INTRODUCTION

This was going to be an article about finding a local group and what consists of a good group with local contacts in my local area, but I changed my mind. I figured that there is a lot of information out there about how to find a local group for doing HEMA in whatever particular flavour you are looking for. Less, on the other hand, is said about the solo practitioner and how a person is to go about doing it alone. Luckily we have the internet and faster communications which makes things easier, but there are still times when it is necessary to do things solo.

GOING IT ALONE

Sometimes a group is not convenient to get to. Sometimes the group does not mesh well with you, or is not studying what you are interested in. There are lots of reasons for going it alone. Sometimes it is just necessary for you to start the research into a particular form on your own to get a handle on it before involving other people. Every one of these is a valid reason for going it alone and you should not be ashamed for any of them.

HARD ROAD BUT REWARDING

The first thing that the future solo practitioner should note is that it is a hard road, but it is also rewarding as well. Groups have some support mechanisms which are absent when studying or practicing alone. However there are still support mechanisms that you can use to your advantage. Don't forget about chat groups and other connections, all of these can provide some support when you need it. Just remember to do your research to support (or not) the things which people tell you.

All of the work falls to you, but in the end so do all of the rewards for that work. You can stand there at the end and say that you did it. Each advance is something that you did on your own and each advance is an achievement in its own right. Even the small advances are advances; don't forget this, because sometimes it will get really tough.

MANY CHOICES

In studying alone or practicing alone there are many choices to make, and all of them are open. There is no one to sway you from one path to another or make any other determinations. In the same way there also equally as many chances to be distracted. This is where you need to keep with what you are doing. It will be most easy to be distracted in choices when things become harder in your studies, these are the times when you must stick to what you have chosen and proceed onward. You must finish what you begin to understand it completely otherwise you will only have partial understanding of the information presented. Often partial information is worse than no information as it leads to bad tangents of understanding and makes for confusing conclusions.

FOCUS

The most important thing is that you must keep your focus; it is very easy to get off-track. You need to set yourself a program to follow and then follow it and not be distracted by other things. Elements of life will get in the way, when they do you need to get them done and then get back to what you were doing. Unlike in a group you will not have others to keep you focussed it is up to you. You will also have to make time to practice what you have learnt. This will be more difficult than with a group as there will be no group training. Take some time out of every day to do your training and your study and make it a routine so that people that live with you understand that this is what you do. It will make things easier on everyone around you also. This way it will also make it easier for them to plan things around your study time.

MY OWN EXPERIENCE

In my own experience, I spent the early years of my rapier career as a solo practitioner. For my part I spent much of my time studying anything and everything I could get my hands on. This meant the history of the weapon, curatorial elements, social elements, *everything*. At that time period manuals were somewhat rare and as such I only had a few to look at, and whatever pictures from others that I could scrounge from other sources. They say that a picture tells a thousand words, well sometimes it is the wrong ones.

Studying just from pictures can lead to some really interesting interpretations. These days, knowing what I know now, I look back at my interpretations and a lot of it is just plain *wrong*. Learning just from pictures is difficult, but it does give you some idea of movements and positions of the fencers. This will at least give you an idea to begin with of where you are going, or whether the particular style of combat may suit you or not.

READ, READ AND READ SOME MORE

Most importantly, read. Read a lot. Find information about what you are studying and read it, note it. Study the subject to death. Find actions which fall in line with what you are doing in the mainstream and do exercises which will complement it. Walking is always good for building your cardio-vascular health; if you can get drills out of your manual, even better. This is even better if they are based on the plays which are in the manual. At least then you are using the movements which are described.

CONCLUSION

The study of the solo practitioner is a hard path. It is not impossible though, it just takes time to achieve a result. The greatest problem is no partner to train with, thus no chance to see actions in motion. If you get the chance to try your skills out with someone do it. This will help evaluate whether you are on the right path.

Remember about the wider community which is easy to contact via the internet. Ask questions, get suggestions and help. Most people are more than willing to assist you in your studies. They will benefit from the work that you do from the feedback that you give them as to whether or not their suggestions have worked or not. More than likely they will give the same to their own students to help them. Don't give up. It will be worth it in the end. It will also give you a lot of satisfaction when you get there as well.

Cross-Training and Other Groups

INTRODUCTION

I have spent some time in a single group following their rules and guidelines as to how I should fence. In later years I have begun to engage with other groups who have similar but differing perspectives on the same activities. This has resulted in some interesting scenarios and some opening of my mind as to how swordplay works. This discussion is focussed on the idea of cross-training with other groups and how this can benefit the swordsman regardless of the weapon form which is chosen.

EXPERIENCE GAINED

The most useful benefit in engaging with other groups in swordplay is experience. It introduces the fencer to another approach to the same or similar weapons that the individual may not have experienced before. All which is learnt in this particular scenario is useful for the future of the fencer regardless of whether any blades are actually crossed. This leads to another aspect of the experience in that not all groups will have the same approach in their training or their goals and seeing swordplay from a different perspective can also be useful for a different approach in their own dealings. No group should be judged from the outside, all have something to share with regard to this, and the experience of engaging with these other groups can only be of benefit to the fencer and the wider fencing community.

In that even sword groups who share the same weapons do not train the same and sometimes they do not even have the same overriding principles behind their swordplay, the experience of crossing blades with different schools can show the fencer different problems and approaches which can be presented in the actual form and conduct of combat. This can only benefit the fencer as it may give them some ideas about how to solve similar problems in future encounters with other fencers as well.

Experience in crossing blades with other schools gives some idea about how they approach the combat form and this can be intellectually stimulating in a big way, especially if the system being used is different from the system that the fencer is most commonly used to. This experience can open new ideas about how the weapon can be moved and also how the body can be moved in concert with the weapon.

Elements from other schools can even be incorporated into our own fencing allowing a broadening of the style being used and this is most useful. It is useful as it increases the knowledge of the weapon and also gives the fencer the benefit of a different point of view. All this can be useful if the fencer is willing to use it.

DIFFERENT APPROACHES APPRECIATED

There are some schools of swordplay which have a very rigid approach and there are others which are much more relaxed and fluid in their styles. Both types of school have benefit to the fencer and the wider community. A school may have chosen to focus only on one weapon form or even a single teacher in a single weapon form. Regardless of how rigid the school is knowledge can be gained about what is being taught and this knowledge can be used to benefit the fencer even if it is only from a purely intellectual point of view. One of the important things to examine when looking at a rigid school is their point of view, why they have chosen to approach their swordplay in this manner. The answer to this particular question can be very revealing and will explain the reasons for their particular approach.

Some schools are substantially more fluid in their styles; they do not choose a specific weapon or a particular school of thought. For these schools they take what they can from all weapon forms and all schools and pool it into one universal approach to swordplay. For some this will cause problems for them in that they cannot point to specific source material for every technique which is being demonstrated. Such an approach is more practically based and seeks the truth of the weapon through its use in a more holistic approach to swordplay, and this has its benefits. Being untied to a specific school/master/approach they can explore swordplay in a very practical method taking and leaving from what can be found in documentation. This usually results in a very rough and ready approach, but an intellectual side cannot be denied as this is actually usually based on a conglomeration of different approaches.

CONCLUSION

Cross-training and social sparring with different schools can only benefit the fencer, regardless of whether any of the new techniques learnt can be brought back to their original school. The experience of crossing blades with another swordsman from a different approach can only enhance the experience and knowledge of the fencer and encourage them to seek more. Threats about brutalising or mishandling a style due to its contact with others should be put behind for the experience gained by the fencer in the approach swordplay. The experience gained from the encounter with different fencers and their approach will far outweigh any issues.

We should all seek out those people who study the art of the sword and engage with them in a positive function. Friendly bouting and sparring can only do the fencing community good, especially where this begins real dialogue about swordplay in general. The important thing throughout this is that the players involved in this interaction need to be open-minded enough to see the benefit in the first place and willing enough to put themselves out of their comfort zones enough to participate completely. Often some negotiation is required for two members of disparate schools to safely engage in swordplay, but the achievement of such negotiations along with the resulting social and intellectual potential is something which every scholar of the blade should find worth in.

Being a Good Training Partner

INTRODUCTION

This is a subject, which we all need to consider, because sooner or later we will all be involved in a partnered drill, or in a partnered situation. This may be at our regular practice or at a convention or at some other sort of gathering. The partner may be someone who you have fenced with for years, or you may have literally just met them. All of the same stuff applies. All of it will make your partnered experience much more fruitful and much more fulfilling.

1. DON'T HURT YOUR PARTNER

Seems pretty obvious that we do not want to hurt the person that we are fencing with, right? It seems not to be the case with some. Some seem that they need to put a little bit more emphasis in on their strikes and other offensive actions. There is no need for it. If you continue to do this, you will simply run out of people who will be your partner and you will run out of people to train and spar with. Strike your partner only as hard as you would want to be struck yourself. Apply the same rule to all offensive actions.

2. FOLLOW THE DRILLS

This means that if you are doing a parry and riposte drill and you are attacking, you *are* going to get hit. That is your part of the drill. The only reason why you should not get hit is if your partner misses, and even then you should assist them so that you do. You should see what they are doing and assist them by correcting their mistake so that you can do and learn your part of the drill. You need to do your part of the drill as faithfully as possible to ensure that the learning experience is fulfilling for your partner. You should be practicing your actions at the same time to make sure that they are correct. If you don't follow the drill you and your partner will not learn what is supposed to be learnt. If you continually not follow drills people will not want partner with you and you again will run out of people to train with.

3. NO ADDITIONS

Even if you know what's coming next in the next drill don't make any additions to the drill. Wait until the trainer teaches the additional part of the drill. Your partner may not know about the new part and will become confused, and will also want to focus on the current part. This also means that you should not really experiment with other options available as you may miss the point of the drill. If added defences so you don't get hit are not part of the drill, don't add them. If you are supposed to get hit as part of the drill, you get hit. Additions to drills just show you as unwilling to follow instruction or arrogant, and not a good student. If you complete the drill early you should wait patiently for the next part of the lesson.

4. REMAIN IN CONTROL

Some drills will be done at slow speed; some drills will be done at faster speeds. This will be determined by your instructor. It is up to you to remain in control of your actions. If you are supposed to be performing a drill at slow speed and your partner speeds up, do not follow them but remain at slow speed. You may even encourage them to slow down. Your instructor will have told you to do the drills at slow speed for a reason. Speeding up so that you can make a hit only cheats you.

5. BE TRUTHFUL

Cheating in drills and bouts only cheats you. Being truthful in drills gives a true evaluation of how your learning is going and whether or not you need more practice at the skills or not. Changing at the last minute or speeding up to hide a mistake that you have made is a cheat, and even if it allows you to strike your target you lose because you have cheated yourself. You have cheated yourself in training and therefore from learning a lesson. By making mistakes we learn. By cheating so mistakes are not made, you cheat yourself of that learning, and also your partner as well.

6. REMOVE THE EGO

Some people feel that when they are struck it is a personal insult and their ego is somehow damaged. This is a very toxic attitude and you should avoid these people. Especially when training you need to remove the ego from the equation. Training is the best time to make mistakes as it is the best time to learn from them. Your instructors do not point out your mistakes to beat you down, but to help you learn. Your partners in learning are the same they are helping you so that they can learn too, assisting a partner helps them too. If you get hit, ask how it happened so you can correct what you did wrong, do not be insulted and lose the lesson.

7. RESPECT FOR YOUR PARTNER

Finally, and this is most important, respect your partner. While a certain amount of training can be done alone and much more can be learnt by crossing swords with another. By respecting your partner you allow both of you to learn and thus both of you to grow as swordsmen. With respect for your partner much of what has already been said already will come into play. Regardless of your partner's skill level, ability, history, age or gender, all of them need to be respected. This is essential. You can learn from *all* of your partners.

CONCLUSION

Being the best training partner you can be is an ability which all swordsmen should train toward. This is something which will enhance your fencing career and also allow you to meet many interesting people in the process. It will also allow you to gain the most out of your learning experience.

We have all experienced "that person" who deviates from the drills and will not follow instruction. This person is a nuisance and no one wants to partner them. The best thing is to not be "that person" and you will have a much finer experience. If you end up with "that person" as a partner you should do your best to be a good partner to them and try your best to stick with what you are supposed to be doing, in the end you may be able to drag them back in line.

You can train and learn alone for your entire fencing career, but having a partner will make things easy; even if it is only to bounce ideas of them and try out techniques with them. That one person who challenges you to be a better swordsman is a boon and an asset and you should always remember that. They can only make you a better swordsman in the end.

Disability Aspects in Fencing

INTRODUCTION

Disability is a subject which comes up with regard to fencing on a semi-infrequent basis. This is mainly due to the highly physical nature of fencing that it is often assumed that the participants are in a relative degree of health. However, it is an important aspect which must be considered. This discussion will address various aspects with regard to fencing and disability and some of how the less able fencers are able to compete in fencing and also enjoy the experience of fencing itself despite physical infirmities.

One of the most trying things for a fencer is becoming somehow less able than before. This can occur due to a great deal of reasons, injury, sickness and operations being the most common reasons. What can happen here is that a fencer may be reduced in capacity to operate. The most important thing is that this is not the end. In a lot of cases it is possible to get back to where you were.

BACKGROUND

The first question that will be asked by the reader of this blog is what sort of authority is the author speaking from and how would they know what is going on in this situation. From my own point of view, I have a medical condition called Fibromyalgia (FM), which is closely related to both arthritis and Chronic Fatigue Syndrome (CFS). I suffer from joint pain and immobility as part of my condition and I would be lying if I said that this does not affect my fencing.

From this point of view it is of interest to me to give people some ideas about how I deal with a lack of mobility. What is also important about this article is that I am not a qualified Occupational Therapist (OT) or other health-care professional, though some of the ideas that I will present do come from people with such qualifications. Hopefully this may give you some ideas about how you can get back to fencing or in some cases start fencing in the first place.

ADVANCES MADE

With regards to fencing literature which has been published and the great advances made towards the various aspects of disability with regard to fencing, there has been a lot of focus on the lack of mobility on the part of some fencers and how they can still compete. To this end wheelchair fencing was developed for use in sport fencing and this appears in the Paralympics. This can be easily found by doing a search on "wheelchair fencing". There has been, however somewhat of a lack of any sort of address with regard to other aspects which may affect fencers, or potential fencers.

WORKING AROUND IT

These particular aspects need to be taken into account as there are many different ways to assist an individual with a physical infirmity of various kinds to get them fencing, or back to fencing. In all cases, this will work on the same sorts of principles. There are many disability aspects that can be worked around with the right approach.

First Part: The Decision

The first part of the process of getting back to fencing, or starting fencing, is deciding to do it in the first place. This needs to be a firm decision on the part of the person as it will require effort on their part, in much the same way as the first, and following lessons, took effort, or will take effort. What you must understand, is that it is not necessary to have a sword in your hand from the start, there are much more gentle ways to start.

One of the easiest ways is to watch others fence and see what you can see. This establishes the mind-game of fencing in its initial phase. See what comes back to you as you are watching. You may be surprised what you can see and actually remember. This is especially the case for those who have not fenced in a while.

Second Part: Think Like a Fencer

The next part of the process is to actually think about fencing. From the movement of the sword, to the movement of the feet, all are important. This is all about reading the opponent, something that all fencers should do anyway. The actual thought processes of going through this are just as important as doing the actions. Find a notebook and write your thoughts down. Think of ways to practice and improve without requiring actual practice. It is the next part of the process, which takes the real effort.

Third Part: What Can You Do

The most important part of the physical part of fencing is looking at it from an OT point of view. It is important to focus on those things that you can do with regard to fencing rather than focusing on those things that you cannot do. This requires you to focus on the positive aspects with regard to the process. This mental aspect of the process is of a lot of importance as it is this sort of motivation that will assist you to get past hurdles that will be placed in your path.

Examine the physical parts of fencing and see what you can and cannot do, and also ways that you can assist yourself to attempt those things that you may not be able to do. Find out about how you can help yourself through the use of various aids and also exercises. One example of an aid for those with problems with weak wrists is the wrist strap, or martingale. All of these things will help you increase your capacity to fence.

UNDERSTAND YOUR LIMITS

The first part of the physical element of fencing and returning to it is to understand your own limits. It is important that you are able to start within these limits, but also to stay active within your own capacity. You must increase this capacity to do things steadily but slowly. Rushing the process will only hurt more and get you less. In the beginning it is best to rest frequently and to stop before you are too tired and/or sore. This sounds like a bit of a cop out but this is not the case. If you keep going until you are unable to move you will have a harder time getting back into it later.

With regard to work and rest, both are important. Work increases your capacity, but rest is essential to give your body time to recover to be able to do more. This is especially the case during the times of activity. You must rest before becoming exhausted, short breaks are important during activity. Short breaks during the activity will actually enable you to do more than attempting to push through.

BETWEEN FEAR AND DISREGARD

With regard to your capacity it is important to be able to both test your limits and also increase them, but not at the expense of doing damage to yourself. Pain is the best indicator in the world about when you should stop. Ignoring this cue will lead to your detriment, but having a fear of pain will also limit you. In this you need to have a balance in your regard for pain. Somewhere between fear and disregard, there is respect and this is where the balance is found. If you become afraid of pain you will stagnate and will not improve, but also if you disregard pain you will cause yourself damage.

Fear —> Respect <— Disregard

You should exercise to fatigue but before pain occurs. This is how the OTs say it. You must consider the overall effect of what you are doing. Only by attempting more is it possible to increase your fitness, but this must be done through exercise and not pain. In my case I would say that you should be aiming to increase your capacity by a factor of about 5% and no more. Once the 5% has been achieved, stop. You should only push yourself to this point and not further. This way you will increase your ability bit by bit without the threat of doing damage to yourself.

JOINT STRESS

Stress is important. Some things are more stressful than others and some things will stress your joints and other affect portions more than others. Do those, which exercise but do not stress your joints or other affected parts of the body. If something becomes too stressful on your joint, stop. Here it is important to know your own limits. It is necessary to stress the joint or other part of your body a little but not too much. Relaxation is also an important part of the process. This is vital for removing stress. What is also important is that you take as much time as you need to. There is no need to rush, it is better that you proceed slowly and steadily.

SLOWLY INCREASE YOUR CAPACITY

You need to consider what you can do that is within your capacity that will gradually increase your ability to fence. In the case of a person with a mobility issue this could include fencing from a chair. For a fencer with a problem with the ability to hold a weapon due to weight, it could be the use of a lighter weapon or using a wrist strap to reduce the stress and weight of the weapon. For a fencer with cardio-vascular issues this may be too slowly increase their ability to fence by increasing fitness over a period of time through an increase in fitness. These are just some suggestions that the fencer can think about.

There are many others that can be used to deal with different problems. For those fencers with joint issues, you should do exercises that will build muscle around the affected joint. This increase in muscle will help to support the joint and enable you to do more. This is best achieved through the use of low impact exercises so that the muscles are being worked, but the joint is not being stressed.

SEE A HEALTH CARE PROFESSIONAL

It is important that the fencer also discuss with their health care professional about their decision to go back to fencing. They ask about what things they can do to increase their capacity to fence. The fencer should heed this advice so that they do not cause themselves more issues by going back and fencing too early. It is important that the fencer consider that their health to be the highest priority in all considerations. You should also discuss your decision to go back to fencing, or start fencing with your trainer. Talk with them and see what they can do to help you. They may be able to find some stretches or exercises that will assist you, or may be able to find some sort of aid for you that may assist your progression.

FOR TRAINERS

For trainers, if you have a student with a physical infirmity it is important that you examine what the problem is and see if you can figure out ways to get around it. You should sit down and have a long chat with the student about what they can and cannot do in order that you are able to tailor their training program around what they are and are not able to do. You need to be positive in this approach as your support will be vital to assist the student to continue or begin fencing. Focus on what the student can do and assist them in their capacity to do things that they cannot. You need to be open-minded in this approach.

CONCLUSION

The focus of this particular discussion has been the increase in ability for those fencers with disability issues. Remember to start slowly and work on increasing your capacity, do not try to rush in and do too much at once. This whole process also applies to those who have been away from fencing for any longer period of time for any reason. Ease yourself back into the motions of fencing. It is better that you take time, than rush the process and do yourself an injury. No one can be expected to be back at their full form after months of "down-time" at their first practice back.

If you are having issues with joint pain or other forms of disability, I advise you to speak to a health care professional before it gets any worse. They can help you devise a program that will improve your quality of life and will also, in the long run, improve your fencing at a base level. Take their advice to heart. If you have a specific condition, especially with your joints, it is more than likely that some fencer has had similar issues. Share your concerns and ideas about dealing with the issues.

It is my hope that this article will help some, give some ideas to some, and increase everybody's awareness of the importance of their joints. If you are having some sort of issue with your body, there is no doubt a trainer or another fencer who will be able to help you around it. Do not be afraid to ask for help. Remember, you only have one set of joints – look after them.

On a final note I must say that fencing is actually great for mobility, especially for those with joint and/or muscle issues. I have been fencing now for about two decades and it has been remarked by several health care professionals that it is one of the things that has kept me so mobile. The most important thing to remember with regard to disability and fencing is that there are things that you can do, and you can fence. You need the courage and determination to strive through the obstacles placed in your path, and you need the willpower and motivation to do this. You need to want to fence. Have a look at your situation if you are interested in fencing, give it a go, you never know until you try.

Females and Fencing

INTRODUCTION

The following article is based on a lesson I delivered this year at a "local" event and I use the word "local" very loosely as it is now recognised as a national one. That event was Swordplay '15 (SP15). Essentially it was designed to get all of the female combatants together and have a chat about HEMA, tournaments and the whole gambit of things as they relate to being women and the simple thing that they are not alone and that they needed to talk more to one another to share their experiences, more on this later.

While at the event in the position of Safety Marshal I was in a great position to see a lot of fighting at the event and see how everybody was doing. One of the things that I noticed was that the female combatants were attempting to fight like the males, with some achievement it has to be said. The obvious problems associated related directly and indirectly to the method and approach to the fighting is what sparked the idea for the lesson.

Before I go into much detail there are a couple of things that I have to say. I know that this post is possibly going to cause some issues that I am talking about females in fencing and I am a male, but this is all from my point of view and based upon my training and my experiences training females. I hope that this post will help rather than hinder women in HEMA. I know it is a little arrogant to be speaking on the subject, but please bear with me. Finally, this is probably going to be a pretty hefty sort of article so get ready for a solid sort of a read.

FACTS AND SITUATIONS

So we have the situation that women most often taught by men and men most often do not know how women work physically and mentally. This is simply because most of the more experienced members of the community are male, a simple statement of fact. This presents problems in training for the women who are participating in the training and, for the most part, these problems are kept to themselves. I would like to highlight these "problems" and demonstrate them not as "problems" but as "differences" and differences which trainers need to take into account. The following will be divided up into various sections so that areas can be highlighted for discussion

PHYSICAL

So men and women are different physically. Well done, Captain Obvious! Tell us something we don't know. This simple fact is something we need to take into account when training. It is something which I have indicated in another article. The other article was mostly indicated at different body shapes as in short versus tall, broad versus thin and so forth. For this discussion, we need to go more deeply into the discussion and examine how the male and female forms differ and how they move differently.

Hips

To start with we need to examine hip shape. The hips control the centre of mass and also control the legs which make them essential for movement. If you do not have free movement through this you are bound to have problems. Well, males and females are markedly different here, especially the way that the legs join up with the hips. The way that the leg joints are positioned in men and women are different; this can be seen in the on guard position. Let us take the generic terza (third) guard.

The right foot is forward the left is to the rear, many guards in HEMA will begin like this. Many will actually be a little broader with the rear foot a little further outward and a little more forward. This will immediately put the hips in a diagonal position if this position is adopted, which for a male suits them perfectly, due to the way their leg joints are shaped. For the female, she will have all sorts of trouble keeping her front foot pointing at the opponent and the knee aligned, this is because her hips do not want to do this. So what we need to do here is make a change in position to make it more comfortable and more moveable for the female. It is not radical it is a change in position from diagonal to horizontal, from the male position to the female position.

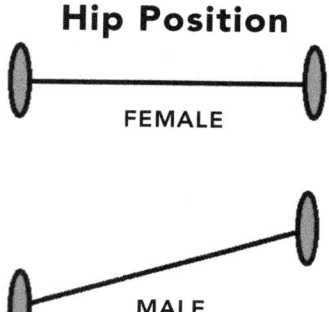

In the case of the image to the left it is from the lower image to the upper image. In the first instance you do this you may need to physically move your hip into this position. In the case of a trainer you may need to move the student's hip into the correct position, make sure you ask permission to do so first. The change in position may require a broadening of the stance, and a slight withdrawal of the foot, that is fine. The ease of movement will have its own reward.

Different Movement

While we are on movement, we might as well stay there for a while. The female combatant will also move differently from the male combatant. This you will see in their actions with the weapon, but also in their movement across the ground. The woman can also access a lot more mobility in their hips and waist than the male can for the movement of their body for voiding and other actions than most men will be able to and this is a great advantage, and one that should be used.

As a female, in general, you will simply not compete with the raw power of the male, so you should not try to. However there are different ways to approach the combat through movement and being lighter on your feet. Against the stronger opponent use their strength against them, slip off their attacks; redirect their power to other directions. Use the lightness that you have to simply avoid the power that your opponent possesses, and with the extra movement indicated already, this will be even easier.

The Breast

Now we come to one final attribute of the female form which most trainers often forget to take into account in their training, the female breast. The Parry of Fourth, the Parry to the High Inside Line, any time your arms have to cross your body close they get in the way, and the trainer will often not take this into account because he doesn't have them.

Breast protection just doesn't help the situation; in fact it even often makes it worse. How do I know? First, I listen. Second, I wear a chest plate myself. How do we get around this particular problem? We look at the assets again and see what we can use to our advantage. Once again it comes down to the hips and waist. In the case of the Parry of Fourth, or High Inside Line, turn your body at the same time you make the parry. This will give you some more clearance for the parry and also some more room. In fact, as far as this "problem" goes this is the primary way around it, use the other attributes of mobility to get around it.

PSYCHOLOGICAL

After dealing with the physical differences we need to look deeper and have a look at the more mental differences. This means having a look at the psychological differences between males and females and seeing how this will affect them in training and also in a combative situation. These need to be taken into account as they are deeply embedded in our minds and are not easily dealt with.

"Feminine Characteristics"

To begin the so-called "feminine characteristics" portray the female as passive and shy. I know this not the case for everyone, but it is the general outlook and for some it is true. Added on top of this is that from the beginning, for the most part, females are given nurturing roles. This means that they are not supposed to hit people, this idea is, in many cases driven from their make-up.

What is the result of this? It means that the female trainee and combatant will often have difficulty starting and often continuing with training as the idea of striking someone else with an object is foreign to their internal make-up. For the trainer this will take time to encourage them that it is fine for them to do this and it is actually what is expected of them. No trainee should be discouraged, male or female, because this is part of their make-up.

More so, it should be emphasised not just by trainers but by other members of the class that it is okay to strike their opponent and partner at the right time and place. If you are having a real problem with this idea of hitting other people there is a way to get around it, it is a little mathematical in idea. Think of it as a set of simple actions, you are extending your weapon into a position in space and your opponent just happens to be occupying that position.

The "Jitters"

Now we need to discuss the "jitters" that horrible feeling in the pit of your stomach that comes up during training and especially at tournaments or examinations when the pressure is on. This is the feeling that you do not belong here, all the training you have done has been a waste of time, all the other combatants hit harder and are better than you, and there is nothing you can do about it. First thing that I am going to say is that *everyone* has had this feeling, and that anyone who denies ever having had this feeling before a tournament or training session is either lying to other people, or lying to themselves which is worse. The question is how to deal with them.

Each person has their own way of dealing with this feeling, and you need to find a way for dealing with your own. I will give some suggestions that may help you, but it is a personal process that you must think through. First we will start with Pre-Tournament, then Tournament, and then Post-Tournament. Each one is slightly different to suit the different situation. In this I will be using the word "tournament" to signify whatever event is being discussed, be it a training session, examination or tournament.

Pre-Tournament

On the way to the location of the tournament I like to listen to music that either puts me in a good mood or music which is appropriate to the tournament. I am a bit of a metal-head but I have found that Iron Maiden's "Flash of the Blade" or "The Duellists" works for me. If you are looking for something a little slower Dire Straits "Brothers in Arms" also works. I have also found that anything classical with some "drive" behind it works Beethoven, Bach, or Tchaikovsky for examples.

Once I have arrived, I make a point of finding someone I know and saying "Hello." This is to realise that I am not there alone. If you are at an event for the first time, be sure that you are not the only one. Go and find someone to say "Hello" to. This is a great way to release some tension. Following this, go and do all the mundane things, signing in and all that business. Go find the Officials of the event and introduce yourself and thank them for being there, they will be happy about it, trust me on this one.

Unpack. Find a comfortable spot. This may be with others, it may not be. It needs to be comfortable for you. Have a good look at each piece of gear as you take it out. Get it *all* out and have a good look. Then walk away for a little while.

Come back and in a relaxed fashion put your protective gear on. Start internal and work external, start from the ground work up. Start from the body and work out to the arms. Hand protection last. Trust me on this one. Once you are in your protective equipment, move about and get used to being in your kit, without your weapon. Next pick up your weapon and go through some simple solo drills, finally go find someone you know to warm-up with. By this time you should be suitably warm and much more comfortable.

Tournament

Regardless of the result of a round, examine how you fought and what you did in response to the opponent's actions. Have a look at you did well and be happy with this. Breathe. Next examine where you did not do so well, remember this because you can ask your trainer about it at your next training. Breathe. You should always look at crossing blades with an opponent as a chance to learn something about yourself and your opponent. Do not miss this chance. Breathe. Victories fade the lessons live on.

In between rounds, if you have time, make sure that you take off your hand protection, mask/helm and neck protection. This will let a lot of the heat out. Breathe. Drink liquid. People say drink water; I say liquid as you should also be concerned about your sugar levels dropping too low. Go for a little walk if you need to, but not too far. Breathe. Watch the other opponents for what they are doing and learn from what they are and are not doing. This is a prime time to learn. Listen to what other combatants are saying. Breathe. Do not think about the next round until it is announced, and even then do not focus on it unless you have seen the opponent and learnt something useful about the way they fight. Did I mention *Breathe*? You need to stay analytical about the process; this will help you calm you. Remember all the things you did right and celebrate them.

Post-Tournament

Why? The tournament is over, why would this be the case that you get jitters? This would be the case that you still have a lot of adrenaline running through your system and also probably endorphins as well. Once again it is a matter of settling yourself. Breathe. Take your time. Have a drink. Get rid of the mask/helm, neck protection and hand protection as before. Put the weapons down with your gear. Go for a little walk. Breathe. Have a chat to some of the other combatants. Breathe. The most important thing here is to relax. If there is a presentation made after the tournament and you have placed high enough to be a part of this enjoy the experience, you deserve it.

YOU ARE NOT ALONE

While the numbers of female combatants in HEMA may be smaller than those of their male counter-parts, the important thing for the female combatants to realise, and even the male combatants need to realise is, you are not alone. Without a doubt there is another combatant out there going through the same problems as you are having, and working through them just like you are. The feeling of loneliness is one that can kill your fighting spirit in no time at all and it is one that you need to purge. You are not alone; there are people out there to help you.

So, the first thing that you are going to tell me is that you are the only female in a class of all males. You are still not alone. Your first point of call should always be your trainer. If they cannot help then you can find help elsewhere. So, you are not a member of any formal organisation and you are studying as a singular individual. You are still not alone. Thanks to the internet there are multiple sources to consult and people often are more than willing to help people and share their own insights and research. In fact, for the most part the harder task is to get us to shut up so you can get a word in. Below you will find a list of links to various Facebook groups where you can link up with other women in HEMA.

Ostensibly, I began the class at Swordplay to demonstrate to the group of ladies that they needed to move differently to the male fighters who were competing in the competition. Something more grew from the conversation that I had with the ladies who were there (Yes, I am calling you all ladies). It was the realisation that most of them had not talked to one another about HEMA and how it worked for them, and how it affected them. This was actually quite a shock to me.

Guys tend to sit and chat about technique, this master over that master, and what protective gear suits and protects us better, so I assumed that it would be the same with the ladies. I was wrong, for this I apologise. I just hope that the class which turned into more of a discussion got people talking and that this series of posts will also get people talking, and especially the ladies. Oh, and in case you are wondering, Yes, I will be checking up on you.

FACEBOOK LINKS

AUS/NZ HEMA/WMA ladies group
https://www.facebook.com/groups/1732046537016304/
Started by Evangelina Corona it is a place for AUS/NZ HEMA/WMA ladies to share their thoughts, meet new friends and change the face of women in Australian and New Zealand Sword play groups. "I began this after SP15, feeling there was a need for we ladies down under to be able to share things solely with each other."

Esfinges
https://www.facebook.com/groups/esfingeshema/
The worldwide group, this group was made for women who practice fencing, to unite

them and let them get to know one other.

Ladybits
https://www.facebook.com/groups/565948176761635/
A group where ladies share... Well, they are ladies, doing ladies things!

WHAT YOU CAN DO (CONCLUSION?)

Note that there is a question mark after the word conclusion. This is there because I am not actually sure that this is the end of the subject at all. I would not be surprised if there are further articles on this subject, possibly inspired by future events or comments. Another thing is that this process is one that needs to continue. Some of what follows will question the way things are done and I expect a certain amount of contention, but I believe that lively intellectual discussion and argument is healthy.

As combatants we all have a role to play to ensure that our female combatants are included and not side-lined in any form. This will begin with a change in attitude. We need to remove some of the negative expressions which we have grown up with such as, "You hit like a girl." and "Stop acting like a girl." All of these put our female combatants in a negative light and this is not healthy for us and definitely not for them. Rather we need to promote the positive nature of their participation in HEMA. Further to this we also need to promote the levelling nature of martial arts in general.

With regard to this I need to approach our first contentious issue the idea of the "Ladies Tournament". I would question whether or not this is actually a healthy idea or not. Is having such a tournament an inclusive or exclusive thing? Sure it is inclusive as it involves the female combatants in a tournament, but it is also exclusive as it side-lines them to another tournament, and almost makes it feel like that they are not welcome to participate in more "general" combats. In my own opinion the nature of HEMA provides a level playing field in which all can compete, thus there is really no need for this separation, but this is a question that no doubt will be debated for some time to come.

Trainers. You are at the forefront of including individuals in HEMA regardless of whether they are male or female, or indeed of their physical nature. I have already written on the nature of bio-mechanics and body-shape, and indeed already on disabilities and fencing. Now we need to look at the male-female dichotomy. These posts are as important for you to realise the differences between the male and female student as they are for the female student to realise their own differences.

You need to approach these differences as simply that, differences, not problems. You need to consider the differences in body shape and approaches to combat. The benefits for taking this into consideration will outweigh the extra work that you will have to put in to making sure that you get it right. Take note of how your female students' bodies want to move and adapt their training to suit that, not the other way around. They will be much more comfortable, and much more successful.

Well, this series of posts has been a lot longer than I ever thought it would have been. I thank those ladies who participated in my class for the information which they gave me. It has enabled me to further understand how the female combatant operates and thinks and thus allowed me to produce these posts without you this would have been a lot more difficult. So thanks go out to: Eva, Sam, Lois, Bec, Sharon, Emma, Rosie, Tristyn and Jessica (if I have forgotten anyone I apologise). I also need to send a big thank you to

Zebee Johnstone for putting me on the right path.

I hope that all of my readers are able to pull something useful from the information which has been presented here. I apologise if there is anything here which has offended you, but I have attempted to do something which I thought needed to be done. I also apologise for some of the rambling nature of the information as I tend to write it how it comes, but then you needed to expect that considering the title of my entire blog, and also this book.

Building Co-ordination in Fencing

INTRODUCTION

Co-ordination is important in fencing as such this article will be discussing the development of co-ordination in its relationship to fencing. This will be partially written from a personal point of view as I have had (and still do have) some co-ordination problems myself. It is hoped that this discussion will assist those with some co-ordination issues and realise it is an obstacle that can be surmounted given time and patience. The discussion proper will discuss the question of co-ordination in fencing from two points of view, the mental and the physical. Both of these are important to get over this particular hurdle.

Co-ordination or lack thereof can be a real problem in fencing. A lack of co-ordination can lead to elements in fencing being substantially more difficult than they otherwise would be. In the realm of the positive is the fact that it is possible to defeat this particular problem given the time and the patience applied to it. The trick is actually taking the time to figure out what is actually happening. Surprisingly enough for some, all fencing students will feel the bite of a lack of co-ordination some time in their fencing career. For some it may not last long for others it will last for a longer period of time.

SOME PERSPECTIVE

It can be as simple as something that just does not work for some inexplicable reason. A lack of co-ordination is something that can be fought against and that can be defeated. While I do not tend to get very personal in these blogs, for this particular subject I think it is important that I explain some things about myself and the reason why I believe that this problem can be beaten.

I am actually naturally uncoordinated. I have a history of being exceptionally clumsy and accident prone, and believe me when I say that I have the hospital records and scars to prove it. In my earlier years as a child I was clumsy enough that it was important enough for my parents to send me along to physiotherapy to get some physical therapy to help the problem. This is something that has plagued my whole life and still does to a point, the FM does not help things. The important thing here is that with time and patience it is something that you can overcome in fencing, it may just take a little more effort than other people.

TWO ASPECTS TO THE PROBLEM

There are two different aspects that need to be taken into account when considering the nature of being uncoordinated. The first is the mental side of things and the second is the physical side of things. Both of these aspects need to be acknowledged for the process of dealing with the problem can start. The correct physical processes will train the body how to move. The correct thought processes will train the brain how to think about what is going on and what to do about it. It is the two working in combination that allows a person to master the problem presented.

THE MENTAL PROCESS

The mental process of dealing with this particular problem is of great importance. The process, the way that I see things, has four elements or parts which are all important to the process. The first is acknowledgement. You need to acknowledge that there is a problem with what is going on. For some this can be an issue as they don't want to acknowledge that they have a problem. Without this step it is impossible to move on to solving the problem. Of course at the other end of the scale are those who obsess about the particular problem and is equally unhelpful; this moves on to the second part of the mental process.

The second part of the mental process is a positive outlook. You must be able to see the light at the end of the tunnel so to speak. It is not enough to believe that you can do it; you need to know that you can. This is the way that you fight frustration. You acknowledge each little victory. Take one step at a time and keep looking at where you are going. Without the positive mental outlook there is no point in starting the process as it is this that will enable you to keep going through the processes required. Of course, beating up on yourself won't help either.

The next part of the mental process is to start dealing with those negative thoughts that you may have about the process and your ability. You should only be thinking positive things about yourself in this process. Words like "clumsy" should not be used to describe yourself. These negative thoughts can poison the whole process of development of the skills required to beat the problem. It is actually quite difficult to stay positive about yourself the entire time.

Yes, mistakes need to be acknowledged, but they also need to be turned around and used. Mistakes are just another way of not achieving the goal, and thus are a learning process. The reason why which is behind it is more important. This requires concentration, and this is something that is required.

Most of the time, in life, we do not particularly concentrate on what we are doing. This is because we already know what we are supposed to be doing and how the body is supposed to move. This is because these particular things have been learnt and practiced to the point that we don't have to think about them anymore. To defeat uncoordinated feelings, it is important that the focus needs to be on what you are trying to do. Each part of the action needs to be focused upon for it to all come together.

Often when mistakes are made it is because the concentration has drifted somewhere else for a brief period of time. It is important for the learning process that the brain is trained to concentrate on what is happening. Distractions in this process can lead to problems with the action and also frustrations. In order to achieve the end desired we must be focused on the action being performed.

THE PHYSICAL PROCESS

Once the elements of the mental process are dealt with, it is then possible to look at the physical. What is important is that the aspects of the mental process will reappear in the physical process. These two sets of concepts must work together for the end to be achieved. The physical aspects are about training the body so that it can do what it is supposed to when it is supposed to. The important thing about this is that the actions have to be mentally set in the mind. You need to think about the action and focus upon it. Then the physical side of the action can be dealt with.

In the case of any action in fencing, or any action for that matter, you need to learn the action. In this particular process you need to be focusing on the movements that are being made. For some, it will require listening to the description of what is required, and for others, it will require watching the action closely. In this process it is important to pay attention to the small movements being made as well as the large ones. This focus will place the action into your mind before you attempt the action.

The first time you attempt the action, do it slowly and have someone watch you doing it. Once you get the action correctly then it is time to practice and drill. At first it is best to practice the action alone so that you can train your muscles and tendons exactly what they are supposed to be doing. At the same time you should be going through the description of the action in your mind and making sure it matches up with what your body is doing. Practice the action slowly over and over until you are comfortable with it.

Once you can do it comfortably alone you should be able to move on to doing the same action with a partner. Drill the action slowly with a partner to see how your action relates to theirs and how your movement relates to theirs. Once you are performing the correct response at slow speed you should begin to speed up. You should be remaining focused on the action that you are doing. Responses to this action and counters will come later. Remember it is all parts of the action that need to be thought about, the small actions and the large actions. Each element of the action needs to be learnt, practiced and drilled.

In the process of learning an action it is important to think about what you are doing and focus on this. All the elements of the action are important and you need to be able to feel how you are moving. To get these movements right you need to be focused on these actions rather than anything else. Find a partner who is willing to allow you to drill slowly so that you can feel the response of the opponent's blade as well. Be approaching the fencing action in this way you will be training both your mind and your body simultaneously. This will make it much easier to learn the action and get over any awkwardness in the action.

DIVIDE THE ACTION

The unity of hands and feet in fencing is important they should be moved together and this may take some time for you to get your head around this concept, and get your body to do this. It takes some practice to get them to work together and if you only focus on one element the other will be left behind. In training a skill it is important that you get one movement completed first and then work on the other. In general while the hand should always move before the foot, training the feet first has its advantages. Work on the foot movement of the technique so that you are comfortable moving in this manner. Once you are comfortable with this move on to the hand movement, first alone and then in combination with the foot movement. This division of an action into single movements is a great advantage when learning and this process can be applied to all actions in fencing.

All fencing actions can be divided into separate movements. This goes for the simplest as well as the most complex. For example, the thrust is actually the combination of the movement of the shoulder and the movement of the wrist. The shoulder moves the arm and the wrist moves the point to the appropriate target. The movement can be practiced as two actions and then worked together to form a single motion.

Movements in fencing should be stacked like bricks one building on the other, in this way you can focus on a single movement which will add to another and another until the technique is completed as a complete movement. This takes more time than attempting to do the whole technique as a single action, but it is better for the assimilation of the movement into a fencing routine. During this process it is important to accept the achievement of getting the technique right. This praise is useful as it motivates you to move on to more complex actions.

CONCLUSION

Being uncoordinated in fencing can be extremely frustrating as this may result in taking much more time to learn an action. The important thing is that with work it is not an insurmountable obstacle. It is important that you get your mind in the right place first and also your body.

Work on the actions from a mental as well as a physical point of view. Work on the actions in simple terms, dividing a technique into individual actions and this will assist your process to learning them greatly. Take the time needed to learn the action before moving on to other things. There are people who can help you with this and who will be willing to take the time required, all you need to do is be able to find them, and also be strong enough in yourself to be able to ask for help in the learning of the actions.

Relax and Fence

INTRODUCTION

We all know that muscles need oxygen, so we need to breathe when we are exercising. This would be the reason why there is an article about the necessity of standing up straight in the on guard position, which you will find in this book. What you will notice about this post is that there is an element of the relaxation point in here as well. This element will be the focus in this article.

Relaxation in fencing plays a vital part in fencing, more than people give credit for it. A relaxed fencer will perform better and will be more comfortable with the actions that they are performing. A relaxed fencer will have a much better time fencing also. Some of this is due to mental processes but some of it is also physical, both aspects need to be taken into account for you to be completely relaxed when you are fencing and thus to fence at your best and with the greatest amount of efficiency.

TENSE = ENERGY LOST

First point, when you are tense, your muscles tense unconsciously. This burns energy, so you are burning fuel without doing anything, so relaxing will increase your endurance when you fence. Further when your muscles are tense before action they move slower, when they are relaxed before action they move faster. Also if you tense your muscles before you move, an observant opponent will notice and thus be aware of your action before you make it, if your muscles are relaxed until just before the action is made the fore-warning is not present.

TENSE = STOP BREATHING

When people tense up one of the first things they stop doing is breathing when they make an action in fencing and it is often restricted and jerky. When you relax, you will breathe properly, this means that your muscles will become oxygenated properly this also means that your muscles will, for the most part, move much more smoothly and freely. It also means that you will have more endurance, as indicated previously. There are certain muscles which move better when deprived of oxygen, but breathing in the current situation is important, so we will be moving further along with this thinking. When people tense up another thing they stop doing is thinking and this is never good. The rigidity in the body leads to rigidity in the mind of the fencer, thus the physical elements lead to psychological elements.

RELAX AND JUST FENCE

Relax. Take a breath and just fence. "Well that's easy for you to say." Why? What is *so* important? Are you going to *die* if your opponent hits you? Most of the pressures that are built up, we build up ourselves and it is up to us to remove them. It is not easy and it will take time. Most importantly someone else cannot do this for us, we must do it ourselves.

Practice

Practice is for *practice*. This means that you are supposed to try new things. It also means that you are supposed to make mistakes because the things that you are trying are new. The most important thing is that you learn from those mistakes; if you are not getting hit while bouting at practice, then you are not learning and you are not progressing. If you have just learnt a new action or skill in a lesson, you are supposed to be trying it out in bouting. Talk to your opponent and tell them what you want to practice; maybe they will want to practice something too and then you can help them. This is the only real opportunity you are going to get to do this. An opponent in a tournament sure won't give you the same opportunity.

RELEASE THE PRESSURE

Release the pressure. Find out what is causing the pressure in your fencing. Find a way to release it and relax. Talk to your teacher. Talk to other fencers. Sometimes a little pressure to push us forward is good, but when it restricts what we are doing then it becomes a detriment to our fencing, and can even become a detriment to our character. Sometimes releasing the pressure will give new life and focus to your pursuit as you will realise the bigger picture and different ways to attain your goals. It is great to be focused on a goal, but not to the exclusion of *all* of life that goes on around you. Remember to live life to the fullest as well. Take time to have some fun, and take some time to not fence.

RELAXING = IMPROVEMENT

Your fencing will improve when you relax. Your actions will become smoother and more natural because you are not forcing them to happen. You are utilising a skill when it is most appropriate, when the conditions are presented to you, not even waiting for them to be presented to you. A relaxed attitude in your fencing relies on your confidence in your skills; this means that you also need to practice what you have learnt. This relaxed attitude and form of fencing can also be passed along to your partners and this will improve your experience.

There is a nice feeling between two fencers when they are both relaxed and can perform their skills. This can be seen by those watching. The bout can still be very technical and also very intense, but because the fencers are both relaxed with what they are doing it will also have a good feel to it. It will be smooth with the action of one flowing into the action of the other. This will be different to two fencers who just go at one another, simply trying to be first to strike the other one. The bout will also be intense but for different reasons. In this case there will also be tension, unlike the previous one.

CONCLUSION

A relaxed attitude and relaxed nature and approach to fencing will lead to better and more comfortable fencing. This takes time. You need to be comfortable with what you are doing. You need to be comfortable with who you are fencing with. You even need to be comfortable with the equipment that you are using to a certain point. The most important part of this process is that it has to start with you.

You have to want to do this. You have to need to change. You have to need to develop your skills. You have to accept that you need practice. You have to accept that you will get hit. You need to relax and just fence.

Move Slow, Learn Fast

INTRODUCTION

The meme of moving slow and learning fast is one which has been around for a long time. For the most part, it is a principle which I like and can easily relate to, however I will be presenting this idea from a slightly different point of view as my main focus will be fencing. Odd? A little in some ways, but as will be demonstrated below; the slow movement principle applies more to the use of the sword, even in the western variations, than many would think.

Fencing for the most part is a quick, energetic form of combat or sport, depending on what your weapon is. This means that the actions are quick and precise, and responses to actions are likewise. With this in mind, for some, it will be difficult to understand how practicing actions slowly will help them progress when in the end they are going to have to perform the same actions at speed. This is something which you will find will come from the newer students for the most part, but some advanced students as well. It will require some explanation as to how it all works and what follows will assist with that.

BACKGROUND

In the SCA, the heavy combatants, i.e. fully-armoured combatants use what is known as "quarter-speed" this is slow movement of the weapon and body for warming up for the most part and also for practice without armour. Essentially this is moving at a slow speed where both combatants can see the weapons moving and thus there is a less likelihood of injury even when not wearing any armour. This same technique, or something like it, can also be applied to fencing.

PURPOSE

The first place that explanation needs to be made with regard to this is purpose. The purpose of this slow-moving action is not to win but to practice movement. It is to encourage the body to move in the correct way so that the weapon will move in the correct way. The opponent, in this particular case is merely there to act as a kind of random stimulus for actions to respond to, and both partners are the same to one another. If one of the individuals speeds up to land a blow and thus "win" they only cheat themselves. The tendency to speed up during slow motions is this blurring of the purpose of the drill; both partners need to focus on what it is *really* about.

EASY TO SEE

The use of slow work allows us to see the body and weapon moving. This is something which is much more difficult to see at full-speed when bouting. What this means is that the combatant and any observer can see how the combatant is moving his or her weapon and body. This can allow a person to see where a possible change in footwork, body movement, or hand movement can make a difference to their technique.

As a diagnostic tool, slow speed performance of technique is very useful. Much smaller movements can be seen at slower speeds and thus changed, if required, to improve technique. Also with technique at slow speed, it can be easily remembered and repeated so combatants can see what happened and change their response to the action. This increases their ability to vary responses to different actions of the opponent.

CORRECTION AND MUSCLE MEMORY

Even in training and especially for drills the movement at slow speed is very useful. Corrections to technique are more easily made at slower speed than they are at faster speeds. A student can develop a lot of muscle memory by moving slowly because they can focus on the movement of individual parts of their body to make the technique being performed more efficient.

Movement at slower speed allows the muscles to remember the actions more finely thus more accurately. This brings more accuracy to technique and more accuracy to muscle memory. This increases the technical efficiency of the fencer. A trainer can see the movement of each part in slow speed and make corrections to engagement and position of the student so that they are learning the correct techniques. At slow speed the muscles can more accurately remember the movements, and the feeling of the weapons against one another, thus gain a better image of exactly what's happening.

BALANCE AND EFFICIENCY

Movement at slow speeds is obviously slowed as compared to that at faster speeds. What this means is that a combatant needs to be balanced in their movements. This is because the combatant will have to remain stable in the same position for an extended period of time than at a quicker speed. The knowledge of balance transfers through to the use of the same action at faster speeds.

Sure there are some actions which are difficult, but the movements which are allowed become more comfortable at slow speed. Part of this comfort will have to do with the balance of the individual and also the efficiency of the action which can be fine-tuned at slower speeds. If the movement is not comfortable they can be corrected until they are. Slow speed movement promotes efficiency in motion as pure speed is removed. Efficiency results in better movements in combat and also better balance.

CONCLUSION

The use of slow speed combat as a learning tool is something which should be embraced by all combatants. Eastern schools have demonstrated its utility in arts such as Tai Chi, which promote movement of the body and health. As western martial artists, should we not take advantage of proven theory to improve ourselves?

Movement at slow speed promotes balance and efficiency in movement both of which are a great asset to the fencer. Practice at slower speeds promotes correct technique, balance, efficiency and accuracy each of which is a boon to the fencer. Fencers should be encouraged to practice at slower speeds to promote these ideas and also to enhance their own understanding of their own movements. Such use of slower speeds in training can only be an asset, especially in the longer term.

The Myth of Speed

INTRODUCTION

Interested in learning how to be amazingly fast, performing actions faster than your opponents? Do you want to know the secrets? Are you ready to put hours in at the gym lifting weights drinking secret formulas?

Unfortunately the secrets are not really secrets. In fact, there are no secret methods or practices to make you faster. There are a couple of exercises which can help, which you can do at home, but it all comes from practice.

MUSCLE ADDS ONLY SO MUCH

Now, it is true that muscle use does have a part to play and this has an effect upon the skill being performed. Building some muscle tone in areas of the body which are used in fencing does help, but where the muscles end the real hard work begins. There is only a finite amount of power that can be added to an action before it starts to be a problem.

Too much power added to the action can actually decrease the efficiency of the action. The focus of the action then changes to one of power rather than efficiency meaning that the body is trying to strike hard rather than efficiently. This is may seem like a problem of the mind, but it is also one of the body as well. There are different muscle fibres in the body which allow the muscles to do different things and it is important to train the correct ones. It is the "quick" muscle fibres that need to be trained for fencing for the most part rather than the "slow", and powerful, ones. This is one of the reasons why you should take care in your gym and muscle-building routines to build the correct type of muscle.

Practicing the action allows control to be added to the equation thus the right amount of power is added. If you want to build some muscle to assist you, use a light dumb-bell (nothing over 1kg) and practice your fencing actions as a part of your exercise routine. Using the same dumb-bell while watching TV or at the computer is also a good way to sneak in some extra practice without having to worry about hitting anyone accidentally with a weapon. Squeezing a stress-ball is also good for developing hand strength so that you can hold your weapon for more extended periods of time. Of course, as has been said before, nothing beats practicing the actions which you will use with your weapon.

MORE PRACTICE, MORE EFFICIENT

The reason that the more experienced, especially the real veteran combatants, seem to move faster is that they have had more practice. The result of the practice is that the actions of the combatant become efficient thus making the action seem faster. The connections between their brains and their muscles are closer with regard to their fencing actions because they have practiced them so much. This is partially due to "muscle memory" and partially due to "pattern recognition".

"Pattern Recognition"

"Pattern Recognition" is a skill which comes from seeing the same things over and over again which means that the brain remembers them and often what comes after them. This is a skill which is built up over time after facing different combatants and seeing how different people move. After a while the brain recognises that a sword from a position will move to another position and will remember this. This piece of information is then stored and then brought to the fore when the fencer's brain recognises the pattern again.

Needless to say, if a fencer knows what an opponent is going to do and can intercept the action of the opponent; it is going to make them seem a lot faster. This skill is one which takes time to build and takes time to perfect as there are some fencers who will not follow the same patterns as others. This is the more experienced fencer's brain being more efficient than a newer fencer's.

"Muscle Memory"

If you practice the same thing about 500 times it will get locked into your "muscle memory". This means in response to this stimulus you will do the action without thinking. A fencer who has been fencing for a longer period of time has practiced his actions a lot more than a newer one, thus they are closer to being locked in thus they are more automatic. Thus the more experienced fencer will seem faster when using these skills which have been practiced.

There are at least two problems with "muscle memory". Firstly, once something is locked in it is very difficult to over-write it. In fact it takes 50,000 repetitions to over-write something in "muscle memory" so it is important that you get it right the first time or it is very difficult to get rid of a bad habit. Secondly, it makes actions very reactive in nature and thus difficult to change. This means it can sometimes limit a person's tactical options if they let their "muscle memory" simply lead them along.

So practicing the skills, and gaining experience against other opponents regardless of winning or losing, is one of the most important elements in becoming more efficient. Most people focus on the winning element, but losing is not a bad thing unless you do not learn from the experience. If you think that a loss when you are doing your best is a learning experience, then you will never really lose.

TIMING

Of course, there is one more element which a fencer can only develop over time and through experience, and that is timing. Timing is about knowing when to perform an action, when to defend, when to strike, even when to move and when to stay still. Timing is developed through engagement with other opponents, thus through fencing.

This is a comparative scale worked out in the mind between the actions of the fencer and the actions of the opponents. This builds a record of patterns of actions and reactions, and the time it takes for these to occur. It is a skill which works with "pattern recognition" which was discussed previously. Timing is using the correct action at the correct time. Through the use of timing a fencer can appear as if they have used multiple actions, or moved large distances. Timing is placing your target in exactly the right place at exactly the right time for you to strike.

CONCLUSION

All of these elements will build together to create a fencer which will seem to be faster to other combatants, but as can be seen, it is actually the result of practice and experience. There is a certain amount of pure speed used in fencing and a certain amount of fitness required, this cannot be denied. The fitter that you are while you are fencing the better off you will be, but this should not be your only focus.

It is in the skills of fencing where you will find the true speed. The skills of fencing need to be practiced and used against other opponents so that they develop and become a normal part of your fencing, and not some add-on. Each skill which you learn needs the same attention as each other skill, thus each needs the same amount of practice. Once you have learnt it, you need to practice it.

There is no point in looking for ways to develop your timing if you have not practiced your skills because you will not be able to put yourself in the right place at the right time to strike. Work on your skills with your "muscle memory" first, then work on your "pattern recognition" in bouting with other opponents, timing will come as a result of working and seeing how opponents move and recognising where their vulnerabilities lie.

Speed lies in practice and lots of it. There is no secret. There is no short cut.

Are You Using or Teaching a System?

INTRODUCTION

Every now and then we must look at what we are teaching and what it is based on. In some cases this may not be as pretty a picture as what we may like it to be but it still must be done. The question remains especially for us looking into the fields of HEMA are we really practicing what we set out to? Are we really teaching what we are claiming to be studying? Are we teaching a system? Or merely tips and tricks?

WHAT IS A SYSTEM?

A system is has a foundation based on the principles of fence. This means that the actions make sense according to the rules of Time and Distance. It means that what we are teaching, when performed purely according to these rules will work. This system does not have to be based in any one "School" or based on the works of any one "Master". Indeed, what I teach in my foundation course is based upon the works of several theorists from at least two different "Schools". What need to be present are the principles upon which the actions are based upon, and these need to be based on the principles of fence.

ESSENTIAL MECHANICS

A system has essential mechanics. These are foundation mechanics which every student knows and every student must learn to progress through to the next stage. The progression of the students must be based upon the training method which is set in place. Each one of the lessons should build upon some part of the lessons which came before it. Every student should progress through these lessons in some form or another. At the end of these lessons, indeed part way through some of these lessons there should be some sort of system of evaluation.

You should be able to evaluate the students and see where they are in their progression to see what they have learnt and what they need to re-learn. This does not need to be formal, but some sort of recognition of the student is always a boon to them. The evaluation process is a boon to the student as it recognises their achievement in progressing through the previous lessons which have been learnt. This evaluation also informs the teacher as to whether their teaching method is effective or not, or whether some changes need to be made so that the students can learn the lessons better, thus it is a two-way process. Both learn from the process of evaluation.

RESPONSES TO ATTACKS

A system has a set of attacks and also responses to attacks. Too often attacks are taught, and there are no responses taught to defend against attacks, leaving fencers with the idea that there is no response. There is always some way to respond to every action of an opponent. These attacks and their responses need to be based upon fencing theory to ensure that they are correct and ensure the safety of the fencer.

There should also be a generalised solutions to situations based on fencing theory to answer general questions of attack and response, and these too need to be founded in fencing theory. From these generalised solutions there should also be specific techniques and specific solutions to specific techniques based on fencing theory. This gives the student informed knowledge how to deal with a situation where they are on the receiving end of the attacks that they have just been learning. The attack-response dichotomy is a complete method and necessary to any system which is being taught. The teacher should always be considering how an attack can be defeated when they are teaching it and be ready to teach its counter also.

ADVANTAGES OF A SYSTEM

These are the elements of a system. A person who teaches the principles of fencing to their students gives them the ability to extrapolate from what they have been taught to learn more. A person who teaches a system gives their student the ability to learn another system due to the foundation knowledge that they have given them based on the theory and principles which have been taught. Someone who teaches tips and tricks gives another some neat ways to answer a couple of attacks here and there but no foundation.

A student with a sound knowledge of the principles of fencing can take a system which is foreign to them, examine it to see how it works, and take it apart to see how it works based on the principles of their own knowledge. From this they should see where the system has elements which they can use to their advantage to defeat it. The knowledge of principles of fencing gives the student a foundation for all methods of fencing so that no new system which they learn will be totally foreign to them.

Thus they will find a level of kinship with other swordsmen and be able to compare and contrast what they have learnt with them finding similarities and differences in approach and technique. This can only lead to a greater understanding on the part of both combatants. It is the greatest advantage of teaching a true system of swordsmanship over single elements taken from individual ones and integrated into another which does not have the essential principles.

CONCLUSION

There are many ways to teach swordsmanship. Some will teach from a single school or master. Others will teach from multiple sources using elements of each to complete a homogeneous system which is still based on the essential principles of fence. Yet others will assemble elements from various masters which seem efficient and useful, but will not use the essential principles to understand them and will use trial and error to integrate them into their own method.

The result of each method will be different. The first will result in a focussed system in which methods are limited to only that school or master. The second will result in a less focussed system, yet it will still be a system due to being based on the principles of fencing. The third will result in a method which is more based on movement rather than any system. They will learn the principles by accident more than by method or understanding and will find the more complex aspects of swordsmanship more difficult to understand. Of the three only the first two can really be seen to be teaching a system. The third will simply not have the understanding of the principles of fencing which the first two will have from the study of the masters or schools which they have examined. Thus when it comes to understanding a foreign school or master they will have a much harder time understanding and countering its actions. Thus they will have lost out on the greatest advantage of studying a system, the principles which flow through all methods of fence.

"Hot" Drills

INTRODUCTION

The article which follows is about drills, more accurately it's about "Hot" drills and getting the most out of your drills. Most people do not like drills as they feel monotonous and unfulfilling, however they do fulfil and important part of the training process so that skills are learnt properly in a practical manner. The problem is that most drills which are performed, while they are effective, they are not as effective as they could be.

What follows below is about taking simple drills using simple and essential skills which fencers should know and increasing their intensity. This means increasing the speed of the drills to "combat speed" to apply pressure. This will seem somewhat contradictory to one of the previous articles, but remember these are performed once the students know the skills and are designed for a purpose.

NORMAL DRILLS

Most drills are performed at slow speeds, and for beginning drills this is important. The slow drill allows the body to understand the movement in a slow and controlled fashion. The slow drill also allows the teacher to correct any issues in the performance of the action before it causes any issues for the fencer. Once a drill is learnt then the drill is sped up, not much but it is. These drills are done at a comfortable speed often without armour and without intensity. These will teach the individuals participating in the drills the mechanics of the action but it lacks something in the execution.

"HOT" DRILLS

"Hot" drills are about taking the essential drills and adding an element of intensity to them so that the drill can be performed under conditions which are closer to the performance of the action in a combative situation. This is designed to discover what the students performing the drill have actually learnt and what actually rests in their muscle memory. To put pressure on people and see how they really react.

5 POINTS BEFORE STARTING

1. Protective gear is essential for these drills as there is too high a chance that the face or another part of the body may be struck with weapon moving at a high speed.
2. These drills should only really be performed with those students who are in a condition where they are ready to face an opponent in full-speed bouting.
3. The focus of these drills is what the student has actually learnt rather than the perfection of form demonstrated.
4. The drills must be kept simple so that the participants still have suitable control remaining to perform the actions associated.
5. The drills must be performed at combat speed to be true "Hot" drills and to be effective.

FIRST DRILL

The best drill to start with involves simple footwork movements and the retention of distance. One fencer advances while the other retreats. The idea here is that the fencer who is retreating must not allow the fencer who is advancing to catch them, but should be doing their best to maintain good distance. Once the fencers have proven that they can do this you can move on to the second one.

SECOND DRILL

The second drill adds a parry into it. One fencer advances and thrusts to a single line. The other fencer must parry or be hit while retreating. Of course the parry with the hand should be made first with the retreat as a back-up. The retreat is also designed to maintain distance. This should be done against a single line only, but can be repeated with all four lines. The goal of this is for the attacking fencer to strike the defender, and of course for the defender it is to defend the line successfully. A successful defence is the goal.

THIRD DRILL

The third drill and the most complex that should be used, is to add a riposte to the drill. One fencer advances and thrusts, the other must parry and riposte while using a retreat. As with the previous this should be against a single line. In this the distance is vital and is a test to see about the maintenance of distance between the two fencers. Once again the goal of the attacker is to strike against the line, and the goal of the defender is to parry and make a riposte. The defence is the highest importance here; the riposte should be still made for a counter-attack in order to train the instinct into the fencer.

2 ACTIONS MAXIMUM COMPLEXITY

"Hot" drills should get no more complex than two actions of the blade performed by one fencer and a single action performed by the other. The simple advance and retreat mechanic is useful for those steps as they are simple. Adding other steps could over-complicate the drill. "Hot" drills are designed to be drills with real intensity added to them to reveal the true condition of the student's training. It also works as a good warm-up.

CONCLUSIONS

"Hot" drills are a very useful training tool when they are utilised and performed properly. The important thing here is that they reveal in fencers what they will actually do under the pressure. They should only be used with fencers who have the skill capacity to perform them and also those who have or are ready to be performing at full-speed.

For experienced combatants, "Hot" drills can be a useful warm-up before a tournament, or even a warm-up before training. Students in the performance of "Hot" drills should be only evaluated on the skills which are being used to refine training for them. They very rarely reveal perfect form. Use the drills for what they are designed for and they can be a very useful tool in the training arsenal.

What's Next?

INTRODUCTION

Much has been presented in this book and others about weapon forms and what we should be doing about training, and a myriad of other topics. These topics are all important and should have attention paid to them; however there is another topic which needs addressing. A school curriculum is only so long and the completion of such a curriculum is important and an achievement of note, however the question remains when this curriculum is completed... what's next?

LAY A FOUNDATION

A good school will teach the basics in a formal or at least semi-formal manner so that the student can build their skills gradually. Regardless of the weapon form chosen, this process will teach the student the basic operations of the weapon and set a foundation for the student so that they can participate in the martial aspects of the school. Once this foundation is laid then the student will, or should, after a while, ask "What's next?"

MORE ADVANCED TECHNIQUES

So the student will progress on to more advanced techniques. These may involve more advanced techniques on the same weapon and/or may include the addition of other weapons. Once again, based on the foundation laid in the beginnings of training, the skills of the student will develop. This is the purpose of the training at this point in time to develop and hone the skills. This will, no doubt, take some time if the student really wants to understand the weapons properly.

Once, after some time, the more advanced techniques are learnt the student will eventually come to the end of the curriculum. At this point in time the student will be fully involved in the martial aspects of the school. The swordsman is well-developed and on their way. However, just as at the end of the foundation elements the same question should remain, "What's next?"

TRAINING THE TRAINERS

Up to this point in time, for the most part, the student has been fed techniques and principles from senior students and trainers. Now the student can count themselves amongst the senior students. The trainers at this point in time should be asking this student to help with training and to learn how to become a trainer.

This is not an easy process and the student to trainer development will take time. Indeed this process should start while the student is undertaking the advanced training syllabus. So the student becomes a trainer, over period of time. They are teaching new students, and even the more advanced students. This is not the end of the road, the question remains, "What's next?"

SELF-MOTIVATION

Once the student has progressed to the rank of senior student and trainer at a school they should be looking at things more broadly. Maybe they want to go back and examine techniques which they have already learnt, or further their own studies into different areas or weapon forms. By the time a student gets to this stage, their search should be self-motivated, they should not need a trainer prodding them along to find topics, topics should emerge from their own experimentations. By this point in time the student should have realised that there are many different ways and many different schools of thought about how the sword can be used. The ever-burning question should be alight in them, "What's next?"

CONCLUSION

The swordsman should always attempt to keep sharp. This applies to mind and body. Basic drills should be a normal part of the regimen along with combats against other opponents. These keep the body sharp but to keep the mind sharp more is required. To stay motivated the swordsman should always be looking for new projects and new things to learn. This can be broad or focused dependent on the interest at the time. There is always something which can be learnt for fencing or something which can be refined. There is always something new to be discovered or something new to learn. The swordsman should always be thinking, "What's next?"

SECTION 6.
Mind Games

Why Do Renaissance Fencing?

INTRODUCTION
What a question. This is a big question that needs to be asked both of the beginner and the more experienced fencer. For those at the beginning, the answer is a reason to start and stick with the training. For those more experienced fencers, the answer is a reason to keep going with the training. This discussion will bring up some of the reasons for starting fencing and also some of the reasons to continue with it. The important thing about the answer that is given to this question is that it must satisfy *you* more than anyone else.

WHY FENCE?
The most interesting and often most difficult question to answer especially for the practitioner of Renaissance fencing is why fence? What is the use of fencing? Why bother going to all the effort? In a way, points have to be conceded to this sort of questioning. For the Renaissance fencer, it is an "outdated" style of combat, which belongs to a period up to 500 or so years ago. For most fencers, there are no gold medals at the end of it, and not to mention the many confusing issues that abound with the recreation of this martial art. The original purpose of learning to fence has gone, people do not generally wander around in public with swords at their sides, and it is not likely you will be challenged to a duel either. This is a question of outsiders to the fencing community and members of the community also. The question is often best answered by each individual practitioner. But we can highlight some general points of relevance in answer to this perplexing question.

INFLUENCES
There are many influences, which may cause a person to become interested in fencing, these all have an impact on the individual. The media, especially in regard to movies often influences people in this. A person may see a movie and become

interested due to the flair, which is shown by the characters in the movie. With special attention to rapier combat, movies such as "The Three Musketeers", "The Mask of Zorro" and "The Musketeer" all show rapier combat as a combat art with much skill. Unfortunately, these movies do not show the hard work that is required to develop such a level of skill. Learning how to fence and learning how to do it properly takes a lot of time and effort.

People are also influenced by friends and family, especially those who are already involved in groups which do fence. A person may become influenced by the skills demonstrated by a relation or friend. Others may become interested because of a search for something new; these people often have a background in sport fencing and wish to explore new skills. Still others are interested in fencing because of the different styles and approaches, which are possible, and some become interested because of a level of competition that is not found in other sports. The reasons for starting to fence may actually not be the same reasons that a fencer will continue with it. This notes a change in mind-set in the fencer over time.

VALUES AND PASSIONS

A person's own individual values and passions also influence a person's interest. Values expressed in fencing and not so much in other combat arts. Others simply develop a passion for the arts of their own culture, and especially those from older times. It is often these passions and values, which will sustain a person through the long process of training. While oriental martial arts have a lot of mysticism associated with them, western martial arts do not, or not as much.[15]

The important thing is that something deeper can be found in these martial arts and amongst the community who performs them, if only the fencer will look deeper than what is seen on the surface. The culture of the sword does have an effect upon the western practices of the sword and it needs to be noted. We salute our opponents at the beginning of a bout and at the end to show respect, and this only scratches the very surface of a culture which extends back in time and deep in thought. To discover the culture which is hidden here is to explain much of the history of the western world.

A NEW VIEW

Fencing not only teaches new skills but also teaches control, among other things. It also teaches a new approach on how the world should be viewed through the teaching of the social elements that are important. Though some teachers may neglect this particular aspect of fencing, it is something which should be taught. In some cases the student may have to simply go out and discover these aspects for themselves. Fencing also teaches strategy, strategy which is not only useful when fencing but also in other aspects of one's life. These things that fencing teaches are of benefit to all, and not just those who fence.

---

15   There is some mysticism, it is just more related to the philosophy and science of fence, which is bound more in the Classical foundations of many of the treatises.

REASONS

The reasons for learning to fence are many. Some people learn to improve their fitness, and fencing does supply some of the requirements for this. Some people learn to gain a new set of skills, and fencing does teach those. The reasons for learning to fence are personal, but learning how to fence does teach many things.

Fencing gives both intellectual and physical pursuits. On the intellectual side, fencing teaches new ways of thinking, and opens many avenues for intellectual research, and these often improve the physical side. The physical side is much more obvious in the skills, which are learnt and used. Renaissance fencing especially is much closer to a combat art than sport fencing and it does supply a lot of the intensity without the downside of physical harm. Fencing teaches gracefulness in its movements, style in its actions and finesse. These all translate into things outside of fencing.

THE WHY AND HOW OF WINNING

Renaissance fencing, when it comes to tournaments, is competitive. The important thing that needs to be questioned here is why a person should win and also how. There are reasons for this, and each must be considered. Winning can supply a sense of achievement, and an enjoyment of victory, this must be tempered with grace and consideration. It can supply recognition from fellow fencers and this is also a good thing. It can elevate a person's esteem and prestige; there is a certain amount of glory achieved in winning. Most of all, it demonstrates excellence in a combat art and performance of the skills that have been learned.

With winning comes responsibility. The winning of the tournament may not confer responsibility, but the method of winning the tournament in the first place does. What is important here? The method by which you win is important. A person who wins with brute skill and force will not be as respected as a person who wins with grace and style will. It is the influence of the "perpetual gentleman" which changes a person from a duellist into a gentleman.

To exhibit courtesy to one's opponent displays a certain good nature, which the rapier combatant should possess. This will be influenced by a person's values, and will develop a view of the person by others. This consideration of courtesy should be at the fore whenever a person takes the field in tournaments or in sparring. Is it not more of an achievement to win with grace, style and courtesy than to win by brute force? This should be at the forefront of every rapier combatant's mind. We are attempting to recreate a gentleman's art, so shouldn't we also act like gentlemen in the execution of this art? Consider your own impact upon the arts of defence; do you promote a positive or negative image?

CONCLUSION

Renaissance Fencing, HEMA, Western Martial Arts (WMA), or whichever name-tag it happens to be called by in your particular instance has the ability to give back a lot. The trick is that it requires you to do the hard work to put things in so you can get things back. Someone or something may influence you to fence, and that's great. You get hooked on what is being taught, even better. What is going to keep you going? The important thing is that while the tangible goals are minimal the intangible goals are manifest, if you look hard enough and train hard enough. This is a path travelled which really has no end for the true swordsman as there is always something to learn.

What is a Master?

INTRODUCTION

There have been questions with regard to the idea of the "master" and "mastery" floating around in various forms for some time. Being that I write quite a bit about fencing and I am known by some, I thought it was time that I set the record straight as to what I think of the concept. Hopefully I will also be able to address some of the mysteries of this word and some of the ideas surrounding it, at least from my point of view. Please remember as you read that this is my own point of view.

MYSELF AS A "MASTER"

In some circles I am referred to as a "master". I thought that it would be most useful to address my own position before discussing a more general pattern and thought process. In my particular case there is two times where I might be referred to by the title "master". It will be noted that in each circumstance these are with regard to a specific field of expertise and are specific to the setting in which they are found. Neither have any claims of anything more grand or over-reaching.

The first title of "master" is within the Lochac Royal Guild of Defense, and this is as a Guildmaster or Guild Master as the case may be. This is a teaching organisation formed within Australia as part of the SCA in which each rank is tested. This rank is an accepted level of competence in western martial arts, and more so as an established teacher and researcher of western martial arts. The important part here is that it points these individuals out as teachers, not necessarily as great fencers, even though each is in their own particular way in their own particular right. This title is for the most part only recognised within the SCA, and in many ways only in Australia.[16]

In the second instance of the use of the title of "master" it is Master of the School of Historical Defense Arts (SHDA). This is a title adopted for the school to denote the highest rank in the school, and as an administrative title which could be easily replaced with President or Chairman or similar things. For the most part, however this is to indicate the head trainer of the school and in many ways I get tempted to replace it with a more Elizabethan title in "Schole Maister" in order to be specific as to what the title means. It means that I am the highest rank teacher in the school; once again, no claims of anything aside from being a teacher and researcher.

You will notice that in both instances the words "teacher" and "researcher" are present with regard to the title of "master" in both instances. I think that this is vital. I know I have much to learn, and I am extremely happy about this. Every practitioner should and must keep learning for many reasons. The main answer for all of them is that it is better for the practitioner and also better for others who the practitioner comes into contact with. I make no claims with regards to my titles other than those which have been presented here, and I am quite happy to discuss this.

---

[16] I have since writing this, been elevated to the Order of Defence, which has the title of "Master" with it again this is a title only within the SCA.

"THE MASTER"

Hopefully in this part of the discussion I may be able to shed some light on what it means to be a "master" of western martial arts. As far as I am concerned the following statement is accurate: A Master is a researcher and teacher. A Master is not necessarily the most excellent fencer in the world. Therefore the creation of a master in the community of western martial artists is an excellent thing. But this gives little explanation.

In the thoughts of the "general public" a master is an unbeatable, mysterious teacher, a possessor of mystic arts only passed on to dedicated and appropriate students. This is more related to martial arts movies than real expectations. This is one which has been crossed over due to many Eastern Martial Arts movies and even the Star Wars franchise. In these instances people who are referred to as "master" possess mystical martial and other skills and abilities not possessed by normal people.

The title of mastery states an expectation of a certain level of skill at teaching and also period of learning and teaching, nothing more. This is an expectation of time spent engaging with weapons, learning from manuals, researching forms and many hours of practice. It does not state any mystical ability, aside from the ability to pass on the skills of the weapons to others, which is yet a powerful ability indeed.

WHY SHYING AWAY?

There are some HEMA organisations which shy away from the idea of the title "master" to avoid the entire process. I think that this is foolish. These organisations have accepted levels, as above for mastery and every other level. If you are the head teacher and/or administrator of a martial arts group with a school-ish approach to learning and skill levels, why should you not claim the title? The attainment of this level does not imply any ability to sit back and finish your learning, but encourages you to continue so that you can pass on more to your students.

How is it a bad thing to create a "master" if the level is pointed toward the teaching aspect? This merely recognises more teachers within the community, and more opportunity for students to learn and learn more. The possession of the title of "master" should encourage someone to do more rather than less, to learn more to keep ahead of the students, and to teach the students more so that they can become better at their art. So some organisation creates a "master", how does it affect us anyway? If it is not an over-reaching organisation? If it is not an applicable organisation? If no expectations are present? The only time a person should be concerned is where this organisation has the ability to affect what you do or what your school does.

The USFCA (United States Fencing Coaches Association) has created an historical martial arts mastery qualification. Firstly I live in Australia, so it does not affect me other than demonstrate a forward-looking approach and an attempt to create some pedagogy for western martial arts. Secondly I am not a member which is in any way affiliated with the USFCA, so it does not affect me. As far as I can see, so long as it is bestowed for continued and continuing teaching and researching it cannot be a bad thing.

CONCLUSION

Take a step back and do some research. Have a look at what mastery means to you. Have a look at what becoming a master means to you. These are important questions that every western martial artist should look at. We as western martial artists need to stand up for teaching and research and things which encourage them. We should stand up for aspects which encourage pedagogical approaches to learning western martial arts. If this means making masters, based on demonstrated progression in a pedagogical sense, in organisations, then that is what we need to do. In my particular case as long as "masters" are created within the western martial arts community to promote the art, and they are given to people with demonstrated teaching and research I can't see it being a bad thing.

Fencing Mind Game - The Long Path

INTRODUCTION

The fencing mind game is our key to a longer path in fencing. Once all of the physical aspects are put aside, fencing is a battle of minds and of wills; this is where the real battle is fought. So that we can utilise this aspect of fencing various things are necessary and this discussion will be addressing some of the important points about this and also examining how it is possible to seek the longer path so that we are able to enrich our fencing experience. In this discussion I will be making particular reference to one most useful source, Maestro Nick Evangelista's book, *The Inner Game of Fencing: Excellence in Form, Technique, Strategy, and Spirit*.

FINESSE AND STRENGTH

With regard to development in fencing it is undeniable that the technical and physical aspects play an important part in the process. It is useless for us to be able to think about actions that we would like to be able to perform without the necessary skill to do so, but in this it is also important to look at the application of these techniques in practice. Fencing requires a degree of finesse and this comes about through the correct application of force in fencing, if we rely on pure force and strength this finesse can be lost. "Whatever you do, keep muscle out of your fencing game. It is the over-balancer, the killer of finesse." (Evangelista, 2000:147).

It is essential therefore that we consider what we are doing and how we are applying force in the use of technique, it is much more important to perform the skill correctly, rather than substituting force for where technical skill is lacking. This is a part of the learning process and cannot be ignored. Only through the correct application of skills is it possible to see how they truly work and develop ourselves towards some sort of mastery of the art.

TECHNICAL SKILLS AND MASTERY

Mastery is an interesting word in and of itself, in some ways it is compared to perfection, though this is not the same thing. A technique can be performed perfectly but without mastery. Mastery requires us to use the skill at the right time and for the right reason in our encounter with our opponent, the perfection here is seen in the perfect performance whereas the mastery is the application of the skill to the correct situation. Skills need to be practiced until they are known well so that we can perform them when they are required in the situation, but this requires more than mere repetition of the skill in drills, it requires a situation in which they need to be performed and one way the sport fencing community achieves this is through the use of what are called "conventionals".

> "Conventionals have a way of illuminating the modus operandi of fencing. ... conventionals were designed to provide the fencer with an analytical atmosphere, as opposed to a competitive one." (Evanglista, 2000:8).

Conventionals provide particular situations that arise in fencing where the skill being learnt or practiced is applied to the situation. These need to be performed where both participants know their roles in the situation so that the skill can be applied correctly and thus learnt in the fencing context. The use of such simulations allows us to see how the skill functions in a situation in fencing without the opponent directly opposing the skill. A lot of practice is required for these to be useful, and even more experience is required so that the same skill can be performed in a more antagonistic scenario, it is in this that mastery lies, but it needs to be not over a single skill but all of the skills learnt in fencing. Such pure technical skill developed in fencing, is of great use but it is the mind that also needs to be harnessed so that we can seek to achieve mastery of the art.

The skills that are learnt and perfected in practice give us the technical tools that we use to defeat our opponent through their application in the encounter with them. This is only one part of the picture and it is important to realise this to truly progress and develop in fencing, we must also cultivate the skills of the mind so that we can apply such skills correctly to the situation.

DEVELOPMENT OF THE MIND

> "no matter how good a fencer's technical skill is, if he doesn't know how to apply it effectively and efficiently, he'll never evolve beyond a simple poker. The mind of the fencer is his most important tool," (Evangelista, 2000:xviii).

It is the cultivation of the mind of the fencer that truly opens the options for research, investigation and development of the fencer. This is beyond the mere physical aspects of the game and delves into the mental side of the game which is how fencing can develop further than just the physical side of the game. While the physical side of fencing is important, it is the mere bare bones of it without the mental side.

The title of this article implies that the fencing mind game is a long path, and truly it is. The physical side will supply some of what the fencer needs but to truly develop and become the best that you can be it is important that the mind is also developed. This is the long path that the true fencer will eventually seek and it exists far beyond the simple application of the skills to a particular situation. Unfortunately it is true that it is a long path that is not easy and will not eventuate with a lot of work; this is what Evangelista refers to as the "inner game".

> "For those who find the inner game, only death interrupts the connection. Unfortunately the truths of fencing do not come quickly nor without much work." (Evangelista, 2000:xix).

Development of the physical and technical skills of fencing merely consists of learning and practicing these skills and in some part learning how they are applied to particular situations. The development of the mind is not so simple. The development of the mind takes self-analysis, investigation and an attempt to find out the thought processes that are involved in fencing so that they are better understood. It is connecting with the mind of the opponent and using the information which is found there not only to defeat them but in some part to understand them to achieve this goal. While this is seen in the application of the physical skills, it is the process of fencing rather than the result which is the most fascinating,

> "the process is what gives fencing depth, personality, and life. It is what makes fencing more than just racking up points. If you think this is true, you will end up finding a game in fencing that will take you to the end of your days and will never cease to fascinate you." *(Evanglista, 2000:88)*

THE PROCESS OF DEVELOPMENT

This is a long and slow process that will not come about without a lot of work. This is the path that a true student of the blade will seek and follow not only to improve their skill but also themselves as an entire fencer rather than merely a physical one. The situation in the modern world is that people will seek instant gratification from the effort that they put in and few are willing to seek the longer term goal.

This is mostly seen in dedicated intellectuals who spend a lifetime trying to understand particular aspects in their own fields; it is rarely seen in the more physical pursuits. "It is the rare individual who chooses some distant reward over instant results. Instant results are very seductive." (Evanglista, 2000:109). This is unfortunately the same for most fencers, it is the win that they are after; the result at the end of the bout which is the goal, and not some far flung goal that so often seems so out of reach.

There are no real trophies at the end of this path, and no tangible rewards in most instances. The only benefit that is truly gained through this process is a person's own development as a fencer and also as a human being. The long path will not only affect the fencer's fencing, but will reveal itself subtly in other aspects of the person's life. This is the path of the true student of the blade and to do this you must open your mind to the possibilities available to you.

OPEN YOUR MIND: DIFFERENT POINTS OF VIEW

It is important that we examine our art not through a single view. You need to open your mind to different possibilities to truly grasp what the real truths are in fencing. This means taking yourself out of your comfort zone and going out and challenging yourself and your beliefs. The answers that you will find will not always be what you are looking for and they may not always fit. This does not mean that they should be cast aside. This involves digging deep and researching the more theoretical aspects of the game and finding deeper meaning in the process of fencing.

> "The teacher or student who hasn't the time or inclination to delve beneath the surface of his game has robbed himself of something valuable to his fencing and his life." *(Evangelista, 2000:XiX).*

As teachers we should encourage our students to investigate and discover for themselves. As students we should also do the same. Only through research and investigation of what we do through the broadest point of view can we see the entire picture. While one school of thought does not approach things the way that you do does not mean that their point of view is useless to you, it gives you a different perspective through which you can see what you do and others do.

> "The history of fencing thought is a history of thought directed to a single purpose: how to most effectively place a sword into an enemy's body to produce the most damaging results without being hit at the same time." *(Evangelista, 2000:2).*

This means that anything which is written on fencing; be it sport, rapier or kendo can be useful to us if it is viewed correctly. Each piece of information and point of view is valuable and should be embraced for how it can show us different things. One of the places this reveals itself is in the discussion of fencing tactics.

TACTICS

Tactics and their application are part mind and part body. The mind must realise how it can apply the body to the situation and the body must recognise what the mind sees and be able to perform what is required of it. This is not a one-way street, not in the relationship between the body and the mind and not in the relationship between a fencer and the opponent. There must be a level of knowledge on the part of the fencer of not only what they want to do but also of what the opponent may do in response or what they might do.

> "A fencer needs to be able to mentally connect to his opponent on the fencing strip; to make contact, to observe, to work in conjunction with, to blend strategy and technique into what he sees in front of him. This is what fencing is really about." *(Evangelista, 2000:xix).*

If a technique is developed that relies upon the action of the opponent, it will not work without the action of the opponent, and it also must be the right one. Each technique performed in fencing is connected in some way or another and not only connected to the actions of the fencer who performs them, but also to the actions of the opponent. To each question there is an answer and a counter-point and a counter-point to this, each one is linked in a singular manner one can lead to the next, and is reliant on the one beforehand. It is this logic that the fencer must see to deal effectively and tactically with the opponent. "Everything, offensively and defensively, is connected by a fine web of logic and common sense. Ideas overlap, intermingle, play off of one another." (Evangelista, 2000:xvi). To break this web is to invite disaster upon the situation.

Fencing has been described as an argument with statement, argument and counter-point. Just as an argument or discussion must follow a logical fashion so must the tactical thinking of the fencer. There is no point in starting with the statement and going to the counter-point without the opponent making the argument. This is where many complex actions and compound attacks will fail. This is where tactics lie in fencing. It is a relationship between the two combatants played out for a result based on the information gained by the fencers and used against the opponent in a logical manner. To be truly effective in fencing the idea of strategy and tactics are vital.

> "Strategy is how you relate to your opponent ... This is the science of fencing. How successful you are in strategy will underscore your effectiveness as a fencer. A good strategic game adds much depth and variety to your fencing."
> (Evanglista, 2000:192).

THE ART AND SCIENCE OF FENCING

There is a science of fencing and there is an art of fencing. Both are related and both are different. "It is the art that gives us the ability to fight with control. It is science that unlocks the puzzle presented by one's opponent." (Evanglista, 2000:60). In this way the science of fencing is more about the purely physical aspects of fencing and the art is the more mental side of it.

Another way to look at it is that the science of fencing are the skills that the fencer is given to use against the opponent and the art is how the skills are used against the opponent. In some ways it could also be seen that the science of fencing is how it appears in the manuals and the art of fencing is how it is actually performed, usually with much less scientific accuracy. This sets the paradigm between the art of fencing and the science of fencing, and how they are also intimately related. To truly understand fencing it is important to understand both these aspects of the game.

The science of fencing is a science in its truest form with theory and experimentation. This is most easily revealed in the examination of any bout. There is experimentation in the use of actions to form a hypothesis and then this hypothesis is tested against the opponent. In this way the science of fencing is not only a physical aspect of fencing but also a mental one and defines how two fencers relate to one another in their bout.

> "The science of fencing is the mental side of fencing. It is about effectively relating to your opponent ... It is about figuring out the other guy, about manipulation, about the logical and practical strategic implementation of your art." (Evanglista, 2000:194).

This is where some of the aspects of the tactical approach discussed above are revealed. This aspect of fencing is reliant upon the art of fencing to be performed effectively.

The art of fencing is about the mental side of fencing, but more to the point about the mental side of the fencer. This is about the application of the purely physical aspects of the science of fencing on a mental scale. It is also about the discipline within to wait for the opportune moment and to perform the correct action at the correct moment in the correct manner. In this way it can be seen that it is important to master the science of fencing for the art of fencing to flourish.

> "The art of fencing is about gaining control over your own actions. It is about self-discipline. It is mastery of form and technique, which leads to the effective and efficient maneuverings of body and weapon" (Evanglista, 2000:115).

These two are related on such a scale and that neither can be ignored if the fencer truly wants to succeed in their art. The highest art of fencing is demonstrated in the application of tactical theory using the skills developed by the fencer in the correct manner in the correct form for the situation. It is difficult to remove one from the other and they need to be seen as a whole and it is the whole picture of fencing that allows us to develop a philosophy of fencing.

A PHILOSOPHY OF FENCING

The idea of a philosophy for fencing will seem an alien point of view to some, but what these people do not realise is that they use a philosophy in their fencing without even realising it. The philosophy that you follow may be extremely simple, or it may be extremely complex, but the way that this philosophy is formed and its application to fencing is the important part, even if it is not clearly stated. "A philosophy will color both your approach to the learning process of fencing and your bouting." (Evanglista, 2000:259).

The philosophy applied and used by the fencer will reflect in how they do things and how they approach training. In the case of teachers it will affect how the students learn and what they consider important in the learning process. If the philosophy is about winning at all costs, this will be reflected in the performance of the fencers both on and off their chosen field. Where the focus is on the win, the philosophy may be lax in other areas such as sportsmanship which is vital so that the fencer can grow as a fencer and as a person.

> *"Sportsmanship is the cleansing agent of fencing. It anchors the spirit, gives depth and meaning to action, and promotes growth. It elevates rather than demeans, supports rather than condemns."*
> *(Evangelista, 2000:63).*

We must consider how we reflect the aspects of sportsmanship both in actual fencing and in our relationships with other people; it will reflect a lot of us. The importance of sportsmanship to the fencer is underpinned by their philosophy and their approach to fencing and learning. If the physical aspects are all that matters to the fencer then much of the mental aspects will be lost to them, and this can stunt their growth. Where the more social aspects of fencing are missing this can also stunt their growth and can lead to a lack of respect from their opponents and others who are observing them. All of these aspects hidden in the philosophy will reveal themselves in the encounter between one fencer and another. "On a fencing strip, the sportsman and the bore become obvious, as well as the master and the poker." (Evanglista, 2000:268)

CONCLUSION

The long path has many important aspects and it was the purpose of this article to highlight some of them and to bring them to light for discussion and thought. We must all consider where our path in fencing is leading us and also why this is so. If we really want to succeed and flourish as fencers who are complete in all senses it is important that we examine what we are doing to achieve this.

The real way for the fencer to truly flourish is to examine and consider the long path and consider not the end result but the path it presents. This will determine how long our fencing careers are and what sort of fulfilment we are able to gain in the end. It should be noted that the long path is not easy and it is not simple, it asks a great deal of us to follow it, and seems like it gives very little back in the short term, but in the long term it demonstrates great benefits that will assist in promoting the best of us and encouraging us to search for what we seek, the mastery of the art, and the fulfilment it presents.

Psychology of Fencing: Things to Consider

INTRODUCTION

There are many psychological factors which have a great influence on your fencing. These need to be considered when you are fencing. Before the bout there are aspects which you should take into account, but there are also factors which will impact during the bout. The following discussion is an introduction to the idea of the psychology of fencing and will introduce some of the aspects that should be considered. Not all of the aspects will be considered here, but it will touch on some important points for consideration.

BEFORE THE BOUT

Before a bout there are various things that should be considered. The preparation before a bout with an opponent is important and there are advantages that can be gained before a person steps out on to the field. Some of these things are quite simple and are often overlooked by fencers. The usual thing is that people tend to throw their armour on and then go onto the field. For the more experienced fencers, these other aspects may come normally, but for others, they may not be so natural and thus must be considered as to what needs to be done, rather than just appearing on the field in a state of semi-readiness.

Previous Bouts

Information can be gained about the opponent before the bout which can be of great use. Observe the opponent in previous bouts if you can, the skills that they use will tell you something about them. Do they rely on the same techniques each time? Is there any restriction that they have placed upon themselves due to this preference? What gaps does this leave?

Handedness

The handedness of the opponent is also important as this will change how the opponent should be approached. Are they left-handed or right-handed? This is one that is often forgotten. A left-handed opponent may be able to close certain lines less easily than a right-handed opponent and will approach the opponent differently to a right-handed opponent.

Weapons

The weapons that the opponent chooses to take upon the field are important as this will give you some ideas about the options that they have. This needs to be considered in relation to the weapons that you have chosen to take out on the field. It is not necessary to change your choice to match them. This is especially the case if you are less comfortable with their combination. Unless it is some part of the tournament set-up, you should take the weapons you are most comfortable with.

Equipment
What are they wearing? Will their clothing slow them down? What about footwear? Will it restrict their foot movement? Boots will tend to restrict a person's footwork, whereas shoes will tend to leave them freer to move about. What does their clothing tell you about them? Does it look well-fitting? This will affect how they will be able to move. The condition of their equipment can also tell you somethings about your opponent.

Announcement
Listen to the announcement of your opponent. Are there any titles or positions that have been announced? This can give you some idea of their skill level, and sometimes how to approach the opponent. You should not be frightened if the opponent has impressive titles as everyone has the ability to beat any opponent as long as they use their skills properly.

Physical
The purely physical aspects of the opponent can also tell you things about them. How tall are they? How long are their limbs? How is this in proportion to their weapon? You should go and introduce yourself to your opponent. The simple handshake can tell you something about their strength, and can also allow you to compare yourself to them physically. It is also a good way to break the ice.

Warming Up
Warming up is useful. Fencers will stretch and warm their muscles up before the bout. In some instances this is all that they will do, but this leaves a great deal that is not done. Warming up on the physical side should also be the movement of the weapons allowing you to see how they will move and how to follow from one action to another.

Body and Brain
You should also be considering how you will respond to the actions of the opponent. Pushing all of this to the forebrain will allow you much easier access to it during the bout. The movement of the weapons around will also assist in the mental preparation for the bout, which is also important. The bout before you are supposed to take the field, you should take some time to yourself to prepare properly. This is important so that you can relax and prepare properly.

RELAX
Relaxing in fencing has great benefits that can be attained through its use. This particular aspect covers various things which have already been discussed, but also adds some more into the discussion. Having the ability to relax will allow you to move more freely and do a great deal more. It is important that you consider this, both before you take the field and also while you are on the field and engaged with your opponent.

Self-Confidence
Being able to relax comes from self-confidence. This confidence must be placed in your own abilities as they are the ammunition that you take into the encounter. Remember all the work that you have put in to get you as far as you have, be confident in the ability that you have and that you know how to respond to the actions of the opponent. Do not let it grow to over-confidence lest this blinds you to the true ability

of the opponent and also inflates your own to a situation where it is of no use to you. This confidence in your own ability will allow you to relax more easily.

TENSION

Tension is important, but it must be tension used at the correct moment, rather than tension that has been built up. You need to be able to use and release the tension whenever you need to. An excess of tension will be detriment to you. This tension needs to be considered not only of the body but also of the mind. If you are tense in your mind you will end up tense in your body. A tension of the body will lead to a restriction in movement and a slowing down of the actions that you are making due to the muscles already being tense.

One of the places where this tension can most easily be seen is in the on guard stance. If you are hunched over, your muscles in your shoulders are already working as there is tension in them. This will restrict the movement of your arms. If you stand up properly and broaden your chest, the tension in your shoulders will be released. In a proper standing up position you will also be able to breathe more easily which means that you will have more energy.

BREATHE

Breathing is important. Breathing gives more oxygen to the muscles which allows them to move more freely. Breathing can also be used to relax you. This can be done before and even during the bout. Before, you should take relaxed breaths; breathe as deeply as you can. During the bout, you should take the time to breathe and relax and release tension. To do this you should break off from your opponent and out of distance, then take some deep breaths and relax yourself. This will allow you to release tension in your mind and your body.

ENJOY IT

One of the key ways to relax when fencing is to enjoy the encounter. If you are at training doing bouting, you are there to learn about yourself and your opponent. It does not matter if you are struck so long as you learn something from the encounter. If you do, you win.

Your focus needs to be on the bout itself and not any prize or reward that may or may not come afterward. You should be focussed on the skills that you are using and the skills that the opponent is using. In a tournament or examination you need to be aware of your opponent and deal with what they throw at you. You need to deal with what is in front of you and enjoy what you are doing. This will allow you to relax.

You need to consider what is truly on the line in the encounter. Each bout is the matching of the skills of two fencers against one another, and this is how they should be approached. It is a chance to explore your own skills and demonstrate what you have learnt. To truly relax you need to enjoy the encounter between you and your opponent, with this relaxation you will be able to do a great deal more.

CONCLUSION

The psychology of fencing is important for any person who participates in it, but it is often not considered by the fencers. It is important that you do consider what is going on to understand it better and be prepared for what may come. The points which have been raised are things to consider. This in no way covers all of the aspects that you should be aware of, but is designed to highlight some to be thought about. Fencing is both a set of physical skills but also a set of mental skills. These need to be combined so that you are the most effective that you can be. The psychology of fencing is something which is often pushed to the side by some, but it needs to be considered as it is of great importance.

Pressure in Fencing

INTRODUCTION

Pressure is something that we all have to deal with in our everyday lives. This article is primarily aimed at the idea of pressure in fencing and more to the point suggestions of how it can be dealt with. In fencing pressure can build up for many different reasons and some of these are self-influenced. The result of this pressure is what happens when it actually begins to affect people. The pressure will affect people in different ways and we need to be aware of this, but more importantly is how to deal with the pressure.

MANY REASONS...

Pressure is exerted on people in fencing for different reasons and each one of these reasons has a particular impact on the individual. Any form of examination, whether it is verbal or physical, exerts pressure on the fencer as they are expected to perform. The success of this examination will allow them to progress further, the failure of which will restrict their progress. It is these thoughts which form a great part of the pressure. In the case of tournaments pressure is exerted because of the drive in the individual to win. Even if it is not to win the expectation of a certain level of performance is present.

EXPECTATIONS

Expectations form one of the most pervasive forms of pressure placed on the individual. This pressure can either be an internal thing or an external thing. The pressure exerted from others may be explicit or implicit. A teacher or someone else may come up and tell the individual that they expect them to do well in this particular situation, as much as this is encouragement, it is also a form of pressure. The implicit pressure is merely from an expectation that the student has learnt a great deal and should do well because of this.

Expectations which come from the self are actually much more pervasive than those from the outside. These exert more pressure because there is an expectation which has become a part of our own thoughts and thus while the expectations of others can be ignored to a point, the internal ones are ever-present and in our thoughts. This is also how the external pressures can become internal.

PERSONAL RESULTS OF PRESSURE

There are three primary results due to pressure being exerted on the individual. Some people go to absolute pieces, some people focus harder on their task, and others do not seem to be affected at all. Obviously the people who go to pieces seem to be feeling the pressure of the situation the most out of the three, but this is not to say that pressure does not affect the other two, even subtly.

Pieces
The people who go to pieces when the pressure is exerted, it hits a particular mark and then they go to pieces, all that they have learnt leaves their brain, and sometimes they go catatonic. In this situation the pressure will move on toward panic, and the situation will get worse for them.

Focus
The people who focus, tend to internalise the pressure and use it as a focus for the task which is at hand. They tend to end up so focussed that other that everything else is forgotten or just pushed to one side.

Unaffected
The people, who do not seem to be affected, actually are affected, but they have internalised it so far that it is just a normal thing for them and nothing to be thought about. The result of this is usually they end up blasé about the situation, and this can lead to a lack of focus.

Identifying which type of individual you are is the first step in dealing with it.

RESULTS OF PRESSURE

Mental Effects
Pressure exerted on the fencer can result in some specific things and some general things. For some it would seem that they have a loss of ability. They can't seem to perform the techniques which they have learnt effectively. A further stage of this is what I refer to as the "brain-melt". In this situation they have a complete loss of ability and they have no response to the actions of their opponent. This is usually one of the most catastrophic results of the exertion of pressure on a fencer.

Physical Effects
There are also physical effects that the fencer will notice in them. There is a large flow of adrenaline to the individual. This gives them more energy, but can result in being "twitchy" or the hands shaking. Another result of the boost of adrenaline is an increase in heart rate. Sometimes the increase in heart-rate will actually happen before the burst of adrenaline.

This particular causality is the result of the human being's in-built fight or flight response. The increase blood-flow and adrenaline is so that the individual can either fight or fly. The amusing thing about this is that for a large portion of people the brain is programmed toward the flight response. This is not particularly helpful for the fencer. There are other effects that may be noticed, but these are the most common.

DEALING WITH PRESSURE

Understanding
The first step toward dealing with pressure is understanding your natural response to it. There are important elements of this that must be taken into account. Many people will focus on the physical aspects of the increase in pressure, but will forget the psychological ones. It is important that both aspects of the situation must be taken into account. The attempt to deal with either of the sets of symptoms alone is futile. Once your own symptoms have been identified then it is possible to move on to dealing with these symptoms.

Relaxation

When pressure takes hold of the individual and the physical symptoms start manifesting, these are usually a result of the psychological ones being in full swing. The first approach is relaxation; deep breathing to slow the heart-rate down and to conserve energy. This actually works very effectively as the blood gets flushed with oxygen allowing the heart to work more easily thus slowing it down and the rest of the body with it.

Examine Thought Processes

The next part of the process is examining the thought process and removing all of those things which will not have an impact immediately. In this situation, it is especially negative thoughts that need to be removed. The focus on the individual needs to be on the current situation and not what may or may not happen. For the fencer, it is simply dealing with the problem presented by the other fencer. This allows the mind to be cleared and the focus placed on the present.

Harness the Energy

The other way to deal with pressure is to harness the energy supplied by the physical effects of the pressure applied. This approach works especially well for those who tend to focus rather than the other ones, but this is not to say that they cannot. The increased heart rate and adrenaline supply the body with more energy. This particular approach harnesses this energy and uses it for the current process.

Energy is wasted in such things as shaking hands and other twitches; this energy needs to be directed to the purpose at hand. To do this the fencer needs to focus on what they are doing and to use the energy supplied on what they are doing. This may require holding some of it back while waiting. Having a constant flow of energy is much more useful than sharp spikes of energy.

Of course, it also requires the fencer to allow themselves some leeway to open themselves up to more possibilities in their fencing. The important thing is that the energy needs to be focussed at what they are doing rather than being wasted. This can be a difficult approach especially for big tournaments where there are large breaks, but it is possible.

CONCLUSION

Pressure is present in fencing, the important thing is to know where and why the pressure is being felt. Once that is known then it is possible to go about dealing with the pressure being exerted. It is important that in any approach to dealing with pressure that both aspects, physical and psychological, must be taken into account in order to get the best answer to the situation.

The approaches presented are designed to give some ideas about how pressure can be dealt with by the fencer. It is important in all cases that the energy supplied is used effectively so that it is not wasted, or the energy of the fencer runs out before they have achieved their end. Look at pressure in fencing as one of the problems to deal with, and a challenge to surmount. Just remember that like any one opponent, it can be beaten.

On Winning

INTRODUCTION

Everyone likes to win. Everyone likes the feeling of defeating an opponent and feeling the sense of victory. This is a positive feeling that surpasses many. It is highly addictive as many will attest. What needs to be noted, and will be demonstrated in this post is that there are two paths to victory and greatness, and these two paths result in two different results.

The results of these paths may not be immediately apparent, and often by the time that they are, it is difficult, though not impossible, to change the path that a fencer is on, at least according to public opinion. Interestingly, often it is public opinion that may make a person change which path they are on once they discover that one is not as fulfilling as they once thought it may have been. More often though, it takes an entire shift within a person to change path and this is a much bigger step as the driving forces which decide how we approach victory and its attainment come from within. We should all consider what path we are on and whether or not we are willing to live with the consequences of this choice.

TWO PATHS TO GREATNESS

To describe these two paths to greatness I will use the philosophies and use the names and headings of two great writers of the Renaissance. The first is Niccolo Machiavelli, and in this I will focus on his famous book *The Prince*. The other is Baldassare Castiglione, the writer of the famous book of etiquette *The Book of the Courtier*. What should be noted in my treating of both of these authors is that both of their philosophies are treated from the most rudimentary form possible. Both have a lot more to be said of them and I encourage everyone to read them both to gain a greater and fuller understanding of them. Each one will be used to present a different set of principles and a different approach to victory.

MACHIAVELLIAN

> *"Lisa: ... Ralph Wiggum lost his shin guard! Hack the bone! Hack the bone!"*
> *("Lisa on Ice" - Episode 6, Season 6 - "The Simpsons")*

The general reading of Machiavelli's *The Prince* is of a sanguine individual who will do anything to keep his principality alive. Machiavelli is a very practical man and for the most part his book is about political survival. I would encourage all to read his insightful book. However, using the generally accepted view, it discusses anything for a win.

The Machiavellian combatant will find the opponent's weakness any way that he can and use it against him regardless of what it is. This combatant is often brutal in his attacks and will exploit weaknesses in armour as well as in defences. The Machiavellian combatant is ruthless in his combats and often skates on the edges of the rules with regards to legalities to achieve his ends.

The Machiavellian combatant will be noted for his practical manner of his fighting rather than finesse. While having skill in his method, there will be a lack of flair in his method, and there will be little satisfaction fighting this combatant as his methods will always be focussed on the gaining of victory rather than the pleasure of crossing swords with an opponent. There will be no testing of new technique to find new ways of doing things unless something is not being effective against a particular opponent.

The Machiavellian combatant always fights at his full capacity and never lets up, regardless of the situation, regardless of the combatant. There is always a reason behind his combats and that is to defeat his opponent. This combatant will be respected for his ability to win, and his fighting prowess, but not respected as an honourable combatant, thus for the most part he will earn notoriety rather than renown in his exploits.

CASTIGLIONIAN

"The art of fencing is about gaining control over your own actions. It is about self-discipline. It is mastery of form and technique, which leads to the effective maneuvering of body and weapon"

Maestro Nick Evangelista

Baldassare Castiglione's *The Book of the Courtier* was heralded as *the* book of etiquette for the Renaissance gentleman, and is often still referenced for opinions with regard to the subject of gentlemanly qualities. It presents an individual imbued with qualities which will make him the flavour of the upper crust of society, and an all-round generally pleasant individual to be around.

The Castiglionian combatant will seek a quality engagement with all of his opponents, regardless of their skill level. His focus is not primarily about winning but about the presentation and performance of his skills. This combatant will use timing and precision to defeat his opponents. This combatant will stay well within the confines of any rule system and seek to do so especially in his combats.

The Castiglionian combatant will be noted for his finesse in the manner of his fighting, along with his timing and application. There will be flair and also the correct application of skill, there will be lots of satisfaction in fighting this combatant as his methods will focus more on the performance on skill rather than winning the engagement, and the pleasure of the encounter. He will attempt new skills in his encounters with opponents to test his own skills against them as his focus is to be better than his old self rather than his opponents.

The Castiglionian combatant will match skill for skill with his opponent to keep a fight equal as much as he can to allow the opponent to learn something from the encounter. His reason for fighting is the pleasure of crossing blades with his opponents. This combatant will be respected regardless of whether he wins or loses due to his application of skill, and his method. He will be respected as an honourable combatant and for the most part will earn renown for his exploits.

CONCLUSION

There has been stark contrast drawn between the Machiavellian and Castiglionian combatants, however at times we will all drift between the two of them. The Machiavellian combatants we see all of the time in sport fencing, especially at the highest level of competition. This is where competition is at its highest and where the fencers have been pushed so that winning is their only focus. It is here that we see that the idea of the

Castiglionian combatant has completely been eclipsed.

Consider where you are now in your fencing and what your focus is. What is your opinion on the importance of winning? If placed in a position to win but based on dubious grounds, would you take the opportunity? These are the questions which we need to ask ourselves.

We should all do our best to focus more on the Castiglionian and the gaining of renown as this will outlast regardless of our victories. Take care in your actions as there is always someone watching. This counts as much in your training and a social bout as it does for tournaments and public events.

Ego: The Good, the Bad and the Ugly

INTRODUCTION

Your personality will have an effect on how you fence and how you approach it. This is an important point that must be considered with regards to all aspects in your fencing. This discussion is an examination of the effects of personality on fencing, and more to the point an examination of the effects of ego on fencing. The information below will address various aspects of personality and ego and its impact on training and competition. It is something that we should all consider as to how our own personality and ego will affect the way that we train and the way that we fence. The discussion will address both the positive and negative effects of personality and ego upon the fencing process including training and competition.

Your personality will have an impact on your training it will affect the way that you approach your fencing and how you perform on the field and this is an important point that we must all realise. There are good aspects that will promote the best in us and there will be negative effects that will detract from what we do and how we are perceived in our fencing. Both of these aspects need to be taken into account and the positive enhanced and the negative reduced as much as possible.

APPROACH

> *"You must keep egotism out of your fencing. Egotism has no place in your training, ... or your fencing persona. It is an ugly, misleading companion."*
> *(Evangelista, 2000:219)*

Your personality will affect your approach to fencing. This is more focussed on our personal philosophy that grounds the reasons for fencing. The reasons for fencing are many and it is these reasons that will drive us to succeed or not. If our aim is simply to beat every opponent that we encounter on the field, this will have a different effect than if our goal is to further our search for the truths in swordplay.

A person whose simple goal is to beat every opponent on the field may reject certain approaches in their fencing to enhance their ability to win. In most cases once this person has found what will work best for them on the field they will stop learning and just attempt to enhance these skills. A person who is seeking the truth in swordplay, however, will seek more than the simple win, and will search out better technique and train this.

This will lead this individual to learn more and more and thus enhance their knowledge of the art that they have chosen to pursue. Thus it can be seen that the overall approach is affected by our personality and approach.

CONDUCT

Personality will affect your conduct on the field, especially where it is purely driven by ego, any hit against you will feel like an assault on your ego. On the other hand if this is approached as a learning experience any hit against you will be seen as a chance to learn something from the experience. Thus in this approach every encounter with an opponent is a learning experience and benefits the fencer regardless of the result. The person who seeks to enhance their experience in fencing will take every chance to learn and this will benefit them in the long run. This will also affect the way the person trains, seeking to learn from every encounter and every lesson so that they can become a more complete swordsman. We must examine how our personality affects or performance and approach to every encounter.

NECESSARY ELEMENT

"I'm not sure if I can stress enough how important having confidence is to your success at fencing (or life in general). What I'm talking about is not brash, loud, empty bravado or egotism, but the quiet assuredness you can feel emanating from people who are secure in themselves and their abilities."
(Kellner, 2009)

Ego is a necessary thing in fencing. It is what drives our aspirations in fencing; it is what enables us to succeed, and also to accept successes. Having the effect of ego is a necessary and good thing for the fencer, but this must be tempered by the fencer's approach to what they are doing and learning. The ego must be balanced with the knowledge that fencing is a learning experience, thus the ego must realise that there will be elements where you will not succeed the first time. These times must be taken as a chance to learn rather than a personal affront. In this way, with the ego kept in check and used to drive a person to succeed through the best methods, ego can actually be a good thing. Of course, as with everything there is a negative side which must be taken into account.

NEGATIVE SIDE

"there is a point when ego takes a step beyond the normal scheme of things, when feeling good about yourself and having aspirations become self-inflating conceits. When this happens, you will most certainly get in the way of your own progress." (Evangelista, 2000:219)

Egotism and ego to excess is a bad thing for the fencer. This will lead the fencer to be conceited and arrogant. This is not good for fencing and not good for the fencer. Conceit on its own will prevent learning, as the fencer will feel that they have learnt everything that there is need to be learnt. This may be promoted by a long stretch of wins against their opponents. At this point in time where conceit has taken firm root in the fencer, they will stop learning and stop progressing because they feel that they have learnt all that they need. Conceit will also be expressed in the fencer's attitude to other fencers and this will not be favourable at all. Arrogance is closely related to conceit in its effect upon the fencer. This is an aspect that the fencer should avoid as much as possible. These two aspects will result in the fencer thinking that they are the measure of all their opponents. This will lead them to stop learning. Egotism in the fencer is a detriment to them and will prevent successes that they would have otherwise had access to.

TRAINING

> "You stop measuring when you think you are the ruler by which all things are measured. And when you stop measuring, you stop thinking."
> (Evangelista, 2000:219)

Ego has an effect on training, both what the fencer will learn and also how the fencer will learn it, or not. A fencer who has a lack of confidence or ego at all will mean that they do not have the will to succeed and will stop at the first problem. On the other hand a fencer who has too much ego will derail the learning process and will find it difficult to learn anymore. In this way too much ego and too little will be a detriment to fencing.

The fencer needs to have enough ego that they will continue trying and learning, but not so much that they become arrogant nor so little that they stumble at the first problem that they encounter in their training. In this way the ego needs to be balanced in training with other factors such as the want to learn and the acceptance that they have not learnt everything possible. To progress we must learn, and learning is a process in which the fencer needs to be a full participant and thus needs the will to go further and the self-check to keep on learning. This ego issue is also reflected in the encounters between the fencer and their opponents.

TOURNAMENTS

> "If you allow egotism to take over, you will underestimate every opponent you meet. You will overestimate yourself. ... Don't ever believe you can fall back on your reputation to create victories." (Evangelista, 2000:220)

Ego has a place in tournament and bouting. The same effects of too much and too little can be seen in bouting and in tournaments. Too much and the fencer will underestimate the opponent, too little and the fencer will give up before the bout has started. Arrogance as an expression of an over-abundance of ego will be expressed by the fencer both on and off the field.

Off the field it will be seen as disdain toward other fencers and a complete lack of consideration for them at all. On the field it will be seen in the way the fencer approaches the opponent and how they deal with the opponent. Arguments about hits, especially against them where a discussion is not warranted will surface. There will be complaints about how the judges dealt with a hit where they are used, there will be complaints about how the opponent fences, and various other aspects such as this. A prime place where this can be seen is especially in sport fencing at the highest levels. There are arguments about the hits and the conduct of the bout. Large outbursts by the fencers are a perfect example, whether this is due to a victory or about a defeat. Classical fencing rejects these ideas about the ego and attempts to focus on the form of the fencing rather than the result.

EGO AND HONOUR

> *"While a Classical Fencer places honour above all, even when it might cost him/her a touch, or bout or a tournament title, it is equally vital that fencing students come to appreciate the difference between "ego" and "honour." Ego says "Whatever I do is right." Honour says "Whatever is right, I will do." (You may recognize in this, as I do, the distinction between nationalism and patriotism.)" (Crown, 2006)*

Crown (2006) expresses the difference between ego and honour in a succinct way, and it is a point that we should all consider in our fencing regardless of the form that takes. The points he raises are equally relevant to the Renaissance fencer and also the sport fencer. We all know when we have been struck by the opponent, whether that hit is acknowledged or not. This is something that we need to consider in our approach to fencing, is our ego driving our fencing or is it something else?

CONCLUSION

There has been much said in this discussion about personality and ego and they are important aspects which we must all consider as fencers. Does your ego drive your fencing or is it the search for the truths about swordplay? We should all at the highest and most expressed levels present ourselves as searching for the truths about swordplay, but we must also acknowledge the effect that our egos have upon ourselves and others as well. Approach your fencing as a learning experience in all accounts, and a long road is opened ahead of you. Approach your fencing as the pure desire to defeat all opponents and the road is shortened considerably. We must keep our egos under control at all times, use them to progress in fencing, but not so much that they are all that drive us. We all need to consider the effect that our fencing has on our fencing and also the fencing of those around us.

Renown Versus Notoriety

INTRODUCTION

Renown and notoriety are two words which some may have heard and some may have not. They are how a fencer may be talked about, even if the people doing the talking do not even know the words or what they mean. This post is designed to bring these two words into the light of examination and show how the actions of a swordsman can determine the reactions that he will get from other swordsmen and even non-combatants. They are integrally linked to a swordsman's reputation.

DEFINITIONS

The first thing to do is to define these words and to do that definitions have been taken from www.merriam-webster.com. Thus the definitions of the words are:

> *Renown:* a state of being widely acclaimed and highly honoured
> *Notoriety:* the condition of being famous or well-known especially for something bad: the state of being notorious

Clearly they both have something in common in that in both cases a person with renown and a person who has notoriety are well-known. This is the common element that links them. The difference is that one is respected and praised while the other is known for something less than positive. It is in this difference where the importance lies.

Ironically as soon as you say "notorious" people begin to have some idea about what you are talking about as this word is used a lot more in the modern world than "renown" is, and that is truly a sad state of affairs. That the negative is somehow seen as a positive is truly something which society needs to look long and hard at for answers and reasons. Now that we have the definitions and the beginnings of an explanation, we can begin to relate them to the swordsman.

FOR THE SWORDSMAN

There are two sides to fame. We all know of celebrities who are famous for doing good things and staying that way, but we all know of celebrities who are good at what they do, but are known also for bad things. The former have renown, the latter have notoriety. Too often we see celebrities making front page news for doing the wrong thing and it being almost celebrated, it should not. Notoriety should be shunned.

> *"How you win is ... important, if not more important, than any individual victory. You must win decisively, cleanly, and gallantly."*
>
> (Evangelista, 2000:301)

In relation to the swordsman, the swordsman who has renown is respected on and off the field regardless of the result of his bouts or tournaments, or even whether he even participates in tournaments. When he fights he fights with grace and skill, acknowledging the skill of his opponent, a truly positive influence on the community. This swordsman is often a pleasant individual to be around as well as most often the true character of an individual is reflected in their use of the sword.

The swordsman who has notoriety is respected on the field for his skill and his ability to defeat opponents, but there is as far as it extends. His influence only lasts as long as his victories do. This swordsman is often over-bearing, and often arrogant.

What is interesting about renown and notoriety is that, like fame, it is in other people's hands. It is determined by what others see the person do and how this is reported to others and how this news is spread, exactly like reputation. This means that for the swordsman, they should always assume that someone is watching them bout and in tournaments as word will spread of their exploits for good or not.

PUBLIC ACCLAIM

"At the end of every bout, whether you win or lose, salute, shake hands, smile, and say, "Thank you." No one should be able to tell from your expression, tone, gesture, or manner, whether you have just won or lost." (Evangelista, 2000:302)

The most interesting thing about renown and notoriety is that you cannot seek either one, but you will gain one or the other. There are things, however that you can do to sway your chances one way or the other. What the choice will come down to is your consideration on the field and how you act when you are fencing. It will also be how you act when you are not fencing as well, thus your social interactions with people.

For the most part the part off the field is merely being of good manner and treating everyone in a friendly manner and at all times. This is regards to spectators, officials and also other swordsmen. All of these people are important to allow you to compete with other swordsmen even if you do not see it. Each one of them will have an influence on how all the others will see you.

"When you get hit, instead of taking it personally, acknowledge the skilful maneuver and congratulate your opponent on an excellent bit of fencing."
(Evangelista, 2000:221)

The part of the actual combats is a little more interesting for some, and can be quite difficult for others. It may even require a slight shift in thinking. In this case it is to focus more on the process of fencing rather than the result, making each action precise and clean. This will also help anyone who has to marshal your combat as well. This process is also acknowledging the validity of the hit of the opponent if he strikes you. Don't focus on the hit, acknowledge it, congratulate him and move on. Talk with your opponent, converse with steel and words. It makes for a much more relaxed bout for both of you.

To gain renown you must demonstrate that it is for the art of the sword that you cross swords with your opponent and no other reason. This means that any thought of winning or losing must be completely gone from your mind. You should be focussing on the actions of your opponent anyway rather than winning or losing. Do your best to make your bouts with your opponents as clean as possible. Talk to your opponent through the bout and make sure that they are comfortable. This is a way to demonstrate the more gentlemanly aspects of the sword and thus possibly gain you renown.

Regardless of what we do, there are certain things which we must acknowledge are out of our hands. Public opinion about us as swordsmen is one of them. Of course, as has been indicated, we can shift the flow of this one way or another to see that our side is seen a little better.

CONCLUSION

Renown is a word which is not used much in the modern world and should be. Notoriety is a word which is used much more and should not be as a good thing. The fact that we have so-called celebrities happily stating that they are notorious for particular acts and go out of their way because of the publicity it creates for them is not a good thing.

For the swordsman there should be no choice he should always attempt to gain renown where he can, thus increase the respect for himself and his school.

Think about what you are doing and how this reflects not only on yourself but also on your school, your teacher, and other swordsmen. Be a good ambassador for what we all love and do. Bring renown to what we do and not give others the image we are merely thugs with swords.

Reasons Why I Do Not Do Sport Fencing

INTRODUCTION

I have a fencing history which begins officially back in my late teens. Of course I played with swords when I was a child however it was only in my late teens and my first adventure to university that anything official happened with regard to this. This first adventure into the world of swordplay was to join my university fencing club, which, of course was teaching sport fencing. Due to leaving the university, I had to stop attending the club, however after sometime, and finding other areas of swordplay I decided I did not want to go back. This entry discusses the reasons for this.

Now, admittedly my adventure into this form of fencing was not long, relatively. So, there will be those that this was not a real investment or investigation into the art of fencing. However, from what I have seen as it is presented both in the media, but also as it is presented by those who promote this particular art, I believe that my reasons for not coming back or taking it up were well-founded.

HIT AND NON-HIT

The first area I would like to highlight in this particular explanation of my choice is aims. It would seem that to strike the opponent is the primary aim of what happens in sport fencing. In no place is this more emphasised that in épée where the difference between a «hit» and a «non-hit» is something in the vicinity of 0.25 of a second. The idea of avoiding being struck in the process of striking the opponent seems to have been lost as long as your hit scores first. This seems to go against everything I know and feel about fencing. My belief is that you should be seeking to strike while not being struck yourself, or maybe my focus is a little off.

What has been discussed above focuses on the essential principle of fencing being that it is to defend yourself first and then to strike the opponent. This is the primary principle of fencing and it seems to have been pushed aside for «as long as you strike your opponent first». I will be examining this concept a little further later on with regard to another concept and reason.

PRINCIPLES

The principles of fencing seem to be something which are taught to beginners and then pushed aside. The other principle which is most evidently lost is the principle of distance and knowing it. In many pictures of fencers, they are standing on one another's toes, much too close. It would seem then rather than re-adjusting distance the idea is to contort arms etc. to strike the opponent. If this foundation principle seems to be missing, what else could be?

FORM

My next point that I would raise can be described in one word, "ugly". This comprises two areas. The first I have dealt with a little and that is the "anything for a hit" concept; this bothers me a lot as it allows a lot into the "game" which would seem not to fit into an art which was once practiced by gentlemen and ladies. The idea allows a fencer to perform whatever action he can to lay his point or edge on to the opponent, rather than sticking with the forms and functions of the weapon which he is using, which leads to the second area "form".

In manuals we see pictures of fencers upright and standing with arms extended. In lessons we see the same things being taught to beginners. It would seem, however, that once you become more advanced, this all goes out the window. A person investigates fencing and is confronted with pictures of bodies twisted in horrible angles to strike their opponent. We see fencers airborne and twisting to avoid being struck while at the same time attempting to strike the opponent. The form and function of the actions seems to have been lost by those who practice this art, and most often it s these pictures which newer sport fencers emulate as they are usually pictures of those at the top of their game. This ugliness is not what the art is about for me.

DOUBLE-HIT

Sport fencing has truly gone into the realms of sport and has left combat behind. The original purpose of the weapons which are being used has been lost along with the realisation of the weapons and the effects of them which were found in the originals. When swords were sharp and men fought with them in the infancy of fencing, a double-hit meant that both combatants were dead, or injured, regardless of what time passed between one hit and the other. This is something which I have alluded to in one of my previous statements. The issue of the double-hit has been indicated, but the effect of the single or double hit seems to be absent in the minds of sport fencers. The lethality of the weapon has faded from significance.[17]

A FOIL'S PURPOSE

The foil is seen as a premiere weapon of the sport fencing world. It is seen as the expression of form and function in fencing, and taught right it is. However, as a weapon, it is a mere practice item. The history of the weapons and their practice has been lost. The rules for the use of the foil, and indeed the weapon itself, came about for safety reasons. The idea of priority was to stop students stabbing one another simultaneously and also to emphasise defense. The idea of taking the head "off-target" was so that students would not die from being struck in the head. The weapon was made light so that it could be used for an extended period of time so that students could have the time to learn with it without their arms getting too sore. Hence, the height of the art of fencing has come from a practice item. It almost defines the new focus of sport fencing, practice without ever really performing the real art.

---

17 In many instances it has also faded from the thoughts of those competing in tournaments for HEMA.

CONCLUSION

The reasons which I have given are those which have prompted me to stay doing what I am doing. Should the opportunity come for me to investigate "classical fencing" there is a good chance that I will have a look at it as it would seem that these principles are still present.[18] We must all examine exactly what we are doing and find out the reasons why we continue with what we are doing. At this point in time, I prefer historical weapons which, in some form represent their historical predecessors and are used in a form which at least closely recreates them as they were used in the past, obviously not as tournament weapons. For me, the principles of the art must be present and some idea about the weapon which is being used and its former potential for damage. These are principles which should underlie any pursuit of good swordsmanship.

Martial Art Versus Martial Sport

INTRODUCTION

Regardless of the organisation, regardless of the weapon we use, at some point in time we need to sit back and have a look at what we are doing. We need to do this with a critical eye. Unfortunately as we become attached to a certain way of doing things in a certain group, we tend to become blind to alternatives which are just as valid, or in some instances even more valid than our own.

This does not mean that we should change groups, or even methods, every time we find this, but we should at least look at what we are doing and with a critical eye. The purpose of this article is to ask question of whether that form of combat we are involved in is a "martial art" or a "martial sport". Both have their valid forms, but as stated we need to look at what we are doing with a critical eye to find the truth.

CONSEQUENCES

The first question to look at and one which will come up again and again is the question of consequences. In their original form the weapons and techniques used have an inherent lethality to them and the consequences for failure were for the most part dire. The presence of this level of threat, whether inferred or real is an important part of the form of combat. In the comparison between the martial art and the martial sport, this is a good place to start.

In the martial sport, there is really little consequence for being struck, a combatant is struck, a point is awarded and the combatants re-start until a time limit is reached or one combatant scores a certain amount of points. This form is found in its extreme form in sport fencing. In the martial art, there are consequences present for the combatant who is struck, these are mostly simulated due to the nature of the real weapons, but are still present. A combatant who is struck with a lethal blow is considered killed, a strike to a limb results in the limb being useless for at least the rest of the bout, or the bout is considered concluded.

---

18 *I have been investigating and training with smallsword, and it is most interesting. This is the origin weapon of the épée and also the foil. It has allowed for some use of the foil for its original purpose.*

FURTHER CONSEQUENCES: THE DOUBLE-KILL

In further discussion of the idea of consequences in the combat, there is the question of the double-kill. Two combatants strike one another with equally lethal blows, what happens as a result of this determines the difference between the martial art and the martial sport. In the sport version both combatants are awarded points each or zero points, the combatants then re-set and then continue the bout. In the martial art, both combatants are considered "dead" and the bout is ended with a loss recorded for both combatants. There is no reward and definite consequences for both combatants striking and failing to consider their defense.

The question of the double-kill and the highlighting of the importance of the defence over the offence is a place where the martial art is presented against the martial sport. In the martial art, the defence is considered prime and striking the opponent is only considered once the combatant is secure to do so. In the martial sport, the consideration for striking the opponent often overrides the importance of the combatant remaining untouched by the opponent resulting in them sacrificing themselves to strike their opponent. In a situation with real weapons this second situation would be quite far from a person's thoughts as the threat of actual injury would off-set any goal gained by striking the opponent, in most instances. This aspect will be raised again later in the question of the teaching approach.

TEACHING APPROACH

In the approach to the combat there is also a difference between the martial art and the martial sport. This is most often seen in how the form of combat is taught and what the focus is in the result. In the martial art the best thing is to strike without being struck, defensive skills are the focus of the art with the offense only coming out of a sure offense. In the martial sport as long as you strike the opponent first, it does not matter if the opponent strikes you as well. This has more of the offensive nature placed first where striking the opponent is more important than avoiding being struck.

The principles of the sword are more likely to be found and taught both explicitly and implicitly in a martial art than in a martial sport. In the martial sport they are more likely to be seen only through the eyes of tactical advantage gained over an opponent through some technique rather than explained in any depth. These principles which underlie the use of weapons are unavoidable thus are taught regardless, but it is the manner and explanation of them which is important in this context. Where they are taught superficially they can only be registered as such, where they are taught in more depth, they can be understood and utilised by the swordsman to a much greater degree.

PURPOSE

Another place where the martial art and the martial sport differ is in the purpose of the pursuit. This is the reason behind what is going on in the activity. In the martial sport the reason is the results of competition, the hits, kills or wins in these competitions, besting opponents. In the martial art there is a more holistic approach to the pursuit, the lethal intent of the art is appreciated, and it is the skills which are taught which are the source of achievement. Most swordsmen like to cross blades with one another to test their skill against another person. It is the manner and purpose of this encounter which is the important factor, is it simple competition against an opponent, or a chance to test your skill and learn from the encounter? This is the important difference. The "martial sportist" is on a search to prove that he is better than his fellow man. The "martial artist" is on a search to prove that he is better than his former self.

CONCLUSION

A real encounter with swords, where there is lethal intent behind their use in the modern world, is unlikely. Bouting is our most common avenue for using our skills. The most important thing to remember here is the purpose behind what we are doing and an appreciation of the martial art and original intent of the art which is what makes the difference between the martial art and the martial sport. The important thing is that if a person is getting what they want out of a martial sport, then there is nothing wrong with them continuing this pursuit, but they should remember what is behind it, and realise what they are doing.

The critical eye is important in all considerations of what we are doing as swordsmen. Each individual has a responsibility to evaluate, for themselves, what they are doing and see if it is what they want to do and where they want to go. Each must put a critical eye to the approach that they take to what they are doing and evaluate if it will get them to where they want to be. If it will, then they should continue with what they are doing. If it will not, then it is time to make a change. This critical thinking is the responsibility of every thinking individual, not just swordsmen.

A Question of Ethics

The entire following article is based upon a post made by Guy Windsor which can be found here: http://guywindsor.net/blog/2015/06/ethics/. In this article he asks seven questions about the ethics of swordsmanship which I feel are significant and that each and every individual who picks up a sword or any other weapon should consider, regardless of purpose. Had I been a little more prompt, the answers to these questions and this post would have appeared earlier. Of course these are my answers to these questions. You need to find your own answers to these questions as they are very personal.

THE QUESTIONS:

1) When is it ok to stab someone in the face with a sword?

I have found two answers to this question, firstly in **self-defence**. This would, of course, be a rare situation where I would find myself defending my life or the lives of those whom I care about. It would have to be in a situation where life was actually threatened, thus the aggressor in the situation would always be the opponent.

The second would be in the practice of **martial arts** where the stab to the face is an essential part of the practice presented in many of the period manuals, and I would make sure that my partner is suitably armoured to ensure the safe practice of such an attack. In this situation there is no aggressor as the two combatants are engaging in an activity for the mutual purpose of learning a martial art rather than in the previous situation where the combatants are one is actively trying to injure the other and the other is defending and replying.

2) What is the one thing you find most useful about swordsmanship training outside the salle?

It is difficult to nail down a single thing which is most useful, as there are multiple; tactics, awareness, or the simple health benefits such as muscle strength and cardio-vascular fitness. For me the essential comes from the ability to problem-solve by looking at things from different angles attributed to reading my opponents.

The health benefits of swordsmanship training have been touted by various masters in their works repeatedly. This is often found in the beginning of the manual where they are justifying what they are doing, and for the most part they are true. For me the problem-solving which swordsmanship supplies come from the multiple different approaches to the same situation that it opens, the same is applied to other problems and applying the same theory of using different assets to solve the problem at hand.

3) How important is history to you in your practice of swordsmanship

The study of history is essential to the practice of swordsmanship as the texts must be placed in the background in which they are placed if they are to be completely understood. From the simplest point of view, language; even the Elizabethan texts written in English have seemingly common words which do not have the same meaning as their modern counter-parts.

The sword itself is out of place in the modern world it needs to be placed in an historical context to be understood for its use. Duels were fought with these weapons and the weapons were sharp, drew blood and killed. These days it is very rare that this happens, so the threat of the real weapon must be placed in an historical context so we can better understand the manuals from which the instructions come.

4) Can a duel settle a matter of honour?

A duel can settle a matter of honour so long as the two combatants approach the combat with the right frame of mind and are set to do so. The duel is a confrontation between two individuals used to settle a point of honour. This is a definition which covers the vital aspects of what it is about.

The point of honour can even be settled without drawing blood so long as the combatants have the correct frame of mind. According to some cultures so long as the individual turns up, pick up a weapon, and places themselves opposite the other they are considered to have satisfied honour. If the combat ensues, they also need to act within the combat itself in a manner which gains them honour rather than reducing it.

5) Can violence be beautiful?

When performed with skill, grace, style and form it can. Where it is two people bludgeoning one another into submission it is simply not. This is the difference between the classical fencer of old and the new sport fencing champion. This is the difference between the fencer and the poker, and often the gentleman and the duellist.

6) To what extent is the practice of swordsmanship the cultivation of virtue?

The practice of swordsmanship cultivates virtue by teaching virtues in its learning. It teaches patience through its practice and repetition. It teaches honour through its teachings. Other virtues are gained in similar fashion through the use of the sword and the lessons learnt both from the teacher and the opponent. Where a teacher is present these virtues are more learnt through the teacher than anywhere else.

Here the influence of the student's teacher can be seen in the student. The student will learn from the teacher even where the teacher is not directly teaching the student.

They will learn from the teacher by the way they teach other students and also by the way they deal with other people. This includes when the teacher is bouting as well. Through this it is important that the teacher is aware of the influence that they will have on their students. If the teacher does not cultivate virtues the student will not learn them.

7) Is the study of ethics necessary for martial artists?

The study of ethics is not just necessary, it is essential. Regardless of the sword being blunt or not, it is a weapon. Thus there are responsibilities which come with this weapon. These responsibilities are taught in the question of ethics. There are also the responsibilities that each person who wields the sword has to all other martial artists. In our day and age no one really has to die by the sword (literally), nor do people have to use them in anger. The person who does, especially while claiming to be a swordsman or martial artist affects the whole community and stains us all.

CONCLUSION

I must stress that these are my personal answers to these particular questions and I am willing to discuss and debate any of them with any who would wish to do so. I believe that the questions which Guy Windsor has proposed are extremely important for all combatants and should be given more than a simple cursory glance. We should look past the simple actions which make up the martial components and look deeper into questions of ethics and history which are inevitably bound to the arts which are practised. Each of us should look at these questions and answer them, not to see them published for others to read but for ourselves to see what we are thinking and where our own thoughts are leading us. Hopefully it is down true paths to true answers.

What Does Fencing Give the Fencer?

INTRODUCTION

The fencer puts a lot of effort into training, acquiring the correct equipment and various other aspects if they want to become a better fencer. How much the fencer puts into this is the measure of their dedication to the art. The question that needs to be asked is, after all of the effort put in by the fencer what do they get back from it? This article will address some of those things that the fencer gets back from doing fencing. Some of these things will be obvious and others will not be so obvious.

In our dollar-emphasised, capitalist, modern society, the question is always what do I get out of this? It is a question that is asked in the workplace and even in social situations. In the workplace it is pretty easy to see, it is perks, benefits, and a regular payday. In the social situation it can be a little blurry, and for the fencer some of the results of the effort put into their fencing can be very difficult to see.

Clearly, some rewards are obvious, these are usually in the form of such things as trophies, accolades, awards and other prizes usually awarded after a tournament or a period of service to fencing. Depending on what sort of fencing and what sort of structure will depend on which apply to you. These things are nice to get but in many cases they are fleeting in nature. The question that needs to be asked is whether there are more than these "pretty" things.

PHYSICAL EFFECTS

There are some physical aspects that the fencer will gain without having to win any tournament whatsoever. It is these physical aspects which are the most obvious rewards for the fencer. Fencing will, over time, improve the fitness of the fencer. This is especially the case if they are doing it on a regular basis.

The simple cardio-vascular activity which goes on inside the body during fencing will improve the health of the fencer. While the health aspects are some which are the most obvious results of fencing, there are some health aspects which are over-looked. Such things as improvement in self-worth due to the acknowledgement of the skills which have been learnt, and the achievement associated with this. Then there are the skills learnt while fencing. These skills have their most obvious application while fencing, but the fencer will also notice other changes due to these skills being learnt. Their movements will be more fluid and more accurate. This actually leads on to the mental aspects as well.

MENTAL EFFECTS

The fencer actually does develop some mental attributes which are not clearly apparent in a short amount of time to the fencer, but these will surface over time. The fencer will begin to look at things from a different point of view. The thinking fencer especially will begin to notice the movements of their opponent and in some instances be able to predict what the opponent will do without thinking about it. This will begin to be apparent in times outside fencing as well. The important thing is that these mental aspects need to be developed while fencing. Problem solving will also be improved, and one that links with the physical aspects is the movements of the body in a thinking manner. The fencer who develops these mental skills will begin to see them appear more and more in daily life and not just in their fencing.

SOCIAL EFFECTS

There are also some social aspects which are present as a result of fencing. Many long-term and indeed life-long friendships can be developed due to a mutual interest in fencing. These friends become such not only in the fencing environment, but also outside of it. There are also other social attributes which are developed. Due to the expected performance of the fencer in social situations notions of manners are also developed if the fencer takes the time to acknowledge their importance. This particular aspect increases their ability to deal with people in the wider community as well. Clearly some accolades received fencing will also carry over into the social aspect of people's lives, but these are not as regular as the other rewards which have been mentioned.

CONCLUSION

While the bulk of the rewards from fencing are hidden, they are present. The important thing is that for these things to develop in the fencer, they must put in the effort to develop them. The mental aspects will not develop unless the fencer is actually thinking about what they are doing when fencing. The physical aspects will not be developed without some effort put in and some pushes made. The social aspects will not develop unless the fencer takes on the ideals of fencing etiquette and is willing to express these in the correct situation. Without these more hidden prizes for the fencing, there is very little for the fencer to strive for, and it is often due to this that we see fencers drop off. Instant gratification is not what fencing is about in the long run. True gratification in fencing takes time and it takes effort on the part of the fencing. If this effort is put in then the rewards increase and never end. More of the gains for the fencer will be discussed in the following discussion.

Virtues Gained from Swordsmanship

INTRODUCTION

Based on some of what I said in a previous article on the ethics of swordsmanship, I had a request from one of my readers to write something about what virtues are gained from studying and performing swordsmanship. For your interest, the original article called "A Question of Ethics" can also be found in this same book. So, what I am going to do is have a little chat about these virtues gained from swordsmanship. To begin with I will have a look at some primary sources. Then I will have a look at some of the things from my own point of view, some of which will refer back to the post indicated above.

PRIMARY SOURCES

Call me biased, I am only going to be using manuals and masters which are written in English because I only speak/read English. This makes for much easier translation on my part. First we start with one of my own favourites, di Grassi.

> *"For this cause I beseech the gentle Reader to show himself such a one in the reading of this my present work, assuring himself by so reading it, to reap profit and honour thereby. And not doubting but that he (who is sufficiently furnished with this knowledge, and has his body proportionally exercised thereunto) shall far surmount any other although he be imbued with equal force and swiftness."*
>
> *Giacomo di Grassi (1594) His True Arte of Defence*

In essence, first thing that Giacomo di Grassi focuses on is profit and honour from following what is written in his book. This is the result of training. Further that the reader will be able to defeat any other opponent who is of equal physical ability. So, in essence, di Grassi claims that his method will give you honour through defeating your opponents if you study hard and this will result in profit of some kind. This is not particularly specific.

> *"I speak not against Masters of Defence indeed, they are to be honored, nor against the Science, it is noble, and in my opinion to be preferred next to Divinity, for as Divinity preserves the soul from Hell and the Devil, so does this Noble Science defend the body from wounds and slaughter. And moreover, the exercising of weapons puts away aches, griefs, and diseases, it increases strength, and sharpens the wits. It gives a perfect judgement, it expels melancholy, choleric and evil conceits, it keeps a*

man in breath, perfect health, and long life. It is unto him that has the perfection thereof, a most friendly and comfortable companion when he is alone, having but only his weapon about him. It puts him out of fear, & in the wars and places of most danger, it makes him bold, hardy and valiant.

George Silver (1599) Paradoxes of Defence

George Silver, as I have noted previously, is a character and a half, and his claims about his method are just as characteristic. He claims that the swordsmanship will "defend the body from wounds and slaughter" as one would expect, but then he goes on to list a long list of health benefits of swordsmanship. These health benefits which he lists are not just physical, as one might expect, but they are also mental. The significance of the idea of the benefit to both mind and body is often passed over by many.

"This irresistible power of practice does not only master and overcome the unflexibleness of our bodily members, but also affects and prevails very much, even over our more dull and ignorant judgements."

Sir William Hope (1707) A New Short, and Easy Method of Fencing: Or the Art of the Broad and Small sword Rectified and Compendiz'd

Sir William Hope, much like Silver also highlights the benefits of swordsmanship to the swordsman as being to both the mind and the body. This idea of swordsmanship being as much a mental pursuit as a physical one is something which must be realised for the greatest benefits of it to be attained.

"[Fencing] which justly forms part of the education of persons of rank; giving them additional strength of body, proper confidence, grace, activity and address; enabling them, likewise, to pursue other exercises with greater facility."

Domenico Angelo (1787) The School of Fencing With a General Explanation of the Principle Attitudes and Positions Peculiar to the Art

Domenico Angelo is focusing on an address to a particular clientele, thus insisting that it is an important part of their education. Further to this he also explains further health benefits much like the previous examples which have been presented. Angelo expands his list to include benefits to the social sphere and interactions with others.

There have been four sources cited four evidence of virtues which are gained from the training in swordsmanship. They have elucidated several in the process of the justification of their arts, and it is exactly what they are doing. These men had to justify what they were doing as profitable to the Realm to seek patronage from great men for their livelihoods. From here I will present my own that I have noticed developing along my own path.

MY STUFF
Physical

The first thing that will be easily noted is that fencing does supply health benefits. It does improve cardio-vascular fitness, it does increase musculature (even if it does this in some interesting spots), in general it will improve your general health overall. From my own point of view, if I had not taken up and continued fencing my own personal health issues most likely would have rendered me to a wheelchair for a period of time. But this is not really what this is all about.

Mental Benefits

The virtues which really need to be talked about are those which cannot be seen directly but their effects can be felt in other ways. They can be felt personally by the fencer and felt by others by the actions of the fencer, these are the more important virtues which we should really concern ourselves with. While the physical attributes allow us to perform and live longer lives and thus enable us to learn more it is the other virtues beyond the mere physical which are more important.

Fencing and learning has been related to the treating of depression and other mental illnesses, and indeed physical illnesses. Increased levels of adrenaline and endorphins from the victories whether they are large or small can be related to an increase in positivity in the student. This can be only beneficial to a student's well-being. Such heightened positivity also increases the yearning in the student for more knowledge, which can only be a good thing. Fencing, done properly, is a thinking man's game.

Broadening Thought Processes

Fencing broadens the thought processes. What? Yes. Fencing allows you to think about things from different perspectives rather than thinking about things only from a single perspective. The primary source for this in fencing is in tactical thinking. Each opponent is a tactical puzzle and you must solve that puzzle. One way to do this is to figure out what they are going to do against you. This same process can be applied outside of fencing to allow you a different point of view on all sorts of things, and not just arguments.

Similarly the idea of awareness comes from a similar source. While fencing, you do not have time to check around you, but you become familiar with things around you, including your opponent's position. This can also be useful in other situations. This awareness can be applied to situations outside of fencing also, and not just finding your keys in the dark.

Not only can fencing teach you about these things, but it can also teach you about problem-solving. The obvious one is in dealing with an opponent, as above. This is a purely tactical idea, which can be applied to all sorts of other situations, but it can also apply to us and our own problems. We can look at different ways to get around problems that we all have as opponents, and thus look at ways to defeat them.

Increased Capacity for Thought

Next we move on to the idea of the increased capacity for thought. Once again, I am going to expect people to look at their screens incredulously. A fencer who looks at fencing as more than just a game of physical actions performed can really miss out. The other fencer who is willing to read and learn more can open a door to a much wider world where there are more possibilities than they ever realised, this fencer has a true relationship with the swordsmen of the past.

Most of the time, when fencing manuals are read, the first parts are skipped over for the "good" parts, the parts where the action starts. The problem is that in these earlier parts of the manuals you will find the author's thought processes, what he was actually thinking as he was assembling the manual. This can lead you into the reasons why he produced the manual and thus the reasons why or why not certain techniques may or may not be present. Our two English Gentlemen George Silver and Joeseph Swetnam are perfect examples of this.

As martial artists carrying weapons the concept of ethics must come up somewhere along the line, and thus must come up in the thought process. For many, as soon as they have done the safety brief they think they are done, but it should stretch further than there. We are carrying weapons, we are delivering blows and thrusts which have the potential to do serious damage and even kill. The concept of ethics is vital. In carrying any sort of weapon, you have a responsibility to others, and you also have a responsibility to yourself. This actually goes for all martial artists and all weapons. Any time either is seen in the media in a negative way, it is a black mark against us all.

CONCLUSION: THE CULTIVATION OF VIRTUE

Most of all the virtues which have been discussed must be cultivated. They cannot just grow on their own. We must teach patience, we must teach honour. These virtues are gained through teaching and combat. Sure some of the thought processes can be learnt through the student engaging in reading but we must all teach them also. "But I am not a teacher/trainer/master." It doesn't matter. How you act, what you do, and what you say, will inform newer students and people around them how they should act, and there is always someone newer than you.

The Renaissance period, through which we find many of our sources for rapier and longsword combat, was the time of Humanism and Humanistic thought. This is of great benefit to us. It is because these thoughts are imprinted in the pages of the manuals. You will find these thoughts in the so-called "boring" bits at the beginning of the manuals. Humanistic thought believes in the capacity for the individual to grow and become something better, and it is something which we need to embrace, regardless of in which particular period our particular weapon preference is found.

The virtues of honour and the Gentleman or Gentle-woman (Yes, an anachronism) need to be emphasised. We need to find the highest standards found here and push these to the limit and beyond. We need to push these ideas and make them our own and present ourselves as we would wish ourselves always to be seen. I believe that once we have done this then we will truly be on the way to performing our Arts as the Masters we so dearly cling to would have, and then we will truly find that the virtues gained from swordsmanship are vast, and beyond anything we thought possible.

Time and Distance

INTRODUCTION

The article which follows is about Time and Distance as will be noted by the title, will be a discussion about these concepts and will examine the various elements involved in each of them. First the importance of these concepts to fencing will be discussed. Along with an important realisation about them that must be highlighted to understand them properly. Following this will be a discussion of each one of the concepts in some detail so that each one of the parts of Time and Distance can be understood.

KEY CONCEPTS

Time and Distance are key concepts in fencing and indeed all martial arts. Any form of martial art which involves the engagement of two combatants with one another will involve elements of Time and Distance. They are so important that they should be included in some way in every lesson that is taught in fencing. They are also important to the development of the fencer as without them their understanding of what they are doing will be severely limited.

Only with a complete understanding of these concepts and how they apply to fencing will the fencer be able to excel. One of the most important realisations of these concepts is that they are relative and not concrete. This means that they cannot be measured in increments of seconds for time or metres or feet and inches for distance.

TIME

Time is also known as *tempo*, but in many ways these two terms are interchangeable, so when one is spoken about so is the other. A *tempo* is an action, but it is discussed relative to the movements of the individual and the opponent. This is important as often Time is discussed only with the movement of the individual. It is important that the movements of the opponent must also be taken into account to understand this principle completely.

Efficient

It was stated by di Grassi that every movement is accomplished in Time. What he is stating is that each movement takes time. This is a basic understanding of the concept. What most do not take into account is that he is also pointing towards efficiency of action that an efficient action takes less time than a less efficient one, but it fails to bring to light that it is not only movement that must be taken into account but stillness as well.

Aristotelian Time

A motion of stillness or the lack of movement is also a tempo; thus when counting the tempos it is important that an action must be completed and there is a stillness there. For example, the parry and riposte are counted as such, there is one tempo for the start of the movement, a stillness; there is a tempo involved in the action of the parry, a movement; there is a tempo in the completion of the parry, a stillness. There is a tempo involved in the beginning movement of the riposte, a movement; and finally a tempo in the completion of the riposte; a stillness. In this there will be counted five tempos used. This method of counting the stillness as well as the movement is an Aristotelian method of counting the tempos.

Timing

Time is a concept, Timing is the action performed in relation to an opponent. In this it must be noted that while time describes all actions in fencing, Timing discusses the actions of fencing in relation to an opponent's actions. It is vital that both of these are understood. Time is the overall concept but, Timing is also necessary as it describes the movements in action against an opponent who is also moving. With regard to this Time must be understood as a concept, while Timing must be felt while fencing against an opponent.

Dui Tempo

There are some elements that must be understood with regard to Time for it to be completely understood. In general for the starting student most of their actions as described by the teacher will be completed in *dui tempo*, or double time. This means that they will be encouraged to make a solid defence before attempting to make any sort of counter against their opponent. This ensures that the combatant is safe from their opponent's attack before any counter is made.

Stesso Tempo

Stesso tempo, often called single time, literally means "same time". This is an action which combines the action of defence and counter-attack in a single motion, hence often being referred to as single time. This motion is often developed from the smooth motion of a fencer who knows *dui tempo* well and is able to combine the two actions into a single one. What is important with regard to this concept is that there's a defence made, but it is done in combination with the counter-offensive action.

Contra-tempo

Contra-tempo, means against time. This means that an attack is launched when the fencer should be parrying the opponent's attack. What is important in this particular concept is that the attack is not launched without any concept of defence, the defence is usually ensured by displacement of the body or the blade engagement with the opponent. Without this defence in place it would be highly likely that both fencers will be struck.

Mezzo tempo

Mezzo tempo, or half time, is one of the more difficult concepts to understand. What it means is that an action is performed in the middle of the opponent's action to counter it. This is often confused with *contra-tempo*. The most common action performed in *mezzo tempo* is an attack to the opponent's hand or arm as it is moved forward in the attack, a stop hit to this part of the body. This effectively counters the opponent's attack before it is completed. This is the primary goal of the *mezzo tempo* action, to arrest the action of the opponent before it is completed. It also includes a stop it to the head or body as this also arrests the action of the opponent.

Comparisons

The slowest form of time is *dui tempo* as more tempos are spent in its action, but it is also the safest from the straight attack. *Stesso tempo* is highly effective when used and very fast as it uses very few tempos in its execution. The same could be said of *contra-tempo* as a similar action is often being performed when compared to *stesso tempo*. Of the times *mezzo tempo* is actually the fastest as it counters the opponent's action before it is allowed to be completed, this in half time. What needs to be taken into account with regard to these concepts is how they affect fencing and how each of them uses time to their advantage, and what each advantage gains the opponent. This is one of the keys to developing Timing.

Time of the Hand and Foot

With regard to Time there is also the concept of the Time of the Hand and the Time of the Foot, these being the two most dominant. The Time of the Hand is any movement involving the use of the hand or the arm. The Time of the Foot is any movement of the feet. This also includes the body, which follows the feet.

The Time of the Hand is faster than the Time of the Foot, and this needs to be taken into account. The hand should always be moved before the foot, this sounds contradictory to the speeds which have been described, but it is important that the defence or offence of the weapon is in place before the foot moves the body. This is most important in the lunge. If the foot is moved forward first the body is presented as a target. If the hand is moved forward first then a threat is aimed at the opponent, which they must deal with before being able to attack. The same things apply in defence. A parry should be made before a retreat is made to control the opponent's weapon for the same reason that the hand is moved first in the lunge.

DISTANCE

Distance, also known as measure or *misura*, these terms are interchangeable and as with Time it is a relative measurement which is dependent on the movements of both the individual and the opponent. Both of the combatants can and often do affect the measure. Every movement of the fencers either increases or decreases the measure. If only one moves then the measure is changed, if both move the measure may or may not be changed. It is the movement of the body through the use of footwork that increases or decreases measure. The choice of whether to move to increase or decrease the measure is dependent on the particular situation and the preference of the combatants.

Misura stretta and Misura larga

With regard to measure there are two main Distances which are discussed, *stretta* and *larga*, narrow and wide distance. *Misura stretta*, narrow distance, is where the combatants can reach one another by a simple extension of the arm, with or without the assistance of the body. *Misura larga*, wide distance, is where the combatants can only reach one another through the movement of the feet and the extension of the arm, with or without the assistance of body movement. These are two important concepts as they are integrally involved in the motions of fencing. Most simple attacks will be made at the *misura stretta* where a simple thrust is sufficient to strike the opponent, whereas more complex actions are required for use of an attack at *misura larga*. A fencer's on guard position should be adopted at the *misura larga* because the opponent requires foot movement to attack and this is more easily visible than a simple hand movement. This is related to the Time of the Hand and Foot which were discussed previously. Essentially, *misura larga* is at the Time of the Foot whereas *misura stretta* is all at the Time of the Hand.

Closer and Further

Two Distances which are often not discussed as much as narrow and wide distance are close distance and out of distance. Close distance is a measure inside that of *misura stretta*, while out of distance is a distance outside that of *misura larga*. Close distance is often the result of two combatants closing with one another while at *misura stretta*, while out of distance is usually the result of one of the combatants retreating while at *misura larga*.

Close distance as described is referred to by Capo Ferro as extra narrow distance or *misura strettissima* and is most often used for the execution of the *mezzo tempo* attack as described above, but it can also be used to refer to the situation as described above. Out of distance or *fuori misura*, is where the fencers cannot reach one another even with the use of a foot movement.

Distance Preference

Some fencers may have a preference for a particular distance. This is often based on where they feel that they can gain the greatest advantage out of the situation. This consideration should be made dependent on the opponent rather than any personal preference. It would be foolish to close with an opponent who prefers to fight close, and it would be foolish to stay at range with an opponent who prefers that distance. With regard to this any preference for distance can actually limit the fencer, in all cases the fencer should be adept at using distance to their advantage and use the distance which is most appropriate to the situation and opponent.

CONCEPTS INTERTWINED

Just as Time is affected by Distance, so too is Distance affected by Time; at the *misura stretta* all actions are at the Time of the Hand, this makes for very fast movements and often single tempos being used. At *misura larga* actions are at the Time of the Foot, and thus two tempos are required for the effective use of an action, one of the foot and one of the hand to reach the opponent. At *misura strettissima*, half tempo actions are used this can make for a very messy situation if the combatants are struggling with one another. In general, when combatants are at *fuori misura* actions are much to slow to be performed against the opponent due to the time taken to close the distance. These examples describe the important relationship between the two concepts, and it must be realised that they should not be talked about separately as they are so intertwined.

CONCLUSION

Time and Distance are two concepts without which a true understanding of fencing is not possible. They should be integrated into every lesson that is taught by the teacher so that the students get used to using the terms and how they affect fencing. It is important that the concepts which have been presented are understood not only alone but also in association with one another. Time and Distance are very much intertwined and to discuss one means discussing the other. More than understanding the concepts the fencer must also be able to apply these and understand where they are present while actually fencing. This develops a feeling for the concepts while they are in motion and with this feeling the fencer will have a great advantage over an opponent who does not understand them and cannot feel them in motion.

Tactics in Fencing

INTRODUCTION

> *"Fencing is a competitive sport. The will-power and the intelligence of the opponent have to be reckoned with in it. In such a sport tactics, stratagems have equal weight and an equal role with technique. One without the other is worth nothing. The fencer's performance cannot be productive, however brilliant the development of his technical skill, if he is utterly lacking in tactical imagination,"*
>
> (Beke and Polgár, 1963:29)

The title of this article, as you can see above is tactics in fencing. This is a very important consideration for all fencers. Some of this was discussed in a previous article about the thinking game. This article will be a more in-depth discussion of fencing tactics and the details associated with them. The first thing to examine in this discussion is to see exactly what fencing tactics means.

MEANING

> *"The process of fencing is your blueprint for producing touches. It is the combining of the mental and physical components of fencing into an effective whole."*
> (Evangelista, 2000:88)

As stated by Evangelista (2000) above tactics is a part of the process of fencing and provides the blueprint of how you may strike your opponent, of course without being struck yourself. It is tactics which makes fencing a thinker's game as it involves the fencer examining the situation, evaluating what is going on, formulating a solution for the situation, and then acting on it. This involves a level of thought by the fencer to perform. Fencing tactics is more than just reaction, they are planned actions and show the difference between the thinking fencer and those who just react to the actions of the opponent.

> *"Strategy is how you relate to your opponent ... This is the science of fencing. How successful you are in strategy will underscore your effectiveness as a fencer. A good strategic game adds much depth and variety to your fencing."*
> (Evangelista, 2000:192)

Tactics demonstrates and shows the relationship between the actions of the fencer and the opponent. Not only do your tactics need to take into account what you want to do, but it also must take into account how your opponent will respond to your actions. Your tactics are answers to the questions posed by the opponent in the actions that they perform against you. These answers are made on the basis of the evidence supplied by the actions of the opponent.

> *"Tactics are the brainwork of fencing; they are based upon observation and analysis of the opponent and upon intelligent choices of actions against him."*
> (Palffy-Alpar, 1967:47)

MORE BRAINS

There are tactics in fencing at all levels, from the purely responsive actions of the physical fencer to the complex and detailed actions of the thinking fencer in response to the opponent. The level of thinking behind the actions defines where in this scale the actions of the fencer are positioned. We need to strive for the higher end of this scale so that we are more successful in fencing, and this requires thinking, *"more than anything a good fencer has brains."* (Barth and Barth, 2003:84). This thought process supplies the preparatory material for compound actions performed by the opponent.

Any complex action performed by the fencer requires a level of thought behind it. This means evidence gathered by the fencer and used to plan a response to the opponent's actions. There are requirements to use fencing tactics and these requirements will be discussed next.

LEARN AND PRACTICE SKILLS FIRST

"This [tactical application] requires cool judgement, anticipation, opportunism, bluff and counter-bluff and the ability to think at least on move ahead, combined with courage and controlled reaction of muscles and limbs which enables the fencer to carry out simple or complex movements of his weapon as required by the situation at any given moment."

(De Beaumont, 1960:197)

The first requirement for fencing tactics is the ability to perform the actions required. This means that the fencer needs to learn the fencing skills and gain technical competence in them before he can perform them at will, on demand. Without the technical ability firmly in place, the fencer can see what he wants to do, can plan ahead to perform it, but if he does not have the technical skills to perform the action, then the process is a waste of time. This highlights the importance of practicing the fencing skills so that they can be called upon to be used at a moment's notice. Of course this is the first requirement, to add to this, there are others.

THINK!

"A fencer poor in tactical thinking is like a well-trained army with a poor general, lacking imaginative leadership."

(Beke and Polgár, 1963:30)

What is being spoken about here is simply the ability to think, the use of the fencer's brain. It is necessary for the fencer to be able to use their brain to use tactics and fence well. The purely physical fencer can do quite well, but will be defeated most often by the fencer who has progressed past the physical and into the mental side of fencing.

The ability to think while fencing enables you to use the information that you gain from your opponent to plan how you will deal with him, in other words form tactics. Without the thought process in action tactics can only be used at their most basic, reactive level. In combination with raw intellectual power, there is more. There psychological aspects which are involved in fencing as well and these abilities are also necessary.

"Among the psychological qualities we must also emphasize diligence and will-power. The development of these ensures that the physical and psychological inhibitions arising in a competitive fencer can be overcome."

(Beke and Polgár, 1963:30)

DILIGENCE

Diligence is being attentive to what is going on. A diligent student can overcome almost any obstacle which is placed in their path. Only the diligent student of fencing will really grasp what fencing is all about and be able to see the importance of the skills that are being learnt. A fencer with diligence can utilise those skills which they are most proficient at and reduce the importance of those skills which they are not so talented at, but they need to be aware of this. Tactically the student needs to be diligent to pay attention to all which is going on around them and to be aware of these things so that they can act on them. The thinking process is enhanced by willpower as it is what drives us to succeed where we may fail.

WILLPOWER

> "Will-power, with which we can overcome the physical and psychological inhibitions is more important in fencing than physical dexterity and flexibility, because psychological inhibitions play a major role in fencing."
> (Beke and Polgár, 1963:31)

Willpower is of great importance to fencing not only for the sake of tactics but to drive us to succeed. This is most important in those situations where one fencer is clearly more experienced than the other. Where the less experienced combatant has the willpower he can through striving and using his skill actually overcome the opponent. Willpower in fencing is about having the strength to fight even where the odds are not in our favour and also giving all we can to succeed.

PATIENCE

> "In life, patience is considered a virtue. In fencing, it is a necessity – both in the learning process and on the fencing strip." (Evangelista, 2000:216)

Patience is important to fencing. It takes time to develop skills and as such this requires patience on our part to take the time to learn and practice the skills so that they can be used to their full potential. With regard to tactics, patience is necessary so that we take the time to properly read the opponent and gauge their actions. Patience is also about waiting for the correct response from the opponent, or waiting for a good opening or position to act upon. If the process is rushed the tactics may not be formulated properly and this will lead into hasty decisions and bad tactical choices.

DO NOTHING WHICH IS OF NO USE

> "Use your brain. Gauge your actions. See if they are drawing the desired response out of your opponent. If what you are doing produces nothing, stop doing it!" (Evangelista, 2000:97)

To use tactics in fencing you must be able to observe, read and predict what the opponent will do. The observation portion of this is the first part of the process, taking in what you can see of the opponent. This is the simplest form of reading the opponent. The next part of the process is examining what is reading the opponent which involves examining not only what you can see but also the responses the opponent gives to your actions and also what you can feel through the use of *sentiment du fer* or *senso di ferro*. All of these elements are important. Once you have gained the information about the opponent, this needs to be applied logically to predict what the opponent will do. It is from all of these elements that tactics are based, and each element is important to the process.

ACT WITH PURPOSE

There are tactics which are of use and there are tactics which are of no use. It is the former that we should be aiming for as fencers and the latter that we should be avoiding at all costs. Each action that is performed must have a purpose. The purpose may be to see the reaction of the opponent or much simpler being a final blow in the tactical approach. It is the purpose behind the action which is important. A lack of purpose means the usage of energy where it is not used fruitfully against the opponent, and also wasted effort, this can lead to downfall and defeat at the hands of the opponent. The action should be thought about before it is performed and its purpose known before it is performed. No action should be performed without a purpose in mind.

TACTICAL FAILURE

The failure of a tactic used against the opponent supplies information, even if this information is as simple as that the approach did not work. The failures should be examined to see where the fault lies so that a reason for their failure is realised. A failed tactic should not be used against the same opponent again straight after the tactic has failed. It may be used again later in the bout, but only if the evidence serves that the tactic may work the second time. A tactic should not be used a third time, especially if it has failed before.

TACTICAL APPROACH

The idea of fencing is to dominate the opponent and therefore the bout. This should be the aim of the tactics which are created there should be no other reason behind them. If you can dominate the opponent this is achieved through the use of effective tactics. How to dominate the opponent is revealed in the information gained from reading the opponent and this can tell us when and how to attack the opponent. The timing and placement of the attack must be based upon the information gained about the opponent for it to succeed.

THREE STEP PROCESS

The three step approach to fencing tactics needs to happen, and does happen, even if you do not realise it. The simplest tactic, a hole in the opponent's defence is observed, the weapon is brought on-line and the thrust is made. This is a very simple example of the process in action. In more advanced forms of the process there is a great more detail in the process. The detail is what creates the more complex tactical approaches. The three step process is actually missing a step and that is one which comes after the execution and that is evaluation. It is necessary to see whether the tactic worked against the opponent. This is important so that a failed tactic is not repeated if the same evidence is presented. In some ways this can also be added to the analysis part of the approach where the process is used for a second, or further, approach to the opponent.

Observe
The first part of the process is analysis where the opponent is observed and information is gained about the opponent. This information is analysed to find where the opponent is weak and what approach would be best against the opponent. This analysis process must be detailed so that the best planning may be made.

Prepare
The preparation phase of the process is preparing for the approach to the opponent and preparing for using the tactic against the opponent. The last part of this process is getting in the correct position for the first action to be performed.

Execute and Evaluate
The execution part of the process is putting the tactic into action against the opponent. This must be performed correctly for the tactic to be effective. This is the most active part of the process. Finally there is the evaluation to find the final outcome to the use of the tactic against the opponent. This part of the process is important as it tells us what the result of the tactic was and how effective it was against the opponent. This part of the process should lead to the analysis part of the next tactical approach used against the opponent.

CONCLUSION
While this article gave no specific details about individual fencing tactics, this article focussed on the process and requirements for fencing tactics to be used along with other details of a similar nature. These founding principles are those upon which fencing tactics should be based. There are a different tactics for different approaches for different opponents. This means that if a person was to write about tactics specifically much would have to be taken into account. This would mean that a person could write a great deal on the subject, but it is more important for us to be able to use the process of developing fencing tactics so that it can be used against all the opponents that we may face.

Motivation and Fencing

INTRODUCTION
We all have our own reasons for taking up fencing in the first place. For some we have seen something in the media and thought it would be cool to do it. For some we have been influenced by friends and family who fence and have decided to fence ourselves. For others we were looking for a pastime that would last a long time, and for others it is a simple search for the secrets of swordplay in all its forms. Whatever your reason for learning to fence in the first place, it will become a factor in your motivation to continue.

Your fencing instructor or teacher will attempt to keep you motivated by introducing new skills for you to learn and encouraging you, but when it comes down to it, the motivation must become internalised if you want to really get anywhere. You need to decide where fencing sits in your priorities and this will decide how much energy you will be willing to put in.

WHAT DO YOU DO?

Do your lessons end at the end of your training session, or do you do extra research? Do you practice alone at home to improve your skill at and understanding of the things you have learnt at the lesson? Do you do extra research into things related to fencing to understand more of what is out there? All of these things relate to personal motivation. If you are truly motivated, you should have answered "Yes" to all of the questions. If you really want to succeed in fencing these things are the key and they are requiring motivation on your part. Your teacher will have information about these things and can give you direction, but in the end it is up to you. Personal motivation in fencing is expressed not only in seeking the things which I have mentioned above but also in simple things. Simple things such as turning up to your practice before it starts so that you are prepared to go when the practice starts, making sure that all of your equipment is present at the training session, making sure that all of your equipment is in good working order, finally, and a big one is being at the training session and being prepared and interested in learning. All of these things express a level of personal motivation and it will be noticed by your teacher.

TEACHERS CAN *ASSIST*

Your teacher will attempt to supply some motivation to you by attempting to keep the training sessions interesting and encouraging you when you do well. This support is much easier to give where the student is personally motivated also. Where the students are less motivated, the teacher is less likely to give extra information and classes as in many ways the teacher's interest in teaching the students is dependent on their interest in learning. If there is no interest, why should the teacher bother? If you want interesting lessons where you can get the maximum benefit you must understand that your interest is one of the keys to this. If you turn up late, don't have the right equipment, show little interest, distract other students, or similar things, the teacher will notice. This will affect what sort of classes you will get, especially in the future.

YOUR SUCCESSES

Your success in fencing is up to you. You do the work. You learn the skills. You fight the bouts. You put the skills into practice. There is only so much that the teacher can do. So, what happens if the teacher is unavailable for a training session? Do you go home? Do you find something else to do? Or do you go out and practice the skills that you have already learnt with other students to improve them? This is a choice and displays personal motivation, or a lack of it. The teacher should not have to be there for you to do drills in things that you have already learnt. Getting other students out on the field and practicing skills with them demonstrates interest and motivation on your part and will be noticed by the teacher. You need to consider what you are doing to further your fencing career.

CONCLUSION

In the end, success in fencing requires personal motivation. Your teacher can teach you the skills and give you the information, but it is you who puts them into practice. You need to be willing to put in the effort if you want to get anywhere with any form of fencing. Drills can be boring, but in the end the benefits will show. Go out seek information, seek new skills, and improve the ones you already have, but remember in the end it is all up to you.

afencersramblings.blogspot.com

Fencing and Dedication to the Art... Too Much to Ask?

INTRODUCTION

In all our endeavours we must sit back and have a look at where we are going and where we want to go. It is the same with fencing, and it doesn't matter which form of fencing you are talking about. We need to have a look at our motivations and where we want to go, but also what this will require of all of us as students and teachers. The question that is raised here is our level of dedication to the Art.

The following article will address this particular facet of the Art that we have all chosen to pursue and ask just how dedicated we really are to it. Is it too much to ask for our students and teachers to be dedicated to what they are doing? What does it mean to be dedicated? It will also investigate the idea of whether or not it is too much to ask a student or teacher to be dedicated to what they are doing. First there is the question of a meaning to the word "dedication".

MEANING

Dedication: "the willingness to give a lot of time and energy to something because it is important:" [19]

First of all it is important to figure out what is meant by "dedication". There is a dictionary definition above, but while this one does explain some, it gives no "real world" examples or explanation, as most do not. There are many grades of this particular word and many different interpretations that may be used.

For some dedication brings ideas about travelling vast distances in horrible weather to get somewhere. For others it simply means that they always put their mind to a single task. With regard to fencing and this discussion, there is a mid-point between these two.

Dedication means putting in the effort to get somewhere and use the teaching that the teacher has supplied. It is also about being regular to training and putting in the effort while being present at the training session. Sure, it is understood that things do not always go the way that they are supposed to. Injuries and illnesses will hamper the ability of the fencer, but aside from these there are certain things that are expected of the student.

Most of the things that people are dedicated to in the modern world are those things which are most relevant to their existence. For example, people go to work each day and do what they need to do because this is relevant to their existence. So, with this in mind, could the fencer be on the wrong track, as skill with a sword in the modern world is not particularly relevant? Can this be used as a valid reason for the student to be slack, or the teacher to not give the students their full attention? This is clearly not the case. If the person has decided that fencing is what they need to do, and it is not just another hobby, then a certain level of dedication should be able to be expected.

---

19 https://dictionary.cambridge.org/dictionary/english/dedication

NEEDS AND WANTS

Next we have the question of needs and wants. Do you want to fence, or do you need to fence? There is a distinct difference between the two. A person who merely wants to fence is stating that it is something which is not really necessary to them; a person who needs to fence is stating that it is something that they cannot do without. To be dedicated to fencing you have to need to fence. It has to be so much a part of what you are and what you do that its absence is felt in a very deep manner. This will determine your willingness to go out of your way to do things to enhance your fencing, and follow the path you have chosen.

THE SPIRIT OF FENCING

The Spirit of Fencing is something that we must ask ourselves whether we have or not. This is about whether the Art is within us and has been made a part of us or whether it is just another pastime that we do. This encompasses many questions that we must ask ourselves whether or not the spirit of fencing is within us or not.

Is fencing just another game or is it something else? Could you just as well be playing tennis or doing some other hobby? This is an important question as it tells us just how far we are willing to go with what we are doing. This also questions the level of thinking we have toward fencing, is it just something that we like doing or something that is more important to us than that? If we are truly dedicated to the Art then nothing will be able to take its place, and nothing will fill the hole that is left by the absence of fencing. For those who are truly dedicated to what they are doing fencing is something that cannot be put down and picked up, it must be held on to and utilised and followed.

LEARNING

We need to have a close look at the actual fencing that we do, and how we achieve the end that we seek. Winning is nice and is something which should be considered, but you need to ask yourself if the final result is more important than how you got there. Is it better to win by any means necessary, or is it better to stick to our form and win using skill and style? This is a question of dedication to what we are doing.

Learning to fence is hard and winning by the use of pure skills and techniques looks hard in the beginning, but it will improve your fencing overall. Only a fencer who is dedicated to what they are doing will spend the time to ensure that they win using skill and not brute force or some trick. This leads well into the subject of learning and how important it is to the process and our level of dedication to the art.

Learning is important to progressing in the Art, and it is something that we need to be dedicated to progress fully. It is important that we must always be learning to progress, and learning to improve our fencing. The only way to progress is to keep learning, while this can be a more difficult process as we progress in skill, there is always something new to learn and dedication to this process must be made if we truly want to excel in out Art. It is important that we take the opportunity to learn from anyone who is willing to teach us something, a different point of view is always useful. This is the case even across the various disciplines, and this should not be underestimated. Even our students can teach us something, even if it is just a different point of view. This learning process does take dedication, and remembering why we are there and what we are doing.

afencersramblings.blogspot.com

EXPECTATIONS

Expectations are something which we have put on us and also are personally placed. The athletically gifted individual has a great advantage over someone who is not so gifted, it could be said that this person has a lot of potential. The same could be said of a person who picks skills up quickly and is able to put them into practice. Both of these people would be expected to do well, but only if they are willing to put in the work. Regardless of a student's potential, the student still needs to be putting in the same amount of effort as the student with less potential.

The expectation of a teacher is for the student to come along to classes regularly and participate to their fullest capacity. The student's expectation is that the teacher will come along prepared to teach and give the students their full attention. Aside from this there are other expectations which can be present such as the expectation that both the student and teacher will do things "out of class" to further themselves. Unless both the student and the teacher meet these simple expectations, how can they be seen to be dedicated to what they are doing?

Is fencing just another hobby, or is it something more? Other hobbies expect that a person participating will put in a certain amount of time and effort for the person participating to achieve anything. The same can be said for fencing. Of course it can also be said that there are those hobbies which have much lower expectations of the person, but there are also those which have much higher ones also. The question that the fencer has to ask is whether or not fencing is just another hobby or whether it is something that he or she truly wants to be dedicated to. It can be easily expected that the more dedicated a person is and the more effort put in, the more benefit the person will get.

PROGRESSION

Progression is important and the amount of progression in a period of time is actually irrelevant. We must be dedicated to progression to progress. If we are not we stagnate. Progression itself needs dedication also to push us past those times where the progression is hard.

Everyone hits plateaus in their progression, in fencing, in music, and in most pursuits. It is important to stay dedicated and work through this particular phase to progress. The progression may seem slow at these times, but it is important that we stick with the process. With regard to plateaus it will be noted that the early stages the plateaus are infrequent and short, as we progress and our skill level increases, these plateaus will become more frequent and longer. We must be dedicated enough to push through these periods in order to continue to progress. This will take a great deal of time and patience.

In the question of measuring progression there are different approaches. One is a physical evaluation based upon wins and results of encounters; the other is a more internal process which is based upon the increase of knowledge and its expression. The first one is what often drives sport fencers and those who are more interested in winning than the pursuit of the Art.

The second gives a much broader playing field and progression can be noted in the form of the skill presented and the ability of the fencer to achieve their goal through the use of their skills. This enables the fencer to see progression in different places, from the performance of a skill against an opponent, to the realisation of a concept or the application of a piece of fencing theory. The measurement of success and progression is important.

PROGRAM OF PROGRESSION

Progression is necessary as has been stated, but how it is achieved is also important. To progress we must stay dedicated to the Art which we are learning. This means progressing through the lessons, drills and bouts associated in a methodical manner. A training program for yourself will help in this particular aspect so you can see where you are going. This needs to be based on a set of goals, short term, and long term ones as well. Once you achieve a particular goal, it needs to be recognised in proportion. This is important as it recognises the successes that you have had. It is important to push through those lessons which seem difficult and those times where progression is not immediately evident. These are the times where your dedication will be tested. If you can push through this you will achieve a much greater result than if you give up and get distracted part way through.

EXPRESSIONS

Dedication or a lack of dedication is expressed in many ways. Some of these expressions are very subtle and some are quite overt. The first and most overt expression of dedication is attendance. A person who attends all the training sessions and tournaments that they can get their hands on is a person who is clearly dedicated to learning and performance of their Art. A person who is less frequent at training and tournaments may display a much lower level of dedication to the Art that they have chosen to pursue.

Mere attendance is not the only method of expression, there is also the performance at these training sessions. A person who just hangs around and talks at training sessions and only participates to the minimum amount even though they are attending training sessions is clearly less motivated than the person who engages in these sessions to their full capacity. As for tournaments, it cannot be expected that a fencer will win every tournament that they enter into, as this is reliant on many different things, but if they do not do their best at the tournament and fight their hardest and this will be seen.

Another expression of dedication can be seen in the fencer's equipment. If the fencer's gear is left in a state of disrepair or if they forget parts of their equipment, then it is clear that they are not as dedicated to what they are doing as a person who turns up with their gear in good working order, and all present. This also goes for the acquisition of equipment to use at tournaments and training sessions. A person who is constantly borrowing gear from other students or the fencing school rather than going out and buying their own equipment is clearly less dedicated than the person who obtains their own equipment at the first chance that they are able to.

Dedication can also be seen in the preparation for lessons; this has physical and psychological elements which are all important in the person's level of dedication to fencing. Part of the preparation for a lesson is ensuring that all the appropriate gear is in good working order and is present and packed before leaving for the lesson. Forgetting some part of the equipment shows a lack of dedication as this should have been checked before the person left for the lesson, and ensured that the gear is in good working order.

ATTITUDE

Next to look at are less overtly expressed elements in the preparation and attendance at training sessions and tournaments. Attitude has a great part to play in the student's ability to learn and also the way that they approach the lessons and tournaments. If they have the attitude that they have already learnt what they need to learn, then it is less likely that they will pay close attention to the class being taught.

Ego is an element which needs to be controlled and kept in check; this was already discussed in one of the other articles but relates very much to dedication. If the ego is used to fence rather than the skills learnt, this says something about the fencer, and alludes to their level of dedication to the learning process and thus the Art overall. Obviously to participate completely in the lessons, a person needs to have the willingness to learn what the teacher is imparting at the lessons. The willingness to learn is expressed in how they approach the lessons themselves, but this is something which starts before the lesson starts. This willingness needs to be enshrined in the individual before they leave for the lesson, and is one of the most important elements. It relates very much back to the question of attitude and ego.

CONCLUSION

The dedication to the Art of fence is something that each person needs to consider on their own part and to what level they are truly dedicated to the Art that they have chosen. This dedication will be expressed in many ways and it is up to the individual to ensure that this dedication is enhanced to gain the greatest benefit from the Art. Dedication will determine how far we will be able to go more than pure physical ability. Skills can be learnt. Concepts can be learnt. Theory can be learnt, but the fencer has to be willing to put in the hard work that is required to gain these things and this will take dedication. It is dedication that will see us through the hard parts of the fencing process, and only dedication that will assist us to surmount the largest obstacles in our path. As a fencer, dedication is something that we must all consider personally as it will determine how far we are able to progress within the Art.

So it comes to the time where the question must be asked, is dedication too much to be asked of the fencer in the modern world? Or is dedication more of a personal thing? Dedication is clearly related to the amount of effort a person is willing to put into a thing, thus if the person is willing to put in the effort then they could be considered to be dedicated. Each fencer needs to ask themselves, how dedicated am I really to what I am doing? How much effort am I willing to put in to get what I want out of this? Sure, there will be those people with their own expectations of what a dedicated fencer will or will not do, but it is up to the individual. Regardless of the potential of the individual, with the right level of dedication the fencer has the potential to do well.

The Way Forward...

INTRODUCTION

In studying the western martial arts many of us tend to blunder a bit of our way through, letting chance guide our way from one discovery of a new manual to the next. For the western martial arts to have a real future, this future needs some real consideration as to where we are going and the direction or directions in which we are heading in. We need to consider what our schools are doing and what they are creating in the process and where this fits into the scheme of things, without this direction, we will continue to blunder through, with successes and failures along the way, but ultimately it will lead to a "boom and bust" kind of future which has been seen already. The problem is that if certain people in our society have their way, we may not recover from the "bust".

TWO WAYS FORWARD

In my view I see two ways forward, following the manuals and recreating them as they are, and taking what we can from the manuals applying these techniques and developing our own ways. In some ways this is like the emergence of eastern martial arts in the 70's and 80's. We need to get on board with this emergence and enthusiasm and take hold of it to ensure that western martial arts can take a hold in a similar manner that eastern martial arts did. From the point of view of the two methods what needs to be realised by all is that both approaches have their benefits and issues and that both sides need to be accepted.

HISTORICAL EUROPEAN MARTIAL ARTS

The first is an historical recreation of skills expressed by previous masters which keeps the examination of period masters alive and the history associated. This method is what could be most closely called HEMA as it takes the historical works of the masters and then recreates them as close as possible to how they are presented in the treatises which were left behind. The practitioners of this method tend to focus on the methods and nomenclature of single schools or geographical regions in their investigations. These investigators use the core principles which are presented in the treatises and also the other methods and apply them as they are presented in the treatises to situations which are presented to them.

The problem with this method for some is that it tends to feel somewhat artificial in that the methods do not seem to apply to what occurs when practitioners cross weapons in the current period. For others the problem is that some get so obsessed about what is said in the manual that they refuse to accept anything which is not present in one of the manuals and thus refuse to accept new ideas. The benefit of this method is that it is the recreation of an actual period martial art as it is depicted in a manual from when it was used and that most of the secrets are present in the manual. Another thing is that the information which is discovered by this approach often fuels the second approach with new ideas and new approaches tactically and technically.

OF WORDS...

Before more is said, HEMA and WMA have been for a long time used to mean the same thing. For myself, there are two different things which are similar, but do things differently. The HEMA groups approach things with the historical in mind, looking at manuals and treatises using them and following what is written in them. The WMA groups have what could be termed a more bio-mechanical or "practical" point of view. They examine the manuals and treatises for what works to be more efficient and effective in the use of the sword. This is the difference that I draw between the two and how I determine the difference in the two ways forward.

WESTERN MARTIAL ARTS

The second approach uses manuals but in a different manner taking core principles and techniques to enhance new approaches. This is more focussed towards the WMA approach and thus a much more practical one. The focus of the practitioner here is to become more efficient and effective at using his weapon, but the expression of this is seen in a very practical sense. For the most part these schools will often use a manual to the point of finding new techniques to make them more effective in what they already know, but not to learn an entire system. The investigations are focussed toward how the techniques apply as applied to an opponent before them.

The problem with this method is that techniques tend to get selected from various manuals and from various regions meaning they do not necessarily hang together meaning that there is no real system taught, core principles but no real system. The lack of a real system means that they often lack longevity. There is little understanding of the historical foundation of the weapons and therefore little understanding of how the weapons actually worked. The advantage of this method is that its core principles are easily learnt and that there is always something to learn. These groups do not tend to get bogged down with nomenclature and other issues which can cause problems in their HEMA brethren.

CONCLUSION

What is important in this is that both approaches need to be encouraged as each one fuels the other. The first approach finds period manuals and investigates them to see how the techniques work and the second uses the techniques and encourages further investigation. In both approaches the investigation needs to be a broad overlook, not narrowing into a singular school or approach. The only way for all to benefit is for all to share with one another and thus benefit all.

For HEMA and WMA to survive they must work together and fuel themselves off one another and also elements of popular culture which allow them to. Such elements as "Game of Thrones" and other sword-wielding shows excite the public and will draw people to different groups and it is up to those groups to show them what they have got. If they are not interested in what you have got, show them to another group, not away. Another person in another group, HEMA or WMA is of benefit to both regardless of which they go into. Most of all the way forward is to support one another in our endeavours, even if it is not yours.

SECTION 7.
Teaching

What is the role of the teacher and the student in fencing?

INTRODUCTION
What follows is a discussion of the roles of the student and teacher and the relationship between them. Both of these groups of individuals have a role to play in fencing, and especially fencing training. They are actually both important to one another and it is this relationship and how sound it is that will determine how effective the training is and also the ability to excel on both parts. There is always a teacher and a student in every situation, even if periodically these roles are swapped.

TWO SIDES OF THE SAME COIN
The first thing is that both the teacher and the student have important roles to play in the training process and this cannot be ignored. The roles are two sides of the same coin. One does not happen without the other in an effective environment. A person cannot be a student without there being a teacher of some sort, and a teacher cannot be a teacher really without there being a student to teach. Now, in some instances, the student and the teacher will be the same person, but still the same applies, or the roles may swap in some groups where they are small.

One is reliant on the other. The student is reliant on the teacher to be taught what is required, but the teacher is also relying on the student to learn what is being taught so that the relationship between the two is fruitful. In this it is important both fulfil the roles that they have in their best capacity for the best outcome for the situation and the training process.

If one slacks off there is the highly likely chance that the other will slack off. This will result in a reduction in the level of learning. This is where it is best seen that they have a reciprocal relationship. If the teacher is lacking in enthusiasm for what is being taught, then the student will also slack off as they will see what is being taught as not important and also will reduce their efforts to learn what is being taught. If the student is lacking in enthusiasm for what is being taught, the teacher will recognise this and will not put in as much effort in the teaching process which will lead to a reduction in the learning. In this way it is vital that both put in the maximum amount of effort in their roles to achieve the best outcome from the training situation. This also leads on to questions of what it means to be a student or teacher in fencing.

WHAT ARE THE ROLES OF THE STUDENT AND TEACHER?

The role of the teacher is to teach. The role of the student is to learn. It is as simple as that, or is it? Does this mean that the teacher may only teach and is precluded from learning, even from the student? Does this mean that the student may only learn and is precluded from teaching? The simple answer to this is "No."

This is best seen in the situation where fencing or particular parts of fencing are being learnt alone. In this situation the individual is both student and teacher rolled into one. The individual must not only teach but also learn. Where there are two or more individuals the same applies. The teacher should also be learning, even if it is only learning how to teach better. The student must also be willing to teach, even if it is to teach the teacher a different perspective. We should all be seeking to learn at all times, and from everyone who has information to part with. The learning experience should never stop and we should never become only teachers as there is so much to learn and to do this you must be a student.

What has been discussed is the relationship between the student and the teacher. It is also important to examine what it means to be a student and what it means to be a teacher in fencing. This was a subject that was going to be left for another article, but it fits too well into the current one to be left separate. This is because to understand the roles of these two it is important to understand what it means to be a student or teacher.

What does it mean to be a teacher in fencing?

The simplest answer to this question is simply that you teach, but it must be taken further so that the complete role is understood. It is true that the teacher's primary role is to teach, but it must not stop there. The teacher must also be able to understand. Understand where the student is coming from and understand why they may be having problems. This is another place where there is a division between the teacher and the instructor. It also means that you are willing to learn to improve your ability to teach.

The learning process of the teacher is more aimed at improving what is being taught to the students, but it must not stop here. In some ways the teacher must also be able to talk with the student so that they can understand where the student is coming from and possibly assist the student in dealing with some of the problems that they may be having. For some teachers this will be limited to how this problem is associated with their fencing, for others this is not necessarily true. The important thing here is that the teacher must draw a line between where they are a friend of the student and where they are the teacher.

What does it mean to be a student in fencing?

What does it mean to be a student in fencing? The simplest answer to this is that you learn. It is true that the primary goal of the student in fencing is to learn so that they become better at their craft. To be a true student in fencing also means that you will go out and learn whatever you can from whomever you can to improve your fencing.

Every piece of information is important and every piece in its own way will assist in improving the skills and understanding of fencing overall. This means that the student should also go out and seek such information that will improve their fencing. This also means that for the true student, they will pay attention to what is being taught and approach this process with enthusiasm so that they can get the maximum benefit out of the relationship with their teacher. Being a student is also about being willing in some part to teach at some stage. A person learns a lot from teaching and this process can actually solidify what the student knows as it is important that you know something before you teach it.

CONCLUSION

Once these roles are understood then the relationship between the two can be more completely understood. It is important that both the student and the teacher completely understand what their roles is and what it means for them. The relationship between the two is of great importance and the boundaries that are set between the two must be clear so that both are able to act correctly in their roles. So that students and teachers can perform to their maximum capacity both roles must be fulfilled and performed at their maximum capacity, once this is achieved then the maximum can be gained both from the relationship and from the fencing training.

Teacher vs Instructor

INTRODUCTION

The issue of the teacher versus the instructor is one to be debated. This may be an issue for some, and a matter of semantics for others, but I think that it is something that needs to be looked at both from the teacher/instructor point of view and also the student's point of view. What I am talking about is the difference between a teacher and an instructor, and consequently teaching versus instruction.

SIMPLY PUT...

To put it simply, and in my own opinion, the difference between the two is the relationship the two have with the student. This relationship, depending on which the individual delivering the information is, will affect the method of delivery and also how the student will approach the person delivering the information and also the relationship that the two will have between one another. This will also determine whether or not the student receives the most complete information possible from the individual delivering the information.

SEMANTICS

Now first we have a look at the words, a teacher teaches, and an instructor instructs; pretty simple really. The question is which one has the most benefit for both the student and the teacher/instructor. In essence I would like to look at it this way, instruction involves the giving of a set of techniques which the student follows, the instructor says and the student does, this is the essence of instruction. It is a single path of communication from instructor to student.

Teaching differs from this; a teacher teaches the student the technique and explains what it is based upon and how it fits into fencing overall. This involves a two way form of communication something that instruction is missing. The teacher teaches and explains, the student questions, and the teacher responds giving more information and deeper insight into the techniques. This is a much deeper relationship than that between the instructor and the student.

ARE YOU A TEACHER OR AN INSTRUCTOR?

So the big question here is do we want to be instructors or teachers? Or another way to look at it, are you a teacher or an instructor? Teaching involves explanation of what is happening in the technique. Instruction just deals with the technique and perfecting it.

Now, there has to be some element of instruction in the teaching to pass the information along, but there has to be more than that for it to be teaching. How is only one question that can be asked of a technique, there is also why and when, which are relevant to understanding a technique properly. The teacher should be able to answer these questions. The instructor will not worry about them as all he is interested in is the how of the technique. The teacher provides background and foundation to the techniques which are being taught. Much more information than what the instructor provides.

Instruction is easy, teaching is hard. The question here is whether we have the willingness to put in the effort to improve ourselves and our students as a result. Any person can tell another how to perform most fencing actions and make sure that they can do it properly. It takes someone more dedicated to teach the person the action as there is a fuller explanation of the action.

We should all strive to become teachers of fence rather than instructors as this will result in better students and further on better fencers. This requires us to seek the deeper answers about the techniques that we teach and to understand the theory upon which they are founded. Rather than just knowing the techniques, we must understand the techniques and the reasons why they are performed.

WHAT DO YOU HAVE?

From the student's point of view you must ask, do I have an instructor or a teacher? Am I being given instruction or am I being taught? A student needs to have the fullest explanation of every element of the fencing actions that are being taught, rather than just being instructed how to do it. You need to seek a teacher of fence more than an instructor. The instructor will perfect your technique, but the teacher will give you the full explanation and explain how this action fits with all the others.

Of course sometimes you simply need to follow the instruction and learn the technique and learn the why of the technique and when of the technique as you progress. In these instances the teacher may withhold the information so that you will not confuse you with information which you do not yet understand. Be patient in these times, the answers will come when you are ready for them.

CONCLUSION

This is an element which some think about, and more should. Have a think, are you being instructed or taught? Are you a teacher or an instructor? What answers can you get about the techniques that you are taught? Of course you should also ask whether you are at a stage of your training where you are ready for the answers to these questions. Still in the end it is always better to have a teacher than an instructor as the teacher will have a more complete understanding of the techniques that you are being taught.

The relationship between the student and the instructor is different than the student and the teacher. The instructor instructs, delivers the message, delivers the technique, improves the technique and then moves on to the next one. The teacher, delivers the message, explains the message, delivers the technique, explains the technique, and then only moves on to the next one once the questions about the current one have been answered. There is a distinct one-way information flow with the instructor, and a two-way flow with the teacher. Here is the difference, if the information is there and relevant to the lesson, the teacher will give it. The instructor is more interested in making sure the mechanics work.

Beginning to Teach

INTRODUCTION

Beginning to teach can be one of the scariest endeavours a fencer can put themselves through. Just like all other aspects of fencing it is a skill which needs to be learnt. The decision to teach really needs to be a voluntary one and not something which is forced on the fencer. There has been a great deal said about teaching and the process of teaching. The following will be of use to the beginner teacher as it looks at the process of beginning to teach and where to start.

PREACH WHAT YOU PRACTICE

The expression "practice what you preach" is most useful for correcting your own techniques, but there is also a situation where the reverse of the process is actually more useful for the fencer who is beginning to teach. The skills which the fencer uses in bouting are the ones which they will know the best. They understand these particular techniques and subconsciously understand why they work. This is where the teaching process should start from, hence "preach what you practice".

The skills which you have honed over your time fencing are those which you will know the best. It is of little use attempting to teach things that you do not know so the best thing is to start with those things that you do know. For example, a fencer who does not use a great deal of blade engagement techniques should not be attempting to teach this. More he should be looking at how he manages with blade engagement in bouting and teaching this, possibly teaching absence of the blade or something similar. This is the sort of thing that you should be looking at when you begin to teach.

THE BASICS

Each fencer will have been taught the basics at some point in time. This may have come from a more qualified teacher, or it may have actually come from another fencer. The basics are those lessons which we have drilled the most in our fencing careers. Footwork and the simple elements of defence and attack are perfect examples of the basics. This is a great place for the beginning teacher to start teaching.

The basics should keep your prospective students occupied for some period of time. These particular formative lessons are the most important lessons a fencer learns. If there is something missing from these particular lessons then there is the good chance that something will go amiss in the future of the fencer. The simple fact that these lessons should also be very familiar will help with any concerns about confidence with regard to teaching the lessons.

RESEARCH

Do research. Fill in those gaps in your fencing knowledge which you know you have. Begin to research how some lessons are put together and also information about the skills being learnt. This will help a great deal in the teaching process. The more that you learn, the more you will be able to impart. The more you understand, the better able you will be able to teach your students. Research is something which all teachers should do.

You should even consider examining where your teacher got their information from to understand it better too. Some teachers will have a "tried and true" method of teaching which has worked for them for many years. This does not mean it is the only way to teach. Find a set of skills and lessons which are more comfortable for you and the way that you teach. You have to be comfortable teaching them.

YOUR FIRST LESSON

You will be nervous, expect it. You will make mistakes that is fine, *everyone* does. If you do not know the answer to a question say "I don't know." It is better than attempting to bluff your way through. Tell them that you will go and find out and get back to them. Bluffing your way through give the students false information and this undermines their confidence in you *when* they find out that you didn't know the answer.

Start with something you know, as has been explained previously. So, it is often best to start with one of the basic lessons for beginners. This is one of the parts of fencing you should know well, thus you will be more at ease teaching it. Before you teach the lesson, even if there is one already planned, make your own lesson plan. This is so you know what you are going to say and the main points. Having a copy with you will help you if you get bogged down or lost somewhere in the lesson. Remember that your audience, the students, are interested in what you are going to teach them and they need to know it.

CONCLUSION

Teaching can be one of the most fulfilling experiences that a fencer can have, or it can be one of the most harrowing. In most situations it is the level of preparation that the teacher has had that will determine the result of the lesson. Think about what you are going to teach, see what the vital elements are, and stick to them.

Experienced teachers should be explaining why they teach the things that they do and how they do it. In this way the information can be passed along. If you are interested in teaching, talk to your teacher if you have one and discuss it. Get together and consider some lesson plans. Most of all when you begin to teach; be prepared to learn, teaching is the greatest learning experience. You learn about fencing and you also learn about yourself. It will teach you a different perspective and what you really know about fencing.

Conduct of Training

INTRODUCTION

Training is a vital aspect of all sports and martial arts. It is something that we all need to do. The teacher in the lesson must construct a training session that has all the elements necessary for the students to learn what they need to learn in their lesson. This discussion will focus on the conduct of training, from the planning to the execution, and dealing with some of the problems that will arise in training. Hopefully this will be of interest to students and teachers alike so that you can examine your own training sessions and see how they compare to what is written here.

OVERALL PLAN

For the teacher the training session needs to start before they turn up for training. Planning needs to be the first stage of any training session; this is a necessary process especially to remain in control of the training session and to ensure that you can teach all of what the students need to learn. The first thing you need to look at in the planning stage is the overall plan for training. You need to look at how the students will progress from the beginning stages to the end where they are able to fence with a level of competence and then further to include more advanced techniques. You don't need to plan out the entirety of the student's career, more you need to give them the skills to progress in that direction. This is the first stage of the planning process.

LESSON PLANS

Once you have an overall plan for the training sessions on the whole you need to have a look at the individual lessons. The lessons should build upon one another like building blocks. This means that the first lessons establish the foundation for the student's fencing and then the others build on top of this. What this means is that the first lessons are some of the most important as if the basic skills are not established to begin with it will be difficult to build upon these to get to more advanced techniques.

Each one of the lessons should be connected to the others in some way. Obviously they are all connected due to what is being learnt, but the connections need to be on a more specific level as well. Basic techniques should lead to more advanced ones as the basics are the foundation of the more advanced techniques. This needs to be established in the planning process for the training program. The next part of the process is to look at the individual lesson or lessons that will be taught on a particular night.

HOW MUCH TO TEACH

The decision of how much to teach in a single training session is an important one and needs to be considered. There is a sliding scale from teaching not enough in the session all the way up to teaching too much. In general it is best to focus on one particular area in a lesson, though in some instances this can be branched out into more. This is highly dependent on the lessons being taught. For example, lessons on footwork all link together and may be taught as a single block as they are all related to how the feet move, but trying to link a lesson on footwork to some aspect of the use of the hands is probably not a good idea to start with.

In general you should teach a maximum of two lessons per training session otherwise you will give the students problems in remembering all of the information that you have presented. This is, of course, highly dependent on the lessons themselves and also the students being taught. Look at how the lesson relates to others as has been noted before. This will allow you to decide whether the lesson is best taught alone or in conjunction with another lesson. Some lessons will tend to lead to other ones and this should be noted as it will give some directions as to how the lessons should be taught. Remember though, that each lesson should have a particular area of focus and this should be what is being aimed at for the lesson. If this is not clear then the students will get confused as to what they are supposed to be learning and this is not good.

THE TRAINING SESSION: PLANNED OR NOT?

The next part of the process is examining the content of the lesson and what will be taught in the training session. This can be approached in one of two ways really. You can have a lesson planned out as to what will be taught or you can see what the students want to learn and then focus on that for the session. Both methods have their advantages and disadvantages.

The second gives the students what they want, but if the entire program is based in this method then the program tends to be very disjointed and aspects can be missed in the process. This is a very spontaneous form of lessons and should really only be used for more advanced students and the more experienced teachers as it does not allow much time for planning. The first is good as there is a structure which is followed lesson by lesson, this method does, however lack spontaneity. This means if a particular problem comes up it is somewhat difficult to deal with that problem instantly without deviating from the program. It does, however, have the advantage of planning what will be taught in a particular training session. The most important part is regardless of what method you use, you should focus on one aspect of the training per lesson and ensure the students understand which aspect is the focus of the lesson in order that some structure is maintained.

INTERESTING CONTENT

The lessons need to have content which is interesting to the students. This means that in most cases the lessons will be dominantly practical in nature. Lessons with a lot of theory and very little practical aspect to them tend to be seen as rather boring by students. You should try to include some aspect of a practical nature in the lesson to keep the students interested in what is going on. The only way to keep the students' attention is to make the lesson interesting to them.

The lesson may be very important to their progress, but if it is not interesting to them their attention will waver and they may miss important parts of the lesson. The theory lessons should be directly related to practical aspects. In this way the theory is demonstrated to be something that has great benefit in what is going on in actual fencing. Keeping the students interested in what is going on is important and should be considered carefully when planning a lesson and also teaching it.

TRAINING SESSION STRUCTURE

The organisation of the training session is important. You need to structure it in such a way that each element leads on to another one. This structure is important so that the students can see what is going on and then be able to follow this. You need to consider what should be the start of the session and how you will engage the students and keep their attention.

Warm-Up

Warming up is an important part of the training session. Not only does it prepare the body for the practical aspects in the lesson it also increases blood flow and thus improves the thinking capacity and attention span of the students. Training sessions are usually held at night or on weekends. In both these instances people will have just relaxed after working and will need some motivation to get them moving so that they can fully participate in the lesson. The warm-up is a good way to get people enthusiastic and get them moving again.

Theory

The next part of the training session should be the theory, the information about what is being taught in the lesson. Some believe that this should be before the warm-up as the body will cool while doing the theory. The warm-up gets the student excited and willing to learn, thus it will improve the retention of the theory that is taught. As long as the theory aspect does not go too long the students should not cool down too much. Once the theory is done you should move on to the practical aspects.

Practical

The practical aspects of the lesson will keep the students interested in what is going on but these needs to be done in a way that the information is retained by the student. An action being learnt should be demonstrated at full-speed by the teacher, and then again at slower speed so that the students can see what is going on. The students should be then shown how the action is done in parts. This is how the action should be taught, in parts. Once they can do the parts slowly you should then speed things up.

Drills and Coached Bouting

Once the students are able to do the action at speed, you should move on to drills which use the particular skill which has been learnt. These drills should reflect a situation in fencing in a controlled manner. Once the drills have been done and the students can perform the technique, you should move them on to controlled or coached bouting. This bouting focuses on the use of the new technique. In a bouting situation the technique the student learns when the appropriate time for the use of the skill is. This bouting should be controlled so that the skill is used, but also let go so that it reflects normal fencing better.

Free Bouting

Free bouting should always come at the end of the lesson as it is a way for the students to practice their skills and also have some fun. This should be included in the training sessions as many times as possible to keep their enthusiasm up. Free bouting is a great way to release tension, but this should come at the end of the training session.

PROBLEMS

In everything that is attempted there will be problems and training sessions are no different. Some of the problems will be easy to deal with and some will not be so easy. Some of these problems are generated by the students and some by the teacher. Both need to take responsibility for their impact upon the training session.

Trouble-makers

Trouble-makers are abounded and they should be dealt with promptly so that they do not disrupt the entire session. The method use depends on what the person is doing and what the teacher is permitted to do within their structure. Some will be easily dealt with and others won't.

A lack of interest

A lack of interest in the lesson can be dealt with in one of two ways. You either abandon the lesson and move on to something else, or you continue on with the lesson and attempt to generate interest in the lesson through demonstrating its importance to the process. The choice of which depends on the particular lesson.

Moving too fast

The other end of this is the student attempting to move on to fast. The initiative of the student should be praised, but it should also be explained as to what the lesson is trying to achieve and that what they are doing comes later and they should wait for this. This leads to problems in the session.

Too Much or Not Enough?

If it seems that you are giving the students too much to learn at once, you should stop and evaluate the situation. It would be better to stop the lesson and try again at a different session than to continue and have the lesson not properly learnt. On the other end of the scale is not giving the students enough to learn. This usually results in them getting more bouting at the end of the session which is not necessarily a bad thing, but for the next session more should be included.

Too Advanced?

The content of the lesson may be too advanced for some students so they will not understand what is going on. Attempt to describe the technique a different way to the student so that they may understand what is going on. If this does not work a physical demonstration of the skill can be helpful. Correction of technique is part and parcel of the process, this need to be done with encouragement, but not too much. If the technique is too difficult for the student to master at that point in time, you should come back to it later on.

CONCLUSION

Training sessions are important as is their conduct. The best conducted sessions are those in which the teacher has the most control over what is going on. This means that the teacher needs to plan what is going to happen before-hand in most instances. Experienced teachers will be able to teach lessons from their experience, but until this skill is attained it is better to plan the session out, and in some detail.

Training sessions give a chance for the students to learn what they need to learn and for the teacher to also learn, in a lot of instances. This is important in the process of learning fencing for both students and teachers. Only through the learning process will both become better at what they are doing and expand their knowledge. You should consider your impact on the training session and see whether this is a positive or negative influence. Consider your training session carefully and see what you can do to improve it.

Drill Design and Construction

INTRODUCTION

Drills are an important part of the learning process for students and it is important that teachers know what they are for, how they are constructed and their inner workings to get the greatest potential from them. This article is about drills, sometimes called "conventionals" in sport fencing. It will address some of the issues associated with the construction and use of drills in a training situation. Whether you are a teacher or student of fencing, the information provided will hopefully provide you with some thinking points with regard to this most useful tool in fencing.

PURPOSE OF DRILLS

Before we can look at drills in any sort of detailed way it is necessary to examine the purpose of drills as a training tool. Drills are most useful for the practicing of skills which have been learnt in a lesson. By using this method the theory present and the isolated form of the skill or skills that have been taught can be seen together working both with and against other skills. This is essentially seeing the skill in a practical situation, or in another way of thinking, seeing the technique in action against the movements of an opponent.

Through the use of drills and their repetitive fashion muscle memory is also built, designed to instil the skills in the muscles and subconscious of the student. In this way the student will know how to respond to the stimulus presented by the opponent by use of the skill learnt in the drill. This is important as it then frees the fencer's mind up to be thinking about what he will do against his opponent once the action has been completed.

DRILL EXAMINATION

Next it is important to look at drills specifically. To do this without detailing all examples of skills and their drills, more general terms will be used in the address of their purpose. In all cases a drill should highlight the importance of the skill being drilled, and it should also highlight the importance of the correct performance of that skill against an opponent.

Purpose of the Drill

There needs to be a reason for the drill being performed, it needs to be more than just a mere repetition of a particular skill for no seen purpose. Purpose must be injected into the drill so that the student will understand what both the skill and the drill are designed to achieve. This purpose must be specific to the skill and also the drill rather than the general terms which have already been discussed in the previous paragraph. The next part of this is the actual design of the drill itself. This must relate directly to the skill being taught and must place the skill in a situation where it is the best option available. This design phase of the drill is important and must be thought about carefully for the drill to achieve its purpose.

DRILL DESIGN
A Specific Skill
In designing a drill the focus of the drill must be upon the specific skill being trained or learnt by the student. Without this focus the student will become confused about the purpose of both the drill and also the purpose of the skill. While in many cases the drill will involve the use of other skills, the focus must be on a specific skill.

For a drill to be effective the other skills being used in the drill must be skills that the student already has so that the drill is not side-tracked on to the attached skills rather than the particular focus skill of the drill. This is an element which is of great importance in the design and development of a drill. For example, if the drill involves the use of a particular footwork step along with a blade action, which is the focus of the drill, the footwork needs to be already known to the student for the drill to work.

The Last Thing
The drills will stack upon one another in a similar way that the skills will. With this in mind design the drill so that the focus is upon the new skill being learnt, and in a way that this is possible. The drill should end with the skill being learnt so that it is the last thing that the student does in the drill and thus it will become the most significant action in the drill. Use simple steps in the construction of the drill so that there is little confusion with regard to the drill.

SPEED
Speed is always a factor with regard to fencing and choosing the speed at which a drill should be performed is of great importance. The drill should always start by being performed slowly so that the skill is developed and examined in a very specific way. This will enable the student to focus on the technique of the skill rather than the result of the skill. The student should understand that the goal of the drill is the correct performance of the skill rather than whether or not they can hit their partner. If the student can perform the skill and the drill correctly striking an opponent should come about as a result of the correct performance, if that is appropriate to the skill being learnt.

Drills, in most cases, should result with a full speed version of the drill being performed. This will enable the student to see the action in practice. This should only be done once they are able to perform the technique properly at slower speeds. Full speed drills are necessary for those drills where the skill will be use in a full combat situation. Without these drills the student will perform the action slowly but will not do the same at full speed, thus it can be seen that drills at full speed are necessary. There are times where the slow drill actually achieves its goal; this is most evidently seen in the physical demonstration of time. It is much easier to see tempos at slow speed than it is to see them at full speed. This form of drill is more aimed at the student understanding the concept behind what is happening more than the skills being used.

STUDENTS FOLLOW THE DRILL
For drills to work properly and achieve their goals various things are required. First of all the students must have been taught the skills involved in the drill, and

most importantly the skill being drilled. Next is that the participants in the drills must participate completely in the drill. This means following the drill according to what has been directed by the teacher. This means that the participants need to stick with the drill as it has been directed and sticking with the purpose of the drill. There should be very little deviation in the action of the drill, save those points where the participant is having trouble and needs help.

Deviations from the drill detract from the purpose and focus of the drill and make it less useful to the participants in the drill. Deviation in the drill should not be tolerated by the teacher and this is why the drills should be observed closely by the teacher of the class. Deviation such as countering the final action by one partrer does not allow the skill being taught to be successfully completed and therefore learnt properly, this should be discouraged. This is especially the case where a counter is taught against the action in a later drill.

Changes in footwork should be avoided as well so that the positions and distance are not changed for the drill. These elements can be added in later on, if it is appropriate to the skill being taught. Each participant must know their purpose in the drill for it to be used successfully. In a parry and riposte drill the attacker should simply thrust and wait for the response. Their purpose in the drill is to thrust and be struck and nothing more. Only where the two participants in a drill are completing their participation in the drill completely will the drill be effective. With regards to this drills must be done at the correct distance and all actions must be completed with purpose. This enables the responding participant to also perform their actions properly against it.

DRILLS AND BOUTING

Drills are a good accompaniment to bouting. There are really two forms of bouting, free bouting and structured bouting. Free bouting involves the two combatants engaging with no restriction on technique or target. Structured bouting applies specific restrictions to the bout so that particular skill-sets may be the focus of the bout. These are most useful when accompanied by the drills which use the appropriate skills. Bouting should be used for the students to use the skills that they have learnt against an opponent. This is the prime time for the students to figure out where any problems in their use of the skill may be, and also different ways and times in which the skill may be applied. It is important that drills are accompanied by bouting in order that the students have the chance to test out their new skills against different opponents.

CONCLUSION

Drills are a most useful tool for teachers, if they are utilised properly. So that this can happen it is also important that the drills are formed properly as well. This requires that the drills be designed with a purpose in mind. They need to be focusing on a single skill or skill-set to be effective and the participants need to fulfil their role in the drill and nothing more. Deviation from drills is a distraction which will detract from the drill and its purpose. In this each participant has a responsibility in their participation in the drill and this is of great importance. Think when you design or participate in drills exactly what your purpose is. You need to be considering what the drill is designed to teach and how this relates to the whole picture of fencing that you are learning.

Building Self-Confidence

INTRODUCTION

Going by the title of this particular article one could assume that this is going to be some sort of "make people happy" discussion. Actually, that is not the focus of this one. In this particular case the subject of self-confidence will be addressed from two points of view. Firstly it will be examined from the student's point of view and then from the teacher's point of view. The purpose of this piece is to address the idea of how both the teacher and the student can build the student's self-confidence. This is a necessary process that both the student and the teacher need to be aware of for the student to excel.

STUDENTS

From the student's point of view, there are three main points that will be raised. Firstly that training is a learning process and mistakes will be made. Secondly, the importance of practice and how it builds skill and thus confidence, and finally being comfortable in what you are doing. Each one of these particular points is vital and needs to be addressed for the student to build confidence in them.

Training is Learning

Fencing and training is a learning process, in this there will be mistakes made by the student in what they are doing. The student needs to learn from these mistakes. In this way the mistake made is not a failure but a chance for the student to learn and improve what they are doing.

The learning process takes time. The student must acknowledge that it will take time to learn skill-sets and use them effectively in fencing. Fencing is a long road if it is approached from the correct point of view and they will never stop learning. When something is done well it should be celebrated. The student should take pride in all of their achievements, no matter how small they might be, but this must be in proportion to the level of the achievement, and also through this not become over-confident. This achievement should spur them on to want to do more.

Practice Builds Confidence

It is practice that builds skill, and skill that builds confidence. Needless to say, practice is required for all of the skills in fencing so that they can be called upon and used at any time that the student requires them. In this practice the student needs to be practicing the correct action so that the correct action is learnt. The teacher should be correcting them in order that this is possible, and to a point the student should also be correcting themselves.

The action performed must be completed. Where the drill involves a parry and riposte, both actions need to be completed for the student to learn the correct thing. Where the parry is missed, the student should correct the parry, and then make the appropriate riposte. This is the same for all actions. It is this sort of repetition that builds muscle memory and allows a student to perform an action without thinking about it. Much in these articles has already been said about practice, but it is something which is vital for the student to keep progressing.

Comfortable

Being comfortable in what a person is doing is about several things. Firstly it is necessary for them to understand what they are doing and what it is supposed to achieve. Next it is important to understand the effect of the action and the parts that are involved in the action. This understanding will enable the student to have a better grasp of what they are doing and thus be more comfortable with it. Once the mind is prepared it is important for the body to feel what is happening.

Performing an action slowly will allow the student to feel the activation of muscles and other parts of their body. This will enable them to perform the action properly at faster speeds once they can feel what their body is doing during the performance of the action. Each student will find things that feel more comfortable for them. In some cases there may be some modification in the action required for the action to work for them, and this is fine.

It is important for the student to discover what works for them and thus enable them to develop a level of comfort for themselves in their actions. Of course, the development of this level of comfort in an action will take time, especially for a new action. It is important that the teacher allows the student to take the time that they need for them to become comfortable with an action. An action which is comfortable for the student will more readily be used by them.

TEACHERS

From the teacher's point of view, there are also three main points that will be raised. The teacher's purpose in training is an important factor in building self-confidence in the student. Next is encouragement and how it can be effective in building self-confidence through building the student. Lastly is the idea of relaxation on the part of the student so that they can more freely learn what needs to be learnt. Rather than specific points of reference for the teacher, it will be a general discussion focussed on the particular sub-topics presented.

Purpose

The purpose of the teacher needs to be something that the teacher is aware of. In teaching their purpose is to develop skill in the student, rather than simply demonstrating how good they are to the student. It is important that this focus is maintained by the teacher so that they do not get side-tracked into simply contradicting the actions of the student.

Along with this, the teacher must get hit. The hit should be the result of a correct technique performed by the student and not simply the teacher just standing there. This may be required for the most timid of the students, but in general the hit should result from a correctly performed technique. In this particular aspect, once the teacher has taught a student a particular technique, and they are getting them to perform the action, they should never counter the correct technique as this builds negative reinforcement associated with the technique.

If there is a counter, this should be taught as a separate section. The student should be allowed to complete the action as described. The teacher must allow the student to complete the action and to perform it as it was taught, if there are problems, the teacher should correct them once the action is complete. Being that it s the training of the student, which is the focus; the teacher must also know the difference between training and bouting. Training is designed to reinforce a particular action, in this the person who is supposed to get hit, should. This is the same for drills as well; the action needs to be completed. This is where the focus of the teacher must be toward teaching the student.

Encouragement

Encouragement is important and necessary. The student should be praised for a skill well performed. This encourages the student to complete action and gives them a boost to move on to the next action. It is important that the encouragement is not over-used, but measured in proportion to the achievement of the student. This will also reinforce the validity of the action taught and performed.

Encouragement is especially necessary where a student is having problems. This may be problems with a particular technique, or overall. In both cases, the teacher needs to find little victories to encourage the student to continue along their path, without this encouragement the student may give up. When an action is performed as per a drill, the action must be allowed to be completed, unimpeded by the teacher. Encouragement should be given for the performance of the action completed. Encouragement goes a large way toward building confidence in the student, and especially confidence in their skills.

Relaxation

For some students, relaxation in the performance of skills is difficult, but it is also vital so that they can perform the action without hesitation and more fluidly. It is important that the student is focussed on what they are doing, but not so much that they become tense. This tension needs to be relieved in some manner or other.

Tension will be built by the student over-thinking an action. This often comes from looking outside the technique being taught. It is important that the students focus on the particular technique being taught, rather than worrying about what comes next or what might happen. Over-thinking an action will increase tension which will make the action more difficult to perform.

If the muscles are relaxed, and thus lack tension, the action will be much easier to perform. This is the primary reason that relaxation is important, it allows for better performance of actions. Of course true relaxation comes from confidence, and this must be built. This confidence needs to be built one technique at a time, and then stacked in order to complete the picture.

CONCLUSION

Self-confidence is important for both the student and the teacher, without it neither could perform. It is also important that both are able to improve the level of self-confidence by both their actions and also their attitude toward training and the training process. The student needs to consider how what they are doing can build their own confidence in what they are doing, but the teacher also has a role to play in this.

Victories need to be celebrated, especially where the road toward it has been difficult for the student and the teacher. Of course, such victories need to be celebrated in proportion to their merit otherwise over-confidence will build and this will be to the detriment of the student and the teacher. Fencers all need to consider how they affect and are affected by the actions of ourselves and others in the building of self-confidence. The students in a class all have a role to play for themselves and one another. The building of self-confidence in the student needs to be a partnership between the student and the teacher.

Biomechanics and the Effects of Body Shape

INTRODUCTION

Bio-mechanics is something that we, as fencers, often ignore. There are many elements of bio-mechanics which can be very useful to the fencer if they are understood, being that fencing is the actions performed by the body and this is affected by bio-mechanics. This article will be addressing some of the elements of bio-mechanics from a very basic point of view which affect the fencer. It is more designed to encourage the fencer to consider bio-mechanics and their effect. This is especially important for teachers as the effects of body shape can be seen in different actions in fencing.

NECESSARY CONSIDERATION

Bio-mechanics is something which most fencers will not take into account in their fencing, but it is something that cannot really be ignored. This particular element affects all of the actions on fencing and needs to be considered, even if it is only to examine it from a personal point of view about how the individual moves. For the teacher, bio-mechanics becomes more important especially in dealing with students of different body shapes. A brief study in the elements of bio-mechanics can greatly assist in fencing, and also the teaching of fencing, especially where this takes into account body shape. The awareness of bio-mechanics and how it can affect your fencing will greatly enhance the fencer's ability to perform.

PERCEIVED ADVANTAGES AND DISADVANTAGES

There are some supposed advantages and disadvantages in body shape when fencing is considered. The tall fencer with the long arms, in general, is supposed to have an advantage over the shorter individual with shorter arms. This is due to the range that the tall individual has and their ability to move because of their long limbs. Even with this taken into account, it does not mean that the shorter individual has no hope of excelling in fencing, actually quite the opposite.

While the longer limbed individual has an advantage at range and this can be taken away, both the advantages and the disadvantages must be taken into account when considering body shape and its effect on bio-mechanics. The shorter fencer, for example, will have an advantage once inside the reach of the taller advantage due to a lower centre of gravity, and optimum distance. Each fencer needs to use their body shape to their advantage, and needs to consider how bio-mechanics can enhance their advantages while compensating for some of the disadvantages.

GUARD

It has already been stated that bio-mechanics will have an effect on all the movement elements of fencing, but it will have an effect even on the individual's on guard position. In the on guard position, especially for Renaissance fencers, there are choices to be made with regard to the on guard position. Even when considering the basic on guard position with the weapon held in the natural on guard position of third or terza, there are elements which can come into effect which will affect the way the fencer moves.

The first choice is with regard to the feet, sword foot forward or off-hand foot forward. This will affect the body position in the on guard position and change the options available, and affect those options which are available. The refused stance promotes the off-hand for use in defence. The forward stance promotes the sword. The refused stance withdraws the body; the forward pushes it more forward along with the weapon. Next is the consideration of whether the weapon is extended or more withdrawn; this will affect the way the weapon will be used and also the timing of the actions. All of these elements, even in the on guard stance, are affected by bio-mechanics.

ACTIONS

Bio-mechanics also has an effect on the actions of fencing. This is because all of the actions are the result of the movement of the body and therefore are reliant on bio-mechanics for their effect. If a person understands how bio-mechanics affects their actions they can learn how to do them better, and one of the keys to this is flowing through the action. The action performed needs to be moved through and completed in a fluid motion.

Some fencers will attempt to use their strength in the performance of the action, where the action is performed fluidly and accurately there is very little strength required for the action to be effective. This is a perfect example of how bio-mechanics affects the performance of an action, and how it is the body movement of the fencer that really needs to be considered in the action. This needs to relate to the fencer and how they move naturally.

CHOICE OF ACTION AND BIO-MECHANICS

The choice of which action to perform against the action of the opponent will come down to personal preference in all cases, but if the bio-mechanics of the individual are understood this choice can be more informed and thus more suited to the situation and the individual. The choice of how to approach a particular situation should be dependent on what the individual knows works best for them. This is mostly based on bio-mechanics and what actions they will prefer to perform against an opponent. In the performance of an action the fencer should consider what will give them the greatest advantage over the opponent.

In all cases a mechanical advantage should be gained, this is also based on bio-mechanics. It does not rely on strength; in fact the use of a lack of strength against a strong opponent can be very effective. This particular effect can also be seen in the choice of measure. The shorter individual will need to get closer to the opponent to strike, thus there must be a consideration of how they can get there safely. The taller person will want to keep the opponent at range. These two choices are purely based on bio-mechanics.

SUIT THE INDIVIDUAL

Some of the effects of bio-mechanics on fencing have been discussed. The actions can be modified to suit the individual. Each teacher will teach actions in a particular way; these are the base elements that need to be considered in the actions. Where the bio-mechanics of the individual have an effect on the action is where a consideration needs to be made as to how the action can be changed to suit the individual. It is important to utilise the advantages that you have and minimise the disadvantages.

If something does not work for the fencer they need to consider why and how their own personal bio-mechanics will affect the action being performed. The action should then be modified to suit the individual in order that they can be more effective in their movements. One of the most important things here is that the fencer needs to fight the game that suits them and not let their opponent dominate what is happening. The fencer needs to move and to perform those actions which will give them and advantage over their opponent. This will take practice.

CONCLUSION

Bio-mechanics affects all the actions of the fencer and this need to be considered, even if on the most basic level. A person who can utilise these particular principles will have an advantage over the opponent who has not considered them. Fencers need to examine their own movements and consider how they move and why they perform the actions of fencing in the way that they do.

Once this is completed, elements can be considered as to how they can change this to suit their own body and thus move more effectively. Teachers need to take bio-mechanics into account in their teaching so that they can teach their students to be more effective in their movements and also teach each student to take the advantages that they have and increase them. While it is often not considered on any conscious level, bio-mechanics is important to the fencer and needs to be considered.

SECTION 8.
Equipment and Curatorial Discussions

Buying a Sword

INTRODUCTION
The purchase of a sword is something which is often not talked about very much. Usually the only concern for people is the potential financial burden that may occur in the purchase. What this does not take into account is the other aspects of the purchase of a sword that the swordsman should take into account. This article will address the concept of buying a sword and present some considerations that should be made by the buyer.

AN INVESTMENT
Buying a sword is an investment, but it is one that many fencers take quite lightly. This should not actually be the case. The purchase of a sword is also an event, which should signify something to both the purchaser of the weapon and also to the teacher and club to which they belong. No one is ever expected that they will turn up to their first fencing practice with a weapon and other gear already bought. The opposite is a very rare occurrence. What this means is that for a period of time the fencer will borrow a weapon. It may belong to a club, or it may belong to another fencer. The purchase of a sword should signify that the person is ready to commit to the enterprise to which they have undertaken, of course this is not the only thing that a fencer should be concerned about when buying a sword.

In previous centuries, and even relatively recently, a sword was not simply purchased "off the rack" or out of a collection of examples present, as is mostly the case these days. The fencer was measured for a sword. This was because the swordsman would be relying on that particular weapon to save their life in an armed encounter. For the fencer today fighting someone where there is the potential for serious injury or death is not so much of a concern. In these previous days the make of the sword would also give some indication of the wealth of the owner of the weapon and also their taste as it was worn as a piece of costume jewellery. Once again, this is not the case today. However, some of the considerations made in these previous days should be made by the modern swordsman.

LENGTH

There are examples in treatises by various masters and theorists of the Renaissance and middle ages about the correct length of a sword. Ridolfo Capo Ferro, for example, determined that the correct length of the sword should be twice the length of the arm, and there were others who proposed that the weapon should be longer, or shorter. Needless to say the length of the weapon was proportional to the individual who was using it. For the most part, weapons these days are sold at set lengths or at different ones by special request. While there are many different theories about how long or short a weapon should be, the important thing for the fencer is comfort. This is the most important consideration.

COST

For the most part a sword these days will cost somewhere more than $400. Sure there are some which can be obtained for cheaper, and sure there are those which are substantially more than this, it is a ball-park figure. For some this will be a significant investment on their part and this in itself is significant. A fencer does not want to go out, spend a deal of money and purchase a sword just to find out that it is too heavy, or light, or short, or long. This will result in the sword having to be modified or even replaced, which is another expense on the part of the fencer. To avoid this some planning and investigation should be made.

FEEL THE WEAPON

The only real way to see how a sword feels is to pick up the weapon and use it. Of course many shops will not allow you to use the merchandise unless you intend to buy the one that you are using. So long as you are not causing problems for other customers or stock, some merchants will allow you to do this. Taking the weapon and feeling its weight is a good start, being able to move the sword around is also a good thing. For the most part fencers are a reasonable bunch of individuals who will allow you to look and feel a weapon in their possession. Of course you should *always* ask before handling another person's weapon. This should allow you, once again, to get a feel for the weapon. If the fencer is generous they may even allow you to have a couple of bouts with the weapon to get a better feel of it. This is the best way, currently, to get an idea of the feel of different weapons. For the most part, you can then find the same weapon at a merchant.

QUALITY

When selecting a weapon for purchase, a consideration should be made about quality. For the most part a cheaper weapon will not be as high quality as a weapon which is more expensive. This should be a concern for the buyer as the higher quality weapon will last longer than a cheaper weapon, based on quality of manufacture, and as a general rule. Of course, the fencer must also be concerned with what happens to fall into the fencer's own budget as well. It is advised however, that a fencer spend on the upper limit rather than the lower limit of their budget to obtain a weapon of quality.

Known Manufacturers

Of course when a weapon is on sale then the price is not necessarily a good guide. It is then up to the fencer to talk to others about their weapons and how well they have lasted; or to start investigating weapon manufacturers in order to get some idea about the quality of the workmanship of various weapons. Two particularly well-known manufacturers of weapons are Darkwood Armory [20] and Castille Armory. [21] Both of these manufacturers are commonly known to sell quality weapons. There are others out there, but it is up to the fencer to discover what they want and where from. You can also some on-sellers of the original manufacturers who sell their products. The fencer may even find an individual experienced in sword manufacture and purchase a weapon this way.

Sword & Dagger. Image supplied by Darkwood Armory

CONCLUSION

The purchase of a weapon for the fencer is a significant investment regardless of how much the actual weapon costs. For the most part this will, or should, be the last piece of equipment that the fencer will purchase to complete their basic kit. The fencer should have some serious consideration about what weapon and where they are going to get it from before actually purchasing a weapon. The fencer should be comfortable with the weapon as fighting the weapon to get it to do something will reduce the ability of the fencer. A comfortable weapon, comfortable to use, which does not strain the individual is the goal. Be careful when buying a weapon, do your research and consider what you really want *before* buying.

---

20 http://www.darkwoodarmory.com/

21 http://www.castillearmory.com/

Glove Preparation

INTRODUCTION

One of the most important pieces of equipment and indeed protective equipment that a fencer needs to obtain is gloves. This is regardless of the type of fencing that the person is engaging in. This article addresses the idea of new gloves primarily and how to make them more usable to the fencer, or how to prepare a pair of gloves so that they can be used.

CHOICE

The first thing that needs to be discussed is glove choice. In this there are many different pieces of advice that can be given and many different types of glove to choose from. There are fencing gloves of various kinds, gardening gloves of various kinds, and of course all manner of glove in between. So the fencer needs to make a choice as to what is best for them.

The first piece of advice that I will give is go for a leather pair that is leather in some fashion. Leather has the advantage of being natural and also hardy in nature for the most part. These are two attributes which will serve you well in the long run. Natural has the advantage of being able to breathe and thus allow some of the sweat from your hands to dissipate. Hardy means that they will last a longer amount of time than if they were not. As such avoid artificial or constructed materials such as vinyl in your gloves.

FIT

The next piece of advice which is important is fit. Some styles of gloves only come in certain sizes and it is important that you choose a style of glove which suits your hand shape and size. Sure there is some leeway, but they have to start with a reasonable fit to start with if you are to have any hope of being comfortable. This is the second factor they need to be comfortable, it is not much good if you want to take them off the instant you put them on.

CONSTRUCTION

Some gloves start of quite supple due to their construction and material. Some gloves start of quite stiff and will need quite a bit of working to get them supple. The irony is that the stiffer gloves will take longer to prepare, but will also last longer. The ones which are suppler to begin with will be easy to use and prepare but are less likely to last as long. These are all considerations that should be made in your glove choice.

PREPARATION

The primary focus for the preparation of the gloves in this blog will be toward welding gloves. This is because these are the type of glove which I favour myself and have been using for years. However the points which are raised here will pertain to other types of glove as well. However, consider how the preparation suggested may affect your particular type of glove before applying it.

New welding gloves are stiff and they are most often quite thick. What this means is that the fencer will have a hard time moving their hands freely and also feeling through them. Both of these things are bad for the fencer as it will lead to them holding their weapon too tight, and this is just for starters.

The softening of gloves is best done with no mechanical devices assisting in the stretching of the glove. If a mechanical device is used it may over-stretch the glove or force it into the wrong shape. The softening of the gloves is best done with your own hands or more to the point the hands that will wear the gloves once they are prepared. This will result in the glove conforming better to the shape of the hand that is to wear the glove. It is one of those times when it really is better to do it yourself.

The gloves can be loosened through the use of water or similar natural substances or appropriate liquids or without them. In the case of welding gloves I advise the use of water as it aids in the breaking of the fibres and thus the loosening of the gloves.

In this, firstly run water to as hot a temperature as you can stand to put your hands in. Second put your hands into the gloves and then put them in the water. Once you can feel that your hands are wet and thus the gloves are soaked through, start making movements with your fingers while still in the water. Once they have loosened a little you can then include movements of the hands and wrists. Move the hands in movements similar to those expected to be done in normal use of the gloves.

Once you have done this for a bit, take your gloves out of the water while your hands are still in them and continue to move them about until most of the water has run out of them. Keep moving until the gloves are only a little wet. Take the gloves off and roll them up to the wrist, then unroll them. Place your hands back in the gloves and move them again. Once they have gone back to the form of your hands hang them up to dry.

This is an initial shaping and is only the beginning of the process. The best way to improve your gloves is to use them as they will develop their own shape as they are used and will more and more conform to your hands. The irony of all of this is that your gloves will improve (for the most part) right up until they need to be replaced and will be at their peak just beforehand.

CONCLUSION

Gloves are often forgotten for comfort and importance in favour of the mask or helm, or even the weapon. The gloves should not be forgotten as they are an essential piece of equipment that no fencer can do without. Look after your gloves and use them well and they will serve you well. Remember all new gloves, regardless of their form or construction need some breaking in.

The Perfect Weapon Length: A Discussion of Weapon Proportion

INTRODUCTION

The original thought for what follows was to seek weapons of perfect length for my own purposes. Not to go out and actually acquire said weapons, but to examine the lengths and compare them to the ones that I am currently using. Instead, I thought it would be more useful to examine various theorists' preferences for weapon length, and it will be noted that what follows is not an exhaustive list of weapons or theorists. This can then move on to a discussion of other things related to weapon length such as weapon proportion and its importance.

With regard to weapon length preference, there is a general organisation between determined and proportional for the examination of the theorist's preferences. There will also be the question of the importance of choosing a weapon length as several theorists do not designate a weapon preference, the reasons for the choice of weapon length, and how the weapon length relates to both the form of combat and its foundation.

With regard to the evidence presented, some will come from primary texts and others will come from secondary texts, based on primary texts. The conclusions drawn from the evidence and discussion made with regard to reasons for these choices of weapon length are, however, my own and based upon my own understanding of the various weapons and their use. Please excuse the lack of bibliographical details where they have not been included, in most cases period works simply are referenced by author and date.

LENGTH DETERMINED

What is most interesting is that some theorists discussed weapon length while others did not. More interestingly is that there is a clear trend for theorists not to discuss the dimensions of the weapon rather than to discuss them. This could come down to a couple of reasons, either the length of the weapon was not considered important, or that the student should be appropriately fitted for his weapon before consulting with the teacher. Another reason could also be is that the weapon length could be decided for a duel, so weapon length would be up to the chooser and thus not appropriate to be discussed in the context of learning. In any case, what will be found below is a mix of weapons proportional and also simply determined.

The length of a weapon could be chosen for different reasons. The proportional measurement of weapons makes most sense as this fits the weapon to the individual who would be using it and thus, by rationale make it the most suitable weapon for the individual to use. Other measurements of weapons however are simply determined by the author. Swetnam states "thy weapon fowre foot long or there about," (Swetnam, 1617). He gives no rationale simply a statement of fact. It would be assumed that this length of weapon is the one that either he is most comfortable with or has found most suitable for what he is teaching. What is most interesting is that a similar determination for length is also made with regard to the Iberian Tradition.

While Swetnam gives a weapon length approximate and would seem to indicate a weapon length which may be longer, the Spanish seem to go in the other direction determining the maximum length of the weapon. "According to the canonical authors, the length of the weapon should be no longer than 5/4 vara. That's an upper limit just a bit over 41 inches." (Curtis, 2010). This indicates that a weapon should have a maximum length, but a preference for a shorter one. The weapon length determined here is echoed by Pacheco de Narváez and Francisco Lórenz de Rada (Curtis, 2010). This would indicate that for the Spanish tradition it is better to have a weapon shorter than longer, this weapon preference and choice of form and method of play have a clear relation to one another.

LENGTH PROPORTIONAL

To broaden the scope and moving on to a shorter, but equally essential weapon, examination needs to be made of Vadi's determination for dagger length. The length of this weapon is proportional to the user, as are all Vadi's weapons. He states that "The length of the dagger should be just to the elbow, with an edge and two corners. The grip should be the length of the fist, as the shape is shown depicted here below." (Windsor, 2012:173). This keeps the dagger proportional to the user, a shorter dagger would not cover the forearm for some of Vadi's defences and a longer one would likely get in the way.

Vadi applies a similar reasoning with regard to proportionality with regard to his primary weapon the longsword, "proportionate to the wielder, reaching from the ground to the armpit, with a long hilt, rounded pommel and an equally long, squared and pointed cross guard." (Porzio and Mele, 2002:12). Clearly the weapon is proportional to the user of the weapon as determined by the length of the weapon overall. What is also noted is that such proportionality in the weapon is further highlighted in the formation of the hilt. The handle is determined to be a span long, and the cross guard, the same length as the handle and pommel together (Porzio and Mele, 2002:45).

Even George Silver states that the two-handed sword needs to be proportional to the user's other weapons, "The perfect length of your two handed sword is, the blade to be the length of the blade of your single sword." (Silver, 1599). It should be noted that there was little considered difference between the long and two-handed swords in their description in the treatises. Needless to say, with all of his vehemence against the long Italian weapons, he makes clear statement as to the perfect length of his single sword.

> "To know the perfect length of your sword, you shall stand with your sword and dagger drawn, as you see this picture, keeping out straight your dagger arm, drawing back your sword as far as conveniently you can, not opening the elbow joint of your sword arm, and look what you can draw within your dagger, that is the just length of your sword, to be made according to your own stature." (Silver, 1599)

In some ways, and at the other end of the length question is found Ridolfo Capo Ferro, whose determination for the length of a weapon is at the highest end of length of all weapons. Capo Ferro's weapon is quite long and eminently suited to the point-orientated system which he presents in his treatise. For him the weapon can be determined by three different measurements.

> "Thus the length of the sword must be twice that of one's arm, or as much as my extraordinary step, the length whereof corresponds equally to the distance from my armpit down to the sole of my foot."
> (Capo Ferro, 1610)

Once again the weapon is proportional to the user of the weapon, however in his measurements, some of them do not always correspond to one another and the reader is left to either determine which is best or average out the results. Regardless of the mathematical determination, the weapon ends up being quite long and most suited to the form of fencing which is presented in his manual.

In a similar method of measurement Girard Thibault determines that the cross-guard should be at the navel of the fencer and the blade length goes so that the tip touches the floor (Thibault, 1628). Obviously this makes a clearly shorter weapon than Capo Ferro however it does present a weapon proportional to the user. The shorter weapon can also be attributed to Thibault's use of the Spanish system of fence.

CONCLUSION

The perfect weapon length was either determined by a specific length, as described by Swetnam and some of the Spanish, or left to be measured to be proportional to the user, as described by Vadi, Silver, Capo Ferro and Thibault. These two methods of determining weapon length result in different weapons used for different purposes. Even within these determinations there are clear differences in preference for weapon length, the clearest being the shorter weapon of Silver and the much longer weapon of Capo Ferro, both determined by proportionality.

Essentially one determination of dagger length, two for longsword and a couple more have been presented for the single handed sword, rapier or otherwise. This is not a complete catalogue of weapons in any way shape or form. Nor is it a complete catalogue of all of the theorists and their various measurements of weapons and off-hand devices. What have been presented are some ideas about why the various lengths and determining factors were used by various theorists. How this information is used is entirely up to the reader, practitioner, and swordsman.

The search for the perfect weapon length is a slow process, and for the most part while information can be found in manuals of the period, it is really up to the user to determine the weapon which is the most appropriate to their use at the time, and in the style which they are using. This is evident by the clear difference in length as determined by the proponents of the various schools which have been presented. Finding your own perfect weapon length is a matter of using different weapons and finding the one which suits you best. Advice can be gained from different sources, but in the end it is your weapon and you will be using it.

EQUIPMENT & CURATORIAL DISCUSSIONS

Saviolo's Weapons

INTRODUCTION

I took it upon myself to examine the depictions given by Vincentio Saviolo, or at least his artist, [22] of the two combatants and their weapons so that I might discern the length of the weapons though proper by Saviolo for the practice of his art, or at least something in the vicinity of them. While Saviolo gives no indication of the length of his weapons in his text, nor gives any particular preference to the length of the weapon desired by him, the depiction of the weapons gives some idea of what these weapons might be like. The following details the short bit of research that I embarked upon in the search for the weapons of Saviolo.

WHY?

The first question is why? Or more to the point, why bother? To this I answer that having some idea of the length of the weapons is useful due to the effect which the length of a weapon has upon the combat in which it is involved. Clearly a weapon's make-up will have an effect on the combat. Weapons designed for cutting thrust less well, and vice versa. Thus gaining some idea of the length of the weapons in Saviolo will assist in the understanding of his combat, along with the proportion of the weapon to the user, which also has an effect.

INACCURACIES

What needs to be noted and accepted is that there are some inaccuracies that need to be taken into account. These inaccuracies will become apparent because of the method used and also some of the data collected from external sources. However, even with these factors the results of this examination are useful as it will give at least an approximate answer to the question.

AVERAGE MALE HEIGHT

First of all the "average" height of a male of the Renaissance period was researched in order to give some way to transfer the data from the page and into a "real world" setting. By the research performed on this particular subject the average height was established at approximately 5'5" or approximately 165-cm. The second part was to decide on what images to use to gain the data. So four images were selected, the first four given in the manual, thus there is the depiction of the three single rapier and one from rapier and dagger. With this information gained it was then possible to start examining the images.

SOURCE IMAGES

All of the images were scaled so that they were all from a common source. These images were then placed upon the screen and measurements taken of the height of the

---

22   It should be pointed out that I have noted some rather large discrepancies between what Saviolo states in his words and what his artis presents.

individual, the length of their sword arm, and the length of the weapons. Clearly using a ruler and measuring them off the screen would result in some inaccuracies, and some differences in the measurements given. As a result averages were made across the data. Not to mention any inaccuracies of the artist who produced the images.

TO THE REAL WORLD

The result of the averaging gave some single numbers to generally reflect the height of the individuals depicted; the lengths of their sword arms; and the lengths of their weapons. In order to bring these measurements into the real world, the average height was measured to the "real world" average height. The result of this calculation resulted in an average height in the real world and a multiplication factor to be applied to the average lengths of arms and weapons.

WEAPON LENGTHS

Assuming that the images depict and individual of average height, the swords depicted in the images have a total length of 118-cm or 46", with a blade length of 104-cm or 41". The total dagger length was 43-cm or 17", with a blade length of 30-cm or 12". Further, due to the calculations given, proportions of weapon to height and weapon to arm length are also possible. The sword was approximately twice the length of the arm, measured from shoulder to wrist, and approximately 70% of the height of the person.

CONCLUSION

I will in no way claim that this *the* definitive answer to either weapon length or proportion to the individual as preferred by Saviolo, nor will I claim that these are the lengths of weapons used in his art. However, they are useful as an experiment as they do give us some idea of the length of weapons used in the period. This alone is useful as it allows us to tailor our weapons to a length which is more appropriate to the art which is being performed.

Of course averages could have been taken from sword data, however, swords are very personal things and each person will have their preference, thus the variations would have been much wilder. Further investigation is required in this particular matter. However, the information presented is useful in giving a "ball park" and encouraging the use of weapons of an appropriate length for the art being performed.

A Discussion of the Form of the Longsword

INTRODUCTION

What follows is a discussion about the longsword. This is a curatorial examination rather than a practical "how to" discussion of the weapon. This is designed to introduce the reader to the form of the weapon and encourage some thought as to the weapons actually being used to recreate what is presented in the manuals.

EQUIPMENT & CURATORIAL DISCUSSIONS

"a most noble weapon which once had high significance in the minds of men, and fulfilled the most vital and personal service in their hands." (Oakeshott, 1998:11)

The question of the sword is one which has delighted the minds of many for many years. For some reason this weapon above all others has excited and interested people of all kinds for many years, even into ancient history. There is no other weapon which, even cross-culturally, has achieved the level of attention of the sword.

There are many different types of swords over the ages to cover all of these swords over all of these times takes a lot of time. It is better that efforts are more focused on single types of weapons and to this point, and as the title has indicated, the focus here will be the longsword. Some will question the time period of the weapon, and as such the focus will be on the medieval longsword, taking a lot of the information from the Oakeshott Typology of swords. This would seem to miss out the longsword of the Renaissance, but the weapon passes through into this age, the weapon was changed to the purpose to which it was suited, as will be demonstrated.

What needs to be emphasised is that what is presented here is foundation research. It lays the foundation for much a much more in depth study of the weapon, both as an artefact, but also as a weapon of use. The both of these are connected in that the form of the weapon will determine the most appropriate and effective use, this a weapon which is primarily designed for less armoured targets will do less well than a weapon which is designed for it. Thus, part of the aim of what is presented is to address practitioners and encourage them to investigate the weapon which is being used and consider whether or not the form of the longsword which they have chosen to use is actually the most appropriate for the actions and the form of combat that they have chosen.

What will follow in the body of the discussion is three parts, each pertaining to the longsword in their own way. Each of the three sections is significant for the understanding of the weapon and to see the weapon in a different way. The order of the discussion proceeds from more general ideas about the longsword to the more specific elements present in the weapon.

The first part of the discussion is about terminology so that the longsword may be found with regard to the terms used for it. This is so that the weapon which is being discussed may be understood from a literary, and will address the varied names given to the weapon. This is followed by a general discussion of the form of the weapon from different points of view and will present some of the issues with regard to the classification of weapons by type and date. The final and most technically specific part of the discussion will look at Oakeshott's Typology of the sword, and address the longsword by the type of weapon as specified in this typology.

As has been stated already this is an overview of the longsword as a weapon, and much more information can be found on this weapon in many different texts. Indeed more than what is being presented can be found in the Oakeshott sources and in museum pieces. This discussion presents the longsword not as a standardised weapon but one of many different forms which changed over time to suit the circumstances in which they were used. The changes in the weapon are as significant, if not more so, than what stayed the same as this also marks different usage of the weapon, affected by the form of the weapon and vice versa. These considerations should be significant for any person interested in the weapon either from a curatorial point of view or a more practical one.

A QUESTION OF TERMINOLOGY: WHAT IS A LONGSWORD?

> *"Sword types tend to blend into each other:"*
> *(Windsor, 2013:30)*

In the discussion of the longsword, one of the greatest issues is one of terminology. The issue of the of sword types blending into one another means it is difficult to identify the longsword, or even terms which mean similar or the same weapon. Unlike some weapons, there is no one single form of the weapon; so many terms are created to describe them. What is presented in this part of the investigation into the longsword is an introduction to terminology.

The following discussion will attempt to clear up some of the issues with the identification of the longsword, especially with regard to terminology. What will be evident in this discussion is that the terminology which is presented here will re-appear in other sections of the investigation, and some other terminology, explained in the parts where they are found, will also emerge. The first discussion that will be made with regard to terminology is the difference between the longsword, the bastard sword and the two-hand sword. This will be followed by a more practical approach to the definition of the weapon from a certain point of view. These two questions, for the most part will cover the foundation questions with regard to the weapon and assist in its identification so that the form of the weapon can be discussed in a later section.

Sword Type Terms

To begin with the weapon needs to be described at least in general. The weapon being discussed here is one which has a handle which can accommodate the use of one or two hands which has a blade which is of a length to be suited for this use and may be used for both cutting and thrusting. With this general idea of the weapon established, terms can be discussed. There are five terms which are often used with this form of weapon: longsword, bastard or hand-and-a-half sword, war sword, great sword and two-hand or two-handed sword. The fact that there are five terms would indicate five different weapons however this is not necessarily the case.

> *"In fifteenth-century English "longsword" referred to a two-handed sword. What we call a longsword today was, in English up to quite recently (late twentieth-century), usually called a hand-and-a-half sword, or bastard sword."*
> *(Windsor, 2013:30)*

Already three of the terms have been used above to describe a single weapon; the first referring to the form of the weapon as being used with two hands, as it is referred to in the few English treatises on the weapon, and the other two being used to describe the weapon in a similar sense. It would seem by this that the terms have all been used either replacing or being used at the same time as one another to describe the same weapon. The clearest delineation in this with regard to the terms is the presence of one or two hands on the weapon, however as will be demonstrated this is not necessarily a clear line drawn, and it would seem neither is the purposed use of the weapon.

EQUIPMENT & CURATORIAL DISCUSSIONS

> "We may perhaps take it, since there are as many references to "swords of war" as there are to "great swords" and since both seem to indicate the same sort of weapon that it was indeed so—the type was used in war, and was not the everyday sword of the knight such as might be shown on his monument." (Oakeshott, 1998:46)

So the terms "war sword" and "great sword" are also introduced into the question of terminology. As is stated above, at least it is indicated that both of these terms refer to the same sort of weapon, a weapon suited for use in war. These weapons would be indicated to be large, hence the use of the word "great" in their description, however this does not divorce them from any of the terms previous, thus also having these terms refer to the same weapons which have already been indicated previously.

> "Thus it seems that the war-sword was not regarded as a two-hander. What other, then, can it be but this very big sword of a kind which, in its later forms, is familiar as the Bastard or hand-and-a-half sword? We find it distinguished in a class of its own, for instance, in the inventory of the effects of Humphrey de Bohun (ob. 1319)" (Oakeshott, 1998:43)

So, it would seem that the war sword, and great sword by association of the terms, bastard or hand-and-a-half sword are the same weapon, and by association this would also mean that they are also longswords and two-handed swords as indicated above. Thus it would seem that all of these terms, rather than referring to separate weapons, actually refer to the same ones, or do in this particular case. Evidence for this is further supported by Philippo Vadi's referring to his weapon as a "de ſpada da dui mane." a two-handed sword (Porzio and Mele, 2002:44). A note should be made that this weapon is not to be confused with the much larger cousin of the longsword, which was a purpose-built weapon designed to be used with two hands, not the longsword, a weapon which could be comfortably used with one or two.

What needs to be stated here is that there are five terms which have been indicated, and each has been used to describe the weapon about which this investigation is being made. Where a hand-use is indicated would imply the only time where some level of specificity may be made. For example a bastard, or hand-and-a-half sword, would indicate a weapon which has a handle which may accommodate one or two hands and be used with one or two hands, where as a two-hand sword would indicate a weapon which has a longer handle and thus is more suited to be used with two hands. This being said, in this particular context, both weapons could be referred to as longswords, or great swords, or even war swords, depending on their use. With this being said it is necessary that a practical definition of the longsword based upon its use, and clearly defining it, is most helpful.

A Practical Definition

> "For convenience, I prefer to define them by the length of their handles. An arming sword's handle con only comfortably fit one hand; a longsword can fit two, but the weapon is light enough and the handle short enough, to be wielded with one hand (a very long handle gets in the way if your

> *other hand is not on it), and a two-handed sword has a handle and mass that clearly requires both hands."* (Windsor, 2013:30)

Windsor (2013) describes the weapons from the single-handed sword, increasing in size to the two-handed sword. These definitions are based upon the use of the weapon and thus are useful, as it is the use of the weapon which gives us the best definition of the weapon. Curatorial descriptors can only do so much, especially for the practitioner. Windsor's definition of the longsword is broad enough that it does cover the five terms which have been indicated, and focuses on the use of the weapon, which leads to the form of the weapon, which is often the best way to describe the weapon.

There are many terms which are used to describe weapons of many different forms, not just the longsword. There is a certain assumption in the discussion that the reader will already understand the parts of the sword, and thus no description or explanation has been of these. These parts of the weapon are an inevitable part of the discussion as are other terms and elements which have not been described here. Where necessary, these terms will be indicated and discussed within the text as it follows. What has been presented is the idea of the weapon which is being discussed and the terms which have been used, and are being used to describe it indicated. With this foundation laid it is possible to move on to the general form of the weapon.

THE FORM OF THE LONGSWORD

The terminology which was discussed in the previous section lays a simple literary foundation for the discussion of the longsword. The aspect of the weapon which will be addressed in this part is the form of the longsword, its actual physical form. This is being presented to give a general idea of the form of the weapon used. It should be noted that there are many different forms of longsword, and many of these will be dealt with in a later section.

The following is a general introduction to the longsword, to give its basic form. This will address its physical characteristics in a general sense and also examine a very brief examination of its usage and how this affects the form of the weapon. The different forms of longsword and the changes and developments of the longsword, affected by changes in armour and usage, will be addressed also. The final element which will be examined is the classification and dating of the longsword as a curatorial artefact. This will lead on to a more in depth discussion of the particular forms of the longsword in the section which follows this examination of the general form of the longsword.

Usage Affects Form

The use of a weapon will affect its form. A military weapon will have to take into account any sort of armour that the opponent may be wearing. Likewise, if the weapon is to be worn there is the question of length and size which needs to be taken into account. With regard to this Guy Windsor (2013) demonstrates how effectively the longsword was taken into civilian circles due to its form, and of course this affected its form.

> *"As a civilian side-arm, the longsword had many advantages. It was the longest weapon that could reasonably be worn at the hip. Indeed, the ideal length for your longsword is the longest on that you can draw in one movement from a belt-slung scabbard. This gives you*

> *the maximum reach for your point, and the maximum tip-speed for your cuts ... The sword being primarily used with two hands, and manoeuvrable enough for a strong defence, ... The beauty of this weapon is that being light enough for single-handed use, the left arm was available for disarms, locks and throws."* (Windsor, 2013:31)

In his description Windsor highlights certain aspects of the longsword which need to be taken into account when considering the weapon. The length of the weapon is one which was discussed, and will have more detail given to it further along in this discussion. More importantly in discussing the form is the description of the weapon being able to be used both single and double-handed. This specifies a weapon which is purpose-designed to be used alone. "The longsword was probably the first sword designed primarily to be enough on its own." (Windsor, 2013:33), Needless to say the weapon had to be suitable to be used for both attack and defence in simple or complex motions. This indicates a weapon which is not overtly heavy or cumbersome, likewise that was suited to defend and attack alone without the use of any other device, "it should be light enough to be used with ease and to come back easily into guard." (Porzio and Mele, 2002:12).

Weight

The description above given by Windsor indicates a weapon which is reasonably light, so that it can be moved relatively easily. More to the point it is a weapon which can be advantageously wielded both single and double-handed; this simple characteristic limits the weight of the weapon to a certain degree for the swordsman to achieve this. The concept of the heavy, cumbersome medieval weapon has been disregarded as false thanks to research made.

> *"In fact the average weight of these swords is between 2 lbs. and 3 lbs., and they were balanced (according to their purpose) with the same care and skill in the making as a tennis racket or a fishing-rod. The old belief that they are unwieldable is as absurd and out-dated,"* (Oakeshott, 1998:12)

The weight indicated above by Oakeshott (1998), who made great strides in the understanding of medieval swords, and swords in general, means that the longsword as depicted was actually quite light in comparison to some weapons. This lightness allowed for a better balance in the weapon and also better handling. Along with the question of weight is the length of the weapon, especially as one affects the other quite markedly.

Measure of Weapon

The measure or length of the weapon is important as this will determine its best use and how effectively the owner of the weapon may use it. For the most part, many masters of the longsword do not describe how long the weapon should be, possibly due to inherited weapons or that it may be the swordsmith's job to know the appropriate size of the weapon, or it may be determined by the conditions of a duel.

However, Filippo Vadi does specify the weapon to be, "proportionate to the wielder, reaching from the ground to the armpit, with a long hilt, rounded pommel and an equally long, squared and pointed cross guard." (Porzio and Mele, 2002:12). This means that the weapon should be not too long or too short for the wielder being fitted to the user. He does give further details as to the form of the weapon which is most interesting, he states that the handle should be a hand span, and the cross to be the same length as the handle and pommel together (Porzio and Mele, 2002:45). This gives all the measurements a student would need to order a weapon which is appropriate according to Vadi.

Change in Weapons Due to Armour

Weapons change to suit the armour against which they are fighting against, as has been indicated previously. In the case of the longsword, the weapon was to change to suit the circumstance to deal with armour. "During the latter part of the thirteenth century a type of blade whose chief purpose was to thrust had come into use." (Oakeshott, 1996:301). This thrust-orientated weapon was designed to deal with the developments in armour at the time however the change in weapons would match the change in armour, so much so that the form of the longsword changed radically in the medieval period.

> "During the transitional period between 1320-50, when more and more pieces of reinforcing plate were being added to the old harness of mail, blades of a transitional type were developed too, though the old blunt-ended cutting blades were still popular. These transitional forms combine the acute, rigid points capable of effective thrusting with the wide, flat, fullered section in the old manner."
> (Oakeshott, 1996:302)

What can be seen in these transitional blades is an attempt to combine the advantages of the thrusting point with a cutting edge in order to achieve a more rounded weapon; one that could be used effectively for both cutting and thrusting. As more and more plate was added to armour, the cutting weapon lost its effectiveness against such armoured targets, so once again the thrusting longsword re-emerged. "After 1350, when the complete harness of plate was universal, blades became instruments designed almost entirely for thrusting;" (Oakeshott, 1996:303). These weapons were clearly biased to thrusting in their form, and had very little cutting edge, if any at all. The dominance of the thrust-orientated weapon, with very little cutting ability was not to remain, but was to be over-shadowed, once again by the dual-function weapon designed for both cut and thrust.

> "During the second quarter of the fifteenth century swords seem to have reverted to the dual function of cut and thrust. A type of blade which appears early in this century gives an admirable all-purpose sword, much lighter than the massive late fourteenth-century thrusting swords (about 2½ to 3 lb. as against 4 to 5 lb.) with very sharp points but of sufficient breadth at the centre of percussion, and a flat enough section, to provide perfect cutting edges. This blade, with minor variations of breadth and taper, was used extensively throughout the fifteenth century and remained popular until the eighteenth." (Oakeshott, 1996:303)

The chronology and form of the longsword will be presented in some detail in the next section which addresses those weapons appropriately identified as longswords from the Oakeshott Typology. This would indicate that the weapon, due to its form is a relatively easy piece to identify and place in a particular period of history. This is simply not the case, the classification and dating of swords is not as cut and dried as it may seem.

EQUIPMENT & CURATORIAL DISCUSSIONS

Classification and Dating

> *"when we consider sword types of the later Middle Ages we have to reckon with many differing blade forms which have an all-important bearing on classification:"*
> (Oakeshott, 1996:203)

What needs to be stated here is that it is blade classification more than any other part of the sword which is the key to identification of the weapon. The hilt may be changed from one to another. The blade is where the work of the sword happens and thus is the more significant part. So dating should be a simple matter of identification and placement, this is not actually the case.

> *"Though it has been possible to classify the European sword into clearly defined types and sub-types, it is not possible with the knowledge and material at present available to lay down any precise definitions of date or place."*
> (Oakeshott, 1998:14)

The types and sub-types, which will be described and had significant detail presented in the next part of the discussion, are a way to classify the weapons and get a general idea about where the weapon belongs. This does not necessarily give a confirmed date as to when the sword was made or used. A perfect example of one of the complications with regard to this is the concept of generational sword-passing. The passing of a sword from father to son means that a sword may be passed down generations from when the sword was originally made.

> *"in trying to date a sword or a sword-type, it is perhaps more practical to look for a period during which it could have been in use, though this might cover a span of time too long to be of value."*
> (Oakeshott, 1998:16)

This means that weapons can be classified by type in some form but dates are much more difficult to come by which are useful. A generationally passed weapon may be hundreds of years old by the time it is laid to rest. Further to this complication is that as communications increased in the medieval period so too did the passing of weapons. "In the High Middle Ages we do not even have these regional classifications to help us." (Oakeshott, 1998:19). A blade forged in Spain may have an Italian hilt attached to it and then presented to a noble of England. This makes the original location of the weapon difficult.

Those in the archaeological community would claim that the weapon should be dated and located by where it was found. This is not necessarily as useful as it might seem and Oakeshott (1998) clearly states, "So I firmly adhere to the archaeological heresy that knowledge of the find-place of any sword is utterly valueless in dating or placing it." (Oakeshott, 1998:20). A weapon may be found in a particular place, but was it dropped, buried or placed in that particular position. Misdating of weapons has occurred due to the location and association of other items found in the same location.

Further to the classification and related dating of weapons it should be noted that the popularity of a weapon form may emerge and then dissipate and then re-emerge. This can be found in at least two classifications of weapons identified by Oakeshott and then had these weapons follow the exact pattern which has been described.

> "Another thing to remember is that certain types – particularly XIII and XIV – lasted for a very long time. In the last two decades of the fifteenth century, for instance, Type XIII became very popular again, so much so that many old blades of the early fourteenth century were re-mounted in fashionable hilts;"
> (Oakeshott, 1996:212)

Needless to say much care must be taken in the classification of the longsword to a particular period. The form of the longsword existed over centuries and changed over this period. The significant thing is that there is a general form of the longsword and more specific classifications as well. The indicated weapon is one which is of an appropriate length to be used with a single or double-hand action, weighted and balanced to be suitable to be used alone. The length of the weapon is dependent on its form. This is a general idea of the longsword.

Much more detail will be presented using the Oakeshott Typology in the next part in order to give a clearer, more curatorial and academic examination of the weapon. This information is useful even to the practitioner in order to find the most appropriate weapon to the style which is being performed with the weapon as function is important to the form of the weapon.

OAKESHOTT'S TYPOLOGY

> "So the following typologies are based purely and simply upon an aesthetic standard, form and proportion being the only criteria. This may seem to be a serious archaeological heresy; the only excuse I can offer for it is that it works."
> (Oakeshott, 1998:22)

Oakeshott's Typology has become the standard for the classification of the medieval sword at least. One of the reasons for this is the fact that the typology works for the higher proportion of weapons, more to the point it is based upon the actual form of the weapon and in comparison to other weapons rather than some arbitrary classification. These two keys to the classification of the weapons takes into account not only their form but also their use and this is because it is based upon blade forms.

Blade Classification

The previous section on the form of the longsword introduced the idea of the classification of the sword and indicated that this was based on blade classification. The blade is used because it is the truly operational part of the weapon, "for the form of their blades gives the essential key to any classification. In fact, to attempt to classify these later weapons on hilt forms alone is impossible;" (Oakeshott, 1998:21). This is especially the case as hilts could be removed and replaced. A weapon of one nationality could

EQUIPMENT & CURATORIAL DISCUSSIONS

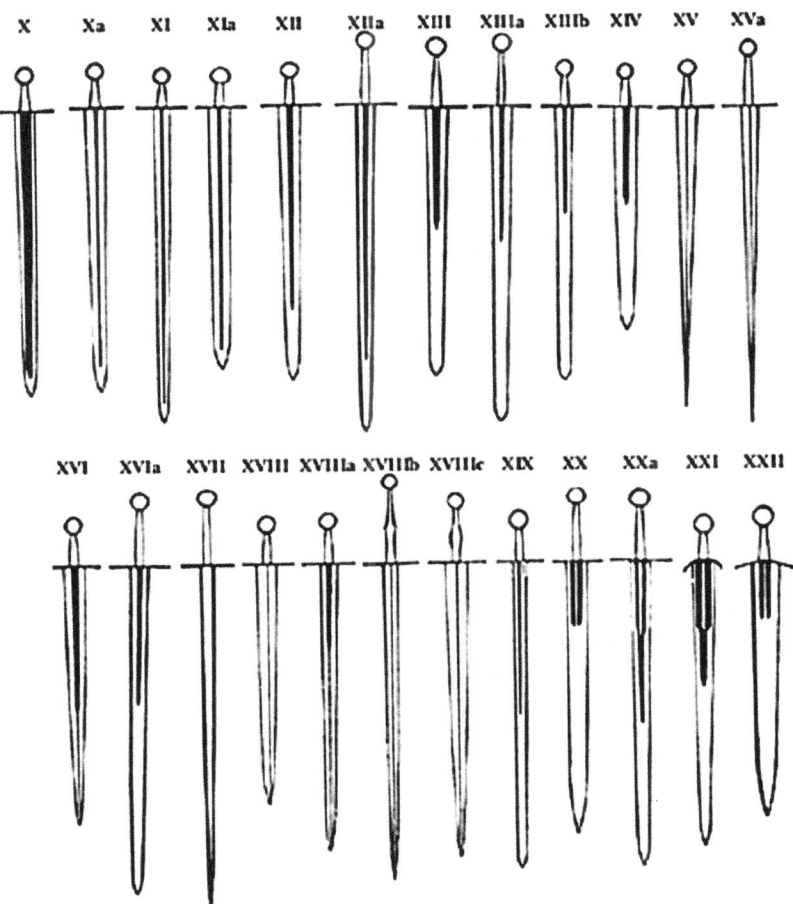

The Oakeshott Typology

be re-hilted with a hilt from an entirely different region, and especially in the case of generational swords, could be replaced to suit the current fashion. Thus the classification of "the sword itself must depend upon its blade-form and the relative proportions of its parts," (Oakeshott, 1998:22). Of course, even with this foundation for the basis of classification, it does not mean that external factors may not alter the form of a blade and thus possibly its classification.

> "one thing about these sword-blades needs to be said: the variations in their form for the most part are very subtle, especially between Types XII and XIV; many surviving swords cannot be pigeon-holed into a type at all, because the shape of their blade's outline has been changed either by corrosion or by grinding." *(Oakeshott, 1996:212)*

The fact that there are subtle differences between the types in many instances, and changes in the blade through various factors can change the classification means that some weapons are difficult to classify as one or the other type. This makes dating and classification somewhat difficult and the examiner of the weapon needs to take into account various factors in the classification of any single weapon, and in some cases the weapon cannot be classified due to these external factors.

Weapon Types

> "The typology of swords may seem to have serious omissions, but these are deliberate. It is for the straight, two-edged, cross-hilted sword of the kind which is generally (and very rightly, if somewhat romantically) called "Knightly". ... Two-hand swords, before about 1520, are only very big examples of some of the ordinary types,"
>
> (Oakeshott, 1998:23)

In some ways this simple statement should invalidate much of what is presented, especially in relation to the longsword, however the typology is still useful even for the longsword, as will be demonstrated, as even though double-handed weapons seem to be omitted, they are present in the typology and it will be these weapons which are the focus of this investigation. More to the point, as has been previously presented the longsword is clearly not simply a two-handed weapon but one which may be use with one or two hands.

The process of the investigation will highlight those types found in the typology which are most clearly weapons of the appropriate type to be called longswords and will highlight their characteristics. This will enable the reader to get an appreciation of the development of the weapon over time in somewhat more detail than has been previously presented. These weapons will be presented in the same order as they are found in Oakeshott's typology.

Type XII

While the Type XII is not identified as a longsword per se, and is clearly a single-handed weapon, "The grip is a little longer than in the preceding types, averaging about 4½"." (Oakeshott, 1998:37). This weapon could indicate a pre-cursor weapon to the longsword having a blade of the same length as a single-handed weapon but a longer handle to accommodate the use of a second hand. This general shape and development in the style of the weapon is continued into the Type XIII.

Type XIII

> "Swords of Type XIII are of a very striking and individual shape; some of them are very large – "swords of war" they were called in the time of their popularity between about 1280 and 1340. These Epées de Guerre are massive weapons, but are not to be confused with two-handed swords. There were a few such as early as 1350, but they were considerably bigger and were always referred to as Epées a deux Mains or even "Twahandswerds". The War Sword had a blade some 36 in. to 40 in. long with a very long hilt, from 6 in. to 8 in. between cross and

> pommel, but it can be wielded in one hand, though provision is made for using it with both. Most Type XIII swords are large like this, but there are several of more ordinary dimensions, though they have hilts long in proportion to their blades. These are broad and flat, with edges running nearly parallel to a spatulate point;"
> (Oakeshott, 1996:207)

The Type XIII is clearly in a longsword form, this is evident by the image in the typology, but also by the description of the weapon given. These war swords were clearly a development to allow the use of a second hand on the weapon, as indicated in their description. What needs to be noted here is the clearly defined difference, as asserted by Oakeshott between these weapons and the Renaissance two-handed sword. The naming of two-hand here is based upon the use of the weapon; indeed the weapon described above is clearly a longsword.

The blade length of these weapons along with the handle length means that the weapon could be comfortably used with either a single or two hands, thus falling into the definition of a longsword as established. This weapon shows the clear progression toward a weapon which was purposefully designed for the dual use of either one-handed or two-handed operation. Further to this particular element is the form of the weapon itself, tending toward a weapon which has a dual purpose of cut and thrust.

> "During the second quarter of the fifteenth century swords seem to have reverted to the dual function of cut and thrust. A type of blade which appears early in this century gives an admirable all-purpose sword, much lighter than the massive late fourteenth-century thrusting swords (about 2½ to 3 lb. as against 4 to 5 lb.) with very sharp points but of sufficient breadth at the centre of percussion, and a flat enough section, to provide perfect cutting edges. This blade, with minor variations of breadth and taper, was used extensively throughout the fifteenth century and remained popular until the eighteenth."
> (Oakeshott, 1996:303)

The indicated weapon is one which fell out and came back into favour due to its shape and its ability to be used for both cut and thrust. What will be found in this discussion is that some weapons were clearly biased toward one direction or another, obviously to deal with armour however the dominant weapon form will be one which serves the dual purpose of both cut and thrust. The weight of the weapon is significant as indicated in the form previously, the fact that these weapons were lighter means that they could more easily be wielded by the combatant, and thus used more effectively. The form of the weapon clearly indicates a multi-purpose weapon designed to be used single- or double-handed.

> "A broad blade, nearly as wide at the tip as at the hilt. Most examples show a distinct widening immediately below the hilt, thereafter the edges run with an imperceptible taper to a spatulate point. The fuller generally occupies a little more than half of the blade's length. The grip is long in proportion to the blade—average length 6"."
> (Oakeshott, 1998:41)

Type XIIIa

The separation of Type XIII and Type XIIIa is a matter of size. The Type XIIIa is a larger sword as depicted in the image for the typology presented in the early part of this presentation. "This is generally the same shape as Type XIII, only much larger. The blade, of similar form, is generally from 37" to 40" long, while the grip ranges from 6½" to 9" in length." (Oakeshott, 1998:42). The separation between Type XIII and Type XIIIa would seem to be a piece of pedantry however the size difference is significant as this would affect the operation of the weapon. This is one of the few times in the typology in which the size is the determining factor for the type.

> "The size of a sword has not hitherto determined its type, but here, and in swords of the 14th and 15th centuries, it will be found to do so. The reason here is partly that the XIIIa's are very big weapons, partly because in their own time they were distinguished from their smaller contemporaries by the term "espées de Guerre" or "Grete Swerdes"."
> (Oakeshott, 1998:42)

The term "great sword" has often been used to refer to a two-handed sword in the spirit of the two-handed sword of the sixteenth century. What is of significance here is that the term is being used to describe a weapon, admittedly large by comparison to other contemporary weapons, but clearly in the same class as the longsword as it has been so far depicted. This idea of the "great sword" is more likely a nomenclature used to describe the size of the weapon in comparison to other weapons of a similar period, namely single-handed or arming swords.

> "The expression "Grant Espée" would distinguish Types XIIIa from the "epée courte" or "parvus ensis" which may have been the short weapon of Types XIV or XV, better known by its 15th century name of "arming sword"."
> (Oakeshott, 1998:44)

More to the point, and especially with regard to the relative size of this weapon as compared to other weapons in the "longsword" category, this weapon while clearly larger than some, was clearly one which could be used in a single-handed fashion or a two-handed fashion. Further to the point and going back to the previous description of a longsword as one which could be worn and drawn from the belt there is evidence of this type of sword being worn on a belt (Oakeshott, 1998:45), clearly placing this weapon, while large, in the longsword category. What is even more interesting with regard to this is the evidence presented that not only was this weapon worn and used alone, but also the distinction is clear that the longsword was considered a separate weapon type.

Type XV

"A strongly tapering, acutely pointed blade of four-sided "flattened diamond" section. The edges are straight, and taper without noticeable curves to the point, which may be strongly reinforced. The blade may be broad at the hilt (some 2"–2¼") or quite narrow (about 1¼")."
(Oakeshott, 1998:56)

The Type XV presents a weapon which was clearly biased toward the use of the point, merely due to its shape. This is further evidenced by the reinforced point of the weapon. This is a weapon which was designed to defeat the armour of the day. "Type XV seems first to have appeared in the second half of the thirteenth century." (Oakeshott, 1996:307), about the time that armour was changing and the addition of plates on armour was beginning to occur. This weapon was clearly designed to punch through mail and get in the gaps in plate. This form of weapon has clear trends toward the form of the longsword as depicted.

"Many swords of this type [XV] have long grips, like the war-swords of Type XIII. After about 1350 nine swords out of ten seem to have such grips, and are to-day variously referred to as "Hand-and-a-half" or "Bastard" swords. The latter term was used in the fifteenth century, but it is not certain that it was applied to this particular kind of weapon. "Hand-and-a-half", though modern, is a name far more apt for it; these swords were single-handed weapons, but being furnished with long grips, could at need be wielded easily in both."
(Oakeshott, 1996:308)

The idea of the "bastard sword" is one where the hilt of the weapon was suitable for the use of one or two hands. This obviously would have to be complemented by the rest of the weapon in the form of balance and length for this to be useful. These weapons were referred to as "bastard" due to the hand-and-a-half grip which was neither single- nor two-handed in nature. The advantage in this design was the resulting versatility presented by the use of one or both hands if required.

"All these [Type XV] are hand-and-a-half swords, with grips about 7 in. long, sharply tapering blades of four-sided section about 32 in. long, straight crosses tapering towards the tips, which are abruptly turned downwards and large pommels of Type J." (Oakeshott, 1996:309)

Once again, the description presents a weapon which has a substantial grip presented, which could be used for single or double-handed use. The blade sharply tapers toward the tip giving it a great advantage in the thrust, rather than a broad blade for use in the cut. This is a weapon by its form is able to be used in true longsword-fashion, utilising its shorter blade and longer handle for speed and accuracy, while maintaining the advantage of a double-handed grip should the wielder require.

> "The type [Type XV] seems to have gone out of favour for a time in the early fifteenth century, but after about 1440 it became extremely popular again in its earliest form, particularly in Italy." (Oakeshott, 1996:309)

This is no doubt the type of weapon which Filippo Vadi describes as being his perfect weapon in his treatise, and which Fiore dei Liberi alludes to in his. This is a weapon which is designed for the use of both edge and point, but would seem to bias itself toward the point. The Type XVa which follows is a clear follow on from the principles of this weapon.

Type XVa

> "The blade is similar [to the XV], though generally narrow and slender. The grip is much longer, from 7" to 9" or even 10". Forms of pommel and cross are the same as for Type XV." (Oakeshott, 1998:59)

Once again, as with the Type XV, a weapon with a slender and pointed blade is presented with a longer handle to be used by one or two hands depending on what is required by the user at the time. In this particular instance the weapon is clearly biased toward the use of two hands due to the extended handle as compared to its predecessor. What is even more interesting is that this weapon was heavily biased toward use against armoured opponents in the additions to the form of the weapon.

> "In the Tower of London is another (with a "scent-stopper" pommel) of Type XVa; this is particularly interesting as it has, just below the hilt, a piece about 6" long where the edges are thickened and squared off, forming a long "ricasso". The purpose of this was to enable the wielder to bring his left hand forward to grasp the sword below the cross, so that he could make a powerful two-handed thrust with a shortened blade in close fighting." (Oakeshott, 1998:60)

While this is a specific example of the Type XVa sword, the addition of the ricasso, combined with the already tapered and reinforced point of the weapon heavily biases this weapon toward foot combat between armoured opponents. The two-handed thrust of the weapon in what is known as "half-swording" is evident in many period manuals. This is designed to allow the weapon to be levered into place so that a short hard thrust may be made between plates, or in some instances, to punch through the plates of the opponent. Just like their parent type, the XV, they are well known in form as "bastard swords", having utility for actions with both one and two hands.

> "These swords are of the well-known "Bastard" or "hand-and-a-half" kind. Eight out of ten military effigies and brasses of the period 1360–1420 show swords like this; there is only a limited variety in the forms of hilt, and the blades are long and slender." (Oakeshott, 1998:60)

Type XVI

The Type XVI is a single-handed form of weapon and thus would seem to be out of the scope of this investigation however it does form the basis of the following longsword form which follows it. Thus an examination of this weapon will reveal some of the characteristics which are found in the following type. The first note which needs to be made about this type is in comparison to two previous types the XIV and XV.

> "Type XVI is really a compromise between Types XIV and XV, for the upper half of the blade retains the old flat fullered section while the lower half (the business end of the sword) is four-sided and acutely-pointed."
> (Oakeshott, 1996:309)

This is a weapon which is clearly designed for both cut and thrust actions. It has the tapered point for thrusting actions while retaining a broad blade clearly designed for cutting actions. This demonstrates a shift in ideas about how the weapon can be utilised against an opponent and the realisation that both cut and thrust can be effective.

> "The most striking thing about these blades [Type XVI] is that they seem very clearly to be made to serve the dual purpose of cutting and thrusting. The upper part of the blade is in the old style, while the lower part is acute enough, and stiff enough to thrust effectively." (Oakeshott, 1998:61)

The idea of the utilisation of the weapon for both cut and thrust is one which forms the basis for the following Type XVIa, a larger weapon, formed in such a way that it can be equally used for both cut and thrust. This is weapon is based on the form of the single handed Type XVI, which is presented above. It is necessary to see the foundation of the weapon in order to understand it.

Type XVIa

> "A long tapering blade, broad at the hilt, with a sharp point often strongly reinforced. The fuller is well-marked, often quite short (about 1/3 of the blade's length) rarely more than half the length. The lower part of the blade is not of diamond section, but of a stout, flat hexagonal section. The grip is long, as in Types XIIIa and XVa, the tang of stout rectangular section, often with the fuller running up into it." (Oakeshott, 1998:63)

What can be seen in the description above is a lot of similarities in the form of the weapon between it and the previous XVI. Both have blades which are quite wide at the hilt and with a strongly reinforced point, thus giving the weapon the dual function of both cut and thrust. The grip in the case of the XVIa is long, as can be expected and thus it clearly falls into the idea of the longsword in form. Much has been argued about the origin and dating of these weapons and their relationships to other types.

> "These swords are generally said to belong to the late 14th—early 15th centuries, but the evidence does not uphold this. It might be said that Type XVIa is merely another variety of Type XIIIa, but it does seem, on the whole, to be a development of it, though undoubtedly in use at the same time."
> (Oakeshott, 1998:63)

The questions of dating and form in this particular case highlight the issues of dating and classification in general. The similarities between the Type XVIa and the Type XIIIa bring in questions about the form and the dating of the weapon, and as to whether or not they are too similar not to be ignored. The biggest difference is in the point, where it is tapered and reinforced in the Type XVIa and not so in the Type XIIIa. Further questions arise as to the dating of this particular type.

> "There are many of these swords, nearly all once thought to be of the late 14th or early 15th centuries. The earlier dating which I suggest is well supported by a number of clearly shown swords in Italian paintings of the early 14th century." (Oakeshott, 1998:65)

Regardless of the dating of the weapon, what is presented in the form of the weapon is clearly that the weapon is presented in such a form that it would be utilised for both cut and thrusting effectively by the user of the weapon. The addition of the longer handle and the longer blade from the previous single-handed type, XVI, clearly puts this weapon in the hand-and-a-half or longsword bracket. The type which follows, the Type XVII, is an interesting weapon as it seems to be designed for a single purpose, rather than the dual of the XVIa.

Type XVII

> "Type XVII ... was perhaps the sword most in use during the period 1370-1425. Its section is usually hexagonal and very solid with sometimes a very shallow fuller in its upper half." (Oakeshott, 1996:311)

The fact that this type was most used during this period is fascinating in some ways and quite expected in others. More detail is required to examine the weapon more fully, but needless to say it is the shape of this weapon which is the most significant in this instance. In some ways it is similar to the previous weapon, but there are also significant differences which must also be noted.

> "A long, slender blade acutely tapering. Many are reminiscent of 16th century rapier blades, but others are nearly as broad at the hilt (1½"–2") as some of the XVIa blades. The section is generally hexagonal. Many examples have a shallow fuller in the upper quarter of the blade, though some do not. The grip is always long. The tang usually very stout, of a quadrangular section." (Oakeshott, 1998:65)

EQUIPMENT & CURATORIAL DISCUSSIONS

Being that the blade of the weapon is most significant to the use of the weapon this is the focus of the description above. The form of the cross-guard and pommel has no real significant effect on the use of the weapon, at least in comparison to the blade of the weapon. The slender form of the blade would imply that the primary purpose of this weapon is thrusting. This is further reinforced by the solid shape of the weapon.

The form of the weapon is similar to the XVIa; however this weapon is heavily biased in favour of the thrust, with much less cutting ability. In some ways it is much like an estoc, a specialised thrusting weapon, "It is essentially a thrusting sword, some being more like stout, sharp-pointed bars of steel." (Oakeshott, 1998:65). This is a weapon which is designed to either punch through the armour of an opponent, or have the point moved around the plates to find the gaps in the armour. The idea of using the weapon to thrust with and thus get around armour is reinforced by the presence of the ricasso.

> *"Type XVII with one of these pommels [T3]. Its blade, incidentally, has a ricasso about 6 in. long, the purpose of which seems to have been to allow the left hand of the man wielding it to be brought forward to grasp the blade below the hilt so that the sword can be "shortened" in close fighting on foot." (Oakeshott, 1996:315)*

Clearly this weapon was designed primarily for armoured foot combat against an opponent who had a significant amount of armour and plated at that. The shortened grip on the weapon is designed for a much stronger thrust against an opponent in armour, and images of the weapon used in this fashion can be found in the manuals of the period such as Fiore dei Liberi's *Flos Duellatorum*.

Fiore dei Liberi Flos Duellatorum (1410)

This shortened grip is also designed so that the weapon can be more easily used in close quarters combat for leverage against the opponent's weapon and also to move the point of the weapon into a position to thrust against any gap in the armour. While this is not the common form of the weapon its presence does easily represent this idea and direction in use.

Type XVIII

The Type XVIII is an interesting weapon to say the least. This is one weapon which could be really referred to as general purpose and generic, both in terms of use and also in terms of form, "Type XVIII is a general all-purpose sword which varies a good deal in the shape of its blade's outline as well as in its hilt styles." (Oakeshott, 1996:313). The variation in the weapon is one thing which makes this type difficult to isolate, and thus there are some sub-types present. The weapon is depicted as a single-handed weapon going by the image of the typology, so the question is why is it present in this discussion? The description of the weapon assists with this.

> "A broad blade (2"–2½" at the hilt) of four-sided "flattened diamond" section; the edges taper in graceful curves to a sharp point. The grip is of moderate length (3¾"–4") but some are big swords with grips over 5" long. A feature of the grips of these swords—many are preserved—is a noticeable swelling in the middle (as plate 46D, fig. 75, p. 104)." (Oakeshott, 1998:67)

What the description gives is a weapon which has a hilt which can vary in length, along with variation in the blade length. This means that there are examples of the Type XVIII which quite comfortably fit into the form of the longsword as well as those which do not. The sub-typing of the weapon presented by Oakeshott, some of which will be discussed in the following types assists with classification of this type. The form of the weapon was very much generic in form having various variations depending on the actual weapon.

> "This type [XVIII] of blade was used extensively all through the fifteenth century, some being broad like Henry V's and others much narrower. Most of them had a four-sided section showing a definite mid-rib and slightly concave faces to each of the four sides, but after about 1450 many of them had sharply defined ribs and flat faces, similar to the later blades of Type XV" (Oakeshott, 1996:313)

These variations make it a little difficult to specify exactly the form and attributes of this particular type, however the variations do fall within a general form and thus type of weapon. What should be noted, and is of real interest in the actual use of the weapon, is that unlike the Type XVII which came before it, the XVIII reverts back to the idea of the use of the edge as well as the point, thus cut and thrust in operation, rather than purely thrust.

> "In XVIII, the edges run in curves, and the lower part of the blade looks broader. The type is, in fact, admirably adapted for a cut-and-thrust style of fighting, and seems to be a logical development of Type XVI. The strong midrib gives great rigidity, yet toward the point at the centre of percussion there is plenty of width to each edge." (Oakeshott, 1998:68)

EQUIPMENT & CURATORIAL DISCUSSIONS

The form of the weapon allows it to be used equally effectively for both cutting and thrusting actions, and as indicated, it bears resemblance to the Type XVI which came before it, and carrying much of the same characteristics. Needless to say this generic form of weapon would have great advantages being able to cut and thrust and this would assist in its longevity simply due to its utility. Being that this is the primary weapon and having sub-types, it is of importance that such sub-types, and such a wide variety of sub-types, would have only eventuated had the original type been of such use, and also in such a generic form that modifications could be made from it. Needless to say, as far as types go the XVIII and its sub-types have one of the greatest sustained longevities.

> "This type, and its four sub-types, were the most widely used swords between c. 1410 and 1510 all over Europe. It may well have been in use in the late 14th century, but the earliest date we so far have for it is 1419;" (Oakeshott, 1998:68)

Type XVIIIb

Three of the sub-types of the XVIII will be discussed being XVIIIb, XVIIIc, and XVIIIe. These weapons are the ones which conform to the idea of the longsword the closest. While the others may have similar characteristics, they are missing an element which is necessary for this classification, and thus have been omitted from the discussion. What will be noted are their common characteristics which can be found in the parent-type, the XVIII.

> "A long, slender, acutely pointed blade, generally of "flattened diamond" section, often with the point reinforced. The grip is very long, often as much as 10"–11". The pommel is most frequently of one of the wheel forms, but second to those in popularity seem to have been the scent-stopper and fruit shaped ones of Types T and T5. Crosses are generally long and slender, more often straight than curved. The grip is of a very characteristic shape, with a waisted lower half which merges with a slender upper half."
> (Oakeshott, 1998:70)

The Type XVIIIb has the main characteristics of its parent-type, as can be expected. The reinforced point on this type is one area in which this sub-type varies with the original. This is continued with the extended and waisted shape of the grip on the weapon. The flattened diamond cross-section of the blade allows it to give it the extra length of the weapon while maintaining a true cutting edge. Thus the weapon has equal utility for cutting as it does for thrusting. The characteristics of this weapon clearly place it in the expected form of the longsword as presented previously.

> "One may unhesitatingly say that here [Type XVIIIb] is the very epitome of a "hand-and-a-half" sword of the second half of the 15th century, a German one exactly similar to so many carried by Dürer's saints and knights."
> (Oakeshott, 1998:70)

Type XVIIIc

"A broad, heavy blade, of "flattened diamond" section, the faces nearly always flat or slightly convex, generally about 34" long. The grip is long, rather like those grips of some type XVIII swords with a sharp swelling in the middle. As these big swords are hand-and-a-half weapons, the swelling is nearer to the cross than to the pommel. The pommel is generally of one of the wheel forms."
(Oakeshott, 1998:71)

The Type XVIIIc conforms to the "classic" form of its parent-type. It has the flattened diamond cross-section on the blade. This weapon is a little shorter than the Type XVIIIb, both in the blade and the handle, but it has the same shaped handle with the swelling in the middle of it. The weapon here is broader than the previous one thus giving it more ability to cut, however it retains the tapered point typical to the parent-type, thus also giving it thrusting capability. This weapon has more in common with the parent-type than it does differences.

Type XVIIIe

"A long, narrow blade generally with a long (5"–6") ricasso narrower than the blade itself; occasionally with a fuller running most of the length, but more commonly of "flattened diamond" section. Pommel of pear form, and the cross is curved sharply downward." (Oakeshott, 1998:72)

The basic design of the Type XVIIIe is much the same as the parent-type for the XVIII however it is not all the same. The addition of the ricasso is significant as it allows the user to gain more leverage over the opponent when placing a hand on the weapon, known as half-swording. This idea has been presented previously in the form of the Type XVII. This weapon is more unique in form however and is most likely Danish in origin going by examples of the weapon; this is a different form of weapon, purpose designed (Oakeshott, 1998:73). This makes this type one of the few which can, for the most part, be identified by location. This is rather unique amongst swords, as has been previously indicated. This weapon, purely by its longer shape and the presence of the ricasso would be more likely used for thrusting than cutting, while retaining at least some ability to cut.

Type XX

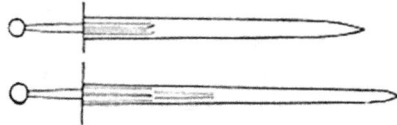

"A large, broad blade sometimes extremely wide at the hilt. Many examples have three shallow fullers in the upper half, two side by side immediately below the hilt, and a single one in the middle of the blade below them. Others may have two very narrow, deep fullers side by side extending about a quarter of the blade length. Hilts are usually long (about 8"–10") with scent-

stopper pommels of Type T. Some may have wheel pommels. Crosses are generally long and slender, curved slightly—or rather, each arm inclines at an angle downward, but remains straight" (Oakeshott, 1998:75)

The reinforcing fullers on the weapon are designed to both strengthen the blade but also to keep it reasonably light in the hand. The longer handle places it clearly in the form of the longsword, being able to be used either with one or two hands. The Type XX has a broad blade, much like the earlier types. This makes the weapon primarily designed for cutting rather than thrusting. "Some of these swords are war-swords, a sort of late development of Type XIIIa, in use at the same time as the late examples of that type." (Oakeshott, 1998:76). This relationship demonstrates how the weapons were very much developed based on the experiences gained from the previous forms.

Longsword "Type"

After examining the thirteen types of sword as presented by Oakeshott, what can be clearly said is that there is no one type of sword which is clearly "the" longsword type. Rather that the longsword came in many different variations and shapes. These shapes were heavily dictated by the use of the weapon, and thus the weapon needs to be classified by the blade of the weapon rather than by any other part. Hilts and other attachments can and often were changed to suit the style at the time.

What have been presented are some different forms of the longsword for examination. What is important is this is merely a glossing over of the information which is presented by Oakeshott and a person should treat it as such. This is an introduction to the Oakeshott's Typology and much more can be said of it. What has been presented here is designed to point the researcher in the right direction as to where to find the longsword in amongst the many weapons which are described, and also to demonstrate that this weapon is present in the Typology even if it is not clearly separated from other weapons.

The modern researcher and indeed the modern recreationalist should take note of which weapon that they are using and how it is being used; ask whether or not it is actually the best weapon to be recreating what they are doing. The information found in more curatorial sources such as Oakeshott's Typology is significant as it details much of the form of the weapon and also approximately when this weapon would have been in use. It is important to be able to match the appropriate weapon to the appropriate use in order to perform the actions presented in manuals of the period properly.

CONCLUSION

The discussion which has been presented has been designed to present the longsword as a weapon and it has been designed to discover the form of the longsword and what the weapon actually is. This means that the discussion, for the most part, has been from a curatorial standpoint in order to classify the weapon and demonstrate its differences and similarities with other weapons.

The first place for identifying the longsword was with regard to terminology. This did not go into the very simple aspects common amongst all swords but kept to terms which are more directly associated with the longsword, and like terms. The result of this was that the weapon now called the longsword was also called a two-handed sword, a hand-and-a-half sword, a bastard sword, a great sword and also a war sword. All of these terms were demonstrated to indicate the same general form of weapon, while having some particular characteristics of their own.

This then moved on to a practical definition of the weapon, one which was based on how the weapon is handled and fits into the hand. In this particular case the longsword was identified as a weapon which had the facility to be wielded with two hands due to the grip, but also had the length and weight characteristics which enabled it to be used with a single hand. Thus the longsword was identified as a weapon of great utility.

The second part moved on to the form of the longsword. This searched for common physical characteristics of the weapon which could be identified easily. The first identifier was that the usage of the weapon affected its form. Thus it was long enough to be used two-handed but short enough to be used single-handed. This measurement characteristic was further emphasised in the weight and length aspects which were identified both as a matter of fact and also advice from one of the masters of the period. This led on to the discussion of the changes in the weapon due to the developments in armour. The weapon changed to suit the situation in which it was found some weapons having distinctive thrusting aspects while many retained the equal ability for both cut and thrust. This led on to the question of classification and dating which set up for the discussion of the Oakeshott Typology.

The Oakeshott Typology has been used, and various weapons selected from the typology to fit into the form which is the longsword, and these types were discussed in some detail. The idea of this was to identify the longsword of various periods in a curatorial form in order that the changes in the weapon could be identified. What should be noted here are the difficulties in clearly stating to which period or even nationality a weapon belongs due to the many influences the weapon may be subject to. Thirteen types were identified as either distinctively longsword in form or at least related to a form which was. These forms give us an idea about how the weapon changed and the various different forms of the longsword. Its place in history and the location and use of a particular type should be at least in the back of a practitioner's mind so that the correct or at least passingly similar form of longsword is used for the method that is being used.

There are many different forms of the weapon which is called the longsword. This investigation has identified a general form of the weapon and also some more specific examples of the weapon. The research presented is designed to introduce the idea of the form of the longsword and what it was, and to clear up some of the confusion with regard to terminology. What is presented is foundation and introductory research; there is much more to be found about the longsword and it is encouraged that further research is made upon this subject.

What is a Rapier?

INTRODUCTION

The question which is asked in this article is one which needs to be considered by anyone who would consider using a rapier, talking about rapiers, or indeed having an interest in rapiers. For the most part the question itself belies the complexity which is involved in such a discussion. There are many elements which need to be discussed to have a complete discussion of this particular topic, and what is presented are some of the arguments toward that discussion.

EQUIPMENT & CURATORIAL DISCUSSIONS

NOT AN EASY QUESTION

What is a rapier? This is a question that has been posed by curators and historians alike, and contrary to some beliefs, it is not exactly the easiest question to answer. The biggest problem is, "it is hard to define something which comes in many shapes and sizes." (Anglo, 2000:99). This is one of the greatest problems associated with answering the question. The fact that the rapier came with many different hilts, blades of different lengths and widths makes defining exactly what a rapier is a very difficult prospect. There are types of rapier which contradict one another in their form as well.

> "the ambiguities of the rapier are, however, in a class of their own. As A.V.B. Norman puts it, with masterly understatement: 'the evidence for what is meant by the word rapier at a particular period is confused'. This would matter little had historians of fencing not tended to equate scientific swordsmanship with the Renaissance,"
> *(Anglo, 2000:99)*

What historians of fencing, especially those with a bias toward the modern sport, feel is that the rapier is an evolutionary step toward perfection found in the foil and epée found in modern fencing. From their point of view, the arts found in the Middle Ages and Renaissance were not particularly well formed and required development. To circumvent this particular problem, it is best to go back to the original sources, but in the case of the rapier, this is not particularly helpful as contemporary definitions are hazy at best, even those which had practical experience with the weapon (Anglo, 2000:101). This creates a real problem in the definition of this particular weapon. The word itself does appear in period, but its presence is very limited.

LIMITED WORD PRESENCE

> "there never was any general agreement as to what a rapier might be. It was only in England and Germany, around the middle decades of the sixteenth century, that rapier came to be used to denote a long sword which, though designed both for cutting and thrusting, placed emphasis on the use of the point rather than the edge: and in neither country has it been possible to establish a conniving etymology." *(Anglo, 2000:99)*

What this means is that there was only two countries and only for a short period of time where the word "rapier" was actually used in a period context.[23] Of course there have been many who have decided that to establish the meaning of the word it is important to look at its origin, and thus establish an etymology of the word and thus find its origin nationally. This would seem to be a great idea, but it has led many curatorial experts and fencing historians along a very interesting path. One of the many sources cites this as the origin.

---

23   Just for interest the German spelling was "rappier".

ETYMOLOGICAL ORIGIN?

> "The origin of the term "rapier", first noted in 1474 in a French document, is believed to be from the Spanish words for costume sword – espada ropera. By the early 16th century the term had come to mean a sword for use by gentlemen; and shortly after the middle of the century is was accepted as meaning a long, pointed and slender fencing sword for use by civilians."
>
> *(Valentine, 1968:7)*

The French term found was *"epee rapiere"* and this was compared to the Spanish term, which has been cited for re-emphasis and legitimisation. What will be noted later on is this is not necessarily the case, and that calling this the origin is not necessarily accurate. Of course through searches of etymological data, several ideas have been expounded. Bull (1990) gives three different origins for the word rapier; from the German *"rappen"* meaning to tear, from the Spanish *"raspar"* meaning to scratch and finally from the Spanish *"espada ropera"* meaning robe sword (Bull, 1990:96). If an examination of the period documents is done, the results put some of these discoveries and theories in a bad light.

The best source currently available for this information about the rapier is Anglo's (2000) *The Martial Arts of Renaissance Europe*, in which he states that the French and Spanish never used *espee rapiere* or *espada ropera* (Anglo, 2000:100). Further in the English translation of many manuals from the period of the popularity of the rapier, especially in England, and later, Italian manuals in which the word *spada*, meaning sword, was used, this is often interpreted as "rapier" (Anglo, 2000:100). This is how such manuals which were translated into English in the Renaissance period such as Di Grassi's *His True Art of Defence* of 1594, were the word *spada* is used and it is translated as "rapier" as this was the weapon commonly used in the period and also the one which was most popular at the time.

WORD NOT USED

What is also important to note is that even in the case of the places where the practice of rapier-play originated, "Italian, French and Spanish authors had several words indicating different types of sword; but rapier was not one of them." (Anglo, 2000:100). This gives us pause for thought at this point in time. Had some other word been used in the English translations, would that be the one that was used now? It is not to say that some of the original words proposed were not used, this is not the case. There is a rare occurrence of *rapiere* in French Renaissance account, keen edge, alludes to cutting sword (Anglo, 2000:100). This is exactly what the rapier was generally not, truly it could cut but it was not primarily a cutting sword.

The Italians did have a different word, which does appear in period texts, for a primarily thrusting sword, but it is not "rapier". This weapon which is described is also often mistakenly said to be the precursor of the rapier, where actually it is not.

> "the only weapon given a specific name was the estoque... occurs only twice in the Valencia documents to indicate on of a number of long, sharp, narrow-bladed thrusting swords" *(Anglo, 2000:100)*

EQUIPMENT & CURATORIAL DISCUSSIONS

These long, sharp, narrow-bladed thrusting swords were designed to be used from horseback against armoured opponents. They were often used as a substitute for the lance or as a sword when the other had broken. This weapon was designed to puncture through the gaps in armour something that the rapier was certainly not designed to do. Also the fact that this was a military weapon and not a civilian one also removes it from contention as the father of the rapier. Some of the reasons for this evolutionary history of fencing have already been given, but to understand this issue, more detail is required.

HISTORIOGRAPHICAL ISSUES

> "central issue for nineteenth-century historians and their followers was the development of the rapier - a notion which they used to denigrate the medieval masters and, indeed, most swordsmanship prior to the seventeenth century. Nowadays the word rapier conjures up visions of a long, thin-bladed, sharp-pointed weapon capable of being wielded with virtuosic speed and dexterity to delude and, ultimately, to run through an opponent." *(Anglo, 2000:99)*

Historiographically, especially with regard to the nineteenth-century historians, they had a particular thought in mind when writing these histories and this needs to be taken into account. The fact that they were attempting to show the medieval and Renaissance masters in a less pleasant light than the later ones who worked with the small-sword and later weapons demonstrates the idea of an evolutionary point of view with regard to the weapons used. The estoc evolved into the rapier, which evolved into the small-sword, which evolved into the epée and other modern weapons. With new research that has been done of late this problem is being addressed, of course problems still persist.

> "the polyglot nature of fencing literature further complicates matters; and, for anyone interested in how people used swords for fighting, curatorial concerns (more with hilts than with blades) are of limited value. It is self-evident that, in order to understand sword play, one must understand the types of sword used."
> *(Anglo, 2000:99)*

The multiple different languages of fencing literature make the discovery of the "true rapier" problematic to say the least. Even in translations of other languages into English the bias of the interpreter needs to be taken into account. For the more practical angle for the Renaissance fencer, studies of hilt types are less useful as how the sword was used is vastly more important. Even where a curatorial study is made, hilts are more the focus, rather than the blades, this gives an incomplete description and often mislabelling of weapons occurs. Blades are far more important as they assist in defining how the weapon was used.

Even in the use of the weapons if that is to be the primary delineation as to what a rapier is and is not there are issues to contend with, "for most of the period with which we are concerned, cutting was as important as thrusting." (Anglo, 2000:99). If the point is the focus, as it was in histories of fencing, those weapons which could also cut effectively were often discarded, even though they may fill the criteria perfectly in other areas. For the purposes of description of the period rapier, it is to the manuals which actually used the weapon where some answers lay.

IN THE MANUALS

How the weapons are described along with those illustrations found in these manuals can give a doorway into discovering an accurate description of the weapon and therefore some answers (Anglo, 2000:101). Of course, in the case of pictures this relies upon the artist depicting the weapons as they actually were and not an interpretation of their own, and in translation it once again relies on the person who actually wrote the book. For those translated into a different language it again relies upon the actual translation.

> "The blades of the single-hand sword shown in Marozzo's Opera nova are all fairly wide at the hilt and generally provided with a side ring and finger ring, while the edges, although not completely parallel, are more or less straight until they suddenly taper to a point."
> *(Anglo, 2000:102)*

This would describe a weapon which has utility for both cutting and thrusting. The hilt design is something close to an earlier rapier also. Of course this is contradicted by the fact that Marozzo describes many cutting actions with these weapons which would eliminate them from being rapiers according to some interpretations. This is one example of the problems associated even when dealing with the weapons from one manual, but this problem actually exists across manuals also. Many different rapiers are depicted by different masters, in some cases different within the same treatises. There is however, a distinct change from broader blades to narrower blades as time progresses, but still there is no uniformity. (Anglo, 2000:102).

CONCLUSION

The result of the above description could be the question of whether or not the rapier in the classical sense actually existed at all. It is important that in the discussion of a weapon assumptions are disregarded and the facts of the matter are stuck to get the most accurate answer presently available.

What needs to happen for any discussion of the weapon to occur in any sort of reasonable way is a common understanding of what this most perplexing weapon is. For the most part this will be dependent on the point of view of the people discussing the weapon. For my own purposes I assume that the rapier is a long-bladed, single-handed weapon, designed for civilian use, which may be used for either cutting or thrusting, but is primarily designed to thrust. This gives a general form of the weapon and how it is used, both of which are significant, needless to say it is vital for a common definition to be made for people to discuss this weapon.

EQUIPMENT & CURATORIAL DISCUSSIONS

What is a Feder?

INTRODUCTION

The question posed above would seem to be answered straight-forwardly and simply enough, but to truly understand this weapon, more digging and research needed to be done. Not only was there the question of the term itself, but there was the question of where this term came from, and what it actually meant, and what it has been interpreted to mean over the years that it has been used. This is without examining the weapon itself.

Unfortunately, there are so few well-structured and efficient reports on the museum pieces which are held. This is not to mention, the simple mismanagement and elements of failure to place them under the correct category, often of predecessors of current curators, that has allowed some to be lost, that has made examining museum pieces difficult for this examination. Thus there is very little if any examination of museum pieces in this study.

What has been studied in this examination is all of the documentation possible to be accessed about this particular weapon, within the authors own limitations on finances and language limits. There has been a lot of research done on this weapon and much to be said from many different sources about it.

One of the results of this investigation is an examination of image sources where the weapon appears and a discussion of what represents this weapon in these images. This alone, should give some pause for thought and remind the reader that though a weapon may be named, its form does not stay static over time. Much of the same consternation occurs when it comes to the question of the rapier.

Organisation

The investigation which follows is rather in-depth as a result it has been divided into parts. There is the introductory part which includes this introduction and the immediately following section giving the short answer to the question proposed. This is designed to introduce the reader to the argument which surrounds this topic.

Following this is a discussion of "Words". These are all discussions of words associated with the weapon; in other words, reasons for it being called a particular thing or other and also discussions of other words which it may or may not be called by. Naming a thing or finding out the name of a thing can cause a lot of grief amongst a community.

The next section consisting of a single discussion is about "Pictures". This is an investigation of how the weapon was depicted in various treatises over the period in which it was used. This gives the reader an image of the weapon in its various different forms and demonstrates that there was no one form which flowed through its entire existence.

The "Objects" section is designed to give a sort of physicality to the weapon, to describe some of the attributed gathered about the weapon and describe it as such. This will also describe some of its uses and proposed uses and then come up with a way it was used the most.

All of this is wrapped up in the Conclusion as any other paper is and that should be no surprise to any reader of this kind of article. This part is designed to take all of the pieces which have been presented and make some sort of sense out of what has been presented. For the most part this will be evident to the reader as it this investigation processes along.

Only German?
There should be parts of this paper which should be of interest to most people that are interested in the longsword, especially the German one. What is of most interest is that there is a distinct German bias when discussing the weapon. There are examples of other nationalities having this weapon from museums from around the world. This is also evident from the broad collection presented by Norling (2012) in his article and the images which accompany it. The German bias found in the following investigation is due to the commonality with the investigations which have preceded this one, that have focused on German sources and naming conventions.

THE SHORT ANSWER
While a long answer will be forth-coming about the federschwert, detailing various arguments about the weapon and discussing what was used for and its history, there is also the short answer to consider as well. The short answers cover such things as literal translations of the name of the sword from German to English. The slightly more in-depth discussions of the weapon lead to further investigations which will be presented further along.

The first place people go for an interpretation of what a foreign thing is will be to translate the name of the object from the native language into English and interpret this into some idea of what this means thus, "federschwert - a lightweight sword. "Feder" is German for "feather," and "schwert" is German for "sword."" (Shackleford, 2010). This would seem to be a logical progression and explanation of the weapon, but leaves the reader with no real explanation of what the weapon is for. This is where an explanation from a more use-approach comes in handy, "A *Federschwert* ("Feather sword") is a foiled practice blade with a large flanged ricasso and a thick but narrow blade used for longsword training." (Wassom, 2016).

Wassom's (2016) explanation of what a feder is begins to explain not only what a federschwert is but also what it is used for. There is also a physical description which is most useful. A further explanation of the form of the weapon is possible and even a hint as to its use,

> "special fencing school longswords called federschwert, with a narrow rapier-like blade and more mass close to the cross, in the area called the schilt or the ricasso." *(Norling, 2011)*

With all this in mind there is the image of a weapon which is relatively light, blunt because it is used for practice in a school-type setting, which has a wide ricasso called a *schilt*, which brings the mass of the weapon close to the hilt, and a narrow but thick blade. This would seem to cover a reasonably good explanation, but there would seem to be a problem.

> "In Sweden we have a saying; "A loved child has many names" and looking at what is today called a federschwert this seems to be true for this type of sword as well, at least if we think of it in general terms as a sword for training." *(Norling, 2013)*

EQUIPMENT & CURATORIAL DISCUSSIONS

There would seem to be a lack of agreement on what this weapon should be called. Again, much like the rapier, the weapon is trapped in a web of confusion as to some naming nomenclature. For some federschwert or feder, is not a suitable term for this weapon, and another needs to be sought. Other names will be discussed.

> *"we can feel quite safe in assuming that federschwert or feder was not a term historically used for training swords other than as a poetic choice of words." (Norling, 2013)*

Not an historical term? Nope. This will also be revealed. The question is whether or not this even matters or not. Does the term as it has been implied and used by the community suit the weapon and thus, being informed of its lack of history, does this really impact its use? The lack of history of this term will also be discussed in more detail. Needless to say, there is no short answer.

A NEOLOGISM

> *"The term federschwert is quite clearly a neologism, i.e. a modern, reinvented term that wasn't used historically with the same meaning as we confer to it today." (Norling, 2013)*

In a nut-shell, a new term is what a neologism is, and federschwert is that. Of course if we have a look at Castle (1885) *Schools and Masters of Fence: From the Middle Ages to the Eighteenth Century*, it is not quite as new as some would like to claim, even if he did misuse the term. For better recognition of the word, and also the most accurate use or the word "federschwert", and thus its diminutive "feder", it is described as a modern word of the 20th century.

> *"The term federschwert (German for "feather sword") is sometimes used to describe these training swords, though it should be noted that this is an incorrect term made up in the early 20th century. Period texts simply describe these as swords." (Grandy, 2003)*

Job Done
What is most interesting about the word is that even though it does not appear in any medieval or Renaissance fechtbuch ("fight book"), it "fills a gap in our vocabulary by not only defining the sword as a training sword, but also as a specific type of training sword with a flared schilt." (Norling, 2013). This means the word has a use and there is really no reason not to use the word. Thus the word does exactly what it is supposed to do providing a term which describes an object which previously did not really have a specific word to describe it. Further, the fact that the word has become part of the modern language to discuss this form of sword means that there is really no reason not to use the word, even if it is new.

> *"Note: The term "federschwert" is a neologism and it is only about a 100 years old, but is in such common use today, that I choose*

> to use it, and although the term Parat Schwert, as Matt Galas has
> suggested, earlier appeared to be suitable, other evidence has shown
> that the term "Fechtschwert" is more appropriate.
> Still, the term federschwert or feder is in such common use
> today that there is really not reason not to use it." (Norling, 2011)

The following discussion of the feder is not designed to deny the use of the term or the existence of the weapon, more to pinpoint the weapon itself, to identify it and to locate it in history and use. At no point in time was it the purpose ever to deny the term being used to describe it, merely to gather evidence about the weapon so as to understand it better.

THE FEDER, A RAPIER?

According to some fencing historians, especially those of the late nineteenth century, the term feder was used in reference to the rapier. There are arguments proposed about this to and fro, and they will be discussed here. Most of these arguments will be based on fencing history and fencing historians. Of course these arguments will also be based on points of view and interpretations.

Partial Evolutionist

> "The Schwerdt – the two-handed sword – the Düsack and the
> broadsword were replaced by the Feder or Rappier. The play was
> oriented more to the Italian than the French school. Nevertheless,
> play with the older weapons did continue and eventually developed
> into the purely cutting play of the Schläger in the nineteenth
> and twentieth centuries." (Wise, 2014:184)

The interesting thing to find here is that Wise (2014) claims that the feder and rapier are one and the same and replaced the sword and düssack, and that play oriented toward the Italian and French play. This is what would be expected from the typical evolutionist explanation of typical fencing historians, what is most interesting is the claim that the older weapons continued and changed to the schläger. The question is where would the idea that the feder and rapier were the same thing come from?

Castle's Term

Castle (1885) is to blame for the confusion that feder was a term used for rapier in the sixteenth century. What is most interesting is that it is not even in the main text, it is a foot note about the Federfechter, "They [Federfechter] derived their name from the "Feder," a slang word for the "Rapier" – the fashion which began to spread about 1570." (Castle, 1885:30 fn.1). This footnote is then reinforced by a further statement in the text where he makes mention that by the end of the sixteenth century the "Feder" or "Rappier" was adopted in all schools of arms in Germany (Castle, 1885:180). Of course in his usual style, Castle leaves the reader with no idea of his sources.

> "However, investigating the historical use of these terms is interesting. The
> word federschwert appears to stem from a paragraph describing the "feder" as
> being the preferred weapon of the Federfechter, in Egerton Castle's Schools and

> Masters of Fencing - From the Middle Ages to the Eighteenth Century of 1885. According to Castle the "feder" was slang for the rapier," (Norling, 2013)

The interesting thing is that Castle can be credited with the use of the slang term feder for federschwert, as being the preferred weapon of the Federfecter. Of course the fact that he uses it in 1885 means that it does not have the Renaissance or medieval history most would like. What can be noted by this investigation and the investigation of others is that Castle was inaccurate in his interpretations.

> "Most likely, Castle's idea of a federschwert, comes from an over-generalization or misunderstanding of poetic comparisons ... comparisons between a sword and a pen, which the craftsmen of the Marxbrüder used to ridicule the students of the Freifechter guild." (Norling, 2013)

What seems to have happened is that Castle has indeed read the original sources and misinterpreted the poetic comparison between the sword and the pen and assumed that they were somehow talking about the rapier, thus inferred that a federschwert was a rapier. This is most interesting as the Germans already had a word for rapier, "Rappier". Thus a feder is not a rapier.

FEDERFECHTER AND MARXBRÜDER

> "The "Federfechter," while taking care to be proficient in the use of the two-handed "Schwerdt," looked upon the "Feder" as their distinctive weapon, and challenged the "Marxbrüder," wherever they met them, "to fight honourably with them, cut and thrust." (Castle, 1885:30)

The description above relies on Castle's (1885) explanation about the feder being a rapier, however, could be interpreted that the feder was some other kind of similar weapon. Castle was perhaps describing a weapon which was just not as large i.e. with a shorter handle, emphasis being on the thrust also being a difference. More likely, as has been discussed previously, with the confusion made and indicated Castle more likely made a mistake in identification of the weapon.

> "Most likely, Castle's idea of a federschwert, comes from an over-generalization or misunderstanding of poetic comparisons ... comparisons between a sword and a pen, which the craftsmen of the Marxbrüder used to ridicule the students of the Freifechter guild." (Norling, 2013)

While such an indication of the weapon inaccuracy is important, so is the indication of a different way of using the weapon with the use of the point. It could also be that the Marxbrüder, or Marx Brothers, were criticising the Federfechter (or Freifechter) for their light, version of the sword, thus a real "feather sword", which was possibly more point-orientated in its use. Needless to say, what is most indicated is that there was a distinct argument between the two schools and a feder lies somewhere in the middle of it, whether it be a sword or a pen.

Feder as "Feather"

"The German word *Feder* means "feather" or "quill", but came to be used of metal springs in the 17th century (i.e. at about the same time as the name of the sparring weapon and possibly influenced by it). The term *Fechtfeder* itself seems to be connected to the name of the Federfechter, i.e. "feather fencers", a guild or brotherhood of fencers formed in 1570 in Prague. It is possible that the term *Feder* for the sparring sword arose in the late 16th century at first as a term of derision of the practice weapon used by the *Federfechter* (who were so called for unrelated reasons, because of a feather or quill used as their heraldic emblem) by their rivals, the Marx Brothers, who would tease the *Federfechter* as "fencing with quills" as opposed to with real weapons, or as scholars or academics supposedly better at "fighting with the quill" than at real fighting (reflecting the different professional backgrounds of the rival fencing guilds). Johann Fischart in his *Gargantua* (1575) already compares the fencing weapon to a "quill" writing in blood." (Wikipedia, 2016)

In its usual way, the Wikipedia (2016) attempts to round things up and simplify things for the reader so it is easy to read. It also attempts to place all of the information in a simple format in the same place at the same time. Of course this is supposed to result in a simple answer for the reader. The problem is that sometimes the scholarship is not as good as it could be, but it does lead the reader in a direction in which to research. The first statement is true about the definition of "feder" being for "quill" or "feather". It has an interesting note that the sparring weapon may have become related to springs which the word became known for also possibly due to the nature of the blade. Then it gets to the interesting and relevant parts.

The Federfechter and the Marxbrüder often came into conflict over rights to operate in towns, or more to the point with the blessing of local lords. Sometimes this would result in a match with blunted weapons other times, not so blunt. Interestingly, sometimes it would also result in arguments via statements made in local publications as well. Due to the heraldic emblem being the feather or quill, the Marxbrüder would often refer to them as better fencing with a quill or pen, or also referring to a lighter weapon. Interestingly, this is a point which will come up as a significant point and where Castle (1885) may have gained his information.

A Class Struggle

"It is also highly intriguing to note, that the various protestant authors often are called "federfechter", ie "quill fencers" in the late 1500s and 1600s, eg. in "Probstein oder Censur des Lutherischen Tractätls..." by Mattias Faber in 1650 and "Lilium Sionaeum Quinquagenâ Prole foecundum..." from 1695, given that there appears to have existed strong connotations between some of the Freyfechter von der Feder and the Calvinist movement.
- Perhaps not so surprisingly, the term federfechter with the meaning of pen fencer is still used in many countries, e.g Germany, Sweden and Belgium."
(Norling, 2013)

The reference above lays the argument firmly in place that the discussion of the feder being discussed here is that of the quill, or pen, being that they are discussing authors of a particular movement. The implication could also be made that such indication could also cross over to other such "federfechter" accusing them of being better with a pen than with a sword. This idea of the pen being more important to the Federfechter could have come from a difference in class status as there was a distinct difference between the two brotherhoods.

> "Given this poetic connotation between federfechter and quill fighting, it is again very interesting to see how the Marxbrüder members (often being furriers or tanners) appear to have ridiculed the Freifechter von der Feder for being scholars and academics (… Because, hear ye, feather thin paper [and] black ink should be found only in a scriptorium,)." *(Norling, 2013)*

The membership of the two different groups, in the modern world, would not be of particular interest, but in the periods in which these groups existed, this difference was quite significant. It essentially meant that the members of the Marxbrüder were more from the lower classes, while the members of the Freifechter were from the upper classes, thus creating an instant class gap and friction between the two groups.

> "This opposition between the "working man's" Marxbrüder and the "academic" Freifechter Guild is corroborated by Heinrich von Gunterrodt stating the same in his 1579 treatise, where he describes how the Marxbrüder, come from dirty professions like tanners and connected crafts and think they are better than the Freyfechter von der Feder just because they have the Imperial Privilege, while the Freyfechter, more often being students of the good sciences and arts clearly are superior in fighting."
>
> *(Norling, 2013)*

From the statement above there is a clear attitude expressed about the difference between the two groups. One is simply better than the other because they come from the "good sciences and arts" and this must make their fencing much better. Needless to say there were quite a few conflicts between the two groups, as already indicated. It should also be noted that with an upper class station it would not be surprising if they did have access to information about the rapier and its fashionable status, and no doubt access to the weapon, this aside, even with the accusation of the lighter weapon and its relation to the pen, could it not have been claimed by the Freifechter?

> "So, perhaps this is where the name originates from, an originally derogatory word, rooted in a constantly growing opposition between artisans and students, an epithet that the Freyfechter came to carry with pride?" *(Norling, 2013)*

FENCERS OF ST. VITUS

> "Feder in German means "feather" or "quill". Grimm et al. postulated that "Feder" also was a slang term for rapier, an assumption that cannot be supported with a shred of evidence. Karl Wassmannsdorff derived the term "Federfechter" from Veiterfechter, or fencers of St. Vitus. This could be

> *adducted by two or three examples. Schmied-Kowarzik and Kufahl, however, point out that the coat of arms of the Federfechter featured a quill, thus rendering etymological calisthenics redundant."*
> (Amberger, 1999:114 fn.127)

While Castle (1885) is the biggest proponent for feder referring to a rapier he is not the only one as can be seen above. Of course, as can be seen above Amberger (1999) denies Grimm's claim due to a lack of evidence, much in the same way that Castle's is by other authors. He then presents evidence to suggest that the idea came from the fencers of St. Vitus, first presenting evidence from Wassmannsdorff in the form of word formation and then the coat of arms presented by Schmied-Kowarzik and Kufahl which seem to seal the evidence with the quill being present on the coat of arms (Amberger, 1999:114 fn.127). The evidence presented would seem to bury once and for all the idea of the feder as a rapier and present the quill being referred to that being the one on the coat of arms of St Vitus. Norling (2013), on the other hand, disputes this claim of the quill.

> *"Another theory that has been suggested is that it refers to what the patron saint of the Freifechter von der Feder and Bohemia, St. Vitus, holds in his hand, but that is simply a misinterpretation of a palm frond, which is a sign of his martyrdom. On the other hand, in his other hand, he holds a rooster, the animal St. Vitus is said to have been boiled alive with and this might partly explain the association with the fanciful feathers of the Freyfechter von der Feder. The rooster is also sometimes used to symbolize the Freyfechter von der Feder, in place of the Griffin which was the official symbol of the Freyfechter Gesellschaft."* (Norling, 2013)

Thus Norling claims that the quill is a palm frond rather than a quill, but states that the association can still be made through the presence of the rooster, thus feathers, which are one symbols of the Freifechter. This all goes to suggest a reason for the naming of the weapon to being a feder, through the naming of the group rather than any direct correlation to the weapon itself. Of course, this link is much less tenuous than any direct link made with the weapon itself, especially as the weapon is seen in the hands of many different figures in many different images, not all necessarily related to the Freifechter.

PARATSCHWERT

The discussion which follows about the *paratschwert* is of another possible name for the feder. The information for this discussion comes from a single author, namely Norling (2013) however he does give the best coverage of the subject. Usually this would be a problem, but in this case Norling has performed extensive research on the subject and covers the areas of importance.

Etymology

> *"Well, the word Parat stems from the Latin paratus / parare which means to prepare / be prepared / be ready. The word is also related to the modern German word bereit (or beredd, bereda in Swedish)."* (Norling, 2013)

EQUIPMENT & CURATORIAL DISCUSSIONS

According to this first account of the word the *paratschwert* is a "ready"-sword, but ready for what? This does not really make much sense alone. Of course a person could read into it to be prepared would be to practice, therefore it is likely that the word could be interpreted as a "practice" sword, as some may have done. Luckily for the reader Norling goes into more detail and explanation.

> "Furthermore, parat *also means both* parrying / floryishing *and* showing off / displaying, *and we know that the fencers carried various arms when processing in a parade and with other associated festivities, like the* Schwerttanz (sword dancing). *Finally we also know that fencers initiated the fencing events called* fechtschulen *by floryishing their weapons to show their skill. All these connotations to the word make full sense, given that the parading and the ceremonial sword dancing all prepare for the main event; the Fechtschulen, with fancy display of arms and skills."*
> *(Norling, 2013)*

The information above presents a weapon which is used for demonstration purposes; to demonstrate their skills and in other parade elements, and not so much for practice as may have been indicated previously. Thus the word does not have the same sort of connotation that even federschwert has even in the modern language, but of more of a weapon with less practical and more demonstration purpose in mind. The information which Norling presents further reinforces this idea.

> *"Well, looking to the sources, the oldest note I have found is in* The Swedish Etymological Wordbook, *which generally is quite reliable. This source actually states that a parate-swerdh, as used in 1563-64, is a sword used for a parade and possibly an especially fine one. Also, the modern Swedish word* paradsvärd *means just that: A sword that you carry in a parade, usually more decorated and not used for anything else."* *(Norling, 2013)*

So from this point of view the *paratschwert* is a parade sword, a finely decorated weapon which is carried in a parade. Thus the idea of the weapon being used for sword dancing and merely being flourished about to demonstrate skill rather than being used in any form of combat, real or simulated, begins to take shape. Clearly this is not a practice weapon. This idea of the weapon being ceremonial in purpose is further reinforced by the following.

> *"in 1589 Christoff Rösener describes the procedure for how a newly approved Meister des Schwerdts receives his masterhood in his treatise* Ehren Tittel und Lobspruch der Ritterlichen Freyen Kunst der fechter ... the Meisterbrief *in a formal ceremony where a paratschwert is used to "knight" him, while he swears himself to never abandon his mastership for the rest of his life. In a sense he has now both* prepareda *and* readied *himself and he is made,* prepared *into a proper master using a specific sword."*
> *(Norling, 2013)*

afencersramblings.blogspot.com

In this case there is definitely the element of the weapon being used as a ceremonial weapon, as it was being used in the ceremony. There was also the element mentioned before about preparing mentioned before as he would have had to prepare himself for the challenges of being a master, and also the use of his weapon. This is more of an aside, but the interpretations do not actually stop here.

Parry or Trick Sword

> "The meaning of the word parat is interesting, but if we interpret it as a parry or a trick, then it gets a bit confusing, since it describes a meaning that I think would fit most weapons and thus becomes redundant for signifying the sword type. I would suggest that the fact that you can do a parat with a sword doesn't make it a paratschwert. Instead, there are other more important factors that decide the naming of the sword type; factors like context and appearance."
> (Norling, 2013)

To attempt to define a sword as a trick or parry sword is very broad, as Norling indicates. This sort of signification for a weapon is more designed to indicate some sort of negative aspect to the weapon, as a "trick sword". This sort of application of idea can really be applied to any sword of any shape if the individual can do a trick with it, or if it was designed to do such. Such indications may be pointers toward those who would like to indicate negative toward the sword in general.

> "Curiously, it has also been suggested that the term paratschwert is derogatory, meaning a sword used by someone who just shows off but knows little about real fencing, although that claim still needs corroboration."
> (Norling, 2013)

The idea of *paratschwert* being a derogatory term because it is against a person who shows off sword work but knows little about actual fencing, pushes the idea of the *paratschwert* back toward it being a parade sword, or ceremonial sword rather than a practice weapon.

> "A paratschwert would still be a blunted but otherwise fully functional sword and could certainly be used for fencing, but this was not its primary function. With that said, we know for certain that sometimes both paratschwerter and fechtschwerter were carried in the very same parades. However, I have thus far not found a single clear instance of a paratschwert being used for actual fencing."
> (Norling, 2013)

For the most part, aside from a couple of side-notes toward some interesting places, it has been noted that the *paratschwert* is a parade or ceremonial sword. This is indicated by the evidence which has been presented above. As a substitute for the frequently used feder indicating a practice sword, it simply does not fill the gap.

FECHTSCHWERT

Fechtschwert is another name by which a feder may be referred, i.e. another option for naming. This is an option which is discussed heavily by Norling (2013), so much so that this will be the only reference which will appear in this part of the discussion. What is most interesting about how describes the naming of the weapon is that it is by the same way that *federschwert* is described and analysed by other authors. What is even more interesting is that this discussion of the optional naming for the feder provides a bridge to another and an overall wrap-up to the naming discussion.

Fechtschwert – "Fight Sword"

> "So what about fechtschwert then? Well fechten simply means fighting, but the word has been combined into various combinations associated with training throughout the centuries. For example, but not limited to:
> Fechtschule - In 1494, 1495, 1512, 1531, 1537 and 1542.
> Fechtschwert - pre 1541, 1550, 1575, 1583, 1620, 1671 and 1676.
> Fechthaus and Fechtboden - In 1594, 1651, 1654 and 1670.
> Fechtdegen (training rapier) - In 1646, 1647, 1653 and 1660.
> Fechthandschuhe (fencing glove) In 1740, 1762 and 1763.
> Fechtrapier - In 1661, 1832, 1849 and 1850.
> Fechtsäbel - in 1847, 1848 and 1851."
> (Norling, 2013)

The one which Norling fails to mention is *fechtbuch* (fight book), the primary reference from which the method for using the weapons comes. With this history and clear evidence for the use of the word "fecht" in relation to various weapons, locations and objects it would seem that it is a better fit for the weapon than feder ever was. It would seem that the weight of history, and particularly printed history, is what has resulted in the prevalence of the use of federschwert over *fechtschwert*.

Fechtschwert for Training

> "we find two interesting sources; Des Christlichen Teutschen Groß-Fürsten Herkules Und Der Böhmischen Königlichen Fräulein Valiska from 1676 and Geschichte der Oranien-Nassauischen Länder und ihrer Regenten from 1816 mention the fechtschwert specifically. The latter describes how in 1550 a fencing master is hired for the court of Duke Konrad von Sickingen and fechtschwerter are purchased for the then 13 year old Duke Georg Wilhelm and the other young nobles of the court." (Norling, 2013)

Clearly the *fechtschwert* is a sword used for training, evidence for which the feder presents by image and association with the word more than in literature as above. This weapon was designed for training as the previous demonstration of language proves; further evidence such as what appears immediately above only further demonstrates further evidence to support the idea in clear documentation, rather than documentation by association. Further to this there is evidence for the use of this weapon.

UN-BLOGGED: A FENCER'S RAMBLINGS

> *"a fechtschwert being described as "being comfortable in the hand". ... sources clearly, refer to the fechtschwert as a training sword used for actual fencing." (Norling, 2013)*

What this means is that there is evidence for the weapon being used, rather than some idea of the weapon being used and some idea about how it was used. That it was used for training and fencing is most interesting in that it gives credence to the idea of the longsword being used in fencing matches in the period but not in duelling. Not saying that the sword would not do damage, quite the opposite, "the Bloß-fechtschwert obviously hurts badly, even blinding the Freyfechter opponent, though most likely from bleeding into the eyes." (Norling, 2013). The head being the primary target for a bleeding wound in these matches, however the rapier had taken preference for duelling, as worn by the gentlemen in the image below.

These gentlemen carry their *fechtschwert* over the shoulder and are equipped with rapiers [24] at the same time. The rapier had taken over the longsword for duelling in this period and the longsword, while still trained in earnest, had been pushed more to the side. In discussing fencers in parades the discussion turns to the *paratschwert* and the *fechtschwert* and their differences.

Fencers parading by Balthasar Kuchler, 1611

Paratschwert and Fechtschert Together – Different Uses

> *"Another interesting source that we have already looked at, the Kurtze und gründliche Beschreibung des Königlichen Einzuges from 1620, by Georg Reutter, describes a Furrier's guild parade, preceding a sword dance with public fencing by fencing masters in Breslau, ... This passage is interesting as we are told that the three boys carry first a Paratschwerdt and then a pair of Fechtschwerter. This I think further reveals a difference in purpose for the two types of swords; the first being a finer sword used for ceremony, the second for training and tournament fighting. The Paratschwert*

---

24 Rapiers, identified by the complex hilt, the clothing of the gentlemen, and the length and shape of the scabbard, thus the blades of the weapons.

> is carried at the very front of the parade, which would seem to indicate
> a certain importance carried by it (alongside of the laurel wreaths),
> perhaps even a certain reverance, similar to a relic or a cross."
>
> (Norling, 2013)

The *paratschwert* is discussed in more detail in another section of this investigation. Needless to say, it is another term vying for a place by which the feder may be called. By the evidence presented above it would appear, however, that this weapon is more of a weapon designed for ceremonial purposes rather than training or fighting with. That the source mentions both types of sword being carried is significant that they can be separated and some idea of their purpose is determined. It would seem to start to separate these types of weapon from one another and start to disentangle at least some of the terms from the confusion.

Too Broad

> "Some may think that the term fechtschwert is too broad, not really
> defining the historical training swords with flared schilts and although
> this is hard to know for sure, since there is a lack of source material on
> the topic, I would also suggest that the term may actually have referred
> to what we today think of as federschwert, considering that the particular
> type of sword possibly has been used as far back as the first quarter
> of the 1400s and were particularly common in Blossfechten (unarmoured
> fencing). In fact, they appear to have been more common than regular,
> blunt longswords, if we are to trust the illustrated treatises."
>
> (Norling, 2013)

The *fechtschwert* and federschwert may have been the same thing, according to the research which has been presented above. This would imply that this word *fechtschwert* is another viable term, perhaps more viable than feder due to the evidence supporting it, though the sources do not specify that it is actually the actual weapon referred to as a feder being spoken about. Though this is true, the greatest criticism against it is that it is too broad. The end result could always be having two names for the same thing due to evidence supporting one and popular use supporting the other.

IMAGE DISCUSSION

There is a selection of 16 images which will be discussed in various depths in this discussion ranging between 1452 and 1623. Each one of the images is designed to present some aspect typical or atypical of the feder as it has been presented by other documentation. Overall this is designed to give an accurate pictorial presentation of the feder as it was presented in treatises and other places.

Technical terms will be used to discuss the weapons, thus some knowledge of the parts of the weapon is required. A special note with regard to this need to be made in that, the term cross-guard will be used rather than quillons as this is the most period- and weapon-appropriate term, being that quillons is a term which is usually used to refer to later period weapons and also mostly to single handed weapons also.

GENERAL DISCUSSION
Presence Eastablished

> *"they [federschwert] go back as far as the mid-15th century at least, and are shown in the "Peter von Danzig"- manuscript of 14522 ..., the Talhoffer Manuscript of 1467 and numerous others."* (Norling, 2011)

That there are so many images present in this discussion over such a wide timeline demonstrates a long period of use of this particular weapon. For the moment the commonly used "feder" and "federschwert" will be used, as nomenclature has been discussed in detail in other places. The presence of this particular item was not denied. There are more interesting things to be said of this practice weapon.

Von Danzig 1452

> *"the so-called "Von Danzig" manuscript of 1452. There are only two images in this manuscript; one showing the four basic Liechtenauer longsword guards Ochs, Pflug, Alber and Vom Tag and the other image, ... portrays a fencing master, which has been suggested to be Johannes Liechtenauer. Both images clearly show fechtschwert."* (Norling, 2011a)

The image is from the "von Danzig" manuscript and will be discussed in more detail below as the first image discussed. This is the seated figure which may or may not be Johannes Liechtenauer; it will be discussed in more detail. He holds the federschwert or fechtschwert in one hand and a stick in the other, pointing toward other weapons. Clearly this is an image of a teacher or fencing master. This is more interesting in that it is more or less the first image of a feder which we have.

Style Changes

> *"We can find examples of these swords in the old Martial Arts Fechtbucher (fight books) from the early 1420s up until the early 17th century, but they might have been in use for a longer period of time. We see many varying styles of Feders as their designs change from Fechtbuch to Fechtbuch."* (Wassom, 2016)

Just like any other weapon in existence they change over time and even at the same time due to style and use. Some people will want to make the weapon better or move differently, or even just want to change the look of the weapon to make it their own. The result of this is changes in the blade shape, length and proportions. This is most useful to the historian as it makes it possible to track the weapon through its changes through cultures and groups. This also goes to examination of how they were depicted.

Blade Depiction

> *"In the early period sources we almost exclusively see swords that have blades that taper towards the point, with some of them even being illustrated as having ridged blades. The clear majority, however, are depicted as having simple flat blades."* (Norling, 2012)

EQUIPMENT & CURATORIAL DISCUSSIONS

The blade of the feder is one of the most interesting parts of the weapon in its depiction as it tells us something of the nature of the weapon. It can even tell us if the author had ideas as to whether the weapon intended was actually a more solid weapon than a feder or possibly even that the feder was made in a similar fashion to a sharp sword thus preserving a more rigid blade. On the other hand this may also just be artists' interpretation. But the blade depiction must take into account more.

Parallel Edges

Parallel edges rather than tapering edges is a characteristic which the feder shows in the more modern form. In the images, this wavers a little, "Quite a few are shown having near parallel edges, especially in the first and second quarter of the 1500s, but also later," (Norling, 2012). It is most interesting that some would waver in their depiction and show edges on the feder which were not parallel.

Parallel edges are depicted on those weapons which are somewhat larger than the longsword. It has been indicated that the feder could have been used for practice at two-handed sword work as well, and the depictions which are supplied of the feder, in general, bear this idea out. These weapons have long, parallel edges on them and are often quite a bit longer than the standard longsword which is depicted.

> *"This seems to coincide with the large, parallel edge, and sometimes quite flexible zweihänder used by Kaiser Maximilian I's Landsknechten. Other examples are the Goliath treatise of 1510, Paurnfeindt hn236 of 1516, "Egonolph" of 1531, Agrippa of 1553 and Leküchner of 1558."*
> *(Norling, 2012)*

Narrow Blades

> *"Not until the very late 1500s and early 1600s (and onwards) do we see very narrow training swords, for instance in Codex Guelf 83.4 August 8° from 1591 and in Thibault's Académie de l'Espée from 1631."* *(Norling, 2012)*

The narrow blade is one of those characteristics which have been indicated by some that would make the feder lighter. In return it has also been stated that the narrowing of the blade is the simple result of the shift of the weight of the blade back toward the hilt to preserve the correct balance. In the depictions, the narrower blades are seen on the later weapons indicating that these may also have been more toward the time when the longsword was bowing out to the rapier thus the art was being preserved, possibly at the expense of some of its martial capability.

Flared Point

> *"From about 1540, we see some rare examples of swords that flare somewhat towards the point, for instance in Paul Hektor Mair, and the Anton Rast Fechtbuch."* *(Norling, 2012)*

The flared point is the clearest indication that this was a practice weapon rather than one which was designed to be used in earnest combat. The flared point is designed to prevent the point from penetrating when practicing a thrust against a partner. This demonstrates that this weapon was clearly designed for practice rather than in an actual conflict.

The Images

The previous discussion has been designed to introduce the topic of the image discussion and give a brief outline of some of the subject material which will be discussed in the following. What will follow is a more in-depth discussion of each of the images which has been selected, focussing on the feder which can be found in the image. At the end an overall discussion will be made highlighting the main points which has been discovered, most of which will support the documentation which has already been presented.

Image from Cod.44.A.8 "Codex Danzig" (1452)

Cod.44.A.8 2v

While the image at left is present in Norling (2012), this image was taken from the treatise for a better example. The captions below the main images will contain their document and the page from which they came, in this case Codex 44.A.8 page 2-verso. In the case of more modern ones they will have the author's name and page number. Further images, enhancing parts of the original may be included in the text to assist.

There has been a lot already said about this image in other discussions, most are discussing whether or not it is or is not Johannes Liechtenauer. This is not the focus of this investigation. For the purposes of this discussion, it is only a small portion of the image which is a concern, and that is the weapon which the seated figure is holding in his right hand.

The weapon has a simple pommel, not quite round and a handle which can accommodate both hands. It has a very simple cross-guard, a broad *schilt*, and a blade, with tapering edges, which ends in a rounded point. This would seem to be an adequate description of the weapon, but more needs to be said. The blade and *schilt* are of particular interest.

The blade here is depicted as being flat. This makes the blade in this image of interest as it demonstrates how the blades may change in their presentation as images. Blades may also be depicted with a taper as is the case in this image or simply rounded when merely parallel. The depiction, it is often stated, is up to the artist, but some credit must be given to the author or authors as well. The same can be said of the length, in this case being longsword, rather than two-handed sword, length. Such depictions may also allude to the use of the weapon.

The *schilt* of this particular weapon is of interest because it is not particularly common. While Norling (2012) managed to present images of federschwert all with similar kinds

EQUIPMENT & CURATORIAL DISCUSSIONS

of *schilt*, this is not actually the case if a closer look is taken. This broad, sloping backward type which is present in this image is not typical of the type which is present. Most of the *schilt* which will be presented will either be squared-off, or have lugs pointing outward or forward toward the point of the weapon. This type is indicative of a minimalist style trying to achieve the same end with the least disruption to the use of the weapon. Changes in type of *schilt* will be noted in the feder which follow.

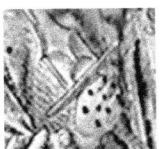

While other aspects of the weapon, such as the handle and pommel shape, and cross-guard size are note-worthy, it is the blade and the *schilt* which are of most note in this investigation, and it is they which most stand out. These parts of the weapon decide really how the weapon handles as the handle needs to be balanced against them, thus need more of the focus. This is especially where a part may interfere or add to the use of the weapon and thus change its characteristics.

Image from Cod.Guelf.78.2 Aug.2° "Wolfenbüttel Sketchbook" (1465 – 1480)

Cod.Guelf.78.2 Aug.2° 7r

The image at left comes from Cod.Guelf.78.2 Aug.2° also known as the "Wolfenbüttel Sketchbook". It depicts to combatants in civilian attire engaged at the longsword. For the purposes of this discussion it is the weapons which are of interest as they are using feder. This is actually a very good depiction of the weapon because in both cases the weapons can be clearly seen and thus easily discussed.

The weapons have a relatively large, tear-drop-shaped pommel, a handle which accommodates the use of two hands as can be seen in both figures. The cross-guard is simple aside from a slight point in the middle extending toward the *schilt*. In this image the *schilt* is relatively small, especially if compared to the previous image discussed. It should also be noted that this *schilt* has lugs or wings extending outward and forward; possibly used to hinder the opponent's weapon.

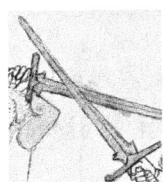

The blade on this weapon is tapered just as with the previous example, and tapers to a rounded point. This rounded point indicates a practice weapon. Unlike the previous example there is the indication of a fuller the middle of both blades which have been depicted. This is less likely to be a ridge as it does not extend all of the way to the tip as can be seen by the weapon in the hands of the figure on the right hand side.

The length and size of the weapon, even with its clearly two-handed grip still indicates a weapon in the longsword class, rather than a weapon in the two-handed class. This is something which is in common with the previous image from the

afencersramblings.blogspot.com   **415**

"Codex Danzig". What makes this codex interesting is that it stretches over a fifteen year period, and as will be noted there are changes in the shape of the weapons over time which will make this seem almost ahead of its time.

Image from Cod.S.554 "Solothurner Fechtbuch" (1470)

Cod.S.554 fig.77

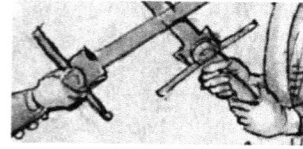

The image at left comes from Cod.S.554 known as the "Solothurner Fechtbuch" of 1470. It depicts two individuals in civilian clothing engaged at the longsword. This image is of note for several reasons which will be made clear in due course. What should be noted is that the weapons are the focus rather than their handling.

The pommels of the weapons are obscured as such nothing can be said of them. The handles can clearly accommodate two hands, and the cross-guard is of very simple design. One point of note, which will be discussed later, is the presence of a *chappe* known as a "rain guard". The *schilt* is square, and the blades taper to a point.

The *schilt* has been noted to be square, more accurately it is oblong, and quite small as compared to previous examples. This would imply that the unseen pommel would have to be relatively large to keep the balance of the weapon. It should also be noted that while it lacks the lugs of the previous example the square shape could serve the same purpose possibly to hinder the opponent's weapon.

Due to its location it is appropriate to talk about the addition of the *chappe* to these weapons. The first thing that should be noted is that this is atypical for German weapons and especially so for feder and even German weapons in general. Of the examples collected there are only two where this is present. This could be seen as an enhancement to the assumed protective capabilities of the *schilt*.

The blade of the weapon is extremely simple. It is flat with no markings at all. The artist is clearly indicating that the figures indicated here are using practice weapons which have no edges or points.

EQUIPMENT & CURATORIAL DISCUSSIONS

From MS Cl. 23842 "Cluny Fechtbuch" (1480s – 1500)

The image at right is from the MS Cl. 23842 known as the "Cluny Fechtbuch" it is dated as 1480s to 1500 and depicts two individuals in civilian clothing combating with longswords. The weapons, which are the prime concern of this investigation, have round pommels and handles with two-handed grips. The cross-guard is simple but with round ends. The *schilt* is long and rectangular and the blade of the weapon is simply depicted as flat with parallel edges and a rounded point.

The *schilt* of the weapon is rectangular. In this case it is a long rectangular section, large and square at the top. This is markedly larger than the *schilts* on the previous examples which have been presented thus far. This would seem to indicate a longer blade, but it is not.

MS Cl. 23842 12r

The blade has parallel edges which come to a rounded point. There is no tapering in the blade at all. There are no markings on the blade to indicate fullers or any other blade features. This indicates a very simple practice blade with no sharp edges and a blunt point. The blade length is within the standard longsword length, despite the larger *schilt* present.

From MS KK5012 "Kunste Zu Ritterlicher Were" (1495)

The first thing that will be noted is that two images (next page) have been selected from this treatise rather than a single one as in previous treatises. This is because the images which have been presented above depict different things which are of importance. Both images depict two combatants in civilian clothing contesting at the longsword and come from the MS KK5012 dated to 1495. While you cannot see the pommels on one image, on the other they are clearly round. The handle is suited to fit two hands, and the cross-guard is very similar to the previous treatise being straight with spherical ends. Both blades are depicted as simple parallel blades with rounded ends, the *schilts* are different and this is of interest.

The blades are depicted as very simple parallel with a rounded point, with no taper at all. There is no marking on the blade to indicate fullers or ridges of any kind. This is definitively indicating a practice weapon with a blunt edge. The blade seems to be the standard length for a longsword.

afencersramblings.blogspot.com

MS KK5012 2r

MS KK5012 16v

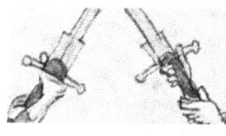

The *schilt* which is found on the first image is rectangular and quite long. This makes it quite similar to the *schilt* found on the swords found in the previous treatise. In this case there is some indication of narrowing on the sword on the right side on the sides of the *schilt*. Overall, it is quite large, as in the previous treatise. This would indicate that the blade should be longer, but as previously indicated it is not. What is most interesting is that this is different to the *schilt* depicted in the second image.

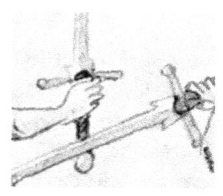

In the second image the *schilt* shape has changed and seems to be more like that found in Cod.Guelf.78.2 Aug.2° 7r which was discussed previously. This type is smaller and has wings extending outward and forward toward the point of the weapon. This would beg the question as to why there was a change in the shape of the *schilt* shape in the treatise, and whether or not it was the author's or the artist's decision.

Another curious note to make about the second image is that the combatant on the left side is holding the blade of the opponent in his grasp, securing the weapon while preparing to strike the opponent. This would indicate that this is a legitimate technique for both practice weapons as indicated by those depicted and also for sharp ones, as that is what they would be practicing for.

The final point of note for these images is the re-appearance of the *chappe* in both cases. This was a feature found in the Cod.S.554 fig.7. This is the other treatise where it was indicated these were present. They are rarely used on these swords.

EQUIPMENT & CURATORIAL DISCUSSIONS

From MS E.1939.65.341 "Glasgow Fechtbuch" (1508)

MS E.1939.65.341 2r

The image which is presented above is from MS E.1939.65.341 of 1508, also known as the "Glasgow Fechtbuch". It depicts two combatants in civilian attire contesting with longswords. The pommel of the sword which can be seen is not the standard round pommel, but a more pointed and complex one. The handles on the weapons can clearly accommodate two hands comfortably and the cross-guard is very simple. The *schilts* on the weapons are of the winged type, and the blades of the weapons are slightly tapered and come to a round point.

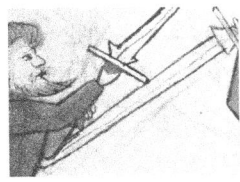

The type of *schilt* which is presented in this image has been seen before in previous images which have been already been presented. The two examples of these presented previously can be found in the "Wolfenbüttel Sketchbook" and the previously examined image MS KK5012 16v. This style of *schilt* becomes especially prevalent from the 1540s onward to about the 1590s.

The blades on these weapons are slightly tapered and come to a rounded point. There is a single line drawn up the middle of each weapon which seems to stop before the point, most likely indicating a fuller rather than a ridge. These are clearly practice weapons. The length of the blades indicates a standard longsword length.

From MS Germ.Quart.2020 "Goliath Fechtbuch" (1510 – 1520)

MS Germ.Quart.2020 31v

The image at left is from MS Germ. Quart.2020 known as the "Goliath Fechtbuch" dated 1510 to 1520, depicts two combatants in civilian clothing contesting with weapons which have proportions which are quite a bit larger than longswords. The weapons have spherical pommels, handles easily fitting two hands, and simple cross-guards. The *schilt* is of the winged kind, but relatively small, the blade is long, parallel and has a round point. The blade is marked with a fuller down the middle. This is most interesting as it depicts a two-handed feder.

The feder has been indicated most predominantly as a practice weapon for the longsword, but it can, and has, also been used as a practice weapon for the two-handed sword as well. This image clearly demonstrates this particular use of the feder. The weapons in this image are clearly larger in proportion to the individuals using the weapons.

The *schilt* of the weapon is quite small, even when taking into account the rest of the weapon, and the enlarged size of the weapon. For a much larger weapon it would almost be expected that the *schilt* would be larger. It is of the winged type which was seen previously, though the extended parts are quite small.

The blades on these weapons are quite long. They are parallel and have rounded points. There is a marking for a fuller down the middle of the blade as has been indicated previously. The most striking feature of these blades is the length of them, which in combination with the extended handles clearly makes them practice weapons for two-handed swords rather than longswords. Practice weapons more so indicated by the rounded point and lack of impact indicated by the blow indicated across the opponent's arms.

EQUIPMENT & CURATORIAL DISCUSSIONS

From Ergrundung Ritterlicher Kunst der Fechterey (1516) by Paurñfeyndt

"Paurñfeyndt 3"

The image above from *Ergrundung Ritterlicher Kunst der Fechterey* in 1516 depicts two combatants contesting with longswords in civilian attire. The weapons have spherical pommels, and handles which can accommodate two hands. The cross-guard is very simple. The *schilt* is square as in some of the previous examples, and the blade is quite broad and parallel and comes to a point at the end. There is the indication of a ridge down the full length of the blade.

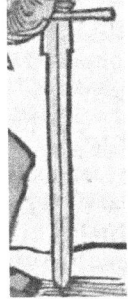

The blade of the weapon is not exemplary aside from it being somewhat broader than most of the previous examples shown. It is parallel all the way until it terminates at the tip of the weapon which is less rounded than in some examples. There is also a single line which has been drawn down the centre of the blade in the image which is likely been used to give the blade some character, thus as indication of a ridge along the blade.

The *schilt* is rectangular and relatively long, but does not stick out very much at the sides. This would seem to be more similar with the earlier depictions such as those found in earlier treatises such as the "Cluny Fechtbuch" and some of those found in the MS KK5012. This may have something to do with the shape of the blade which is broader than later examples of feder presented. What can be said is that this style of *schilt* refers back to previous examples of *schilt* rather than presenting a contemporary style, as compared to the examples already presented.

From Cod.icon. 393 "Opus Amplissimum de Arte Athletica" (1540s)

Cod.icon. 393 48r

Cod.icon.393 37v

The images at left depict two combatants contesting at the longsword. Both are from Cod.icon. 393 entitled "Opus Amplissimum de Arte Athletica" dated to the 1540s. The weapons in both cases have spherical pommels, and grips which can easily accommodate two hands. The cross-guards are very simple in nature. The *schilts* are of a modest winged design. The blades have parallel edges and no point at the end at all; there is some indication of a fuller in the blade. What is most interesting is that one is indicated as drawing blood. This is significant for a practice weapon.

The *schilt* on the weapons is the winged type again, though it is less pronounced as later examples will demonstrate. This will become more standard as the following images will demonstrate. The smaller *schilt* would imply that more of the weight is contained in the pommel and handle the counter-balance the blade.

More of the focus here is on the blade. In this case, the focus is on the image 48r where the blow has drawn blood, yet in 37v there is no blood drawn. This would imply that the blade is not sharp, yet can draw blood if it strikes flesh where it is closely located near the bone. Clearly the blade is not sharp otherwise the individual in 37v who was struck would have also been cut. The blades are parallel and terminate sharply, meaning that they have flat, not rounded ends meaning that there is no chance of a thrust doing anything at all, these are clearly practice weapons. This is one of the few images of feder where the impact draws blood.

EQUIPMENT & CURATORIAL DISCUSSIONS

From MSS Dresd.C.93/C.94 "Opus Amplissimum de Arte Athletica" (1542)

MSS Dresd.C.93/C.94 23r

The image above is from MSS Dresd.C.93/C.94 dated 1542, interestingly, like the previous entry the document is also entitled "Opus Amplissimum de Arte Athletica". Needless to say both treatises display similar things. Depicted here are two combatants engaged with longswords in civilian dress. The weapons' pommels are obscured, but can be assumed to be spherical by the way they are gripped. The handles can fit two hands comfortably, and the cross-guards are simple with spherical ends. The *schilt* are of the winged type, and the blades are parallel with rounded points.

The schilt which is seen on the weapons found in this image is similar to that found in the previous image except that the wings are more accentuated. This form of schilt becomes more the standard which is found on feder as time progresses. The schilt itself is also somewhat enlarged as compared to the previous example.

The blades have parallel edges and come to a rounded point, unlike the previous example where they seem to be simply cut off. Again this demonstrates a weapon without a point. There is no marking on the blade to indicate any fuller or ridge marking of any kind.

From Cod.I.6.2°.4 "Jörg Breu Draftbook" (1545)

Cod.I.6.2o.4 16v

The image above is from the "Jörg Breu Draftbook" dated to 1545 its reference is Cod.I.6.2°.4 and it depicts two combatants combating at the longsword in civilian attire. The weapons' pommels are spherical and there is room for both hands on the handles of the weapons. The cross-guards are of simple construction. The *schilt* are of winged construction and the blades have parallel edges and have rounded points.

Again the winged *schilt* is present in this image as is expected, and noted previously. The wings on the schilt in this case are not as large as the previous example but are not as small as in the Cod. icon.393 examples. This places them somewhere in between the two of them.

The blades of the weapons have parallel edges and rounded points as previously indicated. These are more like the previous example than those found in the Cod.icon.393. This clearly indicates that they are a practice weapon. There is some shading indicated on the blades of these weapons which could indicate a ridge or fuller on the blade, as with a line, but this is not clear so a flat blade could also be possible.

EQUIPMENT & CURATORIAL DISCUSSIONS

From MS A.4⁰.2 "Joachim Meyers Fäktbok" (1560's)

MS A.4°.2 18v

The image above depicts two combatants contesting at the longsword. It is from MS A.4⁰.2 dated to the 1560s, known as "Joachim Meyers Fäktbok". The pommels of the weapons are obscured, but the handles can clearly accommodate the use of two hands. The cross-guard is of simple construction. The *schilt* is of winged construction and the blade is parallel with a rounded point.

 The *schilt* is of the winged type as several of the previous ones have been. What will be noticed about this one is that it is rather short, but broad and that the wings of the *schilt* extend a bit forward. This is something that will be noted especially in Meyer's works.

The blades of the weapons are parallel and they have rounded points, this has already been noted. They also lack any sort of marking on the blades themselves indicating any sort of fuller or ridge on them. In this case the most remarkable point to be made is the bend depicted in the blade of the weapon on the combatant on the left. There has been an addition of a red line to the image to demonstrate the angle of the bend in the blade. It could almost be said that the  action used is designed so that the blade will bend to strike the opponent, thus using the characteristics of the weapon. This could also indicate some tendency of the feder toward being somewhat bendy in nature.

From Gründtliche Beschreibung der Kunst des Fechtens (1600) by Joachim Meyer

"Longsword A"

The image above comes from *Gründtliche Beschreibung der Kunst des Fechtens* which was originally published in 1570 and then re-published in 1600. The image is determined to be "Longsword A" because it is the image that he refers to as "A" when he is discussing the images about longsword. The "A" can be found in the foreground centre.

The image depicts two combatants in civilian clothing in a school scenario combating with longswords. The weapons have spherical pommels and handles which easily accommodate two hands. The cross-guards have a point in the middle toward the *schilt* and also flare towards the ends. The *schilt* is of the winged type, the blade tapers to a rounded point.

This image presents one of the classic examples of the winged *schilt*. It is broad at the top and narrows toward the base and comes in at the top toward the blade giving it its winged shape. The points of this *schilt* extend forward somewhat from the body of the *schilt*. It is a more robust design of the winged *schilt* than found in the previous examples of the same.

The blade is depicted as tapered, and tapers to a rounded point. This is unlike Meyer's previous example of the blade which is parallel. This blade is different and would have different characteristics due to its nature. There is no indication of any fullers or ridges marked on this weapon, and the rounded point clearly points out, along with the setting that this is a practice weapon.

EQUIPMENT & CURATORIAL DISCUSSIONS

From Cod.Guelf.83.4 Aug.8°
"Das Ander Theil Des Newen Kůnstreichen Fechtbůches" (1591)

Cod.Guelf.83.4 Aug.8o 2r

The image above is from Cod. Guelf.83.4 Aug.8° also known as "Das Ander Theil Des Newen Kůnstreichen Fechtbůches" dated 1591 which depicts two combatants contesting at the longsword in civilian clothing. The weapons in this image have spherical pommels, two-handed handles and simple quillons. The *schilt* found on the weapons are of the winged type. The blades are parallel and have rounded points on them. What is remarkable about this image is the cut which has taken place that has drawn blood and the variation in *schilt* shape.

The *schilt* on these weapons is different to the previous winged types seen previously. The *schilt* itself is thinner and the wings are more rounded at the ends. The wings of the *schilt* also start quite a bit later and extend somewhat further toward the point, but this does not necessarily make the *schilt* wider, in fact the whole thing is quite slender. This, it could be assumed to result in a more over-balanced weapon, but as will be seen in the description of the blade, which is to follow, this is not the case as it compensates in its own way for this.

The blades on these weapons are definitely thinner than previous examples of feder, this accounts for how the *schilt* can be thinner also, as previously indicated. The weapon has a definitively rounded point, indicating that it is a practice weapon, yet it is depicted as drawing blood on one of the combatants. There are a couple of possible answers to this particular question. The first answer is that it could be thrown to artistic license, to give the image more impact. Another answer is that it is striking on the outside of the forearm so possibly striking flesh over bone, thus the possibility of drawing blood in this scenario. The only other example of a bleeding wound in these images is presented in Cod.icon. 393 48r, where the blade has struck the head, a likely place where bleeding would occur. In this case it is more likely that it is artistic license, possibly attempting to depict what the sharp weapon would do while depicting the practice weapon in the image.

afencersramblings.blogspot.com

From New Künstliches Fechtbuch (1612) by Jakob Sutor

Sutor (1612, p8)

The image above is from *New Künstliches Fechtbuch* which was published in 1612 and written by Jakob Sutor. It depicts two individuals combating with what longswords. The weapons are not particularly well-drawn. The pommels are spherical and the handles can easily support the use of two hands. The cross-guards are of a relatively simple design flaring at the ends. The *schilt* on the weapons is of a design not seen in the previous images. The blades of the weapons are depicted as parallel but taper to a point.

Sutor is known for his simple plagiarism of other sources and his not particularly good reproduction of other sources which are then claimed as his own work. This image is a perfect example as the proportions of the weapons demonstrate. The pommels of the weapons are distinctively too small for the weapons to be an effective counter-balance, and the handles are very much too thick for the combatants to hold properly.

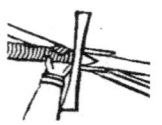

The *schilt* presented in this image is unlike any other which is presented in any other image which has been presented previously. This could be an attempt at reproducing the the *schilt* found in Cod.S.554 or similar, with the rectangular shape and *chappe*, simply misinterpreted. It is more likely from MS KK5012 2r due to the presence of the *chappe*, the rectangular shape of the *schilt* and also the shaping present in the *schilt*.

The blades present in this image are just as badly represented. There is one with no markings on the blade at all and there is one which does have marking on the blade. The blades are both parallel which come to a tapered and then rounded point. This means that the artist is representing them as blunted sharp weapons. One has a marking which extends part way down the blade which could represent a fuller and the other has no markings on it at all.

From Cod.10799 "Būech von fechter Vnnd Ringstückhen zū Ross vnnd Fuoß" (1623)

Cod.10799 19r

The image at left depicts two individuals in civilian clothing contesting with longswords. The image is from Cod.10799 entitled "Būech von fechter Vnnd Ringstückhen zū Ross vnnd Fuoß" dated to 1623. The pommels on these weapons are spherical and the handles accommodate two hands. The cross-guards are straight but have the ends slightly curved toward the point and are enlarged. The *schilt* of the weapons has returned to the simple rectangular shape of earlier designs. The blades are parallel with rounded points. One of the things that make this depiction of the weapons a little odd is the short length of the weapons, and that they are also so small in comparison to the figures, almost as though the figures are more important.

The *schilt* of these weapons has returned to the very simple design that was seen in the much earlier images which were presented. If the whole weapon were to be scaled exactly as it is presented, the *schilt* would barely be required due to the thin nature of the blade. The closest shape to this is found in the "Codex Danzig", Norling or in the Kuchler examples. In this case it almost seems as if the *schilt* is present as a matter of form rather than function.

Of the blades there is nothing remarkable to say. The blades are parallel from *schilt* until they round to the point. It could be claimed that there is some sort of ridge going along the blade going by the shading which is present by the artist, but this would more likely be merely representing the shadow of one figure over another as this is present elsewhere in the image. The thinness of the blades is the only real remarkable thing that could be pointed out being that they are quite thin and thus represent a distinct image of a practice blade rather than any sort of blade for cutting.

CHARACTERISTICS – OLD AND NEW WEAPONS

> *"At this point perhaps I, to avoid further confusion, should clarify that when I speak of "fechtschwert" I do not necessarily mean swords with flexible blades, but rather speak of the shape of the blade, with a broad ricasso and narrower blade."* (Norling, 2011a)

The examination here focuses on the characteristics of the feder, in this case both the extant examples and also the new reproduction examples as they both fall into the same category. Both should carry the same characteristics if the modern practitioner is to be using the correct weapon. The ricasso which is spoken of here is the "schilt", the broadened and blunt section of the blade near the hilt on the feder, which is one of its striking characteristics and makes it stand out from other weapons.

Few Extant Examples

The problem in discussing and examining extant examples of the federschwert is that there are so few examples been found, "However, only 23 confirmed swords are known to be preserved in various collections" (Norling, 2012). For weapons such as the smallsword, or sabre, there are many fine examples of these weapons for curators to examine and for researchers to gain data about however, as indicated there are few examples of the feder available.

> *"The sword consists of a very thin, rounded blade with a large ricasso and a heavy hilt and pommel. Because of this, it has the same weight and center of balance as a real sword, and handles identically. This odd construction also has the effect of moving the sword's center of percussion to a theoretical point beyond its tip. The tip of a Federschwert is spatulated and may have been covered with a leather sleeve to make thrusting safer, though no direct historical evidence exists of such use."*
> (Wikipedia, 2016)

The description above has been cobbled together out of descriptions of multiple weapons no doubt to give a final general description of what feder in general look like. It is most interesting that the *schilt* is referred to as a *ricasso* as in the case of a rapier, the ricasso is often the place where a finger is wrapped to gain more control over the weapon. Clearly the idea of it being a blunted part of the blade is the part of the concept which is being presented here.

Physical Differs From Depicted

With a description based upon the extant examples the characteristics of the feder in its original period should be covered, actually this is a little more complex a problem than that. "The designs of most of the preserved fechtschwerter are quite different from what we see in the period sources of the *fechtbuche*," (Norling, 2012). This means that the primary source material being used to reconstruct the fighting arts for the weapon do not depict weapons which are the same as what are left behind even though they are the same category of weapon. This could seem a mere artist issue, but different aspects of a weapon will change its abilities.

EQUIPMENT & CURATORIAL DISCUSSIONS

> *"In the early period sources we almost exclusively see swords that have blades that taper towards the point, with some of them even being illustrated as having ridged blades. The clear majority, however, are depicted as having simple flat blades."*
> *(Norling, 2012)*

There is a change in the depiction of the weapons, from those which have a rigid blade to those having a simple flat blade. The question the reader needs to ask is whether this was an artist change, or whether the weapons themselves changed. Were earlier feder more rigid and did they have more of a point than the later ones? There is also a question of the form of the blade and the *schilt*, in the depiction, but all of these really need answering in a more specialised discussion. Needless to say, even in the case of the original examples of the feder, their characteristics are well and truly not established.

Modern Production

> *"Modern production of Fechtfedern has been revived in the 21st century for use as sparring weapons and for competition in the context of the Historical European martial arts revival."*
> *(Wikipedia, 2016)*

Modern productions and reproductions of the feder are based on the extant examples of the weapons which have been left behind in museums and collections. The weights and measurements have then been interpreted by modern smiths for construction and use by modern swordsmen. What is most interesting is that the use of the weapon has changed a little, but for a different purpose in most cases. The weapons themselves should be designed to act like their original counter-parts.

"The characteristics of a *good* federschwert include a very lively and agile *point control* and it feels much like a *sharp* sword designed for blossfechten, but due to the design has a little *less punch*, since much mass has been moved closer to the cross. This design causes the often spoken of *centre of percussion (c.o.p.)* to be moved to a theoretical point beyond the actual point of the sword. You simply cannot strike as hard with a federschwert as with a "normal" sword. It should be noted that some federschwert also have flex in the *wrong* part of the blade. Preferably, the blade should flex in the last third or so, but several makers have stretched this flex too close to the cross, causing wobbling in the blade. Also, some federschwert have problems with vibrations in the hilt upon impact." (Norling, 2011)

Norling (2011) describes the characteristics of a "good" feder and points out some of the important aspects which the sword should have. He also notes some of the issues which some of the other swords may have with them should they be constructed without due diligence. The characteristics which have been discussed here should be kept in mind as the discussion proceeds.

SPORT SWORD OR NOT?

"commonly are associated with sports fencing in late 16th century fechtschulen, rather than proper training for combat and duelling. They are simply not seen as "real" swords. Is this really a fair assumption?"
(Norling, 2011a)

Often is the case that the feder is often seen as a sort of "sport longsword". A comparison is often made between the feder and the foil, as in the feder is a sport version of the longsword, just as the foil was the sport or practice version of the smallsword. This is often related to their being seen in primarily school situations, and out of armour. This perspective also comes from the change in dimensions due to the narrower blade and the supposed lighter weapon.

"Of the manuals that show both regular longsword and fechtschwert, there is a clear tendency to use fechtschwert without armour, and in armour, regular longswords are used. Fechtschwert are, with one exception (Ms.Germ.Quart.16), used in blossfechten, i.e. unarmoured fencing."
(Norling, 2011a)

Could this situation not merely be that the situation was that the feder was used in unarmoured combat, civilian combat, rather than armoured combat? This could be a relevant alternative to it being a merely sport weapon. The other alternative is that it was exactly that the feder was fulfilling its role exactly as a practice weapon, thus did not require the weight of the regular longsword, but did require the characteristics of one.

Clearly rigorous practice and art was being practiced as the manuals indicate. The longsword may have been pushed aside by the rapier in prominence for self-defence but the arts were still being taught. Indications of this can be seen in the reprint of longsword manuals in the late sixteenth-century.

NOT JUST FOR LONGSWORD TRAINING?

The feder is most often used for longsword training but it has been indicated by some researchers that they may also be used and have been used for training for other weapons of similar shape, namely the two-handed sword, "some fechtschwert are very close to the bidenhänder with their parierhaken and there may be more connections here than we have realized." (Norling, 2011a). Clearly a lighter weapon of similar proportions would be a god-send to those practicing to use the two-handed sword with its larger form and increased weight, and the feder does demonstrate marked characteristics in similarity to its larger cousin.

"After having studied all the illustrated manuals I have access to, ... it is my belief that some fechtschwert, with widely flared ricassos/schilt, may actually be precursors and/or training versions of the complex-hilt longswords and the bidenhänders, since these three types of swords all offer similar protection for the fingers if you put

EQUIPMENT & CURATORIAL DISCUSSIONS

> *them over the cross, or for the hands in a bind at the strong, by keeping the opponent's blade a few inches from the cross."*
> (Norling, 2011a)

There is further evidence for this supposition in the images which are present in some of the manuals where the weapons seem to be somewhat larger than the standard sort of length a person would expect of a longsword. In further reference to such similarities between the feder depicted in such images and other weapons, there is much similarity to be discovered and discussed in these images and others.

> *"It is also very interesting to compare regular 14th century longswords with leather "rain guards" and early 15th century fechtschwert to 16th century bidenhänder with parierhaken and complex-hilt bastard swords from a functionality perspective. All four types offer similar applications of use and perhaps this is no coincidence?"* (Norling, 2011a)

Not only does this suggest a similar usage of weapon but it also indicates a longer pedigree for the use of the longsword and other weapons of a similar kind. It may even indicate a similar ancestral location for all of these weapons but this may be taking things a little too far. The most important point raised here is that the feder may indeed have been used for practice with more than just the longsword.

RENAISSANCE PRACTICE WEAPON

> *"The Feder (plural Federn; also Fechtfeder, plural Fechtfedern), is a type of training sword used in Fechtschulen (fencing schools) of the German Renaissance. The type has existed since at least the 15th century, but it came to be widely used as a standard training weapon only in the 16th century (when longsword fencing had ceased to have a serious aspect of duelling, as duels were now fought with the rapier), shown extensively in the fighting manuals of the time, particularly those of Paulus Hector Mair and Joachim Meyer, and it remained in use in such Fechtschulen well into the 17th, and in some cases for much of the 18th century."* (Wikipedia, 2016)

The most useful thing about the Wikipedia is its relatively complete and relatively comprehensive explanation of any subject which is examined when it is sought. The above gives the plural and optional naming conventions for the weapon. The focus here, however is that the feder was a Renaissance practice weapon. It was used in fencing schools for practice so that the art of the longsword could survive, as the above indicates the rapier had taken over in aspects of serious duelling.

Renaissance Practice Weapons

> *"In practicing any form of weapon-based martial art, a student must naturally use some form of weapon simulator. The medieval and Renaissance martial artists who trained with the longsword sometimes used wooden swords (known as wasters) for their training, but it was not uncommon for them to also*

> use blunted steel swords. Many of these swords still exist in museums and private collections. They also frequently appear in period fencing treatises from the 15th and 16th centuries. Such swords often had blades with narrow profiles, which was to compensate for the fact that the blades were created thick enough to have a safer edge. In this way the blades did not become too heavy. At the base of the blades there is a wider, winglike ricasso (known as the schilt, or "shield"), which ensures that the tang is not too thin. It also provides a degree of hand protection for practicing certain techniques."
>
> (Grandy, 2003)

Grandy's (2003) introduction to Renaissance practice weapons is most useful as it demonstrates that the feder was not the only practice weapon in existence, which is sometimes forgotten. There were other options which were also commonly used. Wooden swords (wasters) were also a common practice tool, which actually goes back to the Roman period. Grandy also notes the formation and change in the shape of the blade thicker to be safer, but narrower as a result. The *schilt* is used to protect the hands and also reinforce the tang of the sword. These are all important notes to be taken into account.

> "The Federschwert, or Feder sword, is a training sword that was used in fencing schools during the Renaissance. Perfectly designed, the Federschwert served to safely practice full speed combat among practitioners, while reducing the risk of injury. The Federschwert greatest attribute is their similar weight and balance to real swords of the same period. The Federschwert is shown extensively in the fighting manuals of the 16th century, particularly those of Paulus Hector Mair and Joachim Meyer."
>
> (Imperial Swords, 2017)

Again, the presented evidence demonstrates that the idea was to produce a sword which could be used with relative safety, thus reducing injury at full speed. These were obviously practice weapons. Their similar weight and balance attributes to real weapons allowed them to act like real ones for more accurate practice. This documentation also indicates some of their documented presence in manuals.

Documentary Evidence

> "We can find examples of these swords in the old Martial Arts Fechtbucher (fight books) from the early 1420s up until the early 17th century, but they might have been in use for a longer period of time. We see many varying styles of Feders as their designs change from Fechtbuch to Fechtbuch."
>
> (Wassom, 2016)

There are many different examples of the feder found in the manuals, and they also demonstrate a long history of use in these manuals. The designs of the weapons change over time. In some cases the blade profile will change to a shape and then revert back, the *schilt* shape also changes over time as well, with various different shapes being demonstrated.

Practice Weapon – Historical Basis

"we can look to the fencing manuals and see what was used by our predecessors. After all, they ought to have had a good grasp on what tools one should use for good and solid, traditional training that leaves you well-equipped for actual combat. As we shall see later, the fechtschwert have been commonly used for practice since the early 1400s, so there is clearly some merit in practicing with them." (Norling, 2011a)

What is most useful is that not only can the manuals be followed as indicated by their authors but the correct weapon can be used for that manual. Thus the practice weapon has an historical basis presented in the manual itself. This needs to be examined very carefully and the use of the tool also taken very carefully and reminded that the feder is a practice weapon, as the evidence has presented, and that the weapon be used as such. While techniques may be performed with martial intent, the results should not be expected to be the same due to the nature of the weapon.

CONCLUSION

There have been a lot of theories proposed in this investigation. Some of which have results to examine, and some of which will never really have results due to their nature. The important thing with regard to all of these theories is that they have seen the light of investigation and had some time to be dealt with. Many are not afforded the same opportunity.

The investigation into the federschwert can be simply divided into two sections. The first is "Words", in which the meanings and origins of the words which are associated with the weapon are discussed. This was what was discussed in the first half of the investigation. The second is "Objects", in which the feder as an object is discussed, which started with the image discussion and then discussed the more physical aspects of the weapon. While the introduction separated the image discussion from the "Objects" that the images were of the objects and discussed them made them part of the "Object" discussion rather than something separate.

The organisation of the text allowed the separation of the words from the physical nature of the weapon but the nature of the argument meant that there was still links between the two during the discussion. This approach led to a better overall discussion of the weapon. The separation allowed focus where it was required to disentangle items from one another while still addressing the weapon as a whole.

No Short Answer

"The Short Answer" opened the discussion first with the literal translation of the meaning of the word and then more discussion of the weapon it describes from a usage point of view. The second half of this part discussed and opened into the next part of the investigation that the term federschwert and its diminutive feder were terms not used historically and therefore cannot be evaluated from this point of view. This also highlighted one of the arguments central to the discussions to follow, the discussion of the use of the term feder and how it was used.

A Word in Common Usage

The term "federschwert" is a neologism, a modern word invented to fill a hole in the language. The term itself is quite commonly known, especially the simpler more common "feder". This means that it is a word in common usage which refers to a particular thing. When it is said, people know what that thing is that the person is talking about. This means that regardless of it historical background, or lack thereof, it fulfils an important purpose, thus there should be no issue in its use.

Every Man and His Theory

What followed this in the investigation were some interesting points where the term had been used previously, including a claim where the feder was a rapier. Evidence has clearly been put to the contrary with regard to this. Various theories have been placed as to why or why not a particular group may or may not have referred to the practice weapon of the longsword known in the current period as a feder. These were presented to simply present the arguments so that all were clear. Did it refer to the quills that they were using to write their arguments, or the lightness of their weapons? It is hard to tell. Such arguments are tenuous at best and it is best to move on to arguments better founded.

Another Name?

There were two other candidates to replace "federschwert" for the naming of this particular weapon, these being "paratschwert" and "fechtschwert". The first discussed was "paratschwert", as indicated by the order above. This was found to be a parade or ceremonial sword more than one which was actually used, thus not actually really accurate for use or replacement for feder. "Fechtschwert" would seem to be a better option being that its literal definition is a "fight sword", however for some this would seem to be a little broad in its understanding, not indicating a practice weapon specifically, nor the weapon described by feder in particular. The result of this is that federschwert still remains as the more popular and understandable choice for naming of this weapon.

Worth 1000 Words

What is the largest section of this investigation, purely by volume, is the investigation of images from various treatises depicting feder being used. Each one of these images is then scrutinised for how the weapon is depicted and in what sort of scenario. In all cases the combatants are depicted in civilian clothing, which is of note as it leads to the weapon being most noted for being used in unarmoured combat and another weapon being used for armoured combat.

Following this is an examination of the weapons which are being used by the figures that are present in the images, the focus of this investigation. The various pieces of the weapon are noted, pommel, handle, cross-guard, *schilt*, and blade. Basic details are given at first, but then more detail is given about the *schilt* and blade as it is these two items which most determine the status of the feder.

In the case of the *schilt*, it varied in shape from a simple block near the cross-guard to a more extensive winged type in some cases. What was noted in all cases is that it was present in all cases in some form, thus being the purpose of selecting these images. The varying sizes and shape of the *schilt* would have varying effects on the use of the weapon, and this should be noted, as would the shape and make of the blade. To state that there would be any standard form of *schilt* would be far-fetched as the images present.

The blades vary from tapered to parallel edged. From simple flat-bladed depiction to also those which depict fullers and ridges marked on them. This presents an idea that there were various different ideas about what the blade of the feder should be like, and thus how it should act. What is most interesting is that in two cases (Cod.icon. 393 48r and Cod.Guelf.83.4 Aug.8° 2r) the feder is depicted as drawing blood. In the first case it could be logical as it strikes the head where flesh is close to the bone; in the second, not so much. In both cases it could be merely an artist's license or author's emphasis for the impact of the action. This is especially the case as these weapons are considered to be blunt, practice weapons. In all cases the point is rounded or flat, thus the thrust was not an option or, was considered dangerous resulting in extra caution needed.

The result of this pictorial inquest was designed to give an idea of the various shapes of the feder and ways it was presented. Ideas of its use and its physical characteristics can also be formed from these pictures also. They lead the observer to be informed that this weapon did not come in a standard form and that their use was not confined to one area.

Physical Characteristics

The investigation next moved to looking at the physical characteristics of the feder. This discussed both some of the museum examples and also some of the modern reproductions. The intention was both to compare their characteristics and also to demonstrate the overall characteristics of the weapon as a physical object.

One of the biggest problems for the researcher is that there are few extant examples available for research. Norling (2012) points this out quite clearly. With only a small sample of the weapon to go off there are certain biases which are likely to manifest in the data-gathering and this can be detrimental to the research. In some cases there is a stark contrast between those weapons found evident in treatises and those found as examples, artistic impression or survivor bias could easily explain this. Needless to say the researcher should beware any general statements made on such evidence.

Modern reproduction weapons are often based on a few examples of the weapon. This leads to a particular bias toward how the weapon is created and what the final product results in. With the weapons actually in use, the swordsmen give feedback to the swordsmiths and good ones thus change the weapons, just as they would in the period in which they were used formerly. This result in better weapons which actually act how they are supposed to.

A Question of Use

The feder has been accused of being a "longsword foil" or a "sport longsword" by some and it is in the use of the weapon that the true answer to this accusation that we find the answer to this. The longsword in the late sixteenth-century had been replaced by the rapier as the prime weapon for duelling. Thus it was associated as a weapon out of its time, so as a blunt weapon it could only be used for sport, or could it?

The actual case as can be seen by the reprinting of longsword manuals in the late sixteenth-century is that the practice with the feder was actually for longsword combat with sharp longswords. It was still being practiced as a martial art not as some mere sport. It fulfilled its role as a practice weapon for the longsword.

What is also demonstrated especially in the "Goliath Fechtbuch" is that the feder was also used for practicing the two-handed sword. The extended handle of the feder meant that it was in a position to be used for both longsword and two-handed sword training, thus making it a practice weapon of great utility. Further, certain feder were actually constructed for this exact purpose.

Regardless of any other information which is gathered about the federschwert it is determined to be a Renaissance weapon for the practice of longsword and also two-handed sword, should the owner choose. This is the purpose of the weapon and what it was designed for. For the modern martial artist seeking information about European martial arts, the feder is an excellent tool for investigating the martial arts of the Renaissance period, especially with regard to the German region. Should the eye tend toward another area on the other hand, maybe a weapon better suited to this should be chosen. Match the tool to its purpose.

The Rapier: A Curatorial Discussion

INTRODUCTION

The document presented is a curatorial discussion of the rapier. Many historians have examined this weapon from different points of view. Many curatorial discussions result in terms being accepted into common language which are actually artificial, and many assumptions made about the weapon. With regard to the rapier, it is one of the worst for this particular aspect in discussions.

There are two main elements that need to be taken into account when discussing any sword, the hilt and the blade. It is vital that both are addressed with equal importance as one is nothing without the other. With regard to this it will be noted that there is a lot more information available about the hilt of the rapier than there is about the blade. It is only more recently have serious discussions been made about the rapier as a weapon rather than a collector's piece or museum item.

An investigation of the literature available about the rapier is important and as such the first part of the discussion will involve a historiographical discussion. This entails the discussion of the various sources available with regard to the rapier. Through this it is possible to examine the uses of particular sources in comparison to others.

Before any discussion of the rapier is possible, it is important to first establish exactly what is meant by a rapier, or at least for the purposes of this article. Another discussion relating to this exact question can be found in this book, indeed in this section, with all of the detail examined, thus there is no need to repeat it here.

The development of the hilt has often been the focus on the discussion of the rapier. Many assumptions have been made about the development of this particular part of this weapon. The true origin of this particular part of the weapon is often shrouded in assumptions made about the weapon and also the time period. What is important is that the discussion must go back far enough in history to really appreciate and discover its development.

The blade of the rapier is often discarded in discussions of the rapier, this sharpened piece of steel that makes the rapier a weapon. To completely examine the rapier then the blade must be discussed as well as the hilt. Many of the elements will be discussed in very general terms, as this is what information is left to us. The thing here is that this information is important.

The last part of this particular discussion will be about modern recreations of the rapier. Much of this will be done from observances made by the author rather than being from other sources. The rapier as a weapon and especially in association with the Renaissance martial arts of Europe has become very popular. This part of the discussion will be aimed at the importance of finding accurate weapons to accurately recreate the weapon styles which have been chosen.

It should be noted as well that the weapons discussed here will include those up to and including the end of the sixteenth-century, and beginning of the seventeenth-century. This is primarily due to the focus on the weapon during this period but also to avoid any changes in later weapons, which occured after this period.

HISTORIOGRAPHICAL DISCUSSION

In the discussion of the rapier there are many different sources to be examined. Over the past decade this has increased a great deal. This can be attributed to two main things. The first is the growing interest in European martial arts and the other is the Internet. More and more manuals from the period have become available along with research done by many different people. This discussion has focussed on research from books rather than electronic sources though a single one has been used. In this a decision as to the purpose of the investigation must be made.

Most of the research into the rapier in previous years has been more of a curatorial one, and as such there are quite a few books about weapons in general which discuss the rapier from this point of view. They include very general texts such as Harding's (1990) *Weapons: An International Encyclopedia from 5000BC to 2000AD*, which is a discussion of weapons from their earliest stages up to the present, along with more specific texts about arms an armour such as, Bull's (1990) *An Historical Guide to Arms & Armour*, and Norman's (1964) *Arms and Armour*. These texts are all quite useful as they put the rapier in perspective in comparison to other weapons of the same period and also other periods.

Along with these are more sources more specifically concerned with the sword itself. These books are very specific and give a great deal of information about hilt and blade development along with some historical detail associated with these weapons. Wagner's (2004) *Swords and Daggers: An Illustrated Handbook*, is a perfect example of one of these curatorial discussions of swords and associated weapons. Along with these more general curatorial works about swords and hilted weapons are also more specific texts about the rapier itself. Valentine's (1968) *Rapiers: An Illustrated Reference Guide to the Rapiers of the 16th and 17th Centuries, with their Companions*, is one of the most respected and referred texts of this kind. This gives a discussion of the rapier from its beginnings all the way through its period with many examples of the weapons.

Curatorial works are not the only place where useful information about the development of the rapier as a weapon is found. It is important to look further afield for discussions about how the weapon was used in combat. While many of the manuals about how to use the rapier are useful in this search, discussions about the weapon itself in martial arts are more useful. This makes Anglo's (2000) *The Martial Arts of Renaissance Europe*, one of the most useful texts with regard to this particular point of view.

While it has not been possible to include every single source which discusses the rapier from a curatorial point of view, the texts which have been included have been selected for their specific uses to the discussion which will be made. To attempt to include all of the texts available would result in a very long and drawn out discussion of the weapon and would go to such a level of specifics that only a museum curator or weaponsmith would require and this is not the purpose of this discussion.

WHAT IS A RAPIER?

For the purposes of this particular discussion it will be assumed that the rapier is a long-bladed, single-handed weapon, designed for civilian use, which may be used for either cutting or thrusting, but is primarily designed to thrust. This question was addressed in another discussion in this book, thus only a definition of the weapon which is being discussed in this article needs to be given. To give the most complete discussion, earlier, later and contemporary weapons will also be mentioned. This is especially important in the discussion of the development of the hilt.

ASPECTS OF DEVELOPMENT

The development of the hilt of the rapier has often been the focus of curatorial discussions of this particular weapon. As such there is a lot of information available on hilt forms. In this particular discussion, it is important that all of the aspects of the development of the hilt are discussed to examine a deeper reason for the development of the hilt as it did. To do this all of the evidence presented must be examined, from the general development all the way to the reasons and development of specific parts of the weapon.

The first thing that should be noted is that the development of the hilt of a sword in making it more complex is that it is done out of necessity. The development of the overall weapon tends to be included in this sort of discussion, and this is actually useful as it gives a better explanation. The three main causes of the development of the hilt were as such, protection for the forefinger extended over the quillon, a reduction in armour in the use of the sword, especially in the civilian context, and finally the advantage gained through blade length increases (Valentine, 1968:9). The last one pertains to the hilt as the blade had to be balanced by it.

> *"To protect the hand a variety of guards were built on the hilt and the top of the blade was left unsharpened where the forefinger rested on it, as it had to if the fingers were correctly positioned for thrusting."*
> *(Akehurst, 1969:7)*

The development of the hilt and the blade are related. With the development of the ricasso, the unsharpened part of the blade, the finger placed over this area had to be protected in some way, thus through the development of the hilt. Hand protection would previously have been suitable for the protection of the hand and finger, but with more subtle movements of the weapon developing this was being discarded. This was especially the case in the civilian scene where armour was not worn.

> *"After 1500, as the wearing of the sword with civilian dress became more usual and the duel more popular as a way of settling disagreements, more complicated guards developed."* *(Norman, 1964:99)*

What is presented here is a technical and social reason for the development of the hilt. The weapon had to be popularly worn with civilian dress before the requirement for the development of the hilt would be required. Of course it was also the use of the weapon by an unarmoured had that required the hilt to be developed to protect it. The change in use of the sword for the civilian also resulted in a change in the weapon entirely. Both the blade and the hilt were affected by this particular change in focus. This was also affected by choices made by civilians and their attraction for the complex hilts.

> "changes in fencing techniques - especially in the sixteenth century - had considerable effect on the design of swords. The use of the point became more important than the edge, so swords became longer and narrower. By the middle of the fifteenth century the addition of extra guards to the hilt had become more fashionable, and the familiar long rapier is really a development of these hilts. It should be emphasised that the rapier is really a weapon to be worn with civilian dress, ensuite with a dagger."
>
> (Bull, 1990:12)

So far much has been said about the development of the weapon overall, so to address the development of the hilt more directly, the problem of dating such weapons and as such finding their development can be problematical. This is not only due to the lack of a definition of what a rapier is, but also the amount of designs of the hilt of the rapier, "bewildering variety of hilt forms,...[at least] 113 types of hilt" (Bull, 1990:96).

This is a problem for curators, but also for those who would wish to study these weapons. With so many forms of hilt available for the hilt of the rapier it is of little wonder that there are problems with dating and isolating them to a particular area. While this was a problem in the early designs of the rapier, later on it would just become worse, "greater variety than ever before was a characteristic feature of rapier design, particularly from the second quarter of the [16th] century onwards." (Coe et.al., 1996:50). But before it is possible to examine the complex hilt found on the late sixteenth-century rapier, it is important to go back to the start, where this development of the hilt started.

HILT DEVELOPMENT

The development of the rapier is often assumed to be later rather than earlier in the Renaissance period. The development of the hilt found on the rapier started much earlier than it has often been credited. The first thing that should be noted is that this development took place on military weapons, it was only later that these would be adopted for civilian use.

> "It is to fourteenth-century hilts that we must look for the first hints of the changes which led, eventually, to the complicated system of guards characteristic of sixteenth-century rapier hilts."
>
> (Coe et.al., 1996:45)

It is these fourteenth-century hilts that it is possible to find the origins of the hilt found on the rapier in the sixteenth-century. These developments were rather slow but demonstrate a change in the ideas about how the sword was to be used. As plate armour developed, cutting weapons became of less use, and as such thrusting became more important. This is not to say that cutting was abandoned, it was still present in the use of the sword for some time to come.

UN-BLOGGED: A FENCER'S RAMBLINGS

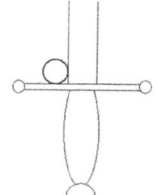

"The forefinger hook, consisting of a bar, rod or branch describing a short loop from the forward quillon to the blade, was added to protect the right forefinger when it was hooked over the forward quillon. This, more than any other feature of fourteenth-century hilts, is considered to be the first step in the evolution of the rapier hilt."
(Coe et.al., 1996:45)

The first development to take place was the addition of some protection to the finger which was extended over the quillon. This simple moving of the finger enabled the person using the weapon to gain more control over the point of the weapon and thus be able to use cutting and thrusting actions with equal ease. This is actually dated quite early in the fourteenth century about 1340 (Coe et.al., 1996:41). This eventually took the form of a simple ring added to one of the quillons.

This simple development allowed the wielder of the weapon to place their finger over the quillon of the weapon. Previously this would be a dangerous prospect as then the finger would be at risk of harm from a blow from the opponent. With the addition of the finger ring this threat was substantially reduced. To further protect the hand from damage, the knuckle guard was developed.

"The next step towards a more developed hilt was the knuckle guard. In its earliest stages, this was formed simply by bending the forward quillon towards and sometimes parallel to the grip. This feature appears on falchions and other cutting swords of the late fourteenth and early fifteenth centuries." (Coe et.al., 1996:46)

The knuckle guard increased the overall protection of the hand. In combination with the finger ring, this development increased the protection of the hand in the use of the weapon, in the manner previously described, immensely. As stated, at this stage the knuckle guard was simply the forward quillon bent forward and downward to form protection for the hand.

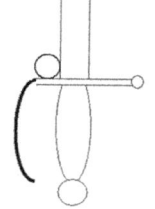

The idea of the protection of the hand by an addition of the knuckle guard was well entrenched. However, at this point in time it meant the sacrifice of the forward quillon, which was reckoned to be suitable still for the protection of the hand. So the next stage of development for the hilt was to have both the knuckle guard present, but also to have the forward quillon still present on the weapon.

"Then the knuckleguard, from being a simple bent quillon, became another branch in addition to the forward quillon and formed an arc from the quillon block to the pommel." (Coe et.al., 1996:46)

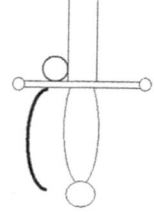

This would all seem to be a direct sort of development of the hilt toward the rapier as it is found in the sixteenth-century. What is most interesting is that this is not necessarily true. While the knuckle guard and finger ring combination was present on weapons early on in the development, it would actually be some time before the knuckle guard was actually adopted. "The earliest examples of the knuckle-guard seem to occur in

EQUIPMENT & CURATORIAL DISCUSSIONS

the last quarter of the 15th century, but it did not appear to be common on rapiers before 1530." (Valentine, 1968:11). Valentine states 1530, but there is other evidence that they were present earlier, but not very much so. This is a most interesting point to be made and deserves special note. Some has been said about quillons, the cross guard as it is sometimes called. This particular development deserves some addressing.

"From the middle of the [15th] century onwards, hilt developments became more and more rapid. Quillons arched more strongly towards the blade and scrolled ends became more common. Straight quillons did not go out of fashion, but towards the end of the century they begin to recurve horizontally. The quillon block with a strong central point extended towards the blade had been quite common since the early part of the century." (Coe et.al., 1996:46)

The question of straight quillons or curved ones is a question which users of the sword have thought about for some time. This particular change to curved quillons and back again to straight ones is notable as the same question would come up again, and still does, as to whether straight or curved quillons are the best to have. Curved quillons are assumed to be able to trap the opponent's weapon better, while the straight one are useful in other ways, especially for protection. This particular question is one that will re-emerge later on. For the rapier, while the knuckle guard would come later, it would be a second ring added that would be the next development.

"The first guard of the rapier hilt was designed to protect the fore-finger, which was placed over the fore-quillon on to the blade. This guard, or ring, first appeared on swords in about 1400, and by about 1450 a corresponding branch for the other quillon appeared, to protect the thumb. ... the two guards then forming what is known as the "arms of the hilt"."

(Valentine, 1968:10)

The "arms of the hilt" was a development to protect the thumb of the user of the weapon. So, for the rapier, rather than the addition of the knuckle guard after the finger ring, it would be the addition of a second ring. While the figure presented represents the two rings as complete this was not necessarily true in all cases. Some were opened toward the blade of the weapon. In this way they were semi-circular in shape. Of course, it would not take long before the knuckle guard was added to the hilt to complete the protection of the hand.

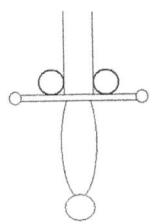

"By about 1450 knuckleguard and forefinger ring were combined on the same hilt, and a second finger ring was added, mirroring the first. These two loops or rings symmetrically flanking the shoulders of the blade are referred to by modern writers as 'the arms of the hilt'. (Coe et.al., 1996:46)

What can be seen here is the development toward the more complete and more common rapier hilt that is known so well. The classic shape of the rapier is beginning to take form with the addition of these developments. It should be noted that these developments result in a profile vertically, when looking from either the pommel or point of a weapon, which is essentially flat in profile. Two of the following developments change this profile quite significantly.

> "By 1475, if not earlier, the knuckleguard was combined with the arms of the hilt, and shortly thereafter the ends of the arms of the hilt were fitted with transverse lugs or a short curved bar which passed horizontally from the end of one arm to the end of the other; this is known as a side ring."
> (Coe et.al., 1996:46)

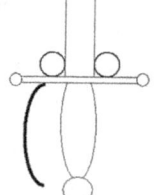

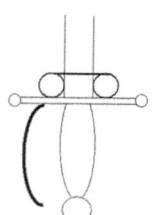

To begin with, this side ring was only added to the outside of the hilt, for the right-hander that is the right side. This was designed to prevent an opponent's blade sliding down the blade across the hilt and into the top of the hand. This simple addition increased the protective capacity of the weapon quite a bit and began to change its profile.

At this point in time, two-dimensional diagrams such as those which have been presented begin to lose their utility. For the further developments of the hilt, it is better that examples of actual weapons are examined. There are many fine examples of these weapons with the hilts described in many sources, and many can be found on the Internet. Returning to the development, the next obvious development of the hilt would be to add an additional side ring mounted on the quillons. This further enhanced the defensive capabilities of the hilt.

> "A further development during the last half of the 15th century was the forward extension of the tips of the arms of the hilt into lugs, or their linking together by what is known as a side-ring. During the early part of the 16th century, hilts were further equipped with an additional side-ring stemming from the centre of the quillons and usually larger than the lower ring."
> (Valentine, 1968:10)

Aside from the knuckle guard most of the developments thus far described have been either in line with the quillons or above them. These developments started the process, but the true incorporation of the hilt also required development of the hilt below the quillons. While the side rings were a simple answer, the counter-guards are something which was much more complex.

> "A guard for the thumb was incorporated at the rear of the quillons in the shape of a diagonal bar connecting the base of one quillon to the lower tip of the opposite arm. A further development of this guard, having two, and later three branches, can often be found on rapiers of the middle of the 16th century ... Some rapiers of the middle to the end of the 16th century simply had a rearguard formed by a semicircular bar, commencing at one side of the lower tip of the arm and finishing in the corresponding position of the other arm."
> (Valentine, 1968:10)

The description from Valentine (1968) above shows how the guards developed. One element was added on to another and then another. While some of the elements may

EQUIPMENT & CURATORIAL DISCUSSIONS

have changed shape or been moved around, the basic elements are still present. Even in the most complex hilts, the basic elements of the arms of the hilt and knuckle guard are still, for the most part, present. These complex additions to the hilt of the rapier resulted in the classic form most recognised as a rapier. Of course, such developments happened on both sides of the hilt. This ensured that the hand was protected to a degree on both sides.

> "Late in the century the hilt sprouted yet another guard in the form of a side ring, post or short block, protruding horizontally from the outer face of the quillon block; this was designed to protect the back of the hand. ... to all intents and purposes, the rapier hilt was born."
> *(Coe et.al., 1996:46)*

A pommel is present on all forms of swords. This is the counter-weight to the weight of the blade, and also holds the sword together. It is a simple element, but one which is of great importance for the weapon to operate properly. As with the other parts of the hilt, "A great variety of pommels were used in the sixteenth century." (Coe et.al., 1996:48). It is not necessary to go through the development of these various types to understand its purpose. The important fact here is that the pommel was an essential part of the weapon and their designs were not quite as varied as the hilt, and often locally fitted and chosen.

> "Ovoid pommels were now more or less universal, except in a few isolated groups of swords, such as those used in Dalmatia, where a square pommel was popular, and in Saxony where conical or pear-shaped pommels were fashionable." *(Norman, 1964:100)*

THE FULLY DEVELOPED HILT

> "The design book of Filippo Orso, in the Victoria and Albert Museum, which is dated 1554, shows the complicated hilts of the period as well as simpler ones which were still the most popular for the full armoured man. These sketches indicate that all the guards found on hilts of the later sixteenth century were already in use. Additional rings sprang from the top of the arms of the hilt outside the hand, a Y-shaped guard linked the knuckle-guard to the same point inside, while the knuckle-guard itself often branched to join the larger of the rings outside the hand."
> *(Norman, 1964:99)*

Some explanation is required of what is meant by inner guards. Most of the focus of the development of the hilt focuses on the outer hilt. The inner hilt is toward the left side of the right hander. Through this development the classical hilt of the rapier can now be seen. This form of hilt became and remained popular from the middle of the sixteenth-century. Examples of such hilts can be seen in the portraits of nobles of the period.

> "the portrait of the future Emperor Maximilian II by Antonio Mor at the Prado, dated 1550, shows a sword with thin, elegant guards and long, straight quillons. The sword of the Archduke Ferdinand of Tyrol is a fine example of the fully developed sword of the mid-sixteenth century"
> (Norman, 1964:100)

Of course with the wide array of different styles of hilt there are examples of particular fashions which were popular with particular countries. These hilts assist in the location of the hilts as to where they were developed and most used. The hilts found in Saxony, for example had particular characteristics, which were common for all the hilts in this particular area.

> "Particularly in Saxony there was a tendency for the sword to have a rather short hilt with long spatulate quillons, a few small ring-guards and no knuckle-bow." (Norman, 1964:101)

It is in this period of the greatest interest in the hilt of the rapier that can be found the classic idea of the 'swept hilt'. This is the most recognised form of the hilt and as such deserves some discussion. What should be noted with regard to this is that the form of the hilt which was to become the 'swept hilt' was actually a development of an earlier form of hilt, as all hilts of the period were.

> "By the second quarter of the sixteenth century the side ring, found on the arms of the hilt from the 1480s, was sometimes found in conjunction with a second side ring mounted on the quillon block. At about the same time the outer face of the hilt sprouted a system of supplementary transverse bars or branches which passed from the root of the quillons to the knuckle guard and, in the opposite direction, to the arms of the hilt. The diagonal sweep of these transverse guards gives rise to the modern term 'swept hilt' rapier. The inner face of the hilt followed suit, and by about 1575 the triple branch inner guard typical of most late rapiers was in place." (Coe et.al., 1996:48)

What can be seen in the swept hilt is the combination of all of the elements of the hilt which have been described through the discussion of the development of the hilt. The arms of the hilt, inner guard, side rings, ricasso and knuckle guard are all present in the form of the swept hilt (Harding, 1990:50). Of course one of the key elements that define the swept hilt as different from other hilts is that the quillons were more often than not bent into an S-shape. This particular shape of the hilt gave it its elegant form which came to be seen as the most elegant form of the hilt in the period. It is in the swept hilt where the discussion of the curved or straight quillon was definitively biased toward the curved.

> "The typical sixteenth-century rapier is sometimes referred to as 'swept hilted' on account of the bold S-shaped sweep of the quillons round the knuckles to the pommel, and at the other end curved forward over the blade." (Akehurst, 1969:7)

EQUIPMENT & CURATORIAL DISCUSSIONS

The final development of the hilt of the rapier that will be discussed, which will lead on to those hilts which extend beyond the sixteenth-century, is the addition of plates to parts of the hilt to provide extra protection. This particular addition became common on these hilts and some military ones from the middle of the sixteenth-century and onwards. The hilts of this form exhibit all of the elements of the fully developed rapier hilt, but also have the addition of plates within the hilt to provide extra protection for the hand.

"By the middle of the [16th] century, long, slender, straight quillons, frequently with recurved finials, became fashionable, but not to the exclusion of other types. By this time the arms of the hilt sometimes supported double side rings, one above the other, the uppermost being inclined toward the grip and sometimes joined to the knuckleguard by a transverse branch. Also it not unusual for one or both of these side rings to be filled by a pierced plate. By the end of the century a pierced plate was also occasionally found between two branches of the transverse inner guard. A solid plate, engraved rather than pierced, was also used in the side rings, especially on silver-hilted Saxon swords." (Coe et.al., 1996:48)

It was the addition of plates to the hilt of the rapier at this time that would eventually result in the development of the cup hilt in which the entire combination of bars was replaced by a single solid plate to protect the hand. This form of hilt is most commonly seen in Spanish examples of the rapier where due to the position of the hand in combat, the addition of this form of hilt was designed to protect the hand from attack. Both the cup hilt and what was to be called the 'Pappenheimer' hilt, with plates on both sides of the hilt, are beyond the purview of this discussion, but needless to say the developments laid in the sixteenth-century eventually saw their development. "The late sixteenth century saw the development of more complicated guards, particularly by the addition of pierced shells on each side of the quillons." (Norman, 1964:101). Before the hilt is completely left as a subject, it is useful to examine some of the decoration of the hilts.

HILT DECORATION

"Great care and ingenuity went into the decoration of these weapons, especially as they were regarded almost as items of costume jewellery. Hilts were chiselled and pierced, damascened in gold, made from precious metal and set with stones, and they were always expensive items."
(Bull, 1990:12)

Rapiers are an elegant weapon in general. The decoration of such a weapon was a consideration that was made by the users of this period in order to further enhance the elegance of the weapon. There were many ways that the hilts were decorated. Before any discussion of the actual decoration of the hilt is made, it is important to look at the reason for this.

> *"The decoration of edged weapons was always an important consideration and a symbol of the status of those who could afford fine arms. ... These swords and others bore witness not only to the high rank but also to the connoisseurship of their owners."*
> (Coe et.al., 1996:57)

As much as the choice of car is for some people, or the choice of jewellery for some ladies, so too the choice of the weapon and its decoration in the Renaissance period was also a serious consideration, and it was class based. Any man could have a weapon made, but only the richest could afford the decoration of the weapon along with it. The weapon and its decoration set the owner of the weapon above others who had less.

The Renaissance, especially the sixteenth-century being such a period of religious consideration and some contention, it would be of little surprise that in some cases this affected the decoration of the weapon. "The names of saints are sometimes carved in the runnels of European rapiers;" (Coe et.al., 1996:7). The blades were engraved as well as the hilts in some instances. Mottos and other such writings were also present on the blades.

> *"With the local manufacture of hilts all over Europe there are innumerable styles, often highly and richly decorated. Fine examples made for European nobility are preserved in many museums,"* (Valentine, 1968:9)

It already has been noted that there were many different designs for the rapier hilt. Often the particular design chosen by an individual would be affected by what was common in his particular area. This was an element of fitting in. The weapons of the nobility present in museums give some idea of the importance of decoration of the rapier for these individuals and some are the most elegant forms of the swordsmith's craft.

> *"Until the sixteenth century the decoration of the hilt usually consisted of plating and engraving, but in the sixteenth and seventeenth centuries the steel of the hilt was often chiselled in high relief with decoration which included all the motifs of contemporary taste. The Orso designs show hilts in the Mannerist taste which he states can be carried out in steel or silver, and many of the engravers who produced books of design at this time included a few for swords. The designs of Pierre Woeiriot of Lyon, c. 1550-60, show hilts almost entirely constructed of nudes, strapwork and grotesques, and the engravings of Virgil Solis also include a few of hilts and mounts decorated with his thin, interlacing strapwork and Mauresques."* (Norman, 1964:101)

Considering the tools available to the artisans at the time, some of the work presented on rapier hilts is magnificent. In fact the work is magnificent regardless of any consideration. These designs were all done by hand without the assistance of mechanical technology found in the modern era. The choice of the decoration of the hilt was influenced by the individual purchasing the weapon, but was often left to the artisan to make decisions about what was suitable. Just as the construction of the hilts was very much a local consideration so too was the decoration of the weapon and differences in decoration can be found amongst the various countries which produced them.

> "The only group systematically studied so far, is the Bavarian court school of which a number of steel chisellers are known by name and their work identified. The earliest of this group was Othmar Wetter who worked at Munich from 1583-89, and then moved to Dresden where he introduced his new style, displacing the rather fussy, over-decorated work of the Torgau smiths. The hilt signed by Wetter and dated 1594, now at Copenhagen, illustrates his style with its characteristic, deeply under-cut figures in niches" (Norman, 1964:102)

Identification of the artist who produced the hilt is often a task which is much more difficult than that of the blade of the weapon. Rarely did the artist leave their mark on the weapon so it could be identified as such. This was most commonly left to word of mouth. The fact that it is possible to follow the development of this particular school of artisans in their production of rapier hilts and their decoration is significant as it makes it substantially easier to date the weapons. This is of great significance to the historical community. Of course, for some nobles such decorations were not enough, and more was required.

> "While chiselled steel hilts of varying quality are not uncommon, only a few of the gold and enamelled hilts worn by the very great have survived. It is clear from the study of portraits that they were never common."
> (Norman, 1964:103)

The use of gold on a hilt is obviously designed to show the wealth of the individual who owns such a weapon. These were more often than not pieces for show as gold is a very soft metal and not very practical for a weapon. For martial purposes a much simpler weapon would have been chosen. Of course a mean in between these two was possible. English hilts in particular demonstrate the combination of gold work along with an element of practicality in their designs.

> "English hilts of the late sixteenth century and early seventeenth century are often decorated with rather characteristic, silver encrusting and very fine, gold damascening"
> (Norman, 1964:103)

The use of precious metal and stones on hilts is most common in those pieces which were designed as gifts for a particular noble. These were most often designed to demonstrate the craft of the artisan in order to possibly gain the patronage of the noble. Of course requests for such fine weapons were also not uncommon. While the rapier is the focus of this investigation, a brief examination of the dagger will demonstrate that such decoration also extended to this companion of the rapier.

> "common way of fencing in the 16th and early 17th centuries was with a rapier in the right hand and a main gauche dagger in the left for parrying an opponent's thrusts. Such daggers were often made in a matching set with the rapier." (Harding, 1990:50)

Matching weapons were designed to demonstrate that the weapons were deliberately designed to match. It would also be a rather strange thing to have an elegantly designed rapier and a dagger which was very much undecorated, as such rapier and dagger designed en suite was not uncommon in the period. While most of the curatorial discussion of the rapier has been focussed on the hilt, the discussion of the blade is most essential in order to understand the weapon and its construction.

OF THE BLADE

The result of the often intense discussion of the hilt, to the detriment of that of the blade, is a lack of information about the development of the blade of the weapon. This is not only restricted to the rapier, but other weapons as well. Often assumptions about the weapon are made and this results in some faulty conclusions.

Faulty conclusions are often the result of a lack of knowledge about the martial arts in which the weapons were involved. "The blade of wonderfully tempered steel, was lighter, more narrow and designed to be used entirely with the point." (Akehurst, 1969:7). Akehurst claims that the rapier's long thin blade was designed entirely for thrusting. This is not actually the case as these weapons actually did have some cutting ability. Of course such broad statements are not only the conclusions that are made about the weapon.

> "Swords of the period, fitted with long, thin blades principally designed for thrusting, were known as rapiers. Their popularity seems due to the dominance of Spanish fashions." (Norman, 1964:100)

Norman makes a similarly broad statement as Akehurst above. He does however, qualify the statement stating that they were used principally for thrusting, allowing some use of the cut into the definition of the weapon, of course that he claims that all swords of the period with such blades, is somewhat inaccurate as the discussion previously proves. The element of fashion is interesting as it would seem that he would be going from a more English point of view where Spanish fashions did dominate during the early sixteenth-century at least. Such information would lead the reader to believe some inaccurate things about the rapier and lead to some bad conclusions.

Where such investigations from a curatorial point of view as presented previously are useful in the investigation of the blade can be found in other aspects where the writer is open to other ideas. Useful information can be found about the makers of the blades of the weapons however. This is useful to a point.

> "The great majority of sword blades were made in a few areas, some of the more famed being Toledo and Valencia in Spain, Milan and Brescia in Italy and Solingen and Passau in Germany. The blades were exported throughout Europe, where they were then locally equipped with hilts." (Valentine, 1968:7)

EQUIPMENT & CURATORIAL DISCUSSIONS

This allows for the origin of the blade to be determined in those cases where the maker's mark is still present on the weapon. Of course the fact that the hilts were locally manufactured and fitted does not allow for the complete documentation of the weapon as the blade may have been exported. Thus to attempt to place the weapon by the blade alone would be inaccurate. Both parts of the weapon must be taken into account making many rapiers a perfect example of international weapons having blades from one country and hilts from another.

To attempt to classify a weapon by the hilt alone would also be a problem. It is simply the case that just because the hilt is of the rapier design, does not necessarily mean that the weapon is either a rapier or necessarily a civilian weapon. This is simply because such hilts could be put on military weapons. This is especially the case for earlier forms of the weapon.

> "However, at the end of the fifteenth century the developed hilt just described [arms, knuckle, side-ring] was usually mounted on a sturdy cut-and-thrust blade. This is at odds with the modern notion of the rapier as a slender thrusting instrument. Such rapiers did indeed develop in the course of the sixteenth century as the wearing of swords with civilian dress became fashionable,"
> (Coe et.al., 1996:46)

The addition of such developed hilts to arming sword blades resulted in the modern period of the term "sword rapier" which is a curatorial term denoting a sword with a rapier hilt and a cutting blade. This particular term gained some popularity in describing those weapons which did not fit into either the niche of the rapier or the military sword. Of course the concept itself is inaccurate. Weapons should be defined by their use rather than any form of the weapon.

As the rapier became more and more popular, there was a break between those weapons for civilian use and those for military use, "the sixteenth century marked a parting of the ways between those swords and rapiers suitable for use on the battlefield and those intended for civilian wear." (Coe et.al., 1996:48). This is significant as it is often assumed that the sword disappeared from the battlefield with the advent of firearms and the development of the rapier, and this is simply not the case. Interestingly the popularity of the rapier actually had a reverse effect on the hilting of the military weapon.

> "as the rapier became more fashionable, from about the second quarter of the [16th] century, so the practice of fitting military swords with rapier-type hilts became more common."
> (Coe et.al., 1996:48)

So, just as earlier forms of the hilt would be placed on more military weapons so too would they return to such military weapons as the popularity of the style of the rapier increased. This is of great significance and explains why rapier hilts can be found on military weapons in the sixteenth-century and later on. This also highlights the importance in classification of the weapon the importance of examining what the weapon was used for rather than any form of the hilt.

afencersramblings.blogspot.com

> "Related to the guard with forefinger ring is the earlier innovation of an unsharpened area at the shoulder of the blade, against which the finger could rest. A rudimentary form of ricasso, as this unsharpened area is called, was in evidence by the mid-twelfth century. Some later blades have a cresentic cut-out in the shoulder of the blade to accommodate the forefinger."
> (Coe et.al., 1996:45)

The ricasso allowed the finger of the user of the weapon to be wrapped around the blade and thus gain more control over the point. This development, as noted earlier in the development of the hilt, happened substantially earlier in the development of the hilt than has often been acknowledged. This particular idea gained in popularity as the years progressed to become an integral part of straight-bladed swords.

> "As for the ricasso, seen with increasing frequency from the mid-fourteenth century onwards, this gradually became thicker and square in cross-section, and remained so for so long as straight sword blades continued to be used."
> (Coe et.al., 1996:47)

What must be recognised in the development of the blade of the rapier is that while its length increased and decreased, and its width decreased, the overall development of the blade was not as varied as that of the hilt. In most cases the shape of the blade of the rapier remained the same. It was long and slender in most cases with a sharply tapering point designed for thrusting and an edge on both sides of the blade which could be used for cutting though cutting was not the blade's primary purpose.

> "The blade of the rapier did not vary to the same degree as its hilt. The distinctive feature of the blade is the ricasso or squared-off section immediately below the grip – which was, of course, encircled by the thumb and finger(s) of the swordsman" (Valentine, 1968:11)

Of course in any such development of a weapon there are some peculiarities which deserve special note, "in the seventeenth century, led to the invention of special rapiers which extended their blades by a foot when a lever was pressed." (Bull, 1990:13). Such developments as this were more peculiarities rather than the rule of the rapier. Other examples of such ideas are present such as a blade which comes out through the pommel for when the wielder was too close to use the other end of the blade. These developments demonstrate a deviation in the development of the weapon and the blade and should be treated as the curiosities that they are.

MODERN RECREATIONS

Every time a movie with swords in it comes out, that particular style of weapon seems to increase in popularity. The movies have a lot to do with the increased popularity in weapons. From this particular situation, companies decide that they will make replicas of these particular weapons. This is often the same for copies of famous swords in history.

What happens in these situations is that the market is flooded, and continues to be,

EQUIPMENT & CURATORIAL DISCUSSIONS

with wall-hangers and replicas. The only possible use for these weapons is as decoration. These weapons are in no way practical. This is due to problems with the particular weapons. This particular situation goes as much for the rapier as other styles of sword.

One of the reasons for the problems that occur with the reproduction of swords is that for the most part they are no longer a practical answer to personal defence. The sword is absent from the battlefield, and people do not rely on these weapons for their personal defence. What this results in is no that the sword-makers are not making weapons for practical purposes.

The weapons are often mass produced in a factory rather than made by an individual. These are often interpretations of the weapons often taken from sources which may or may not be historically accurate. It is from this that often the weapons are not made as they would be or the practical application of the weapon considered.

Because there is no feedback for the most part from those who would use the weapons as there would be in the Renaissance period, the weapons are continually constructed with no consideration for their practical use. The weapons are often much too heavy and their balance is usually not what it should be on the weapon. This results in a sword which has not much more use than for hanging on the wall. In the case of a practical weapon the consideration of weight and balance is important.

> "A rapier is considered to be of perfect balance if the point of the balance occurs 3" from the lowest extremity of the guard; that is, 3" on the offensive parts of the blade not including ricasso."
>
> *(Valentine, 1968:10)*

For the most part in the mass recreations of rapiers, the balance is often somewhere too high up on the sword blade, making it very much point-heavy. In some instances so much so that the sword has no practical use whatsoever. The real weapons were heavier than some would like us to believe. These were purpose-made weapons designed for practical purposes. It is from this sort of information that sword-makers should get their information, and in many instances do not.

What can be said is that due to the increase in interest in Renaissance martial arts in general, and indeed in the use of the rapier, certain companies have begun to examine actual period weapons and to build their weapons based on these actual weapons. The consideration of the use of the weapon is now considered as these modern recreationalists have begun to expect that their weapons are now practical and useable in a simulated combat situation. The result of this has been more purpose-made weapons designed for this form of recreation.

While there are many bad examples of weapons with no thought to their practical use on the market, there has also been an increase in good practical weapons for the use of the Renaissance martial artist. The important thing about this situation is that the person buying the weapon needs some idea about the weapon before buying it to see whether or not the weapon will be of practical use or will just be a piece for decoration. While it is difficult to have an idea about the weapon just from pictures, some things can be noted in this, especially with the virtue of even a brief study in the weapons of the period.

Businesses such as Darkwood Armory and Castille Armory make weapons specifically for the use of the Renaissance martial artist. In these weapons consideration has been made to the practical application of these weapons in the hands of the martial artist. There are also other businesses who are building replicas of actual rapiers based on the data gained from the actual weapon examples of these businesses are Arms and Armour, and Museum Replicas, who make high quality replicas of actual weapons found in the Renaissance period. In all cases, the amount which is paid for the weapon does reflect the level of quality of the weapon purchased. The result of this interest is that quality practical and replica weapons are available for the collector and the martial artist.

For the connoisseur and collector of the rapier, the practical use of the rapier is not a particular consideration, but even in this situation the expectation for a quality reproduction of the original weapon is expected. In the case of the Renaissance martial artist there is now a certain level of quality expected from these weapons. While there is still some discrepancy in the quality of weapons that are made, even by some of the more reputable manufacturers, for the most part there has been an increase in quality and practicality of these weapons. This is due to a sincere interest by these businesses in the reproduction of these weapons, and investigations made by them into the curatorial aspects of the weapons.

CONCLUSION

When the rapier is considered, especially from a curatorial point of view, it is important that all of the aspects of the weapon itself are taken into consideration. This is the only way that it is possible to find out the history and development of this particularly influential weapon. The rapier's influence was found in the civilian market more than in the military, but as has been demonstrated the hilts at least in a form became popular on military weapons as well.

The question of what a rapier is will continue to plague curators, historians, recreationalists and modern Renaissance martial artists alike. The definition of this particular weapon may never be completely established for everyone's benefit. In this particular situation it could be said that finding out what type of rapier is being use would actually be more significant. Whether the weapon is from an earlier or later part of the Renaissance period will affect the use of the weapon. Thus for this particular aspect of the discussion a definition was extracted from the information presented in order to gain a definition which would be suitable to the discussion.

The hilt of the rapier has been the subject of much discussion and is often the focus of curatorial discussions of the rapier. The result of this is that there is a lot of information available about this particular subject. What needs to be recognised in this discussion is that the start of the development of the hilt actually occurred much earlier than some would recognise, and that this development occurred on military weapons.

The development of the hilt of the rapier was made in response to practical reasons. The hilt eventually took the form that it did to present a form of protection for the hand of the swordsman, and not for some aesthetic reason. Each addition made to the hilt of the rapier was made in response to some threat, and to prevent damage from occurring. This particular aspect needs to be considered in any consideration of the construction of one of these hilts. What is considered the fully developed hilt of the later sixteenth-century was a result of practical reasons.

The decoration of the weapon had an aesthetic reason, but also had a social reason. The decoration of the weapon and its form was designed to represent a level of status and wealth in the owner of the weapon. There are many fine examples of hilt decoration found in museums. These were the weapons of the nobles and were often not particularly practical. The rapier for practical use would have a much simpler hilt of more practical use.

The rapier is essentially two parts, the hilt and the blade. Without any sort of discussion of the blade, the weapon is really only half considered. These two parts work together in order to form the complete weapon. The length and width of the blade was actually in some part, determined by the hilt. The relative weight of the hilt to the blade would affect the balance and thus the handling of the weapon. While there seems to be much less information on the blade of the rapier, only through a study of both parts of the weapon is it possible to completely understand it.

There have been many attempts to recreate and present weapons found in the medieval and Renaissance period, some of these are good and others are not. Some of the weapons found for sale are not practical at all and their only use is for hanging on the wall and for decoration, they do not represent the weapon in a practical form. What is also significant to note is that there are businesses and individuals who are interested in producing accurate reproductions and practical weapons. It is these weapons that are the most use to the martial artist and collector. Much of this has been the result of the interest in period forms of martial arts from Europe, and the increase in request for practical weapons.

The rapier is a very contentious weapon which has suffered much abuse at the hands of curators and collectors, the interpretations of the weapon through the eyes of the fencing historian has also not been helpful. The result of this is that the weapon is much understood and there is a great deal of urban myth and plain fallacy present in many discussions of this weapon. Only through rigorous research and examination of actual weapons is it possible to understand this weapon completely and appreciate it for what it was and what it is.

The Broadsword: A Curatorial Discussion

The subject of the broadsword is one which has been of interest to me for a while now, and was prodded along more recently by studying the smallsword, and also the workshops at Swordplay 2016 given by Keith Farrell. There are various arguments that you will find going through this post, some of which will be of interest and some, I hope, will clear some of the myths away. Thanks go to Keith Farrell for his editorial assistance with this piece and correcting me on a few things.

INTRODUCTION

What follows is an examination of the broadsword. It is indicated by the title that this will be a curatorial examination, but this will be a little broader than most curatorial examinations as they are most often concerned with hilt construction. This has often led to this misclassification of weapons. Thus this investigation will concern itself with the entire weapon, but also more than that.

To begin with there is the question of what is and is not a broadsword, to this point a definition will be examined and argued for and against, then another proposed. Following this will be a brief history of the development of the broadsword. The word "development" is used here and not "evolution" as it was a process which was affected by external and internal factors, and also had an effect upon other weapons of similar make. Next will be a discussion of the broadsword and the backsword, two weapons which are often confused, usually as a result of one or both not having a clear definition. Getting even more specific there is the question of the claymore and what is and is not one, a question which has been argued to and fro for many years.

After all these preliminary arguments have been established and some of the background has also been established. Then the weapon will be examined. The previous is necessary so that both writer and reader understand what is being discussed. The broadsword will be discussed in order of hilt, blade and then the weapon in general. This will give the differences in different nationalities of broadsword, specifically, English, German and Scottish and the differences between them.

There will be mentions of other weapons of similar classification. The backsword has already been mentioned above, and will feature in different placed in the investigation. The sabre will also be mentioned in the discussions, but more in passing rather than in any sort of detail. Finally, with regard to use considerations, this can only come from the knowledge of the weapon as a whole. This discussion will only barely scratch the surface of that and give some very vague indications. The focus of this investigation is more about the form, origins and development of the weapon.

DEFINITION

"a broad-bladed sword used for cutting rather than stabbing. Also called backsword" (Collins English Dictionary, 2016)

The definition supplied by the Collins English Dictionary (2016) is rather broad and covers quite a few weapons. It could even cover some forms of medieval sword as well, especially as the definition above does not in any way take into account the form of the hilt. What this means is that the definition needs some refining. The broadsword is most easily defined as a straight-bladed, double-edged, relatively broad-bladed sword with a basket-hilt that protects the hand. What needs to be noted here is that the previous definition did not take into account the hilt of the weapon which is a mistake often made in the curatorship of swords in that often all the weapon is not taken into account.

The change in hilt is significant where the cross-guard was changed to a basket-hilt and is similar to that which is found with regard to the development of the rapier, and for similar reasons. The civilian rapier's hilt developed to protect the unarmoured hand of the civilian. The more military broadsword hilt developed as armour declined as a result of the introduction of effective firearms to the battlefield.

THE BROADSWORD STORY

"they [basket-hilted broadswords] are most closely associated with the 18th-century Scottish Highlander." (Holmes, 2010:106)

When the broadsword is thought of, it is the Scottish Highlander which is first thought of wielding the weapon. The history of the weapon will reveal that they were not the only people to use the weapon, and indeed it could be claimed that they were not even the first. The discussion which follows will follow the development of the broadsword, for the most part, in chronological order. It will start with a more general introduction to the history and then examine the three important centuries of development, the sixteenth, seventeenth and eighteenth centuries. While this is not really designed to be a curatorial discussion, there will be curatorial elements present.

To begin there must be a brief examination of the weapon which came before, and to understand that this was primarily a military weapon, rather than a civilian one, even though it found its way into civilian hands. Its history starts with the knightly sword of war, as armour was lessened the hilt had to develop to protect the hand. These developments are primarily noted in England, the result being that the English hilt is the common ancestor of the basket-hilted claymore and English military pattern (Oakeshott, 2012:176). More of this much-argued weapon will be discussed later on.

There is a lot of argument about the dating of weapons and where they came from. This is for a multitude of reasons firstly weapons are difficult to date due to similarity in design and references found for the pieces themselves (Oakeshott, 2012:177). To accurately date something a design needs to be in print in some form to compare to and when the designs are common across an expanse of time this makes the dating even more difficult. This situation can be complicated even further in the case of many swords not just the broadsword with regard to the idea of re-hilting. In the case of the broadsword re-hilting was common, an old blade would be placed in a new hilt, or rarer old hilt and new blade would be put together (Oakeshott, 2012:179). Needless to say, this results in a weapon, if it manages to date both parts with a date for one part and a date for the other.

Sixteenth Century

Previously it was noted that the broadsword was primarily a military weapon. It was also noted that it was a modification of the knightly war sword, answering the need to protect the hand. After 1520 the knightly war sword acquires a more complex hilt, changes at end of the sixteenth century to the proto-typical forms of broadsword of 17th and 18th centuries (Oakeshott, 2012:126). These developments were in answer to a changing situation on the battlefield where armour was being reduced in answer to its lack of effect against firearms. The speed of which the development came is impressive.

> "One of the earliest basket-hilted swords was recovered from the wreck of the Mary Rose, an English warship lost in 1545. Before the find, the earliest positive dating had been two swords from around the time of the English Civil War. At first the wire guard was a simple design but as time passed it became increasingly sculpted and ornate."
> (Wikipedia, 2016)

In a relatively short amount of time, the hilt of the weapon became more and more complex resulting, by middle of century hand protected and surrounded by plates, bars lined with leather or fabric (Coe, 1996:73). This is not a simple operation as can be told by anyone who has assembled a sword of such complex parts. What needs to be noted here is that the earliest hilt here is not Scottish, but English.

Rather than being nationalistic about where it was invented at this point in time, the important thing to note here is that, the ancestry of broadsword hilts found in those that evolved by 1570s and survived (Oakeshott, 2012:156). It was this pattern of basket-hilt which was spread around and resulted in developments in other places. It should be noted that the beginnings of broadswords of 18th and 19th centuries in German experiments of c.1600 can be seen (Oakeshott, 2012:156).

What is most interesting is that the weapons which were developed by the English would have to wait until toward the end of the century to cross over the borders of the closest neighbours, and thus would gain a new name, and not the one expected. As in the last years of the sixteenth century basket hilts associated with Highland Scots, known as 'Irish hilts' in early seventeenth (Oakeshott, 2012:176). More to the point many of these would be sourced from Continental swordsmiths.

Seventeenth Century

In a typical Victorian fashion many have attempted to classify the broadsword hilts of the seventeenth century to try and see if there are any patterns of development, but not with much success, "Any attempt to specify prototypical patterns for the broadsword hilts of the seventeenth century would be doomed to failure," (Oakeshott, 2012:173). This is for two clear reasons the first of which is that the broadsword hilt spread to different nations and was thus changed and developed as according to their own requirements. The second is that, "Basket hilts underwent various changes during the course of the [17th] century." (Coe, 1996:74), and when these two are combined, there are too many variables to be tracked.

What is known is that, "Basket hilts continued to be used during the seventeenth century, especially in England and Scotland" (Coe, 1996:74), which is of little surprise due to the origins of the hilt itself in the sixteenth century as indicated above. More to the point it is also here where most of the fame for the broadsword is found. While the Scottish hilt seems to dominate in popularity and in form and construction, English hilts of same period are often of fine construction (Coe, 1996:74). The other thing that should be noted with regard to this is that with regard to the origins of this weapon, it has a distinctively English heritage.

> "Scottish it was, even in the seventeenth century, and exclusively Scottish it became, but England has good a claim to it, for it originated in that country. However, since it is always called the 'Scottish' sword ... it is necessary to observe the distinctions." *(Oakeshott, 2012:170)*

One of the most useful things about the popularity of an item in the historical record is that sometimes it makes it easier to track through the historical record because it was more likely to be recorded, and also because it was more likely to be researched and thus the information brought to light. In the case of the Scottish broadsword both are the case.

> "The 1881 *Ancient Scottish Weapons* had this to say: The broadsword first appears in formal record in Scotland in 1643, when, along with the Lochaber axe and the Jedburgh staff, it constitutes part of the equipment of the levies then called out by the Convention of Estates, From 1582 to 1649 a "ribbit gaird" often appears as the "essay" of the armourers of Edinburgh, but in 1649 it was changed to "ane mounted sword, with a new scabbard and an Highland guard."" *(Scottish Tartans Authority, 2016)*

This clearly dates the first official record of the appearance of the "Highland guard", clearly what was to be known as the Scottish hilt later on, and fills in another piece of the puzzle of the history of the broadsword which otherwise would have remained unfound. The seventeenth century served as a kind of formative years for the Scottish hilt in which it developed and took its shape. Needless to say that there were many variations of hilt through the period, as a curatorial discussion will find, but eventually will settle on a single one.

> "The Scottish basket hilt, with its traditional heart-shaped piercings and large square plates, seems to have appeared in the second half of the century [17th] and remained in use for over a hundred years." (Coe, 1996:74)

Eighteenth Century

> "During the 18th century, the fashion of dueling in Europe focused on the lighter smallsword, and fencing with the broadsword came to be seen as a speciality of Scotland. A number of fencing manuals teaching fencing with the Scottish broadsword were published throughout the 18th century." (Wikipedia, 2016)

While the Wikipedia (2016) is not considered the most reliable source the information presented above is accurate. Most of the Continent was focused on the use of the smallsword and thus most of use of the broadsword was left to military matters. Being a more "native" weapon to the Scots, manuals for the use of the broadsword were also published alongside those for the smallsword.

In the case of the broadsword, the stage of full development had arrived, "The basket-hilted sword, in which the entire hand was protected by a leather-lined cage of bars was made in many variations throughout the eighteenth century." (Coe, 1996:85). The complete hand was protected and the weapon was established. In the end, the broadsword would serve more as a military sword rather than a civilian sword and, "The variety of basket hilts found on eighteenth-century military swords is enormous," (Coe, 1996:86). One thing that can be said is that the Scottish type was the more dominant form later due to its developmental stages.

> "As for the 'Scottish' sword, in its earliest forms it as uncompromisingly English, and remained a standard English pattern far into the eighteenth century; only very late in the century did it become exclusively Scottish."
> (Oakeshott, 2012:170)

The Scottish form of broadsword was to dominate in form and function and became the more dominant form of hilt for the military. Even in the backsword form, the "basket-hilted backsword of about 1766. Swords of this pattern were fashionable for officers in the last quarter of the eighteenth century." (Coe, 1996:86). The effect of the popularity of this form of hilt type can be seen in popular culture as for the most part when a basket-hilt is seen it is compared to the Scottish form. Instantly the broadsword is associated with the eighteenth-century Scottish Highlander, and also the Highland Regiments of the British Empire which followed.

BROADSWORD OR BACKSWORD?

To delve into the question of the broadsword is also to come up against all sorts of different questions and be confronted by different weapons which may claim to be the same thing when in fact they are not, and sometimes they are. One of the first stops along this path is the backsword. This is the first question that must be answered, what is the difference between the broadsword and the backsword, where is the line drawn between the two, or is there one to be drawn? The answer to this is actually relatively simple, but some other things have to be taken into account.

> *"The Basket hilted sword was also called the Scottish Broad Sword. There was also a version called the claidheamh cuil which means back sword. The back was blunt with just one sharp edge."* (Watterott, 2016)

What can be seen here is that the concept of the backsword is actually quite found quite far afield. In this case there is Scottish Gaelic for the term backsword meaning a weapon which has only one sharp edge, so in essence the idea stands on firm ground. When it comes to the broadsword it is the Scots who would seem to be the experts, as for questions about the "claymore", they will be answered later on. In our contemporary society ideas of curatorial differences in weapons based on form rather than function still hold true, "Where the blade has only one cutting edge it is known as a backsword." (Akehurst, 1969:8). This does not take into account the use of the weapon merely the form of the weapon.

One of the more interesting discoveries which came out of this research is that the weapons, both the broadsword and backsword were claimed as cavalry weapons (Wagner, 2004:20). This is most interesting as it is the Scots Highland Regiments which were primarily infantry units where the broadsword is most known from, not to mention all of the evidence from manuals which points to using the weapon on foot. Further in the same discussion he claims that the weapon, "had a straight blade, originally two-edged, later only one sharp edge. These weapons were uniform in character," (Wagner, 2004:20). What should be noted is that it is the two-edged broadsword, of the infantry version which will be the primary focus of this study and that in the sources which describe the use of the weapons both terms were used to describe the same weapon meaning the difference is more a question for curators, rather than those interested in its use.

WHAT IS A CLAYMORE?

When the word "claymore" is said two weapons are immediately thought of, a two-handed weapon of medieval origin and also the basket-hilted broadsword more associated with a later period. The question remains as to which is the "claymore". Of course it would be simple just to use a modern definition.

The Merriam-Webster dictionary defines a "claymore" as "a large 2-edged sword formerly used by Scottish Highlanders, *also* their basket-hilted broadsword" (Merriam-Webster, 2016). This is rather confusing as it actually indicates two weapons a large one and also the basket-hilted broadsword. What this means is that the common confusion as to what a claymore actually is continues. The aim of what follows is to bring some of this discussion out and find a solution to this question.

EQUIPMENT & CURATORIAL DISCUSSIONS

> *"Perhaps the most famous version of the broadsword is the Scottish claymore. Though claymores were originally two-handed swords usually with simple cruciform hilts, their most famous incarnations were fitted with basket hilts, these swords became iconic weapons of the Highland Regiments that fought for the British Empire."* (Soud, 2014:53)

Soud (2014) would indicate that both were named "claymore", both the two-handed version and also the basket-hilted version, and that the name was carried through from one weapon to another. Thus for this author it would seem that it is not a matter of naming convention which is the problem, merely that it is a problem with naming the correct era which is being spoken about. For him there would be a "medieval claymore" and a "basket-hilted claymore". Unfortunately, this does not take into account the origins of the word or where the weapon came from.

> *"The long two hander was called a claidheamh dà làimh, translated it literally means two handed sword. … In the romanticised period after the Jacobites the term Claymore was then applied to the long medieval sword."* (Watterott, 2016)

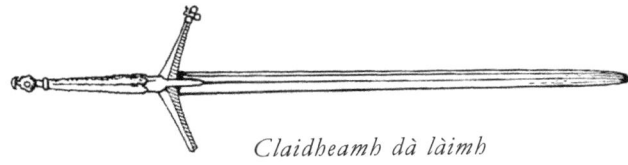

Claidheamh dà làimh

Watterott (2016) examines the native language from which the term "claymore" came from, Scottish Gaelic, presenting the name of the two-handed sword in the language and giving the reason that it was changed to the more familiar one in the later period. This would seem to give more evidence than the previous explanation of giving both weapons the same name. Further to this he explains why the basket-hilted weapon is correctly named "claymore" using similar evidence.

> *"The Scottish version [of the basket-hilted sword] was broader than similar swords of the time. This sword was called a claidheamh-mór. This is Gaelic and translates into Great Sword due to its larger size than its contemporaries. It is well accepted that Claymore is derived from the Gaelic claidheamh-mór."* (Watterott, 2016)

Watterott (2016) uses the original language and demonstrates through history the naming conventions of why the basket-hilted weapon should be called "claymore" and the two-handed weapon should not. Oakeshott (2012) being a respectable historian and curator of weapons gives a much simpler reason and evidence for why the basket-hilted broadsword should be called a "claymore". One based on the weight of history.

> *"the familiar basket-hilted broadsword was called a 'claymore' by the Scots from early in the sixteenth century, and with such respectable contemporary usage behind it, the name may well be allowed to stick."* (Oakeshott, 2012:175)

HILT

The broadsword hilt was not first developed in Scotland, but England, in fact Scotland was last on the list of places for the broadsword to arrive. "The idea of a basket to protect the hand first came to England and then Scotland from Scandinavian and German sword makers." (Scottish Tartans Authority, 2016). What this does is it explains the origins and spread of the broadsword around Europe during the sixteenth and seventeenth centuries as has already been indicated previously, and will also explain the foreign blades found in many Scottish hilts.

What should be noted in the hilts of the weapons are the similarities between those of the late sixteenth century and even those of much later periods, the ancestry of broadsword hilts are found in those which evolved by 1570s and survived (Oakeshott, 2012:156). This is because the foundations were laid by these early weapons and developed over time. One of the more important things about these broadswords is that they were made to last they were often japanned or oxidised to prevent rusting (Oakeshott, 2012:181). These are common methods so that the weapon can be passed down and thus have multiple owners.

German

The German hilts are clearly influenced by the English hilts. In the experimental forms of basket hilt that were being tried around c.1600 and can be seen the beginnings of the broadswords of eighteenth and nineteenth centuries in Germany (Oakeshott, 2012:156). The most contention however comes from the discussion of the differences and similarities between the English and Scottish hilts.

English vs Scottish Hits

There are differences between the English and Scottish hilts and enough that some time needs to be spent examining them. Oakeshott (2012) states that there are three features that differ between the Scottish and the English hilts in the sixteenth century, pommel shape, addition of pair of bars on rear of guards, small linking bar between third and fourth bars inside and outside (Oakeshott, 2012:177). What will be noted from below, as the hilts are examined separately that there are common areas and also some areas where they differ, along with these three which have been noted above.

English

The history of the broadsword notes that the English hilt was in use by the mid-sixteenth century, and a curved quillon form as dated as early as the 1560s (Oakeshott, 2012:175). What this tells us is that the dating for the English form of the broadsword is very early and this needs to be compared to the Scottish form of the broadsword, which will be noted to be somewhat later in the history of the weapon. The fact that the Scottish claymore took over, and the military pattern was designed from the English hilt, or is at least a common ancestor (Oakeshott, 2012:176), places the English hilt as one of importance.

Pommel

Starting with the pommel, it is quite distinctive, it is described as, "a large rounded pommel" (Akehurst, 1969:8). This description of the pommel is not particularly descriptive. It implies that it would be spherical in shape. Luckily there is some more specific information which states that it is apple or bun-shaped (Oakeshott, 2012:177). This means that it is not quite spherical, but more of a slightly compressed sphere.

Guard

With all the focus on the Scottish hilts, being the more famous, English hilts of same periods are often neglected, but are often of fine construction (Coe, 1996:74). This must be the case as has been noted that they formed the bases for many of the guards which followed them. To address the guard more directly, it had, three vertical bars either side, connected by diagonally crossing bar with small circular plate at the join (Oakeshott, 2012:177). This formed the basis of the basket toward the front of the weapon. To the rear there was also protection toward the wrist. This rearward protection consisted of bars which slope sharply from pommel to where rear quillon would be (Oakeshott, 2012:177), noting of course, that in some instances that quillons may still be present.

Scottish

> "By the mid 17th century, ribbon baskets were being made in large quantities and by the turn of the 18th century, the Highland basket was reaching its full pattern. With the addition of the final rear wrist guard at the time of Culloden, it had fully matured. All basket hilt swords after 1746 were of military pattern." *(Scottish Tartans Authority, 2016)*

What appears above is a quite truncated history of the Scottish hilt and broadsword. It does take into account some important parts of its development, which is true, but also leaves out its origins. What can be said is that there is a pattern for the broadsword's development and, "The traditional hilt-pattern, so very well-known, seems to have developed during the late sixteenth century, from an English-designed 'basket' hilt" (Oakeshott, 2012:175). Of course, usually for nationalistic purposes, this inconvenient piece of the history of the hilt is often neglected. What cannot be denied is the link between the hilts.

Pommel

The Scottish hilt has a different pommel, The "Scottish basket hilt with its flattened conical pommel." (Akehurst, 1969:8) is obviously different from the English hilt. This changes the profile of the weapon, even when it is slightly different and is formed as a double cone round (Oakeshott, 2012:177). The conical shape of the pommel remains the same.

Guard

When examining that famous Scottish guard it is best to examine the basic elements and then the more specific ones. The differences between this and the English hilt will be clear. The Scottish guard is constructed of a rectangular plate at where the bars cross on the English hilt, these are decorated; further the rear bars are closer to vertical and an extra shorter one is added to the back of the hilt with an added linking bar (Oakeshott, 2012:177). It is the combination of all of these Elements which gives the Scottish guard all of its characteristics.

The 'beaknose' in which the "basket is formed from a series of welded, flat, ribbon-like strips of metal and is drawn into a kind of beak in front." and is one of earliest Scottish guards c.1600 – 1680 (Oakeshott, 2012:177). This element of the guard remained on the guard for most of the history of the hilt. It could be inferred that this is the remains of the protection for the finger which may be used on the ricasso of the weapon.

The design of the rest of the hilt with regard to the plates on the sides and front of the hilt, were standardised in a fashion. There were exceptions to this, but the mass produced weapons did follow form. Coe (1996) places the appearance of the openwork of hearts and circles on Scottish hilts in late 1600 (Coe,1996:85) or then previously stated that they appeared somewhat later.

> "The Scottish basket hilt, with its traditional heart-shaped piercings and large square plates, seems to have appeared in the second half of the century [17th] and remained in use for over a hundred years."
> (Coe, 1996:74)

What is known for certain is that he states that after 1710 the hilt changed to have rectangular linked bars, pierced and edges filed into serrations (Coe, 1996:85). This denotes a change in the decoration of the hilt. The change in decoration of the hilt can be useful in dating the weapon, at least to before or after 1710, if it follows the standard pattern.

Lining

One thing that is known about the Scottish hilt is that they were lined. This was no doubt for comfort in the use of the weapon. The hilt was most often leather-lined, with thin chamois, covered with velvet or felt and edged with braid, and the base had a thick lining of deer skin (Oakeshott, 2012:181). Examples of these linings can be found on museum examples and good modern reproductions of the weapons.

Blade

> "The chief modern varieties of the curved blade are the Broadsword, the Backsword, the Hanger, and Cutlass, the Scymitar and Düsack, the Yataghan and the Flissa." (Burton, 1987:123)

Burton (1987) classifies the broadsword under a large family of weapons. What is most interesting is that he says that they are curved which they is clearly not the case, however in comparison with the smallsword which would have been the basis of comparison for him at the time of his writing in 1884. There are further issues with the classification of the broadsword, some of which have already been noted. Oakeshott (2012) states that they were mostly double-edged, though back-edged blades were not uncommon (Oakeshott, 2012:178). Clearly there is confusion here between the blade of the broadsword and the backsword, however on the basis that they are both mentioned simultaneously in the manuals this is less of an issue. Similarly the cavalry weapon is similarly confused by Wagner (2004) "It had a straight blade, originally two-edged, later only one sharp edge. These weapons were uniform in character," (Wagner, 2004:20). The cavalry weapon is for a different purpose, so is a different weapon, even if it has a similar hilt. This is the reason why it is important that the entire weapon needs to be taken into account rather than just hilt forms. A similar issue has often been found with the classification of the rapier and similar weapons.

The blades themselves were carefully selected, "preference was given to blades of older origin from workshops of well known blade-makers." (Wagner, 2004:20). Clearly when considering the weapon to be constructed the blade had to be trusted thus an older blade would have shown its worth previously, and well-known blade-makers likewise would have proven their worth. Occasionally the curatorial details will allude to the use of the weapon, and thus give descriptive ideas about the blade, "The blades of such swords were almost invariably for cutting rather than thrusting." (Coe, 1996:74). This would imply a blade which is shorter rather than longer and broader rather than thinner. Soud (2014) gives some detail with regard to this, "Long hacking and slashing blade" (Soud, 2014:53), rather than being short it was long.

With regard to particular nationalities or types of broadsword, Scots weapons have broad blades, often with three fullers (Oakeshott, 2012:178), thus a definitive statement of a broadsword. In comparison, "The British army and many other armies had similar hilted swords but the blades were more slender." (Watterott, 2016). This is an important consideration when considering use characteristics and method of use. The Scottish weapon would have had a heavier cut, based on this description, and it must be remembered that these blades were of some quality, "The Scottish broadswords or backswords have fine springy steel blades, mostly imported from Germany and bearing the 'trade mark' Andrea Ferrara." (Akehurst, 1969:43). This also supports the idea of the broadsword coming to Scotland after having been to the Continent.

WEAPONS

The following will discuss the weapons themselves, and examples of them. There are curatorial issues with regard to dating the weapons, due to similarity and references (Oakeshott, 2012:177). The weapons are often of similar construction and made over such a broad period that reference to a style of hilt or even maker is not necessarily helpful. Further to this, re-hilting was common, old blade with new hilts, and rarer old hilts and new blades (Oakeshott, 2012:179). This means that a blade from an older period can be placed in a newer hilt which means that there is actually two dates, one for the blade and one for the hilt. What can be said about the broadsword, and this often causes problems with dating them, is that there was eventually a uniform shape and ornamentation for whole armies by mid-eighteenth century (Wagner, 2004:20). This is useful for general dating, but not specific.

English

Two examples of broadswords will be presented the first a sixteenth-century basket-hilted sword, the second an eighteenth-century cavalry sword. The first weapon is English and dated to c.1540. It has a full-encompassing hilt which is older than the broad German blade, it weighs 1.36kg and is 1.04m long (Holmes, 2010:104). The second example is English and is dated to c.1750. It has a full- encompassing hilt, a straight broad single-edged blade. It weighs 1.36kg and is 1m long (Holmes, 2010:104). It is most interesting that the weight is consistent as is the length, for the most part, even over the broad expanse of time.

German

This is a single example of a proto-basket hilt sword. What this means is that it is one which most likely would have been copied from the English hilt design. This sword is dated c.1550 and is German. It weighs 1.59kg and is 0.96m long. The blade is double-edged, and the weapon has a simple guard design, which is a "significant improvement over earlier Swiss weapons." (Holmes, 2010:105). Clearly by the weight and length comparison the Germans were in the early development stages.

Scottish

The Scottish hilt of the broadsword is the most well-known of all, and well-developed, "The characteristically Scottish basket-hilt guard was designed to protect the swordsman's hand." (Holmes, 2010:106). There is a single example from the same source which has been used for both the English examples and the German example above, of a Scottish weapon. This broadsword is Scottish and is dated c.1750. The basket is lined with felt-covered leather. It has a wide double-edged blade for cutting and thrusting and a basket-hilt for hand protection. The sword weighs 1.36kg, and is 0.91m long (Holmes, 2010:106).

If the weapons are compared, the Scottish weapon is the shortest of all the weapons which have been described. The Scottish and two English weapons are of equal weight. This would imply that there is more metal in the hilt of the Scottish weapon than the English. This is actually no surprise as in comparison the Scottish hilt would actually cover more of the swordsman's hand and wrist.

CONCLUSION

The broadsword is a weapon which is well-known by many, but often misrepresented or even presented as the wrong weapon. From medieval swords to swords which have similar characteristics but are not the same, each one has been called a "broadsword". Often this is because of the definition given for the weapon. For convenience a definition has been derived as, a straight-bladed, double-edged, relatively broad-bladed sword with a basket-hilt that protects the hand. The definition needs to be specific enough to take into account all of the weapon and not just the hilt. This one is a beginning.

After defining the weapon an examination of its history was made. For some it would sound quite familiar. Due to armour around the hand being reduced, and armour in general being reduced due to the presence of firearms, the hilt was increased. This is actually quite accurate for the broadsword as it was primarily a military weapon, unlike the rapier which was a civilian one in which case the hilt developed to defend the unarmoured hand of the civilian.

More specifically, the English forms of hilt developed first, followed by the German and European, and then the Scottish. In the eighteenth century Scotland became the broadsword fencing centre of Europe, while most of the rest of the nations focussed on the use of the smallsword. Military weapons of the same and later eras were based on the Scottish and English hilt designs.

In the case of the broadsword and the backsword and their differences, the broadsword has two edges, and the backsword has one edge. The mistake of classification of one as the other is usually a result of classification by hilt design. The backsword saw some service in the hands of the cavalry but this was a different weapon again, the problem again being classification by hilt design. For the most part manuals of the period did not discriminate between the broadsword and backsword in use, and it is here where the real definition of the weapon lies.

Next is the question of the claymore and what it is. In Scots Gaelic, the two-handed weapon has a different name as was indicated, meaning that even in the native language of the origin of the weapon it does not mean the larger of the two weapons. More to the point in contemporary usage the Scots themselves were calling the basket-hilted broadsword a "claymore" from the sixteenth century and it results in there being little argument left. The other weapon was only referred to by this name as a result of some romanticised notion of revival after the Jacobite Rebellion.

In the case of the actual curatorial notes which have been made, much of the foundation for the evidence has been laid in the history, with the English hilt influencing all which followed, but the English using the Scottish hilt for the military weapon. Notes about the blade demonstrate more errors of classification due to being based on hilt forms, but demonstrate that the Scottish weapon had the broader blade, and that all had quite long blades even though they were cutting weapons. The weapon examples are more there for interest as they do not provide enough information for any real idea about the weapons, even with images if they had been supplied. It is most important to look at the entire weapon to get idea about it. To classify a weapon by its hilt only is erroneous.

A weapon needs to have a lot of data given about it to give any idea of how the weapon would be used. This is an investigation into the development of the weapon. It is also designed to clear up exactly what weapon is being discussed and to clear up some historical issues with regard to it. The easiest method to do this was a curatorial examination, to look at the form and construction of the weapon.

The Smallsword: A Curatorial Discussion

INTRODUCTION

What follows is a curatorial discussion of the smallsword, this focuses on the various elements which make up the actual weapon. The form of the smallsword is essential to the function of the weapon and as such it is important to understand how the weapon came about, so there will be a discussion of its development as a weapon included in this discussion. The various parts of the weapon need to be discussed in some detail to understand how each affects the way the weapon is used.

There are many people who will simply examine the texts on the use of the weapon and disregard those which discuss the form of the weapon, while some of those which discuss the use of the weapon do discuss recommendations about how the most appropriate weapon should be constructed, this is much too superficial. More detail is required. The weapon needs to be understood as an object and a weapon before its use can be considered, thus a curatorial discussion examining some of the arguments about the weapon is actually useful in the study of the use of a weapon, and this is regardless of what the weapon is. Looking at images of the weapon will give us a feel of what the weapon is like but more detail is required.

The first part of the discussion will examine what has become to be known as the "classic smallsword" this gives us a foundation weapon and a final product and will demonstrate where the development and construction of the weapon is going. Following this is a bibliographical discussion of the often confusing nature of the naming of the weapon to clear up some of the naming conventions of the weapon and the reason why the weapon is so often confused with its predecessor the rapier. This is followed by an examination of the development of the weapon in a general form, an examination of the smallsword as a civilian weapon, and then the various parts of the weapon. Toward the end there is a discussion of some of the construction and decoration of the weapon, and finally recommendations about gaining a modern practice weapon suitable for creating the art described in the manuals in which it is used.

For the most part, curatorial considerations of weapons are left to collectors and curators of museums, as it is these individuals who need to know and are most interested in the individual details of the weapons being described. Pictures and details of weapons are placed in books for the interest of the general public and these are often skipped over by the martial artist as being of little use, but it is necessary to understand the weapon, not just as a weapon, but also as a cultural object and the details about this object, to really understand the way in which the texts describe its use.

THE "CLASSIC SMALLSWORD"

> "What we call French smallsword is a weapon that came in vogue in Europe around the fourth quarter of the 17th Century, although its basic typology had existed already for at least 2 or 3 decades. The smallsword is instantly recognizable for its hilt – which typically features an 8-shaped plate, a single short quillon, two small arms (that get progressively smaller in the course of the 18th Century) and a knucklebow." *(Leoni, 2011)*

The form of the "classic" smallsword is almost instantly recognisable to anyone who is familiar with swords of its period, and indeed swords in general. The hilt with its shell, short, single quillon, knuckle-bow and arms of the hilt, are instantly recognisable. These demonstrate a form which was developed over a period of years as a result of the demands of the individuals who used them and indeed, some due to social pressure for the most elegant form of weapon. What also needs to be noted in this "classic" form is the blade, because a sword is nothing without the blade.

> "hollow ground, with a triangular cross section, such that it was both light and exceptionally strong. Often these blades were fitted to hilts with double-shell guards; the blade would pass through an opening at the center of the guard. This is the classic small sword, and it would become the standard gentleman's sword until the end of the 18th century. Its lightness, quick tip, stiff blade, and tremendous penetration made it deadly in the hand of many a duelist from the late 17th century into the 19th." *(Soud, 2014:79)*

The triangular blade is seen as the blade of the smallsword it is a thrusting blade designed for puncturing the opponent. The edge is barely there if it exists at all this is a weapon which is designed for thrusting, and the later manuals which deal with the smallsword bear this theory out. This triangular section blade would be the foundation upon which the épée would be based, especially as it is essentially the smallsword in practice form. What should be noted, is that the triangular blade is not the only blade that was fitted to the smallsword.

OTHER NAMES

In this modern era we are generally specific when naming things. Something is given a name and for the most part, that is what it is named as. This was not always the case, and the smallsword demonstrates this particular element very much so. Indeed much of these issues with naming have flooded through from the period of the smallsword into our own.

While we would like to separate the rapier and smallsword with a clear defining line this is just not possible, the historical texts do not assist us in this endeavour indeed they complicate it, "it seems that, for a while at least, 'rapier' and 'smallsword' often meant the same thing." (Coe, 1996:58). Indeed in order to maintain the "correct" naming conventions some curators have taken this sort of naming convention and brought it into the present. "1701 Rapier" (Soud, 2014:79), this is a caption which was placed to describe a weapon which is obviously what we would now call a "smallsword", indeed on the same page the author then changes the naming convention top describe another weapon of

EQUIPMENT & CURATORIAL DISCUSSIONS

similar form, "A transitional rapier from 1701, with a hollow-ground, slightly shorter than normal blade with a diamond cross section." (Soud, 2014:79). Thus the number of names for the weapon has not decreased it has actually increased. So, thus we have three names for the weapon, smallsword, rapier, and transitional rapier. Further to these three there is a fourth naming of this particular weapon, Wagner 2004, refers to the smallsword as a "Baroque Rapier" (Wagner, 20014:17). With all the naming conventions present, there is little surprise that things can be a little confusing when studying this particular weapon.

Some of these elements of naming conventions will be cleared up, at least in part, in an examination of the development of the smallsword. For the study of the smallsword it is necessary to focus on the form of the weapon rather than what it has been called by a person. If we acknowledge that the weapons have been called by various different names, and see that in effect that they are the same form of weapon, there can be some solution to this particular puzzle. Allowing for such naming conventions and focusing on form allows for a much clearer path toward the truth and thus the discovery of this weapon.

DEVELOPMENT

The development of the smallsword is a process which is traced from the ending of the rapier through a couple of other forms to the smallsword. What needs to be noted here is that it was not an "evolution" as some theorists would have us believe it was a *development*. The rapier went out of favour due to its length, due to fashion more than anything not a matter of ineffective use. Indeed the first smallswords were short rapiers, "A decade later [1640s] the smallsword, in effect a light rapier, was introduced." (Coe, 1996:58).

Coe 1996 goes further in his development of the smallsword and mentions the scarf sword, which in essence was a court sword worn on a scarf, hence its name. This, like the previously mentioned weapon was based on the form of the rapier, shortened and lightened to suit being worn in a crowded court where the long rapier would be an inconvenience, "The origins of the smallsword are to be found in the light scarf sword or rapier with a double-shell guard and fully developed hilt." (Coe, 1996:66).

What needs to be noted in this development is that the rapier did not instantly disappear, it took time. Indeed the Spaniards persisted with the rapier for at least two centuries after the rest of Europe. This development was not regular or universal (Coe, 1996:66). Time was needed for the weapon to become popular, the smallsword took two decades to become the dominant weapon, "these elegant weapons did not really become fashionable until after 1660." (Coe, 1996:66). This time allowed the swordsmiths to examine the weapon and take the lessons learnt over the years, and indeed those learnt from the rapier to develop a weapon designed for a purpose. This weapon was designed for the gentleman to carry with him as an essential part of his dress, and also to be used to defend him with, it was not originally designed to be used as a military weapon.

> *"By the end of the [17th] century the small-sword, the typical aristocratic weapon of the eighteenth century, was already fully developed. Its guard consisted of the arms of the hilt, already going out of use, a shell on each side of the hilt, a knuckle-guard now fixed to the pommel, and a small rear quillon. A heavier version of this hilt with scroll-guards flanking the knuckle-bow was popular in north-western Europe on cutting blades, and many silver-hilted examples lightly decorated with acanthus foliage exist." (Norman, 1964:103)*

CIVILIAN

The smallsword is primarily a civilian weapon, much as the rapier was, though it saw some military use. "Throughout the eighteenth century there was a close relationship between the civilian smallsword and smallswords designed for military use." (Coe, 1996:84). The close relationship was in the form of similar changes in guard design and form more than changes in use. The military forms of the weapon were much plainer and much more robust than the civilian versions of the smallsword. Clearly the blade of the military version of the military weapon was different to that of the civilian weapon due to the different nature of the combats, though there were still similarities.

The smallsword is defined as a civilian weapon primarily due to the thrusting nature of the weapon. This was less useful on the field of battle, but as noted before, forms of the weapon did see use. The smallsword was primarily a weapon of self-defence, and replaced the rapier in this mode. It became a normal part of dress for the gentleman. "It was a civilian weapon: an essential item of dress for any gentleman that also acted as a duelling sword." (Holmes, 2010:112)

In the eighteenth century the smallsword was seen as *the* duelling weapon and was introduced into England in this period, "The small-sword introduced to England during eighteenth century, only after 1789 it ceased to be universal weapon for affairs of honour" (Burton, 1987:135). After this period the pistol took its place as the primary weapon for duelling.

THE WEAPON

The previous part of the discussion has discussed the social aspects of the weapon and aspects which do not directly relate to the actual weapon itself. These elements are nonetheless necessary for understanding its development however it is the weapon which needs to be the focus of a curatorial discussion of a weapon. The construction and decoration have been left separate so that the parts of the weapon are not obscured by overtly technical elements which may not apply to important elements of the weapon and its use, however important they may be to the weapon and its look.

Hilt

The hilt is the part of the weapon which the swordsman holds and which protects his hand from his opponent, and any swordsman and curator knows this. What is most interesting is that in the curatorship of weapons, this is where most of the interest seems to lie. What needs to be noted in the discussion of the smallsword is that all parts of the weapon need to be taken into account to give a full description and to enable a full understanding of the weapon. The hilt of the smallsword has a look which has been copied by weapons which have followed it and to really understand it, the various elements of the hilt need examination.

These elements will have their technical names in the description and it is not very useful if they cannot be located on the weapon and thus their use known. To aid in this a diagram will accompany the description of the hilt of the smallsword to assist with the naming of the parts of the hilt so it is known where they are located on the hilt of the weapon.

EQUIPMENT & CURATORIAL DISCUSSIONS

Smallsword Hilt - Exploded View

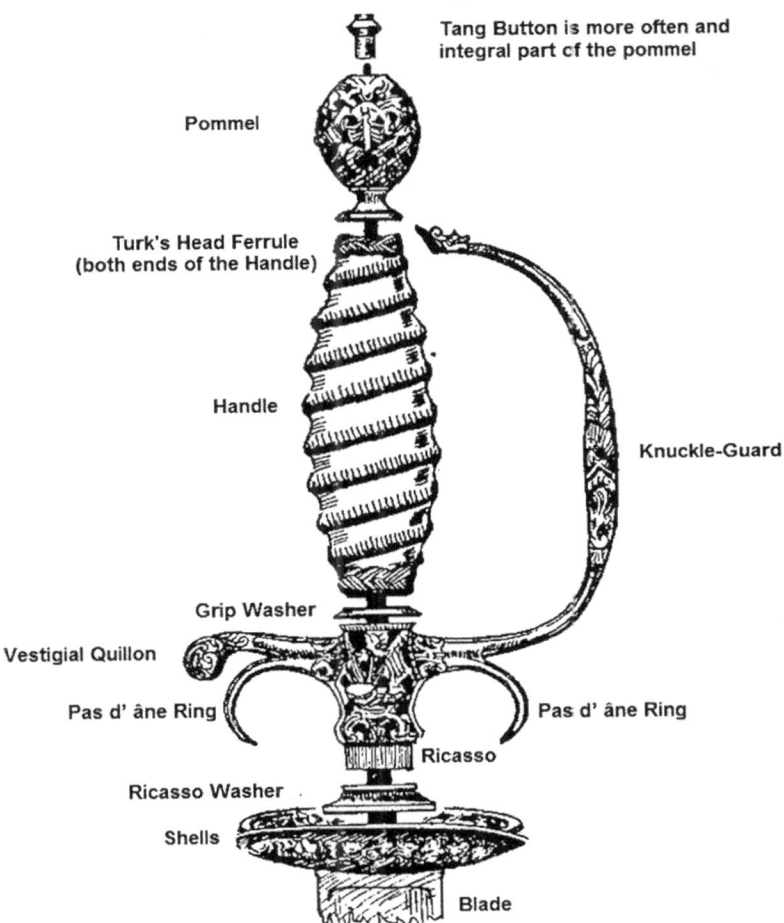

This is what is known as an "exploded" diagram and it shows all of the parts and where they go. It should be noted that the "Pas d' âne Ring" as indicated are sometimes called "arms of the hilt" by some authors. It should also be noted that most sources do not go into such a complete description of the weapon, indeed often it is described as a hand guard of small cup, and finger and knuckle guards (Holmes, 2010:112). The diagram above is for those instances where a more complete description of the various parts of the weapon is given.

This description does not give much to go on with regard to the form of the smallsword as to what it might be, but it gives us an idea of what sort of shape it might take. With regard to the form of the weapon, it is useful to track the changes in the weapon over time. Some of these were due to fashion and some of them were due to changes in the style of combat, as such to call such developments "evolution" is erroneous. The smallsword started to make its appearance in the early seventeenth-century, "The typical, early seventeenth-century civilian sword had short quillons and sometimes a slight shell guard." (Norman, 1964:103)

What should be noted here is this was a change from its predecessor the rapier, which had significant quillons, and more of a cup hilt towards the later part of the period, thus much more complex. The smallsword's hilt was a simplification of the hilt of the rapier. The most interesting thing is that while the rapier's guard changed and varied over its time, the smallsword generally stuck to a similar format from beginning to end with very little change.

> "By 1640 hilts were being made which had a hand guard formed of a double-shell hilt, with the blade passing through an aperture in the centre. This type of guard became a common feature of the later smallsword and continued in use until the nineteenth century." *(Coe, 1996:65)*

It should be noted that it is only the external guard which has been mentioned at this stage, the shell. Internally, the arms of the hilt were present. In the use of the rapier the arms of the hilt were used to protect the finger and enable the forefinger to be wrapped around the ricasso[25] of the weapon to get better control over the weapon in general. However, thought with regard to this in the eyes of some masters was to change, masters in the 1680s did not like fingers in arms of the hilt where they could be injured at close quarters, thus they were there for additional grip rather than protection (Coe, 1996:66). In the case of the smallsword it was pinched by the fingers at the ricasso, its lighter weight enabling the freedom of the fingers.

Despite the advice of these masters not to use the arms of the hilt, they remained as part of the hilt regardless, and no doubt were used by swordsmen in a similar fashion to the way that they were used in the use of the rapier. One of the best descriptions of the smallsword hilt of this period comes from Wagner 2004, who describes the hilt of the smallsword in some detail.

> "In the second half of the seventeenth century the hilt once again began to assume a simpler form. It consisted of a closed shell supported by a bridge, with either two arms and a knuckle bow or a knuckle bow and a back arm of the quillons; the grip was held fast by the pommel, thus holding the whole hilt together." *(Wagner, 2004:17)*

What should be noted in this description is that, while there is more detail about the construction of the smallsword's hilt, the general form of the hilt has not changed since the description given by Coe, 1996. The format, while simplified is much the same. To get into more detail, it is necessary to begin to look at individual elements and see how they changed over time. It is here that subtle changes in the style of the weapon are reflected.

Before 1700 arms of the hilt quite large, knuckle bow is usually straight, pommels globular, pear-shaped or facetted (Coe, 1996:68). Having the arms of the hilt quite

---

25 The unsharpened part of the blade which sat within the hilt of the sword.

large pushes the hand further away from the shell, and also would make the hand more inclined to use the arm to put the finger through, however it is the pommel which is most interesting as there are three different shapes which are indicated. An eccentric style of heart-shaped hilt shell developed 1720s, more popular latter half eighteenth century (Coe, 1996:69). It is most interesting that a shape of hilt would appear early, but be more popular later on in the period of time when a weapon was popular, it almost reflects a change of heart, or an advancement too early for its time.

In the second quarter of the eighteenth century, pommels were pear-shaped and knuckle guard to be broad curve, and arms of hilt were still large (Coe, 1996:69). The pear-shaped pommel seems to be a style which was maintained, along with the larger sized arms of the hilt. The knuckle-bow, it could be suggested developed a broad curve either for more room for the movement of the hand or, for better protection as both would be achieved by this change.

As developments were made on the Continent, so would they affect similar elements in other places such as England. In England from 1760 oval shell-guard, arms of the hilt much smaller (Coe, 1996:71). It should be noted that while the weapons on the Continent persisted with the more figure-8 shaped hilts, those in England were more oval as indicated. So the weapons were different as well. The change in the arms of the hilt in artefacts of the period shows a distinct change in the arms of the hilt to being much smaller. The change in the Neo-classical period to urn-shaped pommels (Coe, 1996:71) can still be seen in some weapons today, especially in cheap foils and replica weapons of the period.

With all of the changes noted and differences in the weapons, it is difficult to know where to look. For the most part the specifics of one type of pommel, versus the shape of the arms of the hilt, versus the shape of the shell, is really only an issue for those who want to date their own weapon or for those in museums. For the swordsman it is how these parts affect the use of the weapon. Thus, in general, while most curatorial discussions focus on hilts, it is blades which are more important. For the most part of the hilt of the smallsword, it needs to be known that, "In its fully developed form the smallsword had two additional guards, [along with the shell] known as arms of the hilt, set in the quillon block, and a large curved knucklebow." (Coe, 1996:66).

Blade

> *"The smallsword blade is generally between 29 and 35 inches long, and may be of flattened diamond, oval or triangular section. The smallsword is almost essentially a thrusting weapon; although records exist of its occasionally being "sharpened as a razor" for dueling (naturally applicable for those blades that could physically take an edge), the major French smallsword instruction treatises focus solely on the thrust." (Leoni, 2011)*

For the swordsman, the blade and its form is much more significant that considerations of the hilt and its form, though it has something to bear with regard to the use of the weapon as has already been noted above. Leoni (2011) above has described a general idea of the form of the smallsword blade and gives a general introduction to its shape and length and indeed its use. What needs to be noted is that there was considerable variety in blades, the narrow flat being used alongside the triangular (Coe, 1996:70), so to state that it is one or the other would be incorrect. Some of the history of the development of the blade is important to understand how these blades came about.

Often early smallswords have shortened rapier blades, in 1660 the hollow-ground triangular section blade from Germany was introduced; it combined strength and lightness (Coe, 1996:69). Thus as indicated in the earlier section about the history of the weapon in general, the weapon was indeed a shortened rapier, thus resulting in the confusion about naming conventions. These earlier blades had an edge which was suitable for cutting, whereas the later blades lost their edge and were designed for thrusting only.

> "By 1700 blades had become much narrower and were designed solely for thrusting. Although they were usually quite at the forte, they taper sharply, giving strength where it was needed, for parrying an opponent's blade."
> *(Coe, 1996:70)*

The statement above refers more to the triangular blade as can be seen by the sharp taper and wide forte described in the blade. The triangular blades were not particularly suited for cutting due to their shape; their edges did not hold a sharpened edge particularly well. With regard to recommendations for blades, at least one master of the period makes a recommendation about which blades should be used and for what Blackwell and also Angelo makes such recommendations of blades.

> "Blackwell recommends against using Spanish tucks. Although they are "the best blades for fencing," "they are too heavy for dueling." He recommends the light German blade. Angelo prefers the hollow blade "because of its lightness and ease in the handling.""
> *(Krishnaraj, 2001:2)*

Colichemarde

> "It [the small-sword] had a curious modification – the Colichemarde blade, so called from its inventor, Count Königsmark." It was heavy near the hilt and light near the tip, invented about 1680, favourite duelling blade, remained in fashion during reign of Louis XIV, then disappeared *(Burton, 1987:135)*

The colichemarde was a unique modification of the smallsword blade which attempted to have the advantage of the broader blade flatter along with the lightness of the triangular blade all rolled into one package. This had a flattened broader blade cross-section on the bottom third of the blade, while it had a narrower triangular cross-section at the top of the blade. This was designed so that the swordsman could have a strong parry with the forte of the blade while enabling quickness with the foible of the blade.

Blade Length

The perfect length of a blade has always been a concern of the swordsman. He needed the weapon long enough to keep the opponent at distance and to be able to attack the opponent, yet short enough that the weapon was light enough to move quickly enough. This question of the perfect length blade is not restricted to the smallsword indeed it has been a question which has been asked of all kinds of swords. "In terms of length, at least two of the masters, Liancour and Blackwell, prescribe 36 inches as being the maximum

EQUIPMENT & CURATORIAL DISCUSSIONS

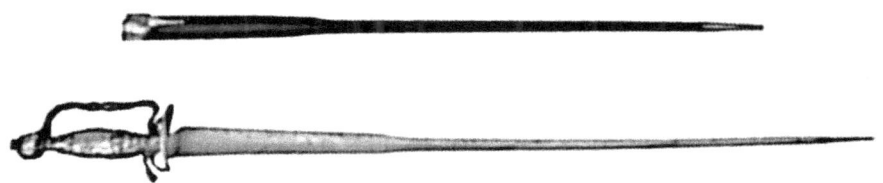

Colichemarde c1745-1746 - Musée national de la Marine from Ancienne collection du musée des phares du Trocadéro (Rama)

blade length." (Krishnaraj, 2001:1). L'Abbat was also concerned with the length of the smallsword, and stated that it should be proportional to the user of the weapon. More of his discussion of length will be dealt with later on.

Testing

Once the length was selected and measured, the measurements discovered however the practitioner and swordsmith agreed upon, it was then important that the blade was tested once the weapon was assembled. This weapon was to be worn by the owner and to be used to defend him for his life so the blade needed to be reliable. Once the hilt is assembled, then it is time for the blade test, looking for flaws across the blade and length-wise, then temper by bending the blade (Krishnaraj, 2001:1).

The last part of the test indicated above, the blade bend was vital. A blade which was too brittle and would not bend would break. A blade which was too soft would bend and remain bent. The best blade will bend in a semi-circle, and then spring back to being straight, but one that does not return to straight but is deformed is better than breaking (Krishnaraj, 2001:1). At least a blade which is soft can be bent back to shape if it is required; a broken blade is useless to the combatant. However in the bending of the blade, it was recommended that some care be taken. "Both Liancour and L'Abbat tell us that we must not force the bend [in the test], as it may cause the blade to be weakened and break upon use." (Krishnaraj, 2001:2)

The destruction test is one that we do not often perform on our own weapons because they are often quite an investment. These weapons are used for martial arts and training purposes, however the smallsword, in its period, was used to defend a man's life, thus it would be a small price to pay to ensure that the blade was properly made. "A second test is recommended by Liancour and L'Abbat, in which they advocate breaking the point." (Krishnaraj, 2001:1). Breaking just the point allows for another point to be ground on to the weapon, but if it was broken further down an entirely new blade would have to be made and the process started again. Once broken the ends of the steel would be inspected for colour, grey for good temper, white for bad temper (Krishnaraj, 2001:2).

WEAPON LENGTH

> *"The length of the blade ought to be proportionate to the Stature of the person who is to use it: the long sword, from point to pommel should reach perpendicularly from the ground to the navel, and the shortest to the waist..." (Monsieur L'Abbat, The Art of Fencing or the Use of the Smallsword.) (Krishnaraj, 2001:1)*

Monsieur L'Abbat has already been noted as having an interest in the length of the blade and it is presented above. He clearly states here that both the weapon and the blade together should be proportional to the user of the weapon. The argument for weapon length follows similar lines to that of blade length, and that should be no surprise as they are part and parcel one and the other.

The idea of the proportionality of the weapon and the blade to the user means that the construction and size of the hilt is also significant and should not be overlooked hence there was some discussion about it. The measurement overall includes the blade and the hilt for the overall weapon length after all. While L'Abbat simply states that the weapon should be proportional, Angelo puts a little more restriction on the overall length of the weapon.

> *"Angelo says that the sword should be proportional to the height and strength of the swordsman and that it should not exceed 38 inches in length from pommel to point."* (Krishnaraj, 2001:1)

So, if a blade is chosen of a particular length then the blade needs to fit in the rest of the length, especially if they are a particularly tall individual, according to Angelo. It would seem that the length of the weapon and the blade is the primary concern of the masters of the time. There seems to be very little consideration with regard to weight, which will be briefly discussed next and balance, which is a product of length and weight together. The balance of the weapon would determine how well the swordsman would be able to move it and how agile it is. Sure, the weight plays some part in this, but the balance point of the weapon can greatly affect the performance of the weapon and this is the result of the correct construction of hilt and blade.

WEIGHT

The weight of the smallsword may surprise some readers, and it will not surprise others. "Weight of a typical French smallsword is around 1 to 1.5lbs." (Leoni, 2011). For those using the metric system, this means a weapon which weighs somewhere between 450 – 680g, which makes for a very light weapon, especially in comparison to its predecessor the rapier.

What makes this weapon move even better is a balance point which suits the movement of the weapon and the use of it by the swordsman. In some ways it is true what the nineteenth-century fencing historians said, the lighter weapon did allow for more complex actions with the weapon alone.[26]

CONSTRUCTION

Having discussed the various bits and pieces of the weapon, almost separate from one another in some cases, a discussion of the construction of the weapon would make some sense to see how the weapon was put together. This will focus on how the hilt was assembled and the blade fitted to it for the final construction.

---

26 More in this instance meaning multiple actions, rather than access to more techniques.

EQUIPMENT & CURATORIAL DISCUSSIONS

"All the masters, except for Blackwell, take great care to emphasize the correct way of mounting a sword. They are especially alert to the danger of filing the tang too thin in order to save time in filing holes in the guard and pommel. The resultant empty space between tang and guard and tang and pommel is filled up with many pieces of wood." (Krishnaraj, 2001:1)

It is not that Blackwell is against the method described, he simply does not mention it at all, and it would seem that he believes that this is a concern for the swordsmith when he measures the sword for the swordsman. The important part with regard to the construction of the hilt of the weapon and the weapon in general is that it is solid and that it does not rattle, or come loose. The parts need to fit together snuggly so there is less chance of movement in the hilt. The wedging of pieces of wood would obviously lead to a reduction in structural solidity due to the nature of the wood being used and the extra effort used. Further to this idea of solidity in hilt construction, "riveting the tang to the pommel is mandatory for Angelo, L'Abbat and Liancour." (Krishnaraj, 2001:1). The pommel holds the blade and hilt and place preventing the weapon from falling apart hence this idea of riveting is important. It would be catastrophic for a weapon to fall apart while it was being used.

DECORATION

The decoration of the weapon was designed to impress those who saw the weapon and reflect the taste of the owner of the weapon. Some weapons were highly decorated, but most practical examples were not so much. The effort to which the decoration of the hilts was made was truly impressive as examples will demonstrate. "Fine quality hilts were encrusted or damascened with silver or gold or more usually chiselled in high relief," (Norman, 1964:103)

The example to the left from the Metropolitan Museum of Art (Accession Number: 26.145.315a,b) dated c.1797-8, demonstrates to some degree some of the artistry that went into some of the more highly decorated examples of the hilts which have been preserved and collected in museums. This would have been a presentation sword, or dress sword, which will be discussed shortly.

There are also examples of plainer designs of weapon designed for war or travelling, such as that from c.1730, these are more heavily built and more solidly designed (Coe, 1996:68), obviously designed for the rigours of combat and general wear. What should be noted is that while

Smallsword c.1787-8 - Metropolitan Museum of Art, Accession Number: 26.145.315a,b

UN-BLOGGED: A FENCER'S RAMBLINGS

Smallsword c1750 - Metropolitan Museum of Art, Accession Number: 2004.525

many of the examples of weapons held in museums and collections are of the highly decorated type, the plain examples would have also been just as numerous, due to their utility for general wear. These plain but practical smallswords survived, have hilts of steel covered with black lacquer, have large arms of the hilt, form of shell suggest first half of 18th century (Coe, 1996:68).

Dress Swords

Dress swords, as typified by the example presented from the Metropolitan Museum of Art from c.1750, were examples of the swordsmiths' highest art.

Often these weapons' hilts, once their basic construction was completed, were sent to jewellers and similar craftsmen in order to place the higher levels of craftsmanship in decoration on the hilts. It was not only smallswords which were used as dress swords, though they are the main topic here, "Dress swords, whether based on small swords, rapiers, or sabres, were often objects of beauty and fascination." (Soud, 2014:90). These weapons demonstrate some of the highest levels of art of the period, even though they are often overlooked in discussions of art in the periods in which they were found.

Above: Smallsword c1730 - Metropolitan Museum of Art, Accession No.: 26.145.325a,b

MODERN PRACTICE WEAPON

"When selecting a practice smallsword, the main things to look for are two, in my opinion. First one is weight: if a smallsword weighs more than 1.5lbs, it's way too heavy. Second is balance. It is fairly common to see smallsword simulators that are too hilt-heavy – you should avoid these and ask your armourer to move the point of balance around an inch/inch-and-a-half from the plate." (Leoni, 2011)

For the modern swordsman interested in recreating the art which is found in the smallsword manuals of the past, an accurate weapon to use to recreate the art is a must. Without an accurate weapon it is difficult to recreate the art as it is described by the masters in their various manuals. There are many different options and the swordsman must weigh these options very carefully to ensure that he has a weapon which is appropriate to the manual or manuals which are being recreated.

The modern foil is often used as a smallsword simulator due to its size and the convenience of accessing the weapon. While the foil was indeed designed for the purpose of practicing smallsword, it is often much too light and the blade is much too flexible to perform the actions which are described. Further, if one selects a manual from the earlier period of the smallsword, the foil has no discernable edge for the cuts which are described. Further to this the modern orthopaedic, or pistol, grip is completely unsuitable as it places the hand in the wrong position for smallsword actions.

The modern épée is an improvement but only on a scale. Its triangular blade is perfectly suited to the later manuals, but its off-set hilt and French grip is a problem as, once again, it will place the hand in the wrong position. It is, however, an improvement on the foil especially for the manuals of the later smallsword period.

The best option is a smallsword simulator, remembering the advice of Leoni, (2011) above. The weapon needs to be suited to you and also suited to the type of smallsword manual that you are using. If you are working from a smallsword manual of the earlier period, it is advised you find something with a blade with an edge, if later, the triangular blade is better. In all cases, when practicing with a partner, the blade should be suitable for the purpose, not sharp, and tipped. It is advised that some sort of rubber blunt is placed on the tip.

CONCLUSION

The purpose of writing this article was not to bore the reader with yet another discussion of particular parts of a weapon which has been discussed again and again. It has been to create a greater understanding of the weapon for the more practically-oriented reader to understand the weapon so that it may be understood better. A better understanding of the weapon can only lead to a better using of the weapon and a better understanding of the writings of those who wrote about using the weapon.

The "classic smallsword" is a weapon with an image which forms in the minds of anyone who has read anything about the weapon. What was important here was to paint a clear picture of what this "classic" smallsword was. This picture often focused on the hilt of the weapon and left the blade to "general understanding". By presenting an image of the blade as well the picture of the weapon became much clearer and thus the use of the weapon was also discovered.

Names are something which historians and curators have always had problems with and the smallsword is no exception. Indeed even in the period in which the smallsword was used it was called different things. So the modern era's idea of calling a thing a specific thing seems to not work here. The smallsword was called: smallsword, rapier, transitional rapier, and Baroque rapier at different times and places and by different people, and not just in ages past, even in the modern period. Thus it is better to focus on the form of the weapon rather than any particular naming convention.

The smallsword developed from the rapier, it did *not* evolve. The smallsword replaced the rapier for the most part due to the forces of fashion. The shorter weapon was more convenient to wear at the crowded courts of the seventeenth and eighteenth centuries. The masters adopted their styles to suit the shortened weapon. There is clear evidence that the weapon developed from the rapier as for the most part the earlier forms were merely shortened rapiers, or had shortened rapier blades on them.

Just like the rapier, the smallsword was primarily a civilian weapon designed to be worn with civilian clothes. It was designed to be used for self-defence in a civilian setting or for settling matters of honour. Indeed it has been referred to by some as the ultimate duelling sword. It is true that forms of the smallsword did see military service, but it was primarily a civilian weapon, for many of the same reasons that the rapier was. The focus on thrusting was simply unsuited to the battlefield.

There was the discussion of the hilt describing its form and parts and how they fit together. Some naming conventions were cleared up, a little at least. This followed a general development of the hilt to its "classic" form found in the eighteenth and nineteenth centuries. Next followed a discussion of the blade, this was much more interesting for the practical swordsman due to its pointing toward the use of the weapon. There were some interesting developments here including the development of the colichemarde. It also had a discussion of how blades were chosen by length and also the best blade found, according to various masters of the period. Most interesting here is that the general agreement was that the blade should be proportional to the user of the weapon.

Just like the blade length, the weapon length was advised by most to be proportional to the user. Interestingly, Blackwell does not bother to give dimensions of the weapon at all. This would be primarily due to a gentleman being measured for his weapon by a swordsmith when it was bought, thus no concern of his. This idea of proportionality demonstrates some of the obsession of the eighteenth century mind with ideas of science.

There are few comments about the weight of weapons to be found, indeed even in museum examples the weight seems to be absent. What needs to be noted is that the weapon was lighter than the rapier. The result of this was that as fencing historians have indicated more actions of the blade were more accessible to the user of the smallsword.

In the construction of the weapon, solidity was the main concern. The hilt of the weapon had to be solidly built to keep the weapon together. A failure here would result in the weapon coming apart, often resulting in dire consequences for the user. The recommendations made highlight this idea and importance of construction of the hilt of the weapon.

Some weapons were highly decorated, as the examples from museum collections presented demonstrate. What needs to be noted is that not all smallswords were so highly decorated. The sword taken travelling or indeed taken to war was much less highly decorated. The more highly decorated weapons were primarily designed as dress weapons or presentation weapons.

The final element discussed was of great importance to the modern swordsman being the selection of a practice weapon. Various ideas were given for weapons suitable for the practice of the art as described by the masters of the period of the smallsword. The most important thing here is that the weapon needs to be suited to the art which is being performed. A weapon which is not suited to the art will cause the practitioner problems, and actions described will be more difficult. Selection of a proper weapon is of vital importance.

What has been presented has been primarily focused on the weapon itself, but it will be noted that there are some very practical elements which need to be noted, along with some social elements which were necessarily related. The form of the weapon will dictate the actions which can be performed with it. A weapon which has a blade which carries no edge obviously is not suitable for thrusting, thus a flatter blade is more suitable for the earlier forms taught in the manuals where some elements of cutting is still present. An understanding of the weapon and how it is constructed and how it came about will increase and understanding of how it was used.

Of Wasters

INTRODUCTION

I have certain opinions with regard to wasters which I believe I need to share with regard to them and also the change in attitude with regard to them. What needs to be noted throughout this discussion is that I am not decrying the use of wasters completely and utterly at all, merely that they are being used incorrectly by some in their current method. Wasters most definitely have their place in HEMA practice, so long as they are used for the purpose that they were designed for. To put some perspective on this discussion, a small piece of history is required.

ROMAN ORIGIN

Wasters have been a part of Western Martial Arts for many years. Their use can be documented as far back as the Roman period where wooden swords (*rudii*, the plural of *rudius*) were used by both legionaries and gladiators for practice. These weapons were used both against the *Palus* or pell, a standing stake and also in mock combats. Wooden weapons were used in these instances to ensure that no permanent injuries came to the combatants, as such for a safe method of training. This idea of using wooden weapons flowed through to the medieval and Renaissance periods and has been adopted in our modern period.

MODERN WASTERS

In the first instances the waster in the modern period was only available in wood, this made for a hard, not very forgiving item meaning that they were best designed for practice with another with control exercised on both sides, and of course use at the pell. The SCA took this one step further and used weapons made out of rattan in their melee combatants as a standard weapon for fighting in armour and so it has continued to this day.

NYLON WASTERS

More recently nylon and other forms of plastic waster have been introduced, these were, in the beginning, somewhat more forgiving and thus allowed more free-play between the combatants so long as a level of control was shown. Indeed with regard to nylon wasters, back in 2011, I participated in some combats using nylon waster longswords in very minimal armour, and thanks to the control of my opponents and myself, the worst the combatants walked away with was a welt here and there.[27]

MIND-SET CHANGE

Due to this particular outing it gave me the idea that if you needed lots of armour to use wasters with an opponent you're doing something wrong. This idea is quite contrary to what I have seen most recently where combatants fighting with wasters having to armour up to the point where they might as well be using steel, as there is not much difference in the armour requirements. Further, in stark contrast to the playful nature of the bouts I was engaged with the injuries sustained have become quite a bit more serious.

In my opinion, this has come about due to a mind-set in the eyes of the combatants

---

27   https://www.youtube.com/watch?v=c9PoU_i--20

using the weapons that they are only plastic so smacking their opponent around as hard as they like is no problem whatsoever. This has resulted in the increase in armour requirements and the increase in injuries from using wasters. The respect which goes from holding a steel weapon in the hand seems to be absent when holding a waster and it is this which needs to be re-introduced. I think part of this comes from realising exactly what a waster is and where it comes from and what it is for.

PURPOSE OF WASTERS

The waster is to the steel sword, the same way the foil was to the smallsword. To be more precise, both the waster and the foil are practice weapons and nothing more and thus should be treated as such. Their original Roman, medieval and Renaissance use needs to be recognised and thus the tool needs to be used the way it is supposed to be. The waster should be used to demonstrate control over a weapon and present technique with the weapon, just as the foil is designed to teach the new fencer the basics of how to use the épée and thus the smallsword.

Armour should be reduced for the use of wasters and the control of the combatants increased. If this requires them to slow their actions down to do this, then that is what is required. Should a tournament be fought with wasters, the aim of the tournament should not only be to find the winner at the end of the tournament, but also who presents the best form with regard to technique and control of the weapon as they deliver blows and also defend against them. In essence, the respect for what a waster is and the tool that it is needs to be recognised and respected for what it is.

CONCLUSION

Should we continue down the path which we are on, what will be the difference in combat with wasters as to steel? For starters, the waster does not act like a steel weapon. It is not as responsive as a steel weapon, and it also does not have an edge like a steel weapon so binds and other actions are much more difficult to perform. The lack of rigidity in most wasters also makes many actions difficult as well so the imitation of steel combat with wasters in effect is fallacious. If combatants are using the same equivalent protective gear when using wasters, they may as well be using steel weapons instead.

What will be the difference in combat with wasters as to what the SCA does? The answer in essence is not a great deal, except the weapon shape and protective gear used. SCA tournaments also tend to be a lot more colourful, and they have had a lot more practice ensuring that the combatants stay safe while practicing it as well.

The purpose of wasters needs to be remembered. They are a practice weapon designed to simulate the use of a steel sword, lightened in most instances so that the fencer does not get as tired using them. These weapons are designed so the combatant gets the feel of swinging a steel weapon with control against an opponent while practicing the actions that they have been taught while not having to wear all of the protective gear that would be otherwise required. Any form of combat using wasters should be made with control emphasised on the part of both combatants with the purpose focussed on the execution of the skills of the form of combat rather than the outcome of the bout. Due to the nature of the weapon anything else will lead the combatants astray from real swordsmanship simply due to the nature of the weapon.

afencersramblings.blogspot.com

Glossary

A - B

aggressive "Ready or likely to confront; characterized by or resulting from aggression" (http://www.oxforddictionaries.com/)
appel a feint using a stomp of the foot designed to startle the opponent
armour AKA protective gear, PPE; for the most part HEMA is conducted with the combatants considered to be unarmoured as such "armour" is actually referring to the gear they wear to protect themselves
assertive "having or showing a confident and forceful personality" (http://www.oxforddictionaries.com/)
assumed armour the amount of real armour a combatant is assumed to be wearing in a particular scenario, or according to a set of rules or conventions; in HEMA unless it is a specifically armour scenario the assumed armour is nil, combatants are assumed to be wearing civilian attire
botta secreta Italian, meaning secret blow; taught by some masters and is a blow which supposedly cannot be parried

C

calibration how hard a combatant must strike another for the struck combatant, or according to a rules set, to call the blow as "good" or effective
cavazione to change from one line to another; AKA cavatiore, a disengage
cavazione di tempo a change of line made around the time of the opponent's blade; AKA cavatione di tempo, time disengage
CFS Chronic Fatigue Syndrome
choreographed combat a staged combat where all the moves of the combatants are already determined by some sort of fight director
coif a hood covering the head and neck, usually of some sturdy material in the case of that designed to go with protective gear
contra-cavazione a change of line made to counter a cavazone; AKA contra-cavatione, a counter-disengage
contra-postura Fabris' (1606) principle of adopting a guard or ward which defends the fencer from the opponent's initial attack while preferably opening a line in the opponent's defence; AKA an opposing position, or a counter-position

contra-tempo literally against time, usually refers to an action which is against the tempo, AKA counter-time
conventionals see partner drills
Cut and Thrust a stream of rapier combat in the SCA which includes percussive cuts

D

debole weak part of the blade furthest from the hilt, extends from the point down to midway; AKA foible, weak
dress sword sword for show, not designed for fighting merely presentation or to go with an outfit
drills two types of drills, solo and partner
  solo drills: exercises in which a fencer is given a specific skill to perform to increase their proficiency in that skill
  partner drills: exercises in which partners are given specific roles and skills to perform to increase their proficiency in those skills

E

Esfinges The worldwide group, this group was made for women who practice fencing, to unite them and let them get to know one other. https://www.facebook.com/groups/esfingeshema/
Esperanto "an artificial language devised in 1887 as an international medium of communication, based on roots from the chief European languages. It retains the structure of these languages and has the advantage of grammatical regularity and ease of pronunciation." (http://www.oxforddictionaries.com/)

F

fencing any system of using a sword where the object of the exercise is to strike the opponent without being struck, primarily while retaining the weapon
FM Fibromyalgia
forte strong part of the blade closest to the hilt, extends to midway up the blade; AKA strong

G

girata a turning void presented in Fabris' (1606) manual
gorget neck protection, should cover the entire neck including cervical vertebrae and hollow of the throat where the collar bones meet the sternum, recommended to be of rigid construction
guard a static position in which one Line is closed
Guild of Defence a teaching organisation within the SCA primarily interested in the research and teaching of the personal combat arts of the medieval and Renaissance period

H - L

HEMA Historical European Martial Arts
"Hot" drills Taking normal drills and adding combat intensity to them
inquartata a void using the movement of the rear foot passing behind and past the front foot to move the body out of the line of attack; AKA volte
lexicon "the vocabulary of a person, language, or branch of knowledge" (http://www.oxforddictionaries.com/)
Lochac A Kingdom within the SCA which includes Australia and New Zealand

M

mezzo middle third of the blade, half forte and half debole
mezzo cavazione a change of line made on the vertical axis, AKA mezzo cavatione, a half-disengage
Minimum Armour a standard by which a combatant is protected to be safe from harm above a recognised level, and if armoured under which it is likely that the combatant will come to harm above the recognised level
misura Italian, meaning measure or distance
misura larga Italian, wide measure, AKA wide distance
misura stretta Italian, narrow measure, AKA narrow distance
muscle memory trained reflexes gained through repetitive drills

N

NCIS Naval Criminal Investigative Service; in this case a TV show based on investigations made by a fictional version of this organisation
notoriety the condition of being famous or well-known especially for something bad: the state of being notorious (www.merriam-webster.com)

O - P

OT Occupational Therapy or Occupational Therapist
Pell Standing pole designed for sword practice, Latin: Palus
PPE Personal Protective Equipment

R

renown a state of being widely acclaimed and highly honoured (www.merriam-webster.com)
ricavazione a change of line made to counter a contra-cavazione; AKA ricavatione, double disengage
Risk Mitigation taking steps to reduce adverse effects and the likelihood of its occurrence
rudius Roman wooden sword, equivalent of a waster, plural is rudii

S

SCA — Society of Creative Anachronisms
senso di ferro — feeling through the steel, gaining knowledge through what is felt through the weapon; AKA sentiment du fer, tacto, Fühlen
SHDA — School of Historical Defense Arts
stringere — gaining the sword, to open a line on the opponent through which to strike, usually countered by a cavatione
SP15 — Swordplay '15, a national HEMA event run in 2015 in Queensland. Swordplay started as a local event and has now grown to one of the premiere events on the national calendar attracting visitors from all over Australia and international visitors.

T

tempo — time, also an action
terza — the third guard, also known as the Low Ward by di Grassi, it is the most commonly taught ward, situated with the sword in the High Outside Line, but hilt and hand usually somewhere near the hip
test cutting — cutting made against targets, both for testing the ability of the sword and also to test the technique of the wielder, common modern targets are tatami mats and water bottles with other more "forensic" targets used for more detailed analysis

U - W

USFCA — United States Fencing Coaches Association
ward — a position from which an attack or defence is launched
waster — practice weapon; of wooden construction in the medieval and Renaissance period; typically same characteristics, or as close to, as the steel weapon; modern reproductions may be made of nylon and other plastics
WMA — Western Martial Arts

Bibliography and Recommended Reading

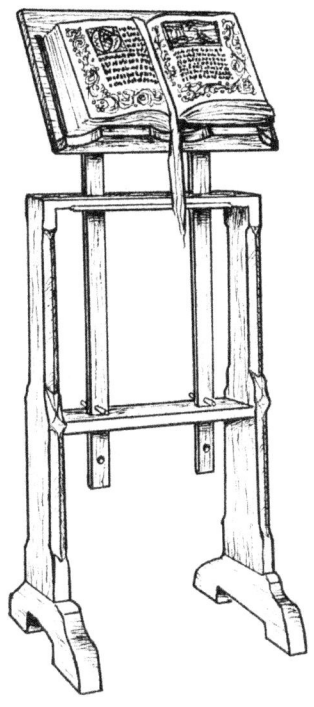

Amberger, J. C. (1999) *The Secret History of the Sword: Adventures in Ancient Martial Arts*, Multi-Media Books Inc.,

Anglo, S. (2000) *The Martial Arts of Renaissance Europe*, Yale University Press, London, UK

Castle, E. (1881) *Schools and Masters of Defense*, G. Bell & Sons, London, pdf Google Books

Castle, E. (1885) *Schools and Masters of Fence: From the Middle Ages to the Eighteenth Century*, George Bell & Sons, London (pdf used from Google Books)

Crown, A. A. (2006) *Why Study Classical Fencing*, http://www.classicalfencing.com/whystudy.php

Farrell, K. (2015) "Western Composers and Western Martial Arts" in Farrell, K. (ed) (2015) *Encased in Steel Anthology I*, Fallen Rook Publishing, Triquetra Services (Scotland), Glasgow

Flavel, M. (2015) "Turn Down the Volume?" in *Australasian Scientist* (Vol. 36, No. 7, Sept. 2015) Central Publications Pty Ltd, Wattle-ree Rd, Australia, pp 14-15

Hutton, A. (2003) *The Sword and the Centuries*, Greenhill Books, London

Kellner, D. (2009) *Building Confidence in Your Fencing*, http://www.sofaemployed.com/?p=1507

Wise, A. (2014) *The History and Art of Personal Combat*, Dover Publications Inc, Mineola, USA

PERIOD SOURCES

Agrippa, C. (2009) *Fencing: A Renaissance Treatise*, Translated by Ken Mondschein, Italica Press, New York, USA

Angelo, D. (1787) The School of Fencing With a General Explanation of the Principle Attitudes and Positions Peculiar to the Art

Capo Ferro, Ridolfo (1610) *Great Representation of the Art of the Use of Fencing*, selections translated by Wm. Jherek Swanger

Caroso da Sermoneta, Fabritio (1581) *Il Ballarino*

Di Grassi, G. (1594) *His True Arte of Defence: Showing how a man without other Teacher or Master may Safelie handle all Sortes of Weapons*, Temple Barre at the Signe of the Hand and Starre, translated from the 1570 manual by I. G., pdf from the Raymond J. Lord Collection

Fiore dei Liberi (1410) *Flos Duellatorum*,

Hope, Sir W. (1707) A New Short, and Easy Method of Fencing: Or the Art of the Broad and Small sword Rectified and Compendiz'd

Kirby, J. (ed.) (2012) *Italian Rapier Combat: Ridolfo Capo Ferro*, Frontline Books, Pen & Sword Books Ltd, Yorkshire, UK

Leoni, T. (2005) *The Art of Dueling: Salvator Fabris' rapier fencing treatise of 1606*, The Chivalry Bookshelf, Highland Village, Texas, USA

Marozzo, A. (1536) *Arte dell' Armi: Books One & Two*, translated by W. E. Wilson

Meyer, Joachim (2006) *The Art of Combat: A German Martial Arts Treatise of 1570*, Greenhill Books, London, UK, Translated by Jeffrey L. Foreng

Musashi, M. (1974) *A Book of Five Rings*, The Overlook Press, Woodstock, New York, USA (Translated by Victor Harris, originally written 1645)

Porzio, L. and Mele, G. (2002) *Arte Gladiatoria Dimicandi: 15th Century Swordsmanship of Master Filippo Vadi*, Chivalry Bookshelf, Union City

Saviolo, V. (1595) His Practise in Two Bookes. The first intreating the use of the Rapier and Dagger. The second, of Honor and honorable Quarrels., London, Printed by John Wolff, pdf from the Raymond J. Lord Collection

Silver, G. (1599) *Paradoxes of Defence*, London, Printed by Edward Blount, pdf from the Raymond J. Lord Collection

Silver, G. (1898) *Brief Instructions on My Paradoxes of Defence*, printed by Captain Cyril G. R. Matthey, British Museum reference: Sloan MS No. 376, html by Greg Lindahl

Swetnam, J. (1617) *The Schole of the Noble and Worthy Science of Defence*, Printed by Nicholas Oakes, London, pdf from Raymond J. Lord Collection

Thibault, G. (1628) *The Academy of the Sword*, Aeon Books, London, Translated by John Michael Greer

Windsor, G. (2012) *Veni Vadi Vici:* A Transcription and Commentary of Philippo Vadi's De Arte Gladiatoria Dimicandi, The School of European Swordsmanship

PRACTICAL MANUALS

Ducklin, K. and Waller, J. (2001) *Sword Fighting: A Manual for Actors & Directors*, Applause Theatre Books, New York, USA

Hutton, Capt. A. (1891) *Old Sword-Play*, H. Grevel & Co, London, pdf by Peter Valentine

Windsor, G. (2013) *The Swordsman's Companion: A Modern Training Manual for Medieval Longsword*, Guy Windsor

MODERN FENCING BOOKS

Barth, Dr. B. and Barth, K. (2003) *Learning Fencing*, Meyer & Meyer Sport Ltd, Oxford, UK

Beke, Z. and Polgár, J. (1963) *The Methodology of Sabre Fencing*, Corvina Press, Budapest, Hungary

De Beaumont, C.L. (1960) *Fencing: Ancient Art and Modern Sport*, Nicholas Kaye, London, UK

BIBLIOGRAPHY & RECOMMENDED READING

Evangelista, N. (2000) *The Inner Game of Fencing: Excellence in Form, Technique, Strategy, and Spirit*, Masters Press, Illinois, USA

Palffy-Alpar, J. (1967) *Sword and Masque*, F. A. Davis Company, Philadelphia, USA

CURATORIAL WORKS

Akehurst, R. (1969) *Antique Weapons for Pleasure and Investment*, Arco Publishing Company Inc., New York, USA

Bull, S. (1990) *An Historical Guide to Arms & Armour*, Victoria and Albert Museum Press, London, UK

Burton, R. (1987) *The Book of the Sword*, Dover Publications Inc, Mineola, New York (originally published 1884)

Coe, M. et. al. (1996) *Swords and Hilt Weapons*, Prion Books Limited, London, UK

Curtis, P. (2010) *Destreza: Choosing a Weapon for the Spanish Tradition* http://www.puckandmary.com/blog_puck/2010/12/destreza-choosing-a-weapon-for-the-spanish-tradition/

Friedman, D. and Cook, E. (1992) *Shield and Weapon Weights*, http://www.pbm.com/~lindahl/cariadoc/shield_and_weapon_weights.html

Grandy, B. (2003) "Hanwei / CAS Iberia *Federschwert* Training Sword", https://myarmoury.com/review_casi_feder.html

Harding, D.(ed) (1990) Weapons: An International Encyclopedia from 5000BC to 2000AD, MacMillian Press Ltd, London, UK

Holmes, R. (2010) *Weapon: A Visual History of Arms and Armour*, Dorling Kindersley, London

Imperial Swords (2017) "Federschwert Sword", http://imperialswords.com/shop/federschwertsword/

Krishnaraj, S. (2001) "Estafilade: Construction of the Smallsword", Association of Historical Fencing (© 2009), www.ahfi.org

Leoni, T. (2011) "Understanding Smallsword", Order of the Seven Hearts, http://www.salvatorfabris.org/UnderstandingSmallsword.shtml

Norling, R. (2011) "Sparring Swords – Introduction", HROARR, https://hroarr.com/reviews/sparring-swords-introduction/

Norling, R. (2011a) "Fechtschert or a Blunt Longsword?", HROARR, https://hroarr.com/article/federschwert-or-a-blunt-longsword/

Norling, R. (2012) "A Call to Arms", HROARR, https://hroarr.com/community-news/a-call-to-arms/

Norling, R. (2013) "The Whatchamacallit-schwert", HROARR, https://hroarr.com/article/the-feder-whatchamacallit/

Norman, V. (1964) *Arms and Armour*, Weidenfeld and Nicolson, London, UK

Oakeshott, R. E. (1996) *The Archaeology of Weapons: Arms and Armour From Prehistory to the Age of Chivalry*, Dover Publications, Inc., New York

Oakeshott, R. E. (1998) *The Sword in the Age of Chivalry*, The Boydell Press, Woolbridge

Oakeshott, E. (2012) *European Weapons and Armour: From the Renaissance to the Industrial Revolution*, The Boydell Press, Woodbridge

Patterson, A. (2009) Fashion and Armour in Renaissance Europe: Proud Lookes and Brave Attire, V&A Publishing, London, UK

Scottish Tartans Authority (2016) "Highland Weapons", http://www.tartansauthority.com/highland-dress/highland-weapons/

Shackleford, S. (2010) *Spirit of the Sword: A Celebration of Artistry and Craftsmanship*, Krause Publications, Iola, USA

Soud, D. (2014) *The Illustrated History of Weapons: Swords, Spears & Maces*, Kingsford Editions, Heatherton, Victoria

Valentine, E. (1968) *Rapiers: An Illustrated Reference Guide to the Rapiers of the 16th and 17th Centuries, with their Companions*, Stackpole Books, Harrisburg, USA

Wagner, E. (2004) *Swords and Daggers: An Illustrated Handbook*, Dover Publications Inc., Mineola, USA

Wassom, D. (2016) "Some Historical Swiss Swords Examined", The Association for Renaissance Martial Arts, http://www.thearma.org/spotlight/swiss-swords.html#.WPge4PmGPIU

Watterott, H. (2016) "Is it a Claymore or a Scottish Basket Hilted Broadsword - History Police 3", http://slaintescotland.com/blog/history-police/item/41-is-it-a-claymore-or-a-scottish-basket-hilted-broadsword-history-police-3.html

REFERENCE

Collins English Dictionary (2016) "Definition of Broadsword", http://www.collinsdictionary.com/dictionary/english/broadsword, Harper Collins Publishers, Glasgow

Evangelista, N. (1995) *Encyclopedia of the Sword*, Greenwood Press, Westport, Connecticut, USA

Merriam-Webster (2016) http://www.merriam-webster.com/dictionary/

Wikipedia (2016) Wikipedia, Wikimedia Foundation, Inc., https://en.wikipedia.org/

INTERNET SOURCES - REFERENCE

Collins' Dictionary:
http://www.collinsdictionary.com/

Cambridge Dictionary:
https://dictionary.cambridge.org/dictionary/
Merriam-Webster Dictionary:
www.merriam-webster.com
Oxford Dictionary:
http://www.oxforddictionaries.com/
Wikipedia:
http://en.wikipedia.org/wiki/
Princeton University WordNet:
wordnetweb.princeton.edu/perl/webwn
HEMA Alliance Wiktenauer:
http://wiktenauer.com

ARMOURIES AND WEAPONSMITHS

Castille Armory:
http://www.castillearmory.com/
Darkwood Armory:
http://www.darkwoodarmory.com/
Fencing.net:
http://fencing.net/
Imperial Swords:
http://imperialswords.com/

ORGANISATIONS

Association for Historical Fencing:
www.ahfi.org
Association for Renaissance Martial Arts:
http://www.thearma.org/
The J. Paul Getty Museum
http://www.getty.edu/museum
HROARR: http://hroarr.com/
My Armoury:
https://myarmoury.com/home.php
http://www.salvatorfabris.org/ - Recently closed down.
Slainte Scotland:
http://slaintescotland.com/blog/history-police/
Scottish Tartans Authority
http://www.tartansauthority.com/

PERSONAL

Guy Windsor's page:
http://guywindsor.net/
Greg Lindahl's page:
http://www.pbm.com/~lindahl/
Puck and Mary Curtis's page:
http://www.puckandmary.com/blog_puck/

BIBLIOGRAPHY & RECOMMENDED READING

About the Author

HENRY WALKER

afencersramblings.blogspot.com

My two greatest passions in life have always been history and swords. Like most boys I pretended to play with swords as a kid and that did not seem to change as I grew older. In 1993 I studied foil at Griffith University, before a change in circumstances caused a necessary break. Soon after however, I became involved in the rapier program within the Society for Creative Anachronism (SCA), an international historical research and recreation group that combined my love of history and swords in a single hobby.

Over the next five years I fought in various fencing competitions within the SCA, wining various championships. I started researching and teaching the art of rapier combat and joined the one of the Guilds of Fence (within the SCA). During that period I played my Prize (levelling system) for Provost in 2001 (think of a brown belt, or assistant instructor, in martial arts).

My interest in Western Martial Arts was piqued during this period and has never diminished. In 2002, I completed Honours in History with a study of the social history of rapier combat. In 2003 I attained the highest rank attainable within the Guild of Fence in the SCA, that of Guild Master. In 2004 I was then awarded with the highest award possible for civilian combat within the SCA at that time, the Order of the White Scarf.

As the SCA has grown and developed, so has the level of research, skill and training within its fields of endeavour. Recognising the influence of the Fencing community across the globe in 2015 the SCA created a new higher level recognition called the Order of Defence. This new award was an international recognition of people considered Masters in period fencing within the SCA. Admittance to this order is by invitation and is a recognition of the highest level knowledge, practical skill and teaching. I was admitted to this Order in 2017.

Since 2009, I have been involved in the planning and creation of a Brisbane-based swordplay convention run by the Australian College of Arms until 2014 when it was taken over by the School of Historical Defense Arts (SHDA). I formed the SHDA in 2013 in order to further my studies of Western Martial Arts and to have a larger platform to share this knowledge to interested individuals with the same passion.

The SHDA is a not-for-profit business dedicated to the teaching of Historical European Martial Arts, under the auspices of the Australasian Living History Federation.

www.ingramcontent.com/pod-product-compliance
Lightning Source LLC
Chambersburg PA
CBHW060910300426
44112CB00011B/1407